28. GILBERT
GALILEO
HARVEY

29. CERVANTES

30. FRANCIS BACON

31. DESCARTES
SPINOZA

32. MILTON

33. PASCAL

34. NEWTON
HUYGENS

35. LOCKE
BERKELEY
HUME

36. SWIFT
STERNE

37. FIELDING

38. MONTESQUIEU
ROUSSEAU

39. ADAM SMITH

40. GIBBON I

41. GIBBON II

42. KANT

43. AMERICAN STATE
PAPERS
THE FEDERALIST
J. S. MILL

44. BOSWELL

45. LAVOISIER
FOURIER
FARADAY

46. HEGEL

47. GOETHE

48. MELVILLE

49. DARWIN

50. MARX
ENGELS

51. TOLSTOY

52. DOSTOEVSKY

53. WILLIAM JAMES

54. FREUD

GREAT BOOKS
OF THE WESTERN WORLD

ROBERT MAYNARD HUTCHINS, *EDITOR IN CHIEF*

38.

MONTESQUIEU

ROUSSEAU

THE SPIRIT OF LAWS

By Charles de Secondat, Baron de Montesquieu

ON THE ORIGIN OF INEQUALITY
ON POLITICAL ECONOMY
THE SOCIAL CONTRACT

By Jean Jacques Rousseau

William Benton, *Publisher*

ENCYCLOPÆDIA BRITANNICA, INC.

CHICAGO · LONDON · TORONTO · GENEVA

THE SPIRIT OF LAWS, TRANSLATED BY THOMAS NUGENT AND REVISED BY J. V. PRICHARD,
IS REPRINTED BY ARRANGEMENT WITH G. BELL & SONS, LTD., LONDON.

THE TEXTS OF ON THE ORIGIN OF INEQUALITY, ON POLITICAL ECONOMY AND
THE SOCIAL CONTRACT, TRANSLATED BY G. D. H. COLE, IN THIS EDITION ARE DERIVED
FROM THE EDITION IN EVERYMAN'S LIBRARY BY PERMISSION OF
J. M. DENT & SONS LTD., LONDON, AND E. P. DUTTON & CO., INC., NEW YORK.

THE UNIVERSITY OF CHICAGO

The Great Books
is published with the editorial advice of the faculties
of The University of Chicago

GENERAL CONTENTS

MONTESQUIEU

BIOGRAPHICAL NOTE

CHARLES DE MONTESQUIEU, 1689–1755

MONTESQUIEU was baptized Charles Louis de la Brède, taking his name from the estate which had been part of his mother's dowry when she married Jacques de Secondat. Born at La Brède, about ten miles from Bordeaux, Montesquieu, like Montaigne, was of Gascon origin, and, like the essayist, he was as an infant placed under the care of a poor man's wife, so that he might know the poor were his brothers. In 1700 he was sent to the college of the Oratorians at Juilly, near Meaux, where he studied classical letters, history, and the sciences. The family had long been associated with the law, and Montesquieu completed his education by preparing for the bar. After the death of his father, he placed himself under the protection of his uncle, the Baron de Montesquieu, and became a counsellor to the Bordeaux Parliament. At his behest he married the heiress of a Huguenot military family in 1715. The following year his uncle died, leaving him his name, his important judicial office of President of the Bordeaux Parliament, and his whole fortune.

Although holding the presidency and acting as a professional jurist, Montesquieu appears to have taken more interest in literature and the vogue of scientific experimentation. He became a member of the Bordeaux Academy of Sciences and between 1717 and 1723 submitted numerous papers on such diverse subjects as the policy of the Romans in matters of religion, the causes of intoxication, intermittent fever, the echo, the transparency and weight of bodies, the movement of the sea, fossil remains, and the flower of the vine. In 1721 he published anonymously at Amsterdam his first extensive literary work, the *Persian Letters*, which, purporting to be exchanged between two Persians traveling in Europe, satirized the follies of French society. Within a year the book had gone through four authorized and numerous pirated editions. His reputation as a wit established, he began to frequent the court and the literary society of the capital. In 1725 he was named to the French Academy, but the King opposed his election, invoking the obsolete rule requiring

residence in Paris. The following year Montesquieu sold the life-tenure of his office in Bordeaux, with the provision that upon his death it revert to his son. He moved to Paris to devote himself to literature and in 1728 obtained membership in the Academy.

Almost immediately afterwards he set out on a tour of Europe to observe men, their customs, and their social and legal institutions, apparently with the project in mind of writing *The Spirit of Laws*. He accompanied the Earl of Waldegrave to Vienna, visited Italy for almost a year, and with Lord Chesterfield returned to England in 1729 by way of Piedmont and the Rhine. During his eighteen months in England he met many notables, including Pope, Walpole, and Swift, and gained a wide acquaintance with English life. Although disliking some traits of the English, he greatly admired their institutions, and on returning to his estate at La Brède he might have seemed to outward appearance to be settling down as a squire. He altered his park in the English fashion, made sedulous inquiries into his own genealogy, arranged an entail, asserted, though not harshly, his seignorial rights, kept the poachers in awe, and generally reorganized his estate.

His principal occupation at La Brède, however, was the preparation of his literary works. In his great study (some sixty feet long by forty wide) he was constantly dictating, making abstracts, revising essays, and in other ways preparing his main book. He may have thought it wise to soften the transition from the *Persian Letters* to *The Spirit of Laws* by interposing a work graver than the former and less elaborate than the latter. *The Considerations on the Causes of the Grandeur and Decadence of the Romans* appeared in 1734. Although the book was eagerly read, the salons, thinking only of the author's reputation as a wit, claimed that the *Persian Letters* and the new book were respectively the "grandeur et decadence" of M. de Montesquieu.

The Spirit of Laws was not formally begun until about 1743, and Montesquieu worked upon it four years before it was completed. He submitted the finished manuscript to a group of friends, including Helvétius, Fontenelle, and Crébillon the Younger. Although they unanimously advised against publication, Montesquieu brought out the work in Geneva in 1748. In France the book met with an unfriendly reception from both the supporters and the opponents of the regime. But in the rest of Europe, and particularly in England, it received the highest praise. The English increased their purchase of the wine made at La Brède, and Montesquieu noted that "the success of my book in that country contributed to the success of my wine, although I think that the success of my wine has done still more for the success of my book."

In revising the final proofs of the book, Montesquieu is reported to have remarked: "This work has nearly killed me, and now I shall rest and labor no more." Although he spent most of his remaining eight years in the country, he still visited Paris, and on one such occasion he procured the release of an admirer who had been imprisoned at the instigation of Voltaire. The romance of *Arsace et Isménie*, a short incomplete treatise on *Taste,* and many of his *Pensées* were composed after the appearance of *The Spirit of Laws.*

At the end of 1754 he went to Paris with the intention of closing his house in the city so that he might retire permanently to La Brède. While there he was stricken with a fever. He died within a fortnight, on February 10, 1755, and was buried in the Church of St. Sulpice. Memorial services were held for him by the French Academy, the Prussian Academy, and the British Royal Society; Frederick the Great paid tribute to him to D'Alembert, and at the instance of Lord Chesterfield the London *Evening Post* lamented his death as the loss of "a friend to mankind."

CONTENTS: The Spirit of Laws

CONTENTS

CONTENTS

CONTENTS

PREFACE

If amidst the infinite number of subjects contained in this book there is anything which, contrary to my expectation, may possibly offend, I can at least assure the public that it was not inserted with an ill intention: for I am not naturally of a captious temper. Plato thanked the gods that he was born in the same age with Socrates: and for my part I give thanks to the Supreme that I was born a subject of that government under which I live; and that it is His pleasure I should obey those whom He has made me love.

I beg one favour of my readers, which I fear will not be granted me; this is, that they will not judge by a few hours' reading of the labour of twenty years; that they will approve or condemn the book entire, and not a few particular phrases. If they would search into the design of the author, they can do it in no other way so completely as by searching into the design of the work.

I have first of all considered mankind; and the result of my thoughts has been, that amidst such an infinite diversity of laws and manners, they were not solely conducted by the caprice of fancy.

I have laid down the first principles, and have found that the particular cases follow naturally from them; that the histories of all nations are only consequences of them; and that every particular law is connected with another law, or depends on some other of a more general extent.

When I have been obliged to look back into antiquity, I have endeavoured to assume the spirit of the ancients, lest I should consider those things as alike which are really different; and lest I should miss the difference of those which appear to be alike.

I have not drawn my principles from my prejudices, but from the nature of things.

Here a great many truths will not appear till we have seen the chain which connects them with others. The more we enter into particulars, the more we shall perceive the certainty of the principles on which they are founded. I have not even given all these particulars, for who could mention them all without a most insupportable fatigue?

The reader will not here meet with any of those bold flights which seem to characterise the works of the present age. When things are examined with never so small a degree of extent, the sallies of imagination must vanish; these generally arise from the mind's collecting all its powers to view only one side of the subject, while it leaves the other unobserved.

I write not to censure anything established in any country whatsoever. Every nation will here find the reasons on which its maxims are founded; and this will be the natural inference, that to propose alterations belongs only to those who are so happy as to be born with a genius capable of penetrating the entire constitution of a state.

It is not a matter of indifference that the minds of the people be enlightened. The prejudices of magistrates have arisen from national prejudice. In a time of ignorance they have committed even the greatest evils without the least scruple; but in an enlightened age they even tremble while conferring the greatest blessings. They perceive the ancient abuses; they see how they must be reformed; but they are sensible also of the abuses of a reformation. They let the evil continue, if they fear a worse; they are content with a lesser good, if they doubt a greater. They examine into the parts, to judge of them in connection; and they examine all the causes, to discover their different effects.

Could I but succeed so as to afford new reasons to every man to love his prince, his country, his laws; new reasons to render him more sensible in every nation and government of the blessings he enjoys, I should think myself the most happy of mortals.

Could I but succeed so as to persuade those who command, to increase their knowledge in what they ought to prescribe; and those who obey, to find a new pleasure resulting from obedience—I should think myself the most happy of mortals.

The most happy of mortals should I think myself could I contribute to make mankind recover from their prejudices. By prejudices I here mean, not that which renders men ignorant of some particular things, but whatever renders them ignorant of themselves.

It is in endeavouring to instruct mankind that we are best able to practise that general virtue which comprehends the love of all. Man, that flexible being, conforming in society to the thoughts and impressions of others, is equally capable of knowing his own nature, whenever it is laid open to his view; and of losing the very sense of it, when this idea is banished from his mind.

Often have I begun, and as often have I laid aside, this undertaking. I have a thousand times given the leaves I had written to the winds: I, every day, felt my paternal hands fall. I have followed my object without any fixed plan: I have known neither rules nor exceptions; I have found the truth, only to lose it again. But when I once discovered my first principles, everything I sought for appeared; and in the course of twenty years, I have seen my work begun, growing up, advancing to maturity, and finished.

If this work meets with success, I shall owe it chiefly to the grandeur and majesty of the subject. However, I do not think that I have been totally deficient in point of genius. When I have seen what so many great men both in France, England, and Germany have said before me, I have been lost in admiration; but I have not lost my courage: I have said with Correggio, "And I also am a painter."

ADVERTISEMENT

1. For the better understanding of the first four books of this work, it is to be observed that what I distinguish by the name of *virtue,* in a republic, is the love of one's country, that is, the love of equality. It is not a moral, nor a Christian, but a political *virtue;* and it is the spring which sets the republican government in motion, as honour is the spring which gives motion to monarchy. Hence it is that I have distinguished the love of one's country, and of equality, by the appellation of political virtue. My ideas are new, and therefore I have been obliged to find new words, or to give new acceptations to old terms, in order to convey my meaning. They, who are unacquainted with this particular, have made me say most strange absurdities, such as would be shocking in any part of the world, because in all countries and governments morality is requisite.

2. The reader is also to notice that there is a vast difference between saying that a certain quality, modification of the mind, or virtue, is not the spring by which government is actuated. and affirming that it is not to be found in that government. Were I to say such a wheel or such a pinion is not the spring which sets the watch going, can you infer thence that they are not to be found in the watch? So far is it from being true that the moral and Christian virtues are excluded from monarchy, that even political virtue is not excluded. In a word, honour is found in a republic, though its spring be political virtue; and political virtue is found in a monarchical government, though it be actuated by honour.

To conclude, the honest man of whom we treat in the third book, chapter 5, is not the Christian, but the political honest man, who is possessed of the political virtue there mentioned. He is the man who loves the laws of his country, and who is actuated by the love of those laws. I have set these matters in a clearer light in the present edition, by giving a more precise meaning to my expression: and in most places where I have made use of the word *virtue* I have taken care to add the term *political.*

THE SPIRIT OF LAWS

Book I. Of Laws in General

1. *Of the Relation of Laws to different Beings.*
Laws, in their most general signification, are
the necessary relations arising from the nature
of things. In this sense all beings have their
laws: the Deity[1] His laws, the material world
its laws, the intelligences superior to man their
laws, the beasts their laws, man his laws.

They who assert that a blind fatality produced the various effects we behold in this world
talk very absurdly; for can anything be more
unreasonable than to pretend that a blind fatality could be productive of intelligent beings?

There is, then, a prime reason; and laws are
the relations subsisting between it and different beings, and the relations of these to one
another.

God is related to the universe, as Creator
and Preserver; the laws by which He created
all things are those by which He preserves
them. He acts according to these rules, because
He knows them; He knows them, because He
made them; and He made them, because they
are in relation to His wisdom and power.

Since we observe that the world, though
formed by the motion of matter, and void of
understanding, subsists through so long a succession of ages, its motions must certainly be
directed by invariable laws; and could we imagine another world, it must also have constant rules, or it would inevitably perish.

Thus the creation, which seems an arbitrary act, supposes laws as invariable as those
of the fatality of the Atheists. It would be absurd to say that the Creator might govern the
world without those rules, since without them
it could not subsist.

These rules are a fixed and invariable relation. In bodies moved, the motion is received,
increased, diminished, or lost, according to the
relations of the quantity of matter and velocity; each diversity is *uniformity*, each change is
constancy.

[1] "Law," says Plutarch, "is the king of mortal
and immortal beings." See his treatise, *A Discourse to an Unlearned Prince.*

Particular intelligent beings may have laws
of their own making, but they have some likewise which they never made. Before there were
intelligent beings, they were possible; they had
therefore possible relations, and consequently
possible laws. Before laws were made, there
were relations of possible justice. To say that
there is nothing just or unjust but what is commanded or forbidden by positive laws, is the
same as saying that before the describing of a
circle all the radii were not equal.

We must therefore acknowledge relations
of justice antecedent to the positive law by
which they are established: as, for instance, if
human societies existed, it would be right to
conform to their laws; if there were intelligent
beings that had received a benefit of another
being, they ought to show their gratitude; if
one intelligent being had created another intelligent being, the latter ought to continue in
its original state of dependence; if one intelligent being injures another, it deserves a retaliation; and so on.

But the intelligent world is far from being
so well governed as the physical. For though
the former has also its laws, which of their own
nature are invariable, it does not conform to
them so exactly as the physical world. This is
because, on the one hand, particular intelligent beings are of a finite nature, and consequently liable to error; and on the other, their
nature requires them to be free agents. Hence
they do not steadily conform to their primitive laws; and even those of their own instituting they frequently infringe.

Whether brutes be governed by the general
laws of motion, or by a particular movement,
we cannot determine. Be that as it may, they
have not a more intimate relation to God than
the rest of the material world; and sensation
is of no other use to them than in the relation
they have either to other particular beings or
to themselves.

By the allurement of pleasure they preserve
the individual, and by the same allurement

1

they preserve their species. They have natural laws, because they are united by sensation; positive laws they have none, because they are not connected by knowledge. And yet they do not invariably conform to their natural laws; these are better observed by vegetables, that have neither understanding nor sense.

Brutes are deprived of the high advantages which we have; but they have some which we have not. They have not our hopes, but they are without our fears; they are subject like us to death, but without knowing it; even most of them are more attentive than we to self-preservation, and do not make so bad a use of their passions.

Man, as a physical being, is like other bodies governed by invariable laws. As an intelligent being, he incessantly transgresses the laws established by God, and changes those of his own instituting. He is left to his private direction, though a limited being, and subject, like all finite intelligences, to ignorance and error: even his imperfect knowledge he loses; and as a sensible creature, he is hurried away by a thousand impetuous passions. Such a being might every instant forget his Creator; God has therefore reminded him of his duty by the laws of religion. Such a being is liable every moment to forget himself; philosophy has provided against this by the laws of morality. Formed to live in society, he might forget his fellow-creatures; legislators have therefore by political and civil laws confined him to his duty.

2. *Of the Laws of Nature.* Antecedent to the above-mentioned laws are those of nature, so called, because they derive their force entirely from our frame and existence. In order to have a perfect knowledge of these laws, we must consider man before the establishment of society: the laws received in such a state would be those of nature.

The law which, impressing on our minds the idea of a Creator, inclines us towards Him, is the first in importance, though not in order, of natural laws. Man in a state of nature would have the faculty of knowing, before he had acquired any knowledge. Plain it is that his first ideas would not be of a speculative nature; he would think of the preservation of his being, before he would investigate its origin. Such a man would feel nothing in himself at first but impotency and weakness; his fears and apprehensions would be excessive; as appears from instances (were there any necessity

of proving it) of savages found in forests,[1] trembling at the motion of a leaf, and flying from every shadow.

In this state every man, instead of being sensible of his equality, would fancy himself inferior. There would therefore be no danger of their attacking one another; peace would be the first law of nature.

The natural impulse or desire which Hobbes attributes to mankind of subduing one another is far from being well founded. The idea of empire and dominion is so complex, and depends on so many other notions, that it could never be the first which occurred to the human understanding.

Hobbes[2] inquires, "For what reason go men armed, and have locks and keys to fasten their doors, if they be not naturally in a state of war?" But is it not obvious that he attributes to mankind before the establishment of society what can happen but in consequence of this establishment, which furnishes them with motives for hostile attacks and self-defence?

Next to a sense of his weakness man would soon find that of his wants. Hence another law of nature would prompt him to seek for nourishment.

Fear, I have observed, would induce men to shun one another; but the marks of this fear being reciprocal, would soon engage them to associate. Besides, this association would quickly follow from the very pleasure one animal feels at the approach of another of the same species. Again, the attraction arising from the difference of sexes would enhance this pleasure, and the natural inclination they have for each other would form a third law.

Beside the sense or instinct which man possesses in common with brutes, he has the advantage of acquired knowledge; and thence arises a second tie, which brutes have not. Mankind have therefore a new motive of uniting; and a fourth law of nature results from the desire of living in society.

3. *Of Positive Laws.* As soon as man enters into a state of society he loses the sense of his weakness; equality ceases, and then commences the state of war.

Each particular society begins to feel its strength, whence arises a state of war between different nations. The individuals likewise of

[1] Witness the savage found in the forests of Hanover, who was carried over to England during the reign of George I.
[2] In pref., *De cive.*

each society become sensible of their force; hence the principal advantages of this society they endeavour to convert to their own emolument, which constitutes a state of war between individuals.

These two different kinds of states give rise to human laws. Considered as inhabitants of so great a planet, which necessarily contains a variety of nations, they have laws relating to their mutual intercourse, which is what we call the *law of nations*. As members of a society that must be properly supported, they have laws relating to the governors and the governed, and this we distinguish by the name of *politic law*. They have also another sort of law, as they stand in relation to each other; by which is understood the *civil law*.

The law of nations is naturally founded on this principle, that different nations ought in time of peace to do one another all the good they can, and in time of war as little injury as possible, without prejudicing their real interests.

The object of war is victory; that of victory is conquest; and that of conquest preservation. From this and the preceding principle all those rules are derived which constitute the *law of nations*.

All countries have a law of nations, not excepting the Iroquois themselves, though they devour their prisoners: for they send and receive ambassadors, and understand the rights of war and peace. The mischief is that their law of nations is not founded on true principles.

Besides the law of nations relating to all societies, there is a polity or civil constitution for each particularly considered. No society can subsist without a form of government. "The united strength of individuals," as Gravina[1] well observes, "constitutes what we call the body politic."

The general strength may be in the hands of a single person, or of many. Some think that nature having established paternal authority, the most natural government was that of a single person. But the example of paternal authority proves nothing. For if the power of a father relates to a single government, that of brothers after the death of a father, and that of cousins-german after the decease of brothers, refer to a government of many. The political power necessarily comprehends the union of several families.

Better is it to say, that the government most

[1] Italian poet and jurist, 1664–1718.

conformable to nature is that which best agrees with the humour and disposition of the people in whose favour it is established.

The strength of individuals cannot be united without a conjunction of all their wills. "The conjunction of those wills," as Gravina again very justly observes, "is what we call the civil state."

Law in general is human reason, inasmuch as it governs all the inhabitants of the earth: the political and civil laws of each nation ought to be only the particular cases in which human reason is applied.

They should be adapted in such a manner to the people for whom they are framed that it should be a great chance if those of one nation suit another.

They should be in relation to the nature and principle of each government; whether they form it, as may be said of politic laws; or whether they support it, as in the case of civil institutions.

They should be in relation to the climate of each country, to the quality of its soil, to its situation and extent, to the principal occupation of the natives, whether husbandmen, huntsmen, or shepherds: they should have relation to the degree of liberty which the constitution will bear; to the religion of the inhabitants, to their inclinations, riches, numbers, commerce, manners, and customs. In fine, they have relations to each other, as also to their origin, to the intent of the legislator, and to the order of things on which they are established; in all of which different lights they ought to be considered.

This is what I have undertaken to perform in the following work. These relations I shall examine, since all these together constitute what I call the *Spirit of Laws*.

I have not separated the political from the civil institutions, as I do not pretend to treat of laws, but of their spirit; and as this spirit consists in the various relations which the laws may bear to different objects, it is not so much my business to follow the natural order of laws as that of these relations and objects.

I shall first examine the relations which laws bear to the nature and principle of each government; and as this principle has a strong influence on laws, I shall make it my study to understand it thoroughly: and if I can but once establish it, the laws will soon appear to flow thence as from their source. I shall proceed afterwards to other and more particular relations.

Book II. Of Laws Directly Derived from the Nature of Government

1. *Of the Nature of the three different Governments.* There are three species of government: republican, monarchical, and despotic. In order to discover their nature, it is sufficient to recollect the common notion, which supposes three definitions, or rather three facts: that a republican government is that in which the body, or only a part of the people, is possessed of the supreme power; monarchy, that in which a single person governs by fixed and established laws; a despotic government, that in which a single person directs everything by his own will and caprice.

This is what I call the nature of each government; we must now inquire into those laws which directly conform to this nature, and consequently are the fundamental institutions.

2. *Of the Republican Government, and the Laws in relation to Democracy.*[1] When the body of the people is possessed of the supreme power, it is called a democracy. When the supreme power is lodged in the hands of a part of the people, it is then an aristocracy.

In a democracy the people are in some respects the sovereign, and in others the subject.

There can be no exercise of sovereignty but by their suffrages, which are their own will; now the sovereign's will is the sovereign himself. The laws therefore which establish the right of suffrage are fundamental to this government. And indeed it is as important to regulate in a republic, in what manner, by whom, to whom, and concerning what, suffrages are to be given, as it is in a monarchy to know who is the prince, and after what manner he ought to govern.

Libanius[2] says that at Athens a stranger who intermeddled in the assemblies of the people was punished with death. This is because such a man usurped the rights of sovereignty.

It is an essential point to fix the number of citizens who are to form the public assemblies; otherwise it would be uncertain whether the whole, or only a part of the people, had given their votes. At Sparta the number was fixed at ten thousand. But Rome, designed by Providence to rise from the weakest beginnings to the highest pitch of grandeur; Rome, doomed to experience all the vicissitudes of fortune; Rome, who had sometimes all her inhabitants without her walls, and sometimes all Italy and a considerable part of the world within them; Rome, I say, never fixed the number;[3] and this was one of the principal causes of her ruin.

The people, in whom the supreme power resides, ought to have the management of everything within their reach: that which exceeds their abilities must be conducted by their ministers.

But they cannot properly be said to have their ministers, without the power of nominating them: it is, therefore, a fundamental maxim in this government, that the people should choose their ministers—that is, their magistrates.

They have occasion, as well as monarchs, and even more so, to be directed by a council or senate. But to have a proper confidence in these, they should have the choosing of the members; whether the election be made by themselves, as at Athens, or by some magistrate deputed for that purpose, as on certain occasions was customary at Rome.

The people are extremely well qualified for choosing those whom they are to entrust with part of their authority. They have only to be determined by things to which they cannot be strangers, and by facts that are obvious to sense. They can tell when a person has fought many battles, and been crowned with success; they are, therefore, capable of electing a general. They can tell when a judge is assiduous in his office, gives general satisfaction, and has never been charged with bribery: this is sufficient for choosing a prætor. They are struck with the magnificence or riches of a fellow-citizen; no more is requisite for electing an edile. These are facts of which they can have better information in a public forum than a monarch in his palace. But are they capable of conducting an intricate affair, of seizing and improving the opportunity and critical moment of action? No; this surpasses their abilities.

Should we doubt the people's natural capacity, in respect to the discernment of merit, we need only cast an eye on the series of sur-

---

[1] Compare Aristotle, *Politics*, vi. 2.
[2] *Declamations*, 17, 18.

[3] See the *Considerations on the Causes of the Grandeur and Decline of the Romans*, 9.

prising elections made by the Athenians and Romans; which no one surely will attribute to hazard.

We know that though the people of Rome assumed the right of raising plebeians to public offices, yet they never would exert this power; and though at Athens the magistrates were allowed, by the law of Aristides, to be elected from all the different classes of inhabitants, there never was a case, says Xenophon,[1] when the common people petitioned for employments which could endanger either their security or their glory.

As most citizens have sufficient ability to choose, though unqualified to be chosen, so the people, though capable of calling others to an account for their administration, are incapable of conducting the administration themselves.

The public business must be carried on with a certain motion, neither too quick nor too slow. But the motion of the people is always either too remiss or too violent. Sometimes with a hundred thousand arms they overturn all before them; and sometimes with a hundred thousand feet they creep like insects.

In a popular state the inhabitants are divided into certain classes. It is in the manner of making this division that great legislators have signalised themselves; and it is on this the duration and prosperity of democracy have ever depended.

Servius Tullius followed the spirit of aristocracy in the distribution of his classes. We find in Livy[2] and in Dionysius Halicarnassus,[3] in what manner he lodged the right of suffrage in the hands of the principal citizens. He had divided the people of Rome into 193 centuries, which formed six classes; and ranking the rich, who were in smaller numbers, in the first centuries, and those in middling circumstances, who were more numerous, in the next, he flung the indigent multitude into the last; and as each century had but one vote,[4] it was property rather than numbers that decided the election.

Solon divided the people of Athens into four classes. In this he was directed by the spirit of democracy, his intention not being to fix those who were to choose, but such as

were eligible: therefore, leaving to every citizen the right of election, he made[5] the judges eligible from each of those four classes; but the magistrates he ordered to be chosen only out of the first three, consisting of persons of easy fortunes.[6]

As the division of those who have a right of suffrage is a fundamental law in republics, so the manner of giving this suffrage is another fundamental.

The suffrage by lot is natural to democracy; as that by choice is to aristocracy.[7]

The suffrage by lot is a method of electing that offends no one, but animates each citizen with the pleasing hope of serving his country.

Yet as this method is in itself defective, it has been the endeavour of the most eminent legislators to regulate and amend it.

Solon made a law at Athens that military employments should be conferred by choice; but that senators and judges should be elected by lot.

The same legislator ordained that civil magistracies, attended with great expense, should be given by choice; and the others by lot.

In order, however, to amend the suffrage by lot, he made a rule that none but those who presented themselves should be elected; that the person elected should be examined by judges[8] and that every one should have a right to accuse him if he were unworthy of the office:[9] this participated at the same time of the suffrage by lot, and of that by choice. When the time of their magistracy had expired, they were obliged to submit to another judgment in regard to their conduct. Persons utterly unqualified must have been extremely backward in giving in their names to be drawn by lot.

The law which determines the manner of giving suffrage is likewise fundamental in a democracy. It is a question of some importance whether the suffrages ought to be public or secret. Cicero observes[10] that the laws[11] which

---

[1] Pp. 691, 692, ed. Wechel, 1596.
[2] Bk. i.
[3] Bk. iv, art. 15 et seq.
[4] See in the Considerations on the Causes of the Grandeur and Decline of the Romans, 9, how this spirit of Servius Tullius was preserved in the republic.
[5] Dionysius Halicarnassus, Eulogium of Isocrates, ii, p. 97, ed. Wechel. Pollux, viii. 10, art. 130.
[6] See Aristotle's Politics, ii. 12.
[7] Ibid, iv. 9.
[8] See the oration of Demosthenes, De Falsa legat., and the oration against Timarchus.
[9] They used even to draw two tickets for each place, one which gave the place, and the other which named the person who was to succeed, in case the first was rejected.
[10] De Leg., i, iii.
[11] They were called leges tabulares; two tablets were presented to each citizen, the first marked with an A, for Antiquo, or I forbid it; and the other with an U and an R, for Uti rogas, or Be it as you desire.

rendered them secret towards the close of the republic were the cause of its decline. But as this is differently practised in different republics, I shall offer here my thoughts concerning this subject.

The people's suffrages ought doubtless to be public;[1] and this should be considered as a fundamental law of democracy. The lower class ought to be directed by those of higher rank, and restrained within bounds by the gravity of eminent personages. Hence, by rendering the suffrages secret in the Roman republic, all was lost; it was no longer possible to direct a populace that sought its own destruction. But when the body of the nobles are to vote in an aristocracy,[2] or in a democracy the senate,[3] as the business is then only to prevent intrigues, the suffrages cannot be too secret.

Intriguing in a senate is dangerous; it is dangerous also in a body of nobles; but not so among the people, whose nature is to act through passion. In countries where they have no share in the government, we often see them as much inflamed on account of an actor as ever they could be for the welfare of the state. The misfortune of a republic is when intrigues are at an end; which happens when the people are gained by bribery and corruption: in this case they grow indifferent to public affairs, and avarice becomes their predominant passion. Unconcerned about the government and everything belonging to it, they quietly wait for their hire.

It is likewise a fundamental law in democracies, that the people should have the sole power to enact laws. And yet there are a thousand occasions on which it is necessary the senate should have the power of decreeing; nay, it is frequently proper to make some trial of a law before it is established. The constitutions of Rome and Athens were excellent. The decrees of the senate[4] had the force of laws for the space of a year, but did not become perpetual till they were ratified by the consent of the people.

3. *Of the Laws in relation to the Nature of Aristocracy.* In an aristocracy the supreme power is lodged in the hands of a certain number of persons. These are invested both with the legislative and executive authority; and the rest of the people are, in respect to them, the same as the subjects of a monarchy in regard to the sovereign.

They do not vote here by lot, for this would be productive of inconveniences only. And indeed, in a government where the most mortifying distinctions are already established, though they were to be chosen by lot, still they would not cease to be odious; it is the nobleman they envy, and not the magistrate.

When the nobility are numerous, there must be a senate to regulate the affairs which the body of the nobles are incapable of deciding, and to prepare others for their decision. In this case it may be said that the aristocracy is in some measure in the senate, the democracy in the body of the nobles, and the people are a cipher.

It would be a very happy thing in an aristocracy if the people, in some measure, could be raised from their state of annihilation. Thus at Genoa, the bank of St. George being administered by the people[5] gives them a certain influence in the government, whence their whole prosperity is derived.

The senators ought by no means to have the right of naming their own members; for this would be the only way to perpetuate abuses. At Rome, which in its early years was a kind of aristocracy, the senate did not fill up the vacant places in their own body; the new members were nominated by the censors.[6]

In a republic, the sudden rise of a private citizen to exorbitant power produces monarchy, or something more than monarchy. In the latter the laws have provided for, or in some measure adapted themselves to, the constitution; and the principle of government checks the monarch: but in a republic, where a private citizen has obtained an exorbitant power,[7] the abuse of this power is much greater, because the laws foresaw it not, and consequently made no provision against it.

There is an exception to this rule, when the constitution is such as to have immediate need of a magistrate invested with extraordinary power. Such was Rome with her dictators, such is Venice with her state inquisitors; these are formidable magistrates, who restore,

[1] At Athens the people used to lift up their hands.
[2] As at Venice.
[3] The thirty tyrants at Athens ordered the suffrages of the *Areopagites* to be public, in order to manage them as they pleased.—Lysias, *Orat. contra Agorat.* 8.
[4] See Dionysius Halicarnassus, iv, ix.
[5] See Mr. Addison, *Travels to Italy,* p. 16.
[6] They were named at first by the consuls.
[7] This is what ruined the republic of Rome. See *Considerations on the Causes of the Grandeur and Decline of the Romans,* 14, 16.

as it were by violence, the state to its liberty. But how comes it that these magistracies are so very different in these two republics? It is because Rome supported the remains of her aristocracy against the people; whereas Venice employs her state inquisitors to maintain her aristocracy against the nobles. The consequence was that at Rome the dictatorship could be only of short duration, as the people acted through passion and not with design. It was necessary that a magistracy of this kind should be exercised with lustre and pomp, the business being to intimidate, and not to punish, the multitude. It was also proper that the dictator should be created only for some particular affair, and for this only should have an unlimited authority, as he was always created upon some sudden emergency. On the contrary, at Venice they have occasion for a permanent magistracy; for here it is that schemes may be set on foot, continued, suspended, and resumed; that the ambition of a single person becomes that of a family, and the ambition of one family that of many. They have occasion for a secret magistracy, the crimes they punish being hatched in secrecy and silence. This magistracy must have a general inquisition, for their business is not to remedy known disorders, but to prevent the unknown. In a word, the latter is designed to punish suspected crimes; whereas the former used rather menaces than punishment even for crimes that were openly avowed.

In all magistracies, the greatness of the power must be compensated by the brevity of the duration. This most legislators have fixed to a year; a longer space would be dangerous, and a shorter would be contrary to the nature of government. For who is it that in the management even of his domestic affairs would be thus confined? At Ragusa[1] the chief magistrate of the republic is changed every month, the other officers every week, and the governor of the castle every day. But this can take place only in a small republic environed[2] by formidable powers, who might easily corrupt such petty and insignificant magistrates.

The best aristocracy is that in which those who have no share in the legislature are so few and inconsiderable that the governing party have no interest in oppressing them. Thus when[3] Antipater made a law at Athens

that whosoever was not worth two thousand drachms should have no power to vote, he formed by this method the best aristocracy possible; because this was so small a sum as to exclude very few, and not one of any rank or consideration in the city.

Aristocratic families ought therefore, as much as possible, to level themselves in appearance with the people. The more an aristocracy borders on democracy, the nearer it approaches perfection: and, in proportion as it draws towards monarchy, the more is it imperfect.

But the most imperfect of all is that in which the part of the people that obeys is in a state of civil servitude to those who command, as the aristocracy of Poland, where the peasants are slaves to the nobility.

4. *Of the Relation of Laws to the Nature of Monarchical Government.* The intermediate, subordinate, and dependent powers constitute the nature of monarchical government; I mean of that in which a single person governs by fundamental laws. I said the intermediate, subordinate, and dependent powers. And indeed, in monarchies the prince is the source of all power, political and civil. These fundamental laws necessarily suppose the intermediate channels through which the power flows: for if there be only the momentary and capricious will of a single person to govern the state, nothing can be fixed, and of course there is no fundamental law.

The most natural, intermediate, and subordinate power is that of the nobility. This in some measure seems to be essential to a monarchy, whose fundamental maxim is: no monarch, no nobility; no nobility, no monarch; but there may be a despotic prince.

There are men who have endeavoured in some countries in Europe to suppress the jurisdiction of the nobility, not perceiving that they were driving at the very thing that was done by the parliament of England. Abolish the privileges of the lords, the clergy and cities in a monarchy, and you will soon have a popular state, or else a despotic government.

The courts of a considerable kingdom in Europe have, for many ages, been striking at the patrimonial jurisdiction of the lords and clergy. We do not pretend to censure these sage magistrates; but we leave it to the public to judge how far this may alter the constitution.

Far am I from being prejudiced in favour of the privileges of the clergy; however, I

[1] Tournefort, *Voyages.*
[2] At Lucca the magistrates are chosen only for two months.
[3] Diodorus, xviii, p. 601, ed. Rhodoman.

should be glad if their jurisdiction were once fixed. The question is not whether their jurisdiction was justly established; but whether it be really established; whether it constitutes a part of the laws of the country, and is in every respect in relation to those laws: whether between two powers acknowledged independent, the conditions ought not to be reciprocal; and whether it be not equally the duty of a good subject to defend the prerogative of the prince, and to maintain the limits which from time immemorial have been prescribed to his authority.

Though the ecclesiastic power be so dangerous in a republic, yet it is extremely proper in a monarchy, especially of the absolute kind. What would become of Spain and Portugal, since the subversion of their laws, were it not for this only barrier against the incursions of arbitrary power? A barrier ever useful when there is no other: for since a despotic government is productive of the most dreadful calamities to human nature, the very evil that restrains it is beneficial to the subject.

In the same manner as the ocean, threatening to overflow the whole earth, is stopped by weeds and pebbles that lie scattered along the shore, so monarchs, whose power seems unbounded, are restrained by the smallest obstacles, and suffer their natural pride to be subdued by supplication and prayer.

The English, to favour their liberty, have abolished all the intermediate powers of which their monarchy was composed. They have a great deal of reason to be jealous of this liberty; were they ever to be so unhappy as to lose it, they would be one of the most servile nations upon earth.

Mr. Law, through ignorance both of a republican and monarchical constitution, was one of the greatest promoters of absolute power ever known in Europe. Besides the violent and extraordinary changes owing to his direction, he would fain suppress all the intermediate ranks, and abolish the political communities. He was dissolving[1] the monarchy by his chimerical reimbursements, and seemed as if he even wanted to redeem the constitution.

It is not enough to have intermediate powers in a monarchy; there must be also a depositary of the laws. This depositary can only be the judges of the supreme courts of justice, who promulgate the new laws, and revive the

obsolete. The natural ignorance of the nobility, their indolence and contempt of civil government, require that there should be a body invested with the power of reviving and executing the laws, which would be otherwise buried in oblivion. The prince's council are not a proper depositary. They are naturally the depositary of the momentary will of the prince, and not of the fundamental laws. Besides, the prince's council is continually changing; it is neither permanent nor numerous; neither has it a sufficient share of the confidence of the people; consequently it is capable of setting them right in difficult conjunctures, or of reducing them to proper obedience.

Despotic governments, where there are no fundamental laws, have no such kind of depositary. Hence it is that religion has generally so much influence in those countries, because it forms a kind of permanent depositary; and if this cannot be said of religion, it may of the customs that are respected instead of laws.

5. *Of the Laws in relation to the Nature of a despotic Government.* From the nature of despotic power it follows that the single person, invested with this power, commits the execution of it also to a single person. A man whom his senses continually inform that he himself is everything and that his subjects are nothing, is naturally lazy, voluptuous, and ignorant. In consequence of this, he neglects the management of public affairs. But were he to commit the administration to many, there would be continual disputes among them; each would form intrigues to be his first slave; and he would be obliged to take the reins into his own hands. It is, therefore, more natural for him to resign it to a vizir,[2] and to invest him with the same power as himself. The creation of a vizir is a fundamental law of this government.

It is related of a pope that he had started an infinite number of difficulties against his election, from a thorough conviction of his incapacity. At length he was prevailed on to accept of the pontificate, and resigned the administration entirely to his nephew. He was soon struck with surprise, and said, "I should never have thought that these things were so easy." The same may be said of the princes of the East, who, being educated in a prison

---

[1] Ferdinand, king of Aragon, made himself grand master of the orders, and that alone changed the constitution.

[2] The Eastern kings are never without vizirs. says Sir John Chardin.

where eunuchs corrupt their hearts and debase their understandings, and where they are frequently kept ignorant even of their high rank, when drawn forth in order to be placed on the throne, are at first confounded: but as soon as they have chosen a vizir, and abandoned themselves in their seraglio to the most brutal passions; pursuing, in the midst of a prostituted court, every capricious extravagance, they would never have dreamed that they could find matters so easy.

The more extensive the empire, the larger the seraglio; and consequently the more voluptuous the prince. Hence the more nations such a sovereign has to rule, the less he attends to the cares of government; the more important his affairs, the less he makes them the subject of his deliberations.

BOOK III. OF THE PRINCIPLES OF THE THREE KINDS OF GOVERNMENT

1. *Difference between the Nature and Principle of Government.* Having examined the laws in relation to the nature of each government, we must investigate those which relate to its principle.

There is this difference between the nature and principle[1] of government, that the former is that by which it is constituted, the latter that by which it is made to act. One is its particular structure, and the other the human passions which set it in motion.

Now, laws ought no less to relate to the principle than to the nature of each government. We must, therefore, inquire into this principle, which shall be the subject of this third book.

2. *Of the Principle of different Governments.* I have already observed that it is the nature of a republican government that either the collective body of the people, or particular families, should be possessed of the supreme power; of a monarchy, that the prince should have this power, but in the execution of it should be directed by established laws; of a despotic government, that a single person should rule according to his own will and caprice. This enables me to discover their three principles; which are thence naturally derived. I shall begin with a republican government, and in particular with that of democracy.

3. *Of the Principle of Democracy.* There is no great share of probity necessary to support a monarchical or despotic government. The force of laws in one, and the prince's arm in the other, are sufficient to direct and maintain the whole. But in a popular state, one spring more is necessary, namely, virtue.

What I have here advanced is confirmed by the unanimous testimony of historians, and is extremely agreeable to the nature of things. For it is clear that in a monarchy, where he who commands the execution of the laws generally thinks himself above them, there is less need of virtue than in a popular government, where the person entrusted with the execution of the laws is sensible of his being subject to their direction.

Clear is it also that a monarch who, through bad advice or indolence, ceases to enforce the execution of the laws, may easily repair the evil; he has only to follow other advice; or to shake off this indolence. But when, in a popular government, there is a suspension of the laws, as this can proceed only from the corruption of the republic, the state is certainly undone.

A very droll spectacle it was in the last century to behold the impotent efforts of the English towards the establishment of democracy. As they who had a share in the direction of public affairs were void of virtue; as their ambition was inflamed by the success of the most daring of their members;[2] as the prevailing parties were successively animated by the spirit of faction, the government was continually changing: the people, amazed at so many revolutions, in vain attempted to erect a commonwealth. At length, when the country had undergone the most violent shocks, they were obliged to have recourse to the very government which they had so wantonly proscribed.

When Sylla thought of restoring Rome to her liberty, this unhappy city was incapable of receiving that blessing. She had only the feeble remains of virtue, which were continually diminishing. Instead of being roused from her lethargy by Cæsar, Tiberius, Caius Claudius, Nero, and Domitian, she riveted ev-

[1] This is a very important distinction, whence I shall draw many consequences; for it is the key of an infinite number of laws.

[2] Cromwell.

ery day her chains; if she struck some blows, her aim was at the tyrant, not at the tyranny.

The politic Greeks, who lived under a popular government, knew no other support than virtue. The modern inhabitants of that country are entirely taken up with manufacture, commerce, finances, opulence, and luxury.

When virtue is banished, ambition invades the minds of those who are disposed to receive it, and avarice possesses the whole community. The objects of their desires are changed; what they were fond of before has become indifferent; they were free while under the restraint of laws, but they would fain now be free to act against law; and as each citizen is like a slave who has run away from his master, that which was a maxim of equity he calls rigour; that which was a rule of action he styles constraint; and to precaution he gives the name of fear. Frugality, and not the thirst of gain, now passes for avarice. Formerly the wealth of individuals constituted the public treasure; but now this has become the patrimony of private persons. The members of the commonwealth riot on the public spoils, and its strength is only the power of a few, and the licence of many.

Athens was possessed of the same number of forces when she triumphed so gloriously as when with such infamy she was enslaved. She had twenty thousand citizens,[1] when she defended the Greeks against the Persians, when she contended for empire with Sparta, and invaded Sicily. She had twenty thousand when Demetrius Phalereus numbered them,[2] as slaves are told by the head in a market-place. When Philip attempted to lord it over Greece, and appeared at the gates of Athens,[3] she had even then lost nothing but time. We may see in Demosthenes how difficult it was to awaken her; she dreaded Philip, not as the enemy of her liberty, but of her pleasures.[4] This famous city, which had withstood so many defeats, and having been so often destroyed had as often risen out of her ashes, was overthrown at Chæronea, and at one blow deprived of all hopes of resource. What does it avail her that Philip sends back her prisoners, if he does not

[1] Plutarch, *Pericles;* Plato, in *Critias.*
[2] She had at that time twenty-one thousand citizens, ten thousand strangers, and four hundred thousand slaves. See Athenæus, vi.
[3] She had then twenty thousand citizens. See Demosthenes in *Aristog.*
[4] They had passed a law, which rendered it a capital crime for any one to propose applying the money designed for the theatres to military service.

return her men? It was ever after as easy to triumph over the forces of Athens as it had been difficult to subdue her virtue.

How was it possible for Carthage to maintain her ground? When Hannibal, upon his being made prætor, endeavoured to hinder the magistrates from plundering the republic, did not they complain of him to the Romans? Wretches, who would fain be citizens without a city, and be beholden for their riches to their very destroyers! Rome soon insisted upon having three hundred of their principal citizens as hostages; she obliged them next to surrender their arms and ships; and then she declared war.[5] From the desperate efforts of this defenceless city, one may judge of what she might have performed in her full vigour, and assisted by virtue.

4. *Of the Principle of Aristocracy.* As virtue is necessary in a popular government, it is requisite also in an aristocracy. True it is that in the latter it is not so absolutely requisite.

The people, who in respect to the nobility are the same as the subjects with regard to a monarch, are restrained by their laws. They have, therefore, less occasion for virtue than the people in a democracy. But how are the nobility to be restrained? They who are to execute the laws against their colleagues will immediately perceive that they are acting against themselves. Virtue is therefore necessary in this body, from the very nature of the constitution.

An aristocratic government has an inherent vigour, unknown to democracy. The nobles form a body, who by their prerogative, and for their own particular interest, restrain the people; it is sufficient that there are laws in being to see them executed.

But easy as it may be for the body of the nobles to restrain the people, it is difficult to restrain themselves.[6] Such is the nature of this constitution, that it seems to subject the very same persons to the power of the laws, and at the same time to exempt them.

Now such a body as this can restrain itself only in two ways; either by a very eminent virtue, which puts the nobility in some measure on a level with the people, and may be the means of forming a great republic; or by an inferior virtue, which puts them at least upon

[5] This lasted three years.
[6] Public crimes may be punished, because it is here a common concern; but private crimes will go unpunished, because it is the common interest not to punish them.

a level with one another, and upon this their preservation depends.

Moderation is therefore the very soul of this government; a moderation, I mean, founded on virtue, not that which proceeds from indolence and pusillanimity.

5. *That Virtue is not the Principle of a Monarchical Government.* In monarchies, policy effects great things with as little virtue as possible. Thus in the nicest machines, art has reduced the number of movements, springs, and wheels.

The state subsists independently of the love of our country, of the thirst of true glory, of self-denial, of the sacrifice of our dearest interests, and of all those heroic virtues which we admire in the ancients, and to us are known only by tradition.

The laws supply here the place of those virtues; they are by no means wanted, and the state dispenses with them: an action performed here in secret is in some measure of no consequence.

Though all crimes be in their own nature public, yet there is a distinction between crimes really public and those that are private, which are so called because they are more injurious to individuals than to the community. Now in republics private crimes are more public, that is, they attack the constitution more than they do individuals; and in monarchies, public crimes are more private, that is, they are more prejudicial to private people than to the constitution.

I beg that no one will be offended with what I have been saying; my observations are founded on the unanimous testimony of historians. I am not ignorant that virtuous princes are so very rare; but I venture to affirm that in a monarchy it is extremely difficult for the people to be virtuous.[1]

Let us compare what the historians of all ages have asserted concerning the courts of monarchs; let us recollect the conversations and sentiments of people of all countries, in respect to the wretched character of courtiers, and we shall find that these are not airy speculations, but truths confirmed by a sad and melancholy experience.

Ambition in idleness; meanness mixed with pride; a desire of riches without industry;

[1] I speak here of political virtue, which is also moral virtue as it is directed to the public good; very little of private moral virtue, and not at all of that virtue which relates to revealed truths. This will appear better in v. 2.

aversion to truth; flattery, perfidy, violation of engagements, contempt of civil duties, fear of the prince's virtue, hope from his weakness, but, above all, a perpetual ridicule cast upon virtue, are, I think, the characteristics by which most courtiers in all ages and countries have been constantly distinguished. Now, it is exceedingly difficult for the leading men of the nation to be knaves, and the inferior sort to be honest; for the former to be cheats, and the latter to rest satisfied with being only dupes.

But if there should chance to be some unlucky honest man[2] among the people, Cardinal Richelieu, in his political testament, seems to hint that a prince should take care not to employ him.[3] So true is it that virtue is not the spring of this government! It is not indeed excluded, but it is not the spring of government.

6. *In what Manner Virtue is supplied in a Monarchical Government.* But it is high time for me to have done with this subject, lest I should be suspected of writing a satire against monarchical government. Far be it from me; if monarchy wants one spring, it is provided with another. Honour, that is, the prejudice of every person and rank, supplies the place of the political virtue of which I have been speaking, and is everywhere her representative: here it is capable of inspiring the most glorious actions, and, joined with the force of laws, may lead us to the end of government as well as virtue itself.

Hence, in well-regulated monarchies, they are almost all good subjects, and very few good men; for to be a good man,[4] a good intention is necessary,[5] and we should love our country, not so much on our own account, as out of regard to the community.

7. *Of the Principle of Monarchy.* A monarchical government supposes, as we have already observed, pre-eminences and ranks, as likewise a noble descent. Now since it is the nature of honour to aspire to preferments and titles, it is properly placed in this government.

Ambition is pernicious in a republic. But in a monarchy it has some good effects; it gives life to the government, and is attended with

[2] This is to be understood in the sense of the preceding note.
[3] We must not, says he, employ people of mean extraction; they are too rigid and morose.—*Testament Polit.*, 4.
[4] This word *good man* is understood here in a political sense only.
[5] *See* Footnote 1.

this advantage, that it is in no way dangerous, because it may be continually checked.

It is with this kind of government as with the system of the universe, in which there is a power that constantly repels all bodies from the centre, and a power of gravitation that attracts them to it. Honour sets all the parts of the body politic in motion, and by its very action connects them; thus each individual advances the public good, while he only thinks of promoting his own interest.

True it is that, philosophically speaking, it is a false honour which moves all the parts of the government; but even this false honour is as useful to the public as true honour could possibly be to private persons.

Is it not very exacting to oblige men to perform the most difficult actions, such as require an extraordinary exertion of fortitude and resolution, without other recompense than that of glory and applause?

8. *That Honour is not the Principle of Despotic Government.* Honour is far from being the principle of despotic government: mankind being here all upon a level, no one person can prefer himself to another; and as on the other hand they are all slaves, they can give themselves no sort of preference.

Besides, as honour has its laws and rules, as it knows not how to submit; as it depends in a great measure on a man's own caprice, and not on that of another person; it can be found only in countries in which the constitution is fixed, and where they are governed by settled laws.

How can despotism abide with honour? The one glories in the contempt of life; and the other is founded on the power of taking it away. How can honour, on the other hand, bear with despotism? The former has its fixed rules, and peculiar caprices; but the latter is directed by no rule, and its own caprices are subversive of all others.

Honour, therefore, a thing unknown in arbitrary governments, some of which have not even a proper word to express it,[1] is the prevailing principle in monarchies; here it gives life to the whole body politic, to the laws, and even to the virtues themselves.

9. *Of the Principle of Despotic Government.* As virtue is necessary in a republic, and in a monarchy honour, so fear is necessary in a despotic government: with regard to virtue, there

[1] See Perry, p. 447.

is no occasion for it, and honour would be extremely dangerous.

Here the immense power of the prince devolves entirely upon those whom he is pleased to entrust with the administration. Persons capable of setting a value upon themselves would be likely to create disturbances. Fear must therefore depress their spirits, and extinguish even the least sense of ambition.

A moderate government may, whenever it pleases, and without the least danger, relax its springs. It supports itself by the laws, and by its own internal strength. But when a despotic prince ceases for one single moment to uplift his arm, when he cannot instantly demolish those whom he has entrusted with the first employments,[2] all is over: for as fear, the spring of this government, no longer subsists, the people are left without a protector.

It is probably in this sense the Cadis maintained that the Grand Seignior was not obliged to keep his word or oath, when he limited thereby his authority.[3]

It is necessary that the people should be judged by laws, and the great men by the caprice of the prince, that the lives of the lowest subject should be safe, and the pasha's head ever in danger. We cannot mention these monstrous governments without horror. The Sophi of Persia, dethroned in our days by Mahomet, the son of Miriveis, saw the constitution subverted before this resolution, because he had been too sparing of blood.[4]

History informs us that the horrid cruelties of Domitian struck such a terror into the governors that the people recovered themselves a little during his reign.[5] Thus a torrent overflows one side of a country, and on the other leaves fields untouched, where the eye is refreshed by the prospect of fine meadows.

10. *Difference of Obedience in Moderate and Despotic Governments.* In despotic states, the nature of government requires the most passive obedience; and when once the prince's will is made known, it ought infallibly to produce its effect.

Here they have no limitations or restrictions, no mediums, terms, equivalents, or re-

[2] As it often happens in a military aristocracy.
[3] Ricaut on the Ottoman Empire. I, ii.
[4] See the history of this revolution by Father du Cerceau.
[5] Suetonius, *Life of Domitian*, viii. His was a military constitution, which is one of the species of despotic government.

monstrances; no change to propose: man is a creature that blindly submits to the absolute will of the sovereign.

In a country like this they are no more allowed to represent their apprehensions of a future danger than to impute their miscarriage to the capriciousness of fortune. Man's portion here, like that of beasts, is instinct, compliance, and punishment.

Little does it then avail to plead the sentiments of nature, filial respect, conjugal or parental tenderness, the laws of honour, or want of health; the order is given, and, that is sufficient.

In Persia, when the king has condemned a person, it is no longer lawful to mention his name, or to intercede in his favour. Even if the prince were intoxicated, or *non compos*, the decree must be executed;[1] otherwise he would contradict himself, and the law admits of no contradiction. This has been the way of thinking in that country in all ages; as the order which Ahasuerus gave, to exterminate the Jews, could not be revoked, they were allowed the liberty of defending themselves.

One thing, however, may be sometimes opposed to the prince's will,[2] namely, religion. They will abandon, nay they will slay a parent, if the prince so commands; but he cannot oblige them to drink wine. The laws of religion are of a superior nature, because they bind the sovereign as well as the subject. But with respect to the law of nature, it is other-wise; the prince is no longer supposed to be a man.

In monarchical and moderate states, the power is limited by its very spring, I mean by honour, which, like a monarch, reigns over the prince and his people. They will not allege to their sovereign the laws of religion; a courtier would be apprehensive of rendering himself ridiculous. But the laws of honour will be appealed to on all occasions. Hence arise the restrictions necessary to obedience; honour is naturally subject to whims, by which the subject's submission will be ever directed.

Though the manner of obeying be different in these two kinds of government, the power is the same. On which side soever the monarch turns, he inclines the scale, and is obeyed. The whole difference is that in a monarchy the prince receives instruction, at the same time that his ministers have greater abilities, and are more versed in public affairs, than the ministers of a despotic government.

11. *Reflections on the preceding Chapters.* Such are the principles of the three sorts of government: which does not imply that in a particular republic they actually are, but that they ought to be, virtuous; nor does it prove that in a particular monarchy they are actuated by honour, or in a particular despotic government by fear; but that they ought to be directed by these principles, otherwise the government is imperfect.

Book IV. That the Laws of Education Ought to be in Relation to the Principles of Government

1. *Of the Laws of Education.* The laws of education are the first impressions we receive; and as they prepare us for civil life, every private family ought to be governed by the plan of that great household which comprehends them all.

If the people in general have a principle, their constituent parts, that is, the several families, will have one also. The laws of education will be therefore different in each species of government: in monarchies they will have honour for their object; in republics, virtue; in despotic governments, fear.

2. *Of Education in Monarchies.* In monarchies the principal branch of education is not

[1] See Sir John Chardin.
[2] *Ibid.*

taught in colleges or academies. It commences, in some measure, at our setting out in the world; for this is the school of what we call honour, that universal preceptor which ought everywhere to be our guide.

Here it is that we constantly hear three rules or maxims, viz., that we should have a certain nobleness in our virtues, a kind of frankness in our morals, and a particular politeness in our behaviour.

The virtues we are here taught are less what we owe to others than to ourselves; they are not so much what draws us towards society, as what distinguishes us from our fellow-citizens.

Here the actions of men are judged, not as virtuous, but as shining; not as just, but as great; not as reasonable, but as extraordinary.

When honour here meets with anything noble in our actions, it is either a judge that approves them, or sophist by whom they are excused.

It allows of gallantry when united with the idea of sensible affection, or with that of conquest; this is the reason why we never meet with so strict a purity of morals in monarchies as in republican governments.

It allows of cunning and craft, when joined with the notion of greatness of soul or importance of affairs; as, for instance, in politics, with finesses of which it is far from being offended.

It does not forbid adulation, save when separated from the idea of a large fortune, and connected only with the sense of our mean condition.

With regard to morals, I have observed that the education of monarchies ought to admit of a certain frankness and open carriage. Truth, therefore, in conversation is here a necessary point. But is it for the sake of truth? By no means. Truth is requisite only because a person habituated to veracity has an air of boldness and freedom. And indeed a man of this stamp seems to lay a stress only on the things themselves, not on the manner in which they are received.

Hence it is that in proportion as this kind of frankness is commended, that of the common people is despised, which has nothing but truth and simplicity for its object.

In fine, the education of monarchies requires a certain politeness of behaviour. Man, a sociable animal, is formed to please in society; and a person that would break through the rules of decency, so as to shock those he conversed with, would lose the public esteem, and become incapable of doing any good.

But politeness, generally speaking, does not derive its origin from so pure a source. It arises from a desire of distinguishing ourselves. It is pride that renders us polite; we are flattered with being taken notice of for behaviour that shows we are not of a mean condition, and that we have not been bred with those who in all ages are considered the scum of the people.

Politeness, in monarchies, is naturalised at court. One man excessively great renders everybody else little. Hence that regard which is paid to our fellow-subjects; hence that politeness, equally pleasing to those by whom, as to those towards whom, it is practised, because it gives people to understand that a person actually belongs, or at least deserves to belong, to the court.

A courtly air consists in quitting a real for a borrowed greatness. The latter pleases the courtier more than the former. It inspires him with a certain disdainful modesty, which shows itself externally, but whose pride insensibly diminishes in proportion to its distance from the source of this greatness.

At court we find a delicacy of taste in everything—a delicacy arising from the constant use of the superfluities of life, from the variety, and especially the satiety, of pleasures, from the multiplicity and even confusion of fancies, which, if they are but agreeable, are sure of being well received.

These are the things which properly fall within the province of education, in order to form what we call a man of honour, a man possessed of all the qualities and virtues requisite in this kind of government.

Here it is that honour interferes with everything, mixing even with people's manner of thinking, and directing their very principles.

To this whimsical honour it is owing that the virtues are only just what it pleases; it adds rules of its own invention to everything prescribed to us; it extends or limits our duties according to its own fancy, whether they proceed from religion, politics, or morality.

There is nothing so strongly inculcated in monarchies, by the laws, by religion and honour, as submission to the prince's will; but this very honour tells us that the prince never ought to command a dishonourable action, because this would render us incapable of serving him.

Crillon refused to assassinate the Duke of Guise, but offered to fight him. After the massacre of St. Bartholomew, Charles IX, having sent orders to the governors in the several provinces for the Huguenots to be murdered, Viscount Dorte, who commanded at Bayonne, wrote thus to the king:[1] "Sire, among the inhabitants of this town, and your majesty's troops, I could not find so much as one executioner; they are honest citizens and brave soldiers. We jointly, therefore, beseech your majesty to command our arms and lives in things that are practicable." This great and generous soul looked upon a base action as a thing impossible.

There is nothing that honour more strongly recommends to the nobility than to serve their prince in a military capacity. And, indeed, this is their favourite profession, because its dangers, its success, and even its miscarriages are the road to grandeur. Yet this very law of its

[1] See d'Aubigny's *History*.

own making honour chooses to explain: and in case of any affront, it requires or permits us to retire.

It insists also that we should be at liberty either to seek or to reject employments, a liberty which it prefers even to an ample fortune.

Honour therefore has its supreme laws, to which education is obliged to conform.[1] The chief of these are that we are permitted to set a value upon our fortune, but are absolutely forbidden to set any upon our lives.

The second is that, when we are raised to a post or preferment, we should never do or permit anything which may seem to imply that we look upon ourselves as inferior to the rank we hold.

The third is that those things which honour forbids are more rigorously forbidden, when the laws do not concur in the prohibition; and those it commands are more strongly insisted upon, when they happen not to be commanded by law.

3. *Of Education in a Despotic Government.* As education in monarchies tends to raise and ennoble the mind, in despotic governments its only aim is to debase it. Here it must necessarily be servile; even in power such an education will be an advantage, because every tyrant is at the same time a slave.

Excessive obedience supposes ignorance in the person that obeys: the same it supposes in him that commands, for he has no occasion to deliberate, to doubt, to reason; he has only to will.

In despotic states, each house is a separate government. As education, therefore, consists chiefly in social converse, it must be here very much limited; all it does is to strike the heart with fear, and to imprint on the understanding a very simple notion of a few principles of religion. Learning here proves dangerous, emulation fatal; and as to virtue, Aristotle[2] cannot think that there is any one virtue belonging to slaves; if so, education in despotic countries is confined within a very narrow compass.

Here, therefore, education is in some measure needless: to give something, one must take away everything, and begin with making a bad subject in order to make a good slave.

---

[1] We mention here what actually is, and not what ought to be; honour is a prejudice, which religion sometimes endeavours to remove, and at other times to regulate.

[2] *Politics,* i. 13.

For why should education take pains in forming a good citizen, only to make him share in the public misery? If he loves his country, he will strive to relax the springs of government; if he miscarries he will be undone; if he succeeds, he must expose himself, the prince, and his country to ruin.

4. *Difference between the Effects of Ancient and Modern Education.* Most of the ancients lived under governments that had virtue for their principle; and when this was in full vigour they performed actions unusual in our times, and at which our narrow minds are astonished.

Another advantage their education possessed over ours was that it never could be effaced by contrary impressions. Epaminondas, the last year of his life, said, heard, beheld, and performed the very same things as at the age in which he received the first principles of his education.

In our days we receive three different or contrary educations, namely, of our parents, of our masters, and of the world. What we learn in the latter effaces all the ideas of the former. This, in some measure, arises from the contrast we experience between our religious and worldly engagements, a thing unknown to the ancients.

5. *Of Education in a Republican Government.* It is in a republican government that the whole power of education is required. The fear of despotic governments naturally arises of itself amidst threats and punishments; the honour of monarchies is favoured by the passions, and favours them in its turn; but virtue is a self-renunciation, which is ever arduous and painful.

This virtue may be defined as the love of the laws and of our country. As such love requires a constant preference of public to private interest, it is the source of all private virtues; for they are nothing more than this very preference itself.

This love is peculiar to democracies. In these alone the government is entrusted to private citizens. Now a government is like everything else: to preserve it we must love it.

Has it ever been known that kings were not fond of monarchy, or that despotic princes hated arbitrary power?

Everything therefore depends on establishing this love in a republic; and to inspire it ought to be the principal business of education: but the surest way of instilling it into children is for parents to set them an example.

People have it generally in their power to communicate their ideas to their children; but they are still better able to transfuse their passions.

If it happens otherwise, it is because the impressions made at home are effaced by those they have received abroad.

It is not the young people that degenerate; they are not spoiled till those of maturer age are already sunk into corruption.

6. *Of some Institutions among the Greeks.* The ancient Greeks, convinced of the necessity that people who live under a popular government should be trained up to virtue, made very singular institutions in order to inspire it. Upon seeing in the life of Lycurgus the laws that legislator gave to the Lacedæmonians, I imagine I am reading the history of the Sevarambes. The laws of Crete were the model of those of Sparta; and those of Plato reformed them.

Let us reflect here a little on the extensive genius with which those legislators must have been endowed, to perceive that by striking at received customs, and by confounding all manner of virtues, they should display their wisdom to the universe. Lycurgus, by blending theft with the spirit of justice, the hardest servitude with excess of liberty, the most rigid sentiments with the greatest moderation, gave stability to his city. He seemed to deprive her of all resources, such as arts, commerce, money, and walls; ambition prevailed among the citizens without hopes of improving their fortune; they had natural sentiments without the tie of a son, husband, or father; and chastity was stripped even of modesty and shame. This was the road that led Sparta to grandeur and glory; and so infallible were these institutions, that it signified nothing to gain a victory over that republic without subverting her polity.[1]

By these laws Crete and Laconia were governed. Sparta was the last that fell a prey to the Macedonians, and Crete to the Romans.[2]

The Samnites had the same institutions, which furnished those very Romans with the subject of four-and-twenty triumphs.[3]

A character so extraordinary in the institutions of Greece has shown itself lately in the dregs and corruptions of modern times.[4] A very honest legislator has formed a people to whom probity seems as natural as bravery to the Spartans. Mr. Penn is a real Lycurgus: and though the former made peace his principal aim, as the latter did war, yet they resemble one another in the singular way of living to which they reduced their people, in the ascendant they had over free men, in the prejudices they overcame, and in the passions which they subdued.

Another example we have from Paraguay. This has been the subject of an invidious charge against a society that considers the pleasure of commanding as the only happiness in life: but it will be ever a glorious undertaking to render a government subservient to human happiness.[5]

It is glorious indeed for this society to have been the first in pointing out to those countries the idea of religion joined with that of humanity. By repairing the devastations of the Spaniards, she has begun to heal one of the most dangerous wounds that the human species ever received.

An exquisite sensibility to whatever she distinguishes by the name of honour, joined to her zeal for a religion which is far more humbling in respect to those who receive than to those who preach its doctrines, has set her upon vast undertakings, which she has accomplished with success. She has drawn wild people from their woods, secured them a maintenance, and clothed their nakedness; and had she only by this step improved the industry of mankind, it would have been sufficient to eternise her fame.

They who shall attempt hereafter to introduce like institutions must establish the community of goods as prescribed in Plato's republic; that high respect he required for the gods; that separation from strangers, for the preservation of morals; and an extensive commerce carried on by the community, and not by private citizens: they must give our arts

[1] Philopœmen obliged the Lacedæmonians to change their manner of educating their children, being convinced that if he did not take this measure they would always be noted for their magnanimity.—Plutarch, *Philopœmen*. See Livy, xxxviii.

[2] She defended her laws and liberty for the space of three years. See the 98th, 99th, and 100th book of Livy, in Florus's epitome. She made a braver resistance than the greatest kings.

[3] Florus, i. 16.

[4] *In fece Romuli.*—Cicero, *Letters to Atticus*, ii. 1.

[5] The Indians of Paraguay do not depend on any particular lord; they pay only a fifth of the taxes, and are allowed the use of firearms to defend themselves.

without our luxury, and our wants without our desires.

They must proscribe money, the effects of which are to swell people's fortunes beyond the bounds prescribed by nature; to learn to preserve for no purpose what has been idly hoarded up; to multiply without end our desires; and to supply the sterility of nature, from whom we have received very scanty means of inflaming our passions, and of corrupting each other.

"The Epidamnians,[1] perceiving their morals depraved by conversing with barbarians, chose a magistrate for making all contracts and sales in the name and behalf of the city." Commerce then does not corrupt the constitution, and the constitution does not deprive society of the advantages of commerce.

7. *In what Cases these singular Institutions may be of Service.* Institutions of this kind may be proper in republics, because they have virtue for their principle; but to excite men to honour in monarchies, or to inspire fear in despotic governments, less trouble is necessary.

Besides, they can take place but in a small state,[2] in which there is a possibility of general education, and of training up the body of the people like a single family.

The laws of Minos, of Lycurgus, and of Plato suppose a particular attention and care, which the citizens ought to have over one another's conduct. But an attention of this kind cannot be expected in the confusion and multitude of affairs in which a large nation is entangled.

In institutions of this kind, money, as we have above observed, must be banished. But in great societies, the multiplicity, variety, embarrassment, and importance of affairs, as well as the facility of purchasing, and the slowness of exchange, require a common measure. In order to support or extend our power, we must be possessed of the means to which, by the unanimous consent of mankind, this power is annexed.

8. *Explanation of a Paradox of the Ancients in respect to Manners.* That judicious writer, Polybius, informs us that music was necessary to soften the manners of the Arcadians, who lived in a cold, gloomy country; that the inhabitants of Cynete, who slighted music, were the cruellest of all the Greeks, and that no other town was so immersed in luxury and debauchery. Plato[3] is not afraid to affirm that there is no possibility of making a change in music without altering the frame of government. Aristotle, who seems to have written his *Politics* only in order to contradict Plato, agrees with him, notwithstanding, in regard to the power and influence of music over the manners of the people.[4] This was also the opinion of Theophrastus, of Plutarch,[5] and of all the ancients—an opinion grounded on mature reflection; being one of the principles of their polity.[6] Thus it was they enacted laws, and thus they required that cities should be governed.

This I fancy must be explained in the following manner. It is observable that in the cities of Greece, especially those whose principal object was war, all lucrative arts and professions were considered unworthy of a freeman. "Most arts," says Xenophon,[7] "corrupt and enervate the bodies of those that exercise them; they oblige them to sit in the shade, or near the fire. They can find no leisure, either for their friends or for the republic." It was only by the corruption of some democracies that artisans became freemen. This we learn from Aristotle,[8] who maintains that a well-regulated republic will never give them the right and freedom of the city.[9]

Agriculture was likewise a servile profession, and generally practised by the inhabitants of conquered countries, such as the Helotes among the Lacedæmonians, the Periecians among the Cretans, the Penestes among the Thessalians, and other conquered[10]

---

[3] *Republic*, iv.   [4] *Politics*, viii. 5.   [5] *Pelopidas*.
[6] Plato, in his seventh book of *Laws*, says that the præfectures of music and gymnic exercises are the most important employments in the city; and, in his *Republic*, iii, Damon will tell you, says he, what sounds are capable of corrupting the mind with base sentiments, or of inspiring the contrary virtues.
[7] *Memorabilia*, v.   [8] *Politics*, iii. 4.
[9] Diophantes, says Aristotle, *Politics*, ii. 7, made a law formerly at Athens, that artisans should be slaves to the republic.
[10] Plato, likewise, and Aristotle require slaves to till the land, *Laws*, viii, *Politics*, vii. 10. True it is that agriculture was not everywhere exercised by slaves: on the contrary, Aristotle observes the best republics were those in which the citizens themselves tilled the land: but this was brought about by the corruption of the ancient governments, which had become democratic: for in earlier times the cities of Greece were subject to an aristocratic government.

[1] Plutarch in his *Questions Concerning the Greek Affairs*, xxix.
[2] Such as were formerly the cities of Greece.

people in other republics.

In fine, every kind of low commerce[1] was infamous among the Greeks; as it obliged a citizen to serve and wait on a slave, on a lodger, or a stranger. This was a notion that clashed with the spirit of Greek liberty; hence Plato[2] in his *Laws* orders a citizen to be punished if he attempts to concern himself with trade.

Thus in the Greek republics the magistrates were extremely embarrassed. They would not have the citizens apply themselves to trade, to agriculture, or to the arts, and yet they would not have them idle.[3] They found, therefore, employment for them in gymnic and military exercises; and none else were allowed by their institution.[4] Hence the Greeks must be considered as a society of wrestlers and boxers. Now, these exercises having a natural tendency to render people hardy and fierce, there was a necessity for tempering them with others that might soften their manners.[5] For this purpose, music, which influences the mind by means of the corporeal organs, was extremely proper. It is a kind of medium between manly exercises, which harden the body, and speculative sciences, which are apt to render us unsociable and sour. It cannot be said that music inspired virtue, for this would be inconceivable: but it prevented the effects of a savage institution, and enabled the soul to have such a share in the education as it could never have had without the assistance of harmony.

Let us suppose among ourselves a society of men so passionately fond of hunting as to make it their sole employment; they would doubtless contract thereby a kind of rusticity and fierceness. But if they happen to imbibe a taste for music, we should quickly perceive a sensible difference in their customs and manners. In short, the exercises used by the Greeks could raise but one kind of passions, viz., fierceness, indignation, and cruelty. But music excites all these; and is likewise able to inspire the soul with a sense of pity, lenity, tenderness, and love. Our moral writers, who declaim so vehemently against the stage, sufficiently demonstrate the power of music over the mind.

If the society above mentioned were to have no other music than that of drums, and the sound of the trumpet, would it not be more difficult to accomplish this end than by the more melting tones of softer harmony? The ancients were therefore in the right when, under particular circumstances, they preferred one mode to another in regard to manners.

But some will ask, why should music be pitched upon as preferable to any other entertainment? It is because of all sensible pleasures there is none that less corrupts the soul. We blush to read in Plutarch[6] that the Thebans, in order to soften the manners of their youth, authorised by law a passion which ought to be proscribed by all nations.

Book V. That the Laws Given by the Legislator Ought To Be in relation to the Principle of Government

1. *Idea of this Book*. That the laws of education should relate to the principle of each government has been shown in the preceding book. Now the same may be said of those which the legislator gives to the whole society. The relation of laws to this principle strengthens the several springs of government; and this principle derives thence, in its turn, a new degree of vigour. And thus it is in mechanics, that action is always followed by reaction.

Our design is, to examine this relation in each government, beginning with the republican state, the principle of which is virtue.

2. *What is meant by Virtue in a political State*. Virtue in a republic is a most simple thing: it is a love of the republic; it is a sensation, and not a consequence of acquired knowledge: a sensation that may be felt by the meanest as well as by the highest person in the state. When the common people adopt good maxims, they adhere to them more steadily than those whom we call gentlemen. It is very rarely that corruption commences with the former: nay, they frequently derive from their imperfect light a stronger attachment to the established laws and customs.

[1] *Cauponatio.*
[2] Book v.
[3] Aristotle, *Politics*, vii–viii.
[4] *Ibid.*, viii. 3.
[5] Aristotle observes that the children of the Lacedæmonians, who began these exercises at a very tender age, contracted thence too great a ferocity and rudeness of behaviour.—*Ibid.*, viii. 4.

[6] *Pelopidas.*

The love of our country is conducive to a purity of morals, and the latter is again conducive to the former. The less we are able to satisfy our private passions, the more we abandon ourselves to those of a general nature. How comes it that monks are so fond of their order? It is owing to the very cause that renders the order insupportable. Their rule debars them from all those things by which the ordinary passions are fed; there remains therefore only this passion for the very rule that torments them. The more austere it is, that is, the more it curbs their inclinations, the more force it gives to the only passion left them.

3. *What is meant by a Love of the Republic in a Democracy.* A love of the republic in a democracy is a love of the democracy; as the latter is that of equality.

A love of the democracy is likewise that of frugality. Since every individual ought here to enjoy the same happiness and the same advantages, they should consequently taste the same pleasures and form the same hopes, which cannot be expected but from a general frugality.

The love of equality in a democracy limits ambition to the sole desire, to the sole happiness, of doing greater services to our country than the rest of our fellow-citizens. They cannot all render her equal services, but they all ought to serve her with equal alacrity. At our coming into the world, we contract an immense debt to our country, which we can never discharge.

Hence distinctions here arise from the principle of equality, even when it seems to be removed by signal services or superior abilities.

The love of frugality limits the desire of having to the study of procuring necessaries to our family, and superfluities to our country. Riches give a power which a citizen cannot use for himself, for then he would be no longer equal. They likewise procure pleasures which he ought not to enjoy, because these would be also repugnant to the equality.

Thus well-regulated democracies, by establishing domestic frugality, made way at the same time for public expenses, as was the case at Rome and Athens, when magnificence and profusion arose from the very fund of frugality. And as religion commands us to have pure and unspotted hands when we make our offerings to the gods, the laws required a frugality of life to enable them to be liberal to our country.

The good sense and happiness of individuals depend greatly upon the mediocrity of their abilities and fortunes. Therefore, as a republic, where the laws have placed many in a middling station, is composed of wise men, it will be wisely governed; as it is composed of happy men, it will be extremely happy.

4. *In what Manner the Love of Equality and Frugality is inspired.* The love of equality and of a frugal economy is greatly excited by equality and frugality themselves, in societies where both these virtues are established by law.

In monarchies and despotic governments, nobody aims at equality; this does not so much as enter their thoughts; they all aspire to superiority. People of the very lowest condition desire to emerge from their obscurity, only to lord it over their fellow-subjects.

It is the same with respect to frugality. To love it, we must practise and enjoy it. It is not those who are enervated by pleasure that are fond of a frugal life; were this natural and common, Alcibiades would never have been the admiration of the universe. Neither is it those who envy or admire the luxury of the great; people that have present to their view none but rich men, or men miserable like themselves, detest their wretched condition, without loving or knowing the real term or point of misery.

A true maxim it is, therefore, that in order to love equality and frugality in a republic, these virtues must have been previously established by law.

5. *In what Manner the Laws establish Equality in a Democracy.* Some ancient legislators, as Lycurgus and Romulus, made an equal division of lands. A settlement of this kind can never take place except upon the foundation of a new republic; or when the old one is so corrupt, and the minds of the people are so disposed, that the poor think themselves obliged to demand, and the rich obliged to consent to a remedy of this nature.

If the legislator, in making a division of this kind, does not enact laws at the same time to support it, he forms only a temporary constitution; inequality will break in where the laws have not precluded it, and the republic will be utterly undone.

Hence for the preservation of this equality it is absolutely necessary there should be some regulation in respect to women's dowries, donations, successions, testamentary settlements, and all other forms of contracting. For were we once allowed to dispose of our property to whom and how we pleased, the will of each individual would disturb the order of the fundamental law.

Solon, by permitting the Athenians, upon failure of issue,[1] to leave their estates to whom they pleased, acted contrary to the ancient laws, by which the estates were ordered to continue in the family of the testator;[2] and even contrary to his own laws, for by abolishing debts he had aimed at equality.

The law which prohibited people having two inheritances[3] was extremely well adapted for a democracy. It derived its origin from the equal distribution of lands and portions made to each citizen. The law would not permit a single man to possess more than a single portion.

From the same source arose those laws by which the next relative was ordered to marry the heiress. This law was given to the Jews after the like distribution. Plato,[4] who grounds his laws on this division, made the same regulation which had been received as a law by the Athenians.

At Athens there was a law whose spirit, in my opinion, has not been hitherto rightly understood. It was lawful to marry a sister only by the father's side, but it was not permitted to espouse a sister by the same venter.[5] This custom was originally owing to republics, whose spirit would not permit that two portions of land, and consequently two inheritances, should devolve on the same person. A man who married his sister only by the father's side could inherit but one estate, namely, that of his father; but by espousing his sister by the same venter, it might happen that this sister's father, having no male issue, might leave her his estate, and consequently the brother who married her might be possessed of two.

Little will it avail to object to what Philo says,[6] that although the Athenians were allowed to marry a sister by the father's side, and not by the mother's, yet the contrary practice prevailed among the Lacedæmonians, who were permitted to espouse a sister by the mother's side, and not by the father's. For I find in Strabo[7] that at Sparta, whenever a woman was married to her brother she had half his portion for her dowry. Plain is it that this second law was made in order to prevent the bad consequences of the former. That the estate belonging to the sister's family might not devolve on the brother's, they gave half the brother's estate to the sister for her dowry.

Seneca,[8] speaking of Silanus, who had married his sister, says that the permission was limited at Athens, but general at Alexandria. In a monarchical government there was very little concern about any such thing as a division of estates.

Excellent was that law which, in order to maintain this division of lands in a democracy, ordained that a father who had several children should pitch upon one of them to inherit his portion,[9] and leave the others to be adopted, to the end that the numbers of citizens might always be kept upon an equality with that of the divisions.

Phaleas of Chalcedon[10] contrived a very extraordinary method of rendering all fortunes equal, in a republic where there was the greatest inequality. This was that the rich should give fortunes with their daughters to the poor, but receive none themselves; and that the poor should receive money for their daughters, instead of giving them fortunes. But I do not remember that a regulation of this kind ever took place in any republic. It lays the citizens under such hard and oppressive conditions as would make them detest the very equality which they designed to establish. It is proper sometimes that the laws should not seem to tend so directly to the end they propose.

Though real equality be the very soul of a democracy, it is so difficult to establish that an extreme exactness in this respect would not be always convenient. Sufficient is it to establish

---

[1] Plutarch, *Solon.*
[2] *Ibid.*
[3] Philolaus of Corinth made a law at Athens that the number of the portions of land and that of inheritances should be always the same.—Aristotle, *Politics,* ii. 7, 12.
[4] *Laws,* xi.
[5] Cornelius Nepos, preface. This custom began in the earliest times. Thus Abraham says of Sarah, "She is my sister, my father's daughter, but not my mother's." The same reasons occasioned the establishing the same law among different nations.

[6] *De specialibus legibus quæ pertinent ad præceptar Decalogi.*
[7] Book x.
[8] *Athenis dimidium licet, Alexandriæ totum.*—Seneca, *De Morte Claudii.*
[9] Plato has a law of this kind, *Laws,* v.
[10] Aristotle, ii. 7.

a census,[1] which shall reduce or fix the differences to a certain point: it is afterwards the business of particular laws to level, as it were, the inequalities, by the duties laid upon the rich, and by the ease afforded to the poor. It is moderate riches alone that can give or suffer this sort of compensation; for as to men of overgrown estates, everything which does not contribute to advance their power and honour is considered by them as an injury.

All inequality in democracies ought to be derived from the nature of the government, and even from the principle of equality. For example, it may be apprehended that people who are obliged to live by their labour would be too much impoverished by a public employment, or neglect the duties attending it; that artisans would grow insolent, and that too great a number of freemen would overpower the ancient citizens. In this case the equality[2] in a democracy may be suppressed for the good of the state. But this is only an apparent equality; for a man ruined by a public employment would be in a worse condition than his fellow-citizens; and this same man, being obliged to neglect his duty, would reduce the rest to a worse condition than himself, and so on.

6. *In what Manner the Laws ought to maintain Frugality in a Democracy.* It is not sufficient in a well-regulated democracy that the divisions of land be equal; they ought also to be small, as was customary among the Romans. "God forbid," said Curius to his soldiers,[3] "that a citizen should look upon that as a small piece of land which is sufficient to maintain him."

As equality of fortunes supports frugality, so the latter maintains the former. These things, though in themselves different, are of such a nature as to be unable to subsist separately; they reciprocally act upon each other; if one withdraws itself from a democracy, the other surely follows it.

True is it that when a democracy is founded on commerce, private people may acquire vast riches without a corruption of morals.

[1] Solon made four classes: the first, of those who had an income of 500 minas either in corn or liquid fruits; the second, of those who had 300, and were able to keep a horse; the third, of such as had only 200; the fourth, of all those who lived by their manual labour.—Plutarch, *Solon.*

[2] Solon excludes from public employments all those of the fourth class.

[3] They insisted upon a larger division of the conquered lands.—Plutarch, *Lives of the ancient Kings and Commanders.*

This is because the spirit of commerce is naturally attended with that of frugality, economy, moderation, labour, prudence, tranquillity, order, and rule. So long as this spirit subsists, the riches it produces have no bad effect. The mischief is, when excessive wealth destroys the spirit of commerce, then it is that the inconveniences of inequality begin to be felt.

In order to support this spirit, commerce should be carried on by the principal citizens; this should be their sole aim and study; this the chief object of the laws: and these very laws, by dividing the estates of individuals in proportion to the increase of commerce, should set every poor citizen so far at his ease as to be able to work like the rest, and every wealthy citizen in such a mediocrity as to be obliged to take some pains either in preserving or acquiring a fortune.

It is an excellent law in a trading republic to make an equal division of the paternal estate among the children. The consequence of this is that how great soever a fortune the father has made, his children, being not so rich as he, are induced to avoid luxury, and to work as he has done. I speak here only of trading republics; as to those that have no commerce, the legislator must pursue quite different measures.[4]

In Greece there were two sorts of republics: the one military, like Sparta; the other commercial, as Athens. In the former, the citizens were obliged to be idle; in the latter, endeavours were used to inspire them with the love of industry and labour. Solon made idleness a crime, and insisted that each citizen should give an account of his manner of getting a livelihood. And, indeed, in a well-regulated democracy, where people's expenses should extend only to what is necessary, every one ought to have it; for how should their wants be otherwise supplied?

7. *Other Methods of favouring the Principle of Democracy.* An equal division of lands cannot be established in all democracies. There are some circumstances in which a regulation of this nature would be impracticable, dangerous, and even subversive of the constitution. We are not always obliged to proceed to extremes. If it appears that this division of lands, which was designed to preserve the people's morals, does not suit the democracy, recourse

[4] In these, the portions or fortunes of women ought to be very much limited.

must be had to other methods.

If a permanent body be established to serve as a rule and pattern of manners; a senate, to which years, virtue, gravity, and eminent services procure admittance; the senators, by being exposed to public view like the statues of the gods, must naturally inspire every family with sentiments of virtue.

Above all, this senate must steadily adhere to the ancient institutions, and mind that the people and the magistrates never swerve from them.

The preservation of the ancient customs is a very considerable point in respect to manners. Since a corrupt people seldom perform any memorable actions, seldom establish societies, build cities, or enact laws; on the contrary, since most institutions are derived from people whose manners are plain and simple, to keep up the ancient customs is the way to preserve the original purity of morals.

Besides, if by some revolution the state has happened to assume a new form, this seldom can be effected without infinite pains and labour, and hardly ever by idle and debauched persons. Even those who had been the instruments of the revolution were desirous it should be relished, which is difficult to compass without good laws. Hence it is that ancient institutions generally tend to reform the people's manners, and those of modern date to corrupt them. In the course of a long administration, the descent to vice is insensible; but there is no reascending to virtue without making the most generous efforts.

It has been questioned whether the members of the senate we are speaking of ought to be for life or only chosen for a time. Doubtless they ought to be for life, as was the custom at Rome,[1] at Sparta,[2] and even at Athens. For we must not confound the senate at Athens, which was a body that changed every three months, with the Areopagus, whose members, as standing patterns, were established for life.

Let this be therefore a general maxim; that in a senate designed to be a rule, and the depository, as it were, of manners, the members

ought to be chosen for life: in a senate intended for the administration of affairs, the members may be changed.

The spirit, says Aristotle, waxes old as well as the body. This reflection holds good only in regard to a single magistrate, but cannot be applied to a senatorial assembly.

At Athens, besides the Areopagus, there were guardians of the public morals, as well as of the laws.[3] At Sparta, all the old men were censors. At Rome, the censorship was committed to two particular magistrates. As the senate watched over the people, the censors were to have an eye over the people and the senate. Their office was to reform the corruptions of the republic, to stigmatise indolence, to censure neglects, and to correct mistakes; as to flagrant crimes, these were left to the punishment of the laws.

That Roman law which required the accusations in cases of adultery to be public was admirably well calculated for preserving the purity of morals; it intimidated married women, as well as those who were to watch over their conduct.

Nothing contributes more to the preservation of morals than an extreme subordination of the young to the old. Thus they are both restrained, the former by their respect for those of advanced age, and the latter by their regard for themselves.

Nothing gives a greater force to the laws than a perfect subordination between the citizens and the magistrate. "The great difference which Lycurgus established between Sparta and the other cities," says Xenophon,[4] "consists chiefly in the obedience the citizens show to their laws; they run when the magistrate calls them. But at Athens a rich man would be highly displeased to be thought dependent on the magistrate."

Paternal authority is likewise of great use towards the preservation of morals. We have already observed that in a republic there is not so coercive a force as in other governments. The laws must therefore endeavour to supply this defect by some means or other; and this is done by paternal authority.

Fathers at Rome had the power of life and death over their children.[5] At Sparta, every

---

[1] The magistrates there were annual, and the senators for life.

[2] Lycurgus, says Xenophon, De Repub. Lacedæm., 10. § 1, 2, ordained that the senators should be chosen from amongst the old men, to the end that they might not be neglected in the decline of life; thus by making them judges of the courage of young people, he rendered the old age of the former more honourable than the strength and vigour of the latter.

[3] Even the Areopagus itself was subject to their censure.

[4] De Repub. Lacedæm., 8.

[5] We may see in the Roman History how useful this power was to the republic. I shall give an instance even in the time of its greatest corruption. Aulus Fulvius was set out on his journey in or-

father had a right to correct another man's child.

Paternal authority ended at Rome together with the republic. In monarchies, where such a purity of morals is not required, they are controlled by no other authority than that of the magistrates.

The Roman laws, which accustomed young people to dependence, established a long minority. Perhaps we are mistaken in conforming to this custom; there is no necessity for so much constraint in monarchies.

This very subordination in a republic might make it necessary for the father to continue in the possession of his children's fortune during life, as was the custom at Rome. But this is not agreeable to the spirit of monarchy.

8. *In what Manner the Laws should relate to the Principle of Government in an Aristocracy.* If the people are virtuous in an aristocracy, they enjoy very nearly the same happiness as in a popular government, and the state grows powerful. But as a great share of virtue is very rare where men's fortunes are so unequal, the laws must tend as much as possible to infuse a spirit of moderation, and endeavour to re-establish that equality which was necessarily removed by the constitution.

The spirit of moderation is what we call virtue in an aristocracy; it supplies the place of the spirit of equality in a popular state.

As the pomp and splendour with which kings are surrounded form a part of their power, so modesty and simplicity of manners constitute the strength of an aristocratic nobility.[1] When they affect no distinction, when they mix with the people, dress like them, and with them share all their pleasures, the people are apt to forget their subjection and weakness.

Every government has its nature and principle. An aristocracy must not therefore assume the nature and principle of monarchy; which would be the case were the nobles to be invested with personal privileges distinct from those of their body; privileges ought to be for

[1] In our days the Venetians, who in many respects may be said to have a very wise government, decided a dispute between a noble Venetian and a gentleman of Terra Firma in respect to precedency in a church, by declaring that out of Venice a noble Venetian had no pre-eminence over any other citizen.

der to join Catiline; his father called him back, and put him to death.—Sallust, *De Bello Catil.,* xxxiv.

the senate, and simple respect for the senators.

In aristocratic governments there are two principal sources of disorder: excessive inequality between the governors and the governed; and the same inequality between the different members of the body that governs. From these two inequalities, hatreds and jealousies arise, which the laws ought ever to prevent or repress.

The first inequality is chiefly when the privileges of the nobility are honourable only as they are ignominious to the people. Such was the law at Rome by which the patricians were forbidden to marry plebeians;[2] a law that had no other effect than to render the patricians on the one side more haughty, and on the other more odious. The reader may see what advantages the tribunes derived thence in their harangues.

This inequality occurs likewise when the condition of the citizens differs with regard to taxes, which may happen in four different ways: when the nobles assume the privilege of paying none; when they commit frauds to exempt themselves;[3] when they engross the public money, under pretence of rewards or appointments for their respective employments; in fine, when they render the common people tributary, and divide among their own body the profits arising from the several subsidies. This last case is very rare; an aristocracy so instituted would be the most intolerable of all governments.

While Rome inclined towards aristocracy, she avoided all these inconveniences. The magistrates never received any emoluments from their office. The chief men of the republic were taxed like the rest, nay, more heavily; and sometimes the taxes fell upon them alone. In fine, far from sharing among themselves the revenues of the state, all they could draw from the public treasure, and all the wealth that fortune flung into their laps, they bestowed freely on the people, to be excused from accepting public honours.[4]

It is a fundamental maxim that largesses are pernicious to the people in a democracy, but salutary in an aristocratic government. The former make them forget they are citizens, the latter bring them to a sense of it.

If the revenues of the state are not distribu-

[2] It was inserted by the decemvirs in the two last tables. See Dionysius Helicarnassus, x.
[3] As in some aristocracies in our time; nothing is more prejudicial to the government.
[4] See in Strabo, xiv., in what manner the Rhodians behaved in this respect.

ted among the people, they must be convinced at least of their being well administered: to feast their eyes with the public treasure is with them the same thing almost as enjoying it. The golden chain displayed at Venice, the riches exhibited at Rome in public triumphs, the treasures preserved in the temple of Saturn, were in reality the wealth of the people.

It is a very essential point in an aristocracy that the nobles themselves should not levy the taxes. The first order of the state in Rome never concerned themselves with it; the levying of the taxes was committed to the second, and even this in process of time was attended with great inconveniences. In an aristocracy of this kind, where the nobles levied the taxes, the private people would be all at the discretion of persons in public employments; and there would be no such thing as a superior tribunal to check their power. The members appointed to remove the abuses would rather enjoy them. The nobles would be like the princes of despotic governments, who confiscate whatever estates they please.

Soon would the profits hence arising be considered as a patrimony, which avarice would enlarge at pleasure. The farms would be lowered, and the public revenues reduced to nothing. This is the reason that some governments, without having ever received any remarkable shock, have dwindled away to such a degree as not only their neighbours, but even their own subjects, have been surprised at it.

The laws should likewise forbid the nobles all kinds of commerce: merchants of such unbounded credit would monopolise all to themselves. Commerce is a profession of people who are upon an equality; hence among despotic states the most miserable are those in which the prince applies himself to trade.

The laws of Venice debar[1] the nobles from commerce, by which they might even innocently acquire exorbitant wealth.

The laws ought to employ the most effectual means for making the nobles do justice to the people. If they have not established a tribune, they ought to be a tribune themselves.

Every sort of asylum in opposition to the execution of the laws destroys aristocracy, and is soon succeeded by tyranny.

They ought always to mortify the lust of dominion. There should be either a temporary or perpetual magistrate to keep the nobles in awe, as the Ephori at Sparta and the State Inquisitors at Venice—magistrates subject to no formalities. This sort of government stands in need of the strongest springs: thus a mouth of stone[2] is open to every informer at Venice—a mouth to which one would be apt to give the appellation of tyranny.

These arbitrary magistrates in an aristocracy bear some analogy to the censorship in democracies, which of its own nature is equally independent. And, indeed, the censors ought to be subject to no inquiry in relation to their conduct during their office; they should meet with a thorough confidence, and never be discouraged. In this respect the practice of the Romans deserved admiration; magistrates of all denominations were accountable for their administration,[3] except the censors.[4]

There are two very pernicious things in an aristocracy—excess either of poverty, or of wealth in the nobility. To prevent their poverty, it is necessary, above all things, to oblige them to pay their debts in time. To moderate the excess of wealth, prudent and gradual regulations should be made; but no confiscations, no agrarian laws, no expunging of debts; these are productive of infinite mischief.

The laws ought to abolish the right of primogeniture among the nobles,[5] to the end that by a continual division of the inheritances their fortunes may be always upon a level.

There should be no substitutions, no powers of redemption, no rights of *Majorasgo,* or adoption. The contrivances for perpetuating the grandeur of families in monarchical governments ought never to be employed in aristocracies.[6]

When the laws have compassed the equality of families, the next thing is to preserve a proper harmony and union among them. The quarrels of the nobility ought to be quickly decided; otherwise the contests of in-

---

[2] The informers throw their scrolls into it.

[3] See Livy, xlix. A censor could not be troubled even by a censor; each made his remark without taking the opinion of his colleague; and when it otherwise happened, the censorship was in a manner abolished.

[4] At Athens the *Logistæ,* who made all the magistrates accountable for their conduct, gave no account themselves.

[5] It is so practised at Venice.—Amelot de la Houssaye, pp. 30, 31.

[6] The main design of some aristocracies seems to be less the support of the state than of their nobility.

[1] Amelot de la Houssaye, *Of the Government of Venice,* part III. The Claudian law forbade the senators to have any ship at sea that held above forty bushels.—Livy, xxi. 63.

dividuals become those of families. Arbiters may terminate, or even prevent, the rise of disputes.

In fine, the laws must not favour the distinctions raised by vanity among families, under pretence that they are more noble or ancient than others. Pretences of this nature ought to be ranked among the weaknesses of private persons.

We have only to cast an eye upon Sparta; there we may see how the Ephori contrived to check the foibles of the kings, as well as those of the nobility and common people.

9. *In what Manner the Laws are in relation to their Principle in Monarchies.* As honour is the principle of a monarchical government, the laws ought to be in relation to this principle.

They should endeavour to support the nobility, in respect to whom honour may be, in some measure, deemed both child and parent.

They should render the nobility hereditary, not as a boundary between the power of the prince and the weakness of the people, but as the link which connects them both.

In this government, substitutions which preserve the estates of families undivided are extremely useful, though in others not so proper.

Here the power of redemption is of service, as it restores to noble families the lands that had been alienated by the prodigality of a parent.

The land of the nobility ought to have privileges as well as their persons. The monarch's dignity is inseparable from that of his kingdom; and the dignity of the nobleman from that of his fief.

All these privileges must be peculiar to the nobility, and incommunicable to the people, unless we intend to act contrary to the principle of government, and to diminish the power of the nobles together with that of the people.

Substitutions are a restraint to commerce, the power of redemption produces an infinite number of processes; every estate in land that is sold throughout the kingdom is in some measure without an owner for the space of a year. Privileges annexed to fiefs give a power very burdensome to those governments which tolerate them. These are the inconveniences of nobility—inconveniences, however, that vanish when confronted with its general utility: but when these privileges are communicated to the people, every principle of government is wantonly violated.

In monarchies a person may leave the bulk of his estate to one of his children—a permission improper in any other government.

The laws ought to favour all kinds of commerce[1] consistent with the constitution, to the end that the subjects may, without ruining themselves, be able to satisfy the continual cravings of the prince and his court.

They should establish some regulation that the manner of collecting the taxes may not be more burdensome than the taxes themselves.

The weight of duties produces labour, labour weariness, and weariness the spirit of indolence.

10. *Of the Expedition peculiar to the Executive Power in Monarchies.* Great is the advantage which a monarchical government has over a republic: as the state is conducted by a single person, the executive power is thereby enabled to act with greater expedition. But as this expedition may degenerate into rapidity, the laws should use some contrivance to slacken it. They ought not only to favour the nature of each constitution, but likewise to remedy the abuses that might result from this very nature.

Cardinal Richelieu[2] advises monarchs to permit no such things as societies or communities that raise difficulties upon every trifle. If this man's heart had not been bewitched with the love of despotic power, still these arbitrary notions would have filled his head.

The bodies entrusted with the deposition of the laws are never more obedient than when they proceed slowly, and use that reflection in the prince's affairs which can scarcely be expected from the ignorance of a court, or from the precipitation of its councils.[3]

What would have become of the finest monarchy in the world if the magistrates, by their delays, their complaints, and entreaties, had not checked the rapidity even of their princes' virtues, when these monarchs, consulting only the generous impulse of their minds, would fain have given a boundless reward to services performed with an unlimited courage and fidelity?

11. *Of the Excellence of a Monarchical Government.* Monarchy has a great advantage

[1] It is tolerated only in the common people. See *Leg. 3, Cod. de comm. et mercatoribus*, which is full of good sense.
[2] *Testament polit.*
[3] *Barbaris cunctatio servilis, statim exequi regium videtur.*—Tacitus, *Annals.*, v. 32.

over a despotic government. As it naturally requires there should be several orders or ranks of subjects, the state is more permanent, the constitution more steady, and the person of him who governs more secure.

Cicero is of opinion that the establishing of the tribunes preserved the republic. "And indeed," says he, "the violence of a headless people is more terrible. A chief or head is sensible that the affair depends upon himself, and therefore he thinks; but the people in their impetuosity are ignorant of the danger into which they hurry themselves." This reflection may be applied to a despotic government, which is a people without tribunes; and to a monarchy, where the people have some sort of tribunes.

Accordingly it is observable that in the commotions of a despotic government, the people, hurried away by their passions, are apt to push things as far as they can go. The disorders they commit are all extreme; whereas in monarchies matters are seldom carried to excess. The chiefs are apprehensive on their own account; they are afraid of being abandoned, and the intermediate dependent powers do not choose that the populace should have too much the upper hand. It rarely happens that the states of the kingdom are entirely corrupted: the prince adheres to these; and the seditious, who have neither will nor hopes to subvert the government, have neither power nor will to dethrone the prince.

In these circumstances men of prudence and authority interfere; moderate measures are first proposed, then complied with, and things at length are redressed; the laws resume their vigour, and command submission.

Thus all our histories are full of civil wars without revolutions, while the histories of despotic governments abound with revolutions without civil wars.

The writers of the history of the civil wars of some countries, even those who fomented them, sufficiently demonstrate the little foundation princes have to suspect the authority with which they invest particular bodies of men; since, even under the unhappy circumstance of their errors, they sighed only after the laws and their duty; and restrained, more than they were capable of inflaming, the impetuosity of the revolted.[1]

Cardinal Richelieu, reflecting perhaps that

he had too much reduced the states of the kingdom, has recourse to the virtues of the prince and of his ministers for the support[2] of government: but he requires so many things, that indeed there is none but an angel capable of such attention, such resolution and knowledge; and scarcely can we flatter ourselves that we shall ever see such a prince and ministers while monarchy subsists.

As people who live under a good government are happier than those who without rule or leaders wander about the forests, so monarchs who live under the fundamental laws of their country are far happier than despotic princes who have nothing to regulate, neither their own passions nor those of their subjects.

12. *The same Subject continued.* Let us not look for magnanimity in despotic governments; the prince cannot impart a greatness which he has not himself; with him there is no such thing as glory.

It is in monarchies that we behold the subjects encircling the throne, and cheered by the irradiancy of the sovereign; there it is that each person filling, as it were, a larger space, is capable of exercising those virtues which adorn the soul, not with independence, but with true dignity and greatness.

13. *An Idea of Despotic Power.* When the savages of Louisiana are desirous of fruit, they cut the tree to the root, and gather the fruit.[3] This is an emblem of despotic government.

14. *In what Manner the Laws are in relation to the Principles of Despotic Government.* The principle of despotic government is fear; but a timid, ignorant, and faint-spirited people have no occasion for a great number of laws.

Everything ought to depend here on two or three ideas; hence there is no necessity that any new notions should be added. When we want to break a horse, we take care not to let him change his master, his lesson, or his pace. Thus an impression is made on his brain by two or three motions, and no more.

If a prince is shut up in a seraglio, he cannot leave his voluptuous abode without alarming those who keep him confined. They will not bear that his person and power should pass into other hands. He seldom therefore wages

[1] *Memoirs of Cardinal de Retz* and other histories.

[2] *Testament polit.*
[3] *Edifying Letters,* coll. ii, p. 315.

war in person, and hardly ventures to entrust the command to his generals.

A prince of this stamp, unaccustomed to resistance in his palace, is enraged to see his will opposed by armed force; hence he is generally governed by wrath or vengeance. Besides, he can have no notion of true glory. War therefore is carried on under such a government in its full natural fury, and less extent is given to the law of nations than in other states.

Such a prince has so many imperfections that they are afraid to expose his natural stupidity to public view. He is concealed in his palace, and the people are ignorant of his situation. It is lucky for him that the inhabitants of those countries need only the name of a prince to govern them.

When Charles XII was at Bender, he met with some opposition from the senate of Sweden; upon which he wrote word home that he would send one of his boots to command them. This boot would have governed like a despotic prince.

If the prince is a prisoner, he is supposed to be dead, and another mounts the throne. The treaties made by the prisoner are void, his successor will not ratify them; and indeed, as he is the law, the state, and the prince: when he is no longer a prince, he is nothing: were he not therefore deemed to be deceased, the state would be subverted.

One thing which chiefly determined the Turks to conclude a separate peace with Peter I was the Muscovites telling the Vizir that in Sweden another prince had been placed upon the throne.[1]

The preservation of the state is only the preservation of the prince, or rather of the palace where he is confined. Whatever does not directly menace this palace or the capital makes no impression on ignorant, proud, and prejudiced minds; and as for the concatenation of events, they are unable to trace, to foresee, or even to conceive it. Politics, with its several springs and laws, must here be very much limited; the political government is as simple as the civil.[2]

The whole is reduced to reconciling the political and civil administration to the domestic government, the officers of state to those of the seraglio.

Such a state is happiest when it can look upon itself as the only one in the world, when it is environed with deserts, and separated from those people whom they call Barbarians. Since it cannot depend on the militia, it is proper it should destroy a part of itself.

As fear is the principle of despotic government, its end is tranquillity; but this tranquillity cannot be called a peace: no, it is only the silence of those towns which the enemy is ready to invade.

Since strength does not lie in the state, but in the army that founded it, in order to defend the state the army must be preserved, how formidable soever to the prince. How, then, can we reconcile the security of the government to that of the prince's person?

Observe how industriously the Russian government endeavours to temper its arbitrary power, which it finds more burdensome than the people themselves. They have broken their numerous guards, mitigated criminal punishments, erected tribunals, entered into a knowledge of the laws, and instructed the people. But there are particular causes that will probably once more involve them in the very misery which they now endeavour to avoid.

In those states religion has more influence than anywhere else; it is fear added to fear. In Mahomedan countries, it is partly from their religion that the people derive the surprising veneration they have for their prince.

It is religion that amends in some measure the Turkish constitution. The subjects, who have no attachment of honour to the glory and grandeur of the state, are connected with it by the force and principle of religion.

Of all despotic governments there is none that labours more under its own weight than that wherein the prince declares himself proprietor of all the lands, and heir to all his subjects. Hence the neglect of agriculture arises; and if the prince intermeddles likewise in trade, all manner of industry is ruined.

Under this sort of government, nothing is repaired or improved.[3] Houses are built only for the necessity of habitation; there is no digging of ditches or planting of trees; everything is drawn from, but nothing restored to, the earth; the ground lies untilled, and the whole country becomes a desert.

Is it to be imagined that the laws which abolish the property of land and the succession of estates will diminish the avarice and

---

[1] Continuation of Pufendorff, *Introduction to the History of Europe*, in the article on Sweden, 10.

[2] According to Sir John Chardin, there is no council of state in Persia.

[3] See Ricaut, *State of the Ottoman Empire*, p. 196.

cupidity of the great? By no means. They will rather stimulate this cupidity and avarice. The great men will be prompted to use a thousand oppressive methods, imagining they have no other property than the gold and silver which they are able to seize upon by violence, or to conceal.

To prevent, therefore, the utter ruin of the state, the avidity of the prince ought to be moderated by some established custom. Thus, in Turkey, the sovereign is satisfied with the right of three per cent on the value of inheritances.[1] But as he gives the greatest part of the lands to his soldiery, and disposes of them as he pleases; as he seizes on all the inheritances of the officers of the empire at their decease; as he has the property of the possessions of those who die without issue, and the daughters have only the usufruct; it thence follows that the greatest part of the estates of the country are held in a precarious manner.

By the laws of Bantam,[2] the king seizes on the whole inheritance, even wife, children, and habitation. In order to elude the cruelest part of this law, they are obliged to marry their children at eight, nine, or ten years of age, and sometimes younger, to the end that they may not be a wretched part of the father's succession.

In countries where there are no fundamental laws, the succession to the empire cannot be fixed. The crown is then elective, and the right of electing is in the prince, who names a successor either of his own or of some other family. In vain would it be to establish here the succession of the eldest son; the prince might always choose another. The successor is declared by the prince himself, or by a civil war. Hence a despotic state is, upon another account, more liable than a monarchical government to dissolution.

As every prince of the royal family is held equally capable of being chosen, hence it follows that the prince who ascends the throne immediately strangles his brothers, as in Turkey; or puts out their eyes, as in Persia; or bereaves them of their understanding, as in the Mogul's country; or if these precautions are not used, as in Morocco, the vacancy of the throne is always attended with the horrors of a civil war.

By the constitution of Russia[3] the Czar may choose whom he has a mind for his successor, whether of his own or of a strange family. Such a settlement produces a thousand revolutions, and renders the throne as tottering as the succession is arbitrary. The right of succession being one of those things which are of most importance to the people to know, the best is that which most sensibly strikes them. Such as a certain order of birth. A settlement of this kind puts a stop to intrigues, and stifles ambition; the mind of a weak prince is no longer enslaved, nor is he made to speak his will as he is just expiring.

When the succession is established by a fundamental law, only one prince is the successor, and his brothers have neither a real nor apparent right to dispute the crown with him. They can neither pretend to nor take any advantage of the will of a father. There is then no more occasion to confine or kill the king's brother than any other subject.

But in despotic governments, where the prince's brothers are equally his slaves and his rivals, prudence requires that their persons be secured; especially in Mahomedan countries, where religion considers victory or success as a divine decision in their favour; so that they have no such thing as a monarch *de jure,* but only *de facto.*

There is a far greater incentive to ambition in countries where the princes of the blood are sensible that if they do not ascend the throne they must be either imprisoned or put to death, than among us, where they are placed in such a station as may satisfy, if not their ambition, at least their moderate desires.

The princes of despotic governments have ever perverted the use of marriage. They generally take a great many wives, especially in that part of the world where absolute power is in some measure naturalised, namely, Asia. Hence they come to have such a multitude of children that they can hardly have any great affection for them, nor the children for one another.

The reigning family resembles the state; it is too weak itself, and its head too powerful; it seems very numerous and extensive, and yet is suddenly extinct. Artaxerxes[4] put all his children to death for conspiring against him.

---

[1] See concerning the inheritances of the Turks, *Ancient and Modern Sparta.* See also Ricaut on the Ottoman empire.

[2] *Collection of Voyages that Contributed to the Establishment of the East India Company,* i. The law of Pegu is less cruel; if there happen to be children, the king succeeds only to two-thirds. *Ibid.,* iii, p. 1.

[3] See the different constitutions, especially that of 1722.

[4] See Justin.

It is not at all probable that fifty children would conspire against their father, and much less that this conspiracy would be owing to his having refused to resign his concubine to his eldest son. It is more natural to believe that the whole was an intrigue of those oriental seraglios, where fraud, treachery, and deceit reign in silence and darkness; and where an old prince, grown every day more infirm, is the first prisoner of the palace.

After what has been said, one would imagine that human nature should perpetually rise up against despotism. But notwithstanding the love of liberty, so natural to mankind, notwithstanding their innate detestation of force and violence, most nations are subject to this very government. This is easily accounted for. To form a moderate government, it is necessary to combine the several powers; to regulate, temper, and set them in motion; to give, as it were, ballast to one, in order to enable it to counterpoise the other. This is a masterpiece of legislation; rarely produced by hazard, and seldom attained by prudence. On the contrary, a despotic government offers itself, as it were, at first sight; it is uniform throughout; and as passions only are requisite to establish it, this is what every capacity may reach.

15. *The same Subject continued*. In warm climates, where despotic power generally prevails, the passions disclose themselves earlier, and are sooner extinguished;[1] the understanding is sooner ripened; they are less in danger of squandering their fortunes; there is less facility of distinguishing themselves in the world; less communication between young people, who are confined at home; they marry much earlier, and consequently may be sooner of age than in our European climates. In Turkey they are of age at fifteen.[2]

They have no such thing as a cession of goods; in a government where there is no fixed property, people depend rather on the person than on his estate.

The cession of goods is naturally admitted in moderate governments,[3] but especially in republics, because of the greater confidence usually placed in the probity of the citizens, and the lenity and moderation arising from a form of government which every subject seems to have preferred to all others.

Had the legislators of the Roman republic established the cession of goods,[4] they never would have been exposed to so many seditions and civil discords; neither would they have experienced the danger of the evils, nor the inconvenience of the remedies.

Poverty and the precariousness of property in a despotic state render usury natural, each person raising the value of his money in proportion to the danger he sees in lending it. Misery therefore pours from all parts into those unhappy countries; they are bereft of everything, even of the resource of borrowing.

Hence it is that a merchant under this government is unable to carry on an extensive commerce; he lives from hand to mouth; and were he to encumber himself with a large quantity of merchandise, he would lose more by the exorbitant interest he must give for money than he could possibly get by the goods. Hence they have no laws here relating to commerce; they are all reduced to what is called the bare police.

A government cannot be unjust without having hands to exercise its injustice. Now, it is impossible but that these hands will be grasping for themselves. The embezzling of the public money is therefore natural in despotic states.

As this is a common crime under such a government, confiscations are very useful. By these the people are eased; the money drawn by this method being a considerable tribute which could hardly be raised on the exhausted subject: neither is there in those countries any one family which the prince would be glad to preserve.

In moderate governments it is quite a different thing. Confiscations would render property uncertain, would strip innocent children, would destroy a whole family, instead of punishing a single criminal. In republics they would be attended with the mischief of subverting equality, which is the very soul of this government, by depriving a citizen of his necessary subsistence.[5]

There is a Roman law[6] against confiscations, except in the case of *crimen majestatis*,

[1] See the book of laws as relative to the nature of the climate, Book xiv, below.

[2] Laquilletière, *Ancient and Modern Sparta*, p. 463.

[3] The same may be said of compositions in regard to fair bankrupts.

[4] There was no such establishment made till the Julian law, *De Cessione bonorum;* which preserved them from prison and from an ignominious division of their goods.—*Cod.*, ii. tit. 12.

[5] They seem to have been too fond of confiscations in the republic of Athens.

[6] *Authentica bona damnatorum.—Cod. de bon. proscript. seu damn.*

or high treason of the most heinous nature. It would be a prudent thing to follow the spirit of this law, and to limit confiscations to particular crimes. In countries where a local custom has rendered real estates alienable, Bodin very justly observes that confiscations should extend only to such as are purchased or acquired.[1]

16. *Of the Communication of Power*. In a despotic government the power is communicated entire to the person entrusted with it. The vizir himself is the despotic prince; and each particular officer is the vizir. In monarchies the power is less immediately applied, being tempered by the monarch as he gives it.[2] He makes such a distribution of his authority as never to communicate a part of it without reserving a greater share to himself.

Hence in monarchies the governors of towns are not so dependent on the governor of the province as not to be still more so on the prince; and the private officers or military bodies are not so far subject to their general as not to owe still a greater subjection to their sovereign.

In most monarchies it has been wisely regulated that those who have an extensive command should not belong to any military corps; so that as they have no authority but through the prince's pleasure, and as they may be employed or not, they are in some measure in the service, and in some measure out of it.

This is incompatible with a despotic government. For if those who are not actually employed were still invested with privileges and titles, the consequence must be that there would be men in the state who might be said to be great of themselves; a thing directly opposite to the nature of this government.

Were the governor of a town independent of the pasha, expedients would be daily necessary to make them agree; which is highly absurd in a despotic state. Besides, if a particular governor should refuse to obey, how could the other answer for his province with his head?

In this kind of government, authority must ever be wavering; nor is that of the lowest magistrate more steady than that of the despotic prince. Under moderate governments, the law is prudent in all its parts, and perfectly well known, so that even the pettiest magistrates are capable of following it. But in a despotic state, where the prince's will is the law, though the prince were wise, yet how could the magistrate follow a will he does not know? He must certainly follow his own.

Again, as the law is only the prince's will, and as the prince can only will what he knows, the consequence is that there are an infinite number of people who must will for him, and make their wills keep pace with his.

In fine, as the law is the momentary will of the prince, it is necessary that those who will for him should follow his sudden manner of willing.

17. *Of Presents*. It is a received custom in despotic countries never to address any superior whomsoever, not excepting their kings, without making them a present. The Mogul[3] never receives the petitions of his subjects if they come with empty hands. These princes spoil even their own favours.

But thus it must ever be in a government where no man is a citizen; where they have all a notion that a superior is under no obligation to an inferior; where men imagine themselves bound by no other tie than the chastisements inflicted by one party upon another; where, in fine, there is very little to do, and where the people have seldom an occasion of presenting themselves before the great, of offering their petitions, and much less their complaints.

In a republic, presents are odious, because virtue stands in no need of them. In monarchies, honour is a much stronger incentive than presents. But in a despotic government, where there is neither honour nor virtue, people cannot be determined to act but through hope of the conveniences of life.

It is in conformity with republican ideas that Plato[4] ordered those who received presents for doing their duty to be punished with death. "They must not take presents," says he, "neither for good nor for evil actions."

A very bad law was that among the Romans[5] which gave the magistrates leave to accept small presents[6] provided they did not exceed one hundred crowns in the whole year. They who receive nothing expect nothing; they who receive a little soon covet more, till at length their desires swell to an exorbitant height.

---

1 *De la République*, v. 3.
2 *Ut esse Phœbi dulcius lumen solet
Jamjam cadentis.*—Seneca, *Troas*, V. i. 1.
3 *Collection of Voyages that Contributed to the Establishment of the East India Company*, i, p. 80.
4 *Laws*, xii.
5 *Leg.* 6, § 2; *Dig. ad leg. Jul. repet.*
6 *Munuscula*.

Besides, it is much easier to convict a man who knows himself obliged to accept no present at all, and yet will accept something, than a person who takes more when he ought to take less, and who always finds pretexts, excuses, and plausible reasons in justification of his conduct.

18. *Of Rewards conferred by the Sovereign.* In despotic governments, where, as we have already observed, the principal motive of action is the hope of the conveniences of life, the prince who confers rewards has nothing to bestow but money. In monarchies, where honour alone predominates, the prince's rewards would consist only of marks of distinction, if the distinctions established by honour were not attended with luxury, which necessarily brings on its wants: the prince therefore is obliged to confer such honours as lead to wealth. But in a republic where virtue reigns —a motive self-sufficient, and which excludes all others—the recompenses of the state consist only of public attestations of this virtue.

It is a general rule that great rewards in monarchies and republics are a sign of their decline; because they are a proof of their principles being corrupted, and that the idea of honour has no longer the same force in a monarchy, nor the title of citizen the same weight in a republic.

The very worst Roman emperors were those who were most profuse in their largesses; for example, Caligula, Claudius, Nero, Otho, Vitellius, Commodus, Heliogabalus, and Caracalla. The best, as Augustus, Vespasian, Antoninus Pius, Marcus Aurelius, and Pertinax, were economists. Under good emperors the state resumed its principles; all other treasures were supplied by that of honour.

19. *New Consequences of the Principles of the three Governments.* I cannot conclude this book without making some applications of my three principles.

1st Question.] It is a question whether the laws ought to oblige a subject to accept a public employment. My opinion is that they ought in a republic, but not in a monarchical government. In the former, public employments are attestations of virtue, depositions with which a citizen is entrusted by his country, for whose sake alone he ought to live, to act, and to think, consequently he cannot refuse them.[1] In the latter, public offices are

testimonials of honour; now such is the capriciousness of honour that it chooses to accept none of these testimonies but when and in what manner it pleases.

The late King of Sardinia[2] inflicted punishments on his subjects who refused the dignities and public offices of the state. In this he unknowingly followed republican ideas: but his method of governing in other respects sufficiently proves that this was not his intention.

2nd Question.] Secondly, it is questioned whether a subject should be obliged to accept a post in the army inferior to that which he held before. Among the Romans it was usual to see a captain serve the next year under his lieutenant.[3] This is because virtue in republics requires a continual sacrifice of our persons and of our repugnances for the good of the state. But in monarchies, honour, true or false, will never bear with what it calls degrading itself.

In despotic governments, where honour, posts, and ranks are equally abused, they indiscriminately make a prince a scullion, and a scullion a prince.

3rd Question.] Thirdly, it may be inquired, whether civil and military employments should be conferred on the same person. In republics I think they should be joined, but in monarchies separated. In the former it would be extremely dangerous to make the profession of arms a particular state, distinct from that of civil functions; and in the latter, no less dangerous would it be to confer these two employments on the same person.

In republics a person takes up arms only with a view to defend his country and its laws; it is because he is a citizen he makes himself for a while a soldier. Were these two distinct states, the person who under arms thinks himself a citizen would soon be made sensible he is only a soldier.

In monarchies, they whose condition engages them in the profession of arms have nothing but glory, or at least honour or fortune, in view. To men, therefore, like these,

---

[1] Plato, in his *Republic*, viii, ranks these refusals among the marks of the corruption of a republic. In his *Laws*, vi, he orders them to be punished by a fine; at Venice they are punished with banishment.

[2] Victor Amadeus.

[3] Some centurions having appealed to the people for the employments which they had before enjoyed, "It is just, my comrades," said a centurion, "that you should look upon every post as honourable in which you have an opportunity of defending the republic."—Livy, dec. 5, xlii, 34.

the prince should never give any civil employments; on the contrary, they ought to be checked by the civil magistrate, that the same persons may not have at the same time the confidence of the people and the power to abuse it.[1]

We have only to cast an eye on a nation that may be justly called a republic, disguised under the form of monarchy, and we shall see how jealous they are of making a separate order of the profession of arms, and how the military state is constantly allied with that of the citizen, and even sometimes of the magistrate, to the end that these qualities may be a pledge for their country, which should never be forgotten.

The division of civil and military employments, made by the Romans after the extinction of the republic, was not an arbitrary thing. It was a consequence of the change which happened in the constitution of Rome; it was natural to a monarchical government; and what was only commenced under Augustus[2] succeeding emperors[3] were obliged to finish, in order to temper the military government.

Procopius, therefore, the competitor of Valens the emperor, was very much to blame when, conferring the pro-consular dignity[4] upon Hormisdas, a prince of the blood royal of Persia, he restored to this magistracy the military command of which it had been formerly possessed; unless indeed he had very particular reasons for so doing. A person that aspires to the sovereignty concerns himself less about what is serviceable to the state than what is likely to promote his own interest.

4th Question.] Fourthly, it is a question whether public employments should be sold. They ought not, I think, in despotic governments, where the subjects must be instantaneously placed or displaced by the prince.

But in monarchies this custom is not at all improper, by reason it is an inducement to engage in that as a family employment which would not be undertaken through a motive of virtue; it fixes likewise every one in his duty, and renders the several orders of the kingdom

more permanent. Suidas very justly observes that Anastasius had changed the empire into a kind of aristocracy, by selling all public employments.

Plato[5] cannot bear with this prostitution: "This is exactly," says he, "as if a person were to be made a mariner or pilot of a ship for his money. Is it possible that this rule should be bad in every other employment of life, and hold good only in the administration of a republic?" But Plato speaks of a republic founded on virtue, and we of a monarchy. Now, in monarchies (where, though there were no such thing as a regular sale of public offices, still the indigence and avidity of the courtier would equally prompt him to expose them to sale) chance will furnish better subjects than the prince's choice. In short, the method of attaining to honours through riches inspires and cherishes industry,[6] a thing extremely wanting in this kind of government.

5th Question.] The fifth question is in what kind of government censors are necessary. My answer is, that they are necessary in a republic, where the principle of government is virtue. We must not imagine that criminal actions only are destructive of virtue; it is destroyed also by omissions, by neglects, by a certain coolness in the love of our country, by bad examples, and by the seeds of corruption: whatever does not openly violate but elude the laws, does not subvert but weaken them, ought to fall under the inquiry and correction of the censors.

We are surprised at the punishment of the Areopagite for killing a sparrow which, to escape the pursuit of a hawk, had taken shelter in his bosom. Surprised we are also that an Areopagite should put his son to death for putting out the eyes of a little bird. But let us reflect that the question here does not relate to a criminal sentence, but to a judgment concerning manners in a republic founded on manners.

In monarchies there should be no censors; the former are founded on honour, and the nature of honour is to have the whole world for its censor. Every man who fails in this article is subject to the reproaches even of those who are void of honour.

Here the censors would be spoiled by the very people whom they ought to correct: they could not prevail against the corruption of a

---

[1] *Ne imperium ad optimos nobilium transferretur, Senatum militia vetuit Gallienus, etiam adire exercitum.*—Aurelius Victor, *De Cæsaribus.*

[2] Augustus deprived the senators, proconsuls, and governors of the privilege of wearing arms.—Dio, xxxiii.

[3] Constantine. See Zozimus, ii.

[4] Ammianus Marcellinus, xxvi, *Et Civilia, more veterum, et bella recturo.*

[5] *Republic,* viii.

[6] We see the laziness of Spain, where all public employments are given away.

monarchy; the corruption rather would be too strong against them.

Hence it is obvious that there ought to be no censors in despotic governments. The example of China seems to derogate from this rule; but we shall see, in the course of this work, the particular reasons of that institution.

Book VI. Consequences of the Principles of Different Governments with Respect to the Simplicity of Civil and Criminal Laws, the Form of Judgments, and the Inflicting of Punishments

1. *Of the Simplicity of Civil Laws in different Governments.* Monarchies do not permit of so great a simplicity of laws as despotic governments. For in monarchies there must be courts of judicature; these must give their decisions; the decisions must be preserved and learned, that we may judge in the same manner to-day as yesterday, and that the lives and property of the citizens may be as certain and fixed as the very constitution of the state.

In monarchies, the administration of justice, which decides not only in whatever belongs to life and property, but likewise to honour, demands very scrupulous inquiries. The delicacy of the judge increases in proportion to the increase of his trust, and of the importance of the interests on which he determines.

We must not, therefore, be surprised to find so many rules, restrictions, and extensions in the laws of those countries—rules that multiply the particular cases, and seem to make of reason itself an art.

The difference of rank, birth, and condition established in monarchical governments is frequently attended with distinctions in the nature of property; and the laws relating to the constitution of this government may augment the number of these distinctions. Hence, among us goods are divided into real estates, purchases, dowries, paraphernalia, paternal and maternal inheritances; movables of different kinds; estates held in fee-simple, or in tail; acquired by descent or conveyance; allodial, or held by soccage; ground rents; or annuities. Each sort of goods is subject to particular rules, which must be complied with in the disposal of them. These things must needs diminish the simplicity of the laws.

In our governments the fiefs have become hereditary. It was necessary that the nobility should have a fixed property, that is, the fief should have a certain consistency, to the end that the proprietor might be always in a capacity of serving the prince. This must have been productive of great varieties; for instance, there are countries where fiefs could not be divided among the brothers; in others, the younger brothers may be allowed a more generous subsistence.

The monarch who knows each of his provinces may establish different laws, or tolerate different customs. But as the despotic prince knows nothing, and can attend to nothing, he must take general measures, and govern by a rigid and inflexible will, which throughout his whole dominions produces the same effect; in short, everything bends under his feet.

In proportion as the decisions of the courts of judicature are multiplied in monarchies, the law is loaded with decrees that sometimes contradict one another; either because succeeding judges are of a different way of thinking, or because the same causes are sometimes well, and at other times ill, defended; or, in fine, by reason of an infinite number of abuses, to which all human regulations are liable. This is a necessary evil, which the legislator redresses from time to time, as contrary even to the spirit of moderate governments. For when people are obliged to have recourse to courts of judicature, this should come from the nature of the constitution, and not from the contradiction or uncertainty of the law.

In governments where there are necessary distinctions of persons, there must likewise be privileges. This also diminishes the simplicity, and creates a thousand exceptions.

One of the privileges least burdensome to society, and especially to him who confers it, is that of pleading in one court in preference to another. Here new difficulties arise, when it becomes a question before which court we shall plead.

Far different is the case of the people under despotic governments. In those countries I can see nothing that the legislator is able to decree, or the magistrate to judge. As the lands belong to the prince, it follows that there are scarcely any civil laws in regard to landed property. From the right the sovereign has to successions, it follows, likewise, that there are none relating to inheritances. The monopolies established by the prince for himself in some countries render all sorts of commercial laws quite useless. The marriages which they usually contract with female slaves are the cause that there are scarcely any civil laws relating to dowries, or to the particular advantage of married women. From the prodigious multitude of slaves, it follows, likewise, that there are very few who have any such thing as a will of their own, and of course are answerable for their conduct before a judge. Most moral actions that are only in consequence of a father's, a husband's, or a master's will, are regulated by them, and not by the magistrates.

I forgot to observe that as what we call honour is a thing hardly known in those countries, the several difficulties relating to this article, though of such importance with us, are with them quite out of the question. Despotic power is self-sufficient; round it there is an absolute vacuum. Hence it is that when travellers favour us with the description of countries where arbitrary sway prevails, they seldom make mention of civil laws.[1]

All occasions, therefore, of wrangling and law-suits are here removed. And to this in part is it owing that litigious people in those countries are so roughly handled. As the injustice of their demand is neither screened, palliated, nor protected by an infinite number of laws, of course it is immediately discovered.

2. *Of the Simplicity of Criminal Laws in different Governments.* We hear it generally said, that justice ought to be administered with us as in Turkey. Is it possible, then, that the most ignorant of all nations should be the most clear-sighted on a point which it most behoves mankind to know?

If we examine the set forms of justice with respect to the trouble the subject undergoes in recovering his property, or in obtaining satisfaction for an injury or affront, we shall find them doubtless too numerous: but if we consider them in the relation they bear to the liberty and security of every individual, we shall often find them too few; and be convinced that the trouble, expense, delays, and even the very dangers of our judiciary proceedings, are the price that each subject pays for his liberty.

In Turkey, where little regard is shown to the honour, life, or estate of the subject, all causes are speedily decided. The method of determining them is a matter of indifference, provided they be determined. The pasha, after a quick hearing, orders which party he pleases to be bastinadoed, and then sends them about their business.

Here it would be dangerous to be of a litigious disposition; this supposes a strong desire of obtaining justice, a settled aversion, an active mind, and a steadiness in pursuing one's point. All this should be avoided in a government where fear ought to be the only prevailing sentiment, and in which popular disturbances are frequently attended with sudden and unforeseen revolutions. Here every man ought to know that the magistrate must not hear his name mentioned, and that his security depends entirely on his being reduced to a kind of annihilation.

But in moderate governments, where the life of the meanest subject is deemed precious, no man is stripped of his honour or property until after a long inquiry; and no man is bereft of life till his very country has attacked him—an attack that is never made without leaving him all possible means of making his defence.

Hence it is that when a person renders himself absolute,[2] he immediately thinks of reducing the number of laws. In a government thus constituted they are more affected with particular inconveniences than with the liberty of the subject, which is very little minded.

In republics, it is plain that as many formalities at least are necessary as in monarchies. In both governments they increase in proportion to the value which is set on the honour, fortune, liberty, and life of the subject.

In republican governments, men are all equal; equal they are also in despotic governments: in the former, because they are everything; in the latter, because they are nothing.

3. *In what Governments and in what Cases the Judges ought to determine according to the express Letter of the Law.* The nearer a government approaches towards a republic, the more the manner of judging becomes settled and fixed; hence it was a fault in the republic of Sparta for the Ephori to pass such arbitrary judgments without having any laws

[1] In Mazulipatam it could never be found out that there was such a thing as a written law. See the *Collection of Voyages that Contributed to the Establishment of the East India Company*, iv., part I, p. 391. The Indians are regulated in their decisions by certain customs. The Vedan and such books do not contain civil laws, but religious precepts. See *Edifying Letters*, coll. xiv.

[2] Cæsar, Cromwell, and many others.

to direct them. The first consuls at Rome pronounced sentence in the same manner as the Ephori; but the inconvenience of this proceeding was soon felt, and they were obliged to have recourse to express and determinate laws.

In despotic governments there are no laws; the judge himself is his own rule. There are laws in monarchies; and where these are explicit, the judge conforms to them; where they are otherwise, he endeavours to investigate their spirit. In republics, the very nature of the constitution requires the judges to follow the letter of the law; otherwise the law might be explained to the prejudice of every citizen, in cases where their honour, property, or life is concerned.

At Rome the judges had no more to do than to declare that the persons accused were guilty of a particular crime, and then the punishment was found in the laws, as may be seen in divers laws still extant. In England the jury give their verdict whether the fact brought under their cognisance be proved or not; if it be proved, the judge pronounces the punishment inflicted by the law, and for this he needs only to open his eyes.

4. *Of the Manner of passing Judgment.* Hence arise the different modes of passing judgment. In monarchies the judges choose the method of arbitration; they deliberate together, they communicate their sentiments for the sake of unanimity; they moderate their opinions, in order to render them conformable to those of others: and the lesser number are obliged to give way to the majority. But this is not agreeable to the nature of a republic. At Rome, and in the cities of Greece, the judges never entered into a consultation; each gave his opinion in one of these three ways: "I absolve," "I condemn," "It does not appear clear to me";[1] this was because the people judged, or were supposed to judge. But the people are far from being civilians; all these restrictions and methods of arbitration are above their reach; they must have only one object and one single fact set before them; and then they have only to see whether they ought to condemn, to acquit, or to suspend their judgment.

The Romans introduced set forms of actions,[2] after the example of the Greeks, and established a rule that each cause should be directed by its proper action. This was necessary in their manner of judging; it was necessary to fix the state of the question, that the people might have it always before their eyes. Otherwise, in a long process, this state of the question would continually change, and be no longer distinguished.

Hence it followed that the Roman judges granted only the simple demand, without making any addition, deduction, or limitation. But the *prætors* devised other forms of actions, which were called *ex bona fide,* in which the method of pronouncing sentence was left to the disposition of the judge. This was more agreeable to the spirit of monarchy. Hence it is a saying among the French lawyers, that in France[3] all actions are *ex bona fide.*

5. *In what Governments the Sovereign may be Judge.* Machiavel[4] attributes the loss of the liberty of Florence to the people's not judging in a body in cases of high treason against themselves, as was customary at Rome. For this purpose they had eight judges: "but the few," says Machiavel, "are corrupted by a few." I should willingly adopt the maxim of this great man. But as in those cases the political interest prevails in some measure over the civil (for it is always an inconvenience that the people should be judges in their own cause), in order to remedy this evil, the laws must provide as much as possible for the security of individuals.

With this view the Roman legislators did two things: they gave the persons accused permission to banish themselves[5] before sentence was pronounced;[6] and they ordained that the goods of those who were condemned should be sacred, to prevent their being confiscated to the people. We shall see in Book XI the other limitations that were set to the judicatory power residing in the people.

Solon knew how to prevent the abuse which the people might make of their power in criminal judgments. He ordained that the Court of Areopagus should re-examine the affair; that if they believed the party accused

---

[1] *Non liquet.*

[2] *Quas actiones ne populus prout vellet institueret, certas solemnesque esse voluerunt.—Dig. de Orig. Jur.,* ii, § 6.

[3] In France a person, though sued for more than he owes, loses his costs if he has not offered to pay the exact debt.

[4] Discourse on the first decade of Livy, i. 7.

[5] This is well explained in Cicero's oration *Pro Cæcina,* towards the end, 100.

[6] This was the law at Athens, as appears by Demosthenes. Socrates refused to make use of it.

was unjustly acquitted,[1] they should impeach him again before the people; that if they believed him unjustly condemned[2] they should prevent the execution of the sentence, and make them rejudge the proceeding—an admirable law, that subjected the people to the censure of the magistracy which they most revered, and even to their own!

In affairs of this kind it is always proper to throw in some delays, especially when the party accused is under confinement; to the end that the people may grow calm and give their judgment coolly.

In despotic governments, the prince himself may be judge. But in monarchies this cannot be; the constitution by such means would be subverted, and the dependent intermediate powers annihilated; all set forms of judgment would cease; fear would take possession of the people's minds, and paleness spread itself over every countenance: the more confidence, honour, affection, and security in the subject, the more extended is the power of the monarch.

We shall give here a few more reflections on this point. In monarchies, the prince is the party that prosecutes the person accused, and causes him to be punished or acquitted. Now, were he himself to sit upon the trial, he would be both judge and party.

In this government the prince has frequently the benefit of confiscation, so that here again, by determining criminal causes, he would be both judge and party.

Further, by this method he would deprive himself of the most glorious attribute of sovereignty, namely, that of granting pardon,[3] for it would be quite ridiculous of him to make and unmake his decisions; surely he would not choose to contradict himself.

Besides, this would be confounding all ideas; it would be impossible to tell whether a man was acquitted, or received his pardon.

Louis XIII being desirous to sit in judgment upon the trial of the Duke de la Valette,[4] sent for some members of the parliament and of the privy council, to debate the matter;

upon their being ordered by the king to give their opinion concerning the warrant for his arrest, the president, De Believre, said "that he found it very strange that a prince should pass sentence upon a subject; that kings had reserved to themselves the power of pardoning, and left that of condemning to their officers; that his majesty wanted to see before him at the bar a person who, by his decision, was to be hurried away into the other world! That the prince's countenance should inspire with hopes, and not confound with fears; that his presence alone removed ecclesiastic censures; and that subjects ought not to go away dissatisfied from the sovereign." When sentence was passed, the same magistrate declared, "This is an unprecedented judgment to see, contrary to the example of past ages—a king of France, in the quality of a judge, condemning a gentleman to death."[5]

Again, sentences passed by the prince would be an inexhaustible source of injustice and abuse; the courtiers by their importunity would always be able to extort his decisions. Some Roman emperors were so mad as to sit as judges themselves; the consequence was that no reigns ever so surprised the world with oppression and injustice.

"Claudius," says Tacitus,[6] "having appropriated to himself the determination of lawsuits, and the function of magistrates, gave occasion to all manner of rapine." But Nero, upon coming to the empire after Claudius, endeavoured to conciliate the minds of the people by declaring "that he would take care not to be judge himself in private causes, that the parties might not be exposed within the walls of a palace to the iniquitous influence of a few freedmen."[7]

"Under the reign of Arcadius," says Zozimus,[8] "a swarm of calumniators spread themselves on every side, and infested the court. Upon a person's decease, it was immediately supposed he had left no children;[9] and, in consequence of this, his property was given away

---

[1] Demosthenes, *Pro Corona*, p. 494, Frankfort, 1604.

[2] See Philostratus, *Lives of the Sophists*, i, Life of Æschines.

[3] Plato does not think it right that kings, who, as he says, are priests, should preside at trials where people are condemned to death, to exile, or to imprisonment.

[4] See the account of the trial of the Duke de la Valette. It is printed in the *Memoirs* of Montresor, ii, p. 62.

[5] It was afterwards revoked. See the same account, ii. p. 236. It was ordinarily a right of the peerage that a peer criminally accused should be judged by the king, as Francis II in the trial of the Prince of Condé, and Charles VII in the case of the Duc d'Alençon. To-day, the presence of the king at the trial of a peer, in order to condemn him would seem an act of tyranny.—*Voltaire.*

[6] *Annals*, xi. 5.

[7] *Ibid.*, xiii. 4.

[8] *Histories*, v.

[9] The same disorder happened under Theodosius the younger.

by a rescript. For as the prince was surprisingly stupid, and the empress excessively enterprising, she was a slave to the insatiable avarice of her domestics and confidants; insomuch that to an honest man nothing could be more desirable than death."

"Formerly," says Procopius,[1] "there used to be very few people at court; but in Justinian's reign, as the judges had no longer the liberty of administering justice, their tribunals were deserted, while the prince's palace resounded with the litigious clamours of the several parties." Everybody knows what a prostitution there was of public judgments, and even of the very laws themselves, at that emperor's court.

The laws are the eye of the prince; by them he sees what would otherwise escape his observation. Should he attempt the function of a judge, he would not then labour for himself, but for impostors, whose aim is to deceive him.

6. *That in Monarchies Ministers ought not to sit as Judges.* It is likewise a very great inconvenience in monarchies for the ministers of the prince to sit as judges. We have still instances of states where there are a great number of judges to decide exchequer causes, and where the ministers nevertheless (a thing most incredible!) would fain determine them. Many are the reflections that here arise; but this single one will suffice for my purpose.

There is in the very nature of things a kind of contrast between a prince's council and his courts of judicature. The king's council ought to be composed of a few persons, and the courts of judicature of a great many. The reason is, in the former, things should be undertaken and conducted with a kind of warmth and passion, which can hardly be expected but from four or five men who make it their sole business. On the contrary, in courts of judicature a certain coolness in requisite, and an indifference, in some measure, to all manner of affairs.

7. *Of a single Magistrate.* A magistracy of this kind cannot take place but in a despotic government. We have an instance in the Roman history how far a single magistrate may abuse his power. Might it not be very well expected that Appius on his tribunal should contemn all laws, after having violated that of his own enacting?[2] Livy has given us the iniquitous

distinction of the Decemvir. He had suborned a man to reclaim Virginia in his presence as his slave; Virginia's relatives insisted that by virtue of his own law she should be consigned to them, till the definitive judgment was passed. Upon which he declared that his law had been enacted only in favour of the father, and that as Virginius was absent, no application could be made of it to the present case.[3]

8. *Of Accusation in different Governments.* At Rome[4] it was lawful for one citizen to accuse another. This was agreeable to the spirit of a republic, where each citizen ought to have an unlimited zeal for the public good, and is supposed to hold all the rights of his country in his own hands. Under the emperors, the republican maxims were still pursued; and instantly appeared a pernicious tribe, a swarm of informers. Crafty, wicked men, who could stoop to any indignity to serve the purposes of their ambition, were sure to busy themselves in the search of criminals whose condemnation might be agreeable to the prince; this was the road to honour and preferment,[5] but luckily we are strangers to it in our country.

We have at present an admirable law, namely, that by which the prince, who is established for the execution of the laws, appoints an officer in each court of judicature to prosecute all sorts of crimes in his name; hence the profession of informers is a thing unknown to us, for if this public avenger were suspected to abuse his office, he would soon be obliged to mention his author.

By Plato's *Laws*,[6] those who neglect to inform or to assist the magistrates are liable to punishment. This would not be so proper in our days. The public prosecutor watches for the safety of the citizens; he proceeds in his office while they enjoy their quiet and ease.

9. *Of the Severity of Punishments in different Governments.* The severity of punishments is fitter for despotic governments, whose principle is terror, than for a monarchy or a republic, whose spring is honour and virtue.

In moderate governments, the love of one's country, shame, and the fear of blame are restraining motives, capable of preventing a multitude of crimes. Here the greatest punish-

---

[1] *Secret History.*
[2] See *Leg.* 2, § 24, *Dig.* ff. *de orig. jur.*

[3] *Quod pater puellæ abesset, locum injuriæ esse ratus.*—Livy, dec. I, iii. 44.
[4] And in a great many other cities.
[5] See in Tacitus the rewards given to those informers.—*Annals,* i. 30.
[6] Book ix.

ment of a bad action is conviction. The civil laws have therefore a softer way of correcting, and do not require so much force and severity.

In those states a good legislator is less bent upon punishing than preventing crimes; he is more attentive to inspire good morals than to inflict penalties.

It is a constant remark of the Chinese authors[1] that the more the penal laws were increased in their empire, the nearer they drew towards a revolution. This is because punishments were augmented in proportion as the public morals were corrupted.

It would be an easy matter to prove that in all, or almost all, the governments of Europe, penalties have increased or diminished in proportion as those governments favoured or discouraged liberty.

In despotic governments, people are so unhappy as to have a greater dread of death than regret for the loss of life; consequently their punishments ought to be more severe. In moderate states they are more afraid of losing their lives than apprehensive of the pain of dying; those punishments, therefore, which deprive them simply of life are sufficient.

Men in excess of happiness or misery are equally inclinable to severity; witness conquerors and monks. It is mediocrity alone, and a mixture of prosperous and adverse fortune, that inspires us with lenity and pity.

What we see practised by individuals is equally observable in regard to nations. In countries inhabited by savages who lead a very hard life, and in despotic governments, where there is only one person on whom fortune lavishes her favours, while the miserable subjects lie exposed to her insults, people are equally cruel. Lenity reigns in moderate governments.

When in reading history we observe the cruelty of the sultans in administration of justice, we shudder at the very thought of the miseries of human nature.

In moderate governments, a good legislator may make use of everything by way of punishment. Is it not very extraordinary that one of the chief penalties at Sparta was to deprive a person of the power of lending out his wife, or of receiving the wife of another man, and to oblige him to have no company at home but virgins? In short, whatever the law calls a punishment is such effectively.

[1] I shall show hereafter that China is, in this respect, in the same case as a republic or a monarchy.

10. *Of the ancient French Laws.* In the ancient French laws we find the true spirit of monarchy. In cases relating to pecuniary mulcts, the common people are less severely punished than the nobility.[2] But in criminal[3] cases it is quite the reverse; the nobleman loses his honour and his voice in court, while the peasant, who has no honour to lose, undergoes a corporal punishment.

11. *That when People are virtuous few Punishments are necessary.* The people of Rome had some share of probity. Such was the force of this probity that the legislator had frequently no further occasion than to point out the right road, and they were sure to follow it; one would imagine that instead of precepts it was sufficient to give them counsels.

The punishments of the regal laws, and those of the Twelve Tables, were almost all abolished in the time of the republic, in consequence either of the Valerian[4] or of the Porcian law.[5] It was never observed that this step did any manner of prejudice to the civil administration.

This Valerian law, which restrained the magistrates from using violent methods against a citizen that had appealed to the people, inflicted no other punishment on the person who infringed it than that of being reputed a dishonest man.[6]

12. *Of the Power of Punishments.* Experience shows that in countries remarkable for the lenity of their laws the spirit of the inhabitants is as much affected by slight penalties as in other countries by severer punishments.

If an inconvenience or abuse arises in the state, a violent government endeavours suddenly to redress it; and instead of putting the old laws in execution, it establishes some cruel punishment, which instantly puts a stop

[2] Suppose, for instance, to prevent the execution of a decree, the common people paid a fine of forty sous, and the nobility of sixty livres.—*Somme Rurale*, ii, p. 198, ed. Goth. 1512; and Beaumanoir, 61, p. 309.
[3] See the *Council* of Peter Defontaines, 13, especially art. 22.
[4] It was made by Valerius Publicola soon after the expulsion of the kings, and was twice renewed, both times by magistrates of the same family. As Livy observes, x, 9, the question was not to give it a greater force, but to render its injunctions more perfect. "*Diligentius sanctum,*" says Livy, *ibid.*
[5] *Lex Porcia pro tergo civium lata.* It was made in the 454th year of the foundation of Rome.
[6] *Nihil ultra quam improbe factum adjecet.*— Livy, *loc. cit.*

to the evil. But the spring of government hereby loses its elasticity; the imagination grows accustomed to the severe as well as the milder punishment; and as the fear of the latter diminishes, they are soon obliged in every case to have recourse to the former. Robberies on the highway became common in some countries; in order to remedy this evil, they invented the punishment of breaking upon the wheel, the terror of which put a stop for a while to this mischievous practice. But soon after robberies on the highways became as common as ever.

Desertion in our days has grown to a very great height; in consequence of which it was judged proper to punish those delinquents with death; and yet their number did not diminish. The reason is very natural; a soldier, accustomed to venture his life, despises, or affects to despise, the danger of losing it. He is habituated to the fear of shame; it would have been therefore much better to have continued a punishment[1] which branded him with infamy for life; the penalty was pretended to be increased, while it really diminished.

Mankind must not be governed with too much severity; we ought to make a prudent use of the means which nature has given us to conduct them. If we inquire into the cause of all human corruptions, we shall find that they proceed from the impunity of criminals, and not from the moderation of punishments.

Let us follow nature, who has given shame to man for his scourge; and let the heaviest part of the punishment be the infamy attending it.

But if there be some countries where shame is not a consequence of punishment, this must be owing to tyranny, which has inflicted the same penalties on villains and honest men.

And if there are others where men are deterred only by cruel punishments, we may be sure that this must, in a great measure, arise from the violence of the government which has used such penalties for slight transgressions.

It often happens that a legislator, desirous of remedying an abuse, thinks of nothing else; his eyes are open only to this object, and shut to its inconveniences. When the abuse is redressed, you see only the severity of the legislator; yet there remains an evil in the state that has sprung from this severity; the minds of the people are corrupted, and become habituated to despotism.

Lysander[2] having obtained a victory over the Athenians, the prisoners were ordered to be tried, in consequence of an accusation brought against that nation of having thrown all the captives of two galleys down a precipice, and of having resolved in full assembly to cut off the hands of those whom they should chance to make prisoners. The Athenians were therefore all massacred, except Adymantes, who had opposed this decree. Lysander reproached Phylocles, before he was put to death, with having depraved the people's minds, and given lessons of cruelty to all Greece.

"The Argives," says Plutarch,[3] "having put fifteen hundred of their citizens to death, the Athenians ordered sacrifices of expiation, that it might please the gods to turn the hearts of the Athenians from so cruel a thought."

There are two sorts of corruptions—one when the people do not observe the laws; the other when they are corrupted by the laws: an incurable evil, because it is in the very remedy itself.

13. *Insufficiency of the Laws of Japan.* Excessive punishments may even corrupt a despotic government; of this we have an instance in Japan.

Here almost all crimes are punished with death,[4] because disobedience to so great an emperor as that of Japan is reckoned an enormous crime. The question is not so much to correct the delinquent as to vindicate the authority of the prince. These notions are derived from servitude, and are owing especially to this, that as the emperor is universal proprietor, almost all crimes are directly against his interests.

They punish with death lies spoken before the magistrate;[5] a proceeding contrary to natural defence.

Even things which have not the appearance of a crime are severely punished; for instance, a man that ventures his money at play is put to death.

True it is that the character of this people, so amazingly obstinate, capricious, and reso-

[1] They slit his nose or cut off his ears.

[2] Xenophon, *Hist.*, iii. 2, §§ 20–22.
[3] *Of Those Who Are Intrusted with the Direction of the State Affairs*, 14.
[4] See Kempfer.
[5] *Collection of Voyages that Contributed to the Establishment of the East India Company*, iii, part I, p. 428.

lute as to defy all dangers and calamities, seems to absolve their legislators from the imputation of cruelty, notwithstanding the severity of their laws. But are men who have a natural contempt for death, and who rip open their bellies for the least fancy—are such men, I say, mended or deterred, or rather are they not hardened, by the continual prospect of punishments?

The relations of travellers inform us, with respect to the education of the Japanese, that children must be treated there with mildness, because they become hardened to punishment; that their slaves must not be too roughly used, because they immediately stand upon their defence. Would not one imagine that they might easily have judged of the spirit which ought to reign in their political and civil government from that which should prevail in their domestic concerns?

A wise legislator would have endeavoured to reclaim people by a just temperature of punishments and rewards; by maxims of philosophy, morality, and religion, adapted to those characters; by a proper application of the rules of honour, and by the enjoyment of ease and tranquillity of life. And should he have entertained any apprehension that their minds, being inured to the cruelty of punishments, would no longer be restrained by those of a milder nature, he would have conducted himself[1] in another manner, and gained his point by degrees, in particular cases that admitted of any indulgence, he would have mitigated the punishment, till he should have been able to extend this mitigation to all cases.

But these are springs to which despotic power is a stranger; it may abuse itself, and that is all it can do: in Japan it has made its utmost effort, and has surpassed even itself in cruelty.

As the minds of the people grew wild and intractable, they were obliged to have recourse to the most horrid severity.

This is the origin, this the spirit, of the laws of Japan. They had more fury, however, than force. They succeeded the extirpation of Christianity; but such unaccountable efforts are a proof of their insufficiency. They wanted to establish a good policy, and they have shown greater marks of their weakness.

We have only to read the relation of the interview between the Emperor and the Deyro at Meaco.[2] The number of those who were suffocated or murdered in that city by ruffians is incredible; young maids and boys were carried off by force, and found afterwards exposed in public places, at unseasonable hours, quite naked, and sewn in linen bags, to prevent their knowing which way they had passed; robberies were committed in all parts; the bellies of horses were ripped open, to bring their riders to the ground; and coaches were overturned, in order to strip the ladies. The Dutch, who were told they could not pass the night on the scaffolds without exposing themselves to the danger of being assassinated, came down, &c.

I shall here give one instance more from the same nation. The Emperor having abandoned himself to infamous pleasures, lived unmarried, and was consequently in danger of dying without issue. The Deyro sent him two beautiful damsels; one he married out of respect, but would not meddle with her. His nurse caused the finest women of the empire to be sent for, but all to no purpose. At length, an armourer's daughter having pleased his fancy,[3] he determined to espouse her, and had a son. The ladies belonging to the court, enraged to see a person of such mean extraction preferred to themselves, stifled the child. The crime was concealed from the Emperor; for he would have deluged the land with blood. The excessive severity of the laws hinders, therefore, their execution: when the punishment surpasses all measure, they are frequently obliged to prefer impunity to it.

14. *Of the Spirit of the Roman Senate.* Under the consulate of Acilius Glabrio and Piso, the Asilian law[4] was made to prevent the intriguing for places. Dio says[5] that the senate engaged the consuls to propose it, by reason that C. Cornelius, the tribune, had resolved to cause more severe punishments to be established against this crime; to which the people seemed greatly inclined. The senate rightly judged that immoderate punishments would strike, indeed, a terror into people's minds, but must have also this effect, that there would be nobody afterwards to accuse or condemn;

[1] Let this be observed as a maxim in practice, with regard to cases where the minds of people have been depraved by too great a severity of punishments.

[2] *Collection of Voyages that Contributed to the Establishment of the East India Company*, v, p. 2.
[3] *Ibid.*
[4] The guilty were condemned to a fine; they could not be admitted into the rank of senators, nor nominated to any public office.—Dio, xxxvi. 21.
[5] *Ibid.*

whereas, by proposing moderate penalties, there would be always judges and accusers.

15. *Of the Roman Laws in respect to Punishments.* I am strongly confirmed in my sentiments upon finding the Romans on my side; and I think that punishments are connected with the nature of governments when I behold this great people changing in this respect their civil laws, in proportion as they altered their form of government.

The regal laws, made for fugitives, slaves, and vagabonds, were very severe. The spirit of a republic would have required that the decemvirs should not have inserted those laws in their Twelve Tables; but men who aimed at tyranny were far from conforming to a republican spirit.

Livy says,[1] in relation to the punishment of Metius Suffetius, dictator of Alba, who was condemned by Tullius Hostilius to be fastened to two chariots drawn by horses, and torn asunder, that this was the first and last punishment in which the remembrance of humanity seemed to have been lost. He is mistaken; the Twelve Tables are full of very cruel laws.[2]

The design of the decemvirs appears more conspicuous in the capital punishment pronounced against libellers and poets. This is not agreeable to the genius of a republic, where the people like to see the great men humbled. But persons who aimed at the subversion of liberty were afraid of writings that might revive its spirit.[3]

After the expulsion of the decemvirs, almost all the penal laws were abolished. It is true they were not expressly repealed; but as the Porcian law had ordained that no citizen of Rome should be put to death, they were of no further use.

This is exactly the time to which we may refer what Livy says[4] of the Romans, that no people were ever fonder of moderation in punishments.

But if to the lenity of penal laws we add the right which the party accused had of withdrawing before judgment was pronounced, we shall find that the Romans followed the spirit which I have observed to be natural to a republic.

Sulla, who confounded tyranny, anarchy, and liberty, made the Cornelian laws. He seemed to have contrived regulations merely with a view to create new crimes. Thus distinguishing an infinite number of actions by the name of murder, he found murderers in all parts; and by a practice too much followed, he laid snares, sowed thorns, and opened precipices, wheresoever the citizens set their feet.

Almost all Sulla's laws contained only the interdiction of fire and water. To this Cæsar added the confiscation of goods,[5] because the rich, by preserving their estates in exile, became bolder in the perpetration of crimes.

The emperors, having established a military government, soon found that it was as terrible to the prince as to the subject; they endeavoured therefore to temper it, and with this view had recourse to dignities, and to the respect with which those dignities were attended.

The government thus drew nearer a little to monarchy, and punishments were divided into three classes:[6] those which related to the principal persons in the state,[7] which were very mild: those which were inflicted on persons of an inferior rank,[8] and were more severe; and, in fine, such as concerned only persons of the lowest condition,[9] which were the most rigorous.

Maximinus, that fierce and stupid prince, increased the rigour of the military government which he ought to have softened. The senate were informed, says Capitolinus,[10] that some had been crucified, others exposed to wild beasts, or sewn up in the skins of beasts lately killed, without any manner of regard to their dignity. It seemed as if he wanted to exercise the military discipline, on the model of which he pretended to regulate the civil administration.

In *The Consideration on the Rise and Declension of the Roman Grandeur,*[11] we find in what manner Constantine changed the mili-

[1] Book i. 28.
[2] We find there the punishment of fire, and generally capital punishments, theft punished with death, &c.
[3] Sulla, animated with the same spirit as the decemvirs, followed their example in augmenting the penal laws against satirical writers.
[4] Book i, 28.
[5] *Pœnas facinorum auxit, cum locupletes eo facilius scelere se obligarent, quod integris patrimoniis exularent.*—Suetonius in *Life of Julius Cæsar,* 162.
[6] See the *Leg.* 3, § *legis, ad leg. Cornel. de sicariis,* and a vast number of others in the *Digest* and in the *Codex.*
[7] *Sublimiores.*
[8] *Medios.*
[9] *Infimos. Leg.* 3, § *legis, ad leg. Cornel. de sicariis.*
[10] Jul. Cap., *Maximini duo,* 8.
[11] Chapter 17.

tary despotism into a military and civil government, and drew nearer to monarchy. There we may trace the different revolutions of this state, and see how they fell from rigour to indolence, and from indolence to impunity.

16. *Of the just Proportion between Punishments and Crimes.* It is an essential point, that there should be a certain proportion in punishments, because it is essential that a great crime should be avoided rather than a smaller, and that which is more pernicious to society rather than that which is less.

"An impostor,[1] who called himself Constantine Ducas, raised a great insurrection at Constantinople. He was taken and condemned to be whipped; but upon informing against several persons of distinction, he was sentenced to be burned as a calumniator." It is very extraordinary that they should thus proportion the punishments between the crime of high treason and that of calumny.

This puts me in mind of a saying of Charles II, King of Great Britain. He saw a man one day standing in the pillory; upon which he asked what crime the man had committed. He was answered, "Please your Majesty, he has written a libel against your ministers." "The fool!" said the King, "why did he not write against me? They would have done nothing to him."

"Seventy persons having conspired against the Emperor Basil, he ordered them to be whipped, and the hair of their heads and beards to be burned. A stag, one day, having taken hold of him by the girdle with his horn, one of his retinue drew his sword, cut the girdle, and saved him; upon which he ordered that person's head to be cut off, for having," said he, "drawn his sword against his sovereign."[2] Who could imagine that the same prince could ever have passed two such different judgments?

It is a great abuse amongst us to condemn to the same punishment a person that only robs on the highway and another who robs and murders. Surely, for the public security, some difference should be made in the punishment.

In China, those who add murder to robbery are cut in pieces:[3] but not so the others; to this

difference it is owing that though they rob in that country they never murder.

In Russia, where the punishment of robbery and murder is the same, they always murder.[4] The dead, say they, tell no tales.

Where there is no difference in the penalty, there should be some in the expectation of pardon. In England they never murder on the highway, because robbers have some hopes of transportation, which is not the case in respect to those that commit murder.

Letters of grace are of excellent use in moderate governments. This power which the prince has of pardoning, exercised with prudence, is capable of producing admirable effects. The principle of despotic government, which neither grants nor receives any pardon, deprives it of these advantages.

17. *Of the Rack.* The wickedness of mankind makes it necessary for the law to suppose them better than they really are. Hence the deposition of two witnesses is sufficient in the punishment of all crimes. The law believes them, as if they spoke by the mouth of truth. Thus we judge that every child conceived in wedlock is legitimate; the law having a confidence in the mother, as if she were chastity itself. But the use of the rack against criminals cannot be defended on a like plea of necessity.

We have before us the example of a nation blessed with an excellent civil government,[5] where without any inconvenience the practice of racking criminals is rejected. It is not, therefore, in its own nature necessary.[6]

So many men of learning and genius have written against the custom of torturing criminals, that after them I dare not presume to meddle with the subject. I was going to say that it might suit despotic states, where whatever inspires fear is the fittest spring of government. I was going to say that the slaves among the Greeks and Romans—but nature cries out aloud, and asserts her rights.

---

[1] *Hist.* of Nicephorus, patriarch of Constantinople.
[2] In Nicephorus' *History.*
[3] Father Du Halde, i, p. 6.

[4] *Present State of Russia,* Perry.
[5] The English.
[6] The citizens of Athens could not be put to the rack (Lysias, *Orat. contra Agorat.*) unless it was for high treason. The torture was used within thirty days after condemnation. (Curius Fortunatus, *Rhetor, scol.,* ii.) There was no preparatory torture. In regard to the Romans, the *Leg.* 3, 4, *ad leg. Jul. majest.,* show that birth, dignity, and the military profession exempted people from the rack, except in cases of high treason. See the prudent restrictions of this practice made by the laws of the Visigoths.

18. *Of pecuniary and corporal Punishments.*
Our ancestors, the Germans, admitted of none
but pecuniary punishments. Those free and
warlike people were of opinion that their
blood ought not to be spilled but with sword
in hand. On the contrary, these punishments
are rejected by the Japanese,[1] under pretence
that the rich might elude them. But are not
the rich afraid of being stripped of their property? And might not pecuniary penalties be
proportioned to people's fortunes? And, in
fine, might not infamy be added to those punishments?

A good legislator takes a just medium; he
ordains neither always pecuniary, nor always
corporal punishments.

19. *Of the Law of Retaliation.* The use of the
law of retaliation[2] is very frequent in despotic
countries, where they are fond of simple laws.
Moderate governments admit of it sometimes;
but with this difference, that the former exercise it in full rigour, whereas among the latter
it ever receives some kind of limitation.

The law of the Twelve Tables admitted
two: first, it never condemned to retaliation,
but when the plaintiff could not be satisfied
in any other manner.[3] Secondly, after condemnation they might pay damages and interest,[4] and then the corporal was changed into a
pecuniary punishment.[5]

20. *Of the Punishment of Fathers for the
Crimes of their Children.* In China, fathers are
punished for the crimes of their children. This
was likewise the custom of Peru[6]—a custom
derived from the notion of despotic power.

Little does it signify to say that in China the
father is punished for not having exerted that
paternal authority which nature has established, and the laws themselves have improved. This still supposes that there is no
honour among the Chinese. Amongst us, parents whose children are condemned by the
laws of their country, and children[7] whose

parents have undergone the like fate, are as
severely punished by shame, as they would be
in China by the loss of their lives.

21. *Of the Clemency of the Prince.* Clemency
is the characteristic of monarchs. In republics,
whose principle is virtue, it is not so necessary.
In despotic governments, where fear predominates, it is less customary, because the great
men are to be restrained by examples of severity. It is more necessary in monarchies,
where they are governed by honour, which
frequently requires what the very law forbids.
Disgrace is here equivalent to chastisement;
and even the forms of justice are punishments. This is because particular kinds of penalty are formed by shame, which on every side
invades the delinquent.

The great men in monarchies are so heavily
punished by disgrace, by the loss (though often imaginary) of their fortune, credit, ac-
quaintances, and pleasures, that rigour in respect to them is needless. It can tend only to
divest the subject of the affection he has for
the person of his prince, and of the respect he
ought to have for public posts and employments.

As the instability of the great is natural to a
despotic government, so their security is in-
terwoven with the nature of monarchy.

So many are the advantages which monarchs gain by clemency, so greatly does it raise
their fame, and endear them to their subjects,
that it is generally happy for them to have an
opportunity of displaying it; which in this
part of the world is seldom wanting.

Some branch, perhaps, of their authority,
but never hardly the whole, will be disputed;
and if they sometimes fight for their crown,
they do not fight for their life.

But some may ask when it is proper to punish, and when to pardon. This is a point more
easily felt that prescribed. When there is danger in the exercise of clemency, it is visible;
nothing so easy as to distinguish it from that
imbecility which exposes princes to contempt
and to the very incapacity of punishing.

The Emperor Maurice made a resolution
never to spill the blood of his subjects. Anastasius[8] punished no crimes at all. Isaac Ange-
lus took an oath that no one should be put to
death during his reign. Those Greek emperors forgot that it was not for nothing they
were entrusted with the sword.

---

[1] See Kempfer.

[2] It is established in the Koran. See the chapter,
Of the Cow.

[3] *Si membrum rupit, ni cum eo pacit, talio esto.*
Aulus Gellius, xx. i.

[4] *Ibid.*

[5] See also the Law of the Visigoths, vi, tit. 4, §§
3, 5.

[6] See Garcilasso, *History of the Civil Wars of
the Spaniards in the West Indies.*

[7] "Instead of punishing them," says Plato, "they
ought to be commended for not having followed
their fathers' example."—*Laws,* ix.

[8] Fragment of Suidas, in Constantine Porphyrogenitus.

Book VII. Consequences of the Different Principles of the Three Governments with respect to Sumptuary Laws, Luxury, and the Condition of Women

1. *Of Luxury*. Luxury is ever in proportion to the inequality of fortunes. If the riches of a state are equally divided there will be no luxury; for it is founded merely on the conveniences acquired by the labour of others.

In order to have this equal distribution of riches, the law ought to give to each man only what is necessary for nature. If they exceed these bounds, some will spend, and others will acquire, by which means an inequality will be established.

Supposing what is necessary for the support of nature to be equal to a given sum, the luxury of those who have only what is barely necessary will be equal to a cipher: if a person happens to have double that sum, his luxury will be equal to one; he that has double the latter's substance will have a luxury equal to three; if this be still doubled, there will be a luxury equal to seven; so that the property of the subsequent individual being always supposed double to that of the preceding, the luxury will increase double, and a unit be always added, in this progression, 0, 1, 3, 7, 15, 31, 63, 127.

In Plato's republic,[1] luxury might have been exactly calculated. There were four sorts of censuses or rates of estates. The first was exactly the term beyond poverty, the second was double, the third triple, the fourth quadruple to the first. In the first census, luxury was equal to a cipher; in the second to one, in the third to two, in the fourth to three: and thus it followed in an arithmetical proportion.

Considering the luxury of different nations with respect to one another, it is in each state a compound proportion to the inequality of fortunes among the subjects, and to the inequality of wealth in different states. In Poland, for example, there is an extreme inequality of fortunes, but the poverty of the whole hinders them from having so much luxury as in a more opulent government.

Luxury is also in proportion to the populousness of the towns, and especially of the capital; so that it is in a compound proportion to the riches of the state, to the inequality of private fortunes, and to the number of people settled in particular places.

In proportion to the populousness of towns, the inhabitants are filled with notions of vanity, and actuated by an ambition of distinguishing themselves by trifles.[2] If they are very numerous, and most of them strangers to one another, their vanity redoubles, because there are greater hopes of success. As luxury inspires these hopes, each man assumes the marks of a superior condition. But by endeavouring thus at distinction, every one becomes equal, and distinction ceases; as all are desirous of respect, nobody is regarded.

Hence arises a general inconvenience. Those who excel in a profession set what value they please on their labour; this example is followed by people of inferior abilities, and then there is an end of all proportion between our wants and the means of satisfying them. When I am forced to go to law, I must be able to fee counsel; when I am sick, I must have it in my power to fee a physician.

It is the opinion of several that the assemblage of so great a multitude of people in capital cities is an obstruction to commerce, because the inhabitants are no longer at a proper distance from each other. But I cannot think so; for men have more desires, more wants, more fancies, when they live together.

2. *Of sumptuary Laws in a Democracy*. We have observed that in a republic, where riches are equally divided, there can be no such thing as luxury; and as we have shown in the 5th Book[3] that this equal distribution constitutes the excellence of a republican government; hence it follows, that the less luxury there is in a republic, the more it is perfect. There was none among the old Romans, none among the Lacedæmonians; and in republics where this equality is not quite lost, the spirit

---

[1] The first census was the hereditary share in land, and Plato would not allow them to have, in other effects, above a triple of the hereditary share. See his *Laws*, v.

[2] "In large and populous cities," says the author of the *Fable of the Bees*, i, p. 133, "they wear clothes above their rank, and, consequently, have the pleasure of being esteemed by a vast majority, not as what they are, but what they appear to be. They have the satisfaction of imagining that they appear what they would be: which, to weak minds, is a pleasure almost as substantial as they could reap from the very accomplishment of their wishes."

[3] Chapters 3, 4.

of commerce, industry, and virtue renders every man able and willing to live on his own property, and consequently prevents the growth of luxury.

The laws concerning the new division of lands, insisted upon so eagerly in some republics, were of the most salutary nature. They are dangerous, only as they are sudden. By reducing instantly the wealth of some, and increasing that of others, they form a revolution in each family, and must produce a general one in the state.

In proportion as luxury gains ground in a republic, the minds of the people are turned towards their particular interests. Those who are allowed only what is necessary have nothing but their own reputation and their country's glory in view. But a soul depraved by luxury has many other desires, and soon becomes an enemy to the laws that confine it. The luxury in which the garrison of Rhegium began to live was the cause of their massacring the inhabitants.

No sooner were the Romans corrupted than their desires became boundless and immense. Of this we may judge by the price they set on things. A pitcher of Falernian wine[1] was sold for a hundred Roman denarii; a barrel of salt meat from the kingdom of Pontus cost four hundred; a good cook four talents; and for boys, no price was reckoned too great. When the whole world, impelled by the force of corruption, is immersed in voluptuousness,[2] what must then become of virtue?

3. *Of sumptuary Laws in an Aristocracy.* There is this inconvenience in an ill-constituted aristocracy, that the wealth centres in the nobility, and yet they are not allowed to spend; for as luxury is contrary to the spirit of moderation, it must be banished thence. This government comprehends, therefore, only people who are extremely poor and cannot acquire, and people who are vastly rich and cannot spend.

In Venice, they are compelled by the laws to moderation. They are so habituated to parsimony that none but courtesans can make them part with their money. Such is the method made use of for the support of industry; the most contemptible of women may be profuse without danger, whilst those who contribute to their extravagance consume their days in the greatest obscurity.

Admirable in this respect were the institutions of the principal republics of Greece. The rich employed their money in festivals, musical choruses, chariots, horse-races, and chargeable offices. Wealth was, therefore, as burdensome there as poverty.

4. *Of sumptuary Laws in a Monarchy.* Tacitus says[3] that the Suiones, a German nation, has a particular respect for riches; for which reason they live under the government of one person. This shows that luxury is extremely proper for monarchies, and that under this government there must be no sumptuary laws.

As riches, by the very constitution of monarchies, are unequally divided, there is an absolute necessity for luxury. Were the rich not to be lavish, the poor would starve. It is even necessary here that the expenses of the opulent should be in proportion to the inequality of fortunes, and that luxury, as we have already observed, should increase in this proportion. The augmentation of private wealth is owing to its having deprived one part of the citizens of their necessary support; this must therefore be restored to them.

Hence it is that for the preservation of a monarchical state, luxury ought continually to increase, and to grow more extensive, as it rises from the labourer to the artificer, to the merchant, to the magistrate, to the nobility, to the great officers of state, up to the very prince; otherwise the nation will be undone.

In the reign of Augustus, a proposal was made in the Roman senate, which was composed of grave magistrates, learned civilians, and of men whose heads were filled with the notion of the primitive times, to reform the manners and luxury of women. It is curious to see in Dio,[4] with what art this prince eluded the importunate solicitations of those senators. This was because he was founding a monarchy, and dissolving a republic.

Under Tiberius, the Ædiles proposed in the senate the re-establishment of the ancient sumptuary laws.[5] This prince, who did not want sense, opposed it. "The state," said he, "could not possibly subsist in the present situation of things. How could Rome, how could the provinces, live? We were frugal, while we

[1] Fragment of the 36th book of Diodorus, quoted by Constantine Porphyrogenitus, in his *Extract of Virtues and Vices.*
[2] *Cum maximus omnium impetus ad luxuriam esset.—Ibid.*

[3] *De Moribus Germanorum,* 44.
[4] Dio Cassius, liv. 16.
[5] Tacitus, *Annals,* iii. 34.

were only masters of one city; now we consume the riches of the whole globe, and employ both the masters and their slaves in our service." He plainly saw that sumptuary laws would not suit the present form of government.

When a proposal was made under the same emperor to the senate, to prohibit the governors from carrying their wives with them into the provinces, because of the dissoluteness and irregularity which followed those ladies, the proposal was rejected. It was said that the examples of ancient austerity had been changed into a more agreeable method of living.[1] They found there was a necessity for different manners.

Luxury is therefore absolutely necessary in monarchies; as it is also in despotic states. In the former, it is the use of liberty; in the latter, it is the abuse of servitude. A slave appointed by his master to tyrannise over other wretches of the same condition, uncertain of enjoying tomorrow the blessings of to-day, has no other felicity than that of glutting the pride, the passions, and voluptuousness of the present moment.

Hence arises a very natural reflection. Republics end with luxury; monarchies with poverty.[2]

5. *In what Cases sumptuary Laws are useful in a Monarchy.* Whether it was from a republican spirit, or from some other particular circumstance, sumptuary laws were made in Aragon, in the middle of the thirteenth century. James the First ordained that neither the king nor any of his subjects should have above two sorts of dishes at a meal, and that each dish should be dressed only one way, except it were game of their own killing.[3]

In our days, sumptuary laws have been also enacted in Sweden; but with a different view from those of Aragon.

A government may make sumptuary laws with a view to absolute frugality; this is the spirit of sumptuary laws in republics; and the very nature of the thing shows that such was the design of those of Aragon.

Sumptuary laws may likewise be established with a design to promote a relative frugality: when a government, perceiving that foreign merchandise, being at too high a price, will require such an exportation of home manufactures as to deprive them of more advantages by the loss of the latter than they can receive from the possession of the former, they will forbid their being introduced. And this is the spirit of the laws which in our days have been passed in Sweden.[4] Such are the sumptuary laws proper for monarchies.

In general, the poorer a state, the more it is ruined by its relative luxury; and consequently the more occasion it has for relative sumptuary laws. The richer a state, the more it thrives by its relative luxury; for which reason it must take particular care not to make any relative sumptuary laws. This we shall better explain in the book on commerce;[5] here we treat only of absolute luxury.

6. *Of the Luxury of China.* Sumptuary laws may, in some governments, be necessary for particular reasons. The people, by the influence of the climate, may grow so numerous, and the means of subsisting may be so uncertain, as to render a universal application to agriculture extremely necessary. As luxury in those countries is dangerous, their sumptuary laws should be very severe. In order, therefore, to be able to judge whether luxury ought to be encouraged or proscribed, we should examine first what relation there is between the number of people and the facility they have of procuring subsistence. In England the soil produces more grain than is necessary for the maintenance of such as cultivate the land, and of those who are employed in the woollen manufactures. This country may be therefore allowed to have some trifling arts, and consequently luxury. In France, likewise, there is corn enough for the support of the husbandman and of the manufacturer. Besides, a foreign trade may bring in so many necessaries in return for toys that there is no danger to be apprehended from luxury.

On the contrary, in China, the women are so prolific, and the human species multiplies so fast, that the lands, though never so much cultivated, are scarcely sufficient to support the inhabitants. Here, therefore, luxury is pernicious, and the spirit of industry and economy is as requisite as in any republic.[6] They are obliged to pursue the necessary arts, and to

---

[1] *Multa duritiei veterum melius et lætius mutata.*—Tacitus, *Annals*, iii. 34.

[2] *Opulentia paritura mox egestatem.*—Florus, iii. 12.

[3] Constitution of James I in the year 1234, art. 6, in *Marca Hispanica*, p. 1429.

[4] They have prohibited rich wines and other costly merchandise.

[5] *Lettres persanes*, 106. See below, xx. 20.

[6] Luxury has been here always prohibited.

shun those of luxury and pleasure.

This is the spirit of the excellent decrees of the Chinese emperors. "Our ancestors," says an emperor of the family of the Tangs,[1] "held it as a maxim that if there was a man who did not work, or a woman that was idle, somebody must suffer cold or hunger in the empire." And on this principle he ordered a vast number of the monasteries of Bonzes to be destroyed.

The third emperor of the one-and-twentieth dynasty,[2] to whom some precious stones were brought that had been found in a mine, ordered it to be shut up, not choosing to fatigue his people with working for a thing that could neither feed nor clothe them.

"So great is our luxury," says Kiayventi,[3] "that people adorn with embroidery the shoes of boys and girls, whom they are obliged to sell." Is employing so many people in making clothes for one person the way to prevent a great many from wanting clothes? There are ten men who eat the fruits of the earth to one employed in agriculture; and is this the means of preserving numbers from wanting nourishment?

7. *Fatal Consequence of Luxury in China.* In the history of China we find it has had twenty-two successive dynasties, that is, it has experienced twenty-two general, without mentioning a prodigious number of particular, revolutions. The first three dynasties lasted a long time, because they were wisely administered, and the empire had not so great an extent as it afterwards obtained. But we may observe in general that all those dynasties began very well. Virtue, attention, and vigilance are necessary in China; these prevailed in the commencement of the dynasties, and failed in the end. It was natural that emperors trained up in military toil, who had compassed the dethroning of a family immersed in pleasure, should adhere to virtue, which they had found so advantageous, and be afraid of voluptuousness, which they knew had proved so fatal to the family dethroned. But after the three or four first princes, corruption, luxury, indolence, and pleasure possessed their successors; they shut themselves up in a palace; their understanding was impaired; their life was short-

[1] In an ordinance quoted by Father Du Halde, ii, p. 497.
[2] History of China, 21st Dynasty, in Father Du Halde's work, i.
[3] In a discourse cited by Father Du Halde, iii, p. 418.

ened; the family declined; the grandees rose up; the eunuchs gained credit; none but children were set on the throne; the palace was at variance with the empire; a lazy set of people that dwelt there ruined the industrious part of the nation; the emperor was killed or destroyed by a usurper, who founded a family, the third or fourth successor of which went and shut himself up in the very same palace.

8. *Of public Continency.* So many are the imperfections that attend the loss of virtue in women, and so greatly are their minds depraved when this principal guard is removed, that in a popular state public incontinency may be considered as the last of miseries, and as a certain forerunner of a change in the constitution.

Hence it is that the sage legislators of republican states have ever required of women a particular gravity of manners. They have proscribed not only vice, but the very appearance of it. They have banished even all commerce of gallantry—a commerce that produces idleness, that renders the women corrupters, even before they are corrupted, that gives a value to trifles, and debases things of importance: a commerce, in fine, that makes people act entirely by the maxims of ridicule, in which the women are so perfectly skilled.

9. *Of the Condition or State of Women in different Governments.* In monarchies women are subject to very little restraint, because as the distinction of ranks calls them to court, there they assume a spirit of liberty, which is almost the only one tolerated in that place. Each courtier avails himself of their charms and passions, in order to advance his fortune: and as their weakness admits not of pride, but of vanity, luxury constantly attends them.

In despotic governments women do not introduce, but are themselves an object of, luxury. They must be in a state of the most rigorous servitude. Every one follows the spirit of the government, and adopts in his own family the customs he sees elsewhere established. As the laws are very severe and executed on the spot, they are afraid lest the liberty of women should expose them to danger. Their quarrels, indiscretions, repugnancies, jealousies, piques, and that art, in fine, which little souls have of interesting great ones, would be attended there with fatal consequences.

Besides, as princes in those countries make a sport of human nature, they allow themselves a multitude of women; and a thousand considerations oblige them to keep those women in close confinement.

In republics women are free by the laws and restrained by manners; luxury is banished thence, and with it corruption and vice.

In the cities of Greece, where they were not under the restraint of a religion which declares that even amongst men regularity of manners is a part of virtue; where a blind passion triumphed with a boundless insolence, and love appeared only in a shape which we dare not mention, while marriage was considered as nothing more than simple friendship;[1] such was the virtue, simplicity, and chastity of women in those cities, that in this respect hardly any people were ever known to have had a better and wiser polity.[2]

10. *Of the domestic Tribunal among the Romans.* The Romans had no particular magistrates, like the Greeks, to inspect the conduct of women. The censors had not an eye over them, as over the rest of the republic.

The institution of the domestic tribunal[3] supplied the magistracy established among the Greeks.[4]

The husband summoned the wife's relatives, and tried her in their presence.[5] This tribunal preserved the manners of the republic; and at the same time those very manners maintained this tribunal. For it decided not only in respect to the violation of the laws, but also of manners: now, in order to judge of the violation of the latter, manners are requisite.

The penalties inflicted by this tribunal ought to be, and actually were, arbitrary: for all that relates to manners, and to the rules of modesty, can hardly be comprised under one code of laws. It is easy indeed to regulate by laws what we owe to others; but it is very difficult of comprise all we owe to ourselves.

The domestic tribunal inspected the general conduct of women: but there was one crime which, beside the animadversion of this tribunal, was likewise subject to a public accusation. This was adultery; whether that in a republic so great a depravation of manners interested the government; or whether the wife's immorality might render the husband suspected; or whether, in fine, they were afraid lest even honest people might choose that this crime should rather be concealed than punished.

11. *In what Manner the Institutions changed at Rome, together with the Government.* As manners were supported by the domestic tribunal, they were also supported by the public accusation; and hence it is that these two things fell together with the public manners, and ended with the republic.[6]

The establishing of perpetual questions, that is, the division of jurisdiction among the prætors, and the custom gradually introduced of the prætors determining all causes themselves,[7] weakened the use of the domestic tribunal. This appears by the surprise of historians, who look upon the decisions which Tiberius caused to be given by this tribunal as singular facts, and as a renewal of the ancient course of pleading.

The establishment of monarchy and the change of manners put likewise an end to public accusations. It might be apprehended lest a dishonest man, affronted at the slight shown him by a woman, vexed at her refusal, and irritated even by her virtue, should form a design to destroy her. The Julian law ordained that a woman should not be accused of adultery till after her husband had been charged with favouring her irregularities; which limited greatly, and annihilated, as it were, this sort of accusation.[8]

Sextus Quintus seemed to have been desir-

---

[1] "In respect to true love," says Plutarch, "the women have nothing to say to it." In his *Treatise of Love*, p. 600. He spoke in the style of his time. See Xenophon in the dialogue intitled *Hiero.*

[2] At Athens there was a particular magistrate who inspected the conduct of women.

[3] Romulus instituted this tribunal, as appears from Dionysius Halicarnassus, ii, p. 96.

[4] See in Livy, xxxix, the use that was made of this tribunal at the time of the conspiracy of the Bacchanalians (they gave the name of conspiracy against the republic to assemblies in which the morals of women and young people were debauched.)

[5] It appears from Dionysius Halicarnassus, ii, that Romulus's institution was that in ordinary cases the husband should sit as judge in the presence of the wife's relatives, but that in heinous crimes he should determine in conjunction with five of them. Hence Ulpian, tit. 6, 9, 12, 13, distinguishes in respect to the different judgments of manners between those which he calls important, and those which are less so: *mores graviores, mores leviores.*

[6] *Judicio de moribus (quod antea quidem in antiquis legibus positum erat, non autem frequentabatur) penitus abolito.* Leg. 11, *Cod. de repud.*

[7] *Judicia extraordinaria.*

[8] It was entirely abolished by Constantine: "It is a shame," said he, "that settled marriages should be disturbed by the presumption of strangers."

ous of reviving the public accusations.[1] But there needs very little reflection to see that this law would be more improper in such a monarchy as his than in any other.

12. *Of the Guardianship of Women among the Romans.* The Roman laws subjected women to a perpetual guardianship, except they were under cover and subject to the authority of a husband.[2] This guardianship was given to the nearest of the male relatives; and by a vulgar expression[3] it appears they were very much confined. This was proper for a republic, but not at all necessary in a monarchy.[4]

That the women among the ancient Germans were likewise under a perpetual tutelage appears from the different codes of the Laws of the Barbarians.[5] This custom was communicated to the monarchies founded by those people; but was not of long duration.

13. *Of the Punishments decreed by the Emperors against the Incontinence of Women.* The Julian law ordained a punishment against adultery. But so far was this law, any more than those afterwards made on the same account, from being a mark of regularity of manners, that on the contrary it was a proof of their depravity.

The whole political system in respect to women received a change in the monarchical state. The question was no longer to oblige them to a regularity of manners, but to punish their crimes. That new laws were made to punish their crimes was owing to their leaving those transgressions unpunished which were not of so criminal a nature.

The frightful dissolution of manners obliged indeed the emperors to enact laws in order to put some stop to lewdness; but it was not their intention to establish a general reformation. Of this the positive facts related by historians are a much stronger proof than all these laws can be of the contrary. We may see in Dio the conduct of Augustus on this occasion, and in what manner he eluded, both in

his prætorian and censorian office, the repeated instances that were made him[6] for that purpose.

It is true that we find in historians very rigid sentences, passed in the reigns of Augustus and Tiberius, against the lewdness of some Roman ladies: but by showing us the spirit of those reigns, at the same time they demonstrate the spirit of those decisions.

The principal design of Augustus and Tiberius was to punish the dissoluteness of their relatives. It was not their immorality they punished, but a particular crime of impiety or high treason[7] of their own invention, which served to promote a respect for majesty, and answered their private revenge. Hence it is that the Roman historians inveigh so bitterly against this tyranny.

The penalty of the Julian law was small.[8] The emperors insisted that in passing sentence the judges should increase the penalty of the law. This was the subject of the invectives of historians. They did not examine whether the women were deserving of punishment, but whether they had violated the law, in order to punish them.

One of the most tyrannical proceedings of Tiberius[9] was the abuse he made of the ancient laws. When he wanted to extend the punishment of a Roman lady beyond that inflicted by the Julian law, he revived the domestic tribunal.[10]

These regulations in respect to women concerned only senatorial families, not the common people. Pretences were wanted to accuse the great, which were constantly furnished by the dissolute behaviour of the ladies.

In fine, what I have above observed, namely, that regularity of manners is not the prin-

---

[1] Sextus Quintus ordained, that if a husband did not come and make his complaint to him of his wife's infidelity, he should be put to death. See Leti, *Life of Sextus V.*

[2] *Nisi convenissent in manum viri.*

[3] *Ne sis mihi patruus oro.*

[4] The Papian law ordained, under Augustus, that women who had borne three children should be exempt from this tutelage.

[5] This tutelage was by the Germans called *Mundeburdium.*

[6] Upon their bringing before him a young man who had married a woman with whom he had before carried on an illicit commerce, he hesitated a long while, not daring to approve or to punish these things. At length recollecting himself, "Seditions," says he, "have been the cause of very great evils; let us forget them." Dio, liv. 16. The senate having desired him to give them some regulations in respect to women's morals, he evaded their petition by telling them that they should chastise their wives in the same manner as he did his; upon which they desired him to tell them how he behaved to his wife. (I think a very indiscreet question.)

[7] Tacitus, *Annals,* iii. 24.

[8] This law is given in the *Digest,* but without mentioning the penalty. It is supposed it was only *relegatio,* because that of incest was only *deportatio. Leg., si quis viduam, ff. de quæst.*

[9] Tacitus, *Annals,* iv. 19.

[10] *Ibid.,* ii. 50.

ciple of monarchy, was never better verified than under those first emperors; and whoever doubts it need only read Tacitus, Suetonius, Juvenal, or Martial.

14. *Sumptuary Laws among the Romans.* We have spoken of public incontinence because it is the inseparable companion of luxury. If we leave the motions of the heart at liberty, how shall we be able to restrain the weaknesses of the mind?

At Rome, besides the general institutions, the censors prevailed on the magistrates to enact several particular laws for maintaining the frugality of women. This was the design of the Fannian, Licinian, and Oppian laws. We may see in Livy[1] the great ferment the senate was in when the women insisted upon the revocation of the Oppian law. The abrogation of this law is fixed upon by Valerius Maximus as the period whence we may date the luxury of the Romans.

15. *Of Dowries and Nuptial Advantages in different Constitutions.* Dowries ought to be considerable in monarchies, in order to enable husbands to support their rank and the established luxury. In republics, where luxury should never reign,[2] they ought to be moderate; but there should be hardly any at all in despotic governments, where women are in some measure slaves.

The community of goods introduced by the French laws between man and wife is extremely well adapted to a monarchical government; because the women are thereby interested in domestic affairs, and compelled, as it were, to take care of their family. It is less so in a republic, where women are possessed of more virtue. But it would be quite absurd in despotic governments, where the women themselves generally constitute a part of the master's property.

As women are in a state that furnishes sufficient inducements to marriage, the advantages which the law gives them over the husband's property are of no service to society. But in a republic they would be extremely prejudicial, because riches are productive of luxury. In despotic governments the profits accruing from marriage ought to be mere subsistence, and no more.

16. *An excellent Custom of the Samnites.* The Samnites had a custom which in so small a republic, and especially in their situation, must have been productive of admirable effects. The young people were all convened in one place, and their conduct was examined. He that was declared the best of the whole assembly had leave given him to take which girl he pleased for his wife; the second best chose after him; and so on.[3] Admirable institution! The only recommendation that young men could have on this occasion was their virtue and the services done their country. He who had the greatest share of these endowments chose which girl he liked out of the whole nation. Love, beauty, chastity, virtue, birth, and even wealth itself, were all, in some measure, the dowry of virtue. A nobler and grander recompense, less chargeable to a petty state, and more capable of influencing both sexes, could scarcely be imagined.

The Samnites were descended from the Lacedæmonians; and Plato, whose institutes are only an improvement of those of Lycurgus, enacted nearly the same law.[4]

17. *Of Female Administration.* It is contrary to reason and nature that women should reign in families, as was customary among the Egyptians; but not that they should govern an empire. In the former case the state of their natural weakness does not permit them to have the pre-eminence; in the latter their very weakness generally gives them more lenity and moderation, qualifications fitter for a good administration than roughness and severity.

In the Indies they are very easy under a female government; and it is settled that if the male issue be not of a mother of the same blood, the females born of a mother of the blood-royal must succeed.[5] And then they have a certain number of persons who assist them to bear the weight of the government. According to Mr. Smith,[6] they are very easy in Africa under female administration. If to this we add the example of England and Russia, we shall find that they succeed alike both in moderate and despotic governments.

[3] Fragment of Nicolaus Damascenus, taken from Stobæus in the collection of Constantine Porphyrogenitus.
[4] He even permits them to have a more frequent interview with one another.
[5] *Edifying Letters,* coll. xiv.
[6] *Voyage to Guinea,* part the second, p. 165, of the kingdom of Angola, on the Golden Coast.

[1] Dec. 4, iv.
[2] Marseilles was the wisest of all the republics in its time; here it was ordained that dowries should not exceed one hundred crowns in money, and five in clothes, as Strabo observes, iv.

Book VIII. Of the Corruption of the Principles of the Three Governments

1. *General Idea of this Book.* The corruption of this government generally begins with that of the principles.

2. *Of the Corruption of the Principles of Democracy.* The principle of democracy is corrupted not only when the spirit of equality is extinct, but likewise when they fall into a spirit of extreme equality, and when each citizen would fain be upon a level with those whom he has chosen to command him. Then the people, incapable of bearing the very power they have delegated, want to manage everything themselves, to debate for the senate, to execute for the magistrate, and to decide for the judges.

When this is the case, virtue can no longer subsist in the republic. The people are desirous of exercising the functions of the magistrates, who cease to be revered. The deliberations of the senate are slighted; all respect is then laid aside for the senators, and consequently for old age. If there is no more respect for old age, there will be none presently for parents; deference to husbands will be likewise thrown off, and submission to masters. This licence will soon become general, and the trouble of command be as fatiguing as that of obedience. Wives, children, slaves will shake off all subjection. No longer will there be any such thing as manners, order, or virtue.

We find in Xenophon's *Banquet* a very lively description of a republic in which the people abused their equality. Each guest gives in his turn the reason why he is satisfied. "Content I am," says Chamides, "because of my poverty. When I was rich, I was obliged to pay my court to informers, knowing I was more liable to be hurt by them than capable of doing them harm. The republic constantly demanded some new tax of me; and I could not decline paying. Since I have grown poor, I have acquired authority; nobody threatens me; I rather threaten others. I can go or stay where I please. The rich already rise from their seats and give me the way. I am a king, I was before a slave: I paid taxes to the republic, now it maintains me: I am no longer afraid of losing: but I hope to acquire."

The people fall into this misfortune when those in whom they confide, desirous of concealing their own corruption, endeavour to corrupt them. To disguise their own ambition, they speak to them only of the grandeur of the state; to conceal their own avarice, they incessantly flatter theirs.

The corruption will increase among the corruptors, and likewise among those who are already corrupted. The people will divide the public money among themselves, and, having added the administration of affairs to their indolence, will be for blending their poverty with the amusements of luxury. But with their indolence and luxury, nothing but the public treasure will be able to satisfy their demands.

We must not be surprised to see their suffrages given for money. It is impossible to make great largesses to the people without great extortion: and to compass this, the state must be subverted. The greater the advantages they seem to derive from their liberty, the nearer they approach towards the critical moment of losing it. Petty tyrants arise who have all the vices of a single tyrant. The small remains of liberty soon become insupportable; a single tyrant starts up, and the people are stripped of everything, even of the profits of their corruption.

Democracy has, therefore, two excesses to avoid—the spirit of inequality, which leads to aristocracy or monarchy, and the spirit of extreme equality, which leads to despotic power, as the latter is completed by conquest.

True it is that those who corrupted the Greek republics did not always become tyrants. This was because they had a greater passion for eloquence than for the military art. Besides there reigned an implacable hatred in the breasts of the Greeks against those who subverted a republican government; and for this reason anarchy degenerated into annihilation, instead of being changed into tyranny.

But Syracuse being situated in the midst of a great number of petty states, whose government had been changed from oligarchy to tyranny,[1] and being governed by a senate[2] scarcely ever mentioned in history, underwent such miseries as are the consequence of a more than

[1] See Plutarch in *Timoleon* and *Dion.*
[2] It was that of the Six Hundred, of whom mention is made by Diodorus, xix. 5.

ordinary corruption. This city, ever a prey to licentiousness,[1] or oppression, equally labouring under the sudden and alternate succession of liberty and servitude, and notwithstanding her external strength, constantly determined to a revolution by the least foreign power—this city, I say, had in her bosom an immense multitude of people, whose fate it was to have always this cruel alternative, either of choosing a tyrant to govern them, or of acting the tyrant themselves.

3. *Of the Spirit of extreme Equality.* As distant as heaven is from earth, so is the true spirit of equality from that of extreme equality. The former does not imply that everybody should command, or that no one should be commanded, but that we obey or command our equals. It endeavours not to shake off the authority of a master, but that its masters should be none but its equals.

In the state of nature, indeed, all men are born equal, but they cannot continue in this equality. Society makes them lose it, and they recover it only by the protection of the laws.

Such is the difference between a well-regulated democracy and one that is not so, that in the former men are equal only as citizens, but in the latter they are equal also as magistrates, as senators, as judges, as fathers, as husbands, or as masters.

The natural place of virtue is near to liberty; but it is not nearer to excessive liberty than to servitude.

4. *Particular Cause of the Corruption of the People.* Great success, especially when chiefly owing to the people, intoxicates them to such a degree that it is impossible to contain them within bounds. Jealous of their magistrates, they soon became jealous likewise of the magistracy; enemies to those who govern, they soon prove enemies also to the constitution. Thus it was that the victory over the Persians in the straits of Salamis corrupted the republic of Athens;[2] and thus the defeat of the Athe-

nians ruined the republic of Syracuse.[3]

Marseilles never experienced those great transitions from lowness to grandeur; this was owing to the prudent conduct of that republic, which always preserved her principles.

5. *Of the Corruption of the Principle of Aristocracy.* Aristocracy is corrupted if the power of the nobles becomes arbitrary: when this is the case, there can no longer be any virtue either in the governors or the governed.

If the reigning families observe the laws, it is a monarchy with several monarchs, and in its own nature one of the most excellent; for almost all these monarchs are tied down by the laws. But when they do not observe them, it is a despotic state swayed by a great many despotic princes.

In the latter case, the republic consists only in the nobles. The body governing is the republic; and the body governed is the despotic state; which forms two of the most heterogeneous bodies in the world.

The extremity of corruption is when the power of the nobles becomes hereditary;[4] for then they can hardly have any moderation. If they are only a few, their power is greater, but their security less: if they are a larger number, their power is less, and their security greater, insomuch that power goes on increasing, and security diminishing, up to the very despotic prince who is encircled with excess of power and danger.

The great number, therefore, of nobles in an hereditary aristocracy renders the government less violent: but as there is less virtue, they fall into a spirit of supineness and negligence, by which the state loses all its strength and activity.[5]

An aristocracy may maintain the full vigour of its constitution if the laws be such as are apt to render the nobles more sensible of the perils and fatigues than of the pleasure of command: and if the government be in such a situation as to have something to dread, while security shelters under its protection, and uncertainty threatens from abroad.

As a certain kind of confidence forms the glory and stability of monarchies, republics, on the contrary, must have something to ap-

---

[1] Upon the expulsions of the tyrants, they made citizens of strangers and mercenary troops, which gave rise to civil wars.—Aristotle, *Politics*, v. 3. The people having been the cause of the victory over the Athenians, the republic was changed.—*Ibid.*, 4. The passion of two young magistrates, one of whom carried off the other's boy, and in revenge the other debauched his wife, was attended with a change in the form of this republic.—*Ibid.*

[2] *Ibid.*

[3] *Ibid.*

[4] The aristocracy is changed into an oligarchy.

[5] Venice is one of those republics that has enacted the best laws for correcting the inconveniences of an hereditary aristocracy.

prehend.[1] A fear of the Persians supported the laws of Greece. Carthage and Rome were alarmed, and strengthened by each other. Strange, that the greater security those states enjoyed, the more, like stagnated waters, they were subject to corruption!

6. *Of the Corruption of the Principle of Monarchy.* As democracies are subverted when the people despoil the senate, the magistrates, the judges of their functions, so monarchies are corrupted when the prince insensibly deprives societies or cities of their privileges. In the former case the multitude usurp the power, in the latter it is usurped by a single person.

"The destruction of the dynasties of Tsin and Soui," says a Chinese author, "was owing to this: the princes, instead of confining themselves, like their ancestors, to a general inspection, the only one worthy of a sovereign, wanted to govern everything immediately by themselves."[2] The Chinese author gives us in this instance the cause of the corruption of almost all monarchies.

Monarchy is destroyed when a prince thinks he shows a greater exertion of power in changing than in conforming to the order of things; when he deprives some of his subjects of their hereditary employments to bestow them arbitrarily upon others; and when he is fonder of being guided by fancy than judgment.

Again, it is destroyed when the prince, directing everything entirely to himself, calls the state to his capital, the capital to his court, and the court to his own person.

It is destroyed, in fine, when the prince mistakes his authority, his situation and the love of his people, and when he is not fully persuaded that a monarch ought to think himself secure, as a despotic prince ought to think himself in danger.

7. *The same Subject continued.* The principle of monarchy is corrupted when the first dignities are marks of the first servitude, when the great men are deprived of public respect, and rendered the low tools of arbitrary power.

It is still more corrupted when honour is set up in contradiction to honours, and when

men are capable of being loaded at the very same time with infamy[3] and with dignities.

It is corrupted when the prince changes his justice into severity; when he puts, like the Roman emperors, a Medusa's head on his breast;[4] and when he assumes that menacing and terrible air which Commodus ordered to be given to his statues.[5]

Again, it is corrupted when mean and abject souls grow vain of the pomp attending their servitude, and imagine that the motive which induces them to be entirely devoted to their prince exempts them from all duty to their country.

But if it be true (and indeed the experience of all ages has shown it) that in proportion as the power of the monarch becomes boundless and immense, his security diminishes, is the corrupting of this power, and the altering of its very nature, a less crime than that of high treason against the prince?

8. *Danger of the Corruption of the Principle of monarchical Government.* The danger is not when the state passes from one moderate to another moderate government, as from a republic to a monarchy, or from a monarchy to a republic; but when it is precipitated from a moderate to a despotic government.

Most of the European nations are still governed by the principles of morality. But if from a long abuse of power or the fury of conquest, despotic sway should prevail to a certain degree, neither morals nor climate would be able to withstand its baleful influence: and then human nature would be exposed, for some time at least, even in this beautiful part of the world, to the insults with which she has been abused in the other three.

9. *How ready the Nobility are to defend the Throne.* The English nobility buried themselves with Charles the First under the ruins

[1] Justin attributes the extinction of Athenian virtue to the death of Epaminondas. Having no further emulation, they spent their revenues in feasts, *frequentius cœnam, quam castra visentes.* Then it was that the Macedonians emerged from obscurity, 9, 1. 6.

[2] Compilation of works made under the Mings, related by Father Du Halde, *Description of China,* ii, p. 648.

[3] During the reign of Tiberius statues were erected to, and triumphal ornaments conferred on, informers; which debased these honours to such a degree that those who had really merited them disdained to accept them. Frag. of Dio, lviii. 14, taken from the *Extract of Virtues and Vices,* by Constantine Porphyrogenitus. See in Tacitus in what manner Nero, on the discovery and punishment of a pretended conspiracy, bestowed triumphal ornaments on Petronius Turpilianus, Nerva, and Tigellinus.—*Annals,* xiv. 72. See likewise how the generals refused to serve, because they condemned the military honours: *pervulgatis triumphi insignibus.*—*Ibid.,* xiii. 53.

[4] In this state the prince knew extremely well the principle of his government.

[5] Herodian.

of the throne; and before that time, when Philip the Second endeavoured to tempt the French with the allurement of liberty, the crown was constantly supported by a nobility who think it an honour to obey a king, but consider it as the lowest disgrace to share the power with the people.

The house of Austria has ever used her endeavours to oppress the Hungarian nobility; little thinking how serviceable that very nobility would be one day to her. She would fain have drained their country of money, of which they had no plenty; but took no notice of the men, with whom it abounded. When princes combined to dismember her dominions, the several parts of that monarchy fell motionless, as it were one upon another. No life was then to be seen but in those very nobles, who, resenting the affronts offered to the sovereign, and forgetting the injuries done to themselves, took up arms to avenge her cause, and considered it the highest glory bravely to die and to forgive.

10. *Of the Corruption of the Principle of despotic Government.* The principle of despotic government is subject to a continual corruption, because it is even in its nature corrupt. Other governments are destroyed by particular accidents, which do violence to the principles of each constitution; this is ruined by its own intrinsic imperfections, when some accidental causes do not prevent the corrupting of its principles. It maintains itself therefore only when circumstances, drawn from the climate, religion, situation, or genius of the people, oblige it to conform to order, and to admit of some rule. By these things its nature is forced without being changed; its ferocity remains; and it is made tame and tractable only for a time.

11. *Natural Effects of the Goodness and Corruption of the Principles of Government.* When once the principles of government are corrupted, the very best laws become bad, and turn against the state: but when the principles are sound, even bad laws have the same effect as good; the force of the principle draws everything to it.

The inhabitants of Crete used a very singular method to keep the principal magistrates dependent on the laws, which was that of Insurrection. Part of the citizens rose up in arms,[1] put the magistrates to flight, and

obliged them to return to a private life. This was supposed to be done in consequence of the law. One would have imagined that an institution of this nature, which established sedition to hinder the abuse of power, would have subverted any republic whatsoever; and yet it did not subvert that of Crete. The reason is this.[2]

When the ancients would cite a people that had the strongest affection for their country, they were sure to mention the inhabitants of Crete: "Our Country," said Plato,[3] "a name so dear to the Cretans." They called it by a name which signifies the love of a mother for her children.[4] Now the love of our country sets everything right.

The laws of Poland have likewise their Insurrection: but the inconveniences thence arising plainly show that the people of Crete alone were capable of using such a remedy with success.

The gymnic exercises established among the Greeks had the same dependence on the goodness of the principle of government. "It was the Lacedaemonians and Cretans," said Plato,[5] "that opened those celebrated academies which gave them so eminent a rank in the world. Modesty at first was alarmed; but it yielded to the public utility." In Plato's time these institutions were admirable:[6] as they bore a relation to a very important object, which was the military art. But when virtue fled from Greece, the military art was destroyed by these institutions; people appeared then on the arena, not for improvement, but for debauch.[7]

Plutarch informs us[8] that the Romans in his

[1] Aristotle, *Politics,* ii. 10.

[2] They always united immediately against foreign enemies, which was called *Syncretism.*— Plutarch *Moralia,* p. 88.

[3] *Republic,* ix.

[4] Plutarch, *Whether a Man Advanced in Years Ought to Meddle with Public Affairs.*

[5] *Republic,* v.

[6] The Gymnic art was divided into two parts, dancing and wrestling. In Crete they had the armed dances of the Curetes; at Sparta they had those of Castor and Pollux; at Athens the armed dances of Pallas, which were extremely proper for those that were not yet of age for military service. Wrestling is the image of war, said Plato *Laws,* vii. He commends antiquity for having established only two dances, the pacific and the Pyrrhic. See how the latter dance was applied to the military art, Plato, *ibid.*

[7] *Aut libidinosæ.*
Ladæas Lacedæmonis palæstras.—Mutual, iv, 55.

[8] Plutarch, in the treatise entitled *Questions Concerning the Affairs of the Romans,* question 40.

time were of opinion that those games had been the principal cause of the slavery into which the Greeks had fallen. On the contrary, it was the slavery of the Greeks that corrupted those exercises. In Plutarch's time,[1] their fighting naked in the parks, and their wrestling, infected the young people with a spirit of cowardice, inclined them to infamous passions, and made them mere dancers. But under Epaminondas the exercise of wrestling made the Thebans win the famous battle of Leuctra.[2]

There are very few laws which are not good, while the state retains its principles: here I may apply what Epicurus said of riches. "It is not the liquor, but the vessel that is corrupted."

12. *The same Subject continued.* In Rome the judges were chosen at first from the order of senators. This privilege the Gracchi transferred to the knights; Drusus gave it to the senators and knights; Sulla to the senators only: Cotta to the senators, knights, and public treasurers; Cæsar excluded the latter; Antony made decuries of senators, knights, and centurions.

When once a republic is corrupted, there is no possibility of remedying any of the growing evils, but by removing the corruption and restoring its lost principles; every other correction is either useless or a new evil. While Rome preserved her principles entire, the judicial power might without any abuse be lodged in the hands of senators; but as soon as this city became corrupt, to whatsoever body that power was transferred, whether to the senate, to the knights, to the treasurers, to two of those bodies, to all three together, or to any other, matters still went wrong. The knights had no more virtue than the senate, the treasurers no more than the knights, and these as little as the centurions.

After the people of Rome had obtained the privilege of sharing the magistracy with the patricians, it was natural to think that their flatterers would immediately become arbiters of the government. But no such thing ever happened.—It was observable that the very people who had rendered the plebeians capable of public offices ever fixed their choice upon the patricians. Because they were virtuous, they were magnanimous; and because they were free, they had a contempt of power.

But when their morals were corrupted, the more power they were possessed of, the less prudent was their conduct, till at length, upon becoming their own tyrants and slaves, they lost the strength of liberty to fall into the weakness and impotency of licentiousness.

13. *The Effect of an Oath among virtuous People.* There is no nation, says Livy,[3] that has been longer uncorrupted than the Romans; no nation where moderation and poverty have been longer respected.

Such was the influence of an oath among those people that nothing bound them more strongly to the laws. They often did more for the observance of an oath than they would ever have performed for the thirst of glory or for the love of their country.

When Quintus Cincinnatus, the consul, wanted to raise an army in the city against the Æqui and the Volsci, the tribunes opposed him. "Well," said he, "let all those who have taken an oath to the consul of the preceding year march under my banner."[4] In vain did the tribunes cry out that this oath was no longer binding, and that when they took it Quintus was but a private person: the people were more religious than those who pretended to direct them; they would not listen to the distinctions or equivocations of the tribunes.

When the same people thought of retiring to the Sacred Mount, they felt some remorse from the oath they had taken to the consuls, that they would follow them into the field.[5] They entered then into a design of killing the consuls; but dropped it when they were given to understand that their oath would still be binding. Now it is easy to judge of the notion they entertained of the violation of an oath from the crime they intended to commit.

After the battle of Cannæ, the people were seized with such a panic that they would fain have retired to Sicily. But Scipio having prevailed upon them to swear they would not stir from Rome, the fear of violating this oath surpassed all other apprehensions. Rome was a ship held by two anchors, religion and morality, in the midst of a furious tempest.

14. *How the smallest Change of the Constitution is attended with the Ruin of its Principles.* Aristotle mentions the city of Carthage

---

[1] *Ibid.*
[2] Plutarch, *Table Propositions,* book ii, question 5.

[3] Book i, pref.
[4] Livy, iii. 20.
[5] *Ibid.,* 32.

as a well-regulated republic. Polybius tells us[1] that there was this inconvenience at Carthage in the second Punic war, that the senate had lost almost all its authority. We are informed by Livy that when Hannibal returned to Carthage he found that the magistrates and the principal citizens had abused their power, and converted the public revenues to their private emolument. The virtue, therefore, of the magistrates, and the authority of the senate, both fell at the same time; and all was owing to the same cause.

Every one knows the wonderful effects of the censorship among the Romans. There was a time when it grew burdensome; but still it was supported because there was more luxury than corruption. Claudius[2] weakened its authority, by which means the corruption became greater than the luxury, and the censorship dwindled away of itself.[3] After various interruptions and resumptions, it was entirely laid aside, till it became altogether useless, that is, till the reigns of Augustus and Claudius.

15. *Sure Methods of preserving the three Principles.* I shall not be able to make myself rightly understood till the reader has perused the four following chapters.

16. *Distinctive Properties of a Republic.* It is natural for a republic to have only a small territory; otherwise it cannot long subsist. In an extensive republic there are men of large fortunes, and consequently of less moderation; there are trusts too considerable to be placed in any single subject; he has interests of his own; he soon begins to think that he may be happy and glorious, by oppressing his fellow-citizens; and that he may raise himself to grandeur on the ruins of his country.

In an extensive republic the public good is sacrificed to a thousand private views; it is subordinate to exceptions, and depends on accidents. In a small one, the interest of the public is more obvious, better understood, and more within the reach of every citizen; abuses have less extent, and of course are less protected.

The long duration of the republic of Sparta was owing to her having continued in the same extent of territory after all her wars. The sole aim of Sparta was liberty; and the sole advantage of her liberty, glory.

It was the spirit of the Greek republics to be as contented with their territories as with their laws. Athens was first fired with ambition and gave it to Lacedæmon; but it was an ambition rather of commanding a free people than of governing slaves; rather of directing than of breaking the union. All was lost upon the starting up of monarchy—a government whose spirit is more turned to increase of dominion.

Excepting particular circumstances,[4] it is difficult for any other than a republican government to subsist longer in a single town. A prince of so petty a state would naturally endeavour to oppress his subjects, because his power would be great, while the means of enjoying it or of causing it to be respected would be inconsiderable. The consequence is, he would trample upon his people. On the other hand, such a prince might be easily crushed by a foreign or even a domestic force; the people might any instant unite and rise up against him. Now as soon as the sovereign of a single town is expelled, the quarrel is over; but if he has many towns, it only begins.

17. *Distinctive Properties of a Monarchy.* A monarchical state ought to be of moderate extent. Were it small, it would form itself into a republic; were it very large, the nobility, possessed of great estates, far from the eye of the prince, with a private court of their own, and secure, moreover, from sudden executions by the laws and manners of the country—such a nobility, I say, might throw off their allegiance, having nothing to fear from too slow and too distant a punishment.

Thus Charlemagne had scarcely founded his empire when he was obliged to divide it; whether the governors of the provinces refused to obey; or whether, in order to keep them more under subjection, there was a necessity of parcelling the empire into several kingdoms.

After the decease of Alexander his empire was divided. How was it possible for those Greek and Macedonian chiefs, who were each of them free and independent, or commanders at least of the victorious bands dispersed throughout that vast extent of conquered land

---

[1] About a hundred years after.

[2] See xi, 12.

[3] See Dio, xxxviii, *Cicero* in Plutarch, Cicero to Atticus, iv. 10, 15. Asconius on Cicero, *De Divinatione.*

[4] As when a petty sovereign supports himself between two great powers by means of their mutual jealousy; but then he has only a precarious existence.

—how was it possible, I say, for them to obey?

Attila's empire was dissolved soon after his death; such a number of kings, who were no longer under restraint, could not resume their fetters.

The sudden establishment of unlimited power is a remedy, which in those cases may prevent a dissolution: but how dreadful the remedy, which after the enlargement of dominion opens a new scene of misery!

The rivers hasten to mingle their waters with the sea; and monarchies lose themselves in despotic power.

18. *Particular Case of the Spanish Monarchy.* Let not the example of Spain be produced against me, it rather proves what I affirm. To preserve America she did what even despotic power itself does not attempt: she destroyed the inhabitants. To preserve her colony, she was obliged to keep it dependent even for its subsistence.

In the Netherlands, she essayed to render herself arbitrary; and as soon as she abandoned the attempt, her perplexity increased. On the one hand the Walloons would not be governed by Spaniards; and on the other, the Spanish soldiers refused to submit to Walloon officers.[1]

In Italy she maintained her ground, merely by exhausting herself and by enriching that country. For those who would have been pleased to have got rid of the king of Spain were not in a humour to refuse his gold.

19. *Distinctive Properties of a despotic Government.* A large empire supposes a despotic authority in the person who governs. It is necessary that the quickness of the prince's resolutions should supply the distance of the places they are sent to; that fear should prevent the remissness of the distant governor or magistrate; that the law should be derived from a single person, and should shift continually, according to the accidents which necessarily multiply in a state in proportion to its extent.

20. *Consequence of the preceding Chapters.* If it be, therefore, the natural property of small states to be governed as a republic, of middling ones to be subject to a monarch, and of large empires to be swayed by a despotic prince; the consequence is, that in order to

[1] See M. Le Clerc, the *History of the United Provinces.*

preserve the principles of the established government, the state must be supported in the extent it has acquired, and that the spirit of this state will alter in proportion as it contracts or extends its limits.

21. *Of the Empire of China.* Before I conclude this book, I shall answer an objection that may be made to the foregoing doctrine.

Our missionaries inform us that the government of the vast empire of China is admirable, and that it has a proper mixture of fear, honour, and virtue. Consequently I must have given an idle distinction in establishing the principles of the three governments.

But I cannot conceive what this honour can be among a people who act only through fear of being bastinadoed.[2]

Again, our merchants are far from giving us any such accounts of the virtue so much talked of by the missionaries; we need only consult them in relation to the robberies and extortions of the mandarins.[3] I likewise appeal to another unexceptional witness, the great Lord Anson.

Besides, Father Perennin's letters concerning the emperor's proceedings against some of the princes of the blood[4] who had incurred his displeasure by their conversion, plainly show us a settled plan of tyranny, and barbarities committed by rule, that is, in cold blood.

We have likewise Monsieur de Mairan's, and the same Father Perennin's, letters on the government of China. I find therefore that after a few proper questions and answers the whole mystery is unfolded.

Might not our missionaries have been deceived by an appearance of order? Might not they have been struck with that constant exercise of a single person's will—an exercise by which they themselves are governed, and which they are so pleased to find in the courts of the Indian princes; because as they go thither only in order to introduce great changes, it is much easier to persuade those princes that there are no bounds to their power, than to convince the people that there are none to their submission.[5]

[2] "It is the cudgel that governs China," says Father Du Halde, *Disc. de la Chine,* ii, p. 134.

[3] Among others, De Lange's account.

[4] Of the Family of Sourniama, *Edifying Letters,* coll. xviii.

[5] See in Father Du Halde how the missionaries availed themselves of the authority of Canhi to silence the mandarins, who constantly declared that by the laws of the country no foreign worship could be established in the empire.

In fine, there is frequently some kind of truth even in errors themselves. It may be owing to particular and, perhaps, very extraordinary circumstances that the Chinese government is not so corrupt as one might naturally expect. The climate and some other physical causes may, in that country, have had so strong an influence on their morals as in some measure to produce wonders.

The climate of China is surprisingly favourable to the propagation of the human species.[1] The women are the most prolific in the whole world. The most barbarous tyranny can put no stop to the progress of propagation. The prince cannot say there like Pharaoh, "Let us deal wisely with them, lest they multiply." He would be rather reduced to Nero's wish, that mankind had all but one head. In spite of tyranny, China by the force of its climate will be ever populous, and triumph over the tyrannical oppressor.

China, like all other countries that live chiefly upon rice, is subject to frequent famines. When the people are ready to starve, they disperse in order to seek for nourishment; in consequence of which, gangs of robbers are formed on every side. Most of them are extirpated in their very infancy; others swell, and are likewise suppressed. And yet in so great a number of such distant provinces, some band or other may happen to meet with success. In that case they maintain their ground, strengthen their party, form themselves into a military body, march up to the capital, and place their leader on the throne.

From the very nature of things, a bad administration is here immediately punished. The want of subsistence in so populous a country produces sudden disorders. The reason why the redress of abuses in other countries is attended with such difficulty is because their effects are not immediately felt; the prince is not informed in so sudden and sensible a manner as in China.

The Emperor of China is not taught like our princes that if he governs ill he will be less happy in the other life, less powerful and less opulent in this. He knows that if his government be not just he will be stripped both of empire and life.

As China grows every day more populous, notwithstanding the exposing of children,[2] the inhabitants are incessantly employed in tilling the lands for their subsistence. This requires a very extraordinary attention in the government. It is their perpetual concern that every man should have it in his power to work, without the apprehension of being deprived of the fruits of his labour. Consequently this is not so much a civil as a domestic government.

Such has been the origin of those regulations which have been so greatly extolled. They wanted to make the laws reign in conjunction with despotic power; but whatever is joined to the latter loses all its force. In vain did this arbitrary sway, labouring under its own inconveniences, desire to be fettered; it armed itself with its chains, and has become still more terrible.

China is therefore a despotic state, whose principle is fear. Perhaps in the earliest dynasties, when the empire had not so large an extent, the government might have deviated a little from this spirit; but the case is otherwise at present.

Book IX. Of Laws in the relation they bear to a Defensive Force

1. *In what Manner Republics provide for their Safety*. If a republic be small, it is destroyed by a foreign force; if it be large, it is ruined by an internal imperfection.

To this twofold inconvenience democracies and aristocracies are equally liable, whether they be good or bad. The evil is in the very thing itself, and no form can redress it.

It is, therefore, very probable that mankind would have been, at length, obliged to live constantly under the government of a single person, had they not contrived a kind of constitution that has all the internal advantages of a republican, together with the external force of a monarchical, government. I mean a confederate republic.

This form of government is a convention by which several petty states agree to become members of a larger one, which they intend to establish. It is a kind of assemblage of societies, that constitute a new one, capable of in-

[1] See *Lettres persanes*, 210.

[2] See the order of Tsongtou for tilling the land, in the *Edifying Letters*, coll. xxi.

creasing by means of further associations, till they arrive at such a degree of power as to be able to provide for the security of the whole body.

It was these associations that so long contributed to the prosperity of Greece. By these the Romans attacked the whole globe, and by these alone the whole globe withstood them; for when Rome had arrived at her highest pitch of grandeur, it was the associations beyond the Danube and the Rhine—associations formed by the terror of her arms—that enabled the barbarians to resist her.

Hence it proceeds that Holland,[1] Germany, and the Swiss cantons are considered in Europe as perpetual republics.

The associations of cities were formerly more necessary than in our times. A weak, defenceless town was exposed to greater danger. By conquest it was deprived not only of the executive and legislative power, as at present, but moreover of all human property.[2]

A republic of this kind, able to withstand an external force, may support itself without any internal corruption; the form of this society prevents all manner of inconveniences.

If a single member should attempt to usurp the supreme power, he could not be supposed to have an equal authority and credit in all the confederate states. Were he to have too great an influence over one, this would alarm the rest; were he to subdue a part, that which would still remain free might oppose him with forces independent of those which he had usurped, and overpower him before he could be settled in his usurpation.

Should a popular insurrection happen in one of the confederate states, the others are able to quell it. Should abuses creep into one part, they are reformed by those that remain sound. The state may be destroyed on one side, and not on the other; the confederacy may be dissolved, and the confederates preserve their sovereignty.

As this government is composed of petty republics, it enjoys the internal happiness of each; and with regard to its external situation, by means of the association, it possesses all the advantages of large monarchies.

2. *That a confederate Government ought to*

be composed of States of the same Nature, especially of the republican Kind. The Canaanites were destroyed by reason that they were petty monarchies, that had no union or confederacy for their common defence; and, indeed, a confederacy is not agreeable to the nature of petty monarchies.

As the confederate republic of Germany consists of free cities, and of petty states subject to different princes, experience shows us that it is much more imperfect than that of Holland and Switzerland.

The spirit of monarchy is war and enlargement of dominion: peace and moderation are the spirit of a republic. These two kinds of government cannot naturally subsist in a confederate republic.

Thus we observe, in the Roman history, that when the Veientes had chosen a king, they were immediately abandoned by all the other petty republics of Tuscany. Greece was undone as soon as the kings of Macedon obtained a seat among the Amphyktyons.

The confederate republic of Germany, composed of princes and free towns, subsists by means of a chief, who is, in some respects, the magistrate of the union, in others, the monarch.

3. *Other Requisites in a confederate Republic.* In the republic of Holland one province cannot conclude an alliance without the consent of the others. This law, which is an excellent one, and even necessary in a confederate republic, is wanting in the Germanic constitution, where it would prevent the misfortunes that may happen to the whole confederacy, through the imprudence, ambition, or avarice of a single member. A republic united by a political confederacy has given itself entirely up, and has nothing more to resign.

It is difficult for the united states to be all of equal power and extent. The Lycian[3] republic was an association of twenty-three towns; the large ones had three votes in the common council, the middling ones two, and the small towns one. The Dutch republic consists of seven provinces of different extent of territory, which have each one voice.

The cities of Lycia[4] contributed to the expenses of the state, according to the proportion of suffrages. The provinces of the United Netherlands cannot follow this proportion; they must be directed by that of their power.

[1] It is composed of about fifty different republics, all different from one another.—M. Janisson, *State of the United Provinces.*

[2] Civil liberty, goods, wives, children, temples, and even burying-places.

[3] Strabo, xiv.

[4] *Ibid.*

In Lycia[1] the judges and town magistrates were elected by the common council, and according to the proportion already mentioned. In the republic of Holland they are not chosen by the common council, but each town names its magistrates. Were I to give a model of an excellent confederate republic, I should pitch upon that of Lycia.

4. *In what Manner despotic Governments provide for their Security.* As republics provide for their security by uniting, despotic governments do it by separating, and by keeping themselves, as it were, single. They sacrifice a part of the country; and by ravaging and desolating the frontiers they render the heart of the empire inaccessible.

It is a received axiom in geometry that the greater the extent of bodies, the more their circumference is relatively small. This practice, therefore, of laying the frontiers waste is more tolerable in large than in middling states.

A despotic government does all the mischief to itself that could be committed by a cruel enemy, whose arms it were unable to resist.

It preserves itself likewise by another kind of separation, which is by putting the most distant provinces into the hands of a great vassal. The Mogul, the king of Persia, and the emperors of China have their feudatories; and the Turks have found their account in putting the Tartars, the Moldavians, the Wallachians, and formerly the Transylvanians, between themselves and their enemies.

5. *In what Manner a Monarchical Government provides for its Security.* A monarchy never destroys itself like a despotic government. But a kingdom of a moderate extent is liable to sudden invasions: it must therefore have fortresses to defend its frontiers; and troops to garrison those fortresses. The least spot of ground is disputed with military skill and resolution. Despotic states make incursions against one another; it is monarchies only that wage war.

Fortresses are proper for monarchies; despotic governments are afraid of them. They dare not entrust their officers with such a command, as none of them have any affection for the prince or his government.

6. *Of the defensive Force of States in general.* [1]*Ibid.*

To preserve a state in its due force, it must have such an extent as to admit of a proportion between the celerity with which it may be invaded, and that with which it may defeat the invasion. As an invader may appear on every side, it is requisite that the state should be able to make on every side its defence; consequently it should be of a moderate extent, proportioned to the degree of velocity that nature has given to man, to enable him to move from one place to another.

France and Spain are exactly of a proper extent. They have so easy a communication for their forces as to be able to convey them immediately to what part they have a mind; the armies unite and pass with rapidity from one frontier to another, without any apprehension of such difficulties as require time to remove.

It is extremely happy for France that the capital stands near to the different frontiers in proportion to their weakness; and the prince has a better view of each part of his country according as it is more exposed.

But when a vast empire, like Persia, is attacked, it is several months before the troops are assembled in a body; and then they are not able to make such forced marches, for that space of time, as they could for fifteen days. Should the army on the frontiers be defeated, it is soon dispersed, because there is no neighbouring place of retreat. The victor, meeting with no resistance, advances with all expedition, sits down before the capital, and lays siege to it, when there is scarcely time sufficient to summon the governors of the provinces to its relief. Those who foresee an approaching revolution hasten it by their disobedience. For men whose fidelity is entirely owing to the danger of punishment are easily corrupted as soon as it becomes distant; their aim is their own private interest. The empire is subverted, the capital taken, and the conqueror disputes the several provinces with the governors.

The real power of a prince does not consist so much in the facility he meets with in making conquests as in the difficulty an enemy finds in attacking him, and, if I may so speak, in the immutability of his condition. But the increase of territory obliges a government to lay itself more open to an enemy.

As monarchs therefore ought to be endued with wisdom in order to increase their power, they ought likewise to have an equal share of prudence to confine it within bounds. Upon removing the inconveniences of too small a territory, they should have their eye constantly on the inconveniences which attend its extent.

7. A Reflection. The enemies of a great prince, whose reign was protracted to an unusual length, have very often accused him, rather, I believe, from their own fears than upon any solid foundation, of having formed and carried on a project of universal monarchy. Had he attained his aim, nothing would have been more fatal to his subjects, to himself, to his family, and to all Europe. Heaven, that knows our true interests, favoured him more by preventing the success of his arms than it could have done by crowning him with victories. Instead of raising him to be the only sovereign in Europe, it made him happier by rendering him the most powerful.

The subjects of this prince, who in travelling abroad are never affected but with what they have left at home; who on quitting their own habitations look upon glory as their chief object, and in distant countries as an obstacle to their return; who disgust you even by their good qualities, because they are tainted with so much vanity; who are capable of supporting wounds, perils, and fatigues, but not of foregoing their pleasures; who are supremely fond of gaiety, and comfort themselves for the loss of a battle by a song upon the general: those subjects, I say, would never have the solidity requisite for an enterprise of this kind, which if defeated in one country would be unsuccessful everywhere else; and if once unsuccessful, would be so for ever.

8. A particular Case in which the defensive Force of a State is inferior to the offensive. It was a saying of the Lord of Coucy to King Charles V that the English are never weaker, nor more easily overcome, than in their own country. The same was observed of the Romans; the same of the Carthaginians; and the same will happen to every power that sends armies to distant countries, in order to reunite by discipline and military force those who are divided among themselves by political or civil interests. The state finds itself weakened by the disorder that still continues, and more so by the remedy.

The Lord of Coucy's maxim is an exception to the general rule, which disapproves of wars against distant countries. And this exception confirms likewise the rule because it takes place only with regard to those by whom such wars are undertaken.

9. Of the relative Force of States. All grandeur, force, and power are relative. Care therefore must be taken that in endeavouring to increase the real grandeur, the relative be not diminished.

During the reign of Louis XIV France was at its highest pitch of relative grandeur. Germany had not yet produced such powerful princes as have since appeared in that country. Italy was in the same case. England and Scotland were not yet formed into one united kingdom. Aragon was not joined to Castile: the distant branches of the Spanish monarchy were weakened by it, and weakened it in their turn; and Muscovy was as little known in Europe as Crim Tartary.

10. Of the Weakness of neighbouring States. Whensoever a state lies contiguous to another that happens to be in its decline, the former ought to take particular care not to precipitate the ruin of the latter, because this is the happiest situation imaginable; nothing being so convenient as for one prince to be near another, who receives for him all the rebuffs and insults of fortune. And it seldom happens that by subduing such a state the real power of the conqueror is as much increased as the relative is diminished.

     ·   ·   ·

BOOK X. OF LAWS IN THE RELATION THEY BEAR TO OFFENSIVE FORCE

1. Of offensive Force. Offensive force is regulated by the law of nations, which is the political law of each country considered in its relation to every other.

2. Of War. The life of governments is like that of man. The latter has a right to kill in case of natural defence: the former have a right to wage war for their own preservation.

In the case of natural defence I have a right to kill, because my life is in respect to me what the life of my antagonist is to him: in the same manner a state wages war because its preservation is like that of any other being.

With individuals the right of natural defence does not imply a necessity of attacking. Instead of attacking they need only have recourse to proper tribunals. They cannot therefore exercise this right of defence but in sudden cases, when immediate death would be the consequence of waiting for the assistance of the law. But with states the right of natural defence carries along with it sometimes the necessity of attacking; as for instance, when one nation sees that a continuance of peace will enable another to destroy her, and that to attack that nation instantly is the only way to prevent her own destruction.

Thence it follows that petty states have oftener a right to declare war than great ones, because they are oftener in the case of being afraid of destruction.

The right of war, therefore, is derived from necessity and strict justice. If those who direct the conscience or councils of princes do not abide by this maxim, the consequence is dreadful: when they proceed on arbitrary principles of glory, convenience, and utility, torrents of blood must overspread the earth.

But, above all, let them not plead such an idle pretext as the glory of the prince: his glory is nothing but pride; it is a passion, and not a legitimate right.

It is true the fame of his power might increase the strength of his government; but it might be equally increased by the reputation of his justice.

3. *Of the Right of Conquest.* From the right of war comes that of conquest; which is the consequence of that right, and ought therefore to follow its spirit.

The right the conqueror has over a conquered people is directed by four sorts of laws: the law of nature, which makes everything tend to the preservation of the species; the law of natural reason, which teaches us to do to others what we would have done to ourselves; the law that forms political societies, whose duration nature has not limited; and, in fine, the law derived from the nature of the thing itself. Conquest is an acquisition, and carries with it the spirit of preservation and use, not of destruction.

The inhabitants of a conquered country are treated by the conqueror in one of the four following ways: Either he continues to rule them according to their own laws, and assumes to himself only the exercise of the political and civil government; or he gives them new political and civil government; or he destroys and disperses the society; or, in fine, he exterminates the people.

The first way is conformable to the law of nations now followed; the fourth is more agreeable to the law of nations followed by the Romans: in respect to which I leave the reader to judge how far we have improved upon the ancients. We must give due commendations to our modern refinements in reason, religion, philosophy, and manners.

The authors of our public law, guided by ancient histories, without confining themselves to cases of strict necessity, have fallen into very great errors. They have adopted tyrannical and arbitrary principles, by supposing the conquerors to be invested with I know not what right to kill: thence they have drawn consequences as terrible as the very principle, and established maxims which the conquerors themselves, when possessed of the least grain of sense, never presumed to follow. It is a plain case that when the conquest is completed, the conqueror has no longer a right to kill, because he has no longer the plea of natural defence and self-preservation.

What has led them into this mistake is, that they imagined a conqueror had a right to destroy the state; whence they inferred that he had a right to destroy the men that compose it: a wrong consequence from a false principle. For from the destruction of the state it does not at all follow that the people who compose it ought to be also destroyed. The state is the association of men, and not the men themselves; the citizen may perish, and the man remain.

From the right of killing in the case of conquest, politicians have drawn that of reducing to slavery—a consequence as ill-grounded as the principle.

There is no such thing as a right of reducing people to slavery, save when it becomes necessary for the preservation of the conquest. Preservation, and not servitude, is the end of conquest; though servitude may happen sometimes to be a necessary means of preservation.

Even in that case it is contrary to the nature of things that the slavery should be perpetual. The people enslaved ought to be rendered capable of becoming subjects. Slavery in conquests is an accidental thing. When after the expiration of a certain space of time all the parts of the conquering state are connected with the conquered nation, by custom, marriages, laws, associations, and by a certain conformity of disposition, there ought to be an end of the slavery. For the rights of the conqueror are founded entirely on the opposition between the two nations in those very articles, whence prejudices arise, and the want of mutual confidence.

A conqueror, therefore, who reduces the conquered people to slavery, ought always to reserve to himself the means (for means there are without number) of restoring them to their liberty.

These are far from being vague and uncertain notions. Thus our ancestors acted, those ancestors who conquered the Roman empire. The laws they made in the heat and transport of passion and in the insolence of victory were gradually softened; those laws were at first severe, but were afterwards rendered impartial. The Burgundians, Goths, and Lombards would have the Romans continue a conquered people; but the laws of Euric, Gundebald, and Rotharis made the Romans and barbarians fellow-citizens.[1]

Charlemagne, to tame the Saxons, deprived them of their liberty and property. Louis the Debonnaire made them a free people,[2] and this was one of the most prudent regulations during his whole reign. Time and servitude had softened their manners, and they ever after adhered to him with the greatest fidelity.

4. *Some Advantages of a conquered People.* Instead of inferring such destructive consequences from the right of conquest, much better would it have been for politicians to mention the advantages which this very right may sometimes give to a conquered people—advantages which would be more sensibly and more universally experienced were our law of nations exactly followed, and established in every part of the globe.

Conquered countries are, generally speaking, degenerated from their original institution. Corruption has crept in, the execution of the laws has been neglected, and the government has grown oppressive. Who can question but such a state would be a gainer, and derive some advantages from the very conquest itself, if it did not prove destructive? When a government has arrived at that degree of corruption as to be incapable of re-

forming itself, it would not lose much by being newly moulded. A conqueror who enters triumphant into a country where the moneyed men have, by a variety of artifices, insensibly arrived at innumerable ways of encroaching on the public, where the miserable people, who see abuses grown into laws, are ready to sink under the weight of impression, yet think they have no right to apply for redress—a conqueror, I say, may make a total change, and then the tyranny of those wretches will be the first thing exposed to his resentment.

We have beheld, for instance, countries oppressed by the farmers of the revenues, and eased afterwards by the conqueror, who had neither the engagements nor wants of the legitimate prince. Even the abuses have been often redressed without any interposition of the conqueror.

Sometimes the frugality of a conquering nation has enabled them to allow the conquered those necessaries of which they had been deprived under a lawful prince.

A conquest may destroy pernicious prejudices, and lay, if I may presume to use the expression, the nation under a better genius.

What good might not the Spaniards have done to the Mexicans? They had a mild religion to impart to them; but they filled their heads with a frantic superstition. They might have set slaves at liberty; they made freemen slaves. They might have undeceived them with regard to the abuse of human sacrifices; instead of that they destroyed them. Never should I have finished, were I to recount all the good they might have done, and all the mischief they committed.

It is a conqueror's business to repair a part of the mischief he has occasioned. The right, therefore, of conquest I define thus: a necessary, lawful, but unhappy power, which leaves the conqueror under a heavy obligation of repairing the injuries done to humanity.

5. *Gelon, King of Syracuse.* The noblest treaty of peace ever mentioned in history is, in my opinion, that which Gelon made with the Carthaginians. He insisted upon their abolishing the custom of sacrificing their children.[3] Glorious indeed! After having defeated three hundred thousand Carthaginians, he required a condition that was advantageous only to themselves, or rather he stipulated in favour of human nature.

The Bactrians exposed their aged fathers to

[1] See the Code of Barbarian Laws, and Book xxviii below.
[2] See the anonymous author of the *Life of Louis le Débonnaire,* in Duchesne's collection, ii, p. 296.
[3] See M. Barbeyrac's collection, art. 112.

be devoured by large mastiffs—a custom suppressed by Alexander, whereby he obtained a signal triumph over superstition.

6. *Of Conquest made by a Republic*. It is contrary to the nature of things that in a confederate government one state should make any conquest over another, as in our days we have seen in Switzerland.[1] In mixed confederate republics, where the association is between petty republics and monarchies, of a small extent, this is not so absurd.

Contrary is it also to the nature of things that a democratic republic should conquer towns which cannot enter into the sphere of its democracy. It is necessary that the conquered people should be capable of enjoying the privileges of sovereignty, as was settled in the very beginning among the Romans. The conquest ought to be limited to the number of citizens fixed for the democracy.

If a democratic republic subdues a nation in order to govern them as subjects, it exposes its own liberty; because it entrusts too great a power to those who are appointed to the command of the conquered provinces.

How dangerous would have been the situation of the republic of Carthage had Hannibal made himself master of Rome? What would he not have done in his own country, had he been victorious, he who caused so many revolutions in it after his defeat?[2]

Hanno could never have dissuaded the senate from sending succour to Hannibal, had he used no other argument than his own jealousy. The Carthaginian senate, whose wisdom is so highly extolled by Aristotle (and which has been evidently proved by the prosperity of that republic), could never have been determined by other than solid reasons. They must have been stupid not to see that an army at the distance of three hundred leagues would necessarily be exposed to losses which required reparation.

Hanno's party insisted that Hannibal should be delivered up to the Romans.[3] They could not at that time be afraid of the Romans; they were therefore apprehensive of Hannibal.

It was impossible, some will say, for them to imagine that Hannibal had been so successful.

But how was it possible for them to doubt it? Could the Carthaginians, a people spread over all the earth, be ignorant of what was transacting in Italy? No: they were sufficiently acquainted with it, and for that reason they did not care to send supplies to Hannibal.

Hanno became more resolute after the battle of Trebia, after the battle of Thrasimenus, after that of Cannæ; it was not his incredulity that increased, but his fear.

7. *The same Subject continued*. There is still another inconvenience in conquests made by democracies: their government is ever odious to the conquered states. It is apparently monarchical: but in reality it is much more oppressive than monarchy, as the experience of all ages and countries evinces.

The conquered people are in a melancholy situation; they neither enjoy the advantages of a republic, nor those of a monarchy.

What has been here said of a popular state is applicable to aristocracy.

8. *The same Subject continued*. When a republic, therefore, keeps another nation in subjection, it should endeavour to repair the inconveniences arising from the nature of its situation by giving it good laws both for the political and civil government of the people.

We have an instance of an island in the Mediterranean, subject to an Italian republic, whose political and civil laws with regard to the inhabitants of that island were extremely defective. The act of indemnity,[4] by which it ordained that no one should be condemned to bodily punishment in consequence of the private knowledge of the governor, *ex informata conscientia,* is still recent in everybody's memory. There have been frequent instances of the people's petitioning for privileges; here the sovereign grants only the common right of all nations.

9. *Of Conquests made by a Monarchy*. If a monarchy can long subsist before it is weakened by its increase, it will become formidable; and its strength will remain entire, while pent up by the neighbouring monarchies.

It ought not, therefore, to aim at conquests beyond the natural limits of its government. So soon as it has passed these limits, it is prudence to stop.

---

[1] With regard to Tockenburg.

[2] He was at the head of a faction.

[3] Hanno wanted to deliver Hannibal up to the Romans, as Cato would fain have delivered up Cæsar to the Gauls.

[4] Of the 18th of October, 1738, printed at Genoa by Franchelli. See also the *Amsterdam Gazette,* Dec. 23, 1738.

In this kind of conquest things must be left as they were found—the same courts of judicature, the same laws, the same customs, the same privileges: there ought to be no other alteration than that of the army and of the name of the sovereign.

When a monarchy has extended its limits by the conquest of neighbouring provinces, it should treat those provinces with great lenity.

If a monarchy has been long endeavouring at conquest, the provinces of its ancient demesne are generally ill-used. They are obliged to submit both to the new and to the ancient abuses; and to be depopulated by a vast metropolis, that swallows up the whole. Now if, after having made conquests round this demesne, the conquered people were treated like the ancient subjects, the state would be undone; the taxes sent by the conquered provinces to the capital would never return; the inhabitants of the frontiers would be ruined, and consequently the frontiers would be weaker; the people would be disaffected; and the subsistence of the armies designed to act and remain there would become more precarious.

Such is the necessary state of a conquering monarchy: a shocking luxury in the capital; misery in the provinces somewhat distant; and plenty in the most remote. It is the same with such a monarchy as with our planet; fire at the centre, verdure on the surface, and between both a dry, cold, and barren earth.

10. *Of one Monarchy that subdues another.* Sometimes one monarchy subdues another. The smaller the latter, the better it is overawed by fortresses; and the larger it is, the better will it be preserved by colonies.

11. *Of the Manners of a conquered People.* It is not sufficient in those conquests to let the conquered nation enjoy their own laws; it is, perhaps, more necessary to leave them also their manners, because people in general have a stronger attachment to these than to their laws.

The French have been driven nine times out of Italy, because, as historians say,[1] of their insolent familiarities with the fair sex. It is too much for a nation to be obliged to bear not only with the pride of conquerors, but with their incontinence and indiscretion; these are, without doubt, most grievous and intolerable, as they are the source of infinite outrages.

[1] See Pufendorff's *Universal History.*

12. *Of a Law of Cyrus.* Far am I from thinking that a good law which Cyrus made to oblige the Lydians to practise none but mean or infamous professions. It is true he directed his attention to an object of the greatest importance: he thought of guarding against revolts, and not invasions; but invasions will soon come, when the Persians and Lydians unite and corrupt each other. I would therefore much rather support by laws the simplicity and rudeness of the conquering nation than the effeminacy of the conquered.

Aristodemus, tyrant of Cumæ,[2] used all his endeavours to banish courage, and to enervate the minds of youth. He ordered that boys should let their hair grow in the same manner as girls, that they should deck it with flowers, and wear long robes of different colours down to their heels; that when they went to their masters of music and dancing, they should have women with them to carry their umbrellas, perfumes, and fans, and to present them with combs and looking-glasses whenever they bathed. This education lasted till the age of twenty—an education that could be agreeable to none but to a petty tyrant, who exposes his sovereignty to defend his life.

13. *Charles XII.* This prince, who depended entirely on his own strength, hastened his ruin by forming designs that could never be executed but by a long war—a thing which his kingdom was unable to support.

It was not a declining state he undertook to subvert, but a rising empire. The Russians made use of the war he waged against them as of a military school. Every defeat brought them nearer to victory; and, losing abroad, they learned to defend themselves at home.

Charles, in the deserts of Poland, imagined himself sovereign of the whole world: here he wandered, and with him in some measure wandered Sweden; while his capital enemy acquired new strength against him, locked him up, made settlements along the Baltic, destroyed or subdued Livonia.

Sweden was like a river whose waters are cut off at the fountain head in order to change its course.

It was not the affair of Pultowa that ruined Charles. Had he not been destroyed at that place, he would have been in another. The casualties of fortune are easily repaired; but who can be guarded against events that incessantly arise from the nature of things?

[2] Dionysius Halicarnassus, vii.

But neither nature nor fortune were ever so much against him as he himself.

He was not directed by the present situation of things, but by a kind of plan of his forming; and even this he followed very ill. He was not an Alexander; but he would have made an excellent soldier under that monarch.

Alexander's project succeeded because it was prudently concerted. The bad success of the Persians in their several invasions of Greece, the conquests of Agesilaus, and the retreat of the ten thousand had shown to demonstration the superiority of the Greeks in their manner of fighting and in their arms; and it was well known that the Persians were too proud to be corrected.

It was no longer possible for them to weaken Greece by divisions: Greece was then united under one head, which could not pitch upon a better method of rendering her insensible to her servitude than by flattering her vanity with the destruction of her hereditary enemy, and with the hopes of the conquest of Asia.

An empire cultivated by the most industrious nation in the world, that followed agriculture from a principle of religion—an empire abounding with every convenience of life, furnished the enemy with all necessary means of subsisting.

It was easy to judge by the pride of those kings, who in vain were mortified by their numerous defeats, that they would precipitate their ruin by their forwardness in venturing battles; and that the flattery of their courtiers would never permit them to doubt of their grandeur.

The project was not only wise, but wisely executed. Alexander, in the rapidity of his conquests, even in the impetuosity of his passion, had, if I may so express myself, a flash of reason by which he was directed, and which those who would fain have made a romance of his history, and whose minds were more corrupt than his, could not conceal from our view. Let us descend more minutely into his history.

14. *Alexander.* He did not set out upon his expedition till he had secured Macedonia against the neighbouring barbarians, and completed the reduction of Greece; he availed himself of this conquest for no other end than for the execution of his grand enterprise; he rendered the jealousy of the Lacedæmonians of no ef-

fect; he attacked the maritime provinces; he caused his land forces to keep close to the sea-coast, that they might not be separated from his fleet; he made an admirable use of discipline against numbers; he never wanted provisions; and if it be true that victory gave him everything, he, in his turn, did everything to obtain it.

In the beginning of his enterprise—a time when the least check might have proved his destruction—he trusted very little to fortune; but when his reputation was established by a series of prosperous events, he sometimes had recourse to temerity. When before his departure for Asia he marched against the Triballians and Illyrians, you find he waged war[1] against those people in the very same manner as Cæsar afterwards conducted that against the Gauls. Upon his return to Greece,[2] it was in some measure against his will that he took and destroyed Thebes. When he invested that city, he wanted the inhabitants to come into terms of peace; but they hastened their own ruin. When it was debated whether he should attack the Persian fleet,[3] it is Parmenio who shows his presumption, Alexander his wisdom. His aim was to draw the Persians from the sea-coast, and to lay them under a necessity of abandoning their marine, in which they had a manifest superiority. Tyre being from principle attached to the Persians, who could not subsist without the commerce and navigation of that city, Alexander destroyed it. He subdued Egypt, which Darius had left bare of troops while he was assembling immense armies in another world.

To the passage of the Granicus, Alexander owed the conquest of the Greek colonies; to the battle of Issus, the reduction of Tyre and Egypt; to the battle of Arbela, the empire of the world.

After the battle of Issus, he suffered Darius to escape, and employed his time in securing and regulating his conquests: after the battle of Arbela, he pursued him so close[4] as to leave him no place of refuge in his empire. Darius enters his towns, his provinces, to quit them the next moment; and Alexander marches with such rapidity that the empire of the world seems to be rather the prize of an Olympian race than the fruit of a great victory.

In this manner he carried on his conquests:

[1] See Arrian, *De Expedit. Alex.*, i.
[2] *Ibid.*
[3] *Ibid.*
[4] *Ibid., iii.*

let us now see how he preserved them.

He opposed those who would have had him treat the Greeks as masters[1] and the Persians as slaves. He thought only of uniting the two nations, and of abolishing the distinctions of a conquering and a conquered people. After he had completed his victories, he relinquished all those prejudices that had helped him to obtain them. He assumed the manners of the Persians, that he might not chagrin them too much by obliging them to conform to those of the Greeks. It was this humanity which made him show so great a respect for the wife and mother of Darius; and this that made him so continent. What a conqueror! He is lamented by all the nations he has subdued! What a usurper! At his death the very family he has cast from the throne is all in tears. These were the most glorious passages in his life, and such as history cannot produce an instance of in any other conqueror.

Nothing consolidates a conquest more than the union formed between the two nations by marriages.[2] Alexander chose his wives from the nation he had subdued; he insisted on his courtiers doing the same; and the rest of the Macedonians followed the example. The Franks and Burgundians permitted those marriages;[3] the Visigoths forbade them in Spain, and afterwards allowed them.[4] By the Lombards they were not only allowed but encouraged.[5] When the Romans wanted to weaken Macedonia, they ordered that there should be no intermarriages between the people of different provinces.

Alexander, whose aim was to unite the two nations, thought fit to establish in Persia a great number of Greek colonies. He built, therefore, a multitude of towns; and so strongly were all the parts of this new empire cemented, that after his decease, amidst the disturbances and confusion of the most frightful civil wars, when the Greeks had reduced themselves, as it were, to a state of annihilation, not a single province of Persia revolted.

To prevent Greece and Macedon from being too much exhausted, he sent a colony of Jews[6] to Alexandria; the manners of those people signified nothing to him, provided he could be sure of their fidelity.

He not only suffered the conquered nations to retain their own customs and manners, but likewise their civil laws; and frequently the very kings and governors to whom they had been subject: the Macedonians[7] he placed at the head of the troops, and the natives of the country at the head of the government, rather choosing to run the hazard of a particular disloyalty (which sometimes happened) than of a general revolt.

He paid great respect to the ancient traditions, and to all the public monuments of the glory or vanity of nations. The Persian monarchs having destroyed the temples of the Greeks, Babylonians, and Egyptians, Alexander rebuilt them:[8] few nations submitted to his yoke to whose religion he did not conform; and his conquests seem to have been intended only to make him the particular monarch of each nation, and the first inhabitant of each city. The aim of the Romans in conquest was to destroy, his to preserve; and wherever he directed his victorious arms, his chief view was to achieve something whence that country might derive an increase of prosperity and power. To attain this end, he was enabled first of all by the greatness of his genius; secondly, by his frugality and private economy;[9] thirdly, by his profusion in matters of importance. He was close and reserved in his private expenses, but generous to the highest degree in those of a public nature. In regulating his household, he was the private Macedonian; but in paying the troops, in sharing his conquests with the Greeks, and in his largesses to every soldier in his army, he was Alexander.

He committed two very bad actions in setting Persepolis on fire and slaying Clitus; but he rendered them famous by his repentance. Hence it is that his crimes are forgotten, while his regard for virtue was recorded: they were considered rather as unlucky accidents than as his own deliberate acts. Posterity, struck with the beauty of his mind, even in the midst of his irregular passion, can view him only with pity, but never with an eye of hatred.

---

[1] This was Aristotle's advice. Plutarch, *Of the Fortune and Virtue of Alexander.*

[2] Arrian, *De Expedit. Alex.,* vii.

[3] See the Law of the Burgundians, tit. 12, art. 5.

[4] See the Law of the Visigoths, iii, tit. 1, § 1, which abrogates the ancient law that had more regard, it says, to the difference of nations than to that of people's conditions.

[5] See the Law of the Lombards, ii, tit. 7, §§ 1, 2.

[6] The kings of Syria, abandoning the plan laid down by the founder of the empire, resolved to oblige the Jews to conform to the manners of the Greeks—a resolution that gave the most terrible shock to their government.

[7] See Arrian, *De Expedit. Alex.,* iii, and others.

[8] *Ibid.*

[9] *Ibid.,* vii.

Let us draw a comparison between him and Cæsar. The Roman general, by attempting to imitate the Asiatic monarch, flung his fellow-citizens into a state of despair for a matter of mere ostentation; the Macedonian prince, by the same imitation, did a thing which was quite agreeable to his original scheme of conquest.

15. *New Methods of preserving a Conquest.* When a monarch has subdued a large country, he may make use of an admirable method, equally proper for moderating despotic power, and for preserving the conquest; it is a method practised by the conquerors of China.

In order to prevent the vanquished nation from falling into despair, the victors from growing insolent and proud, the government from becoming military, and to contain the two nations within their duty, the Tartar family now on the throne of China has ordained that every military corps in the provinces should be composed half of Chinese and half Tartars, to the end that the jealousy between the two nations may keep them within bounds. The courts of judicature are likewise half Chinese and half Tartars. This is productive of several good effects. 1. The two nations are a check to one another. 2. They both preserve the civil and military power, and one is not destroyed by the other. 3. The conquering nation may spread itself without being weakened and lost. It is likewise enabled to withstand civil and foreign wars. The want of so wise an institution as this has been the ruin of almost all the conquerors that ever existed.

16. *Of Conquests made by a despotic Prince.* When a conquest happens to be vastly large, it supposes a despotic power; and then the army dispersed in the provinces is not sufficient. There should be always a body of faithful troops near the prince, ready to fall instantly upon any part of the empire that may chance to waver. This military corps ought to awe the rest, and to strike terror into those who through necessity have been entrusted with any authority in the empire. The emperor of China has always a large body of Tartars near his person, ready upon all occasions. In India, in Turkey, in Japan, the prince has always a body-guard independent of the other regular forces. This particular corps keeps the dispersed troops in awe.

17. *The same Subject continued.* We have observed that the countries subdued by a despotic monarch ought to be held by a vassal. Historians are very lavish of their praises of the generosity of those conquerors who restored the princes to the throne whom they had vanquished. Extremely generous then were the Romans, who made such a number of kings, in order to have instruments of slavery.[1] A proceeding of that kind is absolutely necessary. If the conqueror intends to preserve the country which he has subdued, neither the governors he sends will be able to contain the subjects within duty, nor he himself the governors. He will be obliged to strip his ancient patrimony of troops, in order to secure his new dominions. The miseries of each nation will be common to both; civil broils will spread themselves from one to the other. On the contrary, if the conqueror restores the legitimate prince to the throne, he will of course have an ally; by the junction of whose forces his own power will be augmented. We have a recent instance of this in Shah Nadir, who conquered the Mogul, seized his treasures, and left him in possession of Hindostan.

Book XI. Of the Laws Which Establish Political Liberty, with regard to the Constitution

1. *A general Idea.* I make a distinction between the laws that establish political liberty, as it relates to the constitution, and those by which it is established, as it relates to the citizen. The former shall be the subject of this book; the latter I shall examine in the next.

2. *Different Significations of the word Liberty.* There is no word that admits of more various significations, and has made more varied impressions on the human mind, than that of *liberty.* Some have taken it as a means of deposing a person on whom they had conferred a tyrannical authority; others for the power of choosing a superior whom they are obliged to obey; others for the right of bearing arms, and of being thereby enabled to use violence; others, in fine, for the privilege of being gov-

[1] Tacitus, *Life of Agricola*, 14.

erned by a native of their own country, or by their own laws.[1] A certain nation for a long time thought liberty consisted in the privilege of wearing a long beard.[2] Some have annexed this name to one form of government exclusive of others: those who had a republican taste applied it to this species of polity; those who liked a monarchical state gave it to monarchy.[3] Thus they have all applied the name of liberty to the government most suitable to their own customs and inclinations: and as in republics the people have not so constant and so present a view of the causes of their misery, and as the magistrates seem to act only in conformity to the laws, hence liberty is generally said to reside in republics, and to be banished from monarchies. In fine, as in democracies the people seem to act almost as they please, this sort of government has been deemed the most free, and the power of the people has been confounded with their liberty.

3. *In what Liberty consists.* It is true that in democracies the people seem to act as they please; but political liberty does not consist in an unlimited freedom. In governments, that is, in societies directed by laws, liberty can consist only in the power of doing what we ought to will, and in not being constrained to do what we ought not to will.

We must have continually present to our minds the difference between independence and liberty. Liberty is a right of doing whatever the laws permit, and if a citizen could do what they forbid he would be no longer possessed of liberty, because all his fellow-citizens would have the same power.

4. *The same Subject continued.* Democratic and aristocratic states are not in their own nature free. Political liberty is to be found only in moderate governments; and even in these it is not always found. It is there only when there is no abuse of power. But constant experience shows us that every man invested with power is apt to abuse it, and to carry his authority as far as it will go. Is it not strange,

though true, to say that virtue itself has need of limits?

To prevent this abuse, it is necessary from the very nature of things that power should be a check to power. A government may be so constituted, as no man shall be compelled to do things to which the law does not oblige him, nor forced to abstain from things which the law permits.

5. *Of the End or View of different Governments.* Though all governments have the same general end, which is that of preservation, yet each has another particular object. Increase of dominion was the object of Rome; war, that of Sparta; religion, that of the Jewish laws; commerce, that of Marseilles; public tranquillity, that of the laws of China:[4] navigation, that of the laws of Rhodes; natural liberty, that of the policy of the Savages; in general, the pleasures of the prince, that of despotic states; that of monarchies, the prince's and the kingdom's glory; the independence of individuals is the end aimed at by the laws of Poland; thence results the oppression of the whole.[5]

One nation there is also in the world that has for the direct end of its constitution political liberty. We shall presently examine the principles on which this liberty is founded; if they are sound, liberty will appear in its highest perfection.

To discover political liberty in a constitution, no great labour is requisite. If we are capable of seeing it where it exists, it is soon found, and we need not go far in search of it.

6. *Of the Constitution of England.* In every government there are three sorts of power: the legislative; the executive in respect to things dependent on the law of nations; and the executive in regard to matters that depend on the civil law.

By virtue of the first, the prince or magistrate enacts temporary or perpetual laws, and amends or abrogates those that have been already enacted. By the second, he makes peace or war, sends or receives embassies, establishes the public security, and provides against invasions. By the third, he punishes criminals, or determines the disputes that arise between individuals. The latter we shall call the judici-

[1] "I have copied," says Cicero, "Scævola's edict, which permits the Greeks to terminate their difference among themselves according to their own laws; this makes them consider themselves a free people."
[2] The Russians could not bear that Czar Peter should make them cut it off.
[3] The Cappadocians refused the condition of a republican state, which was offered them by the Romans.

[4] The natural end of a state that has no foreign enemies, or that thinks itself secured against them by barriers.
[5] Inconvenience of the *Liberum veto.*

ary power, and the other simply the executive power of the state.

The political liberty of the subject is a tranquillity of mind arising from the opinion each person has of his safety. In order to have this liberty, it is requisite the government be so constituted as one man need not be afraid of another.

When the legislative and executive powers are united in the same person, or in the same body of magistrates, there can be no liberty; because apprehensions may arise, lest the same monarch or senate should enact tyrannical laws, to execute them in a tyrannical manner.

Again, there is no liberty, if the judiciary power be not separated from the legislative and executive. Were it joined with the legislative, the life and liberty of the subject would be exposed to arbitrary control; for the judge would be then the legislator. Were it joined to the executive power, the judge might behave with violence and oppression.

There would be an end of everything, were the same man or the same body, whether of the nobles or of the people, to exercise those three powers, that of enacting laws, that of executing the public resolutions, and of trying the causes of individuals.

Most kingdoms in Europe enjoy a moderate government because the prince who is invested with the two first powers leaves the third to his subjects. In Turkey, where these three powers are united in the Sultan's person, the subjects groan under the most dreadful oppression.

In the republics of Italy, where these three powers are united, there is less liberty than in our monarchies. Hence their government is obliged to have recourse to as violent methods for its support as even that of the Turks; witness the state inquisitors,[1] and the lion's mouth into which every informer may at all hours throw his written accusations.

In what a situation must the poor subject be in those republics! The same body of magistrates are possessed, as executors of the laws, of the whole power they have given themselves in quality of legislators. They may plunder the state by their general determinations; and as they have likewise the judiciary power in their hands, every private citizen may be ruined by their particular decisions.

The whole power is here united in one body; and though there is no external pomp

[1] At Venice.

that indicates a despotic sway, yet the people feel the effects of it every moment.

Hence it is that many of the princes of Europe, whose aim has been levelled at arbitrary power, have constantly set out with uniting in their own persons all the branches of magistracy, and all the great offices of state.

I allow indeed that the mere hereditary aristocracy of the Italian republics does not exactly answer to the despotic power of the Eastern princes. The number of magistrates sometimes moderates the power of the magistracy; the whole body of the nobles do not always concur in the same design; and different tribunals are erected, that temper each other. Thus at Venice the legislative power is in the *council,* the executive in the *pregadi,* and the judiciary in the *quarantia.* But the mischief is, that these different tribunals are composed of magistrates all belonging to the same body; which constitutes almost one and the same power.

The judiciary power ought not to be given to a standing senate; it should be exercised by persons taken from the body of the people[2] at certain times of the year, and consistently with a form and manner prescribed by law, in order to erect a tribunal that should last only so long as necessity requires.

By this method the judicial power, so terrible to mankind, not being annexed to any particular state or profession, becomes, as it were, invisible. People have not then the judges continually present to their view; they fear the office, but not the magistrate.

In accusations of a deep and criminal nature, it is proper the person accused should have the privilege of choosing, in some measure, his judges, in concurrence with the law; or at least he should have a right to except against so great a number that the remaining part may be deemed his own choice.

The other two powers may be given rather to magistrates or permanent bodies, because they are not exercised on any private subject; one being no more than the general will of the state, and the other the execution of that general will.

But though the tribunals ought not to be fixed, the judgments ought; and to such a degree as to be ever conformable to the letter of the law. Were they to be the private opinion of the judge, people would then live in society, without exactly knowing the nature of their obligations.

[2] As at Athens.

The judges ought likewise to be of the same rank as the accused, or, in other words, his peers; to the end that he may not imagine he is fallen into the hands of persons inclined to treat him with rigour.

If the legislature leaves the executive power in possession of a right to imprison those subjects who can give security for their good behaviour, there is an end of liberty; unless they are taken up, in order to answer without delay to a capital crime, in which case they are really free, being subject only to the power of the law.

But should the legislature think itself in danger by some secret conspiracy against the state, or by a correspondence with a foreign enemy, it might authorise the executive power, for a short and limited time, to imprison suspected persons, who in that case would lose their liberty only for a while, to preserve it for ever.

And this is the only reasonable method that can be substituted to the tyrannical magistracy of the Ephori, and to the state inquisitors of Venice, who are also despotic.

As in a country of liberty, every man who is supposed a free agent ought to be his own governor; the legislative power should reside in the whole body of the people. But since this is impossible in large states, and in small ones is subject to many inconveniences, it is fit the people should transact by their representatives what they cannot transact by themselves.

The inhabitants of a particular town are much better acquainted with its wants and interests than with those of other places; and are better judges of the capacity of their neighbours than of that of the rest of their countrymen. The members, therefore, of the legislature should not be chosen from the general body of the nation; but it is proper that in every considerable place a representative should be elected by the inhabitants.[1]

The great advantage of representatives is, their capacity of discussing public affairs. For this the people collectively are extremely unfit, which is one of the chief inconveniences of a democracy.

It is not at all necessary that the representatives who have received a general instruction from their constituents should wait to be directed on each particular affair, as is practised in the diets of Germany. True it is that by this way of proceeding the speeches of the deputies might with greater propriety be called the voice of the nation; but, on the oth-

[1] See Aristotle, *Politics*, iv. 4.

er hand, this would occasion infinite delays; would give each deputy a power of controlling the assembly; and, on the most urgent and pressing occasions, the wheels of government might be stopped by the caprice of a single person.

When the deputies, as Mr. Sidney well observes, represent a body of people, as in Holland, they ought to be accountable to their constituents; but it is a different thing in England, where they are deputed by boroughs.

All the inhabitants of the several districts ought to have a right of voting at the election of a representative, except such as are in so mean a situation as to be deemed to have no will of their own.

One great fault there was in most of the ancient republics, that the people had a right to active resolutions, such as require some execution, a thing of which they are absolutely incapable. They ought to have no share in the government but for the choosing of representatives, which is within their reach. For though few can tell the exact degree of men's capacities, yet there are none but are capable of knowing in general whether the person they choose is better qualified than most of his neighbours.

Neither ought the representative body to be chosen for the executive part of government, for which it is not so fit; but for the enacting of laws, or to see whether the laws in being are duly executed, a thing suited to their abilities, and which none indeed but themselves can properly perform.

In such a state there are always persons distinguished by their birth, riches, or honours: but were they to be confounded with the common people, and to have only the weight of a single vote like the rest, the common liberty would be their slavery, and they would have no interest in supporting it, as most of the popular resolutions would be against them. The share they have, therefore, in the legislature ought to be proportioned to their other advantages in the state; which happens only when they form a body that has a right to check the licentiousness of the people, as the people have a right to oppose any encroachment of theirs.

The legislative power is therefore committed to the body of the nobles, and to that which represents the people, each having their assemblies and deliberations apart, each their separate views and interests.

Of the three powers above mentioned, the

judiciary is in some measure next to nothing: there remain, therefore, only two; and as these have need of a regulating power to moderate them, the part of the legislative body composed of the nobility is extremely proper for this purpose.

The body of the nobility ought to be hereditary. In the first place it is so in its own nature; and in the next there must be a considerable interest to preserve its privileges—privileges that in themselves are obnoxious to popular envy, and of course in a free state are always in danger.

But as a hereditary power might be tempted to pursue its own particular interests, and forget those of the people, it is proper that where a singular advantage may be gained by corrupting the nobility, as in the laws relating to the supplies, they should have no other share in the legislation than the power of rejecting, and not that of resolving.

By the *power of resolving* I mean the right of ordaining by their own authority, or of amending what has been ordained by others. By the *power of rejecting* I would be understood to mean the right of annulling a resolution taken by another; which was the power of the tribunes at Rome. And though the person possessed of the privilege of rejecting may likewise have the right of approving, yet this approbation passes for no more than a declaration that he intends to make no use of his privilege of rejecting, and is derived from that very privilege.

The executive power ought to be in the hands of a monarch, because this branch of government, having need of despatch, is better administered by one than by many: on the other hand, whatever depends on the legislative power is oftentimes better regulated by many than by a single person.

But if there were no monarch, and the executive power should be committed to a certain number of persons selected from the legislative body, there would be an end then of liberty; by reason the two powers would be united, as the same persons would sometimes possess, and would be always able to possess, a share in both.

Were the legislative body to be a considerable time without meeting, this would likewise put an end to liberty. For of two things one would naturally follow: either that there would be no longer any legislative resolutions, and then the state would fall into anarchy; or that these resolutions would be taken by the

executive power, which would render it absolute.

It would be needless for the legislative body to continue always assembled. This would be troublesome to the representatives, and, moreover, would cut out too much work for the executive power, so as to take off its attention to its office, and oblige it to think only of defending its own prerogatives, and the right it has to execute.

Again, were the legislative body to be always assembled, it might happen to be kept up only by filling the places of the deceased members with new representatives; and in that case, if the legislative body were once corrupted, the evil would be past all remedy. When different legislative bodies succeed one another, the people who have a bad opinion of that which is actually sitting may reasonably entertain some hopes of the next: but were it to be always the same body, the people upon seeing it once corrupted would no longer expect any good from its laws; and of course they would either become desperate or fall into a state of indolence.

The legislative body should not meet of itself. For a body is supposed to have no will but when it is met; and besides, were it not to meet unanimously, it would be impossible to determine which was really the legislative body; the part assembled, or the other. And if it had a right to prorogue itself, it might happen never to be prorogued; which would be extremely dangerous, in case it should ever attempt to encroach on the executive power. Besides, there are seasons, some more proper than others, for assembling the legislative body: it is fit, therefore, that the executive power should regulate the time of meeting, as well as the duration of those assemblies, according to the circumstances and exigencies of a state known to itself.

Were the executive power not to have a right of restraining the encroachments of the legislative body, the latter would become despotic; for as it might arrogate to itself what authority it pleased, it would soon destroy all the other powers.

But it is not proper, on the other hand, that the legislative power should have a right to stay the executive. For as the execution has its natural limits, it is useless to confine it; besides, the executive power is generally employed in momentary operations. The power, therefore, of the Roman tribunes was faulty, as it put a stop not only to the legislation, but likewise to the executive part of government; which was attended with infinite mischief.

But if the legislative power in a free state has no right to stay the executive, it has a right and ought to have the means of examining in what manner its laws have been executed; an advantage which this government has over that of Crete and Sparta, where the Cosmi[1] and the Ephori[2] gave no account of their administration.

But whatever may be the issue of that examination, the legislative body ought not to have a power of arraigning the person, nor, of course, the conduct, of him who is entrusted with the executive power. His person should be sacred, because as it is necessary for the good of the state to prevent the legislative body from rendering themselves arbitrary, the moment he is accused or tried there is an end of liberty.

In this case the state would be no longer a monarchy, but a kind of republic, though not a free government. But as the person entrusted with the executive power cannot abuse it without bad counsellors, and such as have the laws as ministers, though the laws protect them as subjects, these men may be examined and punished—an advantage which this government has over that of Gnidus, where the law allowed of no such thing as calling the Amymones[3] to an account, even after their administration;[4] and therefore the people could never obtain any satisfaction for the injuries done them.

Though, in general, the judiciary power ought not to be united with any part of the legislative, yet this is liable to three exceptions, founded on the particular interest of the party accused.

The great are always obnoxious to popular envy; and were they to be judged by the people, they might be in danger from their judges, and would, moreover, be deprived of the privilege which the meanest subject is possessed of in a free state, of being tried by his peers. The nobility, for this reason, ought not to be cited before the ordinary courts of judicature, but before that part of the legislature which is composed of their own body.

[1] See Aristotle, *Politics*, ii, 10.
[2] *Ibid.*, 9.
[3] These were magistrates chosen annually by the people. See Stephen of Byzantium.
[4] It was lawful to accuse the Roman magistrates after the expiration of their several offices. See in Dionysius Halicarnassus, ix, the affair of Genutius the tribune.

It is possible that the law, which is clear-sighted in one sense, and blind in another, might, in some cases, be too severe. But as we have already observed, the national judges are no more than the mouth that pronounces the words of the law, mere passive beings, incapable of moderating either its force or rigour. That part, therefore, of the legislative body, which we have just now observed to be a necessary tribunal on another occasion, is also a necessary tribunal in this; it belongs to its supreme authority to moderate the law in favour of the law itself, by mitigating the sentence.

It might also happen that a subject entrusted with the administration of public affairs may infringe the rights of the people, and be guilty of crimes which the ordinary magistrates either could not or would not punish. But, in general, the legislative power cannot try causes: and much less can it try this particular case, where it represents the party aggrieved, which is the people. It can only, therefore, impeach. But before what court shall it bring its impeachment? Must it go and demean itself before the ordinary tribunals, which are its inferiors, and, being composed, moreover, of men who are chosen from the people as well as itself, will naturally be swayed by the authority of so powerful an accuser? No: in order to preserve the dignity of the people, and the security of the subject, the legislative part which represents the people must bring in its charge before the legislative part which represents the nobility, who have neither the same interests nor the same passions.

Here is an advantage which this government has over most of the ancient republics, where this abuse prevailed, that the people were at the same time both judge and accuser.

The executive power, pursuant of what has been already said, ought to have a share in the legislature by the power of rejecting, otherwise it would soon be stripped of its prerogative. But should the legislative power usurp a share of the executive, the latter would be equally undone.

If the prince were to have a part in the legislature by the power of resolving, liberty would be lost. But as it is necessary he should have a share in the legislature for the support of his own prerogative, this share must consist in the power of rejecting.

The change of government at Rome was owing to this, that neither the senate, who had one part of the executive power, nor the magistrates, who were entrusted with the other, had the right of rejecting, which was entirely lodged in the people.

Here then is the fundamental constitution of the government we are treating of. The legislative body being composed of two parts, they check one another by the mutual privilege of rejecting. They are both restrained by the executive power, as the executive is by the legislative.

These three powers should naturally form a state of repose or inaction. But as there is a necessity for movement in the course of human affairs, they are forced to move, but still in concert.

As the executive power has no other part in the legislative than the privilege of rejecting, it can have no share in the public debates. It is not even necessary that it should propose, because as it may always disapprove of the resolutions that shall be taken, it may likewise reject the decisions on those proposals which were made against its will.

In some ancient commonwealths, where public debates were carried on by the people in a body, it was natural for the executive power to propose and debate in conjunction with the people, otherwise their resolutions must have been attended with a strange confusion.

Were the executive power to determine the raising of public money, otherwise than by giving its consent, liberty would be at an end; because it would become legislative in the most important point of legislation.

If the legislative power was to settle the subsidies, not from year to year, but for ever, it would run the risk of losing its liberty, because the executive power would be no longer dependent; and when once it was possessed of such a perpetual right, it would be a matter of indifference whether it held it of itself or of another. The same may be said if it should come to a resolution of entrusting, not an annual, but a perpetual command of the fleets and armies to the executive power.

To prevent the executive power from being able to oppress, it is requisite that the armies with which it is entrusted should consist of the people, and have the same spirit as the people, as was the case at Rome till the time of Marius. To obtain this end, there are only two ways, either that the persons employed in the army should have sufficient property to answer for their conduct to their fellow-subjects, and be enlisted only for a year, as was custom-

ary at Rome: or if there should be a standing army, composed chiefly of the most despicable part of the nation, the legislative power should have a right to disband them as soon as it pleased; the soldiers should live in common with the rest of the people; and no separate camp, barracks, or fortress should be suffered.

When once an army is established, it ought not to depend immediately on the legislative, but on the executive, power; and this from the very nature of the thing, its business consisting more in action than in deliberation.

It is natural for mankind to set a higher value upon courage than timidity, on activity than prudence, on strength than counsel. Hence the army will ever despise a senate, and respect their own officers. They will naturally slight the orders sent them by a body of men whom they look upon as cowards, and therefore unworthy to command them. So that as soon as the troops depend entirely on the legislative body, it becomes a military government; and if the contrary has ever happened, it has been owing to some extraordinary circumstances. It is because the army was always kept divided; it is because it was composed of several bodies that depended each on a particular province; it is because the capital towns were strong places, defended by their natural situation, and not garrisoned with regular troops. Holland, for instance, is still safer than Venice; she might drown or starve the revolted troops; for as they are not quartered in towns capable of furnishing them with necessary subsistence, this subsistence is of course precarious.

In perusing the admirable treatise of Tacitus *On the Manners of the Germans*,[1] we find it is from that nation the English have borrowed the idea of their political government. This beautiful system was invented first in the woods.

As all human things have an end, the state we are speaking of will lose its liberty, will perish. Have not Rome, Sparta, and Carthage perished? It will perish when the legislative power shall be more corrupt than the executive.

It is not my business to examine whether the English actually enjoy this liberty or not. Sufficient it is for my purpose to observe that

[1] *De minoribus rebus principes consultant, de majoribus omnes; ita tamen ut ea quoque quorum penes plebem arbitrium est, apud principes pertractentur.*—ix.

it is established by their laws; and I inquire no further.

Neither do I pretend by this to undervalue other governments, nor to say that this extreme political liberty ought to give uneasiness to those who have only a moderate share of it. How should I have any such design, I who think that even the highest refinement of reason is not always desirable, and that mankind generally find their account better in mediums than in extremes?

Harrington, in his *Oceana,* has also inquired into the utmost degree of liberty to which the constitution of a state may be carried. But of him indeed it may be said that for want of knowing the nature of real liberty he busied himself in pursuit of an imaginary one; and that he built a Chalcedon, though he had a Byzantium before his eyes.

7. *Of the Monarchies we are acquainted with.* The monarchies we are acquainted with have not, like that we have been speaking of, liberty for their direct view: the only aim is the glory of the subject, of the state, and of the sovereign. But hence there results a spirit of liberty, which in those states is capable of achieving as great things, and of contributing as much perhaps to happiness as liberty itself.

Here the three powers are not distributed and founded on the model of the constitution above-mentioned; they have each a particular distribution, according to which they border more or less on political liberty; and if they did not border upon it, monarchy would degenerate into despotic government.

8. *Why the Ancients had not a clear Idea of Monarchy.* The ancients had no notion of a government founded on a body of nobles, and much less on a legislative body composed of the representatives of the people. The republics of Greece and Italy were cities that had each their own form of government, and convened their subjects within their walls. Before Rome had swallowed up all the other republics, there was scarcely anywhere a king to be found, no, not in Italy, Gaul, Spain, or Germany; they were all petty states or republics. Even Africa itself was subject to a great commonwealth: and Asia Minor was occupied by Greek colonies. There was, therefore, no instance of deputies of towns or assemblies of the states; one must have gone as far as Persia to find a monarchy.

I am not ignorant that there were confederate republics; in which several towns sent deputies to an assembly. But I affirm there was no monarchy on that model.

The first plan, therefore, of the monarchies we are acquainted with was thus formed. The German nations that conquered the Roman empire were certainly a free people. Of this we may be convinced only by reading Tacitus *On the Manners of the Germans.* The conquerors spread themselves over all the country; living mostly in the fields, and very little in towns. When they were in Germany, the whole nation was able to assemble. This they could no longer do when dispersed through the conquered provinces. And yet as it was necessary that the nation should deliberate on public affairs, pursuant to their usual method before the conquest, they had recourse to representatives. Such is the origin of the Gothic government amongst us. At first it was mixed with aristocracy and monarchy—a mixture attended with this inconvenience, that the common people were bondmen. The custom afterwards succeeded of granting letters of enfranchisement, and was soon followed by so perfect a harmony between the civil liberty of the people, the privileges of the nobility and clergy, and the prince's prerogative, that I really think there never was in the world a government so well tempered as that of each part of Europe, so long as it lasted. Surprising that the corruption of the government of a conquering nation should have given birth to the best species of constitution that could possibly be imagined by man!

9. *Aristotle's Manner of Thinking.* Aristotle is greatly puzzled in treating of monarchy.[1] He makes five species; and he does not distinguish them by the form of constitution, but by things merely accidental, as the virtues and vices of the prince; or by things extrinsic, such as tyranny usurped or inherited.

Among the number of monarchies he ranks the Persian empire and the kingdom of Sparta. But is it not evident that the one was a despotic state and the other a republic?

The ancients, who were strangers to the distribution of the three powers in the government of a single person, could never form a just idea of monarchy.

10. *What other Politicians thought.* To temper monarchy, Arybas, king of Epirus,[2] found

[1] *Politics,* iii. 14.
[2] See Justin, xvii. 3.

no other remedy than a republic. The Molossi, not knowing how to limit the same power, made two kings,[1] by which means the state was weakened more than the prerogative; they wanted rivals, and they created enemies.

Two kings were tolerable nowhere but at Sparta; here they did not form, but were only a part of the constitution.

11. *Of the Kings of the heroic Times of Greece.* In the heroic times of Greece, a kind of monarchy arose that was not of long duration.[2] Those who had been inventors of arts, who had fought in their country's cause, who had established societies, or distributed lands among the people, obtained the regal power, and transmitted it to their children. They were kings, priests, and judges. This was one of the five species of monarchy mentioned by Aristotle;[3] and the only one that can give us any idea of the monarchical constitution. But the plan of this constitution is opposite to that of our modern monarchies.

The three powers were there distributed in such a manner that the people were the legislature,[4] and the king had the executive together with the judiciary power; whereas in modern monarchies the prince is invested with the executive and legislative powers, or at least with part of the legislative, but does not act in a judiciary capacity.

In the government of the kings of the heroic times, the three powers were ill-distributed. Hence those monarchies could not long subsist. For as soon as the people got the legislative power into their hands, they might, as they everywhere did, upon the very least caprice, subvert the regal authority.

Among a free people possessed of the legislative power, and enclosed within walls, where everything tending towards oppression appears still more odious, it is the masterpiece of legislation to know where to place properly the judiciary power. But it could not be in worse hands than in those of the person to whom the executive power had been already committed. From that very instant the monarch became terrible. But at the same time as he had no share in the legislature, he could make no defence against it, thus his power was in one sense too great, in another too little.

They had not as yet discovered that the true function of a prince was to appoint judges, and not to sit as judge himself. The opposite policy rendered the government of a single person insupportable. Hence all these kings were banished. The Greeks had no notion of the proper distribution of the three powers in the government of one person; they could see it only in that of many; and this kind of constitution they distinguished by the name of *Polity*.[5]

12. *Of the Government of the Kings of Rome, and in what Manner the three Powers were there distributed.* The government of the kings of Rome had some relation to that of the kings of the heroic times of Greece. Its subversion, like the latter's, was owing to its general defect, though in its own particular nature it was exceedingly good.

In order to give an adequate idea of this government, I shall distinguish that of the first five kings, that of Servius Tullius, and that of Tarquin.

The crown was elective, and under the first five kings the senate had the greatest share in the election.

Upon the king's decease the senate examined whether they should continue the established form of government. If they thought proper to continue it, they named a magistrate[6] taken from their own body, who chose a king; the senate were to approve of the election, the people to confirm it, and the augurs to declare the approbation of the gods. If any of these three conditions was wanting, they were obliged to proceed to another election.

The constitution was a mixture of monarchy, aristocracy, and democracy; and such was the harmony of power that there was no instance of jealousy or dispute in the first reigns. The king commanded the armies, and had the direction of the sacrifices: he had the power of determining[7] civil and criminal[8] causes; he called the senate together, convened the people, laid some affairs before the latter, and regulated the rest with the senate.[9]

[5] Aristotle, *Politics*, iv. 8.
[6] Dionysius Halicarnassus, ii, p. 120, and iv, pp. 242, 243.
[7] See Tanaquil's Discourse on Livy, i, dec. 1, and the regulations of Servius Tullius in Dionysius Halicarnassus, iv. p. 229.
[8] See Dionysius Halicarnassus, ii, p. 118, and iii, p. 171
[9] It was by virtue of a senatus-consultum that Tullius Hostilius ordered Alba to be destroyed.—*Ibid.*, iii, pp. 167 and 172.

[1] Aristotle, *Politics*, v. 11.
[2] *Ibid.*, iii. 14.
[3] *Ibid.*
[4] See what Plutarch says in the *Theseus*. See likewise Thucydides, i.

The authority of the senate was very great. The kings oftentimes pitched upon senators with whom they sat in judgment; and they never laid any affair before the people till it had been previously debated[1] in that august assembly.

The people had the right of choosing[2] magistrates, of consenting to the new laws, and, with the king's permission, of making war and peace; but they had not the judicial power. When Tullius Hostilius referred the trial of Horatius to the people, he had his particular reasons, which may be seen in Dionysius Halicarnassus.[3]

The constitution altered under[4] Servius Tullius. The senate had no share in his election; he caused himself to be proclaimed by the people; he resigned the power of hearing civil causes,[5] reserving none to himself but those of a criminal nature; he laid all affairs directly before the people, eased them of the taxes, and imposed the whole burden on the patricians. Hence in proportion as he weakened the regal together with the senatorial power, he augmented that of the plebeians.[6]

Tarquin would neither be chosen by the senate nor by the people; he considered Servius Tullius as a usurper, and seized the crown as his hereditary right. He destroyed most of the senators; those who remained he never consulted; nor did he even so much as summon them to assist at his decisions.[7] Thus his power increased: but the odium of that power received a new addition, by usurping also the authority of the people, against whose consent he enacted several laws. The three powers were by these means re-united in his person; but the people at a critical minute recollected that they were legislators, and there was an end of Tarquin.

13. *General Reflections on the State of Rome after the Expulsion of its Kings.* It is impossible to be tired of so agreeable a subject as an-

[1] *Ibid.,* iv, p. 276.
[2] *Ibid.,* ii. And yet they could not have the nomination of all offices, since Valerius Publicola made that famous law by which every citizen was forbidden to exercise any employment, unless he had obtained it by the suffrage of the people.
[3] *Ibid.,* iii, p. 159.
[4] *Ibid.,* iv.
[5] He divested himself of half the regal power, says Dionysius Halicarnassus, iv, p. 229.
[6] It was thought that if he had not been prevented by Tarquin he would have established a popular government.—*Ibid.,* iv, p. 243.
[7] *Ibid.,* iv.

cient Rome: thus strangers at present leave the modern palaces of that celebrated capital to visit the ruins; and thus the eye, after recreating itself with the view of flowery meads, is pleased with the wild prospect of rocks and mountains.

The patrician families were at all times possessed of great privileges. These distinctions, which were considerable under the kings, became much more important after their expulsion. Hence arose the jealousy of the plebeians, who wanted to reduce them. The contest struck at the constitution, without weakening the government; for it was very indifferent as to what family were the magistrates, provided the magistracy preserved its authority.

An elective monarchy, like that of Rome, necessarily supposes a powerful aristocratic body to support it, without which it changes immediately into tyranny or into a popular state. But a popular state has no need of this distinction of families to maintain itself. To this it was owing that the patricians, who were a necessary part of the constitution under the regal government, became a superfluous branch under the consuls; the people could suppress them without hurting themselves, and change the constitution without corrupting it.

After Servius Tullius had reduced the patricians, it was natural that Rome should fall from the regal hands into those of the people. But the people had no occasion to be afraid of relapsing under a regal power by reducing the patricians.

A state may alter in two different ways, either by the amendment or by the corruption of the constitution. If it has preserved its principles and the constitution changes, this is owing to its amendment; if upon changing the constitution its principles are lost, this is because it has been corrupted.

The government of Rome, after the expulsion of the kings, should naturally have been a democracy. The people had already the legislative power in their hands; it was their unanimous consent that had expelled the Tarquins; and if they had not continued steady to those principles, the Tarquins might easily have been restored. To pretend that their design in expelling them was to render themselves slaves to a few families is quite absurd. The situation therefore of things required that Rome should have formed a democracy, and yet this did not happen. There was a necessity that the power of the principal families should be tempered, and that the laws should have a bias to democracy.

The prosperity of states is frequently greater in the insensible transition from one constitution to another than in either of those constitutions. Then it is that all the springs of government are upon the stretch, that the citizens assert their claims, that friendships or enmities are formed amongst the jarring parties, and that there is a noble emulation between those who defend the ancient and those who are strenuous in promoting the new constitution.

14. *In what Manner the Distribution of the three Powers began to change after the Expulsion of the Kings.* There were four things that greatly prejudiced the liberty of Rome. The patricians had engrossed to themselves all public employments whatever; an exorbitant power was annexed to the consulate; the people were often insulted; and, in fine, they had scarcely any influence at all left in the public suffrages. These four abuses were redressed by the people.

1st. It was regulated that the plebeians might aspire to some magistracies; and by degrees they were rendered capable of them all, except that of *Inter-rex*.

2nd. The consulate was dissolved into several other magistracies;[1] prætors were created, on whom the power was conferred of trying private causes; quæstors[2] were nominated for determining those of a criminal nature; ædiles were established for the civil administration; treasurers[3] were made for the management of the public money; and, in fine, by the creation of censors the consuls were divested of that part of the legislative power which regulates the morals of the citizens and the transient polity of the different bodies of the state. The chief privileges left them were to preside in the great meetings[4] of the people, to assemble the senate, and to command the armies.

3rd. The sacred laws appointed tribunes, who had a power of checking the encroachments of the patricians, and prevented not only private but likewise public injuries.

In fine, the plebeians increased their influence in the general assemblies. The people of Rome were divided in three different manners —by centuries, by curiæ, and by tribes; and whenever they gave their votes, they were convened in one of those three ways.

In the first the patricians, the leading men, the rich and the senate, which was very nearly the same thing, had almost the whole authority; in the second they had less; and less still in the third.

The division into centuries was a division rather of estates and fortunes than of persons. The whole people were distributed into a hundred and ninety-three centuries,[5] which had each a single vote. The patricians and leading men composed the first ninety-eight centuries; and the other ninety-five consisted of the remainder of the citizens. In this division therefore the patricians were masters of the suffrages.

In the division into curiæ,[6] the patricians had not the same advantages; some, however, they had, for it was necessary to consult the augurs, who were under the direction of the patricians; and no proposal could be made there to the people unless it had been previously laid before the senate, and approved of by a *senatus-consultum*. But, in the division into tribes they had nothing to do either with the augurs or with the decrees of the senate; and the patricians were excluded.

Now the people endeavoured constantly to have those meetings by curiæ which had been customary by centuries, and by tribes, those they used to have before by curiæ; by which means the direction of public affairs soon devolved from the patricians to the plebeians.

Thus when the plebeians obtained the power of trying the patricians—a power which commenced in the affair of Coriolanus,[7] they insisted upon assembling by tribes,[8] and not by centuries; and when the new magistracies[9] of tribunes and ædiles were established in favour of the people, the latter obtained that they should meet by curiæ in order to nominate them; and after their power was quite settled, they gained[10] so far their point as to assemble by tribes to proceed to this nomination.

15. *In what Manner Rome, in the flourishing*

---

[1] Livy, dec. 1, vi.

[2] *Quæstores parricidii.*—Pomponius, Leg. 2, § 23, ff. *de orig. jur.*

[3] Plutarch, *Poplicola.*

[4] *Comitiis centuriatis.*

[5] See Livy, i, 43; Dionysius Halicarnassus, iv, vii.

[6] Dionysius Halicarnassus, ix, p. 598.

[7] *Ibid.,* vii.

[8] Contrary to the ancient custom, as may be seen: *ibid.,* v, p. 320.

[9] *Ibid.,* pp. 410, 411.

[10] *Ibid.,* ix, p. 605.

State of that Republic, suddenly lost its Liberty. In the heat of the contests between the patricians and the plebeians, the latter insisted upon having fixed laws, to the end that the public judgments should no longer be the effect of capricious will or arbitrary power. The senate, after a great deal of resistance, acquiesced; and decemvirs were nominated to compose those laws. It was thought proper to grant them an extraordinary power, because they were to give laws to parties whose views and interest it was almost impossible to unite. The nomination of all magistrates was suspended; and the decemvirs were chosen in the *comitia* sole administrators of the republic. Thus they found themselves invested with the consular and the tribunition power. By one they had the privilege of assembling the senate, by the other that of convening the people; but they assembled neither senate nor people. Ten men only of the republic had the whole legislative, the whole executive, and the whole judiciary power. Rome saw herself enslaved by as cruel a tyranny as that of Tarquin. When Tarquin trampled on the liberty of that city, she was seized with indignation at the power he had usurped; when the decemvirs exercised every act of oppression, she was astonished at the extraordinary power she had granted.

What a strange system of tyranny—a tyranny carried on by men who had obtained the political and military power, merely from their knowledge in civil affairs, and who at that very juncture stood in need of the courage of those citizens to protect them abroad who so tamely submitted to domestic oppression!

The spectacle of Virginia's death, whom her father immolated to chastity and liberty, put an end to the power of the decemvirs. Every man became free, because every man had been injured; each showed himself a citizen because each had a tie of the parent. The senate and the people resumed a liberty which had been committed to ridiculous tyrants.

No people were so easily moved by public spectacles as the Romans. That of the empurpled body of Lucretia put an end to the regal government. The debtor who appeared in the forum covered with wounds caused an alteration in the republic. The decemvirs owed their expulsion to the tragedy of Virginia. To condemn Manlius, it was necessary to keep the people from seeing the Capitol. Cæsar's bloody garment flung Rome again into slavery.

16. *Of the legislative Power in the Roman Republic.* There were no rights to contest under the decemvirs: but upon the restoration of liberty, jealousies revived; and so long as the patricians had any privileges left, they were sure to be stripped of them by the plebeians.

The mischief would not have been so great had the plebeians been satisfied with this success; but they also injured the patricians as citizens. When the people assembled by curiæ or centuries, they were composed of senators, patricians, and plebeians; in their disputes the plebeians gained this point,[1] that they alone without patricians or senate should enact the laws called *Plebiscita;* and the assemblies in which they were made had the name of *comitia* by tribes. Thus there were cases in which the patricians[2] had no share in the legislative power, but[3] were subject to the legislation of another body of the state. This was the extravagance of liberty. The people, to establish a democracy, acted against the very principles of that government. One would have imagined that so exorbitant a power must have destroyed the authority of the senate. But Rome had admirable institutions. Two of these were especially remarkable: one by which the legislative power of the people was established, and the other by which it was limited.

The censors, and before them the consuls, modelled[4] and created, as it were, every five years the body of the people; they exercised the legislation on the very part that was possessed of the legislative power. "Tiberius Gracchus," says Cicero, "caused the freedmen to be admitted into the tribes, not by the force of his eloquence, but by a word, by a gesture; which had he not effected, the republic, whose drooping head we are at present scarcely able to uphold, would not even exist."

On the other hand, the senate had the power of rescuing, as it were, the republic out

[1] *Ibid.,* xi, p. 725.
[2] By the sacred laws, the plebeians had the power of making the *plebiscita* by themselves, without admitting the patricians into their assembly.—*Ibid.,* vi, p. 410; vii, p. 430.
[3] By the law enacted after the expulsion of the decemvirs, the patricians were made subject to the *plebiscita,* though they had not a right of voting there. Livy, iii. 55, and Dionysius Halicarnassus, xi, p. 725. This law was confirmed by that of Publius Philo the dictator, in the year of Rome 416. Livy, viii. 12.
[4] In the year 312 of Rome the consuls performed still the business of surveying the people and their estates, as appears by Dionysius Halicarnassus, ix.

of the hands of the people, by creating a dictator, before whom the sovereign bowed his head, and the most popular laws were silent.[1]

17. *Of the executive Power in the same Republic.* Jealous as the people were of their legislative power, they had no great uneasiness about the executive. This they left almost entirely to the senate and to the consuls, reserving scarcely anything more to themselves than the right of choosing the magistrates, and of confirming the acts of the senate and of the generals.

Rome, whose passion was to command, whose ambition was to conquer, whose commencement and progress were one continued usurpation, had constantly affairs of the greatest weight upon her hands; her enemies were ever conspiring against her, or she against her enemies.

As she was obliged to behave on the one hand with heroic courage, and on the other with consummate prudence, it was requisite, of course, that the management of affairs should be committed to the senate. Thus the people disputed every branch of the legislative power with the senate, because they were jealous of their liberty; but they had no disputes about the executive, because they were animated with the love of glory.

So great was the share the senate took in the executive power, that, as Polybius[2] informs us, foreign nations imagined that Rome was an aristocracy. The senate disposed of the public money, and farmed out the revenue; they were arbiters of the affairs of their allies; they determined war or peace, and directed in this respect the consuls; they fixed the number of the Roman and of the allied troops, disposed of the provinces and armies to the consuls or prætors, and upon the expiration of the year of command had the power of appointing successors; they decreed triumphs, received and sent embassies: they nominated, rewarded, punished, and were judges of kings, declared them allies of the Roman people, or stripped them of that title.

The consuls levied the troops which they were to carry into the field; had the command of the forces by sea and by land; disposed of the forces of the allies; were invested with the whole power of the republic in the provinces;

gave peace to the vanquished nations, imposed conditions on them, or referred them to the senate.

In the earliest times, when the people had some share in the affairs relating to war or peace, they exercised rather their legislative than their executive power. They scarcely did anything else but confirm the acts of the kings, and after their expulsion those of the consuls or senate. So far were they from being the arbiters of war that we have instances of its having been often declared, notwithstanding the opposition of the tribunes. But growing wanton in their prosperity, they increased their executive power. Thus[3] they created the military tribunes, the nomination of whom till then had belonged to the generals; and some time before the first Punic war, they decreed that only their own body should have the right of declaring war.[4]

18. *Of the judiciary Power in the Roman Government.* The judiciary power was given to the people, to the senate, to the magistrates, and to particular judges. We must see in what manner it was distributed; beginning with their civil affairs.

The consuls had the judiciary power[5] after the expulsion of the kings, as the prætors were judges after the consuls. Servius Tullius had divested himself of the power of determining civil causes, which was not resumed by the consuls, except in some[6] very rare cases, for that reason called *extraordinary*.[7] They were satisfied with naming the judges, and establishing the several tribunals. By a discourse of Appius Claudius, in Dionysius Halicarnassus,[8] it appears that as early as the 259th year of Rome this was looked upon as a settled custom among the Romans; and it is not tracing it very high to refer it to Servius Tullius.

Every year the prætor made a list[9] of such as

---

[1] Such as those by which it was allowed to appeal from the decisions of all the magistrates to the people.
[2] Book vi.

[3] In the year of Rome 444, Livy, dec. 1, ix. 30. As the war against Perseus appeared somewhat dangerous, it was ordained by a *senatus-consultum* that this law should be suspended, and the people agreed to it. Livy, dec. 5, ii.
[4] They extorted it from the senate, says Freinshemius, dec. 2, vi.
[5] There is no manner of doubt but the consuls had the power of trying civil causes before the creation of the prætors. See Livy, dec. 1, ii. 1; Dionysius Halicarnassus, x, pp. 627, 645.
[6] The tribunes frequently tried causes by themselves only, but nothing rendered them more odious.—Dionysius Halicarnassus, xi, p. 709.
[7] *Judicia extraordinaria.* See the *Institutes,* iv.
[8] Book vi, p. 360.
[9] *Album Judicium.*

he chose for the office of judges during his magistracy. A sufficient number was pitched upon for each cause; a custom very nearly the same as that now practised in England. And what was extremely favourable to liberty[1] was the prætor's fixing the judges with the consent[2] of the parties. The great number of exceptions that can be made in England amounts pretty nearly to this very custom.

The judges decided only the questions relating to matter of fact;[3] for example, whether a sum of money had been paid or not, whether an act had been committed or not. But as to questions of law,[4] as these required a certain capacity, they were always carried before the tribunal of the centumvirs.[5]

The kings reserved to themselves the judgment of criminal affairs, and in this were succeeded by the consuls. It was in consequence of this authority that Brutus put his children and all those who were concerned in the Tarquinian conspiracy to death. This was an exorbitant power. The consuls already invested with the military command extended the exercise of it even to civil affairs; and their procedures, being stripped of all forms of justice, were rather exertions of violence than legal judgments.

This gave rise to the Valerian law, by which it was made lawful to appeal to the people from every decision of the consuls that endangered the life of a citizen. The consuls had no longer the power of pronouncing sentence in capital cases against a Roman citizen, without the consent of the people.[6]

We see in the first conspiracy for the restoration of the Tarquins that the criminals were tried by Brutus the consul; in the second the senate and comitia were assembled to try them.[7]

The laws distinguished by the name of sacred allowed the plebeians the privilege of choosing tribunes; whence was formed a body whose pretensions at first were immense. It is hard to determine which was greater, the insolence of the plebeians in demanding, or the condescension of the senate in granting. The Valerian law allowed appeals to the people, that is, to the people composed of senators, patricians, and plebeians. The plebeians made a law that appeals should be brought before their own body. A question was soon after started, whether the plebeians had a right to try a patrician; this was the subject of a dispute to which the impeachment of Coriolanus gave rise, and which ended with that affair. When Coriolanus was accused by the tribunes before the people, he insisted, contrary to the spirit of the Valerian law, that as he was a patrician, none but the consuls had the power to try him; on the other hand, the plebeians, also contrary to the spirit of that same law, pretended that none but their body were empowered to be his judges, and accordingly they pronounced sentence upon him.

This was moderated by the law of the Twelve Tables; whereby it was ordained that none but the great assemblies of the people[8] should try a citizen in capital cases. Hence the body of the plebeians, or, which amounts to the very same, the comitia by tribes, had no longer any power of hearing criminal causes, except such as were punished with fines. To inflict a capital punishment a law was requisite; but to condemn to a pecuniary mulct, there was occasion only for a *plebiscitum*.

This regulation of the law of the Twelve Tables was extremely prudent. It produced an admirable balance between the body of the plebeians and the senate. For as the full judiciary power of both depended on the greatness of the punishment and the nature of the crime, it was necessary they should both agree.

The Valerian law abolished all the remains of the Roman government in any way relating to that of the kings of the heroic times of Greece. The consuls were divested of the power to punish crimes. Though all crimes are public, yet we must distinguish between those which more nearly concern the mutual intercourse of the citizens and those which more immediately interest the state in the relation it bears to its subjects. The first are

---

[1] "Our ancestors," says Cicero, *Pro Cluentio*, "would not suffer any man whom the parties had not agreed to, to be judge of the least pecuniary affair, much less of a citizen's reputation."

[2] See in the fragments of the Servilian, Cornelian, and other laws, in what manner these laws appointed judges for the crimes they proposed to punish. They were often pitched upon by choice, sometimes by lot, or, in fine, by lot mixed together with choice.

[3] Seneca, *De Benefic*. iii. 7, *in fine*.

[4] See Quintilian, iv, p. 54, in fol. ed., Paris, 1541.

[5] *Leg.* 2 ff. *de orig. jur*. Magistrates who were called decemvirs presided in court, the whole under a prætor's direction.

[6] *Quoniam de capite civis Romani, injussu populi Romani, non erat permissum consulibus jus dicere.*—See Pomponius, *Leg.* 2, §6, ff. *de orig. jur.*

[7] Dionysius Halicarnassus, v, p. 322.

[8] The comitia by centuries. Thus Manlius Capitolinus was tried in these comitia.—Livy, Dec. 1, vi. 20.

called private, the second public. The latter were tried by the people; and in regard to the former, they named by particular commission a quæstor for the prosecution of each crime. The person chosen by the people was frequently one of the magistrates, sometimes a private man. He was called the quæstor of parricide, and is mentioned in the law of the Twelve Tables.[1]

The quæstor nominated the judge of the question, who drew lots for the judges, and regulated the tribunal in which he presided.[2]

Here it is proper to observe what share the senate had in the nomination of the quæstor, that we may see how far the two powers were balanced. Sometimes the senate caused a dictator to be chosen, in order to exercise the office of quæstor;[3] at other times they ordained that the people should be convened by a tribune, with the view of proceeding to the nomination of a quæstor:[4] and, in fine, the people frequently appointed a magistrate to make his report to the senate concerning a particular crime, and to desire them to name a quæstor, as may be seen in the judgment upon Lucius Scipio[5] in Livy.[6]

In the year of Rome 604, some of these commissions were rendered permanent.[7] All criminal causes were gradually divided into different parts; to which they gave the name of perpetual questions. Different prætors were created, to each of whom some of those questions were assigned. They had a power conferred upon them for the term of a year, of trying such criminal causes as bore any relation to those questions, and then they were sent to govern their province.

At Carthage the senate of the hundred was composed of judges who enjoyed that dignity for life.[8] But at Rome the prætors were an-

nual; and the judges were not even for so long a term, but were nominated for each cause. We have already shown in the sixth chapter of this book how favourable this regulation was to liberty in particular governments.

The judges were chosen from the order of senators, till the time of the Gracchi. Tiberius Gracchus caused a law to pass that they should be taken from the equestrian order; a change so very considerable that the tribune boasted of having cut, by one rogation only, the sinews of the senatorial dignity.

It is necessary to observe that the three powers may be very well distributed in regard to the liberty of the constitution, though not so well in respect to the liberty of the subject. At Rome the people had the greatest share of the legislative, a part of the executive, and part of the judiciary power; by which means they had so great a weight in the government as required some other power to balance it. The senate indeed had part of the executive power, and some share of the legislative;[9] but this was not sufficient to counterbalance the weight of the people. It was necessary that they should partake of the judiciary power: and accordingly they had a share when the judges were chosen from among the senators. But when the Gracchi deprived the senators of the judicial power,[10] the senate were no longer able to withstand the people. To favour, therefore, the liberty of the subject, they struck at that of the constitution; but the former perished with the latter.

Infinite were the mischiefs that thence arose. The constitution was changed at a time when the fire of civil discord had scarcely left any such thing as a constitution. The knights ceased to be that middle order which united the people to the senate; and the chain of the constitution was broken.

There were even particular reasons against transferring the judiciary power to the equestrian order. The constitution of Rome was founded on this principle, that none should be enlisted as soldiers but such as were men of sufficient property to answer for their conduct to the republic. The knights, as persons of the greatest property, formed the cavalry of the legions. But when their dignity increased, they refused to serve any longer in that capacity, and another kind of cavalry was

---

[1] Pomponius, in *Leg.* 2, *Dig., de orig. jur.*

[2] See a fragment of Ulpian, who gives another of the Cornelian Law: it is to be met with in the *Collation of the Mosaic and Roman Laws*, tit. 1, *De Sicariis et homicidiis.*

[3] This took place, especially in regard to crimes committed in Italy, which were subject chiefly to the inspection of the senate. See Livy, Dec. 1, ix, 26, concerning the conspiracies at Capua.

[4] This was the case in the prosecution for the murder of Posthumius, in the year 340 of Rome. See Livy, iv. 50.

[5] This judgment was passed in the year of Rome 567.

[6] Book viii.

[7] Cicero, in *Brutus.*

[8] This is proved from Livy, book xliii. 46, who says that Hannibal rendered their magistracy annual.

[9] The *senatus-consultums* were in force for the space of a year, though not confirmed by the people.—Dionysius Halicarnassus ix, p. 595; xi, p. 735.

[10] In the year 630.

obliged to be raised: thus Marius enlisted all sorts of people into his army, and soon after the republic was lost.[1]

Besides, the knights were the farmers of the revenue; men whose great rapaciousness increased the public calamities. Instead of giving to such as those the judicial power, they ought to have been constantly under the eye of the judges. This we must say in commendation of the ancient French laws, that they have acted towards the officers of the revenue with as great a diffidence as would be observed between enemies. When the judiciary power at Rome was transferred to the publicans, there was then an end of all virtue, polity, laws, and government.

Of this we find a very ingenious description in some fragments of Diodorus Siculus and Dio. "Mutius Scævola," says Diodorus,[2] "wanted to revive the ancient manners, and the laudable custom of sober and frugal living. For his predecessors having entered into a contract with the farmers of the revenue, who at that time were possessed of the judiciary power at Rome, had infected the province with all manner of corruption. But Scævola made an example of the publicans, and imprisoned those by whom others had been confined."

Dio informs us[3] that Publius Rutilius, his lieutenant, was equally obnoxious to the equestrian order, and that upon his return they accused him of having received some presents, and condemned him to a fine; upon which he instantly made a cession of his goods. His innocence appeared in this, that he was found to be worth a great deal less than what he was charged with having extorted, and he showed a just title to what he possessed: but he would not live any longer in the same city with such profligate wretches.

The Italians, says Diodorus again,[4] bought up whole droves of slaves in Sicily, to till their lands and to take care of their cattle; but refused them a necessary subsistence. These wretches were then forced to go and rob on the highways, armed with lances and clubs, covered with beasts' skins, and followed by large mastiffs. Thus the whole province was laid waste, and the inhabitants could not call anything their own but what was secured by fortresses. There was neither proconsul nor prætor that could or would oppose this disorder, or that presumed to punish these slaves, because they belonged to the knights, who at Rome were possessed of the judiciary power.[5] And yet this was one of the causes of the war of the slaves. But I shall add only one word more. A profession deaf and inexorable, that can have no other view than lucre, that was always asking and never granting, that impoverished the rich and increased even the misery of the poor—such a profession, I say, should never have been entrusted with the judiciary power at Rome.

19. *Of the Government of the Roman Provinces.* Such was the distribution of the three powers in Rome. But they were far from being thus distributed in the provinces. Liberty prevailed in the centre and tyranny in the extreme parts.

While Rome extended her dominions no farther than Italy, the people were governed as confederates, and the laws of each republic were preserved. But when she enlarged her conquests, and the senate had no longer an immediate inspection over the provinces, nor the magistrates residing at Rome were any longer capable of governing the empire, they were obliged to send prætors and proconsuls. Then it was that the harmony of the three powers was lost. The persons appointed to that office were entrusted with a power which comprehended that of all the Roman magistracies; nay, even that of the people.[6] They were despotic magistrates, extremely well adapted to the distance of the places to which they were destined. They exercised the three powers; and were, if I may presume to use the expression, the bashaws of the republic.

We have elsewhere observed[7] that in a commonwealth the same magistrate ought to be possessed of the executive power, as well civil as military. Hence a conquering republic can hardly communicate her government, and rule the conquered state according to her own constitution. And indeed as the magistrate she sends to govern is invested with the executive

---

[1] *Capite censos plerosque.*—Sallust, *De Bello Jugurth,* 84.

[2] Fragment of this author, xxxvi, in the collection of Constantine Porphyrogenitus, *Of Virtues and Vices* [*Historica*].

[3] Fragment of his history, taken from the extract *Of Virtues and Vices* [*Historica*].

[4] Fragment of the book xxxiv in the extract *Of Virtues and Vices* [*Historica*].

[5] *Penes quos Romæ tum judicia erant, atque ex equestri ordine solerent sortito judices eligi in causa Prætorum et Proconsulum, quibus post administratam provinciam dies dicta erat.*

[6] They made their edicts upon entering the provinces.

[7] Book v. 19. See also ii, iii, iv, and v.

power, both civil and military, he must also have the legislative: for who is it that could make laws without him? It is necessary, therefore, that the governor she sends be entrusted with the three powers, as was practised in the Roman provinces.

It is more easy for a monarchy to communicate its government, because the officers it sends have, some the civil executive, and others the military executive power, which does not necessarily imply a despotic authority.

It was a privilege of the utmost consequence to a Roman citizen to have none but the people for his judge. Were it not for this, he would have been subject in the provinces to the arbitrary power of a proconsul or of a propraetor. The city never felt the tyranny which was exercised only on conquered nations.

Thus, in the Roman world, as at Sparta, the freemen enjoyed the highest degree of liberty, while those who were slaves laboured under the extremity of servitude.

While the citizens paid taxes, they were raised with great justice and equality. The regulation of Servius Tullius was observed, who had distributed the people into six classes, according to their difference of property, and fixed the several shares of the public imposts in proportion to that which each person had in the government. Hence they bore with the greatness of the tax because of their proportionable greatness of credit, and consoled themselves for the smallness of their credit because of the smallness of the tax.

There was also another thing worthy of ad-miration, which is, that as Servius Tullius's division into classes was in some measure the fundamental principle of the constitution, it thence followed that an equal levying of the taxes was so connected with this fundamental principle that the one could not be abolished without the other.

But while the city paid the taxes as she pleased, or paid none at all,[1] the provinces were plundered by the knights, who were the farmers of the public revenue. We have already made mention of their oppressive extortions, with which all history abounds.

"All Asia," says Mithridates,[2] "expects me as her deliverer; so great is the hatred which the rapaciousness of the proconsuls,[3] the confiscations made by the officers of the revenue, and the quirks and cavils of judicial proceedings,[4] have excited against the Romans."

Hence it was that the strength of the provinces did not increase, but rather weakened, the strength of the republic. Hence it was that the provinces looked upon the loss of the liberty of Rome as the epoch of their own freedom.

20. *The End of this Book.* I should be glad to inquire into the distribution of the three powers, in all the moderate governments we are acquainted with, in order to calculate the degrees of liberty which each may enjoy. But we must not always exhaust a subject, so as to leave no work at all for the reader. My business is not to make people read, but to make them think.

. . .

BOOK XII. OF THE LAWS THAT FORM POLITICAL LIBERTY, IN RELATION TO THE SUBJECT

1. *Idea of this Book.* It is not sufficient to have treated of political liberty in relation to the constitution; we must examine it likewise in the relation it bears to the subject.

We have observed that in the former case it arises from a certain distribution of the three powers; but in the latter, we must consider it in another light. It consists in security, or in the opinion people have of their security.

The constitution may happen to be free, and the subject not. The subject may be free, and not the constitution. In those cases, the constitution will be free by right, and not in fact; the subject will be free in fact, and not by right.

It is the disposition only of the laws, and even of the fundamental laws, that constitutes liberty in relation to the constitution. But as it regards the subject: manners, customs, or received examples may give rise to it, and particular civil laws may encourage it, as we shall presently observe.

Further, as in most states liberty is more checked or depressed than their constitution requires, it is proper to treat of the particular

[1] After the conquest of Macedonia the Romans paid no taxes.
[2] Speech taken from Trogus Pompeius, and related by Justin, xxxviii. 4.
[3] See the orations against Verres.
[4] It is well known what sort of a tribunal was that of Varus, which provoked the Germans to revolt.

laws that in each constitution are apt to assist or check the principle of liberty which each state is capable of receiving.

2. *Of the Liberty of the Subject.* Philosophic liberty consists in the free exercise of the will; or at least, if we must speak agreeably to all systems, in an opinion that we have the free exercise of our will. Political liberty consists in security, or, at least, in the opinion that we enjoy security.

This security is never more dangerously attacked than in public or private accusations. It is, therefore, on the goodness of criminal laws that the liberty of the subject principally depends.

Criminal laws did not receive their full perfection all at once. Even in places where liberty has been most sought after, it has not been always found. Aristotle[1] informs us that at Cumæ the parents of the accuser might be witnesses. So imperfect was the law under the kings of Rome that Servius Tullius pronounced sentence against the children of Ancus Martius, who were charged with having assassinated the king, his father-in-law.[2] Under the first kings of France, Clotarius made a law[3] that nobody should be condemned without being heard; which shows that a contrary custom had prevailed in some particular case or among some barbarous people. It was Charondas that first established penalties against false witnesses.[4] When the subject has no fence to secure his innocence, he has none for his liberty.

The knowledge already acquired in some countries, or that may be hereafter attained in others, concerning the surest rules to be observed in criminal judgments, is more interesting to mankind than any other thing in the world.

Liberty can be founded on the practice of this knowledge only; and supposing a state to have the best laws imaginable in this respect, a person tried under that state, and condemned to be hanged the next day, would have much more liberty than a pasha enjoys in Turkey.

3. *The same Subject continued.* Those laws which condemn a man to death on the deposi-

tion of a single witness are fatal to liberty. In reason there should be two, because a witness who affirms, and the accused who denies, make an equal balance, and a third must incline the scale.

The Greeks[5] and Romans[6] required one voice more to condemn: but our French laws insist upon two. The Greeks pretend that their custom was established by the gods;[7] but this more justly may be said of ours.

4. *That Liberty is favoured by the Nature and Proportion of Punishments.* Liberty is in perfection when criminal laws derive each punishment from the particular nature of the crime. There are then no arbitrary decisions; the punishment does not flow from the capriciousness of the legislator, but from the very nature of the thing; and man uses no violence to man.

There are four sorts of crimes. Those of the first species are prejudicial to religion, the second to morals, the third to the public tranquillity, and the fourth to the security of the subject. The punishments inflicted for these crimes ought to proceed from the nature of each of these species.

In the class of crimes that concern religion, I rank only those which attack it directly, such as all simple sacrileges. For as to crimes that disturb the exercise of it, they are of the nature of those which prejudice the tranquillity or security of the subject, and ought to be referred to those classes.

In order to derive the punishment of simple sacrileges from the nature of the thing,[8] it should consist in depriving people of the advantages conferred by religion in expelling them out of the temples, in a temporary or perpetual exclusion from the society of the faithful, in shunning their presence, in execrations, comminations, and conjurations.

In things that prejudice the tranquillity or security of the state, secret actions are subject to human jurisdiction. But in those which offend the Deity, where there is no public act, there can be no criminal matter, the whole passes between man and God, who knows the measure and time of His vengeance. Now if

[1] *Politics*, ii. 8.
[2] Tarquinius Priscus. See Dionysius Halicarnassus, iv.
[3] As early as the year 560.
[4] Aristotle, *Politics*, ii. 12. He gave his laws at Thurium in the 84th Olympiad.

[5] See Aristides, *Orat. in Minervam*.
[6] Dionysius Halicarnassus on the judgment of Coriolanus, vii.
[7] *Minervæ calculus*.
[8] St. Louis made such severe laws against those who swore that the pope thought himself obliged to admonish him for it. This prince moderated his zeal, and softened his laws. See his *Ordinances*.

magistrates, confounding things, should inquire also into hidden sacrileges, this inquisition would be directed to a kind of action that does not at all require it: the liberty of the subject would be subverted by arming the zeal of timorous as well as of presumptuous consciences against him.

The mischief arises from a notion which some people have entertained of revenging the cause of the Deity. But we must honour the Deity and leave him to avenge his own cause. And, indeed, were we to be directed by such a notion, where would be the end of punishments? If human laws are to avenge the cause of an infinite Being, they will be directed by his infinity, and not by the weakness, ignorance, and caprice of man.

An historian[1] of Provence relates a fact which furnishes us with an excellent description of the consequences that may arise in weak capacities from the notion of avenging the Deity's cause. A Jew was accused of having blasphemed against the Virgin Mary; and upon conviction was condemned to be flayed alive. A strange spectacle was then exhibited: gentlemen masked, with knives in their hands, mounted the scaffold, and drove away the executioner, in order to be the avengers themselves of the honour of the blessed Virgin. I do not here choose to anticipate the reflections of the reader.

The second class consists of those crimes which are prejudicial to morals. Such is the violation of public or private continence, that is, of the police directing the manner in which the pleasure annexed to the conjunction of the sexes is to be enjoyed. The punishment of those crimes ought to be also derived from the nature of the thing; the privation of such advantages as society has attached to the purity of morals, fines, shame, necessity of concealment, public infamy, expulsion from home and society, and, in fine, all such punishments as belong to a corrective jurisdiction, are sufficient to repress the temerity of the two sexes. In effect these things are less founded on malice than on carelessness and self-neglect.

We speak here of none but crimes which relate merely to morals, for as to those that are also prejudicial to the public security, such as rapes, they belong to the fourth species.

The crimes of the third class are those which disturb the public tranquillity. The punishments ought therefore to be derived from the nature of the thing, and to be in re-

[1] Father Rougerel.

lation to this tranquillity; such as imprisonment, exile, and other like chastisements, proper for reclaiming turbulent spirits, and obliging them to conform to the established order.

I confine those crimes that injure the public tranquillity to things which imply a bare offence against the police; for as to those which by disturbing the public peace attack at the same time the security of the subject, they ought to be ranked in the fourth class.

The punishments inflicted upon the latter crimes are such as are properly distinguished by that name. They are a kind of retaliation, by which the society refuses security to a member who has actually or intentionally deprived another of his security. These punishments are derived from the nature of the thing, founded on reason, and drawn from the very source of good and evil. A man deserves death when he has violated the security of the subject so far as to deprive, or attempt to deprive, another man of his life. This punishment of death is the remedy, as it were, of a sick society. When there is a breach of security with regard to property, there may be some reasons for inflicting a capital punishment: but it would be much better, and perhaps more natural, that crimes committed against the security of property should be punished with the loss of property; and this ought, indeed, to be the case if men's fortunes were common or equal. But as those who have no property of their own are generally the readiest to attack that of others, it has been found necessary, instead of a pecuniary, to substitute a corporal, punishment.

All that I have here advanced is founded in nature, and extremely favourable to the liberty of the subject.

5. Of certain Accusations that require particular Moderation and Prudence. It is an important maxim, that we ought to be very circumspect in the prosecution of witchcraft and heresy. The accusation of these two crimes may be vastly injurious to liberty, and productive of infinite oppression, if the legislator knows not how to set bounds to it. For as it does not directly point at a person's actions, but at his character, it grows dangerous in proportion to the ignorance of the people; and then a man is sure to be always in danger, because the most exceptional conduct, the purest morals, and the constant practice of every duty in life are not a sufficient security against

the suspicion of his being guilty of the like crimes.

Under Manuel Comnenus, the Protestator[1] was accused of having conspired against the emperor, and of having employed for that purpose some secrets that render men invisible. It is mentioned in the life of this emperor[2] that Aaron was detected, as he was poring over a book of Solomon's, the reading of which was sufficient to conjure up whole legions of devils. Now by supposing a power in witchcraft to rouse the infernal spirits to arms, people look upon a man whom they call a sorcerer as the person in the world most likely to disturb and subvert society; and of course they are disposed to punish him with the utmost severity.

But their indignation increases when witchcraft is supposed to have the power of subverting religion. The history of Constantinople[3] informs us that in consequence of a revelation made to a bishop of a miracle having ceased because of the magic practices of a certain person, both that person and his son were put to death. On how many surprising things did not this single crime depend? That revelations should not be uncommon, that the bishop should be favoured with one, that it was real, that there had been a miracle in the case, that this miracle had ceased, that there was a magic art, that magic could subvert religion, that this particular person was a magician, and, in fine, that he had committed that magic act.

The Emperor Theodorus Lascaris attributed his illness to witchcraft. Those who were accused of this crime had no other resource left than to handle a red-hot iron without being hurt. Thus among the Greeks a person ought to have been a sorcerer to be able to clear himself of the imputation of witchcraft. Such was the excess of their stupidity that to the most dubious crime in the world they joined the most dubious proofs of innocence.

Under the reign of Philip the Long, the Jews were expelled from France, being accused of having poisoned the springs with their lepers. So absurd an accusation ought to make us doubt all those that are founded on public hatred.

I have not here asserted that heresy ought not to be punished; I said only that we ought to be extremely circumspect in punishing it.

6. *Of the Crime against Nature.* God forbid that I should have the least inclination to diminish the public horror against a crime which religion, morality, and civil government equally condemn. It ought to be proscribed, were it only for its communicating to one sex the weaknesses of the other, and for leading people by a scandalous prostitution of their youth to an ignominious old age. What I shall say concerning it will in no way diminish its infamy, being levelled only against the tyranny that may abuse the very horror we ought to have against the vice.

As a natural circumstance of this crime is secrecy, there are frequent instances of its having been punished by legislators upon the deposition of a child. This was opening a very wide door to calumny. "Justinian," says Procopius,[4] "published a law against this crime; he ordered an inquiry to be made not only against those who were guilty of it, after the enacting of that law, but even before. The deposition of a single witness, sometimes of a child, sometimes of a slave, was sufficient, especially against such as were rich, and against those of the green faction."

It is very odd that these three crimes, witchcraft, heresy, and that against nature, of which the first might easily be proved not to exist; the second to be susceptible of an infinite number of distinctions, interpretations, and limitations; the third to be often obscure and uncertain—it is very odd, I say, that these three crimes should amongst us be punished with fire.

I may venture to affirm that the crime against nature will never make any great progress in society, unless people are prompted to it by some particular custom, as among the Greeks, where the youths of that country performed all their exercises naked; as amongst us, where domestic education is disused; as amongst the Asiatics, where particular persons have a great number of women whom they despise, while others can have none at all. Let there be no customs preparatory to this crime; let it, like every other violation of morals, be severely proscribed by the civil magistrate; and nature will soon defend or resume her rights. Nature, that fond, that indulgent parent, has strewn her pleasures with a bounteous hand, and while she fills us with delights, she prepares us, by means of our issue, in whom we see ourselves, as it were, reproduced —she prepares us, I say, for future satisfactions

---

[1] Nicetas, *Life of Manuel Comnenus*, iv.
[2] *Ibid.*
[3] Theophylactus, *History of the Emperor Maurice*, 11.

[4] *Secret History.*

of a more exquisite kind than those very delights.

7. *Of the Crime of High Treason.* It is determined by the laws of China that whosoever shows any disrespect to the emperor is to be punished with death. As they do not mention in what this disrespect consists, everything may furnish a pretext to take away a man's life, and to exterminate any family whatsoever.

Two persons of that country who were employed to write the court gazette, having inserted some circumstances relating to a certain fact that was not true, it was pretended that to tell a lie in the court gazette was a disrespect shown to the court, in consequence of which they were put to death.[1] A prince of the blood having inadvertently made some mark on a memorial signed with the red pencil by the emperor, it was determined that he had behaved disrespectfully to the sovereign; which occasioned one of the most terrible persecutions against that family that ever was recorded in history.[2]

If the crime of high treason be indeterminate, this alone is sufficient to make the government degenerate into arbitrary power. I shall descant more largely on this subject when I come to treat[3] of the composition of laws.

8. *Of the Misapplication of the Terms Sacrilege and High Treason.* It is likewise a shocking abuse to give the appellation of high treason to an action that does not deserve it. By an imperial law[4] it was decreed that those who called in question the prince's judgment, or doubted the merit of such as he had chosen for a public office, should be prosecuted as guilty of sacrilege.[5] Surely it was the cabinet council and the prince's favourites who invented that crime. By another law, it was determined that whosoever made any attempt to injure the ministers and officers belonging to the sovereign should be deemed guilty of high treason, as if he had attempted to injure the sovereign himself.[6] This law is owing to

two princes[7] remarkable for their weakness—princes who were led by their ministers as flocks by shepherds; princes who were slaves in the palace, children in the council, strangers to the army; princes, in fine, who preserved their authority only by giving it away every day. Some of those favourites conspired against their sovereigns. Nay, they did more, they conspired against the empire—they called in barbarous nations; and when the emperors wanted to stop their progress the state was so enfeebled as to be under a necessity of infringing the law, and of exposing itself to the crime of high treason in order to punish those favourites.

And yet this is the very law which the judge of Monsieur de Cinq-Mars built upon[8] when endeavouring to prove that the latter was guilty of the crime of high treason for attempting to remove Cardinal Richelieu from the ministry. He says: "Crimes that aim at the persons of ministers are deemed by the imperial constitutions of equal consequence with those which are levelled against the emperor's own person. A minister discharges his duty to his prince and to his country: to attempt, therefore, to remove him, is endeavouring to deprive the former one of his arms,[9] and the latter of part of its power." It is impossible for the meanest tools of power to express themselves in more servile language.

By another law of Valentinian, Theodosius, and Arcadius,[10] false coiners are declared guilty of high treason. But is not this confounding the ideas of things? Is not the very horror of high treason diminished by giving that name to another crime?

9. *The same Subject continued.* Paulinus having written to the Emperor Alexander that "he was preparing to prosecute for high treason a judge who had decided contrary to his edict," the emperor answered, "that under his reign there was no such thing as indirect high treason."[11]

Faustinian wrote to the same emperor that as he had sworn by the prince's life never to pardon his slave, he found himself thereby

---

[1] Father Du Halde, i, p. 43.
[2] Father Parennin in the *Edifying Letters*.
[3] Book xxix.
[4] Gratian, Valentinian, and Theodosius. This is the second in the *Cod. de crimin. sacril.*
[5] *Sacrilegii instar est dubitare an is dignus sit quem elegerit imperator.*—*Cod. de crimin. sacril.* This law has served as a model to that of Roger in the constitution of Naples, tit. 4.
[6] *Leg. 5, ad leg. Jul. Majest.*

[7] Arcadius and Honorius.
[8] *Memoirs* of Montresor, i, p. 238, Cologne, 1723.
[9] *Nam ipsi pars corporis nostri sunt.*—The same law of the *Cod., ad leg. Jul. Majest.*
[10] It is the 9th of the *Cod. Theod. de falsa moneta.*
[11] *Etiam ex aliis causis majestatis crimina cessant meo sæculo.*—*Leg.* 1, *Cod.,* ix, tit. 8, *ad leg. Jul. Majest.*

obliged to perpetuate his wrath, lest he should incur the guilt of *læsa majestas*. Upon which the emperor made answer, "Your fears are groundless,[1] and you are a stranger to my principles."

It was determined by a *senatus-consultum*[2] that whosoever melted down any of the emperor's statues which happened to be rejected should not be deemed guilty of high treason. The Emperors Severus and Antoninus wrote to Pontius[3] that those who sold unconsecrated statues of the emperor should not be charged with high treason. The same princes wrote to Julius Cassianus that if a person in flinging a stone should by chance strike one of the emperor's statues he should not be liable to a prosecution for high treason.[4] The Julian law requires this sort of limitations; for in virtue of this law the crime of high treason was charged not only upon those who melted down the emperor's statues, but likewise on those who committed any such like action,[5] which made it an arbitrary crime. When a number of crimes of *læsa majestas* had been established, they were obliged to distinguish the several sorts. Hence Ulpian, the civilian, after saying that the accusation of *læsa majestas* did not die with the criminal, adds that this does not relate to all the treasonable acts established by the Julian law,[6] but only to that which implies an attempt against the empire, or against the emperor's life.

10. *The same Subject continued.* There was a law passed in England under Henry VIII, by which whoever predicted the king's death was declared guilty of high treason. This law was extremely vague; the terror of despotic power is so great that it recoils upon those who exercise it. In this king's last illness, the physicians would not venture to say he was in danger; and surely they acted very right.[7]

11. *Of Thoughts.* Marsyas dreamed that he had cut Dionysius's throat.[8] Dionysius put him to death, pretending that he would never have dreamed of such a thing by night if he had not

thought of it by day. This was a most tyrannical action: for though it had been the subject of his thoughts, yet he had made no attempt[9] towards it. The laws do not take upon them to punish any other than overt acts.

12. *Of indiscreet Speeches.* Nothing renders the crime of high treason more arbitrary than declaring people guilty of it for indiscreet speeches. Speech is so subject to interpretation; there is so great a difference between indiscretion and malice; and frequently so little is there of the latter in the freedom of expression, that the law can hardly subject people to a capital punishment for words unless it expressly declares what words they are.[10]

Words do not constitute an overt act; they remain only in idea. When considered by themselves, they have generally no determinate signification; for this depends on the tone in which they are uttered. It often happens that in repeating the same words they have not the same meaning; this depends on their connection with other things, and sometimes more is signified by silence than by any expression whatever. Since there can be nothing so equivocal and ambiguous as all this, how is it possible to convert it into a crime of high treason? Wherever this law is established, there is an end not only of liberty, but even of its very shadow.

In the manifesto of the late Czarina against the family of the D'Olgoruckys,[11] one of these princes is condemned to death for having uttered some indecent words concerning her person: another, for having maliciously interpreted her imperial laws, and for having offended her sacred person by disrespectful expressions.

Not that I pretend to diminish the just indignation of the public against those who presume to stain the glory of their sovereign; what I mean is that, if despotic princes are willing to moderate their power, a milder chastisement would be more proper on those occasions than the charge of high treason—a thing always terrible even to innocence itself.[12]

[1] *Alienam sectæ meæ solicitudinem concepisti.*—*Leg.* 2, *Cod.*, iii, tit. 4, ad leg. Jul. Majest.
[2] *Leg.* 4, § 1, ff. ad leg., Jul. Majest., xlviii, tit. 4.
[3] See *Leg.* 5, § 2, ff. ibid.
[4] *Ibid.*, § 1.
[5] *Aliudve quid simile admiserint.*—*Leg.* 6, ff. ad leg. Jul. Majest.
[6] In the last law, ff. ad leg. Jul. de adulteriis.
[7] See Burnet, *History of the Reformation.*
[8] Plutarch, *Dionysius.*

[9] The thought must be joined with some sort of action.
[10] *Si non tale sit delictum in quod vel scriptura legis descendit vel ad exemplum legis vindicandum est,* says Modestinus in *Leg.* 7, § 3, ff. ad leg. Jul. Majest.
[11] In 1740.
[12] *Nec lubricum linguæ ad pœnam facile trahendum est.*—Modestinus, in *Leg.* 7, § 3, ff. ad leg. Jul. Majest.

Overt acts do not happen every day; they are exposed to the eye of the public; and a false charge with regard to matters of fact may be easily detected. Words carried into action assume the nature of that action. Thus a man who goes into a public market-place to incite the subject to revolt incurs the guilt of high treason, because the words are joined to the action, and partake of its nature. It is not the words that are punished, but an action in which words are employed. They do not become criminal, but when they are annexed to a criminal action: everything is confounded if words are construed into a capital crime, instead of considering them only as a mark of that crime.

The Emperors Theodosius, Arcadius, and Honorius wrote thus to Rufinus, who was *præfectus prætorio:* "Though a man should happen to speak amiss of our person or government, we do not intend to punish him:[1] if he has spoken through levity, we must despise him; if through folly, we must pity him; and if he wrongs us, we must forgive him. Therefore, leaving things as they are, you are to inform us accordingly, that we may be able to judge of words by persons, and that we may duly consider whether we ought to punish or overlook them."

13. *Of Writings.* In writings there is something more permanent than in words, but when they are in no way preparative to high treason they cannot amount to that charge.

And yet Augustus and Tiberius subjected satirical writers to the same punishment as for having violated the law of *maiestas.* Augustus,[2] because of some libels that had been written against persons of the first quality; Tiberius, because of those which he suspected to have been written against himself. Nothing was more fatal to Roman liberty. Cremutius Cordus was accused of having called Cassius in his annals the last of the Romans.[3]

Satirical writings are hardly known in despotic governments, where dejection of mind on the one hand, and ignorance on the other, afford neither abilities nor will to write. In democracies they are not hindered, for the very same reason which causes them to be prohibited in monarchies; being generally levelled against men of power and authority, they flatter the malignancy of the people, who are the governing party. In monarchies they are forbidden, but rather as a subject of civil animadversion than as a capital crime. They may amuse the general malevolence, please the malcontents, diminish the envy against public employments, give the people patience to suffer, and make them laugh at their sufferings.

But no government is so averse to satirical writings as the aristocratic. There the magistrates are petty sovereigns, but not great enough to despise affronts. If in a monarchy a satirical stroke is designed against the prince, he is placed on such an eminence that it does not reach him; but an aristocratic lord is pierced to the very heart. Hence the decemvirs, who formed an aristocracy, punished satirical writings with death.[4]

14. *Breach of Modesty in punishing Crimes.* There are rules of modesty observed by almost every nation in the world; now it would be very absurd to infringe these rules in the punishment of crimes, the principal view of which ought always to be the establishment of order.

Was it the intent of those Oriental nations who exposed women to elephants trained up for an abominable kind of punishment—was it, I say, their intent to establish one law by the breach of another?

By an ancient custom of the Romans it was not permitted to put girls to death till they were ripe for marriage. Tiberius found an expedient of having them debauched by the executioner before they were brought to the place of punishment:[5] that bloody and subtle tyrant destroyed the morals of the people to preserve their customs.

When the magistrates of Japan caused women to be exposed naked in the market-places, and obliged them to go upon all fours like beasts, modesty was shocked:[6] but when they wanted to compel a mother—when they wanted to force a son—I cannot proceed; even Nature herself is struck with horror.[7]

---

[1] *Si id ex levitate processerit, contemnendum est; si ex insania, miseratione dignissimum; si ab injuria, remittendum.—Leg. unica, Cod. si quis Imperat. maled.*

[2] Tacitus, *Annals,* i. 72. This continued under the following reigns. See the first law in the *Cod. de famosis libellis.*

[3] Tacitus, *Annals,* iv. 34.

[4] The law of the Twelve Tables.

[5] Suetonius, *Life of Tiberius,* 61.

[6] *Collection of Voyages that Contributed to the Establishment of the East India Company,* v, part II.

[7] *Ibid.,* p. 496.

15. *Of the Enfranchisement of Slaves in order to accuse their Master.* Augustus made a law that the slaves of those who conspired against his person should be sold to the public, that they might depose against their master.[1] Nothing ought to be neglected which may contribute to the discovery of a heinous crime; it is natural, therefore, that in a government where there are slaves they should be allowed to inform; but they ought not to be admitted as witnesses.

Vindex discovered the conspiracy that had been formed in favour of Tarquin; but he was not admitted a witness against the children of Brutus. It was right to give liberty to a person who had rendered so great a service to his country; but it was not given him with a view of enabling him to render this service.

Hence the Emperor Tacitus ordained that slaves should not be admitted as witnesses against their masters, even in the case of high treason:[2] a law which was not inserted in Justinian's compilation.

16. *Of Calumny with regard to the Crime of High Treason.* To do justice to the Cæsars, they were not the first devisers of the horrid laws which they enacted. It was Sulla[3] that taught them that calumniators ought not to be punished; but the abuse was soon carried to such excess as to reward them.[4]

17. *Of the revealing of Conspiracies.* "If thy brother, the son of thy mother, or thy son, or thy daughter, or the wife of thy bosom, or thy friend, which is as thine own soul, entice thee secretly, saying, 'Let us go and serve other gods,' thou shalt surely kill him, thou shalt stone him."[5] This law of Deuteronomy cannot be a civil law among most of the nations known to us, because it would pave the way for all manner of wickedness.

No less severe is the law of several countries which commands the subjects, on pain of death, to disclose conspiracies in which they are not even so much as concerned. When such a law is established in a monarchical government, it is very proper it should be under some restrictions.

It ought not to be applied in its full severity save to the strongest cases of high treason. In those countries it is of the utmost importance not to confound the different degrees of this crime. In Japan, where the laws subvert every idea of human reason, the crime of concealment is applied even to the most ordinary cases.

A certain relation[6] makes mention of two young ladies who were shut up for life in a box thick set with pointed nails, one for having had a love intrigue, and the other for not disclosing it.

18. *How dangerous it is in Republics to be too severe in punishing the Crime of High Treason.* As soon as a republic has compassed the destruction of those who wanted to subvert it, there should be an end of terrors, punishments, and even of rewards.

Great punishments, and consequently great changes, cannot take place without investing some citizens with an exorbitant power. It is, therefore, more advisable in this case to exceed in lenity than in severity; to banish but few, rather than many; and to leave them their estates, instead of making a vast number of confiscations. Under pretence of avenging the republic's cause, the avengers would establish tyranny. The business is not to destroy the rebel, but the rebellion. They ought to return as quickly as possible into the usual track of government, in which every one is protected by the laws, and no one injured.

The Greeks set no bounds to the vengeance they took upon tyrants, or of those they suspected of tyranny; they put their children to death,[7] nay, sometimes five of their nearest relatives;[8] and they proscribed an infinite number of families. By such means their republics suffered the most violent shocks: exiles, or the return of the exiled, were always epochs that indicated a change of the constitution.

The Romans had more sense. When Cassius

---

[1] Dio, in Xiphilin., lv. 5. Tacitus, *Annals*, ii. 30, iii. 67, attributes this law, not to Augustus, but to Tiberius.

[2] Flavius Vopiscus in his Life, 9.

[3] Sulla made a law of majesty, which is mentioned in Cicero's Orations, *Pro Cluentio*, art. 3; *In Pisonem*, art. 21; 2nd against Verres, art. 5. *Familiar Epistles*, iii, 11. Cæsar and Augustus inserted them in the Julian Laws; others made additions to them.

[4] *Et quò quis distinctior accusator, eò magis honores assequebatur, ac veluti sacrosanctus erat.* —Tacitus, *Annals*, iv. 36.

[5] Deut., 13. 6–9.

[6] *Collection of Voyages that Contributed to the Establishment of the East India Company*, v, part II, p. 423.

[7] Dionysius Halicarnassus, *Roman Antiquities*, viii.

[8] *Tyranno occiso quinque ejus proximos cognatione magistratus necato.*—Cicero, *De Invent.* ii. 29.

was put to death for having aimed at tyranny, the question was proposed whether his children should undergo the same fate: but they were preserved. "They," says Dionysius Halicarnassus,[1] "who wanted to change this law at the end of the Marsian and civil wars, and to exclude from public offices the children of those who had been proscribed by Sulla, are very much to blame."

We find in the wars of Marius and Sulla to what excess the Romans had gradually carried their barbarity. Such scenes of cruelty it was hoped would never be revived. But under the triumvirs they committed greater acts of oppression, though with some appearance of lenity; and it is provoking to see what sophisms they made use of to cover their inhumanity. Appian has given us[2] the formula of the proscriptions. One would imagine they had no other aim than the good of the republic, with such calmness do they express themselves; such advantages do they point out to the state; such expediency do they show in the means they adopt; such security do they promise to the opulent; such tranquillity to the poor; so apprehensive do they seem of endangering the lives of the citizens; so desirous of appeasing the soldiers; such felicity, in fine, do they presage to the commonwealth.

Rome was drenched in blood when Lepidus triumphed over Spain: yet, by an unparalleled absurdity, he ordered public rejoicings in that city, upon pain of proscription.

19. *In what Manner the Use of Liberty is suspended in a Republic.* In countries where liberty is most esteemed, there are laws by which a single person is deprived of it, in order to preserve it for the whole community. Such are in England what they call Bills of Attainder.[3]

---

[1] Book viii, p. 547.
[2] *Of the Civil Wars,* iv.
[3] It is not sufficient in the courts of justice of that kingdom that the evidence be of such a nature as to satisfy the judges; there must be a legal proof; and the law requires the deposition of two witnesses against the accused. No other proof will do. Now, if a person who is presumed guilty of high treason should contrive to secrete the witnesses, so as to render it impossible for him to be legally condemned, the government then may bring a bill of attainder against him; that is, they may enact a particular law for that single fact. They proceed then in the same manner as in all other bills brought into parliament; it must pass the two houses, and have the king's consent, otherwise it is not a bill: that is, a sentence of the legislature. The person accused may plead against the bill by counsel, and the members of the house may speak in defence of the bill.

These are in relation to those Athenian laws by which a private person was condemned,[4] provided they were made by the unanimous suffrage of six thousand citizens. They are in relation also to those laws which were made at Rome against private citizens, and were called *privileges.*[5] These were never passed except in the great meetings of the people. But in what manner soever they were enacted, Cicero was for having them abolished, because the force of a law consists in its being made for the whole community.[6] I must own, notwithstanding, that the practice of the freest nation that ever existed induces me to think that there are cases in which a veil should be drawn for a while over liberty, as it was customary to cover the statues of the gods.

20. *Of Laws favourable to the Liberty of the Subject in a Republic.* In popular governments it often happens that accusations are carried on in public, and every man is allowed to accuse whomsoever he pleases. This rendered it necessary to establish proper laws, in order to protect the innocence of the subject. At Athens, if an accuser had not the fifth part of the votes on his side, he was obliged to pay a fine of a thousand drachms. Æschines, who accused Ctesiphon, was condemned to pay this fine.[7] At Rome, a false accuser was branded with infamy[8] by marking the letter K on his forehead. Guards were also appointed to watch the accuser, in order to prevent his corrupting either the judges or the witnesses.[9]

I have already taken notice of that Athenian and Roman law by which the party accused was allowed to withdraw before judgment was pronounced.

21. *Of the Cruelty of Laws in respect to Debtors in a Republic.* Great is the superiority which one fellow-subject has already over another, by lending him money, which the latter borrows in order to spend, and, of course, has no longer in his possession. What must be the consequence if the laws of a republic make a

---

[4] *Legem de singulari aliquo rogato, nisi sex millibus ita visum.*—From Andocidis, *De Mysteriis.* This is what they call Ostracism.
[5] *De privis hominibus latæ.*—Cicero, *De Leg.,* iii. 19.
[6] *Scitum est jussum in omnes.*—*Ibid.*
[7] See Philostratus, i: *Lives of the Sophists:* Æschines. See likewise Plutarch and Phocius.
[8] By the Remnian law.
[9] Plutarch, in a treatise entitled, *How a Person May Reap Advantage from his Enemies.*

further addition to this servitude and subjection?

At Athens and Rome[1] it was at first permitted to sell such debtors as were insolvent. Solon redressed this abuse at Athens[2] by ordaining that no man's body should answer for his civil debts. But the decemvirs[3] did not reform the same custom at Rome; and though they had Solon's regulation before their eyes, yet they did not choose to follow it. This is not the only passage of the law of the Twelve Tables in which the decemvirs show their design of checking the spirit of democracy.

Often did those cruel laws against debtors throw the Roman republic into danger. A man covered with wounds made his escape from his creditor's house and appeared in the forum.[4] The people were moved with this spectacle, and other citizens whom their creditors durst no longer confine broke loose from their dungeons. They had promises made them, which were all broken. The people upon this, having withdrawn to the Sacred Mount, obtained, not an abrogation of those laws, but a magistrate to defend them. Thus they quitted a state of anarchy, but were soon in danger of falling into tyranny. Manlius, to render himself popular, was going to set those citizens at liberty who by their inhuman creditors[5] had been reduced to slavery. Manlius's designs were prevented, but without remedying the evil. Particular laws facilitated to debtors the means of paying;[6] and in the year of Rome 428 the consuls proposed a law[7] which deprived creditors of the power of confining their debtors in their own houses.[8] A usurer, by name Papirius, attempted to corrupt the chastity of a young man named Publius, whom he kept in irons. Sextus's crime gave to Rome its political liberty; that of Papirius gave it also the civil.

Such was the fate of this city, that new crimes confirmed the liberty which those of a

more ancient date had procured it. Appius's attempt upon Virginia flung the people again into that horror against tyrants with which the misfortune of Lucretia had first inspired them. Thirty-seven years after[9] the crime of the infamous Papirius, an action of the like criminal nature[10] was the cause of the people's retiring to the Janiculum,[11] and of giving new vigour to the law made for the safety of debtors.

Since that time creditors were oftener prosecuted by debtors for having violated the laws against usury than the latter were sued for refusing to pay them.

22. *Of Things that strike at Liberty in Monarchies.* Liberty often has been weakened in monarchies by a thing of the least use in the world to the prince: this is the naming of commissioners to try a private person.

The prince himself derives so very little advantage from those commissioners that it is not worth while to change for their sake the common course of things. He is morally sure that he has more of the spirit of probity and justice than his commissioners, who think themselves sufficiently justified by his nomination and orders, by a vague interest of state, and even by their very apprehensions.

Upon the arraigning of a peer under Henry VIII it was customary to try him by a committee of the House of Lords: by which means he put to death as many peers as he pleased.

23. *Of Spies in Monarchies.* Should I be asked whether there is any necessity for spies in monarchies, my answer would be that the usual practice of good princes is not to employ them. When a man obeys the laws, he has discharged his duty to his prince. He ought at least to have his own house for an asylum, and the rest of his conduct should be exempt from inquiry. The trade of a spy might perhaps be tolerable, were it practised by honest men; but the necessary infamy of the person is sufficient to make us judge of the infamy of the thing. A prince ought to act towards his subjects with candour, frankness, and confidence.

---

[1] "A great many sold their children to pay their debts."—Plutarch, *Solon.*

[2] *Ibid.*

[3] It appears from history that this custom was established among the Romans before the Law of the Twelve Tables.—Livy, dec. 1, ii. 23, 24.

[4] Dionysius Halicarnassus. *Roman Antiquities,* vi.

[5] Plutarch, *Furius Camillus.*

[6] See below, xxii. 22.

[7] One hundred and twenty years after the law of the Twelve Tables: *Eo anno plebi Romanæ, velut aliud initium libertatis factum est, quod necti desierunt.*—Livy, viii. 38.

[8] *Bona debitoris, non corpus obnoxium esset.*—*Ibid.*

[9] The year of Rome 465.

[10] That of Plautius who made an attempt upon the body of Veturius.—Valerius Maximus, vi, 1, art. 9. These two events ought not to be confounded; they are neither the same persons nor the same times.

[11] See a fragment of Dionysius Halicarnassus in the extract *of Virtues and Vices [Historica];* Livy's *Epitome,* ii., and Freinshemius, ii.

He that has so much disquiet, suspicion, and fear is an actor embarrassed in playing his part. When he finds that the laws are generally observed and respected, he may judge himself safe. The behaviour of the public answers for that of every individual. Let him not be afraid: he cannot imagine how natural it is for his people to love him. And how should they do otherwise than love him, since he is the source of almost all bounties and favours; punishments being generally charged to the account of the laws? He never shows himself to his people but with a serene countenance; they have even a share of his glory, and they are protected by his power. A proof of his being beloved is that his subjects have confidence in him: what the minister refuses, they imagine the prince would have granted. Even under public calamities they do not accuse his person; they are apt to complain of his being misinformed, or beset by corrupt men. "Did the prince but know," say the people; these words are a kind of invocation, and a proof of the confidence they have in his person.

24. *Of Anonymous Letters.* The Tartars are obliged to put their names to their arrows, that the arm may be known which shoots them. When Philip of Macedon was wounded at the siege of a certain town, these words were found on the javelin, "Aster has given this mortal wound to Philip."[1] If they who accuse a person did it merely to serve the public, they would not carry their complaint to the prince, who may be easily prejudiced, but to the magistrates, who have rules that are formidable only to calumniators. But if they are unwilling to leave the laws open between them and the accused, it is a presumption they have reason to be afraid of them; and the least punishment they ought to suffer is not to be credited. No notice, therefore, should ever be taken of those letters, except in cases that admit not of the delays of the ordinary course of justice, and in which the prince's welfare is concerned. Then it may be imagined that the accuser has made an effort, which has untied his tongue. But in other cases one ought to say, with the Emperor Constantius: "We cannot suspect a person who has wanted an accuser, whilst he did not want an enemy."[2]

25. *Of the Manner of governing in Monarch-*

ies. The royal authority is a spring that ought to move with the greatest freedom and ease. The Chinese boast of one of their emperors who governed, they say, like the heavens, that is, by his example.

There are some cases in which a sovereign ought to exert the full extent of his power; and others in which he should reduce it within narrower limits. The sublimity of administration consists in knowing the proper degree of power which should be exerted on different occasions.

The whole felicity of monarchies consists in the opinion which the subjects entertain of the lenity of the government. A weak minister is ever ready to remind us of our slavery. But granting, even, that we are slaves, he should endeavour to conceal our misery from us. All he can say or write is that the prince is uneasy, that he is surprised, and that he will redress all grievances. There is a certain ease in commanding; the prince ought only to encourage, and let the laws menace.[3]

26. *That in a Monarchy the Prince ought to be of easy Access.* The utility of this maxim will appear from the inconvenience attending the contrary practice. "The Czar Peter I," says the Sieur Perry,[4] "has published a new edict, by which he forbids any of his subjects to offer him a petition till after having presented it to two of his officers. In case of refusal of justice they may present him a third, but upon pain of death if they are in the wrong. After this no one ever presumed to offer a petition to the Czar."

27. *Of the Manners of a Monarch.* The manners of a prince contribute as much as the laws themselves to liberty; like these he may transform men into brutes, and brutes into men. If he prefers free and generous spirits, he will have subjects; if he likes base, dastardly souls, he will have slaves. Would he know the great art of ruling, let him call honour and virtue to attend his person; and let him encourage personal merit. He may even sometimes cast an eye on talents and abilities. Let him not be afraid of those rivals who are called men of merit; he is their equal when once he loves them. Let him gain the hearts of his people, without subduing their spirits. Let him render himself popular; he ought to be

---

[1] Plutarch, *Comparison of some Roman and Greek Histories,* ii, p. 487.
[2] *Leg.* 6, Cod. *Theod. de famosis libellis.*

[3] "Nerva," says Tacitus, "increased the ease of government."
[4] *State of Russia,* p. 173, Paris, 1717.

pleased with the affections of the lowest of his subjects, for they too are men. The common people require so very little condescension, that it is fit they should be humoured; the infinite distance between the sovereign and them will surely prevent them from giving him any uneasiness. Let him be exorable to supplication, and resolute against demands; let him be sensible, in fine, that his people have his refusals, while his courtiers enjoy his favours.

28. *Of the Regard which Monarchs owe to their Subjects.* Princes ought to be extremely circumspect with regard to raillery. It pleases with moderation, because it is an introduction to familiarity; but a satirical raillery is less excusable in them than in the meanest of their subjects, for it is they alone that give a mortal wound.

Much less should they offer a public affront to any of their subjects; kings were instituted to pardon and to punish, but never to insult.

When they affront their subjects, their treatment is more cruel than that of the Turk or the Muscovite. The insults of these are a humiliation, not a disgrace; but both must follow from the insolent behaviour of monarchs.

Such is the prejudice of the eastern nations that they look upon an affront from the prince as the effect of paternal goodness; and such, on the contrary, is our way of thinking that besides the cruel vexation of being affronted, we despair of ever being able to wipe off the disgrace.

Princes ought to be overjoyed to have subjects to whom honour is dearer than life, an incitement to fidelity as well as to courage.

They should remember the misfortunes that have happened to sovereigns for insulting their subjects: the revenge of Chærea, of the eunuch Narses, of Count Julian, and, in fine, of the Duchess of Montpensier, who, being enraged against Henry III for having published some of her private failings, tormented him during her whole life.

29. *Of the civil Laws proper for mixing some portion of Liberty in a despotic Government.* Though despotic governments are of their own nature everywhere the same, yet from circumstances—from a religious opinion, from prejudice, from received examples, from a particular turn of mind, from manners or morals—it is possible they may admit of a considerable difference.

It is useful that some particular notions should be established in those governments. Thus in China the prince is considered as the father of his people; and at the commencement of the empire of the Arabs, the prince was their preacher.[1]

It is proper there should be some sacred book to serve for a rule, as the Koran among the Arabs, the books of Zoroaster among the Persians, the Veda among the Indians, and the classic books among the Chinese. The religious code supplies the civil and fixes the extent of arbitrary sway.

It is not at all amiss that in dubious cases the judges should consult the ministers of religion.[2] Thus, in Turkey, the Cadis consult the Mollahs. But if it is a capital crime, it may be proper for the particular judge, if such there be, to take the governor's advice, to the end that the civil and ecclesiastical power may be tempered also by the political authority.

30. *The same Subject continued.* Nothing but the very excess and rage of despotic power ordained that the father's disgrace should drag after it that of his wife and children. They are wretched enough already without being criminals: besides, the prince ought to leave suppliants or mediators between himself and the accused, to assuage his wrath or to inform his justice.

It is an excellent custom of the Maldivians[3] that when a lord is disgraced he goes every day to pay his court to the king till he is taken again into favour: his presence disarms the prince's indignation.

In some despotic governments[4] they have a notion that it is trespassing against the respect due to their prince to speak to him in favour of a person in disgrace. These princes seem to use all their endeavours to deprive themselves of the virtue of clemency.

Arcadius and Honorius, by a law[5] on which we have already descanted,[6] positively declare that they will show no favour to those who shall presume to petition them in behalf of

---

[1] The Caliphs.

[2] *History of the Tartars*, part III, p. 277, in the remarks.

[3] See Francis Pirard.

[4] As at present in Persia, according to Sir John Chardin, this custom is very ancient. "They put Cavades," says Procopius, "into the castle of oblivion; there is a law which forbids any one to speak of those who are shut up, or even to mention their name."

[5] The fifth law in the *Cod. ad leg. Jul. Majest.*

[6] In the 8th chapter of this book.

the guilty.[1] This was a very bad law indeed, since it is bad even under a despotic government.

The custom of Persia, which permits every man that pleases to leave the kingdom, is excellent; and though the contrary practice derives its origin from despotic power, which has ever considered the subjects as slaves,[2] and those who quit the country as fugitives, yet the Persian practice is useful even to a despotic government, because the apprehension of people's withdrawing for debt restrains or moderates the oppressions of pashas and extortioners.

Book XIII. Of the Relation which the Levying of Taxes and the Greatness of the Public Revenues Bear to Liberty

1. *Of the Public Revenues.* The *public revenues* are a portion that each subject gives of his property, in order to secure or enjoy the remainder.

To fix these revenues in a proper manner, regard should be had both to the necessities of the state and to those of the subject. The real wants of the people ought never to give way to the imaginary wants of the state.

Imaginary wants are those which flow from the passions and the weakness of the governors, from the vain conceit of some extraordinary project, from the inordinate desire of glory, and from a certain impotence of mind incapable of withstanding the impulse of fancy. Often have ministers of a restless disposition imagined that the wants of their own mean and ignoble souls were those of the state.

Nothing requires more wisdom and prudence than the regulation of that portion of which the subject is deprived, and that which he is suffered to retain.

The public revenues should not be measured by the people's abilities to give, but by what they ought to give; and if they are measured by their abilities to give, it should be considered what they are able to give for a constancy.

2. *That it is bad Reasoning to say that the Greatness of Taxes is good in its own Nature.* There have been instances in particular monarchies of petty states exempt from taxes that have been as miserable as the circumjacent places which groaned under the weight of exactions. The chief reason of this is, that the petty state can hardly have any such thing as industry, arts, or manufactures, because of its being subject to a thousand restraints from the great state by which it is environed. The great state is blessed with industry, manufactures, and arts, and establishes laws by which those several advantages are procured. The petty state becomes, therefore, necessarily poor, let it pay never so few taxes.

And yet some have concluded from the poverty of those petty states that in order to render the people industrious they should be loaded with taxes. But it would be a juster inference, that they ought to pay no taxes at all. None live here but wretches who retire from the neighbouring parts to avoid working—wretches who, disheartened by labour, make their whole felicity consist in idleness.

The effect of wealth in a country is to inspire every heart with ambition: that of poverty is to give birth to despair. The former is excited by labour, the latter is soothed by indolence.

Nature is just to all mankind, and repays them for their industry: she renders them industrious by annexing rewards in proportion to their labour. But if an arbitrary prince should attempt to deprive the people of nature's bounty, they would fall into a disrelish of industry; and then indolence and inaction must be their only happiness.

3. *Of Taxes in Countries where Part of the People are Villains or Bondmen.* The state of villainage is sometimes established after a conquest. In that case, the bondman or villain that tills the land ought to have a kind of partnership with his master. Nothing but a communication of loss or profit can reconcile those who are doomed to labour to such as are blessed with a state of affluence.

4. *Of a Republic in the like Case.* When a re-

---

[1] Frederick copied this law in the Constitutions of Naples, i.

[2] In monarchies there is generally a law which forbids those who are invested with public employments to go out of the kingdom without the prince's leave. This law ought to be established also in republics. But in those that have particular institutions the prohibition ought to be general, in order to prevent the introduction of foreign manners.

public has reduced a nation to the drudgery of cultivating her lands, she ought never to suffer the free subject to have the power of increasing the tribute of the bondman. This was not permitted at Sparta. Those brave people thought the Helotes[1] would be more industrious in cultivating their lands, and knowing that their servitude was not to increase; they imagined, likewise, that the masters would be better citizens, when they desired no more than what they were accustomed to enjoy.

5. *Of a Monarchy in the like Case.* When the nobles of a monarchical state cause the lands to be cultivated for their own use by a conquered people, they ought never to have the power of increasing the service or tribute.[2] Besides, it is right the prince should be satisfied with his own demesne and the military service. But if he wants to raise taxes on the vassals of his nobility, the lords of the several districts ought to be answerable for the tax,[3] and be obliged to pay it for the vassals, by whom they may be afterwards reimbursed. If this rule be not followed, the lord and the collectors of the public taxes will harass the poor vassal by turns till he perishes with misery or flies into the woods.

6. *Of a despotic Government in the like Case.* The foregoing rule is still more indispensably necessary in a despotic government. The lord who is every moment liable to be stripped of his lands and his vassals is not so eager to preserve them.

When Peter I thought proper to follow the custom of Germany, and to demand his taxes in money, he made a very prudent regulation, which is still followed in Russia. The gentleman levies the tax on the peasant, and pays it to the Czar. If the number of peasants diminishes, he pays all the same; if it increases, he pays no more; so that it is his interest not to worry or oppress his vassals.

7. *Of Taxes in Countries where Villainage is not established.* When the inhabitants of a state are all free subjects, and each man enjoys his property with as much right as the prince his sovereignty, taxes may then be laid either on persons, on lands, on merchandise, on two

of these, or on all three together.

In the taxing of persons, it would be an unjust proportion to conform exactly to that of property. At Athens the people were divided into four classes.[4] Those who drew five hundred measures of liquid or dried fruit from their estates paid a talent[5] to the public; those who drew three hundred measures paid half a talent; those who had two hundred measures paid ten minæ; those of the fourth class paid nothing at all. The tax was fair, though it was not proportionable: if it did not follow the measure of people's property, it followed that of their wants. It was judged that every man had an equal share of what was necessary for nature, that whatsoever was necessary for nature ought not to be taxed; that to this succeeded the useful, which ought to be taxed, but less than the superfluous; and that the largeness of the taxes on what was superfluous prevented superfluity.

In the taxing of lands it is customary to make lists or registers, in which the different classes of estates are ranged. But it is very difficult to know these differences, and still more so to find people that are not interested in mistaking them. Here, therefore, are two sorts of injustice, that of the man and that of the thing. But if in general the tax be not exorbitant, and the people continue to have plenty of necessaries, these particular acts of injustice will do no harm. On the contrary, if the people are permitted to enjoy only just what is necessary for subsistence, the least disproportion will be of the greatest consequence.

If some subjects do not pay enough, the mischief is not so great; their convenience and ease turn always to the public advantage; if some private people pay too much, their ruin redounds to the public detriment. If the government proportions its fortune to that of individuals, the ease and convenience of the latter will soon make its fortune rise. The whole depends upon a critical moment: shall the state begin with impoverishing the subjects to enrich itself? Or had it better wait to be enriched by its subjects? Is it more advisable for it to have the former or the latter advantage? Which shall it choose—to begin or to end with opulence?

The duties felt least by the people are those on merchandise, because they are not demanded of them in form. They may be so prudently managed that the people themselves shall

---

[1] Plutarch, *Notable Sayings of the Lacedæmonians.*

[2] This is what induced Charlemagne to make his excellent institution upon this head. See the fifth book of the *Capitularies,* art. 303.

[3] This is the practice in Germany.

[4] Pollux, viii. 10, art. 130.

[5] Or 60 minæ.

hardly know they pay them. For this purpose it is of the utmost consequence that the person who sells the merchandise should pay the duty. He is very sensible that he does not pay it for himself; and the consumer, who pays it in the main, confounds it with the price. Some authors have observed that Nero had abolished the duty of the five-and-twentieth part arising from the sale of slaves;[1] and yet he had only ordained that it should be paid by the seller instead of the purchaser; this regulation, which left the impost entire, seemed nevertheless to suppress it.

There are two states in Europe where the imposts are very heavy upon liquors: in one the brewer alone pays the duty, in the other it is levied indiscriminately upon all the consumers; in the first nobody feels the rigour of the impost, in the second it is looked upon as a grievance; in the former the subject is sensible only of the liberty he has of not paying, in the latter he feels only the necessity that compels him to pay.

Further, the obliging the consumers to pay requires a perpetual rummaging and searching into their houses. Now nothing is more contrary than this to liberty; and those who establish these sorts of duties have not surely been so happy as to hit upon the best method of collecting the revenue.

8. *In what Manner the Deception is preserved.* In order to make the purchaser confound the price of the commodity with the impost, there must be some proportion between the impost and the value of the commodity: for which reason there ought not to be an excessive duty upon merchandise of little value. There are countries in which the duty exceeds seventeen or eighteen times the value of the commodity. In this case the prince removes the disguise: his subjects plainly see they are dealt with in an unreasonable manner, which renders them most exquisitely sensible of their servile condition.

Besides, the prince, to be able to levy a duty so disproportioned to the value of the commodity, must be himself the vendor, and the people must not have it in their power to purchase it elsewhere: a practice subject to a thousand inconveniences.

Smuggling being in this case extremely lucrative, the natural and most reasonable penalty, namely, the confiscation of the merchandise, becomes incapable of putting a stop to it;

[1] Tacitus, *Annals*, xiii. 31.

especially as this very merchandise is intrinsically of inconsiderable value. Recourse must therefore be had to extravagant punishments, such as those inflicted for capital crimes.

All proportion then of penalties is at an end. Persons that cannot really be considered as vicious are punished like the most infamous criminals; which of all things in the world is the most contrary to the spirit of a moderate government.

Again, in proportion as people are tempted to cheat the farmer of the revenues, the more the latter is enriched, and the former impoverished. To put a stop to smuggling, the farmer must be invested with extraordinary means of oppressing, and then the country is ruined.

9. *Of a bad Kind of Impost.* We shall here, by the way, take notice of an impost laid in particular countries on the different articles of civil contracts. As these are things subject to very nice disquisitions, a vast deal of knowledge is necessary to make any tolerable defence against the farmer of the revenues, who interprets, in that case, the regulations of the prince, and exercises an arbitrary power over people's fortunes. Experience has demonstrated that a duty on the paper on which the deeds are drawn would be of far greater service.

10. *That the Greatness of Taxes depends on the Nature of the Government.* Taxes ought to be very light in despotic governments: otherwise who would be at the trouble of tilling the land? Besides, how is it possible to pay heavy duties in a government that makes no manner of return to the different contributions of the subject?

The exorbitant power of the prince, and the extreme depression of the people, require that there should not be even a possibility of the least mistake between them. The taxes ought to be so easy to collect, and so clearly settled, as to leave no opportunity for the collectors to increase or diminish them. A portion of the fruits of the earth, a capitation, a duty of so much per cent on merchandise, are the only taxes suitable to that government.

Merchants in despotic countries ought to have a personal safeguard, to which all due respect should be paid. Without this they would be too weak to dispute with the custom-house officers.

11. *Of Confiscations.* With respect to confiscations, there is one thing very particular that,

contrary to the general custom, they are more severe in Europe than in Asia. In Europe not only the merchandise, but even sometimes the ships and carriages, are confiscated; which is never practised in Asia. This is because in Europe the merchant can have recourse to magistrates, who are able to shelter him from oppression; in Asia the magistrates themselves would be the greatest oppressors. What remedy could a merchant have against a pasha who was determined to confiscate his goods?

The prince, therefore, checks his own power, finding himself under the necessity of acting with some kind of lenity. In Turkey they raise only a single duty for the importation of goods, and afterwards the whole country is open to the merchant. Smuggling is not attended with confiscation or increase of duty. In China[1] they never look into the baggage of those who are not merchants. Defrauding the customs in the territory of the Mogul is not punished with confiscation, but with doubling the duty. The princes of Tartary, who reside in towns, impose scarcely any duty at all on the goods that pass through their country.[2] In Japan, it is true, to cheat the customs is a capital crime; but this is because they have particular reasons for prohibiting all communication with foreigners; hence the fraud[3] is rather a contravention of the laws made for the security of the government than of those of commerce.

12. *Relation between the Weight of Taxes and Liberty.* It is a general rule that taxes may be heavier in proportion to the liberty of the subject, and that there is a necessity for reducing them in proportion to the increase of slavery. This has always been and always will be the case. It is a rule derived from nature that never varies. We find it in all parts—in England, in Holland, and in every state where liberty gradually declines, till we come to Turkey. Switzerland seems to be an exception to this rule, because they pay no taxes; but the particular reason for that exemption is well known, and even confirms what I have advanced. In those barren mountains provisions are so dear, and the country is so populous, that a Swiss pays four times more to nature than a Turk does to the sultan.

A conquering people, such as were formerly the Athenians and the Romans, may rid themselves of all taxes as they reign over vanquished nations. Then indeed they do not pay in proportion to their liberty, because in this respect they are no longer a people, but a monarch.

But the general rule still holds good. In moderate governments there is an indemnity for the weight of the taxes, which is liberty. In despotic countries[4] there is an equivalent for liberty, which is the lightness of the taxes.

In some monarchies in Europe there are particular provinces[5] which from the very nature of their civil government are in a more flourishing condition than the rest. It is pretended that these provinces are not sufficiently taxed, because through the goodness of their government they are able to be taxed higher; hence the ministers seem constantly to aim at depriving them of this very government, whence a diffusive blessing is derived, which redounds even to the prince's advantage.

13. *In what Government Taxes are capable of Increase.* Taxes may be increased in most republics, because the citizen, who thinks he is paying himself, cheerfully submits to them, and moreover is generally able to bear their weight, from the nature of the government.

In a monarchy taxes may be increased, because the moderation of the government is capable of procuring opulence: it is a recompense, as it were, granted to the prince for the respect he shows to the laws. In despotic governments they cannot be increased, because there can be no increase of the extremity of slavery.

14. *That the Nature of the Taxes is in Relation to the Government.* A capitation is more natural to slavery; a duty on merchandise is more natural to liberty, by reason it has not so direct a relation to the person.

It is natural in a despotic government for the prince not to give money to his soldiers, or to those belonging to his court; but to dis-

---

[1] Father Du Halde, ii, p. 37.

[2] *History of the Tartars*, part III, p. 290.

[3] Being willing to trade with foreigners without having any communication with them, they have pitched upon two nations for that purpose—the Dutch for the commerce of Europe, and the Chinese for that of Asia; they confine the factors and sailors in a kind of prison, and lay such a restraint upon them as tires their patience.

[4] In Russia the taxes are but small; they have been increased since the despotic power of the prince is exercised with more moderation. See the *History of the Tartars,* part II.

[5] The *Pays d'états,* where the states of the province assemble to deliberate on public affairs.

tribute lands amongst them, and of course that there should be very few taxes. But if the prince gives money, the most natural tax he can raise is a capitation, which can never be considerable. For as it is impossible to make different classes of the contributors, because of the abuses that might arise thence, considering the injustice and violence of the government, they are under an absolute necessity of regulating themselves by the rate of what even the poorest and most wretched are able to contribute.

The natural tax of moderate governments is the duty laid on merchandise. As this is really paid by the consumer, though advanced by the merchant, it is a loan which the latter has already made to the former. Hence the merchant must be considered on the one side as the general debtor of the state, and on the other as the creditor of every individual. He advances to the state the duty which the consumer will some time or other refund: and he has paid for the consumer the duty which he has advanced for the merchandise. It is therefore obvious that in proportion to the moderation of the government, to the prevalence of the spirit of liberty, and to the security of private fortunes, a merchant has it in his power to advance money to the state, and to pay considerable duties for individuals. In England a merchant lends really to the government fifty or sixty pounds sterling for every tun of wine he imports. Where is the merchant that would dare do any such thing in a country like Turkey? And were he so presumptuous, how could he do it with a crazy or shattered fortune?

15. *Abuse of Liberty*. To these great advantages of liberty it is owing that liberty itself has been abused. Because a moderate government has been productive of admirable effects, this moderation has been laid aside; because great taxes have been raised, they wanted to carry them to excess; and ungrateful to the hand of liberty, of whom they received this present, they addressed themselves to slavery, who never grants the least favour.

Liberty produces excessive taxes; the effect of excessive taxes is slavery; and slavery produces a diminution of tribute.

Most of the edicts of the eastern monarchs are to exempt every year some province of their empire from paying tribute.[1] The manifestations of their wills are favours. But in Europe the edicts of princes are disagreeable

even before they are seen, because they always make mention of their own wants, but not a word of ours.

From an unpardonable indolence in the ministers of those countries, owing to the nature of the government, and frequently to the climate, the people derive this advantage, that they are not incessantly plagued with new demands. The public expense does not increase, because the ministers do not form new projects: and if some by chance are formed, they are such as are soon executed. The governors of the state do not perpetually torment the people, for they do not perpetually torment themselves. But it is impossible there should be any fixed rule in our finances, since we always know that we shall have something or other to execute, without ever knowing what it is.

It is no longer customary with us to give the appellation of a great minister to a wise dispenser of the public revenues, but to a person of dexterity and cunning, who is clever at finding out what we call the ways and means.

16. *Of the Conquests of the Mahometans.* It was this excess of taxes[2] that occasioned the prodigious facility with which the Mahometans carried on their conquests. Instead of a continual series of extortions devised by the subtle avarice of the Greek emperors, the people were subjected to a simple tribute which was paid and collected with ease. Thus they were far happier in obeying a barbarous nation than a corrupt government, in which they suffered every inconvenience of lost liberty, with all the horror of present slavery.

17. *Of the Augmentation of Troops.* A new distemper has spread itself over Europe, infecting our princes, and inducing them to keep up an exorbitant number of troops. It has its redoublings, and of necessity becomes contagious. For as soon as one prince augments his forces, the rest of course do the same; so that nothing is gained thereby but the public ruin. Each monarch keeps as many armies on foot as if his people were in danger of being exterminated: and they give the name of peace[3] to this general effort of all

[1] This is the practice of the emperors of China.

[2] See in history the greatness, the oddity, and even the folly of those taxes. Anastasius invented a tax for breathing, *ut quisque pro haustu aeris penderet.*

[3] True it is that this state of effort is the chief support of the balance, because it checks the great powers.

against all. Thus is Europe ruined to such a degree that were private people to be in the same situation as the three most opulent powers of this part of the globe, they would not have necessary subsistence. We are poor with the riches and commerce of the whole world; and soon, by thus augmenting our troops, we shall be all soldiers, and be reduced to the very same situation as the Tartars.[1]

Great princes, not satisfied with hiring or buying troops of petty states, make it their business on all sides to pay subsidies for alliances, that is, generally to throw away their money.

The consequence of such a situation is the perpetual augmentation of taxes; and the mischief which prevents all future remedy is that they reckon no more upon their revenues, but in waging war against their whole capital. It is no unusual thing to see governments mortgage their funds even in time of peace, and to employ what they call extraordinary means to ruin themselves—means so extraordinary indeed, that such are hardly thought of by the most extravagant young spendthrift.

18. *Of an Exemption from Taxes.* The maxim of the great eastern empires, of exempting such provinces as have very much suffered from taxes, ought to be extended to monarchical states. There are some, indeed, where this practice is established; yet the country is more oppressed than if no such rule took place; because as the prince levies still neither more nor less, the state becomes bound for the whole. In order to ease a village that pays badly, they load another that pays better; the former is not relieved, and the latter is ruined. The people grow desperate, between the necessity of paying for fear of exactions, and the danger of paying for fear of new burdens.

A well-regulated government ought to set aside, for the first article of its expense, a determinate sum to answer contingent cases. It is with the public as with individuals, who are ruined when they live up exactly to their income.

With regard to an obligation for the whole amongst the inhabitants of the same village, some pretend[2] that it is but reasonable, because there is a possibility of a fraudulent

combination on their side: but was it ever heard that, upon mere supposition, we are to establish a thing in itself unjust and ruinous to the state?

19. *Which is more suitable to the Prince and to the People, the farming the Revenues, or managing them by Commission.* The managing of the revenues by commission is like the conduct of a good father of a family, who collects his own rents himself with economy and order.

By this management of the revenues the prince is at liberty to press or to retard the levy of the taxes, either according to his own wants or to those of his people. By this he saves to the state the immense profits of the farmers, who impoverish it in a thousand ways. By this he prevents the people from being mortified with the sight of sudden fortunes. By this the public money passes through few hands, goes directly to the treasury, and consequently makes a quicker return to the people. By this the prince avoids an infinite number of bad laws extorted from him by the importunate avarice of the farmers, who pretend to offer a present advantage for regulations pernicious to posterity.

As the moneyed man is always the most powerful, the farmer renders himself arbitrary even over the prince himself; he is not the legislator, but he obliges the legislator to give laws.

I acknowledge that it is sometimes of use to farm out a new duty, for there is an art in preventing frauds, which motives of interest suggest to the farmers, but commissioners never think of. Now the manner of levying it being once established by the farmer, it may afterwards be safely entrusted to a commission. In England the management of the Excise and of the Post-office was borrowed from that of the farmers of the revenue.

In republics the revenues of the state are generally managed by commission. The contrary practice was a great defect in the Roman government.[3] In despotic governments the people are infinitely happier where this man-

[1] All that is wanting for this is to improve the new invention of the militia established in most parts of Europe, and carry it to the same excess as they do the regular troops.

[2] See *A Treatise on the Roman Finances*, 2, Paris, 1740.

[3] Cæsar was obliged to remove the publicans from the province of Asia, and to establish there another kind of regulation, as we learn from Dio, xlii. 6; and Tacitus, *Annals*, i. 76, informs us that Macedonia and Achaia, provinces left by Augustus to the people of Rome, and consequently governed pursuant to the ancient plan, obtained to be of the number of those which the emperor governed by his officers.

agement is established—witness Persia and China.[1] The unhappiest of all are those where the prince farms out his sea-ports and trading cities. The history of monarchies abounds with mischiefs done by the farmers of the revenue.

Incensed at the oppressive extortions of the publicans, Nero formed a magnanimous but impracticable scheme of abolishing all kinds of imposts. He did not think of managing the revenues by commissioners, but he made four edicts:[2] that the laws enacted against publicans, which had hitherto been kept secret, should be promulgated; that they should exact no claims for above a year backward; that there should be a prætor established to determine their pretensions without any formality; and that the merchants should pay no duty for their vessels. These were the halcyon days of that emperor.

20. *Of the Farmers of the Revenues.* When the lucrative profession of a farmer of the revenue becomes likewise a post of honour, the state is ruined. It may do well enough in despotic governments, where this employment is often-times exercised by the governors themselves. But it is by no means proper in a republic, since a custom of the like nature destroyed that of Rome. Nor is it better in monarchies, nothing being more opposite to the spirit of this government. All the other orders of the state are dissatisfied; honour loses its whole value; the gradual and natural means of distinction are no longer respected; and the very principle of the government is subverted.

It is true indeed that scandalous fortunes were raised in former times; but this was one of the calamities of the Fifty Years' War. These riches were then considered as ridiculous; now we admire them.

Every profession has its particular lot. That of the tax-gatherers is wealth; and wealth is its own reward. Glory and honour fall to the share of that nobility who are sensible of no other happiness. Respect and esteem are for those ministers and magistrates whose whole life is a continued series of labour, and who watch day and night over the welfare of the empire.

•   •   •

BOOK XIV. OF LAWS IN RELATION TO THE NATURE OF THE CLIMATE

1. *General Idea.* If it be true that the temper of the mind and the passions of the heart are extremely different in different climates, the laws ought to be in relation both to the variety of those passions and to the variety of those tempers.

2. *Of the Difference of Men in different Climates.* Cold air constringes the extremities of the external fibres of the body;[3] this increases their elasticity, and favours the return of the blood from the extreme parts to the heart. It contracts[4] those very fibres; consequently it increases also their force. On the contrary, warm air relaxes and lengthens the extremes of the fibres; of course it diminishes their force and elasticity.

People are therefore more vigorous in cold climates. Here the action of the heart and the reaction of the extremities of the fibres are better performed, the temperature of the hu-mours is greater, the blood moves more freely towards the heart, and reciprocally the heart has more power. This superiority of strength must produce various effects; for instance, a greater boldness, that is, more courage; a greater sense of superiority, that is, less desire of revenge; a greater opinion of security, that is, more frankness, less suspicion, policy, and cunning. In short, this must be productive of very different tempers. Put a man into a close, warm place, and for the reasons above given he will feel a great faintness. If under this circumstance you propose a bold enterprise to him, I believe you will find him very little disposed towards it; his present weakness will throw him into despondency; he will be afraid of everything, being in a state of total incapacity. The inhabitants of warm countries are, like old men, timorous; the people in cold countries are, like young men, brave. If we reflect on the late wars,[5] which are more recent in our memory, and in which we can better distinguish some particular effects that escape us at a greater distance of time, we shall find

[1] See Sir John Chardin's *Travels through Persia*, vi.

[2] Tacitus, *Annals*, xiii. 51.

[3] This appears even in the countenance: in cold weather people look thinner.

[4] We know that it shortens iron.

[5] Those for the succession to the Spanish monarchy.

that the northern people, transplanted into southern regions,[1] did not perform such exploits as their countrymen who, fighting in their own climate, possessed their full vigour and courage.

This strength of the fibres in northern nations is the cause that the coarser juices are extracted from their aliments. Hence two things result: one, that the parts of the chyle or lymph are more proper, by reason of their large surface, to be applied to and to nourish the fibres; the other, that they are less proper, from their coarseness, to give a certain subtilty to the nervous juice. Those people have therefore large bodies and but little vivacity.

The nerves that terminate from all parts in the cutis form each a nervous bundle; generally speaking, the whole nerve is not moved, but a very minute part. In warm climates, where the cutis is relaxed, the ends of the nerves are expanded and laid open to the weakest action of the smallest objects. In cold countries the cutis is constinged and the papillæ compressed: the miliary glands are in some measure paralytic; and the sensation does not reach the brain, except when it is very strong and proceeds from the whole nerve at once. Now, imagination, taste, sensibility, and vivacity depend on an infinite number of small sensations.

I have observed the outermost part of a sheep's tongue, where, to the naked eye, it seems covered with papillæ. On these papillæ I have discerned through a microscope small hairs, or a kind of down; between the papillæ were pyramids shaped towards the ends like pincers. Very likely these pyramids are the principal organ of taste.

I caused the half of this tongue to be frozen, and, observing it with the naked eye, I found the papillæ considerably diminished: even some rows of them were sunk into their sheath. The outermost part I examined with the microscope, and perceived no pyramids. In proportion as the frost went off, the papillæ seemed to the naked eye to rise, and with the microscope the miliary glands began to appear.

This observation confirms what I have been saying, that in cold countries the nervous glands are less expanded: they sink deeper into their sheaths, or they are sheltered from the action of external objects; consequently they have not such lively sensations.

In cold countries they have very little sen-

[1] For instance, in Spain.

sibility for pleasure; in temperate countries, they have more; in warm countries, their sensibility is exquisite. As climates are distinguished by degrees of latitude, we might distinguish them also in some measure by those of sensibility. I have been at the opera in England and in Italy, where I have seen the same pieces and the same performers: and yet the same music produces such different effects on the two nations: one is so cold and phlegmatic, and the other so lively and enraptured, that it seems almost inconceivable.

It is the same with regard to pain, which is excited by the laceration of some fibre of the body. The Author of nature has made it an established rule that this pain should be more acute in proportion as the laceration is greater: now it is evident that the large bodies and coarse fibres of the people of the north are less capable of laceration than the delicate fibres of the inhabitants of warm countries; consequently the soul is there less sensible of pain. You must flay a Muscovite alive to make him feel.

From this delicacy of organs peculiar to warm climates it follows that the soul is most sensibly moved by whatever relates to the union of the two sexes: here everything leads to this object.

In northern climates scarcely has the animal part of love a power of making itself felt. In temperate climates, love, attended by a thousand appendages, endeavours to please by things that have at first the appearance, though not the reality, of this passion. In warmer climates it is liked for its own sake, it is the only cause of happiness, it is life itself.

In southern countries a machine of a delicate frame but strong sensibility resigns itself either to a love which rises and is incessantly laid in a seraglio, or to a passion which leaves women in a greater independence, and is consequently exposed to a thousand inquietudes. In northern regions a machine robust and heavy finds pleasure in whatever is apt to throw the spirits into motion, such as hunting, travelling, war, and wine. If we travel towards the north, we meet with people who have few vices, many virtues, and a great share of frankness and sincerity. If we draw near the south, we fancy ourselves entirely removed from the verge of morality; here the strongest passions are productive of all manner of crimes, each man endeavouring, let the means be what they will, to indulge his inordinate desires. In temperate climates we find the inhabitants inconstant in their manners, as well as in their vices and virtues: the climate has not a quality determinate enough to fix them.

The heat of the climate may be so excessive as to deprive the body of all vigour and strength. Then the faintness is communicated to the mind; there is no curiosity, no enterprise, no generosity of sentiment; the inclinations are all passive; indolence constitutes the utmost happiness; scarcely any punishment is so severe as mental employment; and slavery is more supportable than the force and vigour of mind necessary for human conduct.

3. *Contradiction in the Tempers of some Southern Nations.* The Indians[1] are naturally a pusillanimous people; even the children[2] of Europeans born in India lose the courage peculiar to their own climate. But how shall we reconcile this with their customs and penances so full of barbarity? The men voluntarily undergo the greatest hardships, and the women burn themselves; here we find a very odd compound of fortitude and weakness.

Nature, having framed those people of a texture so weak as to fill them with timidity, has formed them at the same time of an imagination so lively that every object makes the strongest impression upon them. That delicacy of organs which renders them apprehensive of death contributes likewise to make them dread a thousand things more than death: the very same sensibility induces them to fly and dare all dangers.

As a good education is more necessary to children than to such as have arrived at maturity of understanding, so the inhabitants of those countries have much greater need than the European nations of a wiser legislator. The greater their sensibility, the more it behoves them to receive proper impressions, to imbibe no prejudices, and to let themselves be directed by reason.

At the time of the Romans the inhabitants of the north of Europe were destitute of arts, education, and almost of laws; and yet the good sense annexed to the gross fibres of those climates enabled them to make an admirable stand against the power of Rome, till the memorable period in which they quitted their woods to subvert that great empire.

4. *Cause of the Immutability of Religion, Manners, Customs, and Laws in the Eastern Countries.* If to that delicacy of organs which renders the eastern nations so susceptible of every impression you add likewise a sort of indolence of mind, naturally connected with that of the body, by means of which they grow incapable of any exertion or effort, it is easy to comprehend that when once the soul has received an impression it cannot change it. This is the reason that the laws, manners, and customs,[3] even those which seem quite indifferent, such as their mode of dress, are the same to this very day in eastern countries as they were a thousand years ago.

5. *That those are bad Legislators who favour the Vices of the Climate, and good Legislators who oppose those Vices.* The Indians believe that repose and non-existence are the foundation of all things, and the end in which they terminate. Hence they consider entire inaction as the most perfect of all states, and the object of their desires. To the Supreme Being they give the title of immovable.[4] The inhabitants of Siam believe that their utmost happiness[5] consists in not being obliged to animate a machine, or to give motion to a body.

In those countries where the excess of heat enervates and exhausts the body, rest is so delicious, and motion so painful, that this system of metaphysics seems natural; and Foe,[6] the legislator of the Indies, was directed by his own sensations when he placed mankind in a state extremely passive; but his doctrine arising from the laziness of the climate favoured it also in its turn; which has been the source of an infinite deal of mischief.

The legislators of China were more rational when, considering men not in the peaceful state which they are to enjoy hereafter, but

---

[1] "One hundred European soldiers," says Tavernier, "would without any great difficulty beat a thousand Indian soldiers."

[2] Even the Persians who settle in the Indies contract in the third generation the indolence and cowardice of the Indians. See Bernier on the Mogul, i, p. 182.

[3] We find by a fragment of Nicolaus Damascenus, collected by Constantine Porphyrogenitus, that it was an ancient custom in the East to send to strangle a governor who had given any displeasure; it was in the time of the Medes.

[4] Panamanack: See Kircher.

[5] La Loubère, *Account of the Kingdom of Siam,* p. 446.

[6] Foe endeavoured to reduce the heart to a mere vacuum: "We have eyes and ears, but perfection consists in neither seeing nor hearing; a mouth, hands, &c., but perfection requires that these members should be inactive." This is taken from the dialogue of a Chinese philosopher, quoted by Father Du Halde, iii.

in the situation proper for discharging the several duties of life, they made their religion, philosophy, and laws all practical. The more the physical causes incline mankind to inaction, the more the moral causes should estrange them from it.

6. *Of Agriculture in warm Climates.* Agriculture is the principal labour of man. The more the climate inclines him to shun this labour, the more the religion and laws of the country ought to incite him to it. Thus the Indian laws, which give the lands to the prince, and destroy the spirit of property among the subjects, increase the bad effects of the climate, that is, their natural indolence.

7. *Of Monkery.* The very same mischiefs result from monkery: it had its rise in the warm countries of the East, where they are less inclined to action than to speculation.

In Asia the number of dervishes or monks seems to increase together with the warmth of the climate. The Indies, where the heat is excessive, are full of them; and the same difference is found in Europe.

In order to surmount the laziness of the climate, the laws ought to endeavour to remove all means of subsisting without labour: but in the southern parts of Europe they act quite the reverse. To those who want to live in a state of indolence, they afford retreats the most proper for a speculative life, and endow them with immense revenues. These men, who live in the midst of plenty which they know not how to enjoy, are in the right to give their superfluities away to the common people. The poor are bereft of property; and these men indemnify them by supporting them in idleness, so as to make them even grow fond of their misery.

8. *An excellent Custom of China.* The historical relations[1] of China mention a ceremony[2] of opening the ground which the emperor performs every year. The design of this public and solemn act is to excite the people to tillage.[3]

Further, the emperor is every year informed of the husbandman who has distinguished

himself most in his profession; and he makes him a mandarin of the eighth order.

Among the ancient Persians[4] the kings quitted their grandeur and pomp on the eighth day of the month, called *Chorrem-ruz,* to eat with the husbandmen. These institutions were admirably calculated for the encouragement of agriculture.

9. *Means of encouraging Industry.* We shall show, in the nineteenth book, that lazy nations are generally proud. Now the effect might well be turned against the cause, and laziness be destroyed by pride. In the south of Europe, where people have such a high notion of the point of honour, it would be right to give prizes to husbandmen who had excelled in agriculture; or to artists who had made the greatest improvements in their several professions. This practice has succeeded in our days in Ireland, where it has established one of the most considerable linen manufactures in Europe.

10. *Of the Laws in relation to the Sobriety of the People.* In warm countries the aqueous part of the blood loses itself greatly by perspiration;[5] it must therefore be supplied by a like liquid. Water is there of admirable use; strong liquors would congeal the globules[6] of blood that remain after the transuding of the aqueous humour.

In cold countries the aqueous part of the blood is very little evacuated by perspiration. They may therefore make use of spirituous liquors, without which the blood would congeal. They are full of humours; consequently strong liquors, which give a motion to the blood, are proper for those countries.

The law of Mahomet, which prohibits the drinking of wine, is therefore fitted to the climate of Arabia: and indeed, before Mahomet's time, water was the common drink of the Arabs. The law[7] which forbade the Carthagin-

---

[1] Father Du Halde, *History of China,* i, p. 72.
[2] Several of the kings of India do the same. La Loubère, *Account of the Kingdom of Siam,* p. 69.
[3] Venty, the third emperor of the third dynasty, tilled the lands himself, and made the empress and his wives employ their time in the silkworks in his palace. *History of China.*

[4] Hyde, *Religion of the Persians.*
[5] Monsieur Bernier, travelling from Lahore to Cashmere, wrote thus: "My body is a sieve; scarcely have I swallowed a pint of water, but I see it transude like dew out of all my limbs, even to my fingers' ends. I drink ten pints a day, and it does me no manner of harm."—Bernier, *Travels,* ii, p. 261.
[6] In the blood there are red globules, fibrous parts, white globules, and water, in which the whole swims.
[7] Plato, *Laws,* ii; Aristotle, *Of the Care of Domestic Affairs;* Eusebius, *Evangelical Preparation,* xii. 17.

ians to drink wine was a law of the climate; and, indeed, the climate of those two countries is pretty nearly the same.

Such a law would be improper for cold countries, where the climate seems to force them to a kind of national intemperance, very different from personal ebriety. Drunkenness predominates throughout the world, in proportion to the coldness and humidity of the climate. Go from the equator to the north pole, and you will find this vice increasing together with the degree of latitude. Go from the equator again to the south pole, and you will find the same vice travelling south,[1] exactly in the same proportion.

It is very natural that where wine is contrary to the climate, and consequently to health, the excess of it should be more severely punished than in countries where intoxication produces very few bad effects to the person, fewer to the society, and where it does not make people frantic and wild, but only stupid and heavy. Hence those laws[2] which inflicted a double punishment for crimes committed in drunkenness were applicable only to a personal, and not to a national, ebriety. A German drinks through custom, and a Spaniard by choice.

In warm countries the relaxing of the fibres produces a great evacuation of the liquids, but the solid parts are less transpired. The fibres, which act but faintly, and have very little elasticity, are not much impaired; and a small quantity of nutritious juice is sufficient to repair them; for which reason they eat very little.

It is the variety of wants in different climates that first occasioned a difference in the manner of living, and this gave rise to a variety of laws. Where people are very communicative there must be particular laws, and others where there is but little communication.

11. *Of the Laws in relation to the Distempers of the Climate.* Herodotus[3] informs us that the Jewish laws concerning the leprosy were borrowed from the practice of the Egyptians. And, indeed, the same distemper required the same remedies. The Greeks and the primitive Romans were strangers to these laws, as well as to the disease. The climate of Egypt and Palestine rendered them necessary; and the facility with which this disease is spread is sufficient to make us sensible of the wisdom and sagacity of those laws.

Even we ourselves have felt the effects of them. The Crusades brought the leprosy amongst us; but the wise regulations made at that time hindered it from infecting the mass of the people.

We find by the law of the Lombards[4] that this disease was spread in Italy before the Crusades, and merited the attention of the legislature. Rotharis ordained that a leper should be expelled from his house, banished to a particular place, and rendered incapable of disposing of his property; because from the very moment he had been turned out of his house he was reckoned dead in the eye of the law. In order to prevent all communication with lepers, they were rendered incapable of civil acts.

I am apt to think that this disease was brought into Italy by the conquests of the Greek emperors, in whose armies there might be some soldiers from Palestine or Egypt. Be that as it may, the progress of it was stopped till the time of the Crusades.

It is related that Pompey's soldiers returning from Syria brought a distemper home with them not unlike the leprosy. We have no account of any regulation made at that time; but it is highly probable that some such step was taken, since the distemper was checked till the time of the Lombards.

It is now two centuries since a disease unknown to our ancestors was first transplanted from the new world to ours, and came to attack human nature even in the very source of life and pleasure. Most of the principal families in the south of Europe were seen to perish by a distemper that had grown too common to be ignominious, and was considered in no other light than in that of its being fatal. It was the thirst of gold that propagated this disease; the Europeans went continually to America, and always brought back a new leaven of it.

Reasons drawn from religion seemed to require that this punishment of guilt should be permitted to continue; but the infection had reached the bosom of matrimony, and given the vicious taint even to guiltless infants.

As it is the business of legislators to watch over the health of the citizens, it would have been a wise part in them to have stopped this communication by laws made on the plan of those of Moses.

---

[1] This is seen in the Hottentots, and the inhabitants of the most southern part of Chili.
[2] As Pittacus did, according to Aristotle, *Politics,* ii. 12. He lived in a climate where drunkenness is not a national vice.
[3] Book ii.
[4] Book ii. tit. 1, § 3; tit. 18, § 1.

The plague is a disease whose infectious progress is much more rapid. Egypt is its principal seat, whence it spreads over the whole globe. Most countries in Europe have made exceedingly good regulations to prevent this infection, and in our times an admirable method has been contrived to stop it; this is by forming a line of troops round the infected country, which cuts off all manner of communication.

The Turks,[1] who have no such regulations, see the Christians escape this infection in the same town, and none but themselves perish; they buy the clothes of the infected, wear them, and proceed in their old way, as if nothing had happened. The doctrine of a rigid fate, which directs their whole conduct, renders the magistrate a quiet spectator; he thinks that everything comes from the hand of God, and that man has nothing more to do than to submit.

12. *Of the Laws against Suicides.* We do not find in history that the Romans ever killed themselves without a cause; but the English are apt to commit suicide most unaccountably; they destroy themselves even in the bosom of happiness. This action among the Romans was the effect of education, being connected with their principles and customs; among the English it is the consequence of a distemper,[2] being connected with the physical state of the machine, and independent of every other cause.

In all probability it is a defect of the filtration of the nervous juice: the machine, whose motive faculties are often unexerted, is weary of itself; the soul feels no pain, but a certain uneasiness in existing. Pain is a local sensation, which leads us to the desire of seeing an end of it; the burden of life, which prompts us to the desire of ceasing to exist, is an evil confined to no particular part.

It is evident that the civil laws of some countries may have reasons for branding suicide with infamy: but in England it cannot be punished without punishing the effects of madness.

13. *Effects arising from the Climate of England.* In a nation so distempered by the climate as to have a disrelish of everything, nay, even of life, it is plain that the government most suitable to the inhabitants is that in which they cannot lay their uneasiness to any single person's charge, and in which, being under the direction rather of the laws than of the prince, it is impossible for them to change the government without subverting the laws themselves.

And if this nation has likewise derived from the climate a certain impatience of temper, which renders them incapable of bearing the same train of things for any long continuance, it is obvious that the government above mentioned is the fittest for them.

This impatience of temper is not very considerable of itself; but it may become so when joined with courage.

It is quite a different thing from levity, which makes people undertake or drop a project without cause; it borders more upon obstinacy, because it proceeds from so lively a sense of misery that it is not weakened even by the habit of suffering.

This temper in a free nation is extremely proper for disconcerting the projects of tyranny,[3] which is always slow and feeble in its commencement, as in the end it is active and lively; which at first only stretches out a hand to assist, and exerts afterwards a multitude of arms to oppress.

Slavery is ever preceded by sleep. But a people who find no rest in any situation, who continually explore every part, and feel nothing but pain, can hardly be lulled to sleep.

Politics is a smooth file, which cuts gradually, and attains its end by a slow progression. Now the people of whom we have been speaking are incapable of bearing the delays, the details, and the coolness of negotiations: in these they are more unlikely to succeed than any other nation; hence they are apt to lose by treaties what they obtain by their arms.

14. *Other Effects of the Climate.* Our ancestors, the ancient Germans, lived in a climate where the passions were extremely calm. Their laws decided only in such cases where the injury was visible to the eye, and went no further. And as they judged of the outrages done to men from the greatness of the wound, they

---

[1] Ricaut, *State of the Ottoman Empire*, p. 284.
[2] It may be complicated with the scurvy, which, in some countries especially, renders a man whimsical and unsupportable to himself. See Pirard, *Voyages*, part II, 21.

[3] Here I take this word for the design of subverting the established power, and especially that of democracy; this is the signification in which it was understood by the Greeks and Romans.

acted with no other delicacy in respect to the injuries done to women. The law of the Alemans[1] on this subject is very extraordinary. If a person uncovers a woman's head, he pays a fine of fifty sous; if he uncovers her leg up to the knee, he pays the same; and double from the knee upwards. One would think that the law measured the insults offered to women as we measure a figure in geometry; it did not punish the crime of the imagination, but that of the eye. But upon the migration of a German nation into Spain, the climate soon found a necessity for different laws. The law of the Visigoths inhibited the surgeons to bleed a free woman, except either her father, mother, brother, son, or uncle was present. As the imagination of the people grew warm, so did that of the legislators; the law suspected everything when the people had become suspicious.

These laws had, therefore, a particular regard for the two sexes. But in their punishments they seem rather to humour the revengeful temper of private persons than to administer public justice. Thus, in most cases, they reduced both the criminals to be slaves to the offended relatives or to the injured husband; a free-born woman[2] who had yielded to the embraces of a married man was delivered up to his wife to dispose of her as she pleased. They obliged the slaves,[3] if they found their master's wife in adultery, to bind her and carry her to her husband; they even permitted her children[4] to be her accusers, and her slaves to be tortured in order to convict her. Thus their laws were far better adapted to refine, even to excess, a certain point of honour than to form a good civil administration. We must not, therefore, be surprised if Count Julian was of opinion that an affront of that kind ought to be expiated by the ruin of his king and country: we must not be surprised if the Moors, with such a conformity of manners, found it so easy to settle and to maintain themselves in Spain, and to retard the fall of their empire.

15. *Of the different Confidence which the Laws have in the People, according to the Difference of Climates.* The people of Japan are of so stubborn and perverse a temper that neither their legislators nor magistrates can put any confidence in them: they set nothing before their eyes but judgments, menaces, and chastisements; every step they take is subject to the inquisition of the civil magistrate. Those laws which out of five heads of families establish one as a magistrate over the other four; those laws which punish a family or a whole ward for a single crime; those laws, in fine, which find nobody innocent where one may happen to be guilty, are made with a design to implant in the people a mutual distrust, and to make every man the inspector, witness, and judge of his neighbour's conduct.

On the contrary, the people of India are mild,[5] tender, and compassionate. Hence their legislators repose great confidence in them. They have established[6] very few punishments; these are not severe, nor are they rigorously executed. They have subjected nephews to their uncles, and orphans to their guardians, as in other countries they are subjected to their fathers; they have regulated the succession by the acknowledged merit of the successor. They seem to think that every individual ought to place entire confidence in the good nature of his fellow-subjects.[7]

They enfranchise their slaves without difficulty, they marry them, they treat them as their children.[8] Happy climate which gives birth to innocence, and produces a lenity in the laws!

[5] See Bernier, ii, p. 140.
[6] See in the *Edifying Letters*, coll. xiv, p. 403, the principal laws or customs of the inhabitants of the peninsula on this side the Ganges.
[7] See *Edifying Letters*, coll, ix, p. 378.
[8] I had once thought that the lenity of slavery in India had made Diodorus say that there was neither master nor slave in that country; but Diodorus has attributed to the whole continent of India what, according to Strabo, xv, belonged only to a particular nation.

[1] Chapter 58, §§ 1, 2.
[2] Law of the Visigoths, iii, tit. 4, § 9.
[3] *Ibid.*, § 6.
[4] *Ibid.*, § 13.

Book XV. In What Manner the Laws of Civil Slavery Relate to the Nature of the Climate

1. *Of civil Slavery*. Slavery, properly so called, is the establishment of a right which gives to one man such a power over another as renders him absolute master of his life and fortune. The state of slavery is in its own nature bad. It is neither useful to the master nor to the slave; not to the slave, because he can do nothing through a motive of virtue; nor to the master, because by having an unlimited authority over his slaves he insensibly accustoms himself to the want of all moral virtues, and thence becomes fierce, hasty, severe, choleric, voluptuous, and cruel.

In despotic countries, where they are already in a state of political servitude, civil slavery is more tolerable than in other governments. Every one ought to be satisfied in those countries with necessaries and life. Hence the condition of a slave is hardly more burdensome than that of a subject.

But in a monarchical government, where it is of the utmost importance that human nature should not be debased or dispirited, there ought to be no slavery. In democracies, where they are all upon equality; and in aristocracies, where the laws ought to use their utmost endeavours to procure as great an equality as the nature of the government will permit, slavery is contrary to the spirit of the constitution: it only contributes to give a power and luxury to the citizens which they ought not to have.

2. *Origin of the Right of Slavery among the Roman Civilians*. One would never have imagined that slavery should owe its birth to pity, and that this should have been excited in three different ways.[1]

The law of nations to prevent prisoners from being put to death has allowed them to be made slaves. The civil law of the Romans empowered debtors, who were subject to be ill-used by their creditors, to sell themselves. And the law of nature requires that children whom a father in a state of servitude is no longer able to maintain should be reduced to the same state as the father.

These reasons of the civilians are all false. It is false that killing in war is lawful, unless in a case of absolute necessity: but when a

man has made another his slave, he cannot be said to have been under a necessity of taking away his life, since he actually did not take it away. War gives no other right over prisoners than to disable them from doing any further harm by securing their persons. All nations[2] concur in detesting the murdering of prisoners in cold blood.

Neither is it true that a freeman can sell himself. Sale implies a price; now when a person sells himself, his whole substance immediately devolves to his master; the master, therefore, in that case, gives nothing, and the slave receives nothing. You will say he has a *peculium*. But this *peculium* goes along with his person. If it is not lawful for a man to kill himself because he robs his country of his person, for the same reason he is not allowed to barter his freedom. The freedom of every citizen constitutes a part of the public liberty, and in a democratic state is even a part of the sovereignty. To sell one's freedom[3] is so repugnant to all reason as can scarcely be supposed in any man. If liberty may be rated with respect to the buyer, it is beyond all price to the seller. The civil law, which authorises a division of goods among men, cannot be thought to rank among such goods a part of the men who were to make this division. The same law annuls all iniquitous contracts; surely then it affords redress in a contract where the grievance is most enormous.

The third way is birth, which falls with the two former; for if a man could not sell himself, much less could he sell an unborn infant. If a prisoner of war is not to be reduced to slavery, much less are his children.

The lawfulness of putting a malefactor to death arises from this circumstance: the law by which he is punished was made for his security. A murderer, for instance, has enjoyed the benefit of the very law which condemns him; it has been a continual protection to him; he cannot, therefore, object to it. But it is not so with the slave. The law of slavery can never be beneficial to him; it is in all cases against him, without ever being for his advantage;

[1] Justinian, *Institutes*, i.

[2] Excepting a few cannibals.
[3] I mean slavery in a strict sense, as formerly among the Romans, and at present in our colonies.

and therefore this law is contrary to the fundamental principle of all societies.

If it be pretended that it has been beneficial to him, as his master has provided for his subsistence, slavery, at this rate, should be limited to those who are incapable of earning their livelihood. But who will take up with such slaves? As to infants, nature, who has supplied their mothers with milk, had provided for their sustenance; and the remainder of their childhood approaches so near the age in which they are most capable of being of service that he who supports them cannot be said to give them an equivalent which can entitle him to be their master.

Nor is slavery less opposed to the civil law than to that of nature. What civil law can restrain a slave from running away, since he is not a member of society, and consequently has no interest in any civil institutions? He can be retained only by a family law, that is, by the master's authority.

3. *Another Origin of the Right of Slavery*. I would as soon say that the right of slavery proceeds from the contempt of one nation for another, founded on a difference in customs.

Lopez de Gama[1] relates that the Spaniards found near St. Martha several basketsful of crabs, snails, grasshoppers, and locusts, which proved to be the ordinary provision of the natives. This the conquerors turned to a heavy charge against the conquered. The author owns that this, with their smoking and trimming their beards in a different manner, gave rise to the law by which the Americans became slaves to the Spaniards.

Knowledge humanises mankind, and reason inclines to mildness; but prejudices eradicate every tender disposition.

4. *Another Origin of the Right of Slavery*. I would as soon say that religion gives its professors a right to enslave those who dissent from it, in order to render its propagation more easy.

This was the notion that encouraged the ravagers of America in their iniquity.[2] Under the influence of this idea they founded their right of enslaving so many nations; for these robbers, who would absolutely be both robbers and Christians, were superlatively devout.

Louis XIII[3] was extremely uneasy at a law by which all the negroes of his colonies were to be made slaves; but it being strongly urged to him as the readiest means for their conversion, he acquiesced without further scruple.

5. *Of the Slavery of the Negroes*. Were I to vindicate our right to make slaves of the negroes, these should be my arguments:

The Europeans, having extirpated the Americans, were obliged to make slaves of the Africans, for clearing such vast tracts of land.

Sugar would be too dear if the plants which produce it were cultivated by any other than slaves.

These creatures are all over black, and with such a flat nose that they can scarcely be pitied.

It is hardly to be believed that God, who is a wise Being, should place a soul, especially a good soul, in such a black ugly body.

It is so natural to look upon colour as the criterion of human nature, that the Asiatics, among whom eunuchs are employed, always deprive the blacks of their resemblance to us by a more opprobrious distinction.

The colour of the skin may be determined by that of the hair, which, among the Egyptians, the best philosophers in the world, was of such importance that they put to death all the red-haired men who fell into their hands.

The negroes prefer a glass necklace to that gold which polite nations so highly value. Can there be a greater proof of their wanting common sense?

It is impossible for us to suppose these creatures to be men, because, allowing them to be men, a suspicion would follow that we ourselves are not Christians.

Weak minds exaggerate too much the wrong done to the Africans. For were the case as they state it, would the European powers, who make so many needless conventions among themselves, have failed to enter into a general one, in behalf of humanity and compassion?

6. *The true Origin of the Right of Slavery*. It is time to inquire into the true origin of the right of slavery. It ought to be founded on the nature of things; let us see if there be any cases where it can be derived thence.

In all despotic governments people make no difficulty in selling themselves; the political slavery in some measure annihilates the civil liberty.

[1] *Biblioth. Ang.*, xiii, part II, art. 3.
[2] See Solis, *History of the Conquest of Mexico*, and Garcilasso de la Vega, *History of the Conquest of Peru*.
[3] Labat, *New Voyage to the Isles of America*, iv, p. 114, 1722, 12mo.

According to Mr. Perry,[1] the Muscovites sell themselves very readily: their reason for it is evident; their liberty is not worth keeping.

At Achim every one is for selling himself. Some of the chief lords[2] have not less than a thousand slaves, all principal merchants, who have a great number of slaves themselves, and these also are not without their slaves. Their masters are their heirs, and put them into trade. In those states, the freemen being over-powered by the government, have no better resource than that of making themselves slaves to the tyrants in office.

This is the true and rational origin of that mild law of slavery which obtains in some countries: and mild it ought to be, as founded on the free choice a man makes of a master, for his own benefit; which forms a mutual convention between the two parties.

7. *Another Origin of the Right of Slavery.* There is another origin of the right of slavery, and even of the most cruel slavery which is to be seen among men.

There are countries where the excess of heat enervates the body, and renders men so sloth-ful and dispirited that nothing but the fear of chastisement can oblige them to perform any laborious duty: slavery is there more rec-oncilable to reason; and the master being as lazy with respect to his sovereign as his slave is with regard to him, this adds a political to a civil slavery.

Aristotle[3] endeavours to prove that there are natural slaves; but what he says is far from proving it. If there be any such, I believe they are those of whom I have been speaking.

But as all men are born equal, slavery must be accounted unnatural, though in some countries it be founded on natural reason; and a wide difference ought to be made be-tween such countries, and those in which even natural reason rejects it, as in Europe, where it has been so happily abolished.

Plutarch, in the Life of Numa, says that in Saturn's time there was neither slave nor mas-ter. Christianity has restored that age in our climates.

8. *Inutility of Slavery among us.* Natural slav-ery, then, is to be limited to some particular parts of the world. In all other countries, even the most servile drudgeries may be performed by freemen. Experience verifies my assertion. Before Christianity had abolished civil slav-ery in Europe, working in the mines was judged too toilsome for any but slaves or male-factors: at present there are men employed in them who are known to live comfortably.[4] The magistrates have, by some small privileg-es, encouraged this profession: to an increase of labour they have joined an increase of gain; and have gone so far as to make those people better pleased with their condition than with any other which they could have embraced.

No labour is so heavy but it may be brought to a level with the workman's strength, when regulated by equity, and not by avarice. The violent fatigues which slaves are made to un-dergo in other parts may be supplied by a skil-ful use of ingenious machines. The Turkish mines in the Bannat of Temeswaer, though richer than those of Hungary, did not yield so much; because the working of them depended entirely on the strength of their slaves.

I know not whether this article be dictated by my understanding or by my heart. Possibly there is not that climate upon earth where the most laborious services might not with proper encouragement be performed by freemen. Bad laws having made lazy men, they have been re-duced to slavery because of their laziness.

9. *Several Kinds of Slavery.* Slavery is of two kinds, real and personal. The real annexes the slave to the land, which Tacitus makes[5] the condition of slaves among the Germans. They were not employed in the family: a stated tribute of corn, cattle, or other movables, paid to their master, was the whole of their servi-tude. And such a servitude still continues in Hungary, Bohemia, and several parts of Low-er Germany.

Personal slavery consists in domestic serv-ices, and relates more to the master's person.

The worst degree of slavery is when it is at once both real and personal, as that of the Helotes among the Lacedæmonians. They un-derwent the fatigues of the field, and suffered all manner of insults at home. This helotism is contrary to the nature of things. Real slav-ery is to be found only among nations remark-able for their simplicity of life:[6] all family

1 *Present State of Russia.*
2 Dampier, *Voyages,* iii.
3 *Politics,* i. 5.

4 As may be seen in the mines of Hartz, in Lower Saxony, and in those of Hungary.
5 *De Moribus Germanorum,* 25.
6 Tacitus, *De Moribus Germanorum,* 20, says the master is not to be distinguished from the slave by any delicacy of living.

business being done by the wives and children. Personal slavery is peculiar to voluptuous nations; luxury requiring the service of slaves in the house. But helotism joins in the same person the slavery established by voluptuous nations and that of the most simple.

10. *Regulations necessary in respect to Slavery.* But of whatsoever kind the slavery be, the civil laws should endeavour on the one hand to abolish the abuses of it, and on the other to guard against its dangers.

11. *Abuses of Slavery.* In Mahometan states,[1] not only the life and goods of female slaves, but also what is called their virtue or honour, are at their master's disposal. One of the misfortunes of those countries is that the greatest part of the nation are born only to be subservient to the pleasures of the other. This servitude is alleviated by the laziness in which such slaves spend their days; which is an additional disadvantage to the state.

It is this indolence which renders the eastern seraglios so delightful to those very persons whom they were made to confine.[2] People who dread nothing but labour may imagine themselves happy in those places of indolence and ease. But this shows how contrary they are to the very intent of the institution of slavery.

Reason requires that the master's power should not extend to what does not appertain to his service: slavery should be calculated for utility, and not for pleasure. The laws of chastity arise from those of nature, and ought in all nations to be respected.

If a law which preserves the chastity of slaves be good in those states where an arbitrary power bears down all before it, how much more will it be so in monarchies, and how much more still in republics?

The law of the Lombards[3] has a regulation which ought to be adopted by all governments. "If a master debauches his slave's wife, the slave and his wife shall be restored to their freedom." An admirable expedient, which, without severity, lays a powerful restraint on the incontinence of masters!

The Romans seem to have erred on this head. They allowed an unlimited scope to the master's lusts, and, in some measure, denied

their slaves the privilege of marrying. It is true, they were the lowest part of the nation; yet there should have been some care taken of their morals, especially as in prohibiting their marriage they corrupted the morals of the citizens.

12. *Danger from the Multitude of Slaves.* The multitude of slaves has different effects in different governments. It is no grievance in a despotic state, where the political servitude of the whole body takes away the sense of civil slavery. Those who are called freedmen in reality are little more so than they who do not come within that class; and as the latter, in quality of eunuchs, freedmen, or slaves, have generally the management of all affairs, the condition of a freedman and that of a slave are very nearly allied. This makes it therefore almost a matter of indifference whether in such states the slaves be few or numerous.

But in moderate governments it is a point of the highest importance that there should not be a great number of slaves. The political liberty of those states adds to the value of civil liberty; and he who is deprived of the latter is also bereft of the former. He sees the happiness of a society, of which he is not so much as a member; he sees the security of others fenced by laws, himself without any protection. He perceives that his master has a soul, capable of enlarging itself: while his own labours under a continual depression. Nothing more assimilates a man to a beast than living among freedmen, himself a slave. Such people as these are natural enemies of society; and their number must be dangerous.

It is not therefore to be wondered at that moderate governments have been so frequently disturbed by the revolts of slaves, and that this so seldom happens in despotic states.[4]

13. *Of armed Slaves.* The danger of arming slaves is not so great in monarchies as in republics. In the former, a warlike people and a body of nobility are a sufficient check upon these armed slaves; whereas the pacific members of a republic would have a hard task to quell a set of men who, having offensive weapons in their hands, would find themselves a match for the citizens.

The Goths, who conquered Spain, spread themselves over the country, and soon became very weak. They made three important regu-

---

[1] Sir John Chardin, *Travels to Persia.*
[2] Sir John Chardin, ii, in his description of the market of Izagour.
[3] Book i, tit. 32, § 5.

[4] The revolt of the Mamelukes was a different case; this was a body of the militia who usurped the empire.

lations: they abolished an ancient custom which prohibited intermarriages with the Romans;[1] they enacted that all the freedmen[2] belonging to the Fiscus should serve in war, under penalty of being reduced to slavery; and they ordained that each Goth should arm and bring into the field the tenth part of his slaves.[3] This was but a small proportion: besides, these slaves thus carried to the field did not form a separate body; they were in the army, and might be said to continue in the family.

14. *The same Subject continued.* When a whole nation is of a martial temper, the slaves in arms are less to be feared.

By a law of the Alemans, a slave who had committed a clandestine theft[4] was liable to the same punishment as a freedman in the like case; but if he was found guilty of an open robbery,[5] he was only bound to restore the things so taken. Among the Alemans, courage and intrepidity extenuated the guilt of an action. They employed their slaves in their wars. Most republics have been attentive to dispirit their slaves; but the Alemans, relying on themselves and being always armed, were so far from fearing theirs that they were rather for augmenting their courage; they were the instruments either of their depredations or of their glory.

15. *Precautions to be used in Moderate Governments.* Lenity and humane treatment may prevent the dangers to be apprehended from the multitude of slaves in a moderate government. Men grow reconciled to everything, and even to servitude, if not aggravated by the severity of the master. The Athenians treated their slaves with great lenity; and this secured that state from the commotions raised by the slaves among the austere Lacedæmonians.

It does not appear that the primitive Romans met with any trouble from their slaves. Those civil broils which have been compared to the Punic wars were the consequence of their having divested themselves of all humanity towards their slaves.[6]

A frugal and laborious people generally treat their slaves more kindly than those who are above labour. The primitive Romans used to live, work, and eat with their slaves; in short, they behaved towards them with justice and humanity. The greatest punishment they made them suffer was to make them pass before their neighbours with a forked piece of wood on their backs. Their manners were sufficient to secure the fidelity of their slaves; so that there was no necessity for laws.

But when the Romans aggrandised themselves; when their slaves were no longer the companions of their labour, but the instruments of their luxury and pride; as they then wanted morals, they had need of laws. It was even necessary for these laws to be of the most terrible kind, in order to establish the safety of those cruel masters who lived with their slaves as in the midst of enemies.

They made the Sillanian *Senatus-Consultum,* and other laws,[7] which decreed that when a master was murdered all the slaves under the same roof, or in any place so near the house as to be within the hearing of a man's voice, should, without distinction, be condemned to die. Those who in this case sheltered a slave, in order to save him, were punished as murderers;[8] he whom his master[9] ordered to kill him, and who obeyed, was reputed guilty; even he who did not hinder him from killing himself was liable to be punished.[10] If a master was murdered on a journey, they put to death those who were with him and those who fled.[11] All these laws operated even against persons whose innocence was proved; the intent of them was to inspire their slaves with a prodigious respect for their master. They were not dependent on the civil government, but on a fault or imperfection of the civil government. They were not derived from the equity of civil laws, since they were contrary to the principle of those laws. They were properly founded on the principles of war, with this difference, that the enemies were in the bosom of the state. The Sillanian *Senatus-Consultum* was derived from the law of nations, which requires that a society, however imperfect, should be preserved.

It is a misfortune in government when the magistrates thus find themselves under the

1 Law of the Visigoths, iii, tit. 1, § 1.
2 *Ibid.,* v, tit. 7, § 20.
3 *Ibid.,* ix, tit. 2, § 9.
4 Law of the Alemans, 5, § 3.
5 *Ibid.,* § 5, *per virtutem.*
6 "Sicily," says Florus, "suffered more in the Servile than in the Punic war."—iii. 19.

7 See the whole title of the *senat. cons. Sillan.,* ff.
8 *Leg. Si quis,* § 12, ff. *de senat. cons. Sillan.*
9 When Antony commanded Eros to kill him, it was the same as commanding him to kill himself; because, if he had obeyed, he would have been punished as the murderer of his master.
10 *Leg.* 1, § 22, ff. *de senat. cons. Sillan.*
11 *Leg.* 1, § 31, ff. *ibid.,* xxix, tit. 5.

necessity of making cruel laws; because they
have rendered obedience difficult, they are
obliged to increase the penalty of disobedience, or to suspect the slave's fidelity. A prudent legislator foresees the ill consequences of
rendering the legislature terrible. The slaves
amongst the Romans could have no confidence in the laws; and therefore the laws
could have none in them.

16. *Regulations between Masters and Slaves.*
The magistrates ought to take care that the
slave has his food and raiment; and this should
be regulated by law.

The laws ought to provide that care be tak-
en of them in sickness and old age. Claudius[1]
decreed that the slaves who in sickness had
been abandoned by their masters should, in
case they recovered, be emancipated. This law
insured their liberty; but should not there
have been some care also taken to preserve
their lives?

When the law permitted a master to take
away the life of his slave, he was invested with
a power which he ought to exercise as judge,
and not as master; it was necessary, therefore,
that the law should ordain those formalities
which remove the suspicion of an act of violence.

When fathers, at Rome, were no longer permitted to put their children to death, the magistrates ordained the punishment which the
father would have inflicted.[2] A like custom between the master and his slaves would be
highly reasonable in a country where masters
have the power of life and death.

The law of Moses was extremely severe. If
a man struck his servant so that he died under
his hand, he was to be punished; but, if he
survived a day or two, no punishment ensued,
because he was his money.[3] Strange that a civil institution should thus relax the law of nature!

By a law of the Greeks,[4] a slave too severely
treated by his master might insist upon being
sold to another. In later times there was a law
of the same nature at Rome.[5] A master displeased with his slave, and a slave with his
master, ought to be separated.

When a citizen uses the slave of another ill,

the latter ought to have the liberty of complaining before the judge. The laws of Plato,[6]
and of most nations, took away from slaves
the right of natural defence. It was necessary
then that they should give them a civil defence.

At Sparta slaves could have no justice
against either insults or injuries. So excessive
was their misery, that they were not only the
slaves of a citizen, but also of the public; they
belonged to all, as well as to one. At Rome,
when they considered the injury done to a
slave, they had regard only to the interest of
the master.[7] In the breach of the Aquilian law
they confounded a wound given to a beast and
that given to a slave; they regarded only the
diminution of their value. At Athens,[8] he who
had abused the slave of another was punished
severely, and sometimes even with death. The
law of Athens was very reasonable in not adding the loss of security to that of liberty.

17. *Of Enfranchisements.* It is easy to perceive
that many slaves in a republican government
create a necessity of making many free. The
evil is, if they have too great a number of
slaves they cannot keep them in due bounds;
if they have too many freedmen, they cannot live, and must become a burden to the
republic: besides, it may be as much in danger
from the multitude of freedmen as from
that of slaves. It is necessary, therefore, that
the law should have an eye to these two inconveniences.

The several laws and decrees of the senate
made at Rome, both for and against slaves,
sometimes to limit, and at other times to facilitate, their enfranchisement, plainly show the
embarrassment in which they found themselves in this respect. There were even times
in which they durst not make laws. When, under Nero,[9] they demanded of the senate permission for the masters to reduce again to slavery the ungrateful freedmen, the emperor declared that it was their duty to decide the affairs of individuals, and to make no general
decree.

Much less can I determine what ought to be
the regulations of a good republic in such an
affair; this depends on too many circumstances. Let us, however, make some reflections.

[1] Xiphilin, *In Claudio.*
[2] See *Leg.* 3, in *Cod., De Patriâ potestate,* by the
Emperor Alexander.
[3] Exod., 21. 20, 21.
[4] Plutarch, *On Superstition.*
[5] See the constitution of Antoninus Pius, *Institutes,* i, tit. 7.

[6] *Laws,* Book ix.
[7] This was frequently the spirit of the laws of
those nations who came out of Germany, as may
be seen by their codes.
[8] Demosthenes, *Orat. contra Midian,* p. 610,
Frankfort, 1604.
[9] Tacitus, *Annals,* xiii. 27.

A considerable number of freedmen ought not suddenly to be made by a general law. We known that among the Volsinienses[1] the freedmen, becoming masters of the suffrages, enacted an abominable law, which gave them the right of lying the first night with the young women married to the free-born.

There are several ways of insensibly introducing new citizens into a republic. The laws may favour the acquiring a *peculium,* and put slaves into a condition of buying their liberty: they may prescribe a term to servitude, like those of Moses, which limited that of the Hebrew slaves to six years.[2] It is easy to enfranchise every year a certain number of those slaves who, by their age, health, or industry, are capable of getting a subsistence. The evil may be even cured in its root, as a great number of slaves are connected with the several employments which are given them; to divide among the free-born a part of these employments, for example, commerce or navigation, is diminishing the number of slaves.

When there are many freedmen, it is necessary that the civil laws should determine what they owe to their patron, or that these duties should be fixed by the contract of enfranchisement.

It is certain that their condition should be more favoured in the civil than in the political state; because, even in a popular government, the power ought not to fall into the hands of the vulgar.

At Rome, where they had so many freedmen, the political laws with regard to them were admirable. They gave them very little, and excluded them almost from nothing: they had even a share in the legislature, but the resolutions they were capable of taking were almost of no weight. They might bear a part in the public offices, and even in the dignity of the priesthood;[3] but this privilege was in some sort rendered useless by the disadvantages they had to encounter in the elections. They had a right to enter into the army; but they were to be registered in a certain class of the *census* before they could be soldiers. Nothing hindered the[4] freedmen from being united by marriage with the families of the free-born; but they were not permitted to mix with those of the senator. In short, their children were free-born, though they were not so themselves.

18. *Of Freedmen and Eunuchs.* Thus in a republican government it is frequently of advantage that the situation of the freedmen be but little below that of the free-born, and that the laws be calculated to remove a dislike of their condition. But in a despotic government, where luxury and arbitrary power prevail, they have nothing to do in this respect; the freedmen generally finding themselves above the free-born. They rule in the court of the prince, and in the palaces of the great; and as they study the foibles and not the virtues of their master, they lead him entirely by the former, not by the latter. Such were the freedmen of Rome in the times of the emperors.

When the principal slaves are eunuchs, let never so many privileges be granted them, they can hardly be regarded as freedmen. For as they are incapable of having a family of their own, they are naturally attached to that of another: and it is only by a kind of fiction that they are considered as citizens.

And yet there are countries where the magistracy is entirely in their hands. "In Tonquin,"[5] says Dampier,[6] "all the mandarins, civil and military, are eunuchs." They have no families, and though they are naturally avaricious, the master or the prince benefits in the end by this very passion.

Dampier tells us, too,[7] that in this country the eunuchs cannot live without women, and therefore marry. The law which permits their marriage may be founded partly on their respect for these eunuchs, and partly on their contempt of the fair sex.

Thus they are trusted with the magistracy, because they have no family; and permitted to marry, because they are magistrates.

Then it is that the sense which remains would fain supply that which they have lost; and the enterprises of despair become a kind of enjoyment. So, in Milton, that spirit who has nothing left but desires, enraged at his degradation, would make use of his impotency itself.

We see in the history of China a great number of laws to deprive eunuchs of all civil and military employments; but they always returned to them again. It seems as if the eunuchs of the east were a necessary evil.

[1] Freinshemius, *Supplement,* dec. 2, v.
[2] Exod., 21.
[3] Tacitus, *Annals,* xiii. 27.
[4] Augustus's speech in Dio, lvi.
[5] It was formerly the same in China. The two Mahometan Arabs who travelled thither in the ninth century use the word eunuch whenever they speak of a governor of the city.
[6] Volume iii, p. 91.
[7] *Ibid.,* p. 94.

Book XVI. How the Laws of Domestic Slavery Bear a Relation to the Nature of the Climate

1. *Of domestic Servitude.* Slaves are established for the family; but they are not a part of it. Thus I distinguish their servitude from that which the women in some countries suffer, and which I shall properly call domestic servitude.

2. *That in the Countries of the South there is a natural Inequality between the two Sexes.* Women, in hot climates, are marriageable at eight, nine, or ten years of age;[1] thus, in those countries, infancy and marriage generally go together. They are old at twenty: their reason therefore never accompanies their beauty. When beauty demands the empire, the want of reason forbids the claim; when reason is obtained, beauty is no more. These women ought then to be in a state of dependence; for reason cannot procure in old age that empire which even youth and beauty could not give. It is therefore extremely natural that in these places a man, when no law opposes it, should leave one wife to take another, and that polygamy should be introduced.

In temperate climates, where the charms of women are best preserved, where they arrive later at maturity, and have children at a more advanced season of life, the old age of their husbands in some degree follows theirs; and as they have more reason and knowledge at the time of marriage, if it be only on account of their having continued longer in life, it must naturally introduce a kind of equality between the two sexes; and, in consequence of this, the law of having only one wife.

In cold countries the almost necessary custom of drinking strong liquors establishes intemperance amongst men. Women, who in this respect have a natural restraint, because they are always on the defensive, have therefore the advantage of reason over them.

Nature, which has distinguished men by their reason and bodily strength, has set no other bounds to their power than those of this strength and reason. It has given charms to women, and ordained that their ascendancy over man shall end with these charms: but in hot countries, these are found only at the beginning, and never in the progress of life.

Thus the law which permits only one wife is physically conformable to the climate of Europe, and not to that of Asia. This is the reason why Mahometanism was so easily established in Asia, and with such difficulty extended in Europe; why Christianity is maintained in Europe, and has been destroyed in Asia; and, in fine, why the Mahometans have made such progress in China, and the Christians so little. Human reasons, however, are subordinate to that Supreme Cause who does whatever He pleases, and renders everything subservient to His will.

Some particular reasons induced Valentinian[2] to permit polygamy in the empire. That law, so improper for our climates, was abrogated by Theodosius, Arcadius, and Honorius.[3]

3. *That a Plurality of Wives greatly depends on the Means of supporting them.* Though in countries where polygamy is once established the number of wives is principally determined by the opulence of the husband, yet it cannot be said that opulence established polygamy in those states, since poverty may produce the same effect, as I shall prove when I come to speak of the savages.

Polygamy, in powerful nations, is less a luxury in itself than the occasion of great luxury. In hot climates they have few wants, and it costs little to maintain a wife and children;[4] they may therefore have a great number of wives.

4. *That the Law of Polygamy is an affair that depends on Calculation.* According to the calculations made in several parts of Europe, there are here born more boys than girls;[5] on

[1] "Mahomet married Cadhisja at five, and took her to his bed at eight years old. In the hot countries of Arabia and the Indies, girls are marriageable at eight years of age, and are brought to bed the year after."—Prideaux, *Life of Mahomet.* We see women in the kingdom of Algiers pregnant at nine, ten, and eleven years of age.—Laugier de Tassis, *History of the Kingdom of Algiers,* p. 61.

[2] See Jornandes, *De Regno et tempor. success.,* and the ecclesiastic historians.
[3] See *Leg. 7, Cod., De Judæis et Cælicolis,* and Nov. 18, cap. v.
[4] In Ceylon a man may live on ten sols a month; they eat nothing there but rice and fish. *Collection of Voyages that Contributed to the Establishment of the East India Company,* ii, part I.
[5] Dr. Arbuthnot finds that in England the num-

the contrary, by the accounts we have of Asia, there are there born more girls than boys.[1] The law which in Europe allows only one wife, and that in Asia which permits many, have therefore a certain relation to the climate.

In the cold climates of Asia there are born, as in Europe, more males than females; and hence, say the Lamas,[2] is derived the reason of that law which amongst them permits a woman to have many husbands.[3]

But it is difficult for me to believe that there are many countries where the disproportion can be great enough for any exigency to justify the introducing either the law in favour of many wives or that of many husbands. This would only imply that a majority of women, or even a majority of men, is more conformable to nature in certain countries than in others.

I confess that if what history tells us be true, that at Bantam there are ten women to one man,[4] this must be a case particularly favourable to polygamy.

In all this I only give their reasons, but do not justify their customs.

5. *The Reason of a Law of Malabar.* In the tribe of the Naires, on the coast of Malabar, the men can have only one wife, while a woman, on the contrary, may have many husbands.[5] The origin of this custom is not I believe difficult to discover. The Naires are the tribe of nobles, who are the soldiers of all those nations. In Europe soldiers are forbidden to marry; in Malabar, where the climate requires greater indulgence, they are satisfied with rendering marriage as little burdensome to them as possible: they give one wife amongst many men, which consequently diminishes the attachment to a family, and the cares of house-

keeping, and leaves them in the free possession of a military spirit.

6. *Of Polygamy considered in itself.* With regard to polygamy in general, independently of the circumstances which may render it tolerable, it is not of the least service to mankind, nor to either of the two sexes, whether it be that which abuses or that which is abused. Neither is it of service to the children; for one of its greatest inconveniences is, that the father and mother cannot have the same affection for their offspring; a father cannot love twenty children with the same tenderness as a mother can love two. It is much worse when a wife has many husbands; for then paternal love only is held by this opinion, that a father may believe, if he will, or that others may believe, that certain children belong to him.

They say that the Emperor of Morocco has women of all colours, white, black, and tawny, in his seraglio. But the wretch has scarcely need of a single colour.

Besides, the possession of so many wives does not always prevent their entertaining desires for those of others;[6] it is with lust as with avarice, whose thirst increases by the acquisition of treasure.

In the reign of Justinian, many philosophers, displeased with the constraint of Christianity, retired into Persia. What struck them the most, says Agathias,[7] was that polygamy was permitted amongst men who did not even abstain from adultery.

May I not say that a plurality of wives leads to that passion which nature disallows? for one depravation always draws on another. I remember that in the revolution which happened at Constantinople, when Sultan Achmet was deposed, history says that the people, having plundered the Kiaya's house, found not a single woman; they tell us that at Algiers,[8] in the greatest part of their seraglios, they have none at all.

7. *Of an Equality of Treatment in case of many Wives.* From the law which permitted a plurality of wives followed that of an equal behaviour to each. Mahomet, who allowed of four, would have everything, as provisions, dress, and conjugal duty, equally divided be-

---

ber of boys exceeds that of girls; but people have been to blame to conclude that the case is the same in all climates.

[1] See Kempfer, who relates that upon numbering the people of Meaco there were found 182,072 males, and 223,573 females.

[2] Father Du Halde, *History of China,* iv, p. 4.

[3] Albuzeir-el-hassen, one of the Mahometan Arabs who, in the ninth century, went into India and China, thought this custom a prostitution. And indeed nothing could be more contrary to the ideas of a Mahometan.

[4] *Collection of Voyages that Contributed to the Establishment of the East India Company,* i.

[5] See Francis Pirard, 27. *Edifying Letters,* coll. iii, x, on the Malleami on the coast of Malabar. This is considered as an abuse of the military profession, as a woman, says Pirard, of the tribe of the Bramins never would marry many husbands.

[6] This is the reason why women in the East are so carefully concealed.

[7] *Life and Actions of Justinian,* p. 403.

[8] Laugier de Tassis, *History of the Kingdom of Algiers.*

tween them. This law is also in force in the Maldivian isles,[1] where they are at liberty to marry three wives.

The law of Moses[2] even declares that if any one has married his son to a slave, and this son should afterwards espouse a free woman, her food, her raiment, and her duty of marriage shall he not diminish. They might give more to the new wife, but the first was not to have less than she had before.

8. Of the Separation of Women from Men.

The prodigious number of wives possessed by those who live in rich and voluptuous countries is a consequence of the law of polygamy. Their separation from men, and their close confinement, naturally follow from the greatness of this number. Domestic order renders this necessary; thus an insolvent debtor seeks to conceal himself from the pursuit of his creditors. There are climates where the impulses of nature have such force that morality has almost none. If a man be left with a woman, the temptation and the fall will be the same thing; the attack certain, the resistance none. In these countries, instead of precepts, they have recourse to bolts and bars.

One of the Chinese classic authors considers the man as a prodigy of virtue who, finding a woman alone in a distant apartment, can forbear making use of force.[3]

9. Of the Connection between domestic and political Government.

In a republic the condition of citizens is moderate, equal, mild, and agreeable; everything partakes of the benefit of public liberty. An empire over the women cannot, among them, be so well exerted; and where the climate demands this empire, it is most agreeable to a monarchical government. This is one of the reasons why it has ever been difficult to establish a popular government in the East.

On the contrary, the slavery of women is perfectly conformable to the genius of a despotic government, which delights in treating all with severity. Thus at all times have we seen in Asia domestic slavery and despotic

1 See Pirard, *Voyages*, 12.
2 Exod., 21. 10, 11.
3 "It is an admirable touch-stone, to find by oneself a treasure, and to know the right owner; or to see a beautiful woman in a lonely apartment; or to hear the cries of an enemy, who must perish without our assistance."—Translation of a Chinese piece of morality, which may be seen in Du Halde, iii, p. 151.

government walk hand in hand with an equal pace.

In a government which requires, above all things, that a particular regard be paid to its tranquillity, and where the extreme subordination calls for peace, it is absolutely necessary to shut up the women; for their intrigues would prove fatal to their husbands. A government which has not time to examine into the conduct of its subjects views them with a suspicious eye, only because they appear and suffer themselves to be known.

Let us only suppose that the levity of mind, the indiscretions, the tastes and caprices of our women, attended by their passions of a higher and a lower kind, with all their active fire, and in that full liberty with which they appear amongst us, were conveyed into an eastern government, where would be the father of a family who could enjoy a moment's repose? The men would be everywhere suspected, everywhere enemies; the state would be overturned, and the kingdom overflowed with rivers of blood.

10. The Principle on which the Morals of the East are founded.

In the case of a multiplicity of wives, the more a family ceases to be united, the more ought the laws to reunite its detached parts in a common centre; and the greater the diversity of interests, the more necessary is it for the laws to bring them back to a common interest.

This is more particularly done by confinement. The women should not only be separated from the men by the walls of the house, but they ought also to be separated in the same enclosure, in such a manner that each may have a distinct household in the same family. Hence each derives all that relates to the practice of morality, modesty, chastity, reserve, silence, peace, dependence, respect, and love; and, in short, a general direction of her thoughts to that which, in its own nature, is a thing of the greatest importance, a single and entire attachment to her family.

Women have naturally so many duties to fulfil—duties which are peculiarly theirs—that they cannot be sufficiently excluded from everything capable of inspiring other ideas; from everything that goes by the name of amusements; and from everything which we call business.

We find the manners more pure in the several parts of the East, in proportion as the confinement of women is more strictly observed. In great kingdoms there are necessarily great lords. The greater their wealth, the more enlarged is their ability of keeping their wives in an exact confinement, and of preventing them from entering again into society. Hence it proceeds that in the empires of Turkey, Persia, of the Mogul, China, and Japan, the manners of their wives are admirable.

But the case is not the same in India, where a multitude of islands and the situation of the land have divided the country into an infinite number of petty states, which from causes that we have not here room to mention are rendered despotic.

There are none there but wretches, some pillaging and others pillaged. Their grandees have very moderate fortunes, and those whom they call rich have only a bare subsistence. The confinement of their women cannot therefore be very strict; nor can they make use of any great precautions to keep them within due bounds; hence it proceeds that the corruption of their manners is scarcely to be conceived.

We may there see to what an extreme the vices of a climate indulged in full liberty will carry licentiousness. It is there that nature has a force and modesty a weakness, which exceeds all comprehension. At Patan[1] the wanton desires of the women are so outrageous, that the men are obliged to make use of a certain apparel to shelter them from their designs.[2] According to Mr. Smith,[3] things are not better conducted in the petty kingdoms of Guinea. In these countries the two sexes lose even those laws which properly belong to each.

11. *Of domestic Slavery independently of Polygamy.* It is not only a plurality of wives which in certain places of the East requires

[1] *Collection of Voyages that Contributed to the Establishment of the East India Company,* ii, part II, p. 196.
[2] In the Maldivian isles the fathers marry their daughters at ten and eleven years of age, because it is a great sin, say they, to suffer them to endure the want of a husband. See Pirard, 12. At Bantam, as soon as a girl is twelve or thirteen years old, she must be married, if they would not have her lead a debauched life. *Collection of Voyages that Contributed to the Establishment of the East India Company,* p. 348.
[3] *Voyage to Guinea,* part II, p. 192. "When the women happen to meet with a man, they lay hold of him, and threaten to make a complaint to their husbands if he slight their addresses. They steal into a man's bed, and wake him; and if he refuses to comply with their desires, they threaten to suffer themselves to be caught *in flagranti.*"

their confinement, but also the climate itself. Those who consider the horrible crimes, the treachery, the dark villainies, the poisonings, the assassinations, which the liberty of women has occasioned at Goa and in the Portuguese settlements in the Indies, where religion permits only one wife; and who compare them with the innocence and purity of manners of the women of Turkey, Persia, Hindostan, China, and Japan, will clearly see that it is frequently as necessary to separate them from the men, when they have but one, as when they have many.

These are things which ought to be decided by the climate. What purpose would it answer to shut up women in our northern countries, where their manners are naturally good; where all their passions are calm; and where love rules over the heart with so regular and gentle an empire that the least degree of prudence is sufficient to conduct it?

It is a happiness to live in those climates which permit such freedom of converse, where that sex which has most charms seems to embellish society, and where wives, reserving themselves for the pleasures of one, contribute to the amusement of all.

12. *Of natural Modesty.* All nations are equally agreed in fixing contempt and ignominy on the incontinence of women. Nature has dictated this to all. She has established the attack, and she has established too the resistance; and having implanted desires in both, she has given to the one boldness, and to the other shame. To individuals she has granted a long succession of years to attend to their preservation: but to continue the species, she has granted only a moment.

It is then far from being true that to be incontinent is to follow the laws of nature; on the contrary, it is a violation of these laws, which can be observed only by behaving with modesty and discretion.

Besides, it is natural for intelligent beings to feel their imperfections. Nature has, therefore, fixed shame in our minds—a shame of our imperfections.

When, therefore, the physical power of certain climates violates the natural law of the two sexes, and that of intelligent beings, it belongs to the legislature to make civil laws, with a view to opposing the nature of the climate and re-establishing the primitive laws.

13. *Of Jealousy.* With respect to nations, we

ought to distinguish between the passion of jealousy and a jealousy arising from customs, manners, and laws. The one is a hot raging fever; the other, cold, but sometimes terrible, may be joined with indifference and contempt.

The one, an abuse of love, derives its source from love itself. The other depends only on manners, on the customs of a nation, on the laws of the country, and sometimes even on religion.[1]

It is generally the effect of the physical power of the climate; and, at the same time, the remedy of this physical power.

14. *Of the Eastern Manner of domestic Government.* Wives are changed so often in the East that they cannot have the power of domestic government. This care is, therefore, committed to the eunuchs, whom they entrust with their keys and the management of their families. "In Persia," says Sir John Chardin, "married women are furnished with clothes as they want them, after the manner of children." Thus that care which seems so well to become them, that care which everywhere else is the first of their concern, does not at all regard them.

15. *Of Divorce and Repudiation.* There is this difference between a divorce and a repudiation, that the former is made by mutual consent, arising from a mutual antipathy; while the latter is formed by the will, and for the advantage of one of the two parties, independently of the will and advantage of the other.

The necessity there is sometimes for women to repudiate, and the difficulty there always is in doing it, render that law very tyrannical which gives this right to men without granting it to women. A husband is the master of the house; he has a thousand ways of confining his wife to her duty, or of bringing her back to it; so that in his hands it seems as if repudiation could be only a fresh abuse of power. But a wife who repudiates only makes use of a dreadful kind of remedy. It is always a great misfortune for her to go in search of a second husband, when she has lost the most part of her attractions with another. One of the advantages attending the charms of youth in the female sex is that in an advanced age the husband is led to complacency and love by the remembrance of past pleasures.

It is then a general rule that in all countries where the laws have given to men the power of repudiating, they ought also to grant it to women. Nay, in climates where women live in domestic slavery, one would think that the law ought to favour women with the right of repudiation, and husbands only with that of divorce.

When wives are confined in a seraglio, the husband ought not to repudiate on account of an opposition of manners; it is the husband's fault if their manners are incompatible.

Repudiation on account of the barrenness of the woman ought never to take place except where there is only one wife:[2] when there are many, this is of no importance to the husband.

A law of the Maldivians permitted them to take again a wife whom they had repudiated.[3] A law of Mexico[4] forbade their being reunited under pain of death. The law of Mexico was more rational than that of the Maldivians: at the time even of the dissolution, it attended to the perpetuity of marriage; instead of this, the law of the Maldivians seemed equally to sport with marriage and repudiation.

The law of Mexico admitted only of divorce. This was a particular reason for their not permitting those who were voluntarily separated to be ever reunited. Repudiation seems chiefly to proceed from a hastiness of temper, and from the dictates of passion; while divorce appears to be an affair of deliberation.

Divorces are frequently of great political use: but as to the civil utility, they are established only for the advantage of the husband and wife, and are not always favourable to their children.

16. *Of Repudiation and Divorce amongst the Romans.* Romulus permitted a husband to repudiate his wife, if she had committed adultery, prepared poison, or procured false keys. He did not grant to women the right of re-

---

[1] Mahomet desired his followers to watch their wives; a certain Iman, when he was dying, said the same thing; and Confucius preached the same doctrine.

[2] It does not follow hence that repudiation on account of sterility should be permitted amongst Christians.

[3] They took them again preferably to any other, because in this case there was less expense.— Pirard, *Travels.*

[4] Solis, *History of the Conquest of Mexico,* p. 499.

pudiating their husbands. Plutarch[1] calls this a law extremely severe.

As the Athenian law[2] gave the power of repudiation to the wife as well as to the husband, and as this right was obtained by the women among the primitive Romans, notwithstanding the law of Romulus, it is evident that this institution was one of those which the deputies of Rome brought from Athens, and which were inserted in the laws of the Twelve Tables.

Cicero says that the reasons of repudiation sprang from the law of the Twelve Tables.[3] We cannot then doubt but that this law increased the number of the reasons for repudiation established by Romulus.

The power of divorce was also an appointment, or at least a consequence, of the law of the Twelve Tables. For from the moment that the wife or the husband had separately the right of repudiation, there was a much stronger reason for their having the power of quitting each other by mutual consent.

The law did not require that they should lay open the causes of divorce.[4] In the nature of the thing, the reasons for repudiation should be given, while those for a divorce are unnecessary; because, whatever causes the law may admit as sufficient to break a marriage, a mutual antipathy must be stronger than them all.

The following fact, mentioned by Dionysius Halicarnassus,[5] Valerius Maximus,[6] and Aulus Gellius,[7] does not appear to me to have the least degree of probability: though they had at Rome, say they, the power of repudiating a wife, yet they had so much respect for the auspices that nobody for the space of five hundred and twenty years ever made[8] use of this right, till Carvilius Ruga repudiated his, because of her sterility. We need only be sensible of the nature of the human mind to perceive how very extraordinary it must be for a law to grant such right to a whole nation, and yet for nobody to make use of it. Coriolanus,

setting out on his exile, advised his[9] wife to marry a man more happy than himself. We have just been seeing that the law of the Twelve Tables and the manners of the Romans greatly extended the law of Romulus. But to what purpose were these extensions if they never made use of a power to repudiate? Besides, if the citizens had such a respect for the auspices that they would never repudiate, how came the legislators of Rome to have less than they? And how came the laws incessantly to corrupt their manners?

All that is surprising in the fact in question will soon disappear, only by comparing two passages in Plutarch. The regal law[10] permitted a husband to repudiate in the three cases already mentioned, and "it enjoined," says Plutarch,[11] "that he who repudiated in any other case should be obliged to give the half of his substance to his wife, and that the other half should be consecrated to Ceres." They might then repudiate in all cases, if they were but willing to submit to the penalty. Nobody had done this before Carvilius Ruga,[12] who, as Plutarch says in another place,[13] "put away his wife for her sterility two hundred and thirty years after Romulus." That is, she was repudiated seventy-one years before the law of the Twelve Tables, which extended both the power and causes of repudiation.

The authors I have cited say that Carvilius Ruga loved his wife, but that the censors made him take an oath to put her away, because of her barrenness, to the end that he might give children to the republic; and that this rendered him odious to the people. We must know the genius and temper of the Romans before we can discover the true cause of the hatred they had conceived against Carvilius. He did not fall into disgrace with the people for repudiating his wife; this was an affair that did not at all concern them. But Carvilius had taken an oath to the censors, that by reason of the sterility of his wife he would repudiate her to give children to the republic. This was a yoke which the people saw the censors were going to put upon them. I shall dis-

---

[1] *Romulus.*

[2] This was a law of **Solon.**

[3] *Mimam res suas sibi habere jussit, ex duodecim tabulis causam addidit.*—Philipp, ii. 69.

[4] Justinian altered this, Nov. 117, cap. x.

[5] Book ii.

[6] Book ii. 4.

[7] Book iv. 3.

[8] According to Dionysius Halicarnassus and Valerius Maximus; and five hundred and twenty-three, according to Aulus Gellius. Neither did they agree in placing this under the same consuls.

[9] See the Speech of Veturia in Dionysius Halicarnassus, viii.

[10] Plutarch, *Romulus.*

[11] *Ibid.*

[12] Indeed sterility is not a cause mentioned by the law of Romulus: but to all appearance he was not subject to a confiscation of his effects, since he followed the orders of the censors.

[13] In his comparison between Theseus and Romulus.

cover, in the prosecution of this work,[1] the repugnance which they always felt to regulations of the like kind. But whence can such a contradiction between those authors arise? It is because Plutarch examined into a fact, and the others have recounted a prodigy.

BOOK XVII. HOW THE LAWS OF POLITICAL SERVITUDE BEAR A RELATION TO THE NATURE OF THE CLIMATE

1. *Of political Servitude.* Political servitude does not less depend on the nature of the climate than that which is civil and domestic; and this we shall now demonstrate.

2. *The Difference between Nations in point of Courage.* We have already observed that great heat enervates the strength and courage of men, and that in cold climates they have a certain vigour of body and mind, which renders them patient and intrepid, and qualifies them for arduous enterprises. This remark holds good, not only between different nations, but even in the different parts of the same country. In the north of China[2] people are more courageous than those in the south; and those in the south of Korea[3] have less bravery than those in the north.

We ought not, then, to be astonished that the effeminacy of the people in hot climates has almost always rendered them slaves; and that the bravery of those in cold climates has enabled them to maintain their liberties. This is an effect which springs from a natural cause.

This has also been found true in America; the despotic empires of Mexico and Peru were near the Line, and almost all the little free nations were, and are still, near the Poles.

3. *Of the Climate of Asia.* The relations of travellers[4] inform us "that the vast continent of the north of Asia, which extends from forty degrees or thereabouts to the Pole, and from the frontiers of Muscovy even to the eastern ocean, is in an extremely cold climate; that this immense tract of land is divided by a chain of mountains which run from west to east, leaving Siberia on the north, and Great Tartary on the south; that the climate of Siberia is so cold that, excepting a few places, it is unsusceptible of cultivation; and that, though the Russians have settlements all along the Irtis, they cultivate nothing; that this country produces only some little firs and shrubs; that the natives of the country are divided into wretched hordes or tribes, like those of Canada; that the reason of this cold proceeds, on the one hand, from the height of the land, and on the other from the mountains, which, in proportion as they run from south to north, are levelled in such a manner that the north wind everywhere blows without opposition; that this wind, which renders Nova Zembla uninhabitable, blowing in Siberia makes it a barren waste; that in Europe, on the contrary, the mountains of Norway and Lapland are admirable bulwarks, which cover the northern countries from the wind; so that at Stockholm, which is about fifty-nine degrees latitude, the earth produces plants, fruits, and corn; and that about Abo, which is sixty-one degrees, and even to sixty-three and sixty-four, there are mines of silver, and the land is fruitful enough."

We see also in these relations "that Great Tartary, situated to the south of Siberia, is also exceedingly cold; that the country will not admit of cultivation; that nothing can be found but pasturage for flocks and herds; that trees will not grow there, but only brambles, as in Iceland; that there are, near China and India, some countries where there grows a kind of millet, but that neither corn nor rice will ripen; that there is scarcely a place in Chinese Tartary at forty-three, forty-four, and forty-five degrees where it does not freeze seven or eight months in the year, so that it is as cold as Iceland, though it might be imagined, from its situation, to be as hot as the south of France; that there are no cities, except four or five towards the eastern ocean, and some which the Chinese, for political reasons, have built near China; that in the rest of Great Tartary there are only a few situated in Buchar, Turkestan, and Cathay; that the reason of this extreme cold proceeds from the nature of the nitrous earth, full of saltpetre and sand, and more particularly from the height of the land. Father Verbiest found that a certain place, eighty leagues north of the great wall,

---

[1] Book xxiii, 21.
[2] Father Du Halde, i, p. 112.
[3] The Chinese books make mention of this. *Ibid.*, iv, p. 448.
[4] See *Travels to the North*, viii; the *History of the Tartars;* and Father Du Halde, iv.

towards the source of Kavamhuran, exceeded the height of the sea near Pekin three thousand geometrical paces; that this height[1] is the cause that though almost all the great rivers of Asia have their source in this country, there is, however, so great a want of water that it can be inhabited only near the rivers and lakes."

These facts being laid down, I reason thus: Asia has properly no temperate zone, as the places situated in a very cold climate immediately touch upon those which are exceedingly hot, that is, Turkey, Persia, India, China, Korea, and Japan.

In Europe, on the contrary, the temperate zone is very extensive, though situated in climates widely different from each other; there being no affinity between the climates of Spain and Italy and those of Norway and Sweden. But as the climate grows insensibly cold upon our advancing from south to north, nearly in proportion to the latitude of each country, it thence follows that each resembles the country joining it; that there is no very extraordinary difference between them, and that, as I have just said, the temperate zone is very extensive.

Hence it comes that in Asia, the strong nations are opposed to the weak; the warlike, brave, and active people touch immediately upon those who are indolent, effeminate, and timorous; the one must, therefore, conquer, and the other be conquered. In Europe, on the contrary, strong nations are opposed to the strong; and those who join each other have nearly the same courage. This is the grand reason of the weakness of Asia, and of the strength of Europe; of the liberty of Europe, and of the slavery of Asia: a cause that I do not recollect ever to have seen remarked. Hence it proceeds that liberty in Asia never increases; whilst in Europe it is enlarged or diminished, according to particular circumstances.

The Russian nobility have indeed been reduced to slavery by the ambition of one of their princes; but they have always discovered those marks of impatience and discontent which are never to be seen in the southern climates. Have they not been able for a short time to establish an aristocratic government? Another of the northern kingdoms has lost its laws; but we may trust to the climate that they are not lost in such a manner as never to be recovered.

[1] Tartary is, then, a kind of flat mountain.

4. *The Consequences resulting from this.* What we have now said is perfectly conformable to history. Asia has been subdued thirteen times; eleven by the northern nations, and twice by those of the south. In the early ages it was conquered three times by the Scythians; afterwards it was subdued once by the Medes, and once by the Persians; again by the Greeks, the Arabs, the Moguls, the Turks, the Tartars, the Persians, and the Afghans. I mention only the Upper Asia, and say nothing of the invasions made in the rest of the south of that part of the world which has most frequently suffered prodigious revolutions.

In Europe, on the contrary, since the establishment of the Greek and Phœnician colonies, we know but of four great changes; the first caused by the conquest of the Romans; the second by the inundation of barbarians, who destroyed those very Romans; the third by the victories of Charlemagne; and the last by the invasions of the Normans. And if this be rightly examined, we shall find, even in these changes, a general strength diffused through all the parts of Europe. We know the difficulty which the Romans met with in conquering Europe, and the ease and facility with which they invaded Asia. We are sensible of the difficulties the northern nations had to encounter in overturning the Roman empire; of the wars and labours of Charlemagne; and of the several enterprises of the Normans. The destroyers were incessantly destroyed.

5. *That when the People in the North of Asia and those of the North of Europe made Conquests, the Effects of the Conquest were not the same.* The nations in the north of Europe conquered as freemen; the people in the north of Asia conquered as slaves, and subdued as others only to gratify the ambition of a master.

The reason is that the people of Tartary, the natural conquerors of Asia, are themselves enslaved. They are incessantly making conquests in the south of Asia, where they form empires: but that part of the nation which continues in the country finds that it is subject to a great master, who, being despotic in the south, will likewise be so in the north, and exercising an arbitrary power over the vanquished subjects, pretends to the same over the conquerors. This is at present most conspicuous in that vast country called Chinese Tartary, which is governed by the emperor, with a power almost as despotic as that of China itself, and which he every day extends by his conquests.

We may likewise see in the history of China that the emperors[1] sent Chinese colonies into Tartary. These Chinese have become Tartars, and the mortal enemies of China; but this does not prevent their carrying into Tartary the spirit of the Chinese government.

A part of the Tartars who were conquerors have very often been themselves expelled; when they have carried into their deserts that servile spirit which they had acquired in the climate of slavery. The history of China furnishes us with strong proofs of this assertion, as does also our ancient history.[2]

Hence it follows that the genius of the Getic or Tartarian nation has always resembled that of the empires of Asia. The people in these are governed by the cudgel; the inhabitants of Tartary by whips. The spirit of Europe has ever been contrary to these manners; and in all ages, what the people of Asia have called punishment those of Europe have deemed the most outrageous abuse.[3]

The Tartars who destroyed the Grecian empire established in the conquered countries slavery and despotic power: the Goths, after subduing the Roman empire, founded monarchy and liberty.

I do not know whether the famous Rudbeck, who in his *Atlantica* has bestowed such praises on Scandinavia, has made mention of that great prerogative which ought to set this people above all the nations upon earth; namely, this country's having been the source of the liberties of Europe—that is, of almost all the freedom which at present subsists amongst mankind.

Jornandes the Goth called the north of Europe the forge of the human race. I should rather call it the forge where those weapons were framed which broke the chains of southern nations. In the north were formed those valiant people who sallied forth and deserted their countries to destroy tyrants and slaves, and to teach men that, nature having made them equal, reason could not render them de-

pendent, except where it was necessary to their happiness.

6. *A new physical Cause of the Slavery of Asia, and of the Liberty of Europe.* In Asia they have always had great empires; in Europe these could never subsist. Asia has larger plains; it is cut out into much more extensive divisions by mountains and seas; and as it lies more to the south, its springs are more easily dried up; the mountains are less covered with snow; and the rivers, being not so large, form more contracted barriers.[4]

Power in Asia ought, then, to be always despotic; for if their slavery was not severe they would soon make a division inconsistent with the nature of the country.

In Europe the natural division forms many nations of a moderate extent, in which the ruling by laws is not incompatible with the maintenance of the state: on the contrary, it is so favourable to it, that without this the state would fall into decay, and become a prey to its neighbours.

It is this which has formed a genius for liberty that renders every part extremely difficult to be subdued and subjected to a foreign power, otherwise than by the laws and the advantage of commerce.

On the contrary, there reigns in Asia a servile spirit, which they have never been able to shake off, and it is impossible to find in all the histories of that country a single passage which discovers a freedom of spirit; we shall never see anything there but the excess of slavery.

7. *Of Africa and America.* This is what I had to say of Asia and Europe. Africa is in a climate like that of the south of Asia, and is in the same servitude. America,[5] being lately destroyed and repeopled by the nations of Europe and Africa, can now scarcely display its genuine spirit; but what we know of its ancient history is very conformable to our principles.

8. *Of the Capital of the Empire.* One of the consequences of what we have been mentioning is, that it is of the utmost importance to a great prince to make a proper choice of the seat of his empire. He who places it to the south-

---

[1] As Vouty V, emperor of the fifth dynasty.
[2] The Scythians thrice conquered Asia, and thrice were driven thence. Justin, ii. 3.
[3] This is in no way contrary to what I shall say in book xxviii. 20 concerning the manner of thinking among the German nations in respect to the cudgel; let the instrument be what it will, the power or action of beating was always considered by them as an affront.

[4] The waters lose themselves or evaporate before or after their streams are united.
[5] The petty barbarous nations of America are called by the Spaniards *Indios Bravos* and are much more difficult to subdue than the great empires of Mexico and Peru.

ward will be in danger of losing the north; but he who fixes it on the north may easily preserve the south. I do not speak of particular cases. In mechanics there are frictions by which the effects of the theory are frequently changed or retarded; and policy has also its frictions.

Book XVIII. Of Laws in the Relation They Bear to the Nature of the Soil

1. *How the Nature of the Soil has an Influence on the Laws.* The goodness of the land, in any country, naturally establishes subjection and dependence. The husbandmen, who compose the principal part of the people, are not very jealous of their liberty; they are too busy and too intent on their own private affairs. A country which overflows with wealth is afraid of pillage, afraid of an army. "Who is there that forms this goodly party?" said Cicero to Atticus;[1] "are they the men of commerce and husbandry? Let us not imagine that these are averse to monarchy—these to whom all governments are equal, as soon as they bestow tranquillity."

Thus monarchy is more frequently found in fruitful countries, and a republican government in those which are not so; and this is sometimes a sufficient compensation for the inconveniences they suffer by the sterility of the land.

The barrenness of the Attic soil established there a democracy; and the fertility of that of Lacedæmonia an aristocratic constitution. For in those times Greece was averse to the government of a single person, and aristocracy bore the nearest resemblance to that government.

Plutarch says[2] that the Cilonian sedition having been appeased at Athens, the city fell into its ancient dissensions, and was divided into as many parties as there were kinds of land in Attica. The men who inhabited the eminences would, by all means, have a popular government; those of the flat, open country demanded a government composed of the chiefs; and they who were near the sea desired a mixture of both.

2. *The same Subject continued.* These fertile provinces are always of a level surface, where the inhabitants are unable to dispute against a stronger power; they are then obliged to submit; and when they have once submitted, the spirit of liberty cannot return; the wealth of the country is a pledge of their fidelity. But in mountainous districts, as they have but little, they may preserve what they have. The liberty they enjoy, or, in other words, the government they are under, is the only blessing worthy of their defence. It reigns, therefore, more in mountainous and rugged countries than in those which nature seems to have most favoured.

The mountaineers preserve a more moderate government, because they are not so liable to be conquered. They defend themselves easily, and are attacked with difficulty; ammunition and provisions are collected and carried against them with great expense, for the country furnishes none. It is, then, a more arduous, a more dangerous, enterprise to make war against them; and all the laws that can be enacted for the safety of the people are there of least use.

3. *What Countries are best cultivated.* Countries are not cultivated in proportion to their fertility, but to their liberty; and if we make an imaginary division of the earth, we shall be astonished to see in most ages deserts in the most fruitful parts, and great nations in those where nature seems to refuse everything.

It is natural for a people to leave a bad soil to seek a better, and not to leave a good soil to go in search of worse. Most invasions have, therefore, been made in countries which nature seems to have formed for happiness; and as nothing is more nearly allied than desolation and invasion, the best provinces are most frequently depopulated, while the frightful countries of the north continue always inhabited, from their being almost uninhabitable.

We find by what historians tell us of the passage of the people of Scandinavia along the banks of the Danube that this was not a conquest, but only a migration into desert countries.

These happy climates must therefore have been depopulated by other migrations, though we know not the tragic scenes that happened.

"It appears by many monuments of antiquity," says Aristotle,[3] "that the Sardinians were

[1] Book vii. 7.
[2] *Solon.*
[3] Or he who wrote the book *De Mirabilibus.*

a Grecian colony. They were formerly very rich; and Aristeus, so famed for his love of agriculture, was their law-giver. But they have since fallen to decay; for the Carthaginians, becoming their masters, destroyed everything proper for the nourishment of man, and forbade the cultivation of the lands on pain of death." Sardinia was not recovered in the time of Aristotle, nor is it to this day.

The most temperate parts of Persia, Turkey, Muscovy, and Poland have not been able to recover perfectly from the devastations of the Tartars.

4. *New Effects of the Fertility and Barrenness of Countries.* The barrenness of the earth renders men industrious, sober, inured to hardship, courageous, and fit for war; they are obliged to procure by labour what the earth refuses to bestow spontaneously. The fertility of a country gives ease, effeminacy, and a certain fondness for the preservation of life. It has been remarked that the German troops raised in those places where the peasants are rich, as, for instance, in Saxony, are not so good as the others. Military laws may provide against this inconvenience by a more severe discipline.

5. *Of the Inhabitants of Islands.* The inhabitants of islands have a higher relish for liberty than those of the continent. Islands are commonly of small extent;[1] one part of the people cannot be so easily employed to oppress the other; the sea separates them from great empires; tyranny cannot so well support itself within a small compass: conquerors are stopped by the sea; and the islanders, being without the reach of their arms, more easily preserve their own laws.

6. *Of Countries raised by the Industry of Man.* Those countries which the industry of man has rendered habitable, and which stand in need of the same industry to provide for their subsistence, require a mild and moderate government. There are principally three of this species: the two fine provinces of Kiang-nan and Tsekiang in China; Egypt, and Holland.

The ancient emperors of China were not conquerors. The first thing they did to aggrandise themselves was what gave the highest proof of their wisdom. They raised from beneath the waters two of the finest provinces of the empire; these owe their existence to the labour of man. And it is the inexpressible fertility of these two provinces which has given Europe such ideas of the felicity of that vast country. But a continual and necessary care to preserve from destruction so considerable a part of the empire demanded rather the manners of a wise than of a voluptuous nation, rather the lawful authority of a monarch than the tyrannic sway of a despotic prince. Power was, therefore, necessarily moderated in that country, as it was formerly in Egypt, and as it is now in Holland, which nature has made to attend to herself, and not to be abandoned to negligence or caprice.

Thus, in spite of the climate of China, where they are naturally led to a servile obedience; in spite of the apprehensions which follow too great an extent of empire, the first legislators of this country were obliged to make excellent laws, and the government was frequently obliged to follow them.

7. *Of human Industry.* Mankind by their industry, and by the influence of good laws, have rendered the earth more proper for their abode. We see rivers flow where there have been lakes and marshes: this is a benefit which nature has not bestowed; but it is a benefit maintained and supplied by nature. When the Persians[2] were masters of Asia, they permitted those who conveyed a spring to any place which had not been watered before to enjoy the benefit for five generations; and as a number of rivulets flowed from Mount Taurus, they spared no expense in directing the course of their streams. At this day, without knowing how they came thither, they are found in the fields and gardens.

Thus, as destructive nations produce evils more durable than themselves, the actions of an industrious people are the source of blessings which last when they are no more.

8. *The general Relation of Laws.* The laws have a very great relation to the manner in which the several nations procure their subsistence. There should be a code of laws of a much larger extent for a nation attached to trade and navigation than for people who are content with cultivating the earth. There should be a much greater for the latter than for those who subsist by their flocks and herds. There must be a still greater for these than for such as live by hunting.

[1] Japan is an exception to this, by its great extent as well as by its slavery.

[2] Polybius, x. 25.

9. *Of the Soil of America.* The cause of there being such a number of savage nations in America is the fertility of the earth, which spontaneously produces many fruits capable of affording them nourishment. If the women cultivate a spot of land around their cottages, the maize grows up presently; and hunting and fishing put the men in a state of complete abundance. Besides, black cattle, as cows, buffaloes, &c., thrive there better than carnivorous beasts. The latter have always reigned in Africa.

We should not, I believe, have all these advantages in Europe if the land was left uncultivated; it would scarcely produce anything besides forests of oaks and other barren trees.

10. *Of Population in the Relation it bears to the Manner of procuring Subsistence.* Let us see in what proportion countries are peopled where the inhabitants do not cultivate the earth. As the produce of uncultivated land is to that of land improved by culture, so the number of savages in one country is to that of husbandmen in another: and when the people who cultivate the land cultivate also the arts, this is also in such proportions as would require a minute detail.

They can scarcely form a great nation. If they are herdsmen and shepherds, they have need of an extensive country to furnish subsistence for a small number; if they live by hunting, their number must be still less, and in order to find the means of life they must constitute a very small nation.

Their country commonly abounds with forests, which, as the inhabitants have not the art of draining off the waters, are filled with bogs; here each troop canton themselves, and form a petty nation.

11. *Of savage and barbarous Nations.* There is this difference between savage and barbarous nations: the former are dispersed clans, which for some particular reason cannot be joined in a body; and the latter are commonly small nations, capable of being united. The savages are generally hunters; the barbarians are herdsmen and shepherds.

This appears plain in the north of Asia. The people of Siberia cannot live in bodies, because they are unable to find subsistence; the Tartars may live in bodies for some time, because their herds and flocks may for a time be reassembled. All the clans may then be reunited, and this is effected when one chief has subdued many others; after which they may do two things—either separate, or set out with a design to make a great conquest in some southern empire.

12. *Of the Law of Nations among People who do not cultivate the Earth.* As these people do not live in circumscribed territories, many causes of strife arise between them; they quarrel about waste land as we about inheritances. Thus they find frequent occasions for war, in disputes in relation either to their hunting, their fishing, the pasture for their cattle, or the violent seizing of their slaves; and as they are not possessed of landed property, they have many things to regulate by the law of nations, and but few to decide by the civil law.

13. *Of the Civil Laws of those Nations who do not cultivate the Earth.* The division of lands is what principally increases the civil code. Among nations where they have not made this division there are very few civil laws.

The institutions of these people may be called *manners* rather than *laws*.

Among such nations as these the old men, who remember things past, have great authority; they cannot there be distinguished by wealth, but by wisdom and valour.

These people wander and disperse themselves in pasture grounds or in forests. Marriage cannot there have the security which it has among us, where it is fixed by the habitation, and where the wife continues in one house; they may then more easily change their wives, possess many, and sometimes mix indifferently like brutes.

Nations of herdsmen and shepherds cannot leave their cattle, which are their subsistence; neither can they separate themselves from their wives, who look after them. All this ought, then, to go together, especially as living generally in a flat open country, where there are few places of considerable strength, their wives, their children, their flocks, may become the prey of their enemies.

The laws regulate the division of plunder, and give, like our Salic laws, a particular attention to theft.

14. *Of the political State of the People who do not cultivate the Land.* These people enjoy great liberty; for as they do not cultivate the earth, they are not fixed: they are wanderers and vagabonds; and if a chief should deprive

them of their liberty, they would immediately go and seek it under another, or retire into the woods, and there live with their families. The liberty of the man is so great among these people that it necessarily draws after it that of the citizen.

15. *Of People who know the Use of Money.* Aristippus, being cast away, swam and got safely to the next shore, where, beholding geometrical figures traced in the sand, he was seized with a transport of joy, judging that he was among Greeks, and not in a nation of barbarians.

Should you ever happen to be cast by some adventure among an unknown people; upon seeing a piece of money you may be assured that you have arrived in a civilised country.

The culture of lands requires the use of money. This culture supposes many inventions and many degrees of knowledge; and we always see ingenuity, the arts, and a sense of want making their progress with an equal pace. All this conduces to the establishment of a sign of value.

Torrents and eruptions have made the discovery that metals are contained in the bowels of the earth.[1] When once they have been separated, they have easily been applied to their proper use.

16. *Of Civil Laws among People who know not the Use of Money.* When a people have not the use of money, they are seldom acquainted with any other injustice than that which arises from violence; and the weak, by uniting, defend themselves from its effects. They have nothing there but political regulations. But where money is established, they are subject to that injustice which proceeds from craft—an injustice that may be exercised in a thousand ways. Hence they are forced to have good civil laws, which spring up with the new practices of iniquity.

In countries where they have no specie, the robber takes only bare movables, which have no mutual resemblance. But where they make use of money, the robber takes the signs, and these always resemble each other. In the former nothing can be concealed, because the robber takes along with him the proofs of his conviction; but in the latter it is quite the contrary.

17. *Of political Laws among Nations who have not the Use of Money.* The greatest security of the liberties of a people who do not cultivate the earth is their not knowing the use of money. What is gained by hunting, fishing, or keeping herds of cattle cannot be assembled in such great quantity, nor be sufficiently preserved, for one man to find himself in a condition to corrupt many others: but when, instead of this, a man has a sign of riches, he may obtain a large quantity of these signs, and distribute them as he pleases.

The people who have no money have but few wants; and these are supplied with ease, and in an equal manner. Equality is then unavoidable; and hence it proceeds that their chiefs are not despotic.

If what travellers tell us be true, the constitution of a nation of Louisiana, called the Natches, is an exception to this. Their chief disposes of the goods of all his subjects, and obliges them to work and toil, according to his pleasure.[2] He has a power like that of the grand signior, and they cannot even refuse him their heads. When the presumptive heir enters the world, they devote all the sucking children to his service during his life. One would imagine that this is the great Sesostris. He is treated in his cottage with as much ceremony as an emperor of Japan or China.

18. *Of the Power of Superstition.* The prejudices of superstition are superior to all others, and have the strongest influence on the human mind. Thus, though the savage nations have naturally no knowledge of despotic tyranny, still they feel the weight of it. They adore the sun; and if their chief had not imagined that he was the brother of this glorious luminary, they would have thought him a wretch like themselves.

19. *Of the Liberty of the Arabs and the Servitude of the Tartars.* The Arabs and Tartars are nations of herdsmen and shepherds. The Arabs find themselves in that situation of which we have been speaking, and are therefore free; whilst the Tartars (the most singular people on earth) are involved in a political slavery.[3] I have already given reasons for this,[4] and shall now assign some others.

They have no towns, no forests, and but

---

[1] It is thus that Diodorus, v. 35, tells us the shepherds found gold in the Pyrenean mountains.

[2] *Edifying Letters,* coll. xx.
[3] When a khan is proclaimed, all the people cry that his word shall be as a sword.
[4] Book xvii. 5.

few marshes; their rivers are generally frozen, and they dwell in a level country of an immense extent. They have pasture for their herds and flocks, and consequently property; but they have no kind of retreat, or place of safety. A khan is no sooner overcome than they cut off his head; his children are treated in the same manner,[1] and all his subjects belong to the conqueror. These are not condemned to a civil slavery, for in that case they would be a burden to a simple people, who have no lands to cultivate, and no need of any domestic service. They therefore add to the bulk of the nation; but instead of civil servitude, a political slavery must naturally be introduced among them.

It is apparent that in a country where the several clans make continual war, and are perpetually conquering each other; in a country where, by the death of the chief, the body politic of the vanquished clan is always destroyed, the nation in general can enjoy but little freedom; for there is not a single party that must not have been often subdued.

A conquered people may preserve some degree of liberty when, by the strength of their situation, they are in a state that will admit of capitulating after their defeat. But the Tartars, always defenceless, being once overcome, can never be able to obtain conditions.

I have said, in chapter 2, that the inhabitants of cultivated plains are seldom free. Circumstances have occurred to put the Tartars, who dwell in uncultivated plains, in the same situation.

20. *Of the Law of Nations as practised by the Tartars.* The Tartars appear to be mild and humane among themselves; and yet they are most cruel conquerors: when they take cities they put the inhabitants to the sword, and imagine that they act humanely if they only sell the people, or distribute them among their soldiers.

They have destroyed Asia, from India even to the Mediterranean; and all the country which forms the east of Persia they have rendered a desert.

The law of nations is owing, I think, to the following cause. These people having no towns, all their wars are carried on with eagerness and impetuosity. They fight whenever they hope to conquer; and when they have no such hope, they join the stronger army. With such customs, it is contrary to the law of nations that a city incapable of repelling their attack should stop their progress. They regard not cities as an association of inhabitants, but as places made to bid defiance to their power. They besiege them without military skill, and expose themselves greatly in the attack; and therefore revenge themselves on all those who have spilled their blood.

21. *The Civil Law of the Tartars.* Father Du Halde says that amongst the Tartars the youngest of the males is always the heir, by reason that as soon as the elder brothers are capable of leading a pastoral life they leave the house with a certain number of cattle, given them by their father, and build a new habitation. The last of the males, who continues at home with the father, is then his natural heir.

I have heard that a like custom was also observed in some small districts of England; and we find it still in Brittany, in the duchy of Rohan, where it obtains with regard to ignoble tenures. This is doubtless a pastoral law conveyed thither by some of the people of Britain, or established by some German nation. By Cæsar and Tacitus we are informed that the latter cultivated but little land.

22. *Of a Civil Law of the German Nations.* I shall here explain how that particular passage of the Salic law which is commonly distinguished by the term "the Salic law" relates to the institutions of a people who do not cultivate the earth, or at least who cultivate it but very little.

The Salic law ordains[2] that, when a man has left children behind him, the males shall succeed to the Salic land in preference to the females.

To understand the nature of those Salic lands, there needs no more than to search into the usages or customs of the Franks with regard to lands before they left Germany.

Mr. Echard has very plainly proved that the word *Salic* is derived from *Sala*, which signifies a house; and therefore that the Salic land was the land belonging to the house. I shall proceed further, and examine into the nature of the house, and of the land belonging to the house, among the Germans.

"They dwell not in towns," says Tacitus, "nor can they bear to have their habitations

---

[1] We ought not therefore to be astonished at Mahomet, the son of Miriveis, who, upon taking Ispahan, put all the princes of the blood to the sword.

[2] Tit. 62.

contiguous to those of others; every one leaves a space or small piece of ground about his house, which is enclosed."[1] Tacitus is very exact in this account, for many laws of the Barbarian codes have different decrees against those who threw down this enclosure, as well as against such as broke into the house.[2]

We learn from Tacitus and Cæsar that the lands cultivated by the Germans were given them only for the space of a year, after which they again became public. They had no other patrimony but the house and a piece of land within the enclosure that surrounded it.[3] It was this particular patrimony which belonged to the males. And, indeed, how could it belong to the daughters? They were to pass into another habitation.

The Salic land was then within that enclosure which belonged to a German house; this was the only property they had. The Franks, after their conquests, acquired new possessions, and continued to call them Salic lands.

When the Franks lived in Germany their wealth consisted of slaves, flocks, horses, arms, &c. The habitation and the small portion of land adjoining it were naturally given to the male children who were to dwell there. But afterwards, when the Franks had by conquest acquired large tracts of land, they thought it hard that the daughters and their children should be incapable of enjoying any part of them. Hence it was that they introduced a custom of permitting the father to settle the estate after his death upon his daughter, and her children. They silenced the law; and it appears that these settlements were frequent, since they were entered in the formularies.[4]

Among these formularies I find one of a singular nature.[5] A grandfather ordained by will that his grandchildren should share his inheritance with his sons and daughters. What then became of the Salic law? In those times either it would not be observed, or the continual use of nominating the daughters to an inheritance had made them consider their ability to succeed as a case authorised by custom.

The Salic law had not in view a preference of one sex to the other, much less had it a regard to the perpetuity of a family, a name, or the transmission of land. These things did not enter into the heads of the Germans; it was purely an economical law, which made the house and the land dependent thereon to the males who should dwell in it, and to whom it consequently was of most service.

We need here only transcribe the title of the Allodial Lands of the Salic law; that famous text of which so many have talked, and which so few have read.

"1. If a man dies without issue, his father or mother shall succeed him. 2. If he has neither father nor mother, his brother or sister shall succeed him. 3. If he has neither brother nor sister, the sister of his mother shall succeed him. 4. If his mother has no sister, the sister of his father shall succeed him. 5. If his father has no sister, the nearest relative by the male side shall succeed. 6. Not any part of the Salic land shall pass to the females; but it shall belong to the males; that is, the male children shall succeed their father."[6]

It is plain that the first five articles relate to the inheritance of a man who dies without issue; and the sixth to the succession of him who has children.

When a man dies without children, the law ordains that neither of the two sexes shall have the preference to the other, except in certain cases. In the first two degrees of succession, the advantages of the males and females were the same; in the third and fourth, the females had the preference; and the males in the fifth.

Tacitus points out the source of these extravagances. "The sister's children," says he, "are as dear to their uncle as to their own father. There are men who regard this degree of kindred as more strict, and even more holy. They prefer it when they receive hostages."[7] Hence it proceeds that our earliest historians speak in such strong terms of the love of the kings of the Franks for their sisters and their

---

[1] *Nullas Germanorum populis urbes habitari satis notum est, ne pati quidem inter se junctas sedes; colunt discreti, ut nemus placuit. Vicos locant, non in nostrum morem connexis et cohærentibus ædificiis: suam quisque domum spatio circumdat.—De Moribus Germanorum,* 16.

[2] The Law of the Alemans, 10, and the Law of the Bavarians, tit. 10, §§ 1, 2.

[3] This inclosure is called *curtis* in the charters.

[4] See Marculfus, ii, form. 10, 12. Appendix to Marculfus, form. 49, and the ancient formularies of Sirmondus, form. 22.

[5] Form. 55, in Lindembroch's collection.

[6] *De terra vero Salica in mulierem nulla portio hereditatis transit, sed hoc virilis sexus acquirit, hoc est filii in ipsa hereditate succedunt.—*Tit. 62, § 6.

[7] *Sororum filiis idem apud avunculum quam apud patrem honor. Quidam sanctiorem arctioremque hunc nexum sanguinis arbitrantur, et in accipiendis obsidibus magis exigunt, tanquam ii et animum firmius et domum latius teneant.—De Moribus Germanorum,* 20.

sisters' children.[1] And, indeed, if the children of the sister were considered in her brother's house as his own children, it was natural for these to regard their aunt as their mother.

The sister of the mother was preferred to the father's sister; this is explained by other texts of the Salic law. When a woman became a widow,[2] she fell under the guardianship of her husband's relatives; the law preferred to this guardianship the relatives by the females before those by the males. Indeed, a woman who entered into a family joining herself with those of her own sex, became more united to her relatives by the female than by the male. Moreover, when a man killed another, and had not wherewithal to pay the pecuniary penalty, the law permitted him to deliver up his substance, and his relatives were to supply the deficiency.[3] After the father, mother, and brother, the sister of the mother was to pay, as if this tie had something in it most tender: now the degree of kindred which imposes the burdens ought also to confer the advantages.

The Salic law enjoins that after the father's sister, the succession should be held by the nearest relative male; but if this relative was beyond the fifth degree, he should not inherit. Thus a female of the fifth degree might inherit to the prejudice of a male of the sixth; and this may be seen in the law of the Ripuarian Franks (a faithful interpreter of the Salic law), under the title of Allodial Lands, where it closely adheres to the Salic law on the same subject.[4]

If the father left issue, the Salic law would have the daughters excluded from the inheritance of the Salic land, and determined that it should belong to the male children.

It would be easy for me to prove that the Salic law did not absolutely exclude the daughters from the possession of the Salic land, but only in the case where they were debarred by their brothers. This appears from the letter of the Salic law; which, after having said that the women shall possess none of the Salic land, but only the males, interprets and restrains itself by adding, "that is, the son shall succeed to the inheritance of the father."

2. The text of the Salic law is cleared up by the law of the Ripuarian Franks, which has also a title on allodial lands very conformable to that of the Salic law.[5]

3. The laws of these barbarous nations who all sprang from Germany interpret each other, more particularly as they all have nearly the same spirit. The Saxon law enjoined the father and mother to leave their inheritance to their son, and not to their daughter; but if there were none but daughters, they were to have the whole inheritance.[6]

4. We have two ancient formularies[7] that state the case in which, according to the Salic law, the daughters were excluded by the males; that is, when they stood in competition with their brother.

5. Another formulary[8] proves that the daughter succeeded to the prejudice of the grandson; she was therefore excluded only by the son.

6. If daughters had been generally debarred by the Salic law from the inheritance of land, it would be impossible to explain the histories, formularies, and charters which are continually mentioning the lands and possessions of the females under the first race.

People have been wrong in asserting that the Salic lands were fiefs.[9] 1. This head is distinguished by the title of allodial lands. 2. Fiefs at first were not hereditary. 3. If the Salic lands had been fiefs, how could Marculfus treat that custom as impious which excluded the women from inheriting, when the males themselves did not succeed to fiefs? 4. The charters which have been cited to prove that the Salic lands were fiefs only show that they were freeholds. 5. Fiefs were not established till after the conquest, and the Salic customs existed long before the Franks left Germany. 6. It was not the Salic law that formed the establishment of fiefs, by setting bounds to the succession of females; but it was the establishment of fiefs that prescribed limits to the succession of females, and to the regulations of the Salic law.

After what has been said, one would not imagine that the perpetual succession of males to the crown of France should have taken its rise

[1] See, in Gregory of Tours, viii. 18, 20 and ix, 16, 20, the rage of Gontram at Leovigild's ill-treatment of Ingunda, his niece, which Childebert her brother took up arms to revenge.
[2] Salic Law, tit. 47.
[3] Ibid., tit. 61, § 1.
[4] Et deinceps usque ad quintum genuculum qui proximus fuerit in hereditatem succedat.—Tit. 56, § 6.
[5] Tit. 56.
[6] Tit. 7, § 1: Pater aut mater defuncti, filio non filiæ hereditatem relinquant; § 4, qui defunctus, non filios, sed filias reliquerit, ad eas omnis hereditas pertineat.
[7] In Marculfus, ii, form. 12, and in the Appendix to Marculfus, form. 49.
[8] Lindembroch's collection, form. 55.
[9] Du Cange, Pithou, &c.

from the Salic law. And yet this is a point indubitably certain. I prove it from the several codes of the barbarous nations. The Salic law,[1] and the law of the Burgundians,[2] debarred the daughters from the right of succeeding to the land in conjunction with their brothers; neither did they succeed to the crown. The law of the Visigoths,[3] on the contrary, permitted the daughters to inherit the land with the brothers:[4] and the women were capable of inheriting the crown.[5] Among these people the regulations of the civil law had an effect on the political.

This was not the only case in which the political law of the Franks gave way to the civil. By the Salic law, all the brothers succeeded equally to the land, and this was also decreed by a law of the Burgundians. Thus, in the kingdom of the Franks, and in that of the Burgundians, all the brothers succeeded to the crown, if we except a few murders and usurpations which took place amongst the Burgundians.

23. *Of the regal Ornaments among the Franks.*
A people who do not cultivate the land have no idea of luxury. We may see, in Tacitus, the admirable simplicity of the German nations: they had no artificial elegances of dress; their ornaments were derived from nature. If the family of their chief was to be distinguished by any sign, it was no other than that which nature bestowed. The kings of the Franks, of the Burgundians, and the Visigoths wore their long hair for a diadem.

24. *Of the Marriages of the Kings of the Franks.* I have already mentioned that with people who do not cultivate the earth, marriages are less fixed than with others, and that they generally take many wives. "Of all the barbarous nations the Germans were almost the only people who were satisfied with one

wife,[6] if we except," says Tacitus, "some persons who, not from a dissoluteness of manners, but because of their nobility, had many."[7]

This explains the reason why the kings of the first race had so great a number of wives. These marriages were less a proof of incontinence than a consequence of dignity: and it would have wounded them in a tender point to have deprived them of such a prerogative.[8] This also explains the reason why the example of the kings was not followed by the subjects.

25. *Childeric.* "The laws of matrimony amongst the Germans," says Tacitus, "are strictly observed. Vice is not there a subject of ridicule. To corrupt or be corrupted is not called fashion, or the custom of the age:[9] there are few examples in this populous nation of the violation of conjugal faith."[10]

This was the reason of the expulsion of Childeric: he shocked their rigid virtue, which conquest had not had time to corrupt.

26. *Of the Time when the Kings of the Franks became of age.* Barbarians who do not cultivate the earth have, strictly speaking, no jurisdiction, and are, as we have already remembered, rather governed by the law of nations than by civil institutions. They are, therefore, always armed. Thus Tacitus tells us "that the Germans undertook no affairs either of a public or private nature unarmed."[11] They gave their vote by the sound of their arms.[12] As soon as they could carry them, they were presented to the assembly;[13] they put a javelin into their hands;[14] and from that moment they were out of their minority: they had been a part of the

---

[1] Tit. 62.
[2] Tit. 1, § 3; tit. 16, § 1; tit. 51.
[3] Book iv, tit. 2, § 1.
[4] The German nations, says Tacitus, *De Moribus Germanorum*, 22, had common customs, as well as those which were peculiar to each.
[5] Among the Ostrogoths, the crown twice devolved to the males by means of females; the first time to Athalaricus, through Amalasuntha, and the second to Theodat, through Amalafreda. Not but that the females of that nation might have held the crown in their own right; for Amalasuntha reigned after the death of Athalaricus; nay, even after the election of Theodat, and in conjunction with that prince. See Amalasuntha's and Theodat's letters, in Cassiodorus, x.

[6] *Prope soli Barbarorum singulis uxoribus contenti sunt.—De Moribus Germanorum*, 18.
[7] *Exceptis admodum paucis qui non libidine, sed ob nobilitatem, plurimis nuptiis ambiuntur.—Ibid.*
[8] See Fredegarius, *Chronicle* of the year 628.
[9] *Severa matrimonia . . . nemo illic vitia ridet, nec corrumpere et corrumpi sæculum vocatur.—De Moribus Germanorum*, 19.
[10] *Paucissima in tam numerosâ gente adulteria. —Ibid.*
[11] *Nihil neque publicæ neque privatæ rei nisi armati agunt.—Ibid.*, 13.
[12] *Si displicuit sententia, fremitu aspernantur; sin placuit, frameas concutiunt.—Ibid.*, 11.
[13] *Sed arma sumere non ante cuiquam moris, quam civitas suffecturum probaverit.—Ibid.*, 13.
[14] *Tum in ipso concilio vel principum aliquis, vel pater, vel propinquus, scuto, frameâque juvenem ornant.*

family, now they became a part of the republic.[1]

"The eagles," said the king of the Ostrogoths,[2] "cease to feed their young ones as soon as their wings and talons are formed; the latter have no need of assistance when they are able themselves to seize their prey: it would be a disgrace if the young people in our armies were thought to be of an age unfit for managing their estates or regulating the conduct of their lives. It is virtue that constitutes full age among the Goths."

Childebert II was fifteen years old when Gontram, his uncle, declared that he was of age, and capable of governing by himself.[3] We find in the Ripuarian laws that the age of fifteen, the ability of bearing arms, and majority, went together. It is there said[4] "that if a Ripuarian dies, or is killed, and leaves a son behind him, that son can neither prosecute, nor be prosecuted, till he has completely attained the age of fifteen; and then he may either answer for himself or choose a champion." It was necessary that his mind should be sufficiently formed to be able to defend himself in court; and that his body should have all the strength that was proper for his defence in single combat. Among the Burgundians,[5] who also made use of this combat in their judiciary proceedings, they were of age at fifteen.

Agathias tells us that the arms of the Franks were light: they might, therefore, be of age at fifteen. In succeeding times the arms they made use of were heavy, and they were already greatly so in the time of Charlemagne, as appears by our capitularies and romances. Those who had fiefs,[6] and were consequently obliged to do military service, were not then of age till they were twenty-one years old.[7]

27. *The same Subject continued.* We have seen that the Germans did not appear in their assemblies before they were of age; they were

a part of the family, but not of the republic. This was the reason that the children of Clodomir, king of Orleans, and conqueror of Burgundy, were not proclaimed kings, because they were of too tender an age to be present at the assembly. They were not yet kings, but they had a right to the regal dignity as soon as they were able to bear arms; and in the meantime, Clotildis, their grandmother, governed the state.[8] But their uncles Clotarius and Childebert assassinated them, and divided their kingdom. This was the cause that in the following ages princes in their minority were proclaimed kings immediately after the death of their fathers. Thus Duke Gondovald saved Childebert II from the cruelty of Chilperic, and caused him to be proclaimed king when he was only five years old.[9]

But even in this change they followed the original spirit of the nation; for the public acts did not pass in the name of the young monarch. So that the Franks had a double administration: the one which concerned the person of the infant king, and the other which regarded the kingdom; and in the fiefs there was a difference between the guardianship and the civil administration.

28. *Of Adoption among the Germans.* As the Germans became of age by the wielding of arms, so they were adopted by the same sign. Thus Gontram, willing to declare his nephew Childebert of age and to adopt him for his son, made use of these words: "I have put this javelin into thy hands as a token that I have given thee all my kingdom."[10] Then, turning towards the assembly, he added, "You see that my son Childebert is grown a man; obey him." Theodoric, king of the Ostrogoths, intending to adopt the king of the Heruli, wrote to him thus:[11] "It is a noble custom of ours to be adopted by arms; for men of courage alone deserve to be our children. Such is the efficacy of this act, that whoever is the object of it had rather die than submit to anything ignominious. Therefore, in compliance with the national usage, and because you are a man of courage, we adopt you for our son by these bucklers, these swords,

---

[1] *Hæc apud illos toga, hic primus juventæ honos; ante hoc domni pars videntur, mox reipublicæ.*

[2] Theodoric in Cassiodorus, i. 38.

[3] He was scarcely five years old, says Gregory of Tours, v. 1, when he succeeded to his father, in the year 575. Gontram declared him of age in the year 585; he was, therefore, at that time no more than fifteen.

[4] Tit. 81.

[5] Tit. 87.

[6] There was no change in the time with regard to the common people.

[7] St. Louis was not of age till twenty-one; this was altered by an edict of Charles V in the year 1374.

[8] It appears from Gregory of Tours, iii, that she chose two natives of Burgundy, which had been conquered by Clodomir, to raise them to the see of Tours, which also belonged to Clodomir.

[9] *Ibid.,* v. 1: *Vix lustro ætatis uno jam peracto qui die Dominicæ Natalis regnare cœpit.*

[10] See *Ibid.,* vii. 23.

[11] In Cassiodorus, iv. 2.

these horses, which we send you as a present."

29. *Of the sanguinary Temper of the Kings of the Franks.* Clovis was not the only prince amongst the Franks who had invaded Gaul. Many of his relatives had penetrated into this country with particular tribes; but as he had met with much greater success, and could grant considerable settlements to such as followed him, the Franks flocked to him from all parts, so that the other chiefs found themselves too weak to resist him. He formed a design of exterminating his whole race, and he succeeded.[1] He feared, says Gregory of Tours,[2] lest the Franks should choose another chief. His children and successors followed this practice to the utmost of their power. Thus the brother, the uncle, the nephew, and, what is still worse, the father or the son, were perpetually conspiring against their whole family. The law continually divided the monarchy; while fear, ambition, and cruelty wanted to reunite it.

30. *Of the national Assemblies of the Franks.* It has been remarked above that nations who do not cultivate the land enjoy great liberty.

This was the case of the Germans. Tacitus says that they gave their kings, or chiefs, a very moderate degree of power;[3] and Cæsar adds further that in times of peace they had no common magistrates; but their princes administered justice in each village.[4] Thus, as Gregory of Tours[5] sufficiently proves, the Franks in Germany had no king.

"The princes," says Tacitus, "deliberate on matters of no great concern; while affairs of importance are submitted to the whole nation, but in such a manner that these very affairs which are under the cognizance of the

people are at the same time laid before the princes."[6] This custom was observed by them after their conquests, as may be seen in all their records.[7]

Tacitus says that capital crimes might be carried before the assembly.[8] It was the same after the conquest, when the great vassals were tried before that body.

31. *Of the Authority of the Clergy under the first Race.* The priests of barbarous nations are commonly invested with power, because they have both that authority which is due to them from their religious character, and that influence which among such a people is the offspring of superstition. Thus we see in Tacitus that priests were held in great veneration by the Germans, and that they presided in the assemblies of the people.[9] They alone were permitted[10] to chastise, to bind, to smite; which they did, not by order of the prince, or as his ministers of justice, but as by an inspiration of that Deity ever supposed to be present with those who made war.

We ought not, therefore, to be astonished when, from the very beginning of the first race, we meet with bishops the dispensers of justice,[11] when we see them appear in the assemblies of the nation; when they have such a prodigious influence on the minds of sovereigns; and when they acquire so large a share of property.

---

[1] Gregory of Tours, ii.

[2] *Ibid.*

[3] *Nec Regibus libera aut infinita potestas. Cæterum neque animadvertere, neque vincire, neque verberare, &c.—De Moribus Germanorum,* 7.

[4] *In pace nullus est communis magistratus, sed principes regionum atque pagorum inter suos jus dicunt.—De Bello Gall.,* vi. 22.

[5] Book ii.

[6] *De minoribus principes consultant, de majoribus omnes; ita tamen ut ea quorum penes plebem arbitrium est, apud principes pertractentur.—De Moribus Germanorum,* 11.

[7] *Lex consensu Populi fit et constitutione Regis.* —*Capitularies of Charles the Bald,* year 864, art. 6.

[8] *Licet apud Concilium accusare et discrimen capitis intendere.—De Moribus Germanorum,* 12.

[9] *Silentium per sacerdotes, quibus et coercendi jus est, imperatur.—Ibid.,* 11.

[10] *Nec Regibus libera aut infinita potestas. Cæterum neque animadvertere, neque vincire, neque verberare, nisi sacerdotibus est permissum, non quasi in pœnam, nec Ducis jussu, sed velut Deo imperante, quem adesse, bellatoribus credunt.—Ibid.,* 7.

[11] See the *Constitutions of Clotarius,* year 560, art. 6.

Book XIX. Of Laws in Relation to the Principles Which Form the General Spirit, Morals, and Customs of a Nation

1. *Of the Subject of this Book.* This subject is very extensive. In that crowd of ideas which presents itself to my mind, I shall be more attentive to the order of things than to the things themselves. I shall be obliged to wander to the right and to the left, that I may investigate and discover the truth.

2. *That it is necessary People's Minds should be prepared for the Reception of the best Laws.* Nothing could appear more insupportable to the Germans than the tribunal of Varus.[1] That which Justinian[2] erected amongst the Lazi, to proceed against the murderers of their king, appeared to them as an affair most horrid and barbarous. Mithridates,[3] haranguing against the Romans, reproached them more particularly for their law proceedings.[4] The Parthians could not bear with one of their kings who, having been educated at Rome, rendered himself affable and easy of access to all.[5] Liberty itself has appeared intolerable to those nations who have not been accustomed to enjoy it. Thus pure air is sometimes disagreeable to such as have lived in a fenny country.

Balbi, a Venetian, being at Pegu, was introduced to the king.[6] When the monarch was informed that they had no king at Venice, he burst into such a fit of laughter that he was seized with a cough, and with difficulty could speak to his courtiers. What legislator could propose a popular government to a people like this?

3. *Of Tyranny.* There are two sorts of tyranny: one real, which arises from oppression; the other is seated in opinion, and is sure to be felt whenever those who govern establish things shocking to the existing ideas of a nation.

Dio[7] tells us that Augustus was desirous of

[1] They cut out the tongues of the advocates, and cried, "Viper, don't hiss."—Tacitus.
[2] Agathias, iv.
[3] Justin, xxxviii.
[4] *Calumnias litium.*—Ibid.
[5] Tacitus.
[6] He has described this interview, which happened in 1596, in the *Collection of Voyages that Contributed to the Establishment of the East India Company,* iii, part I, p. 33.
[7] Book liv. 17, p. 532.

being called Romulus; but having been informed that the people feared that he would cause himself to be crowned king, he changed his design. The old Romans were averse to a king, because they could not suffer any man to enjoy such power; these would not have a king, because they could not bear his manners. For though Cæsar, the Triumvirs, and Augustus were really invested with regal power, they had preserved all the outward appearance of equality, while their private lives were a kind of contrast to the pomp and luxury of foreign monarchs; so that when the Romans were resolved to have no king, this only signified that they would preserve their customs, and not imitate those of the African and eastern nations.

The same writer informs us that the Romans were exasperated against Augustus for making certain laws which were too severe; but as soon as he had recalled Pylades the comedian, whom the jarring of different factions had driven out of the city, the discontent ceased. A people of this stamp have a more lively sense of tyranny when a player is banished than when they are deprived of their laws.

4. *Of the general Spirit of Mankind.* Mankind are influenced by various causes: by the climate, by the religion, by the laws, by the maxims of government, by precedents, morals, and customs; whence is formed a general spirit of nations.

In proportion as, in every country, any one of these causes acts with more force, the others in the same degree are weakened. Nature and the climate rule almost alone over the savages; customs govern the Chinese; the laws tyrannise in Japan; morals had formerly all their influence at Sparta; maxims of government, and the ancient simplicity of manners, once prevailed at Rome.

5. *How far we should be attentive lest the general Spirit of a Nation be changed.* Should there happen to be a country whose inhabitants were of a social temper, open-hearted, cheerful, endowed with taste and a facility in communicating their thoughts; who were sprightly and agreeable; sometimes impru-

dent, often indiscreet; and besides had courage, generosity, frankness, and a certain notion of honour, no one ought to endeavour to restrain their manners by laws, unless he would lay a constraint on their virtues. If in general the character be good, the little foibles that may be found in it are of small importance.

They might lay a restraint upon women, enact laws to reform their manners and to reduce their luxury, but who knows but that by these means they might lose that peculiar taste which would be the source of the wealth of the nation, and that politeness which would render the country frequented by strangers?

It is the business of the legislature to follow the spirit of the nation, when it is not contrary to the principles of government; for we do nothing so well as when we act with freedom, and follow the bent of our natural genius.

If an air of pedantry be given to a nation that is naturally gay, the state will gain no advantage from it, either at home or abroad. Leave it to do frivolous things in the most serious manner, and with gaiety the things most serious.

6. *That Everything ought not to be corrected.* Let them but leave us as we are, said a gentleman of a nation which had a very great resemblance to that we have been describing, and nature will repair whatever is amiss. She has given us a vivacity capable of offending, and hurrying us beyond the bounds of respect: this same vivacity is corrected by the politeness it procures, inspiring us with a taste of the world, and, above all, for the conversation of the fair sex.

Let them leave us as we are; our indiscretions joined to our good nature would make the laws which should constrain our sociability not at all proper for us.

7. *Of the Athenians and Lacedæmonians.* The Athenians, this gentleman adds, were a nation that had some relation to ours. They mingled gaiety with business; a stroke of raillery was as agreeable in the senate as in the theatre. This vivacity, which discovered itself in their councils, went along with them in the execution of their resolves. The characteristic of the Spartans was gravity, seriousness, severity, and silence. It would have been as difficult to bring over an Athenian by teasing as it would a Spartan by diverting him.

8. *Effects of a sociable Temper.* The more communicative a people are, the more easily they change their habits, because each is in a greater degree a spectacle to the other and the singularities of individuals are better observed. The climate which influences one nation to take pleasure in being communicative, makes it also delight in change, and that which makes it delight in change forms its taste.

The society of the fair sex spoils the manners and forms the taste; the desire of giving greater pleasure than others establishes the embellishments of dress; and the desire of pleasing others more than ourselves gives rise to fashions. Thus fashion is a subject of importance; by encouraging a trifling turn of mind, it continually increases the branches of its commerce.[1]

9. *Of the Vanity and Pride of Nations.* Vanity is as advantageous to a government as pride is dangerous. To be convinced of this we need only represent, on the one hand, the numberless benefits which result from vanity, as industry, the arts, fashions, politeness, and taste; on the other, the infinite evils which spring from the pride of certain nations, as laziness, poverty, a total neglect of everything—in fine, the destruction of the nations which have happened to fall under their government, as well as of their own. Laziness is the effect of pride;[2] labour, a consequence of vanity. The pride of a Spaniard leads him to decline labour; the vanity of a Frenchman to work better than others.

All lazy nations are grave; for those who do not labour regard themselves as the sovereigns of those who do.

If we search among all nations, we shall find that for the most part gravity, pride, and indolence go hand in hand.

The people of Achim[3] are proud and lazy; those who have no slaves, hire one, if it be only to carry a quart of rice a hundred paces; they would be dishonoured if they carried it themselves.

In many places people let their nails grow,

[1] *Fable of the Bees.*

[2] The people who follow the khan of Malacamber, those of Carnataca and Coromandel, are proud and indolent; they consume little, because they are miserably poor; while the subjects of the Mogul and the people of Hindostan employ themselves, and enjoy the conveniences of life, like the Europeans.—*Collection of Voyages that Contributed to the Establishment of the East India Company,* i, p. 54.

[3] See Dampier, iii.

that all may see they do not work.

Women in the Indies[1] believe it shameful for them to learn to read: this is, they say, the business of their slaves, who sing their spiritual songs in the temples of their pagods. In one tribe they do not spin; in another they make nothing but baskets and mats; they are not even to pound rice; and in others they must not go to fetch water. These rules are established by pride, and the same passion makes them followed. There is no necessity for mentioning that the moral qualities, according as they are blended with others, are productive of different effects; thus pride, joined to a vast ambition and notions of grandeur, produced such effects among the Romans as are known to all the world.

10. *Of the Character of the Spaniards and Chinese.* The characters of the several nations are formed of virtues and vices, of good and bad qualities. From the happy mixture of these, great advantages result, and frequently where it would be least expected; there are others whence great evils arise—evils which one would not suspect.

The Spaniards have been in all ages famous for their honesty. Justin[2] mentions their fidelity in keeping whatever was entrusted to their care; they have frequently suffered death rather than reveal a secret. They have still the same fidelity for which they were formerly distinguished. All the nations who trade at Cadiz trust their fortunes to the Spaniards, and have never yet repented it. But this admirable quality, joined to their indolence, forms a mixture whence such effects result as to them are most pernicious. The rest of the European nations carry on in their very sight all the commerce of their monarchy.

The character of the Chinese is formed of another mixture, directly opposite to that of the Spaniards; the precariousness of their subsistence[3] inspires them with a prodigious activity, and such an excessive desire of gain, that no trading nation can confide in them.[4] This acknowledged infidelity has secured them the possession of the trade to Japan. No European merchant has ever dared to undertake it in their name, how easy soever it might be for them to do it from their maritime provinces in the north.

---

[1] *Edifying Letters*, coll. xil, p. 80.
[2] Book xliii. 2.
[3] By the nature of the soil and climate.
[4] Father Du Halde, ii.

---

11. *A Reflection.* I have said nothing here with a view to lessen that infinite distance which must ever be between virtue and vice. God forbid that I should be guilty of such an attempt! I would only make my readers comprehend that all political are not all moral vices; and that all moral are not political vices; and that those who make laws which shock the general spirit of a nation ought not to be ignorant of this.

12. *Of Customs and Manners in a despotic State.* It is a capital maxim that the manners and customs of a despotic empire ought never to be changed; for nothing would more speedily produce a revolution. The reason is that in these states there are no laws, that is, none that can be properly called so; there are only manners and customs; and if you overturn these you overturn all.

Laws are established, manners are inspired; these proceed from a general spirit, those from a particular institution: now it is as dangerous, nay more so, to subvert the general spirit as to change a particular institution.

There is less communication in a country where each, either as superior or inferior, exercises or is oppressed by arbitrary power, than there is in those where liberty reigns in every station. They do not, therefore, so often change their manners and behaviour. Fixed and established customs have a near resemblance to laws. Thus it is here necessary that a prince or a legislator should less oppose the manners and customs of the people than in any other country upon earth.

Their women are commonly confined, and have no influence in society. In other countries, where they have intercourse with men, their desire of pleasing, and the desire men also have of giving them pleasure, produce a continual change of customs. The two sexes spoil each other; they both lose their distinctive and essential quality; what was naturally fixed becomes quite unsettled, and their customs and behaviour alter every day.

13. *Of the Behaviour of the Chinese.* But China is the place where the customs of the country can never be changed. Besides their women being absolutely separated from the men, their customs, like their morals, are taught in the schools. A man of letters may be known by his easy address.[5] These things being once taught by precept, and inculcated by grave

---

[5] Father Du Halde.

doctors, become fixed, like the principles of morality, and are never changed.

14. *What are the natural Means of changing the Manners and Customs of a Nation.* We have said that the laws were the particular and precise institutions of a legislator, and manners and customs the institutions of a nation in general. Hence it follows that when these manners and customs are to be changed, it ought not to be done by laws; this would have too much the air of tyranny: it would be better to change them by introducing other manners and other customs.

Thus when a prince would make great alterations in his kingdom, he should reform by law what is established by law, and change by custom what is settled by custom; for it is very bad policy to change by law what ought to be changed by custom.

The law which obliged the Muscovites to cut off their beards and to shorten their clothes, and the rigour with which Peter I made them crop, even to their knees, the long cloaks of those who entered into the cities, were instances of tyranny. There are means that may be made use of to prevent crimes; these are punishments: there are those for changing our customs; these are examples.

The facility and ease with which that nation has been polished plainly shows that this prince had a worse opinion of his people than they deserved; and that they were not brutes, though he was pleased to call them so. The violent measures which he employed were needless; he would have attained his end as well by milder methods.

He himself experienced the facility of bringing about these alterations. The women were shut up, and in some measure slaves; he called them to court; he sent them silks and fine stuffs, and made them dress like the German ladies. This sex immediately relished a manner of life which so greatly flattered their taste, their vanity, and their passions; and by their means it was relished by the men.

What rendered the change the more easy was that their manners at that time were foreign to the climate, and had been introduced among them by conquest and by a mixture of nations. Peter I, in giving the manners and customs of Europe to a European nation, found a facility which he did not himself expect. The empire of the climate is the first, the most powerful, of all empires. He had then no occasion for laws to change the manners and customs of his country; it would have been sufficient to have introduced other manners and other customs.

Nations are in general very tenacious of their customs; to take them away by violence is to render them unhappy: we should not therefore change them, but engage the people to make the change themselves.

All punishment which is not derived from necessity is tyrannical. The law is not a mere act of power; things in their own nature indifferent are not within its province.

15. *The Influence of domestic Government on the political.* This alteration in the manners of women will doubtless have a great influence on the government of Muscovy. One naturally follows the other: the despotic power of the prince is connected with the servitude of women; the liberty of women with the spirit of monarchy.

16. *How some Legislators have confounded the Principles which govern Mankind.* Manners and customs are those habits which are not established by legislators, either because they were not able or were not willing to establish them.

There is this difference between laws and manners, that the laws are most adapted to regulate the actions of the subject, and manners to regulate the actions of the man. There is this difference between manners and customs, that the former principally relate to the interior conduct, the latter to the exterior.

These things have been sometimes confounded.[1] Lycurgus made the same code for the laws, manners, and customs, and the legislators of China have done the same.

We ought not to be surprised that the legislators of China and Sparta should confound the laws, manners, and customs; the reason is, their manners represent their laws, and their customs their manners.

The principal object which the legislators of China had in view was to make their subjects live in peace and tranquillity. They would have people filled with a veneration for one another, that each should be every moment sensible of his dependence on society, and of the obligations he owed to his fellow-citizens. They therefore gave rules of the most extensive civility.

[1] Moses made the same code for laws and religion. The old Romans confounded the ancient customs with the laws.

Thus the inhabitants of the villages of China[1] practise amongst themselves the same ceremonies as those observed by persons of an exalted station; a very proper method of inspiring mild and gentle dispositions, of maintaining peace and good order, and of banishing all the vices which spring from an asperity of temper. In effect, would not the freeing them from the rules of civility be to search out a method for them to indulge their own humours?

Civility is in this respect of more value than politeness. Politeness flatters the vices of others, and civility prevents ours from being brought to light. It is a barrier which men have placed within themselves to prevent the corruption of each other.

Lycurgus, whose institutions were severe, had no regard to civility; in forming the external behaviour he had a view to that warlike spirit with which he would fain inspire his people. A people who were in a continual state of discipline and instruction, and who were endued with equal simplicity and rigour, atoned by their virtues for their want of complaisance.

17. *Of the peculiar Quality of the Chinese Government.* The legislators of China went further.[2] They confounded their religion, laws, manners, and customs; all these were morality, all these were virtue. The precepts relating to these four points were what they called rites; and it was in the exact observance of these that the Chinese government triumphed. They spent their whole youth in learning them, their whole life in the practice. They were taught by their men of letters, they were inculcated by the magistrates; and as they included all the ordinary actions of life, when they found the means of making them strictly observed, China was well governed.

Two things have contributed to the ease with which these rites are engraved on the hearts and minds of the Chinese; one, the difficulty of writing, which during the greatest part of their lives wholly employs their attention,[3] because it is necessary to prepare them to read and understand the books in which they are comprised; the other, that the ritual precepts having nothing in them that is spiritual, but being merely rules of common practice, are more adapted to convince and strike the mind than things merely intellectual.

Those princes who, instead of ruling by these rites, governed by the force of punishments, wanted to accomplish that by punishments which it is not in their power to produce, that is, to give habits of morality. By punishments, a subject is very justly cut off from society, who, having lost the purity of his manners, violates the laws; but if all the world were to lose their moral habits, would these re-establish them? Punishments may be justly inflicted to put a stop to many of the consequences of the general evil, but they will not remove the evil itself. Thus when the principles of the Chinese government were discarded, and morality was banished, the state fell into anarchy, and revolutions succeeded.

18. *A Consequence drawn from the preceding Chapter.* Hence it follows that the laws of China are not destroyed by conquest. Their customs, manners, laws, and religion being the same thing, they cannot change all these at once; and as it will happen that either the conqueror or the conquered must change, in China it has always been the conqueror. For the manners of the conquering nation not being their customs, nor their customs their laws, nor their laws their religion, it has been more easy for them to conform by degrees to the vanquished people than the latter to them.

There still follows hence a very unhappy consequence, which is that it is almost impossible for Christianity ever to be established in China.[4] The vows of virginity, the assembling of women in churches, their necessary communication with the ministers of religion, their participation in the sacraments, auricular confession, extreme unction, the marriage of only one wife—all these overturn the manners and customs of the country, and with the same blow strike at their religion and laws.

The Christian religion, by the establishment of charity, by a public worship, by a participation of the same sacraments, seems to demand that all should be united; while the rites of China seem to ordain that all should be separated.

And as we have seen that this separation[5]

---

[1] See Father Du Halde.

[2] See the classic books from which Father Du Halde gives us some excellent extracts.

[3] It is this which has established emulation, which has banished laziness, and cultivated a love of learning.

[4] See the reasons given by the Chinese magistrates in their decrees for proscribing the Christian religion. *Edifying Letters,* coll. xvii.

[5] See iv. 3, xix. 13.

depends, in general, on the spirit of despotism, this will show us the reason why monarchies, and indeed all moderate governments, are more consistent with the Christian religion.[1]

19. *How this Union of Religion, Laws, Manners, and Customs among the Chinese was effected.* The principal object of government which the Chinese legislators had in view was the peace and tranquillity of the empire; and subordination appeared to them as the most proper means to maintain it. Filled with this idea, they believed it their duty to inspire a respect for parents, and therefore exerted all their power to effect it. They established an infinite number of rites and ceremonies to do them honour when living, and after their death. It was impossible for them to pay such honours to deceased parents without being led to reverence the living. The ceremonies at the death of a father were more nearly related to religion; those for a living parent had a greater relation to the laws, manners, and customs: however, these were only parts of the same code; but this code was very extensive.

A veneration for their parents was necessarily connected with a suitable respect for all who represented them; such as old men, masters, magistrates, and the sovereign. This respect for parents supposed a return of love towards children, and consequently the same return from old men to the young, from magistrates to those who were under their jurisdiction, and from the emperor to his subjects. This formed the rites, and these rites the general spirit of the nation.

We shall now show the relation which things in appearance the most indifferent may bear to the fundamental constitution of China. This empire is formed on the plan of a government of a family. If you diminish the paternal authority, or even if you retrench the ceremonies which express your respect for it, you weaken the reverence due to magistrates, who are considered as fathers; nor would the magistrates have the same care of the people, whom they ought to look upon as their children; and that tender relation which subsists between the prince and his subjects would insensibly be lost. Retrench but one of these habits and you overturn the state. It is a thing in itself very indifferent whether the daughter-in-law rises every morning to pay such and such duties to her mother-in-law; but if we

[1] See xxiv. 3.

consider that these exterior habits incessantly revive an idea necessary to be imprinted on all minds—an idea that forms the ruling spirit of the empire—we shall see that it is necessary that such or such a particular action be performed.

20. *Explanation of a Paradox relating to the Chinese.* It is very remarkable that the Chinese, whose lives are guided by rites, are nevertheless the greatest cheats upon earth. This appears chiefly in their trade, which, in spite of its natural tendency, has never been able to make them honest. He who buys of them ought to carry with him his own weights;[2] every merchant having three sorts, the one heavy for buying, another light for selling, and another of the true standard for those who are upon their guard. It is possible, I believe, to explain this contradiction.

The legislators of China had two objects in view: they were desirous that the people should be submissive and peaceful, and that they should also be laborious and industrious. By the nature of the soil and climate, their subsistence is very precarious; nor can it be in any other way secured than by industry and labour.

When every one obeys, and every one is employed, the state is in a happy situation. It is necessity, and perhaps the nature of the climate, that has given to the Chinese an inconceivable greediness for gain, and laws have never been made to restrain it. Everything has been forbidden when acquired by acts of violence; everything permitted when obtained by artifice or labour. Let us not then compare the morals of China with those of Europe. Every one in China is obliged to be attentive to what will be for his advantage; if the cheat has been watchful over his own interest, he who is the dupe ought to be attentive to his. At Sparta they were permitted to steal; in China they are suffered to deceive.

21. *How the Laws ought to have a Relation to Manners and Customs.* It is only singular institutions which thus confound laws, manners, and customs—things naturally distinct and separate; but though they are in themselves different, there is nevertheless a great relation between them.

Solon being asked if the laws he had given to the Athenians were the best, he replied, "I

[2] Lange, *Journal* in 1721 and 1722; in *Voyages to the North,* viii, p. 363.

have given them the best they were able to bear"[1]—a fine expression, that ought to be perfectly understood by all legislators! When Divine Wisdom said to the Jews, "I have given you precepts which are not good," this signified that they had only a relative goodness; which is the sponge that wipes out all the difficulties in the law of Moses.

22. *The same Subject continued.* When a people have pure and regular manners, their laws become simple and natural. Plato[2] says that Rhadamanthus, who governed a nation extremely religious, finished every process with extraordinary despatch, administering only the oath on each accusation. "But," says the same Plato,[3] "when a people are not religious we should never have recourse to an oath, except he who swears is entirely disinterested, as in the case of a judge and a witness."

23. *How the Laws are founded on the Manners of a People.* At the time when the manners of the Romans were pure, they had no particular law against the embezzlement of the public money. When this crime began to appear, it was thought so infamous, that to be condemned to restore[4] what they had taken was considered as a sufficient disgrace: for a proof of this, see the sentence of L. Scipio.[5]

24. *The same Subject continued.* The laws which gave the right of tutelage to the mother were most attentive to the preservation of the infant's person; those which granted it to the next heir were most attentive to the preservation of the state. When the manners of a people are corrupted, it is much better to give the tutelage to the mother. Among those whose laws confide in the manners of the subjects, the guardianship is granted either to the next heir or to the mother, and sometimes to both.

If we reflect on the Roman laws, we shall find that the spirit of these was conformable to what I have advanced. At the time when the laws of the Twelve Tables were made, the manners of the Romans were most admirable. The guardianship was given to the nearest relative of the infant, from a consideration that he ought to have the trouble of the tutelage who might enjoy the advantage of possessing the inheritance. They did not imagine the life

of the heir in danger though it was put into a person's hands who would reap a benefit by his death. But when the manners of Rome were changed, her legislators altered their conduct. "If, in the pupillary substitution," say Gaius[6] and Justinian,[7] "the testator is afraid that the substitute will lay any snares for the pupil, he may leave the vulgar substitution open,[8] and put the pupillary into a part of the testament, which cannot be opened till after a certain time." These fears and precautions were unknown to the primitive Romans.

25. *The same Subject continued.* The Roman law gave the liberty of making presents before marriage; after the marriage they were not allowed. This was founded on the manners of the Romans, who were led to marriage only by frugality, simplicity, and modesty; but might suffer themselves to be seduced by domestic cares, by complacency, and the constant tenor of conjugal felicity.

A law of the Visigoths[9] forbade the man giving more to the woman he was to marry than the tenth part of his substance, and his giving her anything during the first year of their marriage. This also took its rise from the manners of the country. The legislators were willing to put a stop to that Spanish ostentation which only led them to display an excessive liberality in acts of magnificence.

The Romans by their laws put a stop to some of the inconveniences which arose from the most durable empire in the world—that of virtue; the Spaniards, by theirs, would prevent the bad effects of a tyranny the most frail and transitory—that of beauty.

26. *The same Subject continued.* The law of Theodosius and Valentinian[10] drew the causes of repudiation from the ancient manners and customs of the Romans.[11] It placed in the number of these causes the behaviour of the husband who beat his wife[12] in a manner that

[6] *Institutes*, ii. tit. 6, § 2. Ozel's compilation, Leyden, 1658.
[7] *Ibid.*, ii., *De Pupil. substit.* § 3.
[8] The form of the vulgar substitution ran thus: "If such a one is unwilling to take the inheritance, I substitute in his stead," &c.; the pupillary substitution: "If such a one dies before he arrives at the age of puberty, I substitute," &c.
[9] Book iii, tit. 5, § 5.
[10] *Leg.* 8, *Cod.*, *De Repud.*
[11] And the law of the Twelve Tables. See Cicero, *Philipp.*, ii. 69.
[12] *Si verberibus quæ ingenuis aliena sunt, afficientem probaverit.*

[1] Plutarch, *Solon.* [2] *Laws*, xii. [3] *Ibid.*, xii.
[4] *In simplum.*
[5] Livy, xxxviii.

disgraced the character of a free-born woman. This cause was omitted in the following laws:[1] for their manners, in this respect, had undergone a change, the eastern customs having banished those of Europe. The first eunuch of the empress, wife to Justinian II, threatened, says the historian, to chastise her in the same manner as children are punished at school. Nothing but established manners, or those which they were seeking to establish, could raise even an idea of this kind.

We have seen how the laws follow the manners of a people; let us now observe how the manners follow the laws.

27. How the Laws contribute to form the Manners, Customs, and Character of a Nation.

The customs of an enslaved people are a part of their servitude, those of a free people are a part of their liberty.

I have spoken in the eleventh book[2] of a free people, and have given the principles of their constitution: let us now see the effects which follow from this liberty, the character it is capable of forming, and the customs which naturally result from it.

I do not deny that the climate may have produced a great part of the laws, manners, and customs of this nation; but I maintain that its manners and customs have a close connection with its laws.

As there are in this state two visible powers —the legislative and executive, and as every citizen has a will of his own, and may at pleasure assert his independence, most men have a greater fondness for one of these powers than for the other, and the multitude have commonly neither equity nor sense enough to show an equal affection to both.

And as the executive power, by disposing of all employments, may give great hopes, and no fears, every man who obtains any favour from it is ready to espouse its cause; while it is liable to be attacked by those who have nothing to hope from it.

All the passions being unrestrained, hatred, envy, jealousy, and an ambitious desire of riches and honours, appears in their extent; were it otherwise, the state would be in the condition of a man weakened by sickness, who is without passions because he is without strength.

The hatred which arises between the two

parties will always subsist, because it will always be impotent.

These parties being composed of freemen, if the one becomes too powerful for the other, as a consequence of liberty, this other is depressed; while the citizens take the weaker side with the same readiness as the hands lend their assistance to remove the infirmities and disorders of the body.

Every individual is independent, and being commonly led by caprice and humour, frequently changes parties; he abandons one where he left all his friends, to unite himself to another in which he finds all his enemies: so that in this nation it frequently happens that the people forget the laws of friendship, as well as those of hatred.

The sovereign is here in the same case with a private person; and against the ordinary maxims of prudence is frequently obliged to give his confidence to those who have most offended him, and to disgrace the men who have best served him: he does that by necessity which other princes do by choice.

As we are afraid of being deprived of the blessing we already enjoy, and which may be disguised and misrepresented to us; and as fear always enlarges objects, the people are uneasy under such a situation, and believe themselves in danger, even in those moments when they are most secure.

As those who with the greatest warmth oppose the executive power dare not avow the self-interested motives of their opposition, so much the more do they increase the terrors of the people, who can never be certain whether they are in danger or not. But even this contributes to make them avoid the real dangers, to which they may, in the end, be exposed.

But the legislative body having the confidence of the people, and being more enlightened than they, may calm their uneasiness, and make them recover from the bad impressions they have entertained.

This is the great advantage which this government has over the ancient democracies, in which the people had an immediate power; for when they were moved and agitated by the orators, these agitations always produced their effect.

But when an impression of terror has no certain object, it produces only clamour and abuse; it has, however, this good effect, that it puts all the springs of government into motion, and fixes the attention of every citizen. But if it arises from a violation of the funda-

[1] In Nov. 117, cap. xiv.
[2] Chapter 6.

mental laws, it is sullen, cruel, and produces the most dreadful catastrophes.

Soon we should see a frightful calm, during which every one would unite against that power which had violated the laws.

If, when the uneasiness proceeds from no certain object, some foreign power should threaten the state, or put its prosperity or its glory in danger, the little interests of party would then yield to the more strong and binding, and there would be a perfect coalition in favour of the executive power.

But if the disputes were occasioned by a violation of the fundamental laws, and a foreign power should appear, there would be a revolution that would neither alter the constitution nor the form of government. For a revolution formed by liberty becomes a confirmation of liberty.

A free nation may have a deliverer: a nation enslaved can have only another oppressor.

For whoever is able to dethrone an absolute prince has a power sufficient to become absolute himself.

As the enjoyment of liberty, and even its support and preservation, consists in every man's being allowed to speak his thoughts, and to lay open his sentiments, a citizen in this state will say or write whatever the laws do not expressly forbid to be said or written.

A people like this, being always in a ferment, are more easily conducted by their passions than by reason, which never produces any great effect in the mind of man; it is therefore easy for those who govern to make them undertake enterprises contrary to their true interest.

This nation is passionately fond of liberty, because this liberty is real; and it is possible for it, in its defence, to sacrifice its wealth, its ease, its interest, and to support the burden of the heaviest taxes, even such as a despotic prince durst not lay upon his subjects.

But as the people have a certain knowledge of the necessity of submitting to those taxes, they pay them from the well-founded hope of their discontinuance; their burdens are heavy, but they do not feel their weight; whilst in other states the uneasiness is infinitely greater than the evil.

This nation must therefore have a fixed and certain credit, because it borrows of itself and pays itself. It is possible for it to undertake things above its natural strength, and employ against its enemies immense sums of fictitious riches, which the credit and nature of the government may render real.

To preserve its liberty, it borrows of its subjects: and the subjects, seeing that its credit would be lost if ever it were conquered, have a new motive to make fresh efforts in defence of its liberty.

This nation, inhabiting an island, is not fond of conquering, because it would be weakened by distant conquests—especially as the soil of the island is good, for it has then no need of enriching itself by war; and as no citizen is subject to another, each sets a greater value on his own liberty than on the glory of one or any number of citizens.

Military men are there regarded as belonging to a profession which may be useful but is often dangerous, and as men whose very services are burdensome to the nation: civil qualifications are therefore more esteemed than the military.

This nation, which liberty and the laws render easy, on being freed from pernicious prejudices, has become a trading people; and as it has some of those primitive materials of trade out of which are manufactured such things as from the artist's hand receive a considerable value, it has made settlements proper to procure the enjoyment of this gift of heaven in its fullest extent.

As this nation is situated towards the north, and has many superfluous commodities, it must want also a great amount of merchandise which its climate will not produce: it has therefore entered into a great and necessary intercourse with the southern nations; and making choice of those states whom it is willing to favour with an advantageous commerce, it enters into such treaties with the nation it has chosen as are reciprocally useful to both.

In a state where, on the one hand, the opulence is extreme, and on the other the taxes are excessive, they are hardly able to live on a small fortune without industry. Many, therefore, under a pretence of travelling, or of health, retire from among them, and go in search of plenty, even to the countries of slavery.

A trading nation has a prodigious number of little particular interests; it may then injure or be injured in an infinite number of ways. Thus it becomes immoderately jealous, and is more afflicted at the prosperity of others than it rejoices at its own.

And its laws, otherwise mild and easy, may

be so rigid with respect to the trade and navigation carried on with it, that it may seem to trade only with enemies.

If this nation sends colonies abroad, it must rather be to extend its commerce than its dominion.

As men are fond of introducing into other places what they have established among themselves, they have given the people of the colonies their own form of government; and this government carrying prosperity along with it, they have raised great nations in the forests they were sent to inhabit.

Having formerly subdued a neighbouring nation, which by its situation, the goodness of its ports, and the nature of its products, inspires it with jealousy, though it has given this nation its own laws, yet it holds it in great dependence: the subjects there are free and the state itself in slavery.

The conquered state has an excellent civil government, but is oppressed by the law of nations. Laws are imposed by one country on the other, and these are such as render its prosperity precarious and dependent on the will of a master.

The ruling nation inhabiting a large island, and being in possession of a great trade, has with extraordinary ease grown powerful at sea; and as the preservation of its liberties requires that it should have neither strongholds nor fortresses nor land forces, it has occasion for a formidable navy to defend it against invasions; a navy which must be superior to that of all other powers, who, employing their treasures in wars on land, have not sufficient for those at sea.

The empire of the sea has always given those who have enjoyed it a natural pride; because, thinking themselves capable of extending their insults wherever they please, they imagine that their power is as boundless as the ocean.

This nation has a great influence in the affairs of its neighbours; for as its power is not employed in conquests, its friendship is more courted, and its resentment more dreaded, than could naturally be expected from the inconstancy of its government, and its domestic divisions.

Thus it is the fate of the executive power to be almost always disturbed at home and respected abroad.

Should this nation on some occasions become the centre of the negotiations of Europe, probity and good faith would be carried to a greater height than in other places; because the ministers being frequently obliged to justify their conduct before a popular council, their negotiations could not be secret; and they would be forced to be, in this respect, a little more honest.

Besides, as they would in some sort be answerable for the events which an irregular conduct might produce, the surest, the safest way for them would be to take the straightest path.

If the nobles were formerly possessed of an immoderate power, and the monarch had found the means of abasing them by raising the people, the point of extreme servitude must have been that between humbling the nobility and that in which the people began to feel their power.

Thus this nation, having been formerly subject to an arbitrary power, on many occasions preserves the style of it, in such a manner as to let us frequently see upon the foundation of a free government the form of an absolute monarchy.

With regard to religion, as in this state every subject has a free will, and must consequently be either conducted by the light of his own mind or by the caprice of fancy, it necessarily follows that every one must either look upon all religion with indifference, by which means they are led to embrace the established religion, or they must be zealous for religion in general, by which means the number of sects is increased.

It is not impossible but that in this nation there may be men of no religion, who would not, however, bear to be obliged to change that which they would choose, if they cared to choose any; for they would immediately perceive that their lives and fortunes are not more peculiarly theirs than their manner of thinking, and that whoever would deprive them of the one might even with better reason take away the other.

If, among the different religions, there is one that has been attempted to be established by methods of slavery, it must there be odious; because as we judge of things by the appendages we join with them, it could never present itself to the mind in conjunction with the idea of liberty.

The laws against those who profess this religion could not, however, be of the sanguinary kind; for liberty can never inflict such punishments; but they may be so rigorous as to do all the mischief that can be done in cold blood.

It is possible that a thousand circumstances might concur to give the clergy so little credit, that other citizens may have more. Therefore, instead of a separation, they have chosen rather to support the same burdens as the laity, and in this respect to make only one body with them; but as they always seek to conciliate the respect of the people, they distinguish themselves by a more retired life, a conduct more reserved, and a greater purity of manners.

The clergy not being able to protect religion, nor to be protected by it, only seek to persuade; their pens therefore furnish us with excellent works in proof of a revelation and of the providence of the Supreme Being.

Yet the state prevents the sitting of their assemblies, and does not suffer them to correct their own abuses; it chooses thus, through a caprice of liberty, rather to leave their reformation imperfect than to suffer the clergy to be the reformers.

Those dignities which make a fundamental part of the constitution are more fixed than elsewhere; but, on the other hand, the great in this country of liberty are nearer upon a level with the people; their ranks are more separated, and their persons more confounded.

As those who govern have a power which, in some measure, has need of fresh vigour every day, they have a greater regard for such as are useful to them than for those who only contribute to their amusement: we see, therefore, fewer courtiers, flatterers, and parasites; in short, fewer of all those who make their own advantage of the folly of the great.

Men are less esteemed for frivolous talents and attainments than for essential qualities; and of this kind there are but two, riches and personal merit.

They enjoy a solid luxury, founded, not on the refinements of vanity, but on that of real wants; they ask nothing of nature but what nature can bestow.

The rich enjoy a great superfluity of fortune, and yet have no relish for frivolous amusements; thus, many having more wealth than opportunities of expense, employ it in a fantastic manner: in this nation they have more judgment than taste.

As they are always employed about their own interest, they have not that politeness which is founded on indolence; and they really have not leisure to attain it.

The era of Roman politeness is the same as that of the establishment of arbitrary power.

An absolute government produces indolence, and this gives birth to politeness.

The more people there are in a nation who require circumspect behaviour, and care not to displease, the more there is of politeness. But it is rather the politeness of morals than that of manners which ought to distinguish us from barbarous nations.

In a country where every man has, in some sort, a share in the administration of the government, the women ought scarcely to live with the men. They are therefore modest, that is, timid; and this timidity constitutes their virtue: whilst the men without a taste for gallantry plunge themselves into a debauchery, which leaves them at leisure, and in the enjoyment of their full liberty.

Their laws not being made for one individual more than another, each considers himself a monarch; and, indeed, the men of this nation are rather confederates than fellow-subjects.

As the climate has given many persons a restless spirit and extended views, in a country where the constitution gives every man a share in its government and political interests, conversation generally turns upon politics: and we see men spend their lives in the calculation of events which, considering the nature of things and the caprices of fortune, or rather of men, can scarcely be thought subject to the rules of calculation.

In a free nation it is very often a matter of indifference whether individuals reason well or ill; it is sufficient that they do reason: hence springs that liberty which is a security from the effects of these reasonings.

But in a despotic government, it is equally pernicious whether they reason well or ill; their reasoning is alone sufficient to shock the principle of that government.

Many people who have no desire of pleasing abandon themselves to their own particular humour; and most of those who have wit and ingenuity are ingenious in tormenting themselves: filled with contempt or disgust for all things, they are unhappy amidst all the blessings that can possibly contribute to promote their felicity.

As no subject fears another, the whole nation is proud; for the pride of kings is founded only on their independence.

Free nations are haughty; others may more properly be called vain.

But as these men who are naturally so proud live much by themselves, they are commonly bashful when they appear among strangers; and we frequently see them behave for a considerable time with an odd mixture of pride and ill-placed shame.

The character of the nation is more particularly discovered in their literary performances, in which we find the men of thought and deep meditation.

As society gives us a sense of the ridicule of mankind, retirement renders us more fit to reflect on the folly of vice. Their satirical writings are sharp and severe, and we find among them many Juvenals, without discovering one Horace.

In monarchies extremely absolute, historians betray the truth, because they are not at liberty to speak it; in states remarkably free, they betray the truth, because of their liberty itself; which always produces divisions, every one becoming as great a slave to the prejudices of his faction as he could be in a despotic state.

Their poets have more frequently an original rudeness of invention than that particular kind of delicacy which springs from taste; we there find something which approaches nearer to the bold strength of a Michael Angelo than to the softer graces of a Raphael.

Book XX. Of Laws in Relation to Commerce Considered in its Nature and Distinctions

1. *Of Commerce.* The following subjects deserve to be treated in a more extensive manner than the nature of this work will permit. Fain would I glide down a gentle river, but I am carried away by a torrent.

Commerce is a cure for the most destructive prejudices; for it is almost a general rule that wherever we find agreeable manners, there commerce flourishes; and that wherever there is commerce, there we meet with agreeable manners.

Let us not be astonished, then, if our manners are now less savage than formerly. Commerce has everywhere diffused a knowledge of the manners of all nations: these are compared one with another, and from this comparison arise the greatest advantages.

Commercial laws, it may be said, improve manners for the same reason that they destroy them. They corrupt the purest morals.[1] This was the subject of Plato's complaints; and we every day see that they polish and refine the most barbarous.

2. *Of the Spirit of Commerce.* Peace is the natural effect of trade. Two nations who traffic with each other become reciprocally dependent; for if one has an interest in buying, the other has an interest in selling; and thus their union is founded on their mutual necessities.

But if the spirit of commerce unites nations, it does not in the same manner unite individu-

als. We see that in countries[2] where the people move only by the spirit of commerce, they make a traffic of all the humane, all the moral virtues; the most trifling things, those which humanity would demand, are there done, or there given, only for money.

The spirit of trade produces in the mind of a man a certain sense of exact justice, opposite, on the one hand, to robbery, and on the other to those moral virtues which forbid our always adhering rigidly to the rules of private interest, and suffer us to neglect this for the advantage of others.

The total privation of trade, on the contrary, produces robbery, which Aristotle ranks in the number of means of acquiring; yet it is not at all inconsistent with certain moral virtues. Hospitality, for instance, is most rare in trading countries, while it is found in the most admirable perfection among nations of vagabonds.

It is a sacrilege, says Tacitus, for a German to shut his door against any man whomsoever, whether known or unknown. He who has behaved with hospitality to a stranger goes to show him another house where this hospitality is also practised; and he is there received with the same humanity.[3] But when the Germans had founded kingdoms, hospitality had become burdensome. This appears by two laws of the code of the Burgundians;[4] one of which inflicted a penalty on every barbarian who

---

[1] Cæsar said of the Gauls that they were spoiled by the neighbourhood and commerce of Marseilles; insomuch that they who formerly always conquered the Germans had now become inferior to them.—*De Bello Gall.*, vi. 23.

[2] Holland.
[3] *Et qui modo hospes fuerat, monstrator hospitii.—De Moribus Germanorum,* 21. See Cæsar, *De Bello Gall.* vi. 21.
[4] Tit. 38.

presumed to show a stranger the house of a Roman; and the other decreed that whoever received a stranger should be indemnified by the inhabitants, every one being obliged to pay his proper proportion.

3. *Of the Poverty of the People.* There are two sorts of poor; those who are rendered such by the severity of government: these are, indeed, incapable of performing almost any great action, because their indigence is a consequence of their slavery. Others are poor, only because they either despise or know not the conveniences of life; and these are capable of accomplishing great things, because their poverty constitutes a part of their liberty.

4. *Of Commerce in different Governments.* Trade has some relation to forms of government. In a monarchy, it is generally founded on luxury; and though it be also founded on real wants, yet the principal view with which it is carried on is to procure everything that can contribute to the pride, the pleasure, and the capricious whims of the nation. In republics, it is commonly founded on economy. Their merchants, having an eye to all the nations of the earth, bring from one what is wanted by another. It is thus that the republics of Tyre, Carthage, Athens, Marseilles, Florence, Venice, and Holland engaged in commerce.

This kind of traffic has a natural relation to a republican government: to monarchies it is only occasional. For as it is founded on the practice of gaining little, and even less than other nations, and of remedying this by gaining incessantly, it can hardly be carried on by a people swallowed up in luxury, who spend much, and see nothing but objects of grandeur.

Cicero was of this opinion, when he so justly said, "I do not like that the same people should be at once both the lords and factors of the whole earth."[1] For this would, indeed, be to suppose that every individual in the state, and the whole state collectively, had their heads constantly filled with grand views, and at the same time with small ones; which is a contradiction.

Not but that the most noble enterprises are completed also in those states which subsist by economical commerce: they have even an intrepidity not to be found in monarchies. And the reason is this:

One branch of commerce leads to another, the small to the moderate, the moderate to the great; thus he who has gratified his desire of gaining a little raises himself to a situation in which he is not less desirous of gaining a great deal.

Besides, the grand enterprises of merchants are always necessarily connected with the affairs of the public. But, in monarchies, these public affairs give as much distrust to the merchants as in free states they appear to give safety. Great enterprises, therefore, in commerce are not for monarchical, but for republican, governments.

In short, an opinion of greater certainty, as to the possession of property in these states, makes them undertake everything. They flatter themselves with the hopes of receiving great advantages from the smiles of fortune; and thinking themselves sure of what they have already acquired, they boldly expose it in order to acquire more; risking nothing, but as the means of obtaining.

I do not pretend to say that any monarchy is entirely excluded from an economical commerce; but of its own nature it has less tendency towards it: neither do I mean that the republics with which we are acquainted are absolutely deprived of the commerce of luxury; but it is less connected with their constitution.

With regard to a despotic state, there is no occasion to mention it. A general rule: A nation in slavery labours more to preserve than to acquire; a free nation, more to acquire than to preserve.

5. *Of Nations that have entered into an economical Commerce.* Marseilles, a necessary retreat in the midst of a tempestuous sea; Marseilles, a harbour which all the winds, the shelves of the sea, the disposition of the coasts, point out for a landing-place, became frequented by mariners; while the sterility of the adjacent country determined the citizens to an economical commerce.[2] It was necessary that they should be laborious to supply what nature had refused; that they should be just, in order to live among barbarous nations, from whom they were to derive their prosperity; that they should be moderate, to the end that they might always taste the sweets of a tranquil government; in fine, that they should be frugal in their manners, to enable them to subsist by trade—a trade the more certain as it was less advantageous.

[1] Cicero, *De Rep.,* iv.

[2] Justin, xliii. 3.

We everywhere see violence and oppression give birth to a commerce founded on economy, while men are constrained to take refuge in marshes, in isles, in the shallows of the sea, and even on rocks themselves. Thus it was that Tyre, Venice, and the cities of Holland were founded. Fugitives found there a place of safety. It was necessary that they should subsist; they drew, therefore, their subsistence from all parts of the world.

6. *Some Effects of an extensive Navigation.* It sometimes happens that a nation, when engaged in an economical commerce, having need of the merchandise of one country, which serves as a capital or stock for procuring the commodities of another, is satisfied with making very little profit, and frequently none at all, in trading with the former, in expectation of gaining greatly by the latter. Thus, when the Dutch were almost the only nation that carried on the trade from the south to the north of Europe; the French wines which they imported to the north were in some measure only a capital or stock for conducting their commerce in that part of the world.

It is a known fact that there are some kinds of merchandise in Holland which, though imported from afar, sell for very little more than they cost upon the spot. They account for it thus: a captain who has occasion to ballast his ship will load it with marble; if he wants wood for stowage, he will buy it; and, provided he loses nothing by the bargain, he will think himself a gainer. Thus it is that Holland has its quarries and its forests.

Further, it may happen so that not only a commerce which brings in nothing shall be useful, but even a losing trade shall be beneficial. I have heard it affirmed in Holland that the whale fishery in general does not answer the expense; but it must be observed that the persons employed in building the ships, as also those who furnish the rigging and provisions, are jointly concerned in the fishery. Should they happen to lose in the voyage, they have had a profit in fitting out the vessel. This commerce, in short, is a kind of lottery, and every one is allured with the hopes of a prize. Mankind are generally fond of gaming; and even the most prudent have no aversion to it, when the disagreeable circumstances attending it, such as dissipation, anxiety, passion, loss of time, and even of life and fortune, are concealed from their view.

7. *The Spirit of England with respect to Commerce.* The tariff or customs of England are very unsettled with respect to other nations; they are changed, in some measure, with every parliament, either by taking off particular duties, or by imposing new ones. They endeavour by these means still to preserve their independence. Supremely jealous with respect to trade, they bind themselves but little by treaties, and depend only on their own laws.

Other nations have made the interests of commerce yield to those of politics; the English, on the contrary, have ever made their political interests give way to those of commerce.

They know better than any other people upon earth how to value, at the same time, these three great advantages—religion, commerce, and liberty.

8. *In what Manner economical Commerce has been sometimes restrained.* In several kingdoms laws have been made extremely proper to humble the states that have entered into economical commerce. They have forbidden their importing any merchandise, except the product of their respective countries; and have permitted them to traffic only in vessels built in the kingdom to which they brought their commodities.

It is necessary that the kingdom which imposes these laws should itself be able easily to engage in commerce; otherwise it will, at least, be an equal sufferer. It is much more advantageous to trade with a commercial nation, whose profits are moderate, and who are rendered in some sort dependent by the affairs of commerce; with a nation whose larger views and whose extended trade enables them to dispose of their superfluous merchandise; with a wealthy nation, who can take off many of their commodities, and make them a quicker return in specie; with a nation under a kind of necessity to be faithful, pacific from principle, and that seeks to gain, and not to conquer: it is much better, I say, to trade with such a nation than with others, their constant rivals, who will never grant such great advantages.

9. *Of the Prohibition of Commerce.* It is a true maxim that one nation should never exclude another from trading with it, except for very great reasons. The Japanese trade only with two nations, the Chinese and the Dutch. The Chinese[1] gain a thousand per cent upon sug-

[1] Father Du Halde, ii, p. 170.

ars, and sometimes as much by the goods they take in exchange. The Dutch make nearly the same profits. Every nation that acts upon Japanese principles must necessarily be deceived; for it is competition which sets a just value on merchandise, and establishes the relation between them.

Much less ought a state to lay itself under an obligation of selling its manufactures only to a single nation, under a pretence of their taking all at a certain price. The Poles, in this manner, dispose of their corn to the city of Danzig; and several Indian princes have made a like contract for their spices with the Dutch.[1] These agreements are proper only for a poor nation, whose inhabitants are satisfied to forego the hopes of enriching themselves, provided they can be secure of a certain subsistence; or for nations whose slavery consists either in renouncing the use of those things which nature has given them, or in being obliged to submit to a disadvantageous commerce.

10. *An Institution adapted to economical Commerce.* In states that carry on an economical commerce, they have luckily established banks, which by their credit have formed a new species of wealth: but it would be quite wrong to introduce them into governments whose commerce is founded only on luxury. The erecting of banks in countries governed by an absolute monarch supposes money on the one side, and on the other power: that is, on the one hand, the means of procuring everything, without any power; and on the other, the power, without any means of procuring at all. In a government of this kind, none but the prince ever had, or can have, a treasure; and wherever there is one, it no sooner becomes great than it becomes the treasure of the prince.

For the same reason, all associations of merchants, in order to carry on a particular commerce, are seldom proper in absolute governments. The design of these companies is to give to the wealth of private persons the weight of public riches. But in those governments this weight can be found only in the prince. Nay, they are not even always proper in states engaged in economical commerce; for, if the trade be not so great as to surpass the management of particular persons, it is much better to leave it open than, by exclusive privileges, to restrain the liberty of commerce.

11. *The same Subject continued.* A free port may be established in the dominions of states whose commerce is economical. That economy in the government which always attends the frugality of individuals is, if I may so express myself, the soul of its economical commerce. The loss it sustains with respect to customs it can repair by drawing from the wealth and industry of the republic. But in a monarchy a step of this kind must be opposite to reason; for it could have no other effect than to ease luxury of the weight of taxes. This would be depriving itself of the only advantage that luxury can procure, and of the only curb which, in a constitution like this, it is capable of receiving.

12. *Of the Freedom of Commerce.* The freedom of commerce is not a power granted to the merchants to do what they please: this would be more properly its slavery. The constraint of the merchant is not the constraint of commerce. It is in the freest countries that the merchant finds innumerable obstacles; and he is never less crossed by laws than in a country of slaves.

England prohibits the exportation of her wool; coals must be brought by sea to the capital; no horses, except geldings, are allowed to be exported; and the vessels of her colonies trading to Europe must take in water in England.[2] The English constrain the merchant, but it is in favour of commerce.

13. *What it is that destroys this Liberty.* Wherever commerce subsists, customs are established. Commerce is the exportation and importation of merchandise, with a view to the advantage of the state: customs are a certain right over this same exportation and importation, founded also on the advantage of the state. Hence it becomes necessary that the state should be neutral between its customs and its commerce, that neither of these two interfere with each other, and then the inhabitants enjoy a free commerce.

The farming of the customs destroys commerce by its injustice and vexations, as well as by the excess of the imposts: but independent of this, it destroys it even more by the difficul-

---

[1] This was first established by the Portuguese.—Pirard, *Voyages*, part II, 15.

[2] Acts of Navigation, 1660. It is only in time of war that the merchants of Boston and Philadelphia send their vessels directly to the Mediterranean.

ties that arise from it, and by the formalities it exacts. In England, where the customs are managed by the king's officers, business is negotiated with a singular dexterity: one word of writing accomplishes the greatest affairs. The merchant needs not lose an infinite deal of time; he has no occasion for a particular commissioner, either to obviate all the difficulties of the farmers, or to submit to them.

14. *The Laws of Commerce concerning the Confiscation of Merchandise.* The Magna Charta of England forbids the seizing and confiscating, in case of war, the effects of foreign merchants, except by way of reprisals. It is an honour to the English nation that they have made this one of the articles of their liberty.

In the late war between Spain and England, the former made a law which punished with death those who brought English merchandise into the dominions of Spain; and the same penalty on those who carried Spanish merchandise into England.[1] An ordinance like this cannot, I believe, find a precedent in any laws but those of Japan. It equally shocks humanity, the spirit of commerce, and the harmony which ought to subsist in the proportion of penalties; it confounds all our ideas, making that a crime against the state which is only a violation of civil polity.

15. *Of seizing the Persons of Merchants.* Solon made a law that the Athenians should no longer seize the body for civil debts.[2] This law he received from Egypt. It had been made by Boccoris, and renewed by Sesostris.[3]

This law is extremely good with respect to the generality of civil affairs; but there is sufficient reason for its not being observed in those of commerce.[4] For as merchants are obliged to entrust large sums, frequently for a very short time, and to pay money as well as to receive it, there is a necessity that the debtor should constantly fulfil his engagements at the time prefixed; and hence it becomes necessary to lay a constraint on his person.

In affairs relating to common civil contracts, the law ought not to permit the seizure of the person; because the liberty of one citizen is of greater importance to the public than the ease or prosperity of another. But in conventions derived from commerce, the law ought to consider the public prosperity as of greater importance than the liberty of a citizen; which, however, does not hinder the restrictions and limitations that humanity and good policy demand.

16. *An excellent Law.* Admirable is that law of Geneva which excludes from the magistracy, and even from the admittance into the great council, the children of those who have lived or died insolvent, except they have discharged their father's debts. It has this effect: it creates a confidence in the merchants, in the magistrates, and in the city itself. There the credit of the individual has still all the weight of public credit.

17. *A Law of Rhodes.*[5] The inhabitants of Rhodes went further. Sextus Empiricus observes that among those people a son could not be excused from paying his father's debts by renouncing the succession. This law of Rhodes was calculated for a republic founded on commerce. Now I am inclined to think that reasons drawn from commerce itself should make this limitation, that the debts contracted by the father since the son's entering into commerce should not affect the estate or property acquired by the latter. A merchant ought always to know his obligations, and to square his conduct by his circumstances and present fortune.

18. *Of the Judges of Commerce.* Xenophon, in his book of Revenues, would have rewards given to those overseers of commerce who despatched the causes brought before them with the greatest expedition. He was sensible of the need of our modern jurisdiction of a consul.

The affairs of commerce are but little susceptible of formalities. They are the actions of a day, and are every day followed by others of the same nature. Hence it becomes necessary that every day they should be decided. It is otherwise with those actions of life which have a principal influence on futurity, but rarely happen. We seldom marry more than once; deeds and wills are not the work of every day; we are but once of age.

Plato[6] says that in a city where there is no maritime commerce there ought not to be

---

[1] Published in Cadiz in March, 1740.
[2] Plutarch, *Against Lending Upon Usury*, 4.
[3] Diodorus, i, part II, 79.
[4] The Greek legislators were to blame in preventing the arms and plough of any man from being taken in pledge, and yet permitting the taking of the man himself.—*Ibid.*

[5] Hypotiposes, i. 14.
[6] *Laws,* viii.

above half the number of civil laws: this is very true. Commerce brings into the same country different kinds of people; it introduces also a great number of contracts and species of wealth, with various ways of acquiring it.

Thus in a trading city there are fewer judges, and more laws.

19. *That a Prince ought not to engage himself in Commerce.* Theophilus,[1] seeing a vessel laden with merchandise for his wife Theodora, ordered it to be burned. "I am emperor," said he, "and you make me the master of a galley. By what means shall these poor men gain a livelihood if we take their trade out of their hands?" He might have added, Who shall set bounds to us if we monopolise all ourselves? Who shall oblige us to fulfil our engagements? Our courtiers will follow our example; they will be more greedy and more unjust than we: the people have some confidence in our justice, they will have none in our opulence: all these numerous duties, the cause of their wants, are certain proofs of ours.

20. *The same Subject continued.* When the Portuguese and Castilians bore sway in the East Indies, commerce had such opulent branches that their princes did not fail to seize them. This ruined their settlements in those parts of the world.

The viceroy of Goa granted exclusive privileges to particular persons. The people had no confidence in these men; and the commerce declined, by the perpetual change of those to whom it was entrusted; nobody took care to improve it, or to leave it entire to his successor. In short, the profit centred in a few hands, and was not sufficiently extended.

21. *Of the Commerce of the Nobility in a Monarchy.* In a monarchical government, it is contrary to the spirit of commerce that any of the nobility should be merchants. "This," said the Emperors Honorius and Theodosius,[2] "would be pernicious to cities; and would remove the facility of buying and selling between the merchants and the plebeians."

It is contrary to the spirit of monarchy to admit the nobility into commerce. The custom of suffering the nobility of England to trade is one of those things which has there

mostly contributed to weaken the monarchical government.

22. *A singular Reflection.* Persons struck with the practice of some states imagine that in France they ought to make laws to engage the nobility to enter into commerce. But these laws would be the means of destroying the nobility, without being of any advantage to trade. The practice of this country is extremely wise; merchants are not nobles, though they may become so. They have the hopes of obtaining a degree of nobility, unattended with its actual inconveniences. There is no surer way of being advanced above their profession than to manage it well, or with success; the consequence of which is generally an affluent fortune.

Laws which oblige every one to continue in his profession, and to devolve it upon his children, neither are nor can be of use in any but despotic kingdoms; where nobody either can or ought to have emulation.[3]

Let none say that every one will succeed better in his profession when he cannot change it for another: I say that a person will succeed best when those who have excelled hope to rise to another.

The possibility of purchasing honour with gold encourages many merchants to put themselves in circumstances by which they may attain it. I do not take it upon me to examine the justice of thus bartering for money the price of virtue. There are governments where this may be very useful.

In France the dignity of the long robe, which places those who wear it between the great nobility and the people, and without having such shining honours as the former, has all their privileges; a dignity which, while this body, the depositary of the laws, is encircled with glory, leaves the private members in a mediocrity of fortune; a dignity in which there are no other means of distinction but by a superior capacity and virtue, yet which still leaves in view one much more illustrious: the warlike nobility, likewise, who conceive that, whatever degree of wealth they are possessed of, they may still increase their fortunes; who are ashamed of augmenting, if they begin not with dissipating, their estates; who always serve their prince with their whole capital stock, and when that is sunk make room for others, who follow their example; who take

[1] Zonaras.
[2] *Leg., Nobiliores, Cod. de Comm.; Leg. ult. de rescind. vendit.*

[3] This is actually very often the case in such governments.

the field that they may never be reproached with not having been there; who, when they can no longer hope for riches, live in expectation of honours; and when they have not obtained the latter, enjoy the consolation of having acquired glory: all these things together have necessarily contributed to augment the grandeur of this kingdom; and if for two or three centuries it has been incessantly increasing in power, this must be attributed not to Fortune, who was never famed for constancy, but to the goodness of its laws.

23. To what Nations Commerce is prejudicial.

Riches consist either in lands or in movable effects. The soil of every country is commonly possessed by the natives. The laws of most states render foreigners unwilling to purchase their lands; and nothing but the presence of the owner improves them: this kind of riches, therefore, belongs to every state in particular; but movable effects, as money, notes, bills of exchange, stocks in companies, vessels, and, in fine, all merchandise, belong to the whole world in general; in this respect, it is composed of but one single state, of which all the societies upon earth are members. The people who possess more of these movable effects than any other on the globe are the most opulent. Some states have an immense quantity acquired by their commodities, by the labour of their mechanics, by their industry, by their discoveries, and even by chance. The avarice of nations makes them quarrel for the movables of the whole universe. If we could find a state so unhappy as to be deprived of the effects of other countries, and at the same time of almost all its own, the proprietors of the lands would be only planters to foreigners. This state, wanting all, could acquire nothing; therefore, it would be much better for the inhabitants not to have the least commerce with any nation upon earth, for commerce in these circumstances must necessarily lead them to poverty.

A country that constantly exports fewer manufactures or commodities than it receives will soon find the balance sinking; it will receive less and less, until, falling into extreme poverty, it will receive nothing at all.

In trading countries the specie, which suddenly vanishes, quickly returns; because those nations that have received it are its debtors. But it never returns into those states of which we have just been speaking, because those who have received it owe them nothing.

Poland will serve us for an example. It has scarcely any of those things which we call the movable effects of the universe, except corn, the produce of its lands. Some of the lords possess entire provinces; they oppress the husbandmen, in order to have greater quantities of corn, which they send to strangers, to procure the superfluous demands of luxury. If Poland had no foreign trade, its inhabitants would be happier. The grandees, who would have only their corn, would give it to their peasants for subsistence; as their too extensive estates would become burdensome, they would divide them among their peasants; every one would find skins or wool in their herds or flocks, so that they would no longer be at an immense expense in providing clothes; the great, who are ever fond of luxury, not being able to find it but in their own country, would encourage the labour of the poor. This nation, I affirm, would then become more flourishing, at least if it did not become barbarous; and this the laws might easily prevent.

Let us next consider Japan. The vast quantity of what they receive is the cause of the vast quantity of merchandise they send abroad. Things are thus in as nice an equilibrium as if the importation and exportation were but small. Besides, this kind of exuberance in the state is productive of a thousand advantages; there is a greater consumption, a greater quantity of those things on which the arts are exercised; more men employed, and more numerous means of acquiring power; exigencies may also happen that require a speedy assistance, which so opulent a state can better afford than any other. It is difficult for a country to avoid having superfluities; but it is the nature of commerce to render the superfluous useful, and the useful necessary. The state will be, therefore, able to afford necessaries to a much greater number of subjects.

Let us say, then, that it is not those nations who have need of nothing that must lose by trade; it is those who have need of everything. It is not such people as have a sufficiency within themselves, but those who are most in want, that will find an advantage in putting a stop to all commercial intercourse.

Book XXI. Of Laws in Relation to Commerce, Considered in the Revolutions It Has Met with in the World

1. *Some general Considerations.* Though commerce be subject to great revolutions, yet it is possible that certain physical causes, as the quality of the soil, or the climate, may fix its nature for ever.

We at present carry on the trade of the Indies merely by means of the silver which we send thither. The Romans carried annually thither about fifty millions of sesterces;[1] and this silver, as ours is at present, was exchanged for merchandise, which was brought to the west. Every nation that ever traded to the Indies has constantly carried bullion and brought merchandise in return.

It is nature itself that produces this effect. The Indians have their hearts adapted to their manner of living. Our luxury cannot be theirs; nor theirs our wants. Their climate demands and permits hardly anything which comes from ours. They go in a great measure naked; such clothes as they have the country itself furnishes; and their religion, which is deeply rooted, gives them an aversion for those things that serve for our nourishment. They want, therefore, nothing but our bullion to serve as the medium of value; and for this they give us merchandise in return, with which the frugality of the people and the nature of the country furnish them in great abundance. Those ancient authors who have mentioned the Indies describe them just as we now find them, as to their policy, customs, and manners.[2] The Indies have ever been the same Indies they are at present; and in every period of time those who traded with that country carried specie thither and brought none in return.

2. *Of the People of Africa.* The greatest part of the people on the coast of Africa are savages and barbarians. The principal reason, I believe, of this is, because the small countries capable of being inhabited are separated from each other by large and almost uninhabitable tracts of land. They are without industry or arts. They have gold in abundance, which they receive immediately from the hand of nature. Every civilised state is therefore in a condition to traffic with them to advantage, by

[1] Pliny, vi. 23.
[2] See Pliny, vi. 19, and Strabo, xv.

raising their esteem for things of no value, and receiving a very high price in return.

3. *That the Wants of the People in the South are different from those of the North.* In Europe there is a kind of balance between the southern and northern nations. The first have every convenience of life, and few of its wants: the last have many wants, and few conveniences. To one nature has given much, and demands but little; to the other she has given but little, and demands a great deal. The equilibrium is maintained by the laziness of the southern nations, and by the industry and activity which she has given to those in the north. The latter are obliged to undergo excessive labour, without which they would want everything, and degenerate into barbarians. This has neutralised slavery to the people of the south: as they can easily dispense with riches, they can more easily dispense with liberty. But the people of the north have need of liberty, for this can best procure them the means of satisfying all those wants which they have received from nature. The people of the north, then, are in a forced state, if they are not either free or barbarians. Almost all the people of the south are, in some measure, in a state of violence, if they are not slaves.

4. *The principal Difference between the Commerce of the Ancients and the Moderns.* The world has found itself, from time to time, in different situations; by which the face of commerce has been altered. The trade of Europe is, at present, carried on principally from the north to the south; and the difference of climate is the cause that the several nations have great occasion for the merchandise of each other. For example, the liquors of the south, which are carried to the north, form a commerce little known to the ancients. Thus the burden of vessels, which was formerly computed by measures of corn, is at present determined by tuns of liquor.

The ancient commerce, so far as it is known to us, was carried on from one port in the Mediterranean to another; and was almost wholly confined to the south. Now the people of the same climate, having nearly the same things of their own, have not the same need of trading among themselves as with those of a different climate. The commerce of Europe was therefore formerly less extended than at present.

This does not at all contradict what I have said of our commerce to the Indies: for here the prodigious difference of climate destroys all relation between their wants and ours.

5. *Other Differences.* Commerce is sometimes destroyed by conquerors, sometimes cramped by monarchs; it traverses the earth, flies from the places where it is oppressed, and stays where it has liberty to breath: it reigns at present where nothing was formerly to be seen but deserts, seas, and rocks; and where it once reigned now there are only deserts.

To see Colchis in its present situation, which is no more than a vast forest, where the people are every day diminishing, and only defend their liberty to sell themselves by piecemeal to the Turks and Persians, one could never imagine that this country had ever, in the time of the Romans, been full of cities, where commerce convened all the nations of the world. We find no monument of these facts in the country itself; there are no traces of them, except in Pliny[1] and Strabo.[2]

The history of commerce is that of the communication of people. Their numerous defeats, and the flux and reflux of populations and devastations, here form the most extraordinary events.

6. *Of the Commerce of the Ancients.* The immense treasures of Semiramis,[3] which could not be acquired in a day, give us reason to believe that the Assyrians themselves had pillaged other rich nations, as other nations afterwards pillaged them.

The effect of commerce is riches; the consequence of riches, luxury; and that of luxury the perfection of arts. We find that the arts were carried to great perfection in the time of Semiramis;[4] which is a sufficient indication that a considerable commerce was then established.

In the empires of Asia there was a great commerce of luxury. The history of luxury would make a fine part of that of commerce. The luxury of the Persians was that of the Medes, as the luxury of the Medes was that of the Assyrians.

Great revolutions have happened in Asia. The northeast parts of Persia, viz., Hyrcania, Margiana, Bactria, &c., were formerly full of flourishing cities,[5] which are now no more; and the north of this empire,[6] that is, the isthmus which separates the Caspian and the Euxine Seas, was covered with cities and nations, which are now destroyed.

Eratosthenes and Aristobulus[7] learned from Patroclus[8] that the merchandise of India passed by the Oxus into the sea of Pontus. Marcus Varro[9] tells us that at the time when Pompey commanded against Mithridates, they were informed that people went in seven days from India to the country of the Bactrians, and to the river Icarus, which falls into the Oxus; that by this method they were able to bring the merchandise of India across the Caspian Sea, and to enter the mouth of Cyrus; whence it was only five days' passage to the Phasis, a river that discharges itself into the Euxine Sea. There is no doubt but it was by the nations inhabiting these several countries that the great empires of the Assyrians, Medes, and Persians had communication with the most distant parts of the east and west.

An entire stop is now put to this communication. All these countries have been laid waste by the Tartars,[10] and are still infested by this destructive nation. The Oxus no longer runs into the Caspian Sea; the Tartars, for some private reasons, have changed its course, and it now loses itself in the barren sands.[11]

The Jaxartes, which was formerly a barrier between the polite and barbarous nations, has had its course turned in the same manner by the Tartars, and it no longer empties itself into the sea.[12]

Seleucus Nicator formed the project of join-

---

[1] Book vi. 4, 5.
[2] Book xi.
[3] Diodorus, ii.
[4] *Ibid.*, 7, 8, 9.

[5] Pliny, vi. 16, and Strabo, xi.
[6] Strabo, xi.
[7] *Ibid.*
[8] The authority of Patroclus is of great weight, as appears from a passage in Strabo, ii.
[9] Pliny, vi. 17. See also Strabo, xi, upon the passage by which the merchandise was conveyed from the Phasis to the Cyrus.
[10] There must have been very great changes in that country since the time of Ptolemy, who gives us an account of so many rivers that empty themselves into the east side of the Caspian Sea. In the Czar's chart we find only the river of Astrabat; in that of M. Bathalsi there is none at all.
[11] See Jenkinson's account of this, in the *Collection of Voyages to the North,* iv.
[12] I am disposed to think that hence Lake Aral was formed.

ing the Euxine to the Caspian Sea.[1] This project, which would have greatly facilitated the commerce of those days, vanished at his death.[2] We are not certain it could have been executed in the isthmus which separates the two seas. This country is at present very little known; it is depopulated, and full of forests; however, water is not wanting, for an infinite number of rivers roll into it from Mount Caucasus; but as this mountain forms the north of the isthmus, and extends like two arms[3] towards the south, it would have been a grand obstacle to such an enterprise, especially in those times, when they had not the art of making sluices.

It may be imagined that Seleucus would have joined the two seas in the very place where Peter I has since joined them; that is, in that neck of land where the Tanais approaches the Volga; but the north of the Caspian Sea was not then discovered.

While the empires of Asia enjoyed the commerce of luxury, the Tyrians had the commerce of economy, which they extended throughout the world. Bochard has employed the first book of his *Canaan* in enumerating all the colonies which they sent into all the countries bordering upon the sea; they passed the pillars of Hercules, and made establishments on the coasts of the ocean.[4]

In those times their pilots were obliged to follow the coasts, which were, if I may so express myself, their compass. Voyages were long and painful. The laborious voyage of Ulysses has been the fruitful subject of the finest poem in the world, next to that which alone has the preference.

The little knowledge which the greatest part of the world had of those who were far distant from them favoured the nations engaged in the economical commerce. They managed trade with as much obscurity as they pleased; they had all the advantages which the most intelligent nations could take over the most ignorant.

The Egyptians—a people who by their religion and their manners were averse to all communication with strangers—had scarcely at that time any foreign trade. They enjoyed a fruitful soil and great plenty. Their country was the Japan of those times; it possessed everything within itself.

So little jealous were these people of commerce, that they left that of the Red Sea to all the petty nations that had any harbours in it. Here they suffered the Idumeans, the Syrians and the Jews to have fleets. Solomon employed in this navigation the Tyrians, who knew those seas.[5]

Josephus[6] says that this nation, being entirely employed in agriculture, knew little of navigation: the Jews, therefore, traded only occasionally in the Red Sea. They took from the Idumeans Eloth and Eziongeber, from whom they received this commerce; they lost these two cities, and with them lost this commerce.

It was not so with the Phœnicians: theirs was not a commerce of luxury; nor was their trade owing to conquest; their frugality, their abilities, their industry, their perils, and the hardships they suffered, rendered them necessary to all the nations of the world.

Before Alexander, the people bordering on the Red Sea traded only in this sea, and in that of Africa. The astonishment which filled the globe at the discovery of the Indian Sea, under that conqueror, is a sufficient proof of this. I have observed[7] that bullion was always carried to the Indies, and never any brought thence; now the Jewish fleets, which brought gold and silver by the way of the Red Sea, returned from Africa, and not from the Indies.[8]

Besides, this navigation was made on the eastern coast of Africa; for the state of navigation at that time is a convincing proof that they did not sail to a very distant shore.

I am not ignorant that the fleets of Solomon and Jehoshaphat returned only every three years; but I do not see that the time taken up in the voyage is any proof of the greatness of the distance.

Pliny and Strabo inform us that the junks of India and the Red Sea were twenty days in performing a voyage which a Greek or Roman vessel would accomplish in seven.[9] In this proportion, a voyage of one year, made by the fleets of Greece or Rome, would take very nearly three when performed by those of Solomon.

Two ships of unequal swiftness do not perform their voyage in a time proportionate to their swiftness. Slowness is frequently the

[1] Claudius Cæsar, in Pliny, vi. 11.
[2] He was slain by Ptolemy Ceraunus.
[3] See Strabo, xi.
[4] They founded Tartessus, and made a settlement at Cadiz.

[5] I Kings, 9. 26; II Chron., 8. 17.
[6] *Against Appian.*
[7] Chapter 1 of this book.
[8] The proportion between gold and silver, as settled in Europe, may sometimes render it profitable to take gold instead of silver into the East Indies; but the advantage is very trifling.
[9] See Pliny, vi. 22, and Strabo, xv.

cause of much greater slowness. When it becomes necessary to follow the coast, and to be incessantly in a different position, when they must wait for a fair wind to get out of a gulf, and for another to proceed, a good sailor takes the advantage of every favourable moment, while the other still continues in a difficult situation, and waits many days for another change.

The slowness of the Indian vessels, which in an equal time could make but the third of the way of those of the Greeks and Romans, may be explained by what we every day see in our modern navigation. The Indian vessels, which were built with a kind of sea-rushes, drew less water than those of Greece and Rome, which were of wood and joined with iron.

We may compare these Indian vessels to those at present made use of in ports of little depth of water. Such are those of Venice, and even of all Italy in general,[1] of the Baltic, and of the province of Holland.[2] Their ships, which ought to be able to go in and out of port, are built round and broad at the bottom; while those of other nations, who have good harbours, are formed to sink deep into the water. This mechanism renders these last-mentioned vessels able to sail much nearer the wind; while the first can hardly sail, except the wind be nearly in the poop. A ship that sinks deep into the water sails towards the same side with almost every wind; this proceeds from the resistance which the vessel, while driven by the wind, meets with from the water, from which it receives a strong support; and from the length of the vessel which presents its side to the wind, while, from the form of the helm, the prow is turned to the point proposed; so that she can sail very near the wind, or, in other words, very near the point whence the wind blows. But when the hull is round and broad at the bottom, and consequently draws little water, it no longer finds this steady support; the wind drives the vessel, which is incapable of resistance, and can run them but with a small variation from the point opposite to the wind. Whence it follows that broad-bottomed vessels are longer in performing voyages.

1. They lose much time in waiting for the wind, especially if they are obliged frequently to change their course. 2. They sail much

slower, because not having a proper support from a depth of water, they cannot carry so much sail. If this be the case at a time when the arts are everywhere known, at a time when art corrects the defects of nature, and even of art itself; if at this time, I say, we find this difference, how great must that have been in the navigation of the ancients?

I cannot yet leave this subject. The Indian vessels were small, and those of the Greeks and Romans, if we except those machines built for ostentation, much less than ours. Now, the smaller the vessel the greater danger it encounters from foul weather. A tempest that would swallow up a small vessel would only make a large one roll. The more one body surpasses another in size, the more its surface is relatively small. Whence it follows that in a small ship there is a less proportion, that is, a greater difference in respect to the surface of the vessel, compared with the weight or lading she can carry, than in a large one. We know that it is a pretty general practice to make the weight of the lading equal to that of half the water the vessel could contain. Suppose a vessel will contain eight hundred tons, her lading then must be four hundred; and that of a vessel which would hold but four hundred tons of water would be two hundred tons. Thus the largeness of the first ship will be to the weight she carries as 8 to 4, and that of the second as 4 to 2. Let us suppose, then, that the surface of the greater is to the surface of the smaller as 8 to 6; the surface of the latter will be to her weight as 6 to 2,[3] while the surface of the former will be to her weight only as 8 to 4. Therefore as the winds and waves act only upon the surface, the large vessel will, by her weight, resist their impetuosity much more than the small.

7. *Of the Commerce of the Greeks.* The first Greeks were all pirates. Minos, who enjoyed the empire of the sea, was only more successful, perhaps, than others in piracy; for his maritime dominion extended no farther than round his own isle. But when the Greeks became a great people, the Athenians obtained the real dominion of the sea; because this trading and victorious nation gave laws to the most potent monarch of that time,[4] and hum-

---

[1] They are mostly shallow; but Sicily has excellent ports.

[2] I say the province of Holland; for the ports of Zealand are deep enough.

[3] That is, to compare magnitudes of the same kind, the action or pressure of the fluid upon the ship will be to the resistance of the same ship as, &c.

[4] The King of Persia.

bled the maritime powers of Syria, of the isle of Cyprus, and Phœnicia.

But this Athenian lordship of the sea deserves to be more particularly mentioned. "Athens," says Xenophon,[1] "rules the sea; but as the country of Attica is joined to the continent, it is ravaged by enemies while the Athenians are engaged in distant expeditions. Their leaders suffer their lands to be destroyed, and secure their wealth by sending it to some island. The populace, who are not possessed of lands, have no uneasiness. But if the Athenians inhabited an island, and, besides this, enjoyed the empire of the sea, they would, so long as they were possessed of these advantages, be able to annoy others, and at the same time to be out of all danger of being annoyed." One would imagine that Xenophon was speaking of England.

The Athenians, a people whose heads were filled with ambitious projects; the Athenians, who augmented their jealousy instead of increasing their influence; who were more attentive to extend their maritime empire than to enjoy it; whose political government was such that the common people distributed the public revenues among themselves, while the rich were in a state of oppression; the Athenians, I say, did not carry on so extensive a commerce as might be expected from the produce of their mines, from the multitude of their slaves, from the number of their seamen, from their influence over the cities of Greece, and, above all, from the excellent institutions of Solon. Their trade was almost wholly confined to Greece and to the Euxine Sea, whence they drew their subsistence.

Corinth was admirably situated; it separated two seas, and opened and shut the Peloponnesus; it was the key of Greece, and a city of the greatest importance, at a time when the people of Greece were a world, and the cities of Greece nations. Its trade was more extensive than that of Athens, having a port to receive the merchandise of Asia, and another those of Italy; for the great difficulties which attended the doubling Cape Malea, where the meeting of opposite winds causes shipwrecks,[2] induced every one to go to Corinth, and they could even convey their vessels over land from one sea to the other. Never was there a city in which the works of art were carried to so high a degree of perfection. But here religion finished the corruption which their opulence be-

gan. They erected a temple to Venus, in which more than a thousand courtesans were consecrated to that deity; from this seminary came the greatest part of those celebrated beauties whose history Athenæus has presumed to commit to writing.

It seems that in Homer's time the opulence of Greece centred in Rhodes, Corinth, and Orchomenus; "Jupiter," he says, "loved the Rhodians, and made them a very wealthy nation."[3] On Corinth he bestows the epithet of rich.[4] In like manner, when he speaks of cities that have plenty of gold, he mentions Orchomenus, to which he joins Thebes in Egypt. Rhodes and Corinth preserved their power; but Orchomenus lost hers. The situation of Orchomenus in the neighbourhood of the Hellespont, the Propontis, and the Euxine Sea makes us naturally imagine that she was indebted for her opulence to a trade along that maritime coast, which had given rise to the fable of the golden fleece; and, indeed, the name of Minyeios has been given to Orchomenus as well as to the Argonauts.[5] But these seas becoming afterwards more frequented, the Greeks planted along the coasts a greater number of colonies, which traded with the barbarous nations, and at the same time preserved an intercourse with their mother country. In consequence of this, Orchomenus began to decline, till at length it was lost in the crowd of the other cities of Greece.

Before Homer's time the Greeks had scarcely any trade but among themselves, and with a few barbarous nations; in proportion, however, as they formed new colonies, they extended their dominion. Greece was a large peninsula, the capes of which seemed to have kept off the seas, while its gulfs opened on all sides to receive them. If we cast an eye on Greece, we shall find, in a pretty compact country, a considerable extent of sea-coast. Her innumerable colonies formed an immense circle round her; and there she beheld, in some measure, the whole civilised world. Did she penetrate into Sicily and Italy, she formed new nations. Did she navigate towards the sea of Pontus, the coast of Asia Minor, or that of Africa, she acted in the same manner. Her cities increased in prosperity in proportion as they happened to have new people in their neighbourhood. And what was extremely beautiful, she was surrounded on every side

[1] On the Athenian Republic, 2.
[2] See Strabo, viii.
[3] Iliad, ii. 668.
[4] Ibid., 570.
[5] Strabo, ix, p. 414.

with a prodigious number of islands, drawn, as it were, in a line of circumvallation.

What a source of prosperity must Greece have found in those games with which she entertained, in some measure, the whole globe; in those temples, to which all the kings of the earth sent their offerings; in those festivals, at which such a concourse of people used to assemble from all parts; in those oracles, to which the attention of all mankind was directed; and, in short, in that exquisite taste for the polite arts, which she carried to such a height that to expect ever to surpass her would be only betraying our ignorance!

8. *Of Alexander: his Conquests.* Four great events happened in the reign of Alexander which entirely changed the face of commerce: the taking of Tyre, the conquest of Egypt, that likewise of the Indies, and the discovery of the sea which lies south of that country.

The empire of Persia extended to the Indus.[1] Darius, long before Alexander, had sent some vessels, which sailed down this river, and passed even into the Red Sea.[2] How then were the Greeks the first who traded with the Indies by the south? Had not the Persians done this before? Did they make no advantage of seas which were so near them, of the very seas that washed their coasts? Alexander, it is true, conquered the Indies; but was it necessary for him to conquer a country in order to trade with it? This is what I shall now examine.

Ariana,[3] which extended from the Persian Gulf as far as the Indus, and from the South Sea to the mountains of Paropamisus, depended indeed, in some measure, on the empire of Persia; but in the southern part it was barren, scorched, rude, and uncultivated. Tradition relates[4] that the armies of Semiramis and Cyrus perished in these deserts; and Alexander, who caused his fleet to follow him, could not avoid losing in this place a great part of his army. The Persians left the whole coast to the Ichthyophagi,[5] the Oritæ, and other barbarous nations. Besides, the Persians were no great sailors,[6] and their very religion debarred

them from entertaining any such notion as that of a maritime commerce. The voyage undertaken by Darius's direction upon the Indus and the Indian Sea proceeded rather from the capriciousness of a prince vainly ambitious of showing his power than from any settled regular project. It was attended with no consequence either to the advantage of commerce or of navigation. They emerged from their ignorance only to plunge into it again.

Besides, it was a received opinion[7] before the expedition of Alexander that the southern parts of India were uninhabitable.[8] This proceeded from a tradition that Semiramis[9] had brought back thence only twenty men, and Cyrus but seven.

Alexander entered by the north. His design was to march towards the east; but having found a part of the south full of great nations, cities, and rivers, he attempted to conquer it, and succeeded.

He then formed a design of uniting the Indies to the western nations by a maritime commerce, as he had already united them by the colonies he had established by land.

He ordered a fleet to be built on the Hydaspes, then fell down that river, entered the Indus, and sailed even to its mouth. He left his army and his fleet at Patala, went himself with a few vessels to view the sea, and marked the places where he would have ports to be opened and arsenals erected. Upon his return from Patala he separated the fleet, and took the route by land, for the mutual support of fleet and army. The fleet followed the coast from the Indus along the banks of the country of the Oritæ, of the Ichthyophagi, of Carmania and Persia. He caused wells to be dug, built cities, and would not suffer the Ichthyophagi to live on fish,[10] being desirous of having the borders of the sea inhabited by civi-

[1] Strabo, xv.
[2] Herodotus, *Melpomene*, iv. 44.
[3] Strabo, xv.
[4] *Ibid.*, xv.
[5] Pliny, vi. 33, Strabo, xv.
[6] They sailed not upon the rivers, lest they should defile the elements——Hyde, *Religion of the Persians*. Even to this day they have no maritime commerce. Those who take to the sea are treated by them as Atheists.

[7] Strabo, xv.
[8] Herodotus, *Melpomene*, iv. 44, says that Darius conquered the Indies; this must be understood only to mean Ariana; and even this was only an ideal conquest.
[9] Strabo, xv.
[10] This cannot be understood of all the Ichthyophagi, who inhabited a coast of ten thousand furlongs in extent. How was it possible for Alexander to have maintained them? How could he command their submission? This can be only understood of some particular tribes. Nearchus, in his book *Rerum Indicarum,* says that at the extremity of this coast, on the side of Persia, he had found some people who were less Ichthyophagi than the others. I should think that Alexander's prohibition related to these people, or to some other tribe still more bordering on Persia.

lised nations. Nearchus and Onesecritus wrote a journal of this voyage, which was performed in ten months. They arrived at Susa, where they found Alexander, who gave an entertainment to his whole army.

This prince had founded Alexandria, with a view of securing his conquest of Egypt; this was a key to open it, in the very place where the kings his predecessors had a key to shut it;[1] and he had not the least thought of a commerce of which the discovery of the Indian Sea could alone give him the idea.

It even seems that after his discovery he had no new design in regard to Alexandria. He had, indeed, a general scheme of opening a trade between the East Indies and the western parts of his empire; but as for the project of conducting this commerce through Egypt, his knowledge was too imperfect to be able to form any such design. It is true he had seen the Indus, he had seen the Nile, but he knew nothing of the Arabian seas between the two rivers. Scarcely had he returned from India when he fitted out new fleets, and navigated on the Euleus,[2] the Tigris, the Euphrates, and the ocean; he removed the cataracts, with which the Persians had encumbered those rivers; and he discovered that the Persian Gulf was a branch of the main sea. But as he went to view this sea[3] in the same manner as he had done in respect to that of India; as he caused a port to be opened for a thousand ships, and arsenals to be erected at Babylon; as he sent five hundred talents into Phœnicia and Syria, to draw mariners into this service whom he intended to distribute in the colonies along the coast; in fine, as he caused immense works to be erected on the Euphrates, and the other rivers of Assyria, there could be no doubt but he designed to carry on the commerce of India by the way of Babylon and the Persian Gulf.

There are some who pretend that Alexander wanted to subdue Arabia,[4] and had formed a design to make it the seat of his empire: but how could he have pitched upon a place with which he was entirely unacquainted?[5] Besides,

of all countries, this would have been the most inconvenient to him; for it would have separated him from the rest of his empire. The Caliphs, who made distant conquests, soon withdrew from Arabia to reside elsewhere.

9. *Of the Commerce of the Grecian Kings after the Death of Alexander.* At the time when Alexander made the conquest of Egypt, they had but a very imperfect idea of the Red Sea, and none at all of the ocean, which, joining this sea, on one side washes the coast of Africa, and on the other that of Arabia; nay, they thought it impossible to sail round the peninsula of Arabia. They who attempted it on each side had relinquished their design. "How is it possible," said they,[6] "to navigate to the southern coast of Arabia, when Cambyses' army, which traversed it on the north side, almost entirely perished; and the forces which Ptolemy, the son of Lagus, sent to the assistance of Seleucus Nicator at Babylon, underwent incredible hardships, and, upon account of the heat, could march only in the night?"

The Persians were entire strangers to navigation. When they had subdued Egypt, they introduced the same spirit into that country as prevailed in Persia: hence, so great was the supineness of the Persians in this respect, that the Grecian kings found them quite strangers, not only to the commerce of the Tyrians, Idumeans, and the Jews on the ocean, but even to the navigation of the Red Sea. I am apt to think that the destruction of the first Tyre by Nebuchadnezzar, together with the subversion of several petty nations and towns bordering on the Red Sea, had obliterated all their former knowledge of commerce.

Egypt, at the time of the Persian monarchy, did not front the Red Sea; it contained only that long narrow neck of land which the Nile covers with its inundations, and is enclosed on both sides by a chain of mountains.[7] They were, therefore, under the necessity of making a second discovery of the ocean and the Red Sea; and this discovery engaged the curiosity of the Grecian monarchs.

They ascended the Nile, and hunted after elephants in the countries situated between that river and the sea; by this progression they traced the sea-coast; and as the discoveries were made by the Greeks, the names are all Grecian, and the temples are con-

---

[1] Alexandria was founded on a flat shore, called Rhacotis, where, in ancient times, the kings had kept a garrison to prevent all strangers, and more particularly the Greeks, from entering the country.—Pliny, vi. 10; Strabo, xviii.

[2] Arrian, *De Expedit. Alex.* vii.

[3] *Ibid.*

[4] Strabo, vi, towards the end.

[5] Seeing Babylon overflowed, he looked upon the neighbouring country of Arabia as an island.—Aristobulus, in Strabo, xvi.

[6] See *Rerum Indicarum.*

[7] Strabo, xvi.

secrated to Greek divinities.[1]

The Greeks settled in Egypt were able to command a most extensive commerce; they were masters of all the harbours on the Red Sea; Tyre, the rival of every trading nation, was no more; they were not constrained by the ancient superstitions[2] on the country; in short, Egypt had become the centre of the world.

The kings of Syria left the commerce of the south to those of Egypt, and attached themselves only to the northern trade, which was carried on by means of the Oxus and the Caspian Sea. They then imagined that this sea was part of the northern ocean; and Alexander,[3] some time before his death, had fitted out a fleet[4] in order to discover whether it communicated with the ocean by the Euxine Sea, or some other eastern sea towards India. After him, Seleucus and Antiochus applied themselves to make discoveries in it, with particular attention; and with this view they scoured it with their fleets.[5] That part which Seleucus surveyed was called the Seleucidian Sea; that which Antiochus discovered received the name of the Sea of Antiochus. Attentive to the projects they might have formed on that side, they neglected the seas on the south; whether it was that the Ptolemies, by means of their fleets on the Red Sea, had already become the masters of it, or that they discovered an invincible aversion in the Persians against engaging in maritime affairs. The southern coasts of Persia supplied them with no seamen; there had been none in those parts, except towards the latter end of Alexander's reign. But the Egyptian kings, being masters of the Isle of Cyprus, of Phœnicia, and of a great number of towns on the coast of Asia Minor, were possessed of all sorts of conveniences for undertaking maritime expeditions. They had no occasion to force; they had only to follow the genius and bent of their subjects.

I am surprised, I confess, at the obstinacy with which the ancients believed that the Caspian Sea was a part of the ocean. The expeditions of Alexander, of the kings of Syria, of the Parthians and the Romans, could not make them change their sentiments; notwithstanding these nations described the Caspian Sea with wonderful exactness: but men are generally tenacious of their errors. When only the

south of this sea was known, it was at first taken for the ocean; in proportion as they advanced along the banks of the northern coast, instead of imagining it a great lake, they still believed it to be the ocean, that here made a sort of bay: surveying the coast, their discoveries never went eastward beyond the Jaxartes, nor westward farther than the extremity of Albania. The sea towards the north was shallow, and of course very unfit for navigation.[6] Hence it was that they always looked upon this as the ocean.

The land army of Alexander had been in the east only as far as the Hypanis, which is the last of those rivers that fall into the Indus: thus the first trade which the Greeks carried on with the Indies was confined to a very small part of the country. Seleucus Nicator penetrated as far as the Ganges, and thereby discovered the sea into which this river falls, that is to say, the Bay of Bengal.[7] The moderns discover countries by voyages at sea; the ancients discovered seas by conquests at land.

Strabo,[8] notwithstanding the testimony of Apollodorus, seems to doubt whether the Grecian kings of Bactria proceeded farther than Seleucus and Alexander.[9] Were it even true that they went no farther to the east than Seleucus, yet they went farther towards the south; they discovered Siger, and the ports on the coast of Malabar, which gave rise to the navigation I am going to mention.[10]

Pliny informs us that the navigation of the Indies was successively carried on in three different ways.[11] At first they sailed from the Cape of Siagre to the island of Patalena, which is at the mouth of the Indus. This we find was the course that Alexander's fleet steered to the Indies. They took afterwards a shorter and more certain course, by sailing from the same cape or promontory to Siger:[12] this can be no other than the kingdom of Siger mentioned by Strabo,[13] and discovered by the Grecian kings of Bactria. Pliny, by saying that this way was shorter than the other, can mean only that the voyage was made in less time: for, as Siger was discovered by the kings of Bactria, it must

[1] Strabo, xvi.
[2] These gave them an aversion to strangers.
[3] Pliny, ii. 67, vi. 9, 13; Strabo, xi., p. 507; Arrian, *De Expedit. Alex.*, iii, p 74, v, p. 104.
[4] Arrian, *De Expedit. Alex.*, vii.
[5] Pliny, ii. 67.
[6] See the Czar's Chart.
[7] Pliny, vi. 17.
[8] Book xv.
[9] Apollonius Adrumatinus in Strabo, xi.
[10] The Macedonians of Bactria, India, and Ariana, having separated themselves from Syria, formed a great state.
[11] Book vi. 23.
[12] *Ibid.*
[13] *Sigertidis regnum*, xi.

have been farther than the Indus: by this passage they must therefore have avoided the winding of certain coasts, and taken advantage of particular winds. The merchants at last took a third way; they sailed to Canes, or Ocelis, ports situated at the entrance of the Red Sea; whence by a west wind they arrived at Muziris, the first staple town of the Indies, and thence to the other ports. Here we see that instead of sailing to the mouth of the Red Sea as far as Siagre, by coasting Arabia Felix to the north-east, they steered directly from west to east, from one side to the other, by means of the monsoons, whose regular course they discovered by sailing in these latitudes. The ancients never lost sight of the coasts, except when they took advantage of these and the trade-winds, which were to them a kind of compass.[1]

Pliny[2] says that they set sail for the Indies in the middle of summer and returned towards the end of December, or in the beginning of January. This is entirely conformable to our naval journals. In that part of the Indian Ocean which is between the Peninsula of Africa, and that on this side the Ganges, there are two monsoons; the first, during which the winds blow from west to east, begins in the month of August or September; and the second, during which the wind is in the east, begins in January. Thus we set sail from Africa for Malabar at the season of the year that Ptolemy's fleet used to put to sea thence; and we return too at the same time as they.

Alexander's fleet was seven months in sailing from Patala to Susa. It set out in the month of July, that is, at a season when no ship dare now put to sea to return from the Indies. Between these two monsoons there is an interval during which the winds vary; when a north wind, meeting with the common winds, raises, especially near the coasts, the most terrible tempests. These continue during the months of June, July, and August. Alexander's fleet, therefore, setting sail from Patala in the month of July, must have been exposed to many storms, and the voyage must have been long, because they sailed against the monsoon.

Pliny says that they set out for the Indies at the end of summer; thus they spent the time proper for taking advantage of the monsoon

in their passage from Alexandria to the Red Sea.

Observe here, I pray, how navigation has, little by little, arrived at perfection. Darius's fleet was two years and a half in falling down the Indus and going to the Red Sea.[3] Afterwards the fleet of Alexander,[4] descending the Indus, arrived at Susa, in ten months, having sailed three months on the Indus, and seven on the Indian Ocean; at last the passage from the coast of Malabar to the Red Sea was made in forty days.[5]

Strabo,[6] who accounts for their ignorance of the countries between the Hypanis and the Ganges, says there were very few of those who sailed from Egypt to the Indies that ever proceeded so far as the Ganges. Their fleets, in fact, never went thither: they sailed with the western monsoons from the mouth of the Red Sea to the coast of Malabar. They cast anchor in the ports along that coast, and never attempted to get round the peninsula on this side the Ganges by Cape Comorin and the coast of Coromandel. The plan of navigation laid down by the kings of Egypt and the Romans was to set out and return the same year.[7]

Thus it is demonstrable that the commerce of the Greeks and Romans to the Indies was much less extensive than ours. We know immense countries, which to them were entirely unknown; we traffic with all the Indian nations; we even manage their trade and carry on their commerce. But this commerce of the ancients was carried on with far greater facility than ours. And if the moderns were to trade only with the coast of Guzerat and Malabar, and, without seeking for the southern isles, were satisfied with what these islanders brought them, they would certainly prefer the way of Egypt to that of the Cape of Good Hope. Strabo informs us[8] that they traded thus with the people of Taprobane.

10. *Of the Circuit of Africa.* We find from history that before the discovery of the mariner's compass four attempts were made to sail round the coast of Africa. The Phœnicians sent by Necho[9] and Eudoxus,[10] flying from the wrath

[1] The monsoons blow part of the year from one quarter, and part from another; the trade winds blow the whole year round from the same quarter.
[2] Book vi. 23.
[3] Herodotus, *Melpomene,* iv. 44.
[4] Pliny, vi. 23.
[5] *Ibid.*
[6] Book xv.
[7] Pliny, vi. 23.
[8] Book xv.
[9] He was desirous of conquering it.—Herodotus, iv. 42.
[10] Pliny, ii. 67; Pomponius Mela, iii. 9.

of Ptolemy Lathyrus, set out from the Red
Sea, and succeeded. Sataspes[1] sent by Xerxes,
and Hanno by the Carthaginians, set out from
the Pillars of Hercules, and failed in the attempt.

The capital point in surrounding Africa
was to discover and double the Cape of Good
Hope. Those who set out from the Red Sea
found this cape nearer by half than it would
have been in setting out from the Mediterranean. The shore from the Red Sea is not so
shallow as that from the cape to Hercules' Pillars.[2] The discovery of the cape by Hercules'
Pillars was owing to the invention of the compass, which permitted them to leave the coast
of Africa, and to launch out into the vast
ocean, in order to sail towards the island of St.
Helena, or towards the coast of Brazil.[3] It was,
therefore, possible for them to sail from the
Red Sea into the Mediterranean, but not to
set out from the Mediterranean to return by
the Red Sea.

Thus, without making this grand circuit, after which they could hardly hope to return, it
was most natural to trade to the east of Africa
by the Red Sea, and to the western coast by
Hercules' Pillars.

The Grecian kings of Egypt discovered at
first, in the Red Sea, that part of the coast of
Africa which extends from the bottom of the
gulf, where stands the town of Heroum, as far
as Dira, that is, to the strait now known by the
name of Babelmandel. Thence to the promontory of Aromatia, situate at the entrance of
the Red Sea,[4] the coast had never been surveyed by navigators: and this is evident from
what Artemidorus tells us,[5] that they were acquainted with the places on that coast, but
knew not their distances: the reason of which
is, they successively gained a knowledge of
those ports by land, without sailing from one
to the other.

Beyond this promontory, at which the coast

along the ocean commenced, they knew nothing, as we learn from Eratosthenes and Artemidorus.[6]

Such was the knowledge they had of the
coasts of Africa in Strabo's time, that is, in the
reign of Augustus. But after the prince's decease, the Romans found out the two capes
Raptum and Prassum, of which Strabo makes
no mention, because they had not as yet been
discovered. It is plain that both those names
are of Roman origin.

Ptolemy, the geographer, flourished under
Adrian and Antoninus Pius; and the author
of the *Periplus* of the Red Sea, whoever he
was, lived a little after. Yet the former limits
known Africa to Cape Prassum,[7] which is in
about the 14th degree of south latitude; while
the author of the *Periplus*[8] confines it to Cape
Raptum, which is nearly in the tenth degree of
the same latitude. In all likelihood the latter
took his limit from a place then frequented,
and Ptolemy his from a place with which there
was no longer any communication.

What confirms me in this notion is that the
people about Cape Prassum were Anthropo-
phagi.[9] Ptolemy takes notice[10] of a great number of places between the port or emporium
Aromatum and Cape Raptum, but leaves an
entire blank between Capes Raptum and
Prassum. The great profits of the East India
trade must have occasioned a neglect of that
of Africa. In fine, the Romans never had any
settled navigation; they had discovered these
several ports by land expeditions, and by
means of ships driven on that coast; and as at
present we are well acquainted with the maritime parts of Africa, but know very little of
the inland country, the ancients, on the contrary, had a very good knowledge of the inland parts, but were almost strangers to the
coasts.[11]

I said that the Phœnicians sent by Necho
and Eudoxus under Ptolemy Lathyrus had
made the circuit of Africa; but at the time of

[1] Herodotus, *Melpomene*, iv. 43.
[2] Add to this what I shall say in chapter 11 of
this book on the navigation of Hanno.
[3] In the months of October, November, December, and January the wind in the Atlantic Ocean
is found to blow north-east; our ships therefore
either cross the line, and to avoid the wind, which
is there generally east, they direct their course to
the south: or else they enter into the torrid zone,
in those places where the wind is west.
[4] The sea to which we give this name was called
by the ancients the Gulf of Arabia; the name of
Red Sea they gave to that part of the ocean which
borders on this gulf.
[5] Strabo, xvi.

[6] *Ibid.* Artemidorus settled the borders of the
known coast at the place called Austricornu; and
Eratosthenes, Cinnamomiferam.
[7] Strabo, i. 7; iv. 9; table 4 of Africa.
[8] This *Periplus* is attributed to Arrian.
[9] Ptolemy, iv. 9.
[10] Book iv. 7, 8.
[11] See what exact descriptions Strabo and Ptolemy have given us of the different parts of Africa.
Their knowledge was owing to the several wars
which the two most powerful nations in the world
had waged with the people of Africa, to the alliances they had contracted, and to the trade they
had carried on with those countries.

Ptolemy, the geographer, those two voyages must have been looked upon as fabulous, since he places after[1] the *Sinus Magnus*, which I apprehend to be the Gulf of Siam, an unknown country, extending from Asia to Africa, and terminating at Cape Prassum, so that the Indian Ocean would have been no more than a lake. The ancients who discovered the Indies towards the north, advancing eastward, placed this unknown country to the south.

11. *Of Carthage and Marseilles.* The law of nations which prevailed at Carthage was very extraordinary: all strangers who traded to Sardinia and towards Hercules' Pillars this haughty republic sentenced to be drowned. Her civil polity was equally surprising; she forbade the Sardinians to cultivate their lands, upon pain of death. She increased her power by her riches, and afterwards her riches by her power. Being mistress of the coasts of Africa, which are washed by the Mediterranean, she extended herself along the ocean. Hanno, by order of the senate of Carthage, distributed thirty thousand Carthaginians from Hercules' Pillars as far as Cerne. This place, he says, is as distant from Hercules' Pillars as the latter from Carthage. This situation is extremely remarkable. It lets us see that Hanno limited his settlements to the 25th degree of north latitude; that is, to two or three degrees south of the Canaries.

Hanno being at Cerne undertook another voyage, with a view of making further discoveries towards the south. He took but little notice of the continent. He followed the coast for twenty-six days, when he was obliged to return for want of provisions. The Carthaginians, it seems, made no use of this second enterprise. Scylax says[2] that the sea is not navigable beyond Cerne, because it is shallow, full of mud and sea-weeds:[3] and, in fact, there are many of these in those latitudes.[4] The Carthaginian merchants mentioned by Scylax might find obstacles which Hanno, who had sixty vessels of fifty oars each, had surmounted. Difficulties are at most but relative; besides, we

ought not to confound an enterprise in which bravery and resolution must be exerted with things that require no extraordinary conduct.

The relation of Hanno's voyage is a fine fragment of antiquity. It was written by the very man that performed it.

His recital is not mingled with ostentation. Great commanders write their actions with simplicity; because they receive more glory from facts than from words.

The style is agreeable to the subject; he deals not in the marvellous. All he says of the climate, of the soil, the behaviour, the manners of the inhabitants, correspond with what is every day seen on this coast of Africa; one would imagine it the journal of a modern sailor.

He observed from his fleet that in the daytime there was a prodigious silence on the continent, that in the night he heard the sound of various musical instruments, and that fires might then be everywhere seen, some larger than others.[5] Our relations are conformable to this; it has been discovered that in the day the savages retire into the forests to avoid the heat of the sun, that they light up great fires in the night to disperse the beasts of prey, and that they are passionately fond of music and dancing.

The same writer describes a volcano with all the phenomena of Vesuvius; and relates that he captured two hairy women, who chose to die rather than follow the Carthaginians, and whose skins he carried to Carthage. This has been found not void of probability.

This narration is so much the more valuable as it is a monument of Punic antiquity; and hence alone it has been regarded as fabulous. For the Romans retained their hatred of the Carthaginians, even after they had destroyed them. But it was victory alone that decided whether we ought to say the *Punic* or the *Roman* faith.

Some moderns[6] have imbibed these prejudices. What has become, say they, of the cities described by Hanno, of which even in Pliny's time there remained no vestiges? But it would have been a wonder indeed if any such vestiges had remained. Was it a Corinth or Athens that Hanno built on those coasts? He left Carthaginian families in such places as were

[1] Book vii. 3.
[2] See his *Periplus,* under the article on Carthage.
[3] See Herodotus, *Melpomene,* iv. 43, on the obstacles which Sataspes encountered.
[4] See the charts and relations in the first volume of *Collection of Voyages that Contributed to the Establishment of the East India Company,* part 1, p. 201. This weed covers the surface of the water in such a manner as to be scarcely perceived, and ships can only pass through it with a stiff gale.

[5] Pliny, v. 1, tells us the same thing, speaking of Mount Atlas: *Noctibus micare crebris ignibus, tibiarum cantu timpanorumque sonitu strepere, neminem interdiu cerni.*
[6] Mr. Dodwell. See his *Dissertation* on Hanno's *Periplus.*

most commodious for trade, and secured them as well as his hurry would permit against savages and wild beasts. The calamities of the Carthaginians put a period to the navigation of Africa; these families must necessarily then either perish or become savages. Besides, were the ruins of these cities even still in being, who is it that would venture into the woods and marshes to make the discovery? We find, however, in Scylax and Polybius that the Carthaginians had considerable settlements on those coasts. These are the vestiges of the cities of Hanno; there are no others, for the same reason that there are no others of Carthage itself.

The Carthaginians were in the high road to wealth; and had they gone so far as four degrees of north latitude, and fifteen of longitude, they would have discovered the Gold Coast. They would then have had a trade of much greater importance than that which is carried on at present on that coast, at a time when America seems to have degraded the riches of all other countries. They would there have found treasures of which they could never have been deprived by the Romans.

Very surprising things have been said of the riches of Spain. If we may believe Aristotle,[1] the Phœnicians who arrived at Tartessus found so much silver there that their ships could not hold it all; and they made of this metal their meanest utensils. The Carthaginians, according to Diodorus,[2] found so much gold and silver in the Pyrenean mountains, that they adorned the anchors of their ships with it. But no foundation can be built on such popular reports. Let us therefore examine the facts themselves.

We find in a fragment of Polybius, cited by Strabo,[3] that the silver mines at the source of the river Bætis, in which forty thousand men were employed, produced to the Romans twenty-five thousand drachmas a day, that is, about five million livres a year, at fifty livres to the mark. The mountains that contained these mines were called the Silver Mountains:[4] which shows they were the Potosi of those times. At present, the mines of Hanover do not employ a fourth part of the workmen, and yet they yield more. But as the Romans had not many copper mines, and but few of silver; and as the Greeks knew none but the Attic

mines, which were of little value, they might well be astonished at their abundance.

In the war that broke out for the succession of Spain, a man called the Marquis of Rhodes, of whom it was said that he was ruined in gold mines and enriched in hospitals,[5] proposed to the court of France to open the Pyrenean mines. He alleged the example of the Tyrians, the Carthaginians, and the Romans. He was permitted to search, but sought in vain; he still alleged, and found nothing.

The Carthaginians, being masters of the gold and silver trade, were willing to be so of the lead and pewter. These metals were carried by land from the ports of Gaul upon the ocean to those of the Mediterranean. The Carthaginians were desirous of receiving them at the first hand; they sent Himilco to make a settlement in the isles called Cassiterides,[6] which are imagined to be those of Scilly.

These voyages from Bætica into England have made some persons imagine that the Carthaginians knew the compass: but it is very certain that they followed the coasts. There needs no other proof than Himilco's being four months in sailing from the mouth of the Bætis to England; besides, the famous piece of history of the Carthaginian[7] pilot who, being followed by a Roman vessel, ran aground, that he might not show her the way to England,[8] plainly intimates that those vessels were very near the shore when they fell in with each other.

The ancients might have performed voyages that would make one imagine they had the compass, though they had not. If a pilot was far from land, and during his voyage had such serene weather that in the night he could always see a polar star and in the day the rising and setting of the sun, it is certain he might regulate his course as well as we do now by the compass: but this must be a fortuitous case, and not a regular method of navigation.

We see in the treaty which put an end to the first Punic war that Carthage was principally attentive to preserve the empire of the sea, and Rome that of the land. Hanno,[9] in his negotiation with the Romans, declared that they should not be suffered even to wash their hands in the sea of Sicily; they were not permitted to sail beyond the *promontorium pul-*

---

[1] *Of Wonderful Things.*
[2] Book vi.
[3] Book iii.
[4] *Mons argentarius.*

[5] He had some share in their management.
[6] See Festus Avienus.
[7] Strabo, iii, towards the end.
[8] He was rewarded by the senate of Carthage.
[9] Freinshemius, *Supplement to Livy*, dec. 2, vi.

chrum; they were forbidden to trade in Sicily, Sardinia, and Africa, except at Carthage:[1] an exception that proves there was no design to favour them in their trade with that city.

In early times there had been very great wars between Carthage and Marseilles[2] on the subject of fishing. After the peace they entered jointly into economical commerce. Marseilles at length grew jealous, especially as, being equal to her rival in industry, she had become inferior to her in power. This is the motive of her great fidelity to the Romans. The war between the latter and the Carthaginians in Spain was a source of riches to Marseilles, which had now become their magazine. The ruin of Carthage and Corinth still increased the glory of Marseilles, and had it not been for the civil wars, in which this republic ought on no account to have engaged, she would have been happy under the protection of the Romans, who were not the least jealous of her commerce.

12. *The Isle of Delos. Mithridates.* Upon the destruction of Corinth by the Romans, the merchants retired to Delos, an island which from religious considerations was looked upon as a place of safety:[3] besides, it was extremely well situated for the commerce of Italy and Asia, which, since the reduction of Africa and the weakening of Greece, had grown more important.

From the earliest times the Greeks, as we have already observed, sent colonies to Propontis and to the Euxine Sea—colonies which retained their laws and liberties under the Persians. Alexander, having undertaken his expedition against the barbarians only, did not molest these people.[4] Neither does it appear that the kings of Pontus, who were masters of many of those colonies, ever deprived them of their own civil government.[5]

The power of those kings increased as soon as they subdued those cities.[6] Mithridates

found himself able to hire troops on every side; to repair his frequent losses; to have a multitude of workmen, ships, and military machines; to procure himself allies; to bribe those of the Romans, and even the Romans themselves; to keep the barbarians of Asia and Europe in his pay;[7] to continue the war for many years, and of course to discipline his troops, he found himself able to train them to arms, to instruct them in the military art of the Romans,[8] and to form considerable bodies out of their deserters; in a word, he found himself able to sustain great losses, and to be frequently defeated, without being ruined;[9] neither would he have been ruined if the voluptuous and barbarous king had not destroyed, in his prosperous days, what had been done by the great prince in times of adversity.

Thus it was that when the Romans had arrived at their highest pitch of grandeur, and seemed to have nothing to apprehend but from the ambition of their own subjects, Mithridates once more ventured to contest the mighty point, which the overthrow of Philip, of Antiochus, and of Perseus had already decided. Never was there a more destructive war: the two contending parties, being possessed of great power, and receiving alternate advantages, the inhabitants of Greece and of Asia fell a sacrifice in the quarrel, either as foes, or as friends of Mithridates. Delos was involved in the general fatality, and commerce failed on every side: which was a necessary consequence, the people themselves being destroyed.

The Romans, in pursuance of a system of which I have spoken elsewhere,[10] acting as destroyers, that they might not appear as conquerors, demolished Carthage and Corinth; a practice by which they would have ruined themselves had they not subdued the world. When the kings of Pontus became masters of the Greek colonies on the Euxine Sea, they took care not to destroy what was to be the foundation of their own grandeur.

13. *Of the Genius of the Romans as to Maritime Affairs.* The Romans laid no stress on anything but their land forces, who were dis-

[1] In the parts subject to the Carthaginians.
[2] Justin, xliii. 5.
[3] See Strabo, x.
[4] He confirmed the liberty of the city of Amisus, an Athenian colony which had enjoyed a popular government, even under the kings of Persia. Lucullus having taken Sinone and Amisus, restored them to their liberty, and recalled the inhabitants, who had fled on board their ships.
[5] See what Appian writes concerning the Phanagoreans, the Amisians, and the Synopians, in his treatise *Of the War against Mithridates.*
[6] See Appian, in regard to the immense treasures which Mithridates employed in his wars,

[7] See Appian *Of the War against Mithridates.*
[8] *Ibid.*
[9] He lost at one time 170,000 men, yet he soon recruited his armies.
[10] In the *Considerations on the Causes of the Rise and Declension of the Roman Grandeur.*

those which he had buried, those which he frequently lost by the treachery of his own people, and those which were found after his death.

ciplined to stand firm, to fight on one spot, and there bravely to die. They could not like the practice of seamen, who first offer to fight, then fly, then return, constantly avoid danger, often make use of stratagem, and seldom of force. This was not suitable to the genius of the Greeks[1] much less to that of the Romans.

They destined therefore to the sea only those citizens who were not considerable enough to have a place in their legions.[2] Their marines were commonly freedmen.

At this time we have neither the same esteem for land forces nor the same contempt for those of the sea. In the former, art has decreased;[3] in the latter, it has augmented:[4] now things are generally esteemed in proportion to the degree of ability requisite to discharge them.

14. *Of the Genius of the Romans with respect to Commerce.* The Romans were never distinguished by a jealousy for trade. They attacked Carthage as a rival, not as a commercial nation. They favoured trading cities that were not subject to them. Thus they increased the power of Marseilles by the cession of a large territory. They were vastly afraid of barbarians, but had not the least apprehension from a trading people. Their genius, their glory, their military education, and the very form of their government estranged them from commerce.

In the city, they were employed only about war, elections, factions, and law-suits; in the country, about agriculture; and as for the provinces, a severe and tyrannical government was incompatible with commerce.

But their political constitution was not more opposed to trade than their law of nations. "The people," says Pomponius, the civilian,[5] "with whom we have neither friendship, nor hospitality nor alliance, are not our enemies; however, if anything belonging to us falls into their hands, they are the proprietors of it; freemen become their slaves; and they are upon the same terms with respect to us."

Their civil law was not less oppressive. The law of Constantine,[6] after having stigmatised as bastards the children of a mean rank who had been married to those of a superior station, confounds women who retail merchandise with slaves, with the mistresses of taverns, with actresses, with the daughters of those who keep public stews, or who had been condemned to fight in the amphitheatre; this had its origin in the ancient institutions of the Romans.

I am not ignorant that men prepossessed with these two ideas (that commerce is of the greatest service to a state, and that the Romans had the best-regulated government in the world) have believed that these people greatly honoured and encouraged commerce; but the truth is, they seldom troubled their heads about it.

15. *Of the Commerce of the Romans with the Barbarians.* The Romans having erected a vast empire in Europe, Asia, and Africa, the weakness of the people and the tyranny of their laws united all the parts of this immense body. The Roman policy was then to avoid all communication with those nations whom they had not subdued: the fear of carrying to them the art of conquering made them neglect the art of enriching themselves. They made laws to hinder all commerce with barbarians. "Let nobody," said Valens and Gratian,[7] "send wine, oil, or other liquors to the barbarians, though it be only for them to taste." "Let no one carry gold to them," add Gratian, Valentinian, and Theodosius;[8] "rather, if they have any, let our subjects deprive them of it by stratagem." The exportation of iron was prohibited on pain of death.

Domitian, a prince of great timidity, ordered the vines in Gaul to be pulled up,[9] from fear, no doubt, lest their wines should draw thither the barbarians. Probus and Julian, who had no such fears, gave orders for their being planted again.

I am sensible that upon the declension of the Roman empire the barbarians obliged the Romans to establish staple towns, and to trade with them. But even this is a proof that the minds of the Romans were averse to commerce.[10]

16. *Of the Commerce of the Romans with Arabia and the Indies.* The trade to Arabia

---

[1] As Plato has observed, *Laws,* iv.
[2] Polybius, v.
[3] See the *Considerations on the Causes of the Rise and Declension of the Roman Grandeur.*
[4] *Ibid.*
[5] Leg. 5, § 2, *ff. De Captivis.*
[6] *Quæ mercimoniis publice præfuit.—Leg.* 1, *Cod. de natural. liberis.*

[7] *Leg. ad barbaricum, Cod. quæ res exportari non debeant.*
[8] *Leg. 2, Cod. de commerc. et mercator.*
[9] Procopius, *War of the Persians,* i.
[10] See the *Considerations on the Causes of the Rise and Declension of the Roman Grandeur.*

Felix, and that to the Indies, were the two branches, and almost the only ones, of their foreign commerce. The Arabians were possessed of immense riches, which they found in their seas and forests; and as they sold much and purchased little, they drew to themselves the gold and silver of the Romans.[1] Augustus,[2] being well apprised of that opulence, resolved they should be either his friends or his enemies. With this view he sent Ælius Gallus from Egypt into Arabia. This commander found the people indolent, peaceable, and unskilled in war. He fought battles, laid sieges to towns, and lost but seven of his men by the sword; but the perfidy of his guides, long marches, the climate, want of provisions, distempers, and ill-conduct, caused the ruin of his army.

He was therefore obliged to be content with trading to Arabia, in the same manner as other nations; that is, with giving them gold and silver in exchange for their commodities. The Europeans trade with them still in the same manner; the caravans of Aleppo and the royal vessel of Suez carry thither immense sums.[3]

Nature had formed the Arabs for commerce, not for war; but when those quiet people came to be near neighbours to the Parthians and the Romans, they acted as auxiliaries to both nations. Ælius Gallus found them a trading people; Mahomet happened to find them trained to war; he inspired them with enthusiasm, which led them to glory and conquest.

The commerce of the Romans to the Indies was very considerable. Strabo[4] had been informed in Egypt that they employed in this navigation one hundred and twenty vessels; this commerce was carried on entirely with bullion. They sent thither annually fifty millions of sesterces. Pliny[5] says that the merchandise brought thence was sold at Rome at *cent.* per cent profit. He speaks, I believe, too generally; if this trade had been so vastly profitable, everybody would have been willing to engage in it, and then it would have been at an end.

It will admit of a question, whether the trade to Arabia and the Indies was of any advantage to the Romans. They were obliged to export their bullion thither, though they had not, like us, the resource of America, which supplies what we send away. I am persuaded that one of the reasons of their increasing the value of their specie by establishing base coin was the scarcity of silver, owing to the continual exportation of it to the Indies: and though the commodities of this country were sold at Rome at the rate of *cent.* per cent, this profit of the Romans, being obtained from the Romans themselves, could not enrich the empire.

It may be alleged, on the other hand, that this commerce increased the Roman navigation, and of course their power; that new merchandise augmented their inland trade, gave encouragement to the arts, and employment to the industrious; that the number of subjects multiplied in proportion to the new means of support; that this new commerce was productive of luxury, which I have proved to be as favourable to a monarchical government as fatal to a commonwealth; that this establishment was of the same date as the fall of their republic; that the luxury of Rome had become necessary; and that it was extremely proper that a city which had accumulated all the wealth of the universe should refund it by its luxury.

Strabo says[6] that the Romans carried on a far more extensive commerce with the Indies than the kings of Egypt; but it is very extraordinary that those people who were so little acquainted with commerce should have paid more attention to that of India than the Egyptian kings, whose dominions lay so conveniently for it. The reason of this must be explained.

After the death of Alexander, the kings of Egypt established a maritime commerce with the Indies; while the kings of Syria, who were possessed of the more eastern provinces, and consequently of the Indies, maintained that commerce of which we have taken notice in the sixth chapter, which was carried on partly by land, and partly by rivers, and had been further facilitated by means of the Macedonian colonies; insomuch that Europe had communication with the Indies both by Egypt and by Syria. The dismembering of the latter kingdom, whence was formed that of Bactri-

[1] Pliny, vi. 28, and Strabo, xvi.
[2] *Ibid.*
[3] The caravans of Aleppo and Suez carry thither annually to the value of about two millions of livres, and as much more clandestinely; the royal vessel of Suez carries thither also two millions.
[4] Book ii, p. 181, ed. 1587.
[5] Book vi. 23.

[6] He says, book ii, that the Romans employed a hundred and twenty ships in that trade; and, in book xvii, that the Grecian kings scarcely employed twenty.

ana, did not prove in any way prejudicial to this commerce. Marinus the Tyrian, quoted by Ptolemy,[1] mentions the discoveries made in India by means of some Macedonian merchants, who found out new roads, which had been unknown to kings in their military expeditions. We find in Ptolemy[2] that they went from Peter's tower[3] as far as Sera; and the discovery made by mercantile people of so distant a mart, situated in the north-east part of China, was a kind of prodigy. Hence, under the kings of Syria and Bactriana, merchandise was conveyed to the west from the southern parts of India, by the river Indus, the Oxus, and the Caspian Sea; while those of the more eastern and northern parts were transported from Sera, Peter's tower, and other staples, as far as the Euphrates. Those merchants directed their route nearly by the fortieth degree of north latitude, through countries situated to the west of China, more civilised at that time than at present, because they had not as yet been infested by the Tartars.

Now while the Syrian empire was extending its trade to such a distance by land, Egypt did not greatly enlarge its maritime commerce.

The Parthians soon after appeared, and founded their empire; and when Egypt fell under the power of the Romans, this empire was at its height, and had received its whole extension.

The Romans and Parthians were two rival nations, that fought not for dominion but for their very existence. Between the two empires deserts were formed and armies were always stationed on the frontiers; so that instead of there being any commerce, there was not so much as communication between them. Ambition, jealousy, religion, national antipathy, and difference of manners completed the separation. Thus the trade from east to west, which had formerly so many channels, was reduced to one; and Alexandria becoming the only staple, the trade to this city was immensely enlarged.

We shall say but one word of their inland trade. Its principal branch was the corn brought to Rome for the subsistence of the people; but this was rather a political affair than a point of commerce. On this account

the sailors were favoured with some privileges, because the safety of the empire depended on their vigilance.[4]

17. *Of Commerce after the Destruction of the Western Empire.* After the invasion of the Roman empire one effect of the general calamity was the destruction of commerce. The barbarous nations at first regarded it only as an opportunity for robbery; and when they had subdued the Romans, they honoured it no more than agriculture, and the other professions of a conquered people.

Soon was the commerce of Europe almost entirely lost. The nobility, who had everywhere the direction of affairs, were in no pain about it.

The laws of the Visigoths[5] permitted private people to occupy half the beds of great rivers, provided the other half remained free for nets and boats. There must have been very little trade in countries conquered by these barbarians.

In those times were established the ridiculous rights of escheatage and shipwrecks. These men thought that, as strangers were not united to them by any civil law, they owed them on the one hand no kind of justice, and on the other no sort of pity.

In the narrow bounds which nature had originally prescribed to the people of the north, all were strangers to them: and in their poverty they regarded all only as contributing to their riches. Being established, before their conquest, on the coasts of a sea of very little breadth, and full of rocks, from these very rocks they drew their subsistence.

But the Romans, who made laws for all the world, had established the most humane ones with regard to shipwrecks.[6] They suppressed the rapine of those who inhabited the coasts, and what was more still, the rapacity of their treasuries.[7]

18. *A particular Regulation.* The law of the Visigoths made, however, one regulation in favour of commerce.[8] It ordained that foreign merchants should be judged, in the differences that arose among themselves, by the laws and

[1] Book i, 2.
[2] Book i, 13.
[3] Our best maps place Peter's tower in the hundredth degree of longitude, and about the fortieth of latitude.

[4] Suetonius, Life of Claudius, 18; *Leg. 7, Cod. Theodos. de naviculariis.*
[5] Book viii, tit. 4, § 9.
[6] *Toto titulo,* ff. *de incend, ruin. et naufrag.; Cod. de naufragiis; Leg. 3,* ff. *ad leg. Cornel, de sicariis.*
[7] *Leg. 1, Cod. de naufragiis.*
[8] Book xi, tit. 3, § 2.

by judges of their own nation. This was founded on an established custom among all mixed people, that every man should live under his own law—a custom of which I shall speak more at large in another place.

19. *Of Commerce after the Decay of the Roman Power in the East.* The Mahomedans appeared, conquered, extended, and dispersed themselves. Egypt had particular sovereigns; these carried on the commerce of India, and being possessed of the merchandise of this country, drew to themselves the riches of all other nations. The sultans of Egypt were the most powerful princes of those times. History informs us with what a constant and well-regulated force they stopped the ardour, the fire, and the impetuosity of the crusades.

20. *How Commerce broke through the Barbarism of Europe.* Aristotle's philosophy being carried to the west, pleased the subtle geniuses who were the virtuosi of those times of ignorance. The schoolmen were infatuated with it, and borrowed from that philosopher[1] a great many notions on lending upon interest, whereas its source might have been easily traced in the gospel; in short, they condemned it absolutely and in all cases. Hence commerce, which was the profession only of mean persons, became that of knaves; for whenever a thing is forbidden, which nature permits or necessity requires, those who do it are looked upon as dishonest.

Commerce was transferred to a nation covered with infamy, and soon ranked with the most shameful usury, with monopolies, with the levying of subsidies, and with all the dishonest means of acquiring wealth.

The Jews, enriched by their exactions, were pillaged by the tyranny of princes; which pleased indeed, but did not ease, the people.[2]

What passed in England may serve to give us an idea of what was done in other countries. King John[3] having imprisoned the Jews, in order to obtain their wealth, there were few who had not at least one of their eyes plucked out. Thus did that king administer justice. A certain Jew, who had a tooth pulled out every day for seven days successively, gave

ten thousand marks of silver for the eighth. Henry III extorted from Aaron, a Jew at York, fourteen thousand marks of silver, and ten thousand for the queen. In those times they did by violence what is now done in Poland with some semblance of moderation. As princes could not dive into the purses of their subjects because of their privileges, they put the Jews to the torture, who were not considered as citizens.

At last a custom was introduced of confiscating the effects of those Jews who embraced Christianity. This ridiculous custom is known only by the law which suppressed it.[4] The most vain and trifling reasons were given in justification of that proceeding; it was alleged that it was proper to try them, in order to be certain that they had entirely shaken off the slavery of the devil. But it is evident that this confiscation was a species of the right of amortisation, to recompense the prince, or the lords, for the taxes levied on the Jews, which ceased on their embracing Christianity.[5] In those times, men, like lands, were regarded as property. I cannot help remarking, by the way, how this nation has been sported with from one age to another: at one time, their effects were confiscated when they were willing to become Christians; and at another, if they refused to turn Christians, they were ordered to be burned.

In the meantime, commerce was seen to arise from the bosom of vexation and despair. The Jews, proscribed by turns from every country, found out the way of saving their effects. Thus they rendered their retreats for ever fixed; for though princes might have been willing to get rid of their persons, yet they did not choose to get rid of their money.

The Jews invented letters of exchange;[6] commerce, by this method, became capable of eluding violence, and of maintaining everywhere its ground; the richest merchant having none but invisible effects, which he could

---

[1] See Aristotle, *Politics,* i. 9, 10.

[2] See in *Marca Hispanica,* the constitutions of Aragon, in the years 1228 and 1231; and in Brussel, the agreement, in the year 1206, between the King, the Countess of Champagne, and Guy of Dampierre.

[3] Stow, *Survey of London,* iii, p. 54.

[4] The edict passed at Baville, 4th of April, 1392.

[5] In France the Jews were slaves in mortmain, and the lords their successors. Mr. Brussel mentions an agreement made in the year 1206, between the King and Thibaut, Count of Champagne, by which it was agreed that the Jews of the one should not lend in the lands of the other.

[6] It is known that under Philip Augustus and Philip the Long, the Jews who were chased from France took refuge in Lombardy, and that there they gave to foreign merchants and travellers secret letters, drawn upon those to whom they had entrusted their effects in France, which were accepted.

convey imperceptibly wherever he pleased.

The Theologians were obliged to limit their principles; and commerce, which they had before connected by main force with knavery, re-entered, if I may so express myself, the bosom of probity.

Thus we owe to the speculations of the schoolmen all the misfortunes which accompanied the destruction of commerce;[1] and to the avarice of princes, the establishment of a practice which puts it in some measure out of their power.

From this time it became necessary that princes should govern with more prudence than they themselves could ever have imagined; for great exertions of authority were, in the event, found to be impolitic; and from experience it is manifest that nothing but the goodness and lenity of a government can make it flourish.

We begin to be cured of Machiavelism, and recover from it every day. More moderation has become necessary in the councils of princes. What would formerly have been called a master-stroke in politics would be now, independent of the horror it might occasion, the greatest imprudence.

Happy is it for men that they are in a situation in which, though their passions prompt them to be wicked, it is, nevertheless, to their interest to be humane and virtuous.

21. *The Discovery of two new Worlds, and in what Manner Europe is affected by it.* The compass opened, if I may so express myself, the universe. Asia and Africa were found, of which only some borders were known; and America, of which we knew nothing.

The Portuguese, sailing on the Atlantic Ocean, discovered the most southern point of Africa; they saw a vast sea, which carried them to the East Indies. Their danger upon this sea, the discovery of Mozambique, Melinda, and Calicut, have been sung by Camoens, whose poems make us feel something of the charms of the *Odyssey* and the magnificence of the *Æneid.*

The Venetians had hitherto carried on the trade of the Indies through the Turkish dominions, and pursued it in the midst of oppressions and discouragements. By the discovery of the Cape of Good Hope, and those which were made some time after, Italy was no longer the centre of the trading world; it was, if I may be permitted the expression, only a corner of the universe, and is so still. The commerce even of the Levant depending now on that of the great trading nations to both the Indies, Italy even in that branch can no longer be considered as a principal.

The Portuguese traded to the Indies in right of conquest. The constraining laws which the Dutch at present impose on the commerce of the little Indian princes had been established before by the Portuguese.[2]

The fortune of the house of Austria was prodigious. Charles V succeeded to the possession of Burgundy, Castile, and Aragon; he arrived afterwards at the imperial dignity; and to procure him a new kind of grandeur, the globe extended itself, and there was seen a new world paying him obeisance.

Christopher Columbus discovered America; and though Spain sent thither only a force so small that the least prince in Europe could have sent the same, yet it subdued two vast empires, and other great states.

While the Spaniards discovered and conquered the west, the Portuguese pushed their conquests and discoveries in the east. These two nations met each other; they had recourse to Pope Alexander VI, who made the celebrated line of partition, and determined the great suit.

But the other nations of Europe would not suffer them quietly to enjoy their shares. The Dutch chased the Portuguese from almost all their settlements in the East Indies; and several other nations planted colonies in America.

The Spaniards considered these newly-discovered countries as the subject of conquest; while others, more refined in their views, found them to be the proper subjects of commerce, and upon this principle directed their proceedings. Hence several nations have conducted themselves with so much wisdom that they have given a kind of sovereignty to companies of merchants, who, governing these far-distant countries only with a view to trade, have made a great accessory power without embarrassing the principal state.

The colonies they have formed are under a kind of dependence, of which there are but very few instances in all the colonies of the ancients; whether we consider them as holdings of the state itself, or of some trading company established in the state.

---

[1] See *Nov.* 83 of the Emperor Leo, which revokes the law of Basil his father. This law of Basil is in Hermenopulus, under the name of Leo, iii, tit. 7, § 27.

[2] See the account of Pirard, part II, 15.

The design of these colonies is to trade on more advantageous conditions than could otherwise be done with the neighbouring people, with whom all advantages are reciprocal. It has been established that the metropolis,[1] or mother country, alone shall trade in the colonies, and that from very good reason; because the design of the settlement was the extension of commerce, not the foundation of a city or of a new empire.

Thus it is still a fundamental law of Europe that all commerce with a foreign colony shall be regarded as a mere monopoly, punishable by the laws of the country; and in this case we are not to be directed by the laws and precedents of the ancients, which are not at all applicable.[2]

It is likewise acknowledged that a commerce established between the mother countries does not include a permission to trade in the colonies; for these always continue in a state of prohibition.

The disadvantage of a colony that loses the liberty of commerce is visibly compensated by the protection of the mother country, who defends it by her arms, or supports it by her laws.

Hence follows a third law of Europe, that when a foreign commerce with a colony is prohibited, it is not lawful to trade in those seas, except in such cases as are excepted by treaty.

Nations who are, with respect to the whole globe, what individuals are in a state, are governed like the latter by the laws of nature, and by particular laws of their own making. One nation may resign to another the sea, as well as the land. The Carthaginians forbade the Romans to sail beyond certain limits,[3] as the Greeks had obliged the King of Persia to keep as far distant from the sea-coast as a horse could gallop.[4]

The great distance of our colonies is not an inconvenience that affects their safety; for if the mother country, on whom they depend for their defence, is remote, no less remote are those nations who rival the mother country, and by whom they may be afraid of being conquered.

Besides, this distance is the cause that those who are established there cannot conform to the manner of living in a climate so different from their own; they are obliged therefore to draw from the mother country all the conveniences of life. The Carthaginians,[5] to render the Sardinians and Corsicans more dependent, forbade their planting, sowing, or doing anything of the kind, under pain of death; so that they supplied them with necessaries from Africa.

The Europeans have compassed the same thing, without having recourse to such severe laws. Our colonies in the Caribbean islands are under an admirable regulation in this respect; the subject of their commerce is what we neither have nor can produce; and they want what is the subject of ours.

A consequence of the discovery of America was the connecting Asia and Africa with Europe; it furnished materials for a trade with that vast part of Asia known by the name of the East Indies. Silver, that metal so useful as the medium of commerce, became now as merchandise the basis of the greatest commerce in the world. In fine, the navigation to Africa became necessary in order to furnish us with men to labour in the mines, and to cultivate the lands of America.

Europe has arrived at so high a degree of power that nothing in history can be compared with it, whether we consider the immensity of its expenses, the grandeur of its engagements, the number of its troops, and the regular payments even of those that are least serviceable, and which are kept only for ostentation.

Father Du Halde says[6] that the interior trade of China is much greater than that of all Europe. That might be, if our foreign trade did not augment our inland commerce. Europe carries on the trade and navigation of the other three parts of the world; as France, England, and Holland do nearly that of Europe.

22. *Of the Riches which Spain drew from America.* If Europe has derived so many advantages from the American trade, it seems natural to imagine that Spain must have derived much greater.[7] She drew from the newly-

[1] This, in the language of the ancients, is the state which founded the colony.
[2] Except the Carthaginians, as we see by the treaty which put an end to the first Punic war.
[3] Polybius, iii.
[4] The King of Persia obliged himself by treaty not to sail with any vessel of war beyond the Cyanean rocks and the Chelidonean isles.—Plutarch, *Cimon.*

[5] Aristotle, *Of Wonderful Things;* Livy, dec. 2, vii.
[6] Book ii, p. 170.
[7] This has been already shown in a small treatise written by the author about twenty years ago; which has been almost entirely incorporated in the present work.

discovered world so prodigious a quantity of gold and silver, that all we had before could not be compared with it.

But (what one could never have expected) this great kingdom was everywhere baffled by its misfortunes. Philip II, who succeeded Charles V, was obliged to make the celebrated bankruptcy known to all the world. There never was a prince who suffered more from the murmurs, the insolence, and the revolt of troops constantly ill-paid.

From that time the monarchy of Spain has been incessantly declining. This has been owing to an interior and physical defect in the nature of those riches, which renders them vain—a defect which increases every day.

Gold and silver are either a fictitious or a representative wealth. The representative signs of wealth are extremely durable, and, in their own nature, but little subject to decay. But the more they are multiplied, the more they lose their value, because the fewer are the things which they represent.

The Spaniards, after the conquest of Mexico and Peru, abandoned their natural riches, in pursuit of a representative wealth which daily degraded itself. Gold and silver were extremely scarce in Europe, and Spain becoming all of a sudden mistress of a prodigious quantity of these metals, conceived hopes to which she had never before aspired. The wealth she found in the conquered countries, great as it was, did not, however, equal that of their mines. The Indians concealed part of it; and besides, these people, who made no other use of gold and silver than to give magnificence to the temples of their gods and to the palaces of their kings, sought not for it with an avarice like ours. In short, they had not the secret of drawing these metals from every mine; but only from those in which the separation might be made with fire: they were strangers to the manner of making use of mercury, and perhaps to mercury itself.

However, it was not long before the specie of Europe was doubled; this appeared from the price of commodities, which everywhere was doubled.

The Spaniards raked into the mines, scooped out mountains, invented machines to draw out water, to break the ore, and separate it; and as they sported with the lives of the Indians, they forced them to labour without mercy. The specie of Europe soon doubled, and the profit of Spain diminished in the same proportion; they had every year the same quantity of metal, which had become by one-half less precious.

In double the time the specie still doubled, and the profit still diminished another half.

It diminished even more than half: let us see in what manner.

To extract the gold from the mines, to give it the requisite preparations, and to import it into Europe, must be attended with some certain expense. I will suppose this to be as 1 to 64. When the specie was once doubled, and consequently became by one-half less precious, the expense was as 2 to 64. Thus the galoons which brought to Spain the same quantity of gold, brought a thing which really was of less value by one-half, though the expenses attending it had been twice as high.

If we proceed doubling and doubling, we shall find in this progression the cause of the impotency of the wealth of Spain.

It is about two hundred years since they have worked their Indian mines. I suppose the quantity of specie at present in the trading world is to that before the discovery of the Indies as 32 is to 1; that is, it has been doubled five times: in two hundred years more the same quantity will be to that before the discovery as 64 is to 1; that is, it will be doubled once more. Now, at present, fifty quintals of ore yield four, five, and six ounces of gold;[1] and when it yields only two, the miner receives no more from it than his expenses. In two hundred years, when the miner will extract only four, this too will only defray his charges. There will then be but little profit to be drawn from the gold mines. The same reasoning will hold good of silver, except that the working of the silver mines is a little more advantageous than those of gold.

But, if mines should be discovered so fruitful as to give a much greater profit, the more fruitful they may be, the sooner the profit will cease.

The Portuguese in Brazil have found mines of gold so rich[2] that they must necessarily very soon make a considerable diminution in the profits of those of Spain, as well as in their own.

[1] See Frezier, *Voyages.*
[2] According to Lord Anson, Europe receives every year from Brazil two millions sterling in gold, which is found in sand at the foot of the mountains, or in the beds of rivers. When I wrote the little treatise mentioned in the first note of this chapter, the returns from Brazil were far from being so considerable an item as they are at present.

I have frequently heard people deplore the blindness of the court of France, who repulsed Christopher Columbus, when he made the proposal of discovering the Indies. Indeed they did, though perhaps without design, an act of the greatest wisdom. Spain has behaved like the foolish king who desired that everything he touched might be converted into gold, and who was obliged to beg of the gods to put an end to his misery.

The companies and banks established in many nations have put a finishing stroke to the lowering of gold and silver as a sign of representation of riches; for by new fictions they have multiplied in such a manner the signs of wealth, that gold and silver having this office only in part have become less precious.

Thus public credit serves instead of mines, and diminishes the profit which the Spaniards drew from theirs.

True it is that the Dutch trade to the East Indies has increased, in some measure, the value of the Spanish merchandise: for as they carry bullion, and give it in exchange for the merchandise of the East, they ease the Spaniards of part of a commodity which in Europe abounds too much.

And this trade, in which Spain seems to be only indirectly concerned, is as advantageous to that nation as to those who are directly employed in carrying it on.

From what has been said we may form a judgment of the last order of the council of Spain, which prohibits the making use of gold and silver in gildings, and other superfluities; a decree as ridiculous as it would be for the states of Holland to prohibit the consumption of spices.

My reasoning does not hold good against all mines; those of Germany and Hungary, which produce little more than the expense of working them, are extremely useful. They are found in the principal state; they employ many thousand men, who there consume their superfluous commodities, and they are properly a manufacture of the country.

The mines of Germany and Hungary promote the culture of land; the working of those of Mexico and Peru destroys it.

The Indies and Spain are two powers under the same master; but the Indies are the principal, while Spain is only an accessory. It is in vain for politics to attempt to bring back the principal to the accessory; the Indies will always draw Spain to themselves.

Of the merchandise, to the value of about fifty millions of livres, annually sent to the Indies, Spain furnishes only two millions and a half: the Indies trade for fifty millions, the Spaniards for two and a half.

That must be a bad kind of riches which depends on accident, and not on the industry of a nation, on the number of its inhabitants, and on the cultivation of its lands. The king of Spain, who receives great sums from his custom-house at Cadiz, is in this respect only a rich individual in a state extremely poor. Everything passes between strangers and himself, while his subjects have scarcely any share in it; this commerce is independent both of the good and bad fortune of his kingdom.

Were some provinces of Castile able to give him a sum equal to that of the custom-house of Cadiz, his power would be much greater; his riches would be the effect of the wealth of the country; these provinces would animate all the others, and they would be altogether more capable of supporting their respective charges; instead of a great treasury he would have a great people.

23. *A Problem.* It is not for me to decide the question whether, if Spain be not herself able to carry on the trade of the Indies, it would not be better to leave it open to strangers. I will only say that it is for their advantage to load this commerce with as few obstacles as politics will permit. When the merchandise which several nations send to the Indies is very dear, the inhabitants of that country give a great deal of their commodities, which are gold and silver, for very little of those of foreigners; the contrary to this happens when they are at a low price. It would perhaps be of use that these nations should undersell each other, to the end that the merchandise carried to the Indies might be always cheap. These are principles which deserve to be examined, without separating them, however, from other considerations: the safety of the Indies, the advantages of only one custom-house, the danger of making great alterations, and the foreseen inconveniences, which are often less dangerous than those which cannot be foreseen.

Book XXII. Of Laws in Relation to the Use of Money

1. *The Reason of the Use of Money.* People who have little merchandise, as savages, and among civilised nations those who have only two or three species, trade by exchange. Thus the caravans of Moors that go to Timbuctoo, in the heart of Africa, have no need of money, for they exchange their salt for gold. The Moor puts his salt in a heap, and the Negro his dust in another; if there is not gold enough, the Moor takes away some of his salt, or the Negro adds more gold, till both parties are agreed.

But when a nation traffics with a great variety of merchandise, money becomes necessary; because a metal easily carried from place to place saves the great expenses which people would be obliged to be at if they always proceeded by exchange.

As all nations have reciprocal wants, it frequently happens that one is desirous of a large quantity of the other's merchandise, when the latter will have very little of theirs, though with respect to another nation the case is directly opposite. But when nations have money, and proceed by buying and selling, those who take most merchandise pay the balance in specie. And there is this difference, that, in the case of buying, the trade carried on is in proportion to the wants of the nation that has the greatest demands; while in bartering, the trade is only according to the wants of the nation whose demands are the fewest; without which the latter would be under an impossibility of balancing its accounts.

2. *Of the Nature of Money.* Money is a sign which represents the value of all merchandise. Metal is taken for this sign, as being durable,[1] because it is consumed but little by use; and because, without being destroyed, it is capable of many divisions. A precious metal has been chosen as a sign, as being most portable. A metal is most proper for a common measure, because it can be easily reduced to the same standard. Every state fixes upon it a particular impression, to the end that the form may correspond with the standard and the weight, and that both may be known by inspection only.

The Athenians, not having the use of met-

als, made use of oxen,[2] and the Romans of sheep; but one ox is not the same as another ox in the manner that one piece of metal may be the same as another.

A specie is the sign of the value of merchandise, paper is the sign of the value of specie; and when it is of the right sort, it represents this value in such a manner that as to the effects produced by it there is not the least difference.

In the same manner, as money is the sign and representative of a thing, everything is a sign and representative of money; and the state is in a prosperous condition when on the one hand money perfectly represents all things, and on the other all things perfectly represent money, and are reciprocally the sign of each other; that is, when they have such a relative value that we may have the one as soon as we have the other. This never happens in any other than a moderate government, nor does it always happen there; for example, if the laws favour the dishonest debtor, his effects are no longer a representative or sign of money. With regard to a despotic government, it would be a prodigy did things there represent their sign. Tyranny and distrust make every one bury their specie;[3] things therefore are not there the representative of money.

Legislators have sometimes had the art not only to make things in their own nature the representative of specie, but to convert them even into specie, like the current coin. Cæsar, when he was dictator, permitted debtors to give their lands in payment to their creditors, at the price they were worth before the civil war.[4] Tiberius ordered that those who desired specie should have it from the public treasury on binding over their land to double the value.[5] Under Cæsar the lands were the money which paid all debts; under Tiberius ten thousand sesterces in land became as current money equal to five thousand sesterces in silver.

The Magna Charta of England provides

[1] The salt made use of for this purpose in Abyssinia has this defect, that it is continually wasting away.

[2] Herodotus, Bk. i, tells us that the Lydians found out the art of coining money; the Greeks learned it from them: the Athenian coin had the impression of their ancient ox. I have seen one of those pieces in the Earl of Pembroke's cabinet.

[3] It is an ancient custom in Algiers for the father of a family to have a treasure concealed in the earth.—Laugier de Tassis, *History of the Kingdom of Algiers.*

[4] Cæsar, *De Bello Civ.*, iii.

[5] Tacitus, *Annals*, vi. 17.

against the seizing of the lands or revenues of a debtor, when his movable or personal goods are sufficient to pay, and he is willing to give them up to his creditors; thus all the goods of an Englishman represent money.

The laws of the Germans constituted money a satisfaction for the injuries that were committed, and for the sufferings due to guilt. But as there was but very little specie in the country, they again constituted this money to be paid in goods or chattels. This we find appointed in a Saxon law, with certain regulations suitable to the ease and convenience of the several ranks of people. At first the law declared the value of a sou in cattle;[1] the sou of two tremises answered to an ox of twelve months, or to a ewe with her lamb; that of three tremises was worth an ox of sixteen months. With these people money became cattle, goods, and merchandise, and these again became money.

Money is not only a sign of things; it is also a sign and representative of money, as we shall see in the chapter on exchange.

3. *Of ideal Money.* There is both real and ideal money. Civilised nations generally make use of ideal money only, because they have converted their real money into ideal. At first their real money was some metal of a certain weight and standard, but soon dishonesty or want made them retrench a part of the metal from every piece of money, to which they left the same name; for example, from a livre at a pound weight they took half the silver, and still continued to call it a livre; the piece which was the twentieth part of a pound of silver they continued to call a sou, though it is no more the twentieth part of this pound of silver. By this method the livre is an ideal livre, and the sou an ideal sou. Thus of the other subdivisions; and so far may this be carried that what we call a livre shall be only a small part of the original livre or pound, which renders it still more ideal. It may even happen that we have no piece of money of the precise value of a livre, nor any piece exactly with a sou, then the livre and the sou will be purely ideal. They may give to any piece of money the denomination of as many livres and as many sous as they please, the variation may be continual, because it is as easy to give another name to a thing as it is difficult to change the thing itself.

To take away the source of this abuse, it

[1] The Laws of the Saxons, 18.

would be an excellent law for all countries who are desirous of making commerce flourish to ordain that none but real money should be current, and to prevent any methods from being taken to render it ideal.

Nothing ought to be so exempt from variation as that which is the common measure of all.

Trade is in its own nature extremely uncertain; and it is a great evil to add a new uncertainty to that which is founded on the nature of the thing.

4. *Of the Quantity of Gold and Silver.* While civilised nations are the mistresses of the world, gold and silver, whether they draw it from among themselves, or fetch it from the mines, must increase every day. On the contrary, it diminishes when barbarous nations prevail. We know how great was the scarcity of these metals when the Goths and Vandals on the one side, and on the other the Saracens and Tartars, broke in like a torrent on the civilised world.

5. *The same Subject continued.* The bullion drawn from the American mines, imported into Europe, and thence sent to the East, has greatly promoted the navigation of the European nations; for it is merchandise which Europe receives in exchange from America, and which she sends in exchange to the Indies. A prodigious quantity of gold and silver is therefore an advantage, when we consider these metals as merchandise; but it is otherwise when we consider them as a sign, because their abundance gives an alloy to their quality as a sign, which is chiefly founded on their scarcity.

Before the first Punic war,[2] copper was to silver as 960 to 1;[3] it is at present nearly as 73½ to 1. When the proportion shall be as it was formerly, silver will better perform its office as a sign.

6. *The Reason why Interest was lowered one-half after the Conquest of the Indies.* Garcilasso informs us[4] that in Spain after the conquest of the Indies the interest, which was at ten per cent, fell to five. This was a necessary consequence. A great quantity of specie being all of a sudden brought into Europe, much fewer persons had need of money. The price

[2] See chapter 12 of this book.
[3] Supposing a mark of eight ounces of silver to be worth forty-nine livres, and copper twenty sols per pound.
[4] *History of the Civil Wars of the Spaniards in the West Indies.*

of all things increased, while the value of money diminished; the proportion was then broken, and all the old debts were discharged. We may recollect the time of the System,[1] when everything was at a high price except specie. Those who had money after the conquest of the Indies were obliged to lower the price or hire of their merchandise, that is, in other words, their interest.

From this time they were unable to bring interest to its ancient standard, because the quantity of specie brought to Europe has been annually increasing. Besides, as the public funds of some states, founded on riches procured by commerce, gave but a very small interest, it became necessary for the contracts of individuals to be regulated by these. In short, the course of exchange having rendered the conveying of specie from one country to another remarkably easy, money cannot be scarce in a place where they may be so readily supplied with it by those who have it in plenty.

7. *How the Price of Things is fixed in the Variation of the Sign of Riches*. Money is the price of merchandise or manufactures. But how shall we fix this price? or, in other words, by what piece of money is everything to be represented?

If we compare the mass of gold and silver in the whole world with the quantity of merchandise therein contained, it is certain that every commodity or merchandise in particular may be compared to a certain portion of the entire mass of gold and silver. As the total of the one is to the total of the other, so part of the one will be to part of the other. Let us suppose that there is only one commodity or merchandise in the world, or only one to be purchased, and that this is divisible like money; a part of this merchandise will answer to a part of the mass of gold and silver; the half of the total of the one to the half of the total of the other; the tenth, the hundredth, the thousandth part of the one, to the tenth, the hundredth, the thousandth part of the other. But as that which constitutes property among mankind is not all at once in trade, and as the metals or money which are the sign of property are not all in trade at the same time, the price is fixed in the compound ratio of the total of things with the total of signs, and that of the total of things in trade with the total of signs in trade also; and as the things which are

[1] In France, Law's project was called by this name.

not in trade to-day may be in trade to-morrow, and the signs not now in trade may enter into trade at the same time, the establishment of the price of things fundamentally depends on the proportion of the total of things to the total of signs.

Thus the prince or the magistrate can no more ascertain the value of merchandise than he can establish by a decree that the relation 1 has to 10 is equal to that of 1 to 20. Julian's lowering the price of provisions at Antioch was the cause of a most terrible famine.[2]

8. *The same Subject continued*. The Negroes on the coast of Africa have a sign of value without money. It is a sign merely ideal, founded on the degree of esteem which they fix in their minds for all merchandise, in proportion to the need they have of it. A certain commodity or merchandise is worth three macoutes; another, six macoutes; another, ten macoutes; that is, as if they said simply three, six, and ten. The price is formed by a comparison of all merchandise with each other. They have therefore no particular money; but each kind of merchandise is money to the other.

Let us for a moment transfer to ourselves this manner of valuing things, and join it with ours: all the merchandise and goods in the world, or else all the merchandise or manufactures of a state, particularly considered as separate from all others, would be worth a certain number of macoutes; and, dividing the money of this state into as many parts as there are macoutes, one part of this division of money will be the sign of a macoute.

If we suppose the quantity of specie in a state doubled, it will be necessary to double the specie in the macoute; but if in doubling the specie you double also the macoute, the proportion will remain the same as before the doubling of either.

If, since the discovery of the Indies, gold and silver have increased in Europe in the proportion of 1 to 20, the price of provisions and merchandise must have been enhanced in the proportion of 1 to 20. But if, on the other hand, the quantity of merchandise has increased as 1 to 2—it necessarily follows that the price of this merchandise and provisions, having been raised in proportion of 1 to 20, and fallen in proportion of 1 to 2—it necessarily follows, I say, that the proportion is only as 1 to 10.

The quantity of goods and merchandise increases by an augmentation of commerce, the

[2] Socrates, *History of the Church*, ii. 17.

augmentation of commerce by an augmentation of the specie which successively arrives, and by new communications with freshly-discovered countries and seas, which furnish us with new commodities and new merchandise.

9. *Of the relative Scarcity of Gold and Silver.* Besides the positive plenty and scarcity of gold and silver, there is still a relative abundance and a relative scarcity of one of these metals compared with the other.

The avaricious hoard up their gold and silver, for as they do not care to spend, they are fond of signs that are not subject to decay. They prefer gold to silver, because as they are always afraid of losing, they can best conceal that which takes up the least room. Gold therefore disappears when there is plenty of silver, by reason that every one has some to conceal; it appears again when silver is scarce, because they are obliged to draw it from its confinement.

It is then a rule that gold is common when silver is scarce, and gold is scarce when silver is common. This lets us see the difference between their relative and their real abundance and scarcity, of which I shall presently speak more at large.

10. *Of Exchange.* The relative abundance and scarcity of specie in different countries forms what is called the course of exchange.

Exchange is a fixing of the actual and momentary value of money.

Silver as a metal has value like all other merchandise, and an additional value as it is capable of becoming the sign of other merchandise. If it were no more than mere merchandise, it would lose much of its value.

Silver, as money, has a value, which the prince in some respects can fix, and in others cannot.

1. The prince establishes a proportion between a quantity of silver as metal, and the same quantity as money. 2. He fixes the proportion between the several metals made use of as money. 3. He establishes the weight and standard of every piece of money. In fine, 4, he gives to every piece that ideal value of which I have spoken. I shall call the value of money in these four respects its positive value, because it may be fixed by law.

The coin of every state has, besides this, a relative value, as it is compared with the money of other countries. This relative value is established by the exchange, and greatly depends on its positive value. It is fixed by the general opinion of the merchants, never by the decrees of the prince; because it is subject to incessant variations, and depends on a thousand accidents.

The several nations, in fixing this relative value, are chiefly guided by that which has the greatest quantity of specie. If she has as much specie as all the others together, it is then most proper for the others to regulate theirs by her standard: and the regulation between all the others will pretty nearly agree with the regulation made with this principal nation.

In the actual state of the globe, Holland is the nation we are speaking of. Let us examine the course of exchange with relation to her.

They have in Holland a piece of money called a florin, worth twenty sous, or forty half-sous or gros. But, to render our ideas as simple as possible, let us imagine that they have not any such piece of money in Holland as a florin, and that they have no other but the gros: a man who should have a thousand florins should have forty thousand gros; and so of the rest. Now the exchange with Holland is determined by our knowing how many gros every piece of money in other countries is worth; and as the French commonly reckon by a crown of three livres, the exchange makes it necessary for them to know how many gros are contained in a crown of three livres. If the course of exchange is at fifty-four, a crown of three livres will be worth fifty-four gros; if it is at sixty, it will be worth sixty gros. If silver is scarce in France, a crown of three livres will be worth more gros; if plentiful, it will be worth less.

This scarcity or plenty, whence results the mutability of the course of exchange, is not the real, but a relative, scarcity or plenty. For example, when France has greater occasion for funds in Holland than the Dutch of having funds in France, specie is said to be common in France and scarce in Holland: and *vice versâ.*

Let us suppose that the course of exchange with Holland is at fifty-four. If France and Holland composed only one city, they would act as we do when we give change for a crown: the Frenchman would take three livres out of his pocket, and the Dutchman fifty-four gros from his. But as there is some distance between Paris and Amsterdam, it is necessary that he who for a crown of three livres gives me fifty-four gros, which he has in Holland, should give me a bill of exchange for fifty-four gros payable in Holland. The fifty-four gros is not the thing in question, but a bill for that sum. Thus, in order to judge of the scarcity or plenty of specie,[1] we must know if there are in France more bills of fifty-four gros drawn upon Holland than there are crowns drawn upon France. If there are more bills from Holland than there are from France, specie is scarce in France, and common in Holland; it then becomes necessary that the exchange should rise, and that they give for my crown more than fifty-four gros; otherwise I will not part with it; and *vice versâ*.

Thus the various turns in the course of exchange form an account of debtor and creditor, which must be frequently settled, and which the state in debt can no more discharge by exchange than an individual can pay a debt by giving change for a piece of silver.

We will suppose that there are but three states in the world, France, Spain, and Holland; that several individuals in Spain are indebted to France, to the value of one hundred thousand marks of silver; and that several individuals of France owe in Spain one hundred and ten thousand marks: now, if some circumstance both in Spain and France should cause each to withdraw his specie, what will then be the course of exchange? These two nations will reciprocally acquit each other of a hundred thousand marks; but France will still owe ten thousand marks in Spain, and the Spaniards will still have bills upon France, to the value of ten thousand marks; while France will have none at all upon Spain.

But if Holland was in a contrary situation with respect to France, and in order to balance the account must pay her ten thousand marks, the French would have two ways of paying the Spaniards: either by giving their creditors in Spain bills for ten thousand marks upon their debtors in Holland, or else by sending specie to the value of ten thousand marks to Spain.

Hence it follows that when a state has occasion to remit a sum of money to another country, it is indifferent, in the nature of the thing, whether specie be conveyed thither or they take bills of exchange. The advantage or disadvantage of these two methods solely depends on actual circumstances. We must inquire which will yield most gros in Holland—money carried thither in specie, or a bill upon

Holland for the like sum.[2]

When money of the same standard and weight in France yields money of the same standard and weight in Holland, we say that the exchange is at par. In the actual state of specie[3] the par is nearly at fifty-four gros to the crown. When the exchange is above fifty-four gros, we say it is high; when beneath, we say it is low.

In order to know the loss and gain of a state in a particular situation of exchange, it must be considered as debtor and creditor, as buyer and seller. When the exchange is below par, it loses as a debtor, and gains as a creditor; it loses as a buyer and gains as a seller. It is obvious it loses as debtor; suppose, for example, France owes Holland a certain number of gros, the fewer gros there are in a crown the more crowns she has to pay. On the contrary, if France is creditor for a certain number of gros, the less number of gros there are in a crown the more crowns she will receive. The state loses also as buyer, for there must be the same number of gros to purchase the same quantity of merchandise; and while the exchange is low, every French crown is worth fewer gros. For the same reason the state gains as a seller. I sell my merchandise in Holland for a certain number of gros; I receive then more crowns in France, when for every fifty gros I receive a crown, than I should do if I received only the same crown for every fifty-four. The contrary to this takes place in the other state. If the Dutch are indebted a certain number of crowns to France, they will gain; if this money is owing to them, they will lose; if they sell, they lose; and if they buy, they gain.

It is proper to pursue this somewhat further. When the exchange is below par; for example, if it be at fifty instead of fifty-four, it should follow that France, on sending bills of exchange to Holland for fifty-four thousand crowns, could buy merchandise only to the value of fifty thousand; and that on the other hand, the Dutch sending the value of fifty thousands crowns to France might buy fifty-four thousand, which makes a difference of $\frac{4}{54}$, that is, a loss to France of more than one-seventh; so that France would be obliged to send to Holland one-seventh more in specie or merchandise than she would do were the exchange at par. And as the mischief must constantly increase, because a debt of this kind

---

[1] There is much specie in a place when there is more specie than paper; there is little, when there is more paper than specie.

[2] With the expenses of carriage and insurance deducted.

[3] In 1744.

would bring the exchange still lower, France would in the end be ruined. It seems, I say, as if this should certainly follow; and yet it does not, because of the principle which I have elsewhere established;[1] which is that states constantly lean towards a balance, in order to preserve their independency. Thus they borrow only in proportion to their ability to pay, and measure their buying by what they sell; and taking the example from above, if the exchange falls in France from fifty-four to fifty, the Dutch who buy merchandise in France to the value of a thousand crowns, for which they used to pay fifty-four thousand gros, would now pay only fifty thousand, if the French would consent to it. But the merchandise of France will rise insensibly, and the profit will be shared between the French and the Dutch; for when a merchant can gain, he easily shares his profit; there arises then a communication of profit between the French and the Dutch. In the same manner the French, who bought merchandise of Holland for fifty-four thousand gros, and who, when the exchange was at fifty-four, paid for them a thousand crowns, will be obliged to add one-seventh more in French crowns to buy the same merchandise. But the French merchant, being sensible of the loss he suffers, will take up less of the merchandise of Holland. The French and the Dutch merchant will then both be losers, the state will insensibly fall into a balance, and the lowering of the exchange will not be attended with all those inconveniences which we had reason to fear.

A merchant may send his stock into a foreign country when the exchange is below par without injuring his fortune, because, when it returns, he recovers what he had lost; but a prince who sends only specie into a foreign country which never can return, is always a loser.

When the merchants have great dealings in any country, the exchange there infallibly rises. This proceeds from their entering into many engagements, buying great quantities of merchandise, and drawing upon foreign countries to pay for them.

A prince may amass great wealth in his dominions, and yet specie may be really scarce, and relatively common; for instance, if the state is indebted for much merchandise to a foreign country, the exchange will be low, though specie be scarce.

The exchange of all places constantly tends to a certain proportion, and that in the very nature of things. If the course of exchange

[1] See book xx. 23.

from Ireland to England is below par, and that of England to Holland is also under par, that of Ireland to Holland will be still lower; that is, in the compound ratio of that of Ireland to England, and that of England to Holland; for a Dutch merchant who can have his specie indirectly from Ireland, by way of England, will not choose to pay dearer by having it in the direct way. This, I say, ought naturally to be the case; but, however, it is not exactly so. There are always circumstances which vary these things; and the different profit of drawing by one place, or of drawing by another, constitutes the particular art and dexterity of the bankers, which does not belong to the present subject.

When a state raises its specie, for instance, when it gives the name of six livres, or two crowns, to what was before called three livres, or one crown, this new denomination, which adds nothing real to the crown, ought not to procure a single gros more by the exchange. We ought only to have for the two new crowns the same number of gros which we before received for the old one. If this does not happen, it must not be imputed as an effect of the regulation itself, but to the novelty and suddenness of the affair. The exchange adheres to what is already established, and is not altered till after a certain time.

When a state, instead of only raising the specie by a law, calls it in, in order to diminish its size, it frequently happens that during the time taken up in passing again through the mint there are two kinds of money—the large, which is the old, and the small, which is the new; and as the large is cried down as not to be received as money, and bills of exchange must consequently be paid in the new, one would imagine then that the exchange should be regulated by the new. If, for example, in France, the ancient crown of three livres, being worth in Holland sixty gros, was reduced one-half, the new crown ought to be valued only at thirty. On the other hand, it seems as if the exchange ought to be regulated by the old coin; because the banker who has specie, and receives bills, is obliged to carry the old coin to the mint in order to change it for the new, by which he must be a loser. The exchange then ought to be fixed between the value of the old coin and that of the new. The value of the old is decreased, if we may call it so, both because there is already some of the new in trade, and because the bankers cannot keep up to the rigour of the law, having an interest in letting loose the old coin from their chests, and being sometimes obliged to make payments with it. Again, the value of the new specie must rise, because the banker having this finds himself in a situation in which, as we shall immediately prove, he will reap great advantage by procuring the old. The exchange should then be fixed, as I have already said, between the new and the old coin. For then the bankers find it to their interest to send the old out of the kingdom, because by this method they procure the same advantage as they could receive from a regular exchange of the old specie, that is, a great many gros in Holland; and in return, a regular exchange a little lower, between the old and the new specie, which would bring many crowns to France.

Suppose that three livres of the old coin yield by the actual exchange forty-five gros, and that by sending this same crown to Holland they receive sixty, but with a bill of forty-five gros, they procure a crown of three livres in France, which being sent in the old specie to Holland, still yields sixty gros; thus all the old specie would be sent out of the kingdom, and the bankers would run away with the whole profit.

To remedy this, new measures must be taken. The state which coined the new specie would itself be obliged to send great quantities of the old to the nation which regulates the exchange, and, by thus gaining credit there, raise the exchange pretty nearly to as many gros for a crown of three livres out of the country. I say to nearly the same, for while the profits are small the bankers will not be tempted to send it abroad, because of the expense of carriage and the danger of confiscation.

It is fit that we should give a very clear idea of this. Mr. Bernard, or any other banker employed by the state, proposes bills upon Holland, and gives them at one, two, or three gros higher than the actual exchange; he has made a provision in a foreign country, by means of the old specie, which he has continually been sending thither; and thus he has raised the exchange to the point we have just mentioned. In the meantime, by disposing of his bills, he seizes on all the new specie, and obliges the other bankers, who have payments to make, to carry their old specie to the mint; and, as he insensibly obtains all the specie, he obliges the other bankers to give him bills of exchange at a very high price. By this means his profit in the end compensates in a great measure for the loss he suffered at the beginning.

It is evident that during these transactions the state must be in a dangerous crisis. Specie must become extremely scarce—1, because much the greatest part is cried down; 2, because a part will be sent into foreign countries; 3, because every one will lay it up, as not being willing to give that profit to the prince which he hopes to receive himself. It is dangerous to do it slowly; and dangerous also to do it in too much haste. If the supposed gain be immoderate, the inconveniences increase in proportion.

We see, from what has been already said, that when the exchange is lower than the specie, a profit may be made by sending it abroad; for the same reason, when it is higher than the specie, there is profit in causing it to return.

But there is a case in which profit may be made by sending the specie out of the kingdom, when the exchange is at par; that is, by sending it into a foreign country to be coined over again. When it returns, an advantage may be made of it, whether it be circulated in the country or paid for foreign bills.

If a company has been erected in a state with an immense number of shares, and these shares have in a few months risen twenty or twenty-five times above the original purchase value; if, again, the same state established a bank, whose bills were to perform the office of money, while the legal value of these bills was prodigious, in order to answer to the legal value of the shares (this is Mr. Law's System), it would follow, from the nature of things, that these shares and these bills would vanish in the same manner as they arose. Stocks cannot suddenly be raised twenty or twenty-five times above their original value without giving a number of people the means of procuring immense riches in paper: every one would endeavour to make his fortune; and as the exchange offers the most easy way of removing it from home, or conveying it whither one pleases, people would incessantly remit a part of their effects to the nation that regulates the exchange. A continual process of remittances into a foreign country must lower the exchange. Let us suppose that at the time of the System, in proportion to the standard and weight of the silver coin, the exchange was fixed at forty gros to the crown; when a vast quantity of paper became money, they were unwilling to give more than thirty-nine gros for a crown, and afterwards thirty-eight, thirty-seven, &c. This proceeded so far, that after a while they would give but eight gros, and at last there was no exchange at all.

The exchange ought in this case to have regulated the proportion between the specie and the paper of France. I suppose that, by the weight and standard of the silver, the crown of three livres in silver was worth forty gros, and that the exchange being made in paper, the crown of three livres in paper was worth only eight gros, the difference was four-fifths. The crown of three livres in paper was then worth four-fifths less than the crown of three livres in silver.

11. *Of the Proceedings of the Romans with respect to Money.* How great soever the exertion of authority had been in our times, with respect to the specie of France, during the administration of two successive ministers, still it was vastly exceeded by the Romans; not at the time when corruption had crept into their republic, nor when they were in a state of anarchy, but when they were as much by their wisdom as their courage in the full vigour of the constitution, after having conquered the cities of Italy, and at the very time that they disputed for empire with the Carthaginians.

And here I am pleased that I have an opportunity of examining more closely into this matter, that no example may be taken from what can never justly be called one.

In the first Punic war the as,[1] which ought to be twelve ounces of copper, weighed only two, and in the second it was no more than one. This retrenchment answers to what we now call the raising of coin. To take half the silver from a crown of six livres, in order to make two crowns, or to raise it to the value of twelve livres, is precisely the same thing.

They have left us no monument of the manner in which the Romans conducted this affair in the first Punic war; but what they did in the second is a proof of the most consummate wisdom. The republic found herself under an impossibility of paying her debts: the as weighed two ounces of copper, and the denarius, valued at ten ases, weighed twenty ounces of copper. The republic, being willing to gain half on her creditors, made the as of an ounce of copper,[2] and by this means paid the value of a denarius with ten ounces. This proceeding must have given a great shock to the state; they were obliged therefore to break the force of it as well as they could. It was in itself

unjust, and it was necessary to render it as little so as possible. They had in view the deliverance of the republic with respect to the citizens; they were not therefore obliged to direct their view to the deliverance of the citizens with respect to each other. This made a second step necessary. It was ordained that the denarius, which hitherto contained but ten ases, should contain sixteen. The result of this double operation was, that while the creditors of the republic lost one-half,[3] those of individuals lost only a fifth;[4] the price of merchandise was increased only a fifth; the real change of the money was only a fifth. The other consequences are obvious.

The Romans then conducted themselves with greater prudence than we, who in our transactions involved both the public treasure and the fortunes of individuals. But this is not all: their business was carried on amidst more favourable circumstances than ours.

12. *The Circumstances in which the Romans changed the Value of the Specie.* There was formerly very little gold and silver in Italy. This country has few or no mines of gold or silver. When Rome was taken by the Gauls, they found only a thousand-weight of gold.[5] And yet the Romans had sacked many powerful cities, and brought home their wealth. For a long time they made use of none but copper money; and it was not till after the peace with Pyrrhus that they had silver enough to coin money:[6] they made denarii of this metal of the value of ten ases,[7] or ten pounds of copper. At that time the proportion of silver was to that of copper as 1 to 960. For as the Roman denarius was valued at ten ases, or ten pounds of copper, it was worth one hundred and twenty ounces of copper; and as the same denarius was valued only at one-eighth of an ounce of silver,[8] this produced the above proportion.

When Rome became mistress of that part of Italy which is nearest to Greece and Sicily, by degrees she found herself between two rich nations—the Greeks and the Carthaginians. Silver increased at Rome; and as the proportion

[3] They received ten ounces of copper for twenty.
[4] They received sixteen ounces of copper for twenty.
[5] Pliny, xxxiii, art. 5.
[6] Freinshemius, dec. 2, v.
[7] *Ibid.* They struck also, says the same author, half denarii, called quinarii; and quarters, called sesterces.
[8] An eighth, according to Budæus; according to other authors, a seventh.

[1] Pliny, *Natural History*, xxxiii, art. 13.
[2] *Ibid.*

of 1 to 960 between silver and copper could
be no longer supported, she made several regulations with respect to money, which to us
are unknown. However, at the beginning of
the second Punic war, the Roman denarius
was worth no more than twenty ounces of copper;[1] and thus the proportion between silver
and copper was no longer but as 1 to 160. The
reduction was very considerable, since the republic gained five-sixths upon all copper
money. But she did only what was necessary in
the nature of things, by establishing the proportion between the metals made use of as
money.

The peace which terminated the first Punic
war left the Romans masters of Sicily. They
soon entered Sardinia; afterwards they began
to know Spain; and thus the quantity of silver
increased at Rome. They took measures to reduce the denarius from twenty ounces to sixteen,[2] which had the effect of putting a nearer
proportion between the silver and copper;
thus the proportion, which was before as 1 to
160, was now made as 1 to 128.

If we examine into the conduct of the Romans, we shall never find them so great as in
choosing a proper conjuncture for performing
any extraordinary operation.

13. *Proceedings with respect to Money in the
Time of the Emperors.* In the changes made
in the specie during the time of the republic,
they proceeded by diminishing it: in its wants,
the state entrusted the knowledge to the people, and did not pretend to deceive them.
Under the emperors, they proceeded by way
of alloy. These princes, reduced to despair
even by their liberalities, found themselves
obliged to degrade the specie; an indirect
method, which diminished the evil without
seeming to touch it. They withheld a part
of the gift and yet concealed the hand that
did it; and, without speaking of the diminution of the pay, or of the gratuity, it was
found diminished.

We even still see in cabinets a kind of medals which are called plated, and are only pieces
of copper covered with a thin plate of silver.[3]
This money is mentioned in a fragment of the
77th book of Dio.[4]

Didius Julian first began to debase it. We

find that the coin of Caracalla[5] had an alloy of
more than half; that of Alexander Severus of
two-thirds;[6] the debasing still increased, till in
the time of Gallienus nothing was to be seen
but copper silvered over.[7]

It is evident that such violent proceedings
could not take place in the present age; a
prince might deceive himself, but he could deceive nobody else. The exchange has taught
the banker to draw a comparison between all
the money in the world, and to establish its
just value. The standard of money can be no
longer a secret. Were the prince to begin to alloy his silver, everybody else would continue
it, and do it for him; the specie of the true
standard would go abroad first, and nothing
would be sent back but base metal. If, like the
Roman Emperors, he debased the silver without debasing the gold, the gold would suddenly disappear, and he would be reduced to his
bad silver. The exchange, as I have said in the
preceding book,[8] has deprived princes of the
opportunity of showing great exertions of authority, or at least has rendered them ineffec-
tual.

14. *How the Exchange is a Constraint on despotic Power.* Russia would have descended
from its despotic power, but could not. The
establishment of commerce depended on that
of the exchange, and the transactions were inconsistent with all its laws.

In 1745 the Czarina made a law to expel the
Jews, because they remitted into foreign countries the specie of those who were banished into Siberia, as well as that of the foreigners entertained in her service. As all the subjects of
the empire are slaves, they can neither go
abroad themselves nor send away their effects
without permission. The exchange which
gives them the means of remitting their specie
from one country to another is therefore entirely incompatible with the laws of Russia.

Commerce itself is inconsistent with the
Russian laws. The people are composed only
of slaves employed in agriculture, and of
slaves called ecclesiastics or gentlemen, who
are the lords of those slaves; there is then nobody left for the third estate, which ought to
be composed of mechanics and merchants.

[1] Pliny, *Natural History,* xxxiii, art. 13.
[2] *Ibid.*
[3] See Father Joubert, *Science of Medals,* p. 59,
Paris, 1739.
[4] Extract of *Virtues and Vices.*

[5] See Savote, part II, 12, and *Le Journal des
Savants* of the 28th of July, 1681, on a discovery
of fifty thousand medals.
[6] See Savote, *ibid.*
[7] *Ibid.*
[8] Chapter 21.

15. *The Practice of some Countries in Italy.* They have made laws in some part of Italy to prevent subjects from selling their lands in order to remove their specie into foreign countries. These laws may be good, when the riches of a state are so connected with the country itself that there would be great difficulty in transferring them to another. But since, by the course of exchange, riches are in some degree independent of any particular state, and since they may with so much ease be conveyed from one country to another, that must be a bad law which will not permit persons for their own interest to dispose of their lands, while they can dispose of their money. It is a bad law, because it gives an advantage to movable effects, in prejudice to the land; because it deters strangers from settling in the country; and, in short, because it may be eluded.

16. *The Assistance a State may derive from Bankers.* The banker's business is to change, not to lend, money. If the prince makes use of them to change his specie, as he never does it but in great affairs, the least profit he can give for the remittance becomes considerable; and if they demand large profits, we may be certain that there is a fault in the administration. On the contrary, when they are employed to advance specie, their art consists in procuring the greatest profit for the use of it, without being liable to be charged with usury.

17. *Of Public Debts.* Some have imagined that it was for the advantage of a state to be indebted to itself: they thought that this multiplied riches by increasing the circulation.

Those who are of this opinion have, I believe, confounded a circulating paper which represents money, or a circulating paper which is the sign of the profits that a company has or will make by commerce, with a paper which represents a debt. The first two are extremely advantageous to the state: the last can never be so; and all that we can expect from it is that individuals have a good security from the government for their money. But let us see the inconveniences which result from it.

1. If foreigners possess much paper which represents a debt, they annually draw out of the nation a considerable sum for interest.

2. In a nation that is thus perpetually in debt, the exchange must be very low.

3. The taxes raised for the payment of the interest of the debt are an injury to the manu-

factures, by raising the price of the artificer's labour.

4. It takes the true revenue of the state from those who have activity and industry, to convey it to the indolent; that is, it gives facilities for labour to those who do not work, and clogs with difficulties those who do work.

These are its inconveniences: I know of no advantages. Ten persons have each a yearly income of a thousand crowns, either in land or trade; this raises to the nation, at five per cent, a capital of two hundred thousand crowns. If these ten persons employed one-half of their income, that is, five thousand crowns, in paying the interest of a hundred thousand crowns, which they had borrowed of others, that still would be only to the state as two hundred thousand crowns; that is, in the language of the algebraists, 200,000 crowns— 100,000 crowns+100,000 crowns=200,000.

People are thrown perhaps into this error by reflecting that the paper which represents the debt of a nation is the sign of riches; for none but a rich state can support such paper without falling into decay. And if it does not fall, it is a proof that the state has other riches besides. They say that it is not an evil, because there are resources against it; and that it is an advantage, since these resources surpass the evil.

18. *Of the Payment of Public Debts.* It is necessary that there should be a proportion between the state as creditor and the state as debtor. The state may be a creditor to infinity, but it can only be a debtor to a certain degree, and when it surpasses that degree the title of creditor vanishes.

If the credit of the state has never received the least blemish, it may do what has been so happily practised in one of the kingdoms of Europe;[1] that is, it may require a great quantity of specie, and offer to reimburse every individual, at least if they will not reduce their interest. When the state borrows, the individuals fix the interest; when it pays, the interest for the future is fixed by the state.

It is not sufficient to reduce the interest: it is necessary to erect a sinking-fund from the advantage of the reduction, in order to pay every year a part of the capital: a proceeding so happy that its success increases every day.

When the credit of the state is not entire, there is a new reason for endeavouring to form a sinking-fund, because this fund being

[1] England.

once established will soon procure the public confidence.

1. If the state is a republic, the government of which is in its own nature consistent with its entering into projects of a long duration, the capital of the sinking-fund may be inconsiderable; but it is necessary in a monarchy for the capital to be much greater.

2. The regulations ought to be so ordered that all the subjects of the state may support the weight of the establishment of these funds, because they have all the weight of the establishment of the debt; thus the creditor of the state, by the sums he contributes, pays himself.

3. There are four classes of men who pay the debts of the state: the proprietors of the land, those engaged in trade, the labourers and artificers, and, in fine, the annuitants either of the state or of private people. Of these four classes the last, in a case of necessity one would imagine, ought least to be spared, because it is a class entirely passive, while the state is supported by the active vigour of the other three. But as it cannot be higher taxed, without destroying the public confidence, of which the state in general and these three classes in particular have the utmost need; as a breach in the public faith cannot be made on a certain number of subjects without seeming to be made on all; as the class of creditors is always the most exposed to the projects of ministers, and always in their eye, and under their immediate inspection, the state is obliged to give them a singular protection, that the part which is indebted may never have the least advantage over that which is the creditor.

19. *Of lending upon Interest.* Specie is the sign of value. It is evident that he who has occasion for this sign ought to pay for the use of it, as well as for everything else that he has occasion for. All the difference is that other things may be either hired or bought; while money, which is the price of things, can only be hired, and not bought.[1]

To lend money without interest is certainly an action laudable and extremely good; but it is obvious that it is only a counsel of religion, and not a civil law.

In order that trade may be successfully carried on, it is necessary that a price be fixed on the use of specie; but this should be very inconsiderable. If it be too high, the merchant who sees that it will cost him more in interest

[1] We do not speak here of gold and silver considered as a merchandise.

than he can gain by commerce will undertake nothing; if there is no consideration to be paid for the use of specie, nobody will lend it; and here too the merchant will undertake nothing.

I am mistaken when I say nobody will lend; the affairs of society will ever make it necessary. Usury will be established, but with all the disorders with which it has been constantly attended.

The laws of Mahomet confound usury with lending upon interest. Usury increases in Mahometan countries in proportion to the severity of the prohibition. The lender indemnifies himself for the danger he undergoes of suffering the penalty.

In those eastern countries, the greater part of the people are secure in nothing; there is hardly any proportion between the actual possession of a sum and the hopes of receiving it again after having lent it: usury, then, must be raised in proportion to the danger of insolvency.

20. *Of Maritime Usury.* The greatness of maritime usury is founded on two things: the danger of the sea, which makes it proper that those who expose their specie should not do it without considerable advantage, and the ease with which the borrower, by means of commerce, speedily accomplishes a variety of great affairs. But usury, with respect to landmen, not being founded on either of these two reasons, is either prohibited by the legislators, or, what is more rational, reduced to proper bounds.

21. *Of Lending by Contract, and the State of Usury among the Romans.* Besides the loans made for the advantage of commerce, there is still a kind of lending by a civil contract, whence results interest or usury.

As the people of Rome increased every day in power, the magistrates sought to insinuate themselves in their favour by enacting such laws as were most agreeable to them. They retrenched capitals; they first lowered, and at length prohibited, interest; they took away the power of confining the debtor's body; in fine, the abolition of debts was contended for whenever a tribune was disposed to render himself popular.

These continual changes, whether made by the laws or by the *plebiscita*, naturalised usury at Rome; for the creditors, seeing the people their debtor, their legislator, and their judge, had no longer any confidence in their agreements: the people, like a debtor who has lost his credit, could only tempt them to lend by allowing an exorbitant interest, especially as the laws applied a remedy to the evil only from time to time, while the complaints of the people were continual, and constantly intimidated the creditors. This was the cause that all honest means of borrowing and lending were abolished at Rome, and that the most monstrous usury established itself in that city, notwithstanding the strict prohibition and severity of the law.[1] This evil was a consequence of the severity of the laws against usury. Laws excessively good are the source of excessive evil. The borrower found himself under the necessity of paying for the interest of the money, and for the danger the creditor underwent of suffering the penalty of the law.

22. *The same Subject continued.* The primitive Romans had not any laws to regulate the rate of usury.[2] In the contests which arose on this subject between the plebeians and the patricians, even in the sedition on the *Mons Sacer,* nothing was alleged, on the one hand, but justice, and on the other, the severity of contracts.[3]

They then only followed private agreements, which, I believe, were most commonly at twelve per cent per annum. My reason is, that in the ancient language of the Romans, interest at six per cent was called half-usury, and interest at three per cent, quarter-usury.[4] Total usury must, therefore, have been interest at twelve per cent.

But if it be asked how such great interest could be established among a people almost without commerce, I answer that this people, being very often obliged to go to war without pay, were under a frequent necessity of borrowing: and as they incessantly made happy expeditions, they were commonly well able to pay. This is visible from the recital of the contests which arose on this subject; they did not then disagree concerning the avarice of creditors, but said that those who complained might have been able to pay, had they lived in a more regular manner.[5]

They then made laws which had only an influence on the present situation of affairs: they ordained, for instance, that those who enrolled themselves for the war they were engaged in should not be molested by their creditors; that those who were in prison should be set at liberty; that the most indigent should be sent into the colonies; and sometimes they opened the public treasury. The people, being eased of their present burdens, became appeased; and as they required nothing for the future, the senate was far from providing against it.

At the time when the senate maintained the cause of usury with so much constancy, the Romans were distinguished by an extreme love of frugality, poverty, and moderation: but the constitution was such that the principal citizens alone supported all the expenses of government, while the common people paid nothing. How, then, was it possible to deprive the former of the liberty of pursuing their debtors, and at the same time to oblige them to execute their offices, and to support the republic amidst its most pressing necessities?

Tacitus says that the law of the Twelve Tables fixed the interest at one per cent.[6] It is evident that he was mistaken, and that he took another law, of which I am going to speak, for the law of the Twelve Tables. If this had been regulated in the law of the Twelve Tables, why did they not make use of its authority in the disputes which afterwards arose between the creditors and debtors? We find no vestige of this law upon lending at interest; and let us have ever so little knowledge of the history of Rome, we shall see that a law like this could not be the work of the decemvirs.

The Licinian law, made eighty-five years after that of the Twelve Tables,[7] was one of those temporary regulations of which we have spoken. It ordained that what had been paid for interest should be deducted from the principal, and the rest discharged by three equal payments.

In the year of Rome 398, the tribunes Duellius and Menenius caused a law to be passed which reduced the interest to one per cent per annum.[8] It is this law which Tacitus confounds with that of the Twelve Tables,[9] and this was the first ever made by the Romans to fix

[1] Tacitus, *Annals,* vi. 16.
[2] Usury and interest among the Romans signified the same thing.
[3] See Dionysius Halicarnassus, who has described it so well.
[4] *Usuræ semisses, trientes, quadrantes.* See the several titles of the digests and codes on usury, and especially *Leg.* 17, with the note, ff. *de usuris.*
[5] See Appius's speech on this subject, in Dionysius Halicarnassus, v.

[6] *Annals,* vi. 16.
[7] In the year of Rome 388.—Livy, vi. 25.
[8] *Unciaria usura.—Ibid.,* vii. 16.
[9] *Annals,* vi. 16.

the rate of interest. Ten years after,[1] this usury was reduced one-half,[2] and in the end entirely abolished;[3] and if we may believe some authors whom Livy had read, this was under the consulate of C. Martius Rutilius and Q. Servilius, in the year of Rome 413.[4]

It fared with this law as with all those in which the legislator carries things to excess: an infinite number of ways were found to elude it. They enacted, therefore, many others to confirm, correct, and temper it. Sometimes they quitted the laws to follow the common practice; at others, the common practice to follow the laws; but in this case, custom easily prevailed.[5] When a man wanted to borrow, he found an obstacle in the very law made in his favour; this law must be evaded by the person it was made to succour, and by the person condemned. Sempronius Asellus, the prætor, having permitted the debtors to act in conformity to the laws,[6] was slain by the creditors for attempting to revive the memory of a severity that could no longer be supported.[7]

I quit the city, in order to cast an eye on the provinces.

I have somewhere else observed that the Roman provinces were exhausted by a severe and arbitrary government.[8] But this is not all; they were also ruined by a most shocking usury.

Cicero takes notice that the inhabitants of Salamis wanted to borrow a sum of money at Rome, but could not, because of the Gabinian law.[9] We must, therefore, inquire into the nature of this law.

As soon as lending upon interest was forbidden at Rome, they contrived all sort of means to elude the law;[10] and as their allies,[11] and the Latins, were not subject to the civil laws of the Romans, they employed a Latin, or an ally, to lend his name, and personate the creditor. The law, therefore, had only subjected the

creditors to a matter of form, and the public were not relieved.

The people complained of this artifice; and Marius Sempronius, tribune of the people, by the authority of the senate, caused a *plebiscitum* to be enacted to this purport, that in regard to loans the laws prohibiting usury between Roman citizens should equally take place between a citizen and an ally, or a citizen and a Latin.[12]

At that time they gave the name of allies to the people of Italy properly so called, which extended as far as the Arno and the Rubicon, and was not governed in the form of a Roman province.

It is an observation of Tacitus[13] that new frauds were constantly committed, whenever any laws were passed for the preventing of usury. Finding themselves debarred from lending or borrowing in the name of an ally, they soon contrived to borrow of some inhabitant of the provinces.

To remedy this abuse they were obliged to enact a new law; and Gabinius[14] upon the passing of that famous law, which was intended to prevent the corruption of suffrages, must naturally have reflected that the best way to attain his end was to discourage the lending upon interest: these were two objects naturally connected; for usury always increased at the time of elections,[15] because they stood in need of money to bribe the voters. It is plain that the Gabinian law had extended the *Senatus Consultum* of Marcus Sempronius to the provinces, since the people of Salamis could not borrow money at Rome because of that very law. Brutus, under fictitious names, lent them some money[16] at four per cent a month,[17] and obtained for that purpose two *Senatus Consulta;* in the former of which it was expressly mentioned that this loan should not be considered as an evasion of the law,[18] and that the governor of Sicily should determine according to the stipulations mentioned in the bond of the Salaminians.

As lending upon interest was forbidden by the Gabinian law between provincials and

---

[1] Under the consulate of L. Manlius Torquatus and C. Plautius, according to Livy, vii. 27. This is the law mentioned by Tacitus, *Annals*, vi.

[2] *Semiunciaria usura.*

[3] As Tacitus says, *Annals*, vi.

[4] This law was passed at the instance of M. Genucius, tribune of the people.—Livy, vii, towards the end.

[5] *Verteri jam more fœnus receptum erat.*—Appian, *On the Civil War*, i.

[6] *Permisit eos legibus agere.—Ibid.;* and the *Epitome of Livy,* lxiv.

[7] In the year of Rome 663.

[8] Book xi. 19.

[9] *Letters to Atticus,* v. 21.

[10] Livy, xxxv. 7.

[11] *Ibid.*

[12] In the year 561 of Rome.—See Livy, xxv. 7.

[13] *Annals,* vi. 16.

[14] In the year 615 of Rome.

[15] See *Letters to Atticus,* iv. 15, 16.

[16] *Ibid.,* vi. 1.

[17] Pompey having lent 600 talents to King Ariobarzanes, made that prince pay him thirty Attic talents every thirty days.—*Ibid.,* v. 21, vi. 1.

[18] *Ut neque Salaminiis, neque cui eis dedisset, fraudi esset.—Ibid.*

Roman citizens, and the latter at that time had all the money of the globe in their hands, there was a necessity for tempting them with the bait of extravagant interest, to the end that the avaricious might thus lose sight of the danger of losing their money. And as they were men of great power in Rome, who awed the magistrates and overruled the laws, they were emboldened to lend, and to extort great usury. Hence the provinces were successively ravaged by every one who had any credit in Rome: and as each governor, at entering upon his province, published his edict[1] wherein he fixed the rate of interest in what manner he pleased, the legislature played into the hands of avarice, and the latter served the mean purposes of the legislator.

But the public business must be carried on; and wherever a total inaction obtains, the state is undone. On some occasions the towns, the corporate bodies and societies, as well as private people, were under the necessity of borrowing—a necessity but too urgent, were it only to repair the ravages of armies, the rapacity of magistrates, the extortions of collectors, and the corrupt practices daily introduced; for never was there at one period so much poverty and opulence. The senate, being possessed of the executive power, granted, through necessity, and oftentimes through favour, a permission of borrowing from Roman citizens, so as to enact decrees for that particular purpose. But even these decrees were discredited by the law; for they might give occasion to the people's insisting upon new rates of interest, which would augment the danger of losing the capital, while they made a further extension of usury.[3] I shall ever repeat it, that mankind are governed not by extremes, but by principles of moderation.

He pays least, says Ulpian, who pays latest.[4] This decides the question whether interest be lawful; that is, whether the creditor can sell time, and the debtor buy it.

Book XXIII. Of Laws in the Relation They Bear to the Number of Inhabitants

1. *Of Men and Animals with respect to the Multiplication of their Species.*

Delight of human kind,[2] and gods above;
Parent of Rome, propitious Queen of Love;
* * * * * * * *
For when the rising spring adorns the mead,
And a new scene of nature stands display'd;
When teeming buds, and cheerful greens appear,
And western gales unlock the lazy year;
The joyous birds thy welcome first express,
Whose native songs thy genial fire confess:
Then savage beasts bound o'er their slighted food,
Struck with thy darts, and tempt the raging flood:
All nature is thy gift, earth, air, and sea;
Of all that breathes the various progeny,
Stung with delight, is goaded on by thee.
O'er barren mountains, o'er the flow'ry plain,
The leafy forest, and the liquid main,
Extends thy uncontroll'd and boundless reign.
Thro' all the living regions thou dost move,
And scatter'st where thou go'st the kindly seeds of love.

The females of brutes have an almost constant fecundity. But in the human species, the manner of thinking, the character, the passions, the humour, the caprice, the idea of preserving beauty, the pain of child-bearing, and the fatigue of a too numerous family, obstruct propagation in a thousand different ways.

2. *Of Marriage.* The natural obligation of the father to provide for his children has established marriage, which makes known the person who ought to fulfil this obligation. The people[5] mentioned by Pomponius Mela[6] had no other way of discovering him but by resemblance.

Among civilised nations, the father is that person on whom the laws, by the ceremony of marriage, have fixed this duty, because

---

[1] Cicero's edict fixed it to one per cent a month, with interest upon interest at the expiration of the year. With regard to the farmers of the republic, he engaged them to grant a respite to their debtors; if the latter did not pay at the time fixed, he awarded the interest mentioned in the bond.—*Ibid.*, vi. 1.
[2] Dryden, *Lucr.*
[3] See what Lucretius says, in the 21st letter to Atticus, v. There was even a general *Senatus Consultum*, to fix the rate of interest at one per cent per month. See the same letter.
[4] *Leg.* 12, ff. *de verb. signif.*
[5] The Garamantes.
[6] Book i. 8.

they find in him the man they want.[1]

Among brutes this is an obligation which the mother can generally perform; but it is much more extensive among men. Their children indeed have reason; but this comes only by slow degrees. It is not sufficient to nourish them; we must also direct them: they can already live; but they cannot govern themselves.

Illicit conjunctions contribute but little to the propagation of the species. The father, who is under a natural obligation to nourish and educate his children, is not then fixed; and the mother, with whom the obligation remains, finds a thousand obstacles from shame, remorse, the constraint of her sex, and the rigour of laws; and besides, she generally wants the means.

Women who have submitted to public prostitution cannot have the convenience of educating their children: the trouble of education is incompatible with their station; and they are so corrupt that they can have no protection from the law.

It follows from all this that public continence is naturally connected with the propagation of the species.

3. *Of the Condition of Children.* It is a dictate of reason that when there is a marriage, children should follow the station or condition of the father; and that when there is not, they can belong to the mother only.[2]

4. *Of Families.* It is almost everywhere a custom for the wife to pass into the family of the husband. The contrary is without any inconvenience established at Formosa,[3] where the husband enters into the family of the wife.

This law, which fixes the family in a succession of persons of the same sex, greatly contributes, independently of the first motives, to the propagation of the human species. The family is a kind of property: a man who has children of a sex which does not perpetuate it is never satisfied if he has not those who can render it perpetual.

Names, whereby men acquire an idea of a thing which one would imagine ought not to perish, are extremely proper to inspire every family with a desire of extending its duration. There are people among whom names distin-

guish families: there are others where they only distinguish persons: the latter have not the same advantage as the former.

5. *Of the several Orders of lawful Wives.* Laws and religion sometimes establish many kinds of civil conjunctions; and this is the case among the Mahometans, where there are several orders of wives, the children of whom are distinguished by being born in the house, by civil contracts, or even by the slavery of the mother, and the subsequent acknowledgment of the father.

It would be contrary to reason that the law should stigmatise the children for what it approved in the father. All these children ought, therefore, to succeed, at least if some particular reason does not oppose it, as in Japan, where none inherit but the children of the wife given by the emperor. Their policy demands that the gifts of the emperor should not be too much divided, because they subject them to a kind of service, like that of our ancient fiefs.

There are countries where a wife of the second rank enjoys nearly the same honours in a family as in our part of the world are granted to an only consort: there the children of concubines are deemed to belong to the first or principal wife. Thus it is also established in China. Filial respect,[4] and the ceremony of deep mourning, are not due to the natural mother, but to her appointed by the law.

By means of this fiction they have no bastard children; and where such a fiction does not take place, it is obvious that a law to legitimatize the children of concubines must be considered as an act of violence, as the bulk of the nation would be stigmatised by such a decree. Neither is there any regulation in those countries with regard to children born in adultery. The recluse lives of women, the locks, the inclosures, and the eunuchs render all infidelity to their husbands so difficult, that the law judges it impossible. Besides, the same sword would exterminate the mother and the child.

6. *Of Bastards in different Governments.* They have therefore no such thing as bastards where polygamy is permitted; this disgrace is known only in countries in which a man is allowed to marry but one wife. Here they were obliged to stamp a mark of infamy upon concubinage, and consequently they were under a necessity

[1] *Pater est quem nuptiæ demonstrant.*
[2] For this reason, among nations that have slaves, the child almost always follows the station or condition of the mother.
[3] Father Du Halde, i, p. 165.
[4] *Ibid.*, ii, p. 121.

of stigmatising the issue of such unlawful conjunctions.

In republics, where it is necessary that there should be the purest morals, bastards ought to be more degraded than in monarchies.

The laws made against them at Rome were perhaps too severe; but as the ancient institutions laid all the citizens under a necessity of marrying, and as marriages were also softened by the permission to repudiate or make a divorce, nothing but an extreme corruption of manners could lead them to concubinage.

It is observable that as the quality of a citizen was a very considerable thing in a democratic government, where it carried with it the sovereign power, they frequently made laws in respect to the state of bastards, which had less relation to the thing itself and to the honesty of marriage than to the particular constitution of the republic. Thus the people have sometimes admitted bastards into the number of citizens, in order to increase their power in opposition to the great.[1] Thus the Athenians excluded bastards from the privilege of being citizens, that they might possess a greater share of the corn sent them by the King of Egypt. In fine, Aristotle informs us that in many cities where there was not a sufficient number of citizens, their bastards succeeded to their possessions; and that when there was a proper number, they did not inherit.[2]

7. *Of the Father's Consent to Marriage.* The consent of fathers is founded on their authority, that is, on the right of property. It is also founded on their love, on their reason, and on the uncertainty of that of their children, whom youth confines in a state of ignorance and passion in a state of ebriety.

In the small republics, or singular institutions already mentioned, they might have laws which gave to magistrates that right of inspection over the marriages of the children of citizens which nature had already given to fathers. The love of the public might there equal or surpass all other love. Thus Plato would have marriages regulated by the magistrates: this the Lacedæmonian magistrates performed.

But in common institutions, fathers have the disposal of their children in marriage: their prudence in this respect is always supposed to be superior to that of a stranger. Nature gives to fathers a desire of procuring successors to their children, when they have al-

most lost the desire of enjoyment themselves. In the several degrees of progeniture, they see themselves insensibly advancing to a kind of immortality. But what must be done, if oppression and avarice arise to such a height as to usurp all the authority of fathers? Let us hear what Thomas Gage says in regard to the conduct of the Spaniards in the West Indies.[3]

"According to the number of the sons and daughters that are marriageable, the father's tribute is raised and increased, until they provide husbands and wives for their sons and daughters, who, as soon as they are married, are charged with tribute; which, that it may increase, they will suffer none above fifteen years of age to live unmarried. Nay, the set time of marriage appointed for the Indians is at fourteen years for the man, and thirteen for the woman; alleging that they are sooner ripe for the fruit of wedlock, and sooner ripe in knowledge and malice, and strength for work and service, than any other people. Nay, sometimes they force those to marry who are scarcely twelve and thirteen years of age, if they find them well-limbed and strong in body, explaining a point of one of the canons, which alloweth fourteen and fifteen years, *Nisi malitia suppleat ætatem.*"

He saw a list of these taken. It was, says he, a most shameful affair. Thus in an action which ought to be the most free, the Indians are the greatest slaves.

8. *The same Subject continued.* In England the law is frequently abused by the daughters marrying according to their own fancy without consulting their parents. This custom is, I am apt to imagine, more tolerated there than anywhere else from a consideration that as the laws have not established a monastic celibacy, the daughters have no other state to choose but that of marriage, and this they cannot refuse. In France, on the contrary, young women have always the resource of celibacy; and therefore the law which ordains that they shall wait for the consent of their fathers may be more agreeable. In this light the custom of Italy and Spain must be less rational; convents are there established, and yet they may marry without the consent of their fathers.

9. *Of young Women.* Young women who are conducted by marriage alone to liberty and pleasure, who have a mind which dares not

[1] Aristotle, *Politics,* vi. 4.
[2] *Ibid.,* iii. 5.

[3] Thomas Gage, *A New Survey of the West Indies,* p. 345, 3rd ed.

think, a heart which dares not feel, eyes which dare not see, ears which dare not hear, who appear only to show themselves silly, condemned without intermission to trifles and precepts, have sufficient inducements to lead them on to marriage: it is the young men that want to be encouraged.

10. *What it is that determines Marriage.* Wherever a place is found in which two persons can live commodiously, there they enter into marriage. Nature has a sufficient propensity to it, when unrestrained by the difficulty of subsistence.

A rising people increase and multiply extremely. This is, because with them it would be a great inconvenience to live in celibacy; and none to have many children. The contrary of which is the case when a nation is formed.

11. *Of the Severity of Government.* Men who have absolutely nothing, such as beggars, have many children. This proceeds from their being in the case of a rising people: it costs the father nothing to give his heart to his offspring, who even in their infancy are the instruments of this art. These people multiply in a rich or superstitious country, because they do not support the burden of society, but are themselves the burden. But men who are poor, only because they live under a severe government; who regard their fields less as the source of their subsistence than as a cause of vexation; these men, I say, have few children: they have not even subsistence for themselves. How then can they think of dividing it? They are unable to take care of their own persons when they are sick. How then can they attend to the wants of creatures whose infancy is a continual sickness?

It is pretended by some who are apt to talk of things which they have never examined that the greater the poverty of the subjects, the more numerous their families: that the more they are loaded with taxes, the more industriously they endeavour to put themselves in a station in which they will be able to pay them: two sophisms, which have always destroyed and will for ever be the destruction of monarchies.

The severity of government may be carried to such an extreme as to make the natural sentiments destructive of the natural sentiments themselves. Would the women of America have refused to bear children had their masters been less cruel?[1]

[1] *Ibid.,* p. 97, 3rd ed.

12. *Of the Number of Males and Females in different Countries.* I have already observed that there are born in Europe rather more boys than girls.[2] It has been remarked that in Japan there are born rather more girls than boys:[3] all things compared, there must be more fruitful women in Japan than in Europe, and consequently it must be more populous.

We are informed that at Bantam there are ten girls to one boy.[4] A disproportion like this must cause the number of families there to be to the number of those of other climates as 1 to $5\frac{1}{2}$, which is a prodigious difference. Their families may be much larger indeed; but there must be few men in circumstances sufficient to provide for so large a family.

13. *Of Seaport Towns.* In seaport towns, where men expose themselves to a thousand dangers, and go abroad to live or die in distant climates, there are fewer men than women: and yet we see more children there than in other places. This proceeds from the greater ease with which they procure the means of subsistence. Perhaps even the oily parts of fish are more proper to furnish that matter which contributes to generation. This may be one of the causes of the infinite number of people in Japan[5] and China,[6] where they live almost wholly on fish.[7] If this be the case, certain monastic rules, which oblige the monks to live on fish, must be contrary to the spirit of the legislator himself.

14. *Of the Productions of the Earth which require a greater or less Number of Men.* Pasture-lands are but little peopled, because they find employment only for a few. Corn-lands employ a great many men, and vineyards infinitely more.

It has been a frequent complaint in England[8] that the increase of pasture-land dimin-

[2] Book xvi. 4.
[3] See Kempfer, who gives a computation of the people of Meaco.
[4] *Collection of Voyages that Contributed to the Establishment of the East India Company,* i, p. 347.
[5] Japan is composed of a number of isles, where there are many banks, and the sea is there extremely full of fish.
[6] China abounds in rivers.
[7] See Father Du Halde, ii, pp. 139, 142, ff.
[8] The greatest number of the proprietors of land, says Bishop Burnet, finding more profit in selling their wool than their corn, inclosed their estates; the commons, ready to perish with hunger, rose up in arms; they insisted on a division of the lands; the young king even wrote on this sub-

ished the inhabitants; and it has been observed in France that the prodigious number of vineyards is one of the great causes of the multitude of people.

Those countries where coal-pits furnish a proper substance for fuel have this advantage over others, that not having the same occasion for forests, the lands may be cultivated.

In countries productive of rice, they are at vast pains in watering the land: a great number of men must therefore be employed. Besides, there is less land required to furnish subsistence for a family than in those which produce other kinds of grain. In fine, the land which is elsewhere employed in raising cattle serves immediately for the subsistence of man; and the labour which in other places is performed by cattle is there performed by men; so that the culture of the soil becomes to man an immense manufacture.

15. *Of the Number of Inhabitants with relation to the Arts.* When there is an agrarian law, and the lands are equally divided, the country may be extremely well peopled, though there are but few arts; because every citizen receives from the cultivation of his land whatever is necessary for his subsistence, and all the citizens together consume all the fruits of the earth. Thus it was in some republics.

In our present situation, in which lands are unequally distributed, they produce much more than those who cultivate them are able to consume; if the arts, therefore, should be neglected, and nothing minded but agriculture, the country could not be peopled. Those who cultivate, or employ others to cultivate, having corn to spare, nothing would engage them to work the following year; the fruits of the earth would not be consumed by the indolent; for these would have nothing with which they could purchase them. It is necessary, then, that the arts should be established, in order that the produce of the land may be consumed by the labourer and the artificer. In a word, it is now proper that many should cultivate much more than is necessary for their own use. For this purpose they must have a desire of enjoying superfluities; and these they can receive only from the artificer.

The machines designed to abridge art are not always useful. If a piece of workmanship is of a moderate price, such as is equally agree-

able to the maker and the buyer, those machines which would render the manufacture more simple, or, in other words, diminish the number of workmen, would be pernicious. And if water-mills were not everywhere established, I should not have believed them so useful as is pretended, because they have deprived an infinite multitude of their employment, a vast number of persons of the use of water, and great part of the land of its fertility.

16. *The Concern of the Legislator in the Propagation of the Species.* Regulations on the number of citizens depend greatly on circumstances. There are countries in which nature does all; the legislator then has nothing to do. What need is there of inducing men by laws to propagation when a fruitful climate yields a sufficient number of inhabitants? Sometimes the climate is more favourable than the soil; the people multiply, and are destroyed by famine: this is the case of China. Hence a father sells his daughters and exposes his children. In Tonquin,[1] the same causes produce the same effects; so we need not, like the Arabian travellers mentioned by Renaudot, search for the origin of this in their sentiments on the metempsychosis.[2]

For the same reason, the religion of the Isle of Formosa does not suffer the women to bring their children into the world till they are thirty-five years of age:[3] the priestess, before this age, by bruising the belly procures abortion.

17. *Of Greece and the Number of its Inhabitants.* That effect which in certain countries of the East springs from physical causes was produced in Greece by the nature of the government. The Greeks were a great nation, composed of cities, each of which had a distinct government and separate laws. They had no more the spirit of conquest and ambition than those of Switzerland, Holland, and Germany have at this day. In every republic the legislator had in view the happiness of the citizens at home, and their power abroad, lest it should prove inferior to that of the neighbouring cities.[4] Thus, with the enjoyment of a small territory and great happiness, it was easy for the number of the citizens to increase to

ject. And proclamations were made against those who inclosed their lands.—*Abridgment of the History of the Reformation*, pp. 44, 83.

[1] Dampier, *Voyages*, ii, p. 41.
[2] *Ibid.*, p. 167.
[3] See the *Collection of Voyages that Contributed to the Establishment of the East India Company*, v, part I, pp. 182, 188.
[4] In valour, discipline, and military exercises.

such a degree as to become burdensome. This obliged them incessantly to send out colonies,[1] and, as the Swiss do now, to let their men out to war. Nothing was neglected that could hinder the too great multiplication of children.

They had among them republics, whose constitution was very remarkable. The nations they had subdued were obliged to provide subsistence for the citizens. The Lacedæmonians were fed by the Helotes, the Cretans by the Periecians, and the Thessalians by the Penestes. They were obliged to have only a certain number of freemen, that their slaves might be able to furnish them with subsistence. It is a received maxim in our days, that it is necessary to limit the number of regular troops: now the Lacedæmonians were an army maintained by the peasants: it was proper, therefore, that this army should be limited; without this the freemen, who had all the advantages of society, would increase beyond number, and the labourers be overloaded.

The politics of the Greeks were particularly employed in regulating the number of citizens. Plato fixes them at five thousand and forty,[2] and he would have them stop or encourage propagation, as was most convenient, by honours, shame, and the advice of the old men; he would even regulate the number of marriages in such a manner that the republic might be recruited without being overcharged.[3]

If the laws of a country, says Aristotle, forbid the exposing of children, the number of those brought forth ought to be limited.[4] If they have more than the number prescribed by law, he advises to make the women miscarry before the fœtus be formed.[5]

The same author mentions the infamous means made use of by the Cretans to prevent their having too great a number of children— a proceeding too indecent to repeat.

There are places, says Aristotle again[6] where the laws give the privilege of being citizens to strangers, or to bastards, or to those whose mothers only are citizens; but as soon as they have a sufficient number of people this privilege ceases. The savages of Canada burn their prisoners; but when they have empty cottages to give them, they receive them into their nation.

Sir William Petty, in his calculations, supposes that a man in England is worth what he would sell for at Algiers.[7] This can be true only with respect to England. There are countries where a man is worth nothing; there are others where he is worth less than nothing.

18. *Of the State and Number of People before the Romans.* Italy, Sicily, Asia Minor, Gaul, and Germany were nearly in the same state as Greece; full of small nations that abounded with inhabitants, they had no need of laws to increase their number.

19. *Of the Depopulation of the Globe.* All these little republics were swallowed up in a large one, and the globe insensibly became depopulated: in order to be convinced of this, we need only consider the state of Italy and Greece before and after the victories of the Romans.

"You will ask me," says Livy,[8] "where the Volsci could find soldiers to support the war, after having been so often defeated. There must have been formerly an infinite number of people in those countries, which at present would be little better than a desert, were it not for a few soldiers and Roman slaves."

"The Oracles have ceased," says Plutarch, "because the places where they spoke are destroyed. At present we can scarcely find in Greece three thousand men fit to bear arms."

"I shall not describe," says Strabo,[9] "Epirus and the adjacent places, because these countries are entirely deserted. This depopulation, which began long ago, still continues; so that the Roman soldiers encamp in the houses they have abandoned." We find the cause of this in Polybius, who says that Paulus Æmilius, after his victory, destroyed seventy cities of Epirus, and carried away a hundred and fifty thousand slaves.

20. *That the Romans were under the Necessity of making Laws to encourage the Propagation of the Species.* The Romans, by destroying others, were themselves destroyed: incessantly in action, in the heat of battle, and in the most violent attempts, they wore out like a weapon kept constantly in use.

I shall not here speak of the attention with which they applied themselves to procure citi-

[1] The Gauls, who were in the same circumstances, acted in the same manner.
[2] *Laws*, v.
[3] *Republic*, v.
[4] *Politics*, vii. 16.
[5] *Ibid*.
[6] *Ibid*., iii. 5.

[7] Sixty pounds sterling.
[8] Book vi. 12.
[9] Book vii, p. 496.

zens in the room of those they lost,[1] of the associations they entered into, the privileges they bestowed, and of that immense nursery of citizens, their slaves. I shall mention what they did to recruit the number, not of their citizens, but of their men; and as these were the people in the world who knew best how to adapt their laws to their projects, an examination of their conduct in this respect cannot be a matter of indifference.

21. *Of the Laws of the Romans relating to the Propagation of the Species.* The ancient laws of Rome endeavoured greatly to incite the citizens to marriage. The senate and the people made frequent regulations on this subject, as Augustus says in his speech related by Dio.[2]

Dionysius Halicarnassus[3] cannot believe that after the death of three hundred and five of the Fabii, exterminated by the Veientes, there remained no more of this family than one single child; because the ancient law, which obliged every citizen to marry and to educate all his children, was still in force.[4]

Independently of the laws, the censors had a particular eye upon marriages, and according to the exigencies of the republic engaged them to it by shame and by punishments.[5]

The corruption of manners that began to take place contributed vastly to disgust the citizens with marriage, which was painful to those who had no taste for the pleasures of innocence. This is the purport of that speech which Metellus Numidicus, when he was censor, made to the people:[6] "If it were possible for us to do without wives, we should deliver ourselves from this evil: but as nature has ordained that we cannot live very happily with them, nor subsist without them, we ought to have more regard to our own preservation than to transient gratifications."

The corruption of manners destroyed the censorship, which was itself established to destroy the corruption of manners: for when this depravation became general, the censor lost his power.[7]

Civil discords, triumvirates, and proscrip-

tions weakened Rome more than any war she had hitherto engaged in. They left but few citizens,[8] and the greatest part of them unmarried. To remedy this last evil, Cæsar and Augustus re-established the censorship, and would even be censors themselves.[9] Cæsar gave rewards to those who had many children.[10] All women under forty-five years of age who had neither husband nor children were forbidden to wear jewels or to ride in litters;[11] an excellent method thus to attack celibacy by the power of vanity. The laws of Augustus were more pressing;[12] he imposed new penalties on such as were not married,[13] and increased the rewards both of those who were married and of those who had children. Tacitus calls these Julian laws;[14] to all appearance they were founded on the ancient regulations made by the senate, the people, and the censors.

The law of Augustus met with innumerable obstacles, and thirty-four years after it had been made the Roman knights insisted on its being abolished.[15] He placed on one side such as were married, and on the other side those who were not: these last appeared by far the greatest number; upon which the citizens were astonished and confounded. Augustus, with the gravity of the ancient censors, addressed them in this manner:[16]

"While sickness and war snatch away so many citizens, what must become of this state if marriages are no longer contracted? The city does not consist of houses, of porticos, of public places, but of inhabitants. You do not see men like those mentioned in Fable starting out of the earth to take care of your affairs. Your celibacy is not owing to the desire of living alone; for none of you eats or sleeps by himself. You only seek to enjoy your irregularities undisturbed. Do you cite the example of the Vestal Virgins? If you preserve not the laws of chastity, you ought to be punished like them. You are equally bad citizens, whether your example has an influence on the rest of

[8] Cæsar, after the Civil War, having made a survey of the Roman citizens, found there were no more than one hundred and fifty thousand heads of families.—Florus, *Epitome of Livy*, dec. 12.
[9] See Dio, xliii., and Xiphilinus in *August*.
[10] Dio, lib. xliii.; Suetonius, Life of Cæsar, 22; Appian, *On the Civil War*, ii.
[11] Eusebius, *Chronicle*.
[12] Dio, liv. 16.
[13] In the year of Rome 736.
[14] *Julias rogationes.—Annals*, iii. 25.
[15] In the year of Rome 762.—Dio, lvi. 1.
[16] I have abridged this speech, which is of tedious length; it is to be found in Dio, lvi.

[1] I have treated of this in the *Considerations on the Causes of the Rise and Declension of the Roman Grandeur*, 13.
[2] Book lvi.
[3] Book ii.
[4] In the year of Rome 277.
[5] See what was done in this respect in Livy, xlv; the *Epitome of Livy*, lix; Aulus Gellius, i. 6; Valerius Maximus, ii. 9.
[6] It is in Aulus Gellius, i. 6.
[7] See what I have said in Book v. 19.

the world, or whether it be disregarded. My only view is the perpetuity of the republic. I have increased the penalties of those who have disobeyed; and with respect to rewards, they are such as I do not know whether virtue has ever received greater. For less will a thousand men expose life itself; and yet will not these engage you to take a wife and provide for children?"

He made a law, which was called after his name, Julia and Papia Poppæa, from the names of the consuls for part of that year.[1] The greatness of the evil appeared even in their being elected: Dio tells us that they were not married, and that they had no children.[2]

This decree of Augustus was properly a code of laws, and a systematic body of all the regulations that could be made on this subject. The Julian laws were incorporated in it, and received greater strength.[3] It was so extensive in its use, and had an influence on so many things, that it formed the finest part of the civil law of the Romans.

We find parts of it dispersed in the precious fragments of Ulpian,[4] in the Laws of the Digest, collected from authors who wrote on the Papian laws, in the historians and others who have cited them, in the Theodosian code which abolished them, and in the works of the fathers, who have censured them, without doubt from a laudable zeal for the things of the other life, but with very little knowledge of the affairs of this.

These laws had many heads,[5] of which we know thirty-five. But to return to my subject as speedily as possible, I shall begin with that head which Aulus Gellius informs us was the seventh, and relates to the honours and rewards granted by that law.[6]

The Romans, who for the most part sprang from the cities of the Latins, which were Lacedæmonian colonies,[7] and had received a part of their laws even from those cities,[8] had, like the Lacedæmonians, such veneration for old age as to give it all honour and precedence.

When the republic wanted citizens, she granted to marriage and to the number of children the privileges which had been given to age.[9] She granted some to marriage alone, independent of the children which might spring from it: this was called the right of husbands. She gave others to those who had any children, and larger still to those who had three children. These three things must not be confounded. These last had those privileges which married men constantly enjoyed; as, for example, a particular place in the theatre;[10] they had those which could only be enjoyed by men who had children, and which none could deprive them of but such as had a greater number.

These privileges were very extensive. The married men who had the most children were always preferred, whether in the pursuit or in the exercise of honours.[11] The consul who had the most numerous offspring was the first who received the fasces;[12] he had his choice of the provinces:[13] the senator who had most children had his name written first in the catalogue of senators, and was the first in giving his opinion in the senate.[14] They might even stand sooner than ordinary for an office, because every child gave a dispensation of a year.[15] If an inhabitant of Rome had three children, he was exempted from all troublesome offices.[16] The freeborn women who had three children, and the freedwomen who had four, passed out of that perpetual tutelage[17] in which they had been held by the ancient laws of Rome.[18]

As they had rewards, they had also penalties.[19] Those who were not married could receive no advantage from the will of any person that was not a relative;[20] and those who, being married, had no children, could receive only half.[21] The Romans, says Plutarch, marry only

---

[1] Marcus Papius Mutilus and Q. Poppæus Sabinus.—Dio, lvi.

[2] Ibid.

[3] Ulpian, Fragment, tit. 14, distinguishes very rightly between the Julian and the Papian law.

[4] James Godfrey has made a collection of these.

[5] The 35th is cited in Leg. 19, ff. de ritu nuptiarum.

[6] Book ii. 15.

[7] Dionysius Halicarnassus.

[8] The deputies of Rome, who were sent to search into the laws of Greece, went to Athens, and to the cities of Italy.

[9] Aulus Gellius, ii. 15.

[10] Suetonius, Life of Augustus, 44.

[11] Tacitus, ii. 51: Ut numerus liberorum in candidatis præpolleret, quod lex jubebat.

[12] Aulus Gellius, ii. 15.

[13] Tacitus, Annals, xv. 19.

[14] See Leg. 6, § 5, De Decurion.

[15] See Leg. 2, ff. de minorib.

[16] Leg. 1, § 3, Leg. 2, ff. de vacatione et excusat. munerum.

[17] Ulpian, Fragment., tit. 29, § 3.

[18] Plutarch, Numa.

[19] See the Ulpian, Fragment., tit. 14, 15, 16, 17, 18, which compose one of the most valuable pieces of the ancient civil law of the Romans.

[20] Sozomenus, i. 9. They could receive from their relatives.—Ulpian, Fragment., tit. 16, § 1.

[21] Sozomenus, i. 9; and Leg. unic., Cod. Theod. de infirm. pœnis cælib. et orbit.

to *be* heirs, and not to *have* them.[1]

The advantages which a man and his wife might receive from each other by will were limited by law.[2] If they had children of each other, they might receive the whole; if not, they could receive only a tenth part of the succession on the account of marriage; and if they had any children by a former venter, as many tenths as they had children.

If a husband absented himself from his wife on any other cause than the affairs of the republic, he could not inherit from her.[3]

The law gave to a surviving husband or wife two years to marry again,[4] and a year and a half in case of a divorce. The fathers who would not suffer their children to marry, or refused to give their daughters a portion, were obliged to do it by the magistrates.[5]

They were not allowed to betroth when the marriage was to be deferred for more than two years:[6] and as they could not marry a girl till she was twelve years old, they could not be betrothed to her till she was ten. The law would not suffer them to trifle to no purpose;[7] and under a pretence of being betrothed, to enjoy the privileges of married men.

It was contrary to law for a man of sixty to marry a woman of fifty.[8] As they had given great privileges to married men, the law would not suffer them to enter into useless marriages. For the same reason, the Calvisian *Senatus Consultum* declared the marriage of a woman above fifty with a man less than sixty to be unequal:[9] so that a woman of fifty years of age could not marry without incurring the penalties of these laws. Tiberius added to the rigour of the Papian law,[10] and prohibited men of sixty from marrying women under fifty; so

that a man of sixty could not marry in any case whatsoever, without incurring the penalty. But Claudius abrogated this law made under Tiberius.[11]

All these regulations were more conformable to the climate of Italy than to that of the North, where a man of sixty years of age has still a considerable degree of strength, and where women of fifty are not always past childbearing.

That they might not be unnecessarily limited in the choice they were to make, Augustus permitted all the freeborn citizens who were not senators[12] to marry freedwomen.[13] The Papian law forbade the senators marrying freedwomen,[14] or those who had been brought up to the stage; and from the time of Ulpian,[15] freeborn persons were forbidden to marry women who had led a disorderly life, who had played in the theatre, or who had been condemned by a public sentence. This must have been established by a decree of the senate. During the time of the republic they had never made laws like these, because the censors corrected this kind of disorder as soon as it arose, or else prevented its rising.

Constantine made a law[16] in which he comprehended, in the prohibition of the Papian law, not only the senators, but even such as had a considerable rank in the state, without mentioning persons in an inferior station: this constituted the law of those times. These marriages were therefore no longer forbidden, except to the free-born comprehended in the law of Constantine. Justinian, however, abrogated the law of Constantine,[17] and permitted all sorts of persons to contract these marriages; and thus we have acquired so fatal a liberty.

It is evident that the penalties inflicted on such as married contrary to the prohibition of the law were the same as those inflicted on persons who did not marry. These marriages did not give them any civil advantage;[18] for the dowry[19] was confiscated after the death of the wife.[20]

Augustus having adjudged the succession

1 *Of the Love of Fathers towards their Children.*
2 See a more particular account of this in Ulpian, *Fragment.*, tit. 15, 16.
3 *Ibid.*, tit. 16, § 1.
4 *Ibid.*, tit. 14. It seems the first Julian laws allowed three years.—Speech of Augustus, in Dio, lvi; Suetonius, Life of Augustus, 34. Other Julian laws granted but one year: the Papian law gave two.—Ulpian, *Fragment.*, tit. 14. These laws were not agreeable to the people; Augustus, therefore, softened or strengthened them as they were more or less disposed to comply with them.
5 This was the 35th head of the Papian law.—*Leg.* 19, ff. *de ritu nuptiarum.*
6 See Dio, liv, year 736; Suetonius, in *Octavio*, 34.
7 Dio, liv; and in the same Dio, the speech of Augustus, lvi.
8 Ulpian, *Fragment.*, tit. 16, and *Leg.* 27, *Cod. de nuptiis.*
9 Ulpian, *Fragment.*, tit. 16, § 3.
10 See Suetonius, Life of Claudius, 23.
11 *Ibid.*, 23, and Ulpian, *Fragment.*, tit. 16, § 3.
12 Dio, liv; Ulpian, *Fragment.*, tit. 13.
13 Augustus's speech, in Dio, lvi.
14 Ulpian, *Fragment.*, 13, and the *Leg.* 44, ff. *de ritu nuptiarum.*
15 Ulpian, *Fragment.*, tit. 13 and 16.
16 See *Leg.* 1, *Cod. de nat. lib.*
17 Nov. 117.
18 *Leg.* 37, § 7, ff. *de operib. libertorum*, § 7; Ulpian, *Fragment.*, tit. 16, § 2.
19 Ulpian, *Fragment.*, tit. 16, § 2.
20 See book xxvi. 13.

and legacies of those whom these laws had declared incapable, to the public treasury,[1] they had the appearance rather of fiscal than of political and civil laws. The disgust they had already conceived at a burden which appeared too heavy was increased by their seeing themselves a continual prey to the avidity of the treasury. On this account, it became necessary, under Tiberius, that these laws should be softened;[2] that Nero should lessen the rewards given out of the treasury to the informers;[3] that Trajan should put a stop to their plundering;[4] that Severus should also moderate these laws;[5] and that the civilians should consider them as odious, and in all their decisions deviate from the literal rigour.

Besides, the emperors enervated these laws[6] by the privileges they granted of the rights of husbands, of children, and of three children. More than this, they gave particular persons a dispensation from the penalties of these laws.[7] But the regulations established for the public utility seemed incapable of admitting an alleviation.

It was highly reasonable that they should grant the rights of children to the vestals,[8] whom religion retained in a necessary virginity: they gave, in the same manner, the privilege of married men to soldiers,[9] because they could not marry. It was customary to exempt the emperors from the constraint of certain civil laws. Thus Augustus was freed from the constraint of the law which limited the power of enfranchising,[10] and of that which set bounds to the right of bequeathing by testa-

ment.[11] These were only particular cases; but, at last, dispensations were given without discretion, and the rule itself became no more than an exception.

The sects of philosophers had already introduced in the empire a disposition that estranged them from business—a disposition which could not gain ground in the time of the republic,[12] when everybody was employed in the arts of war and peace. Hence arose an idea of perfection, as connected with a life of speculation; hence an estrangement from the cares and embarrassments of a family. The Christian religion coming after this philosophy fixed, if I may make use of the expression, the ideas which that had only prepared.

Christianity stamped its character on jurisprudence; for empire has ever a connection with the priesthood. This is visible from the Theodosian code, which is only a collection of the decrees of the Christian emperors.

A panegyrist of Constantine[13] said to that emperor, "Your laws were made only to correct vice and to regulate manners: you have stripped the ancient laws of that artifice which seemed to have no other aim than to lay snares for simplicity."

It is certain that the alterations made by Constantine took their rise either from sentiments relating to the establishment of Christianity, or from ideas conceived of its perfection. From the first proceeded those laws which gave such authority to bishops, and which have been the foundation of the ecclesiastical jurisdiction; hence those laws which weakened paternal authority[14] by depriving the father of his property in the possessions of his children. To extend a new religion, they were obliged to take away the dependence of children, who are always least attached to what is already established.

The laws made with a view to Christian perfection were more particularly those by which the penalties of the Papian laws were abolished; the unmarried were equally exempted from them, with those who, being married, had no children.

"These laws were established," says an ecclesiastical historian,[15] "as if the multiplication

---

[1] Except in certain cases. See the Ulpian, *Fragment.*, tit. 18, and the only law in *Cod. de Caduc. tollend.*

[2] *Relatum de moderanda Papiâ Poppæâ.*—Tacitus, *Annals*, iii. 25.

[3] He reduced them to the fourth part.—Suetonius, Life of Nero, 10.

[4] See Pliny, *Panegyric.*

[5] Severus extended even to twenty-five years for the males, and to twenty for the females, the time fixed by the Papian law, as we see by comparing Ulpian, *Fragment.*, tit. 16, with what Tertullian says, *Apol.*, 4.

[6] P. Scipio, the censor, complains, in his speech to the people, of the abuses which were already introduced, that they received the same privileges for adopted as for natural children.—Aulus Gellius, v. 19.

[7] See the *Leg.* 31, ff. *de ritu nuptiarum.*

[8] Augustus in the Papian law gave them the privilege of mothers. See Dio, lvi. Numa had granted them the ancient privilege of women who had three children, that is, of having no guardian. —Plutarch, *Numa.*

[9] This was granted them by Claudius.—Dio, lx.

[10] *Leg. apud eum*, ff. *de manumissionib.* § 1.

[11] Dio, lvi.

[12] See, in Cicero, *Offices*, i, his sentiments on the spirit of speculation.

[13] Nazarius, *in panegyrico Constantini*, 321.

[14] See *Leg.* 1,2,3, *Cod. Theod. de bonis maternis, maternique generis*, &c., and *Leg. unic., Cod. Theod. de bonis quæ filiis famil. acquiruntur.*

[15] Sozomenus, i. 9.

of human species was an effect of our care; instead of being sensible that the number is increased or diminished according to the order of Providence."

Principles of religion have had an extraordinary influence on the propagation of the human species. Sometimes they have promoted it, as among the Jews, the Mahometans, the Gaurs, and the Chinese; at others they have put a damp to it, as was the case of the Romans upon their conversion to Christianity.

They everywhere incessantly preached continency; a virtue the more perfect because in its own nature it can be practised but by very few.

Constantine had not taken away the decimal laws which granted a greater extent to the donations between man and wife, in proportion to the number of their children. Theodosius, the younger, abrogated even these laws.[1]

Justinian declared all those marriages valid which had been prohibited by the Papian laws.[2] These laws required people to marry again: Justinian granted privileges to those who did not marry again.[3]

By the ancient institutions, the natural right which every one had to marry and beget children could not be taken away. Thus when they received a legacy,[4] on condition of not marrying, or when a patron made his freedman swear[5] that he would neither marry nor beget children, the Papian law annulled both the condition and the oath.[6] The clauses on continuing in widowhood established among us contradict the ancient law, and descend from the constitutions of the emperors, founded on ideas of perfection.

There is no law that contains an express abrogation of the privileges and honours which the Romans had granted to marriages, and to a number of children. But where celibacy had the pre-eminence, marriage could not be held in honour; and since they could oblige the officers of the public revenue to renounce so many advantages by the abolition of the penalties, it is easy to perceive that with yet greater ease they might put a stop to the rewards.

The same spiritual reason which had permitted celibacy soon imposed it even as necessary. God forbid that I should here speak against celibacy as adopted by religion; but who can be silent when it is built on libertinism; when the two sexes, corrupting each other even by the natural sensations themselves, fly from a union which ought to make them better, to live in that which always renders them worse?

It is a rule drawn from nature, that the more the number of marriages is diminished, the more corrupt are those who have entered into that state; the fewer married men, the less fidelity is there in marriage; as when there are more thieves, more thefts are committed.

22. *Of the Exposing of Children.* The Roman policy was very good in respect to the exposing of children. Romulus, says Dionysius Halicarnassus,[7] laid the citizens under an obligation to educate all their male children, and the eldest of their daughters. If the infants were deformed and monstrous, he permitted the exposing them, after having shown them to five of their nearest neighbours.

Romulus did not suffer them to kill any infants under three years old:[8] by which means he reconciled the law that gave to fathers the right over their children of life and death with that which prohibited their being exposed.

We find also in Dionysius Halicarnassus[9] that the law which obliged the citizens to marry, and to educate all their children, was in force in the 277th year of Rome; we see that custom had restrained the law of Romulus which permitted them to expose their younger daughters.

We have no knowledge of what the law of the Twelve Tables (made in the year of Rome 301) appointed with respect to the exposing of children, except from a passage of Cicero,[10] who, speaking of the office of tribune of the people, says that soon after its birth, like the monstrous infant of the law of the Twelve Tables, it was stifled; the infant that was not monstrous was therefore preserved, and the law of the Twelve Tables made no alteration in the preceding institutions.

"The Germans," says Tacitus,[11] "never expose their children; among them the best manners have more force than in other places the best laws." The Romans had therefore laws against this custom, and yet they did not

[1] *Leg.* 2, 3, *Cod. Theod. de jur. liber.*
[2] *Leg. Sancimus, Cod. de nuptiis.*
[3] *Nov.* 127, cap. iii; *Nov.* 118, cap. v.
[4] *Leg.* 54 ff. *de condit. et demonst.*
[5] *Leg.* 5, § 4, *de jure patronatus.*
[6] Paulus, *Sentences,* iii. tit. 4, § 15.

[7] *Antiquities of Rome,* ii.
[8] *Ibid.*
[9] Book ix.
[10] *De Leg.,* iii. 19.
[11] *De Moribus Germanorum,* 19.

follow them. We find no Roman law that permitted the exposing of children;[1] this was, without doubt, an abuse introduced towards the decline of the republic, when luxury robbed them of their freedom, when wealth divided was called poverty, when the father believed that all was lost which he gave to his family, and when this family was distinct from his property.

23. *Of the State of the World after the Destruction of the Romans.* The regulations made by the Romans to increase the number of their citizens had their effect while the republic, in the full vigour of her constitution, had nothing to repair but the losses she sustained by her courage, by her intrepidity, by her firmness, her love of glory and of virtue. But soon the wisest laws could not re-establish what a dying republic, what a general anarchy, what a military government, what a rigid empire, what a proud despotic power, what a feeble monarchy, what a stupid, weak, and superstitious court had successively pulled down. It might, indeed, be said that they conquered the world only to weaken it, and to deliver it up defenceless to barbarians. The Gothic nations, the Getes, the Saracens and Tartars by turns harassed them; and soon the barbarians had none to destroy but barbarians. Thus, in fabulous times, after the inundations and the deluge, there arose out of the earth armed men, who exterminated one another.

24. *The Changes which happened in Europe with regard to the Number of the Inhabitants.* In the state Europe was in one would not imagine it possible for it to be retrieved, especially when under Charlemagne it formed only one vast empire. But by the nature of government at that time it became divided into an infinite number of petty sovereignties, and as the lord or sovereign, who resided in his village or city, was neither great, rich, powerful, nor even safe but by the number of his subjects, every one employed himself with a singular attention to make his little country flourish. This succeeded in such a manner that notwithstanding the irregularities of government, the want of that knowledge which has since been acquired in commerce, and the numerous wars and disorders incessantly arising, most countries of Europe were better peopled in those days than they are even at present.

I have not time to treat fully of this subject, but I shall cite the prodigious armies engaged in the Crusades, composed of men of all countries. Puffendorf says that in the reign of Charles IX there were in France twenty millions of men.

It is the perpetual reunion of many little states that has produced this diminution. Formerly, every village of France was a capital; there is at present only one large one. Every part of the state was a centre of power; at present all has a relation to one centre, and this centre is in some measure the state itself.

25. *The same Subject continued.* Europe, it is true, has for these two ages past greatly increased its navigation; this has both procured and deprived it of inhabitants. Holland sends every year a great number of mariners to the Indies, of whom not above two-thirds return; the rest either perish or settle in the Indies. The same thing must happen to every other nation concerned in that trade.

We must not judge of Europe as of a particular state engaged alone in an extensive navigation. This state would increase in people, because all the neighbouring nations would endeavour to have a share in this commerce, and mariners would arrive from all parts. Europe, separated from the rest of the world by religion,[2] by vast seas and deserts, cannot be repaired in this manner.

26. *Consequences.* From all this we may conclude that Europe is at present in a condition to require laws to be made in favour of the propagation of the human species. The politics of the ancient Greeks incessantly complain of the inconveniences attending a republic, from the excessive number of citizens; but the politics of this age call upon us to take proper means to increase ours.

27. *Of the Law made in France to encourage the Propagation of the Species.* Louis XIV appointed particular pensions to those who had ten children, and much larger to such as had twelve.[3] But it is not sufficient to reward prodigies. In order to communicate a general spirit, which leads to the propagation of the species, it is necessary for us to establish, like the Romans, general rewards, or general penalties.

---

[1] There is no title on this subject in the Digest; the title of the Code says nothing of it, any more than the Novels.

[2] Mahometan countries surround it almost on every side.

[3] The edict of 1666 in favour of marriages.

28. *By what Means we may remedy a Depopulation.* When a state is depopulated by particular accidents, by wars, pestilence, or famine, there are still resources left. The men who remain may preserve the spirit of industry; they may seek to repair their misfortunes, and calamity itself may make them become more industrious. This evil is almost incurable when the depopulation is prepared beforehand by interior vice and a bad government. When this is the case, men perish with an insensible and habitual disease; born in misery and weakness, in violence or under the influence of a wicked administration, they see themselves destroyed, and frequently without perceiving the cause of their destruction. Of this we have a melancholy proof in the countries desolated by despotic power, or by the excessive advantages of the clergy over the laity.

In vain shall we wait for the succour of children yet unborn to re-establish a state thus depopulated. There is not time for this; men in their solitude are without courage or industry. With land sufficient to nourish a nation, they have scarcely enough to nourish a family. The common people have not even a property in the miseries of the country, that is, in the fallows with which it abounds. The clergy, the prince, the cities, the great men, and some of the principal citizens insensibly become proprietors of all the land which lies uncultivated; the families who are ruined have left their fields, and the labouring man is destitute.

In this situation they should take the same measures throughout the whole extent of the empire which the Romans took in a part of theirs; they should practise in their distress what these observed in the midst of plenty; that is, they should distribute land to all the families who are in want, and procure them materials for clearing and cultivating it. This distribution ought to be continued so long as there is a man to receive it, and in such a manner as not to lose a moment that can be industriously employed.

29. *Of Hospitals.* A man is not poor because he has nothing, but because he does not work. The man who without any degree of wealth has an employment is as much at his ease as he who without labour has an income of a hundred crowns a year. He who has no substance, and yet has a trade, is not poorer than he who, possessing ten acres of land, is obliged to cultivate it for his subsistence. The mechanic who gives his art as an inheritance to his children has left them a fortune, which is multiplied in proportion to their number. It is not so with him who, having ten acres of land, divides it among his children.

In trading countries, where many men have no other subsistence but from the arts, the state is frequently obliged to supply the necessities of the aged, the sick, and the orphan. A well-regulated government draws this support from the arts themselves. It gives to some such employment as they are capable of performing; others are taught to work, and this teaching of itself becomes an employment.

The alms given to a naked man in the street do not fulfil the obligations of the state, which owes to every citizen a certain subsistence, a proper nourishment, convenient clothing, and a kind of life not incompatible with health.

Aurungzebe, being asked why he did not build hospitals, said, "I will make my empire so rich that there shall be no need of hospitals."[1] He ought to have said, "I will begin by rendering my empire rich, and then I will build hospitals."

The riches of the state suppose great industry. Amidst the numerous branches of trade it is impossible but that some must suffer, and consequently the mechanics must be in a momentary necessity.

Whenever this happens, the state is obliged to lend them a ready assistance, whether it be to prevent the sufferings of the people, or to avoid a rebellion. In this case hospitals, or some equivalent regulations, are necessary to prevent this misery.

But when the nation is poor, private poverty springs from the general calamity, and is, if I may so express myself, the general calamity itself. All the hospitals in the world cannot cure this private poverty; on the contrary, the spirit of indolence, which it constantly inspires, increases the general, and consequently the private, misery.

Henry VIII,[2] resolving to reform the Church of England, ruined the monks, of themselves a lazy set of people, that encouraged laziness in others, because, as they practised hospitality, an infinite number of idle persons, gentlemen and citizens, spent their lives in running from convent to convent. He demolished even the hospitals, in which the lower people found subsistence, as the gentlemen did theirs in the monasteries. Since these changes, the spirit of

[1] See Sir John Chardin, *Travels through Persia,* viii.
[2] See Burnet, *History of the Reformation.*

trade and industry has been established in England.

At Rome, the hospitals place every one at his ease except those who labour, except those who are industrious, except those who have land, except those who are engaged in trade.

I have observed that wealthy nations have need of hospitals, because fortune subjects them to a thousand accidents; but it is plain that transient assistances are much better than perpetual foundations. The evil is momentary; it is necessary, therefore, that the succour should be of the same nature, and that it be applied to particular accidents.

Book XXIV. Of Laws in Relation to Religion Considered in Itself, and in Its Doctrines

1. *Of Religion in General.* As amidst several degrees of darkness we may form a judgment of those which are the least thick, and among precipices which are the least deep, so we may search among false religions for those that are most conformable to the welfare of society; for those which, though they have not the effect of leading men to the felicity of another life, may contribute most to their happiness in this.

I shall examine, therefore, the several religions of the world, in relation only to the good they produce in civil society, whether I speak of that which has its root in heaven, or of those which spring from the earth.

As in this work I am not a divine but a political writer, I may here advance things which are not otherwise true than as they correspond with a worldly manner of thinking, not as considered in their relation to truths of a more sublime nature.

With regard to the true religion, a person of the least degree of impartiality must see that I have never pretended to make its interests submit to those of a political nature, but rather to unite them; now, in order to unite, it is necessary that we should know them.

The Christian religion, which ordains that men should love each other, would, without doubt, have every nation blest with the best civil, the best political laws; because these, next to this religion, are the greatest good that men can give and receive.

2. *A Paradox of M. Bayle's.* M. Bayle has pretended to prove[1] that it is better to be an Atheist than an Idolater; that is, in other words, that it is less dangerous to have no religion at all than a bad one. "I had rather," said he, "it should be said of me that I had no existence than that I am a villain." This is only a sophism founded on this, that it is of no importance to the human race to believe that a certain man exists, whereas it is extremely useful for them to believe the existence of a God. From the idea of his non-existence immediately follows that of our independence; or, if we cannot conceive this idea, that of disobedience. To say that religion is not a restraining motive, because it does not always restrain, is equally absurd as to say that the civil laws are not a restraining motive. It is a false way of reasoning against religion to collect, in a large work, a long detail of the evils it has produced if we do not give at the same time an enumeration of the advantages which have flowed from it. Were I to relate all the evils that have arisen in the world from civil laws, from monarchy, and from republican government, I might tell of frightful things. Were it of no advantage for subjects to have religion, it would still be of some, if princes had it, and if they whitened with foam the only rein which can restrain those who fear not human laws.

A prince who loves and fears religion is a lion, who stoops to the hand that strokes, or to the voice that appeases him. He who fears and hates religion is like the savage beast that growls and bites the chain which prevents his flying on the passenger. He who has no religion at all is that terrible animal who perceives his liberty only when he tears in pieces and when he devours.

The question is not to know whether it would be better that a certain man or a certain people had no religion than to abuse what they have, but to know what is the least evil, that religion be sometimes abused, or that there be no such restraint as religion on mankind.

To diminish the horror of Atheism, they lay too much to the charge of idolatry. It is far from being true that when the ancients raised altars to a particular vice, they intended to show that they loved the vice; this signified,

[1] *Thoughts on the Comet, Continuation of Thoughts on the Comet,* ii.

on the contrary, that they hated it. When the Lacedæmonians erected a temple to Fear, it was not to show that this warlike nation desired that he would in the midst of battle possess the hearts of the Lacedæmonians. They had deities to whom they prayed not to inspire them with guilt; and others whom they besought to shield them from it.

3. *That a moderate Government is most agreeable to the Christian Religion, and a despotic Government to the Mahometan.* The Christian religion is a stranger to mere despotic power. The mildness so frequently recommended in the Gospel is incompatible with the despotic rage with which a prince punishes his subjects, and exercises himself in cruelty.

As this religion forbids the plurality of wives, its princes are less confined, less concealed from their subjects, and consequently have more humanity: they are more disposed to be directed by laws, and more capable of perceiving that they cannot do whatever they please.

While the Mahometan princes incessantly give or receive death, the religion of the Christians renders their princes less timid, and consequently less cruel. The prince confides in his subjects, and the subjects in the prince. How admirable the religion which, while it only seems to have in view the felicity of the other life, continues the happiness of this!

It is the Christian religion that, in spite of the extent of the empire and the influence of the climate, has hindered despotic power from being established in Ethiopia, and has carried into the heart of Africa the manners and laws of Europe.

The heir to the empire of Ethiopia[1] enjoys a principality and gives to other subjects an example of love and obedience. Not far thence may we see the Mahometan shutting up the children of the King of Sennar, at whose death the council sends to murder them, in favour of the prince who mounts the throne.

Let us set before our eyes, on the one hand, the continual massacres of the kings and generals of the Greeks and Romans, and, on the other, the destruction of people and cities by those famous conquerors Timur Beg and Jenghiz Khan, who ravaged Asia, and we shall see that we owe to Christianity, in government, a certain political law; and in war, a certain law of nations—benefits which human nature can

never sufficiently acknowledge.

It is owing to this law of nations that among us victory leaves these great advantages to the conquered, life, liberty, laws, wealth, and always religion, when the conqueror is not blind to his own interest.

We may truly say that the people of Europe are not at present more disunited than the people and the armies, or even the armies among themselves were, under the Roman empire when it had become a despotic and military government. On the one hand, the armies engaged in war against each other, and, on the other, they pillaged the cities, and divided or confiscated the lands.

4. *Consequences from the Character of the Christian Religion, and that of the Mahometan.* From the characters of the Christian and Mahometan religions, we ought, without any further examination, to embrace the one and reject the other: for it is much easier to prove that religion ought to humanise the manners of men than that any particular religion is true.

It is a misfortune to human nature when religion is given by a conqueror. The Mahometan religion, which speaks only by the sword, acts still upon men with that destructive spirit with which it was founded.

The history of Sabbaco,[2] one of the pastoral kings of Egypt, is very extraordinary. The tutelar god of Thebes, appearing to him in a dream, ordered him to put to death all the priests of Egypt. He judged that the gods were displeased at his being on the throne, since they commanded him to commit an action contrary to their ordinary pleasure; and therefore he retired into Ethiopia.

5. *That the Catholic Religion is most agreeable to a Monarchy, and the Protestant to a Republic.* When a religion is introduced and fixed in a state, it is commonly such as is most suitable to the plan of government there established; for those who receive it, and those who are the cause of its being received, have scarcely any other idea of policy than that of the state in which they were born.

When the Christian religion, two centuries ago, became unhappily divided into Catholic and Protestant, the people of the north embraced the Protestant, and those of the south adhered still to the Catholic.

The reason is plain: the people of the north have, and will for ever have, a spirit of lib-

---

[1] Description of Ethiopia, by M. Ponce, Physician. *Edifying Letters,* coll. iv, p. 290.

[2] See Diodorus, i. 18.

erty and independence, which the people of the south have not; and therefore a religion which has no visible head is more agreeable to the independence of the climate than that which has one.

In the countries themselves where the Protestant religion became established, the revolutions were made pursuant to the several plans of political government. Luther having great princes on his side would never have been able to make them relish an ecclesiastical authority that had no exterior pre-eminence; while Calvin, having to do with people who lived under republican governments, or with obscure citizens in monarchies, might very well avoid establishing dignities and preferments.

Each of these two religions was believed to be perfect; the Calvinist judging his most conformable to what Christ had said, and the Lutheran to what the Apostles had practised.

6. *Another of M. Bayle's Paradoxes.* M. Bayle, after having abused all religions, endeavours to sully Christianity: he boldly asserts that true Christians cannot form a government of any duration. Why not? Citizens of this profession being infinitely enlightened with respect to the various duties of life, and having the warmest zeal to fulfil them, must be perfectly sensible of the rights of natural defence. The more they believe themselves indebted to religion, the more they would think due to their country. The principles of Christianity, deeply engraved on the heart, would be infinitely more powerful than the false honour of monarchies, than the humane virtues of republics, or the servile fear of despotic states.

It is astonishing that this great man should not be able to distinguish between the orders for the establishment of Christianity and Christianity itself; and that he should be liable to be charged with not knowing the spirit of his own religion. When the legislator, instead of laws, has given counsels, this is because he knew that if these counsels were ordained as laws they would be contrary to the spirit of the laws themselves.

7. *Of the Laws of Perfection in Religion.* Human laws, made to direct the will, ought to give precepts, and not counsels; religion, made to influence the heart, should give many counsels, and few precepts.

When, for instance, it gives rules, not for what is good, but for what is better; not to di-

rect to what is right, but to what is perfect, it is expedient that these should be counsels, and not laws: for perfection can have no relation to the universality of men or things. Besides, if these were laws, there would be a necessity for an infinite number of others, to make people observe the first. Celibacy was advised by Christianity; when they made it a law in respect to a certain order of men, it became necessary to make new ones every day, in order to oblige those men to observe it.[1] The legislator wearied himself, and he wearied society, to make men execute by precept what those who love perfection would have executed as counsel.

8. *Of the Connection between the moral Laws and those of Religion.* In a country so unfortunate as to have a religion that God has not revealed, it is necessary for it to be agreeable to morality; because even a false religion is the best security we can have of the probity of men.

The principal points of religion of the inhabitants of Pegu[2] are, not to commit murder, not to steal, to avoid uncleanliness, not to give the least uneasiness to their neighbour, but to do him, on the contrary, all the good in their power. With these rules they think they should be saved in any religion whatsoever. Hence it proceeds that those people, though poor and proud, behave with gentleness and compassion to the unhappy.

9. *Of the Essenes.* The Essenes[3] made a vow to observe justice to mankind, to do no ill to any person, upon whatsoever account, to keep faith with all the world, to hate injustice, to command with modesty, always to side with truth, and to fly from all unlawful gain.

10. *Of the Sect of Stoics.* The several sects of philosophy among the ancients were a species of religion. Never were any principles more worthy of human nature, and more proper to form the good man, than those of the Stoics; and if I could for a moment cease to think that I am a Christian, I should not be able to hinder myself from ranking the destruction of the sect of Zeno among the misfortunes that have befallen the human race.

[1] Dupin, *Ecclesiastical Library of the Sixth Century,* v.

[2] *Collection of Voyages that Contributed to the Establishment of the East India Company,* iii, part I, p. 63.

[3] Prideaux, *History of the Jews.*

It carried to excess only those things in which there is true greatness—the contempt of pleasure and of pain.

It was this sect alone that made citizens; this alone that made great men; this alone great emperors.

Laying aside for a moment revealed truths, let us search through all nature, and we shall not find a nobler object than the Antoninuses; even Julian himself—Julian (a commendation thus wrested from me will not render me an accomplice of his apostasy)—no, there has not been a prince since his reign more worthy to govern mankind.

While the Stoics looked upon riches, human grandeur, grief, disquietudes, and pleasures as vanity, they were entirely employed in labouring for the happiness of mankind, and in exercising the duties of society. It seems as if they regarded that sacred spirit, which they believed to dwell within them, as a kind of favourable providence watchful over the human race.

Born for society, they all believed that it was their destiny to labour for it; with so much the less fatigue, their rewards were all within themselves. Happy by their philosophy alone, it seemed as if only the happiness of others could increase theirs.

11. *Of Contemplation.* Men being made to preserve, to nourish, to clothe themselves, and do all the actions of society, religion ought not to give them too contemplative a life.[1]

The Mahometans become speculative by habit; they pray five times a day, and each time they are obliged to cast behind them everything which has any concern with this world: this forms them for speculation. Add to this that indifference for all things which is inspired by the doctrine of unalterable fate.

If other causes besides these concur to disengage their affections; for instance, if the severity of the government, if the laws concerning the property of land, give them a precarious spirit—all is lost.

The religion of the Gaurs formerly rendered Persia a flourishing kingdom; it corrected the bad effects of despotic power. The same empire is now destroyed by the Mahometan religion.

12. *Of Penances.* Penances ought to be joined with the idea of labour, not with that of idle-

[1] This is the inconvenience of the doctrine of Foe and Laockium.

ness; with the idea of good, not with that of supereminence; with the idea of frugality, not with that of avarice.

13. *Of inexpiable Crimes.* It appears from a passage of the books of the pontiffs, quoted by Cicero,[2] that they had among the Romans inexpiable crimes:[3] and it is on this that Zozymus founds the narration so proper to blacken the motives of Constantine's conversion; and Julian, that bitter raillery on this conversion in his *Cæsars.*

The Pagan religion indeed, which prohibited only some of the grosser crimes, and which stopped the hand but meddled not with the heart, might have crimes that were inexpiable; but a religion which bridles all the passions; which is not more jealous of actions than of thoughts and desires; which holds us not by a few chains but by an infinite number of threads; which, leaving human justice aside, establishes another kind of justice; which is so ordered as to lead us continually from repentance to love, and from love to repentance; which puts between the judge and the criminal a greater mediator, between the just and the mediator a great judge—a religion like this ought not to have inexpiable crimes. But while it gives fear and hope to all, it makes us sufficiently sensible that though there is no crime in its own nature inexpiable, yet a whole criminal life may be so; that it is extremely dangerous to affront mercy by new crimes and new expiations; that an uneasiness on account of ancient debts, from which we are never entirely free, ought to make us afraid of contracting new ones, of filling up the measure, and going even to that point where paternal goodness is limited.

14. *In what Manner Religion has an Influence on Civil Laws.* As both religion and the civil laws ought to have a peculiar tendency to render men good citizens, it is evident that when one of these deviates from this end, the tendency of the other ought to be strengthened. The less severity there is in religion, the more there ought to be in the civil laws.

Thus the reigning religion of Japan having few doctrines, and proposing neither future rewards nor punishments, the laws to supply these defects have been made with the spirit of

[2] *De Leg.,* ii. 22.
[3] *Sacrum commissum, quod neque expiari poterit, impie commissum est; quod expiari poterit publici sacerdotes expianto.*

severity, and are executed with an extraordinary punctuality.

When the doctrine of necessity is established by religion, the penalties of the laws ought to be more severe, and the magistrate more vigilant; to the end that men who would otherwise become abandoned might be determined by these motives; but it is quite otherwise where religion has established the doctrine of liberty.

From the inactivity of the soul springs the Mahometan doctrine of predestination, and from this doctrine of predestination springs the inactivity of the soul. This, they say, is in the decrees of God; they must therefore indulge their repose. In a case like this, the magistrate ought to waken by the laws those who are lulled asleep by religion.

When religion condemns things which the civil laws ought to permit, there is danger lest the civil laws, on the other hand, should permit what religion ought to condemn. Either of these is a constant proof of a want of true ideas of that harmony and proportion which ought to subsist between both.

Thus the Tartars under Jenghiz Khan,[1] among whom it was a sin and even a capital crime to put a knife in the fire, to lean against a whip, to strike a horse with his bridle, to break one bone with another, did not believe it to be any sin to break their word, to seize upon another man's goods, to do an injury to a person, or to commit murder. In a word, laws which render that necessary which is only indifferent have this inconvenience, that they make those things indifferent which are absolutely necessary.

The people of Formosa believe[2] that there is a kind of hell, but it is to punish those who at certain seasons have not gone naked, who have dressed in calico and not in silk, who have presumed to look for oysters, or who have undertaken any business without consulting the song of birds; while drunkenness and debauchery are not regarded as crimes. They believe even that the debauches of their children are agreeable to their gods.

When religion absolves the mind by a thing merely accidental, it loses its greatest influence on mankind. The people of India believe that the waters of the Ganges have a sanctifying virtue.[3] Those who die on its banks are imagined to be exempted from the torments of the other life, and to be entitled to dwell in a region full of delights; and for this reason the ashes of the dead are sent from the most distant places to be thrown into this river. Little then does it signify whether they had lived virtuously or not, so they be but thrown into the Ganges.

The idea of a place of rewards has a necessary connection with the idea of the abodes of misery; and when they hope for the former without fearing the latter, the civil laws have no longer any influence. Men who think themselves sure of the rewards of the other life are above the power of the legislator; they look upon death with too much contempt. How shall the man be restrained by laws who believes that the greatest pain the magistrate can inflict will end in a moment to begin his happiness?

15. *How false Religions are sometimes corrected by the Civil Laws.* Simplicity, superstition, or a respect for antiquity have sometimes established mysteries or ceremonies shocking to modesty: of this the world has furnished numerous examples. Aristotle says[4] that in this case the law permits the fathers of families to repair to the temple to celebrate these mysteries for their wives and children. How admirable the civil law which in spite of religion preserves the manners untainted!

Augustus[5] excluded the youth of either sex from assisting at any nocturnal ceremony, unless accompanied by a more aged relative; and when he revived the Lupercalia,[6] he would not allow the young men to run naked.

16. *How the Laws of Religion correct the Inconveniences of a political Constitution.* On the other hand, religion may support a state when the laws themselves are incapable of doing it.

Thus when a kingdom is frequently agitated by civil wars, religion may do much by obliging one part of the state to remain always quiet. Among the Greeks, the Eleans, as priests of Apollo, lived always in peace. In Japan,[7] the city of Meaco enjoys a constant peace, as being a holy city. Religion supports this reg-

---

[1] See the account of John Duplan Carpin, sent to Tartary by Pope Innocent IV in the year 1246.
[2] *Collection of Voyages that Contributed to the Establishment of the East India Company,* v, part I, p. 192. [3] *Edifying Letters,* coll. xv.
[4] *Politics,* vii. 17.
[5] Suetonius, Life of Augustus, 31.
[6] *Ibid.*
[7] *Collection of Voyages that Contributed to the Establishment of the East India Company,* iv, part I, p. 127.

ulation, and that empire, which seems to be alone upon earth, and which neither has nor will have any dependence on foreigners, has always in its own bosom a trade which war cannot ruin.

In kingdoms where wars are not entered upon by a general consent, and where the laws have not pointed out any means either of terminating or preventing them, religion establishes times of peace, or cessation from hostilities, that the people may be able to sow their corn and perform those other labours which are absolutely necessary for the subsistence of the state.

Every year all hostility ceases between the Arabian tribes for four months: the least disturbance would then be an impiety.[1] In former times, when every lord in France declared war or peace, religion granted a truce, which was to take place at certain seasons.

17. The same Subject continued.

When a state has many causes for hatred, religion ought to produce many ways of reconciliation. The Arabs, a people addicted to robbery, are frequently guilty of doing injury and injustice. Mahomet enacted this law:[2] "If any one forgives the blood of his brother,[3] he may pursue the malefactor for damages and interest; but he who shall injure the wicked, after having received satisfaction, shall, in the day of judgment, suffer the most grievous torments."

The Germans inherited the hatred and enmity of their near relatives: but these were not eternal. Homicide was expiated by giving a certain number of cattle, and all the family received satisfaction: a thing extremely useful, says Tacitus, because enmities are most dangerous among a free people.[4] I believe, indeed, that their ministers of religion, who were held by them in so much credit, were concerned in these reconciliations.

Among the inhabitants of Malacca,[5] where no form of reconciliation is established, he who has committed murder, certain of being assassinated by the relatives or friends of the deceased, abandons himself to fury, and wounds or kills all he meets.

18. How the Laws of Religion have the Effect of Civil Laws.

The first Greeks were small nations, frequently dispersed, pirates at sea, unjust on land, without government and without laws. The mighty actions of Hercules and Theseus let us see the state of that rising people. What could religion do more to inspire them with horror against murder? It declared that the man who had been murdered was enraged against the assassin, that he would possess his mind with terror and trouble, and oblige him to yield to him the places he had frequented when alive.[6] They could not touch the criminal, nor converse with him, without being defiled:[7] the murderer was to be expelled from the city, and an expiation made for the crime.[8]

19. That it is not so much the Truth or Falsity of a Doctrine which renders it useful or pernicious to Men in civil Government, as the Use or Abuse of it.

The most true and holy doctrines may be attended with the very worst consequences when they are not connected with the principles of society: and on the contrary, doctrines the most false may be attended with excellent consequences when contrived so as to be connected with these principles.

The religion of Confucius disowns the immortality of the soul: and the sect of Zeno did not believe it. These two sects have drawn from their bad principles consequences, not just indeed, but most admirable as to their influence on society. Those of the religion of Tao, and of Foe,[9] believe the immortality of the soul; but from this sacred doctrine they draw the most frightful consequences.

The doctrine of the immortality of the soul falsely understood has, almost in every part of the globe and in every age, engaged women,

[1] See Prideaux, *Life of Mahomet*, p. 64.

[2] Koran, i, chapter "Of the Cow."

[3] On renouncing the law of retaliation.

[4] *De Moribus Germanorum*, 21.

[5] *Collection of Voyages that Contributed to the Establishment of the East India Company*, vii, p. 303. See also *Memoirs* of the Count de Forbin, and what he says of the people of Macassar.

[6] Plato, *Laws*, ix.

[7] Tragedy of *Œdipus at Colonus*.

[8] Plato, *Laws*, ix.

[9] A Chinese philosopher reasons thus against the doctrine of Foe: "It is said in a book of that sect, that the body is our dwelling-place and the soul the immortal guest which lodges there; but if the bodies of our relatives are only a lodging, it is natural to regard them with the same contempt we should feel for a structure of earth and dirt. Is not this endeavouring to tear from the heart the virtue of love to one's own parents? This leads us even to neglect the care of the body, and to refuse it the compassion and affection so necessary for its preservation; hence the disciples of Foe kill themselves by thousands."—Work of an ancient Chinese philosopher, in the Collection of Father Du Halde, iii, p. 52.

slaves, subjects, friends, to murder themselves, that they might go and serve in the other world the object of their respect or love in this. Thus it was in the West Indies; thus it was among the Danes;[1] thus it is at present in Japan,[2] in Macassar,[3] and many other places.

These customs do not so directly proceed from the doctrine of the immortality of the soul as from that of the resurrection of the body, whence they have drawn this consequence, that after death the same individual will have the same wants, the same sentiments, the same passions. In this point of view, the doctrine of the immortality of the soul has a prodigious effect on mankind; because the idea of only a simple change of habitation is more within the reach of the human understanding, and more adapted to flatter the heart, than the idea of a new modification.

It is not enough for religion to establish a doctrine; it must also direct its influence. This the Christian religion performs in the most admirable manner, particularly with regard to the doctrines of which we have been speaking. It makes us hope for a state which is the object of our belief; not for a state which we have already experienced or known: thus every article, even the resurrection of the body, leads us to spiritual ideas.

20. *The same Subject continued.* The sacred books[4] of the ancient Persians say, "If you would be holy instruct your children, because all the good actions which they perform will be imputed to you." They advise them to marry betimes, because children at the day of judgment will be as a bridge, over which those who have none cannot pass. These doctrines were false, but extremely useful.

21. *Of the Metempsychosis.* The doctrine of the immortality of the soul is divided into three branches—that of pure immortality, that of a simple change of habitation, and that of a metempsychosis, that is, the system of the Christians, that of the Scythians, and that of the Indians. We have just been speaking of the first two, and I shall say of the last that as it has been well or ill explained, it has had good or bad effects. As it inspires men with a certain horror against bloodshed, very few

murders are committed in the Indies; and though they seldom punish with death, yet they enjoy a perfect tranquillity.

On the other hand, women burn themselves at the death of their husbands; thus it is only the innocent who suffer a violent death.

22. *That it is dangerous for Religion to inspire an Aversion for Things in themselves indifferent.* A kind of honour established in the Indies by the prejudices of religion has made the several tribes conceive an aversion against each other. This honour is founded entirely on religion; these family distinctions form no civil distinctions; there are Indians who would think themselves dishonoured by eating with their king.

These sorts of distinctions are connected with a certain aversion for other men, very different from those sentiments which naturally arise from difference of rank; which among us comprehends a love for inferiors.

The laws of religion should never inspire an aversion to anything but vice, and above all they should never estrange man from a love and tenderness for his own species.

The Mahometan and Indian religions embrace an infinite number of people; the Indians hate the Mahometans, because they eat cows; the Mahometans detest the Indians because they eat hogs.

23. *Of Festivals.* When religion appoints a cessation from labour it ought to have a greater regard to the necessities of mankind than to the grandeur of the being it designs to honour.

Athens was subject to great inconveniences from the excessive number of its festivals.[5] These powerful people, to whose decision all the cities of Greece came to submit their quarrels, could not have time to despatch such a multiplicity of affairs.

When Constantine ordained that the people should rest on the Sabbath, he made this decree for the cities,[6] and not for the inhabitants of the open country; he was sensible that labour in the cities was useful, but in the fields necessary.

For the same reason, in a country supported by commerce, the number of festivals ought to be relative to this very commerce. Protestant and Catholic countries are situated in

---

[1] See Tho. Bartholin, *Antiquities of the Danes.*
[2] An Account of Japan, in the *Collection of Voyages that Contributed to the Establishment of the East India company.*
[3] Forbin, *Memoirs.*
[4] Hyde, *Religion of the Persians.*

[5] Xenophon, *On the Republic of Athens,* 3, § 8.
[6] *Leg.* 3, *Cod. de feriis.* This law was doubtless made only for the Pagans.

such a manner that there is more need of labour in the former than in the latter;[1] the suppression of festivals is therefore more suitable to Protestant than to Catholic countries.

Dampier observes that the diversions of different nations vary greatly, according to the climate.[2] As hot climates produce a quantity of delicate fruits, the barbarians easily find necessaries, and therefore spend much time in diversions. The Indians of colder countries have not so much leisure, being obliged to fish and hunt continually; hence they have less music, dancing and festivals. If a new religion should be established among these people, it ought to have regard to this in the institution of festivals.

24. *Of the local Laws of Religion.* There are many local laws in various religions; and when Montezuma with so much obstinacy insisted that the religion of the Spaniards was good for their country, and his for Mexico, he did not assert an absurdity; because, in fact, legislators could never help having a regard to what nature had established before them.

The opinion of the metempsychosis is adapted to the climate of the Indies. An excessive heat burns up all the country:[3] they can breed but very few cattle; they are always in danger of wanting them for tillage; their black cattle multiply but indifferently;[4] and they are subject to many distempers. A law of religion which preserves them is therefore more suitable to the policy of the country.

While the meadows are scorched, rice and pulse, by the assistance of water, are brought to perfection; a law of religion which permits only this kind of nourishment must therefore be extremely useful to men in those climates.

The flesh of cattle in that country is insipid,[5] but the milk and butter which they receive from them serve for a part of their subsistence; therefore the law which prohibits the eating and killing of cows is in the Indies not unreasonable.

Athens contained a prodigious multitude of people, but its territory was barren. It was therefore a religious maxim with this people that those who offered some small presents to the gods honoured them more than those who sacrificed an ox.[6]

25. *The Inconvenience of transplanting a Religion from one Country to another.* It follows hence that there are frequently many inconveniences attending the transplanting a religion from one country to any other.

"The hog," says M. de Boulainvilliers,[7] "must be very scarce in Arabia, where there are almost no woods, and hardly anything fit for the nourishment of these animals; besides, the saltness of the water and food renders the people most susceptible of cutaneous disorders." This local law could not be good in other countries,[8] where the hog is almost a universal, and in some sort a necessary, nourishment.

I shall here make a reflection. Sanctorius has observed that pork transpires but little,[9] and that this kind of meat greatly hinders the transpiration of other food; he has found that this diminution amounts to a third.[10] Besides, it is known that the want of transpiration forms or increases the disorders of the skin. The feeding on pork ought rather to be prohibited in climates where the people are subject to these disorders, as in Palestine, Arabia, Egypt, and Libya.

26. *The same Subject continued.* Sir John Chardin says[11] that there is not a navigable river in Persia, except the Kur, which is at the extremity of the empire. The ancient law of the Gaurs which prohibited sailing on rivers was not therefore attended with any inconvenience in this country, though it would have ruined the trade of another.

Frequent bathings are extremely useful in hot climates. On this account they are ordained in the Mahometan law and in the Indian religion. In the Indies it is a most meritorious act to pray to God in the running stream;[12] but how could these things be performed in other climates?

When a religion adapted to the climate of one country clashes too much with the climate of another it cannot be there established; and whenever it has been introduced it has been afterwards discarded. It seems to all human

---

[1] The Catholics lie more toward the south, and the Protestants towards the north.
[2] Dampier, *Voyages,* ii.
[3] See Bernier, *Travels,* ii, p. 137.
[4] *Edifying Letters,* coll. xii, p. 95.
[5] Bernier, *Travels,* ii, p. 137.
[6] Euripides, in Athenæus, ii, p. 40.
[7] Life of Mahomet.
[8] As in China.
[9] *Medicina Statica,* § 3, aphor. 22.
[10] *Ibid.,* aphor. 23.
[11] *Travels into Persia,* ii.
[12] Bernier, *Travels,* ii.

appearance as if the climate had prescribed the bounds of the Christian and the Mahometan religions.

It follows hence, that it is almost always proper for a religion to have particular doctrines, and a general worship. In laws concerning the practice of religious worship there ought to be but few particulars; for instance, they should command mortification in general and not a certain kind of mortification. Christianity is full of good sense; abstinence is of divine institution; but a particular kind of abstinence is ordained by human authority and therefore may be changed.

Book XXV. Of Laws in relation to the Establishment of Religion and Its External Polity

1. *Of Religious Sentiments.* The pious man and the atheist always talk of religion; the one speaks of what he loves, and the other of what he fears.

2. *Of the Motives of Attachment to different Religions.* The different religions of the world do not give to those who profess them equal motives of attachment; this depends greatly on the manner in which they agree with the turn of thought and perceptions of mankind.

We are extremely addicted to idolatry, and yet have no great inclination for the religion of idolaters; we are not very fond of spiritual ideas, and yet are most attached to those religions which teach us to adore a spiritual being. This proceeds from the satisfaction we find in ourselves at having been so intelligent as to choose a religion which raises the deity from that baseness in which he had been placed by others. We look upon idolatry as the religion of an ignorant people, and the religion which has a spiritual being for its object as that of the most enlightened nations.

When with a doctrine that gives us the idea of a spiritual supreme being we can still join those of a sensible nature and admit them into our worship, we contract a greater attachment to religion; because those motives which we have just mentioned are added to our natural inclinations for the objects of sense. Thus the Catholics, who have more of this kind of worship than the Protestants, are more attached to their religion than the Protestants are to theirs, and more zealous for its propagation.

When the people of Ephesus were informed that the fathers of the council had declared they might call the Virgin Mary the Mother of God, they were transported with joy, they kissed the hands of the bishops, they embraced their knees, and the whole city resounded with acclamations.[1]

When an intellectual religion superadds a

[1] St. Cyril's Letter.

choice made by the deity, and a preference for those who profess it over those who do not, this greatly attaches us to religion. The Mahometans would not be such good Mussulmans if, on the one hand, there were not idolatrous nations who make them imagine themselves the champions of the unity of God; and on the other Christians, to make them believe that they are the objects of his preference.

A religion burdened with many ceremonies[2] attaches us to it more strongly than that which has a fewer number. We have an extreme propensity to things in which we are continually employed: witness the obstinate prejudices of the Mahometans and the Jews,[3] and the readiness with which barbarous and savage nations change their religion, who, as they are employed entirely in hunting or war, have but few religious ceremonies.

Men are extremely inclined to the passions of hope and fear; a religion, therefore, that had neither a heaven nor a hell could hardly please them. This is proved by the ease with which foreign religions have been established in Japan, and the zeal and fondness with which they were received.[4]

In order to raise an attachment to religion it is necessary that it should inculcate pure morals. Men who are knaves by retail are extremely honest in the gross; they love morality. And were I not treating of so grave a subject I should say that this appears remarkably

[2] This does not contradict what I have said in the last chapter of the preceding book: I here speak of the motives of attachment of religion, and there of the means of rendering it more general.

[3] This has been remarked over all the world. See, as to the Turks, the Missions of the Levant; the *Collection of Voyages that Contributed to the Establishment of the East India Company*, iii, part I, p. 201 on the Moors of Batavia; and Father Labat on the Mahometan Negroes, &c.

[4] The Christian and the Indian religions: these have a hell and a paradise, which the religion of Sintos has not.

evident in our theatres: we are sure of pleasing the people by sentiments avowed by morality; we are sure of shocking them by those it disapproves.

When external worship is attended with great magnificence, it flatters our minds and strongly attaches us to religion. The riches of temples and those of the clergy greatly affect us. Thus even the misery of the people is a motive that renders them fond of a religion which has served as a pretext to those who were the cause of their misery.

3. *Of Temples.* Almost all civilised nations dwell in houses; hence naturally arose the idea of building a house for God in which they might adore and seek him, amidst all their hopes and fears.

And, indeed, nothing is more comfortable to mankind than a place in which they may find the deity peculiarly present, and where they may assemble together to confess their weakness and tell their griefs.

But this natural idea never occurred to any but such as cultivated the land; those who have no houses for themselves were never known to build temples.

This was the cause that made Jenghiz Khan discover such a prodigious contempt for mosques.[1] This prince examined the Mahometans;[2] he approved of all their doctrines, except that of the necessity of going to Mecca; he could not comprehend why God might not be everywhere adored. As the Tartars did not dwell in houses, they could have no idea of temples.

Those people who have no temples have but a small attachment to their own religion. This is the reason why the Tartars have in all times given so great a toleration;[3] why the barbarous nations, who conquered the Roman empire did not hesitate a moment to embrace Christianity; why the savages of America have so little fondness for their own religion; why, since our missionaries have built churches in Paraguay, the natives of that country have become so zealous for ours.

As the deity is the refuge of the unhappy, and none are more unhappy than criminals, men have been naturally led to think temples

an asylum for those wretches. This idea appeared still more natural to the Greeks, where murderers, chased from their city and the presence of men, seemed to have no houses but the temples, nor other protectors than the gods.

At first these were only designed for involuntary homicides; but when the people made them a sanctuary for those who had committed great crimes they fell into a gross contradiction. If they had offended men, they had much greater reason to believe they had offended the gods.

These asylums multiplied in Greece. The temples, says Tacitus,[4] were filled with insolvent debtors and wicked slaves; the magistrate found it difficult to exercise his office; the people protected the crimes of men as the ceremonies of the gods; at length the senate was obliged to retrench a great number of them.

The laws of Moses were perfectly wise. The man who involuntarily killed another was innocent; but he was obliged to be taken away from before the eyes of the relatives of the deceased. Moses therefore appointed an asylum for such unfortunate people.[5] The perpetrators of great crimes deserved not a place of safety, and they had none:[6] the Jews had only a portable tabernacle, which continually changed its place; this excluded the idea of a sanctuary. It is true that they had afterwards a temple; but the criminals who would resort thither from all parts might disturb the divine service. If persons who had committed manslaughter had been driven out of the country, as was customary among the Greeks, they had reason to fear that they would worship strange gods. All these considerations made them establish cities of safety, where they might stay till the death of the high-priest.

4. *Of the Ministers of Religion.* The first men, says Porphyry,[7] sacrificed only vegetables. In a worship so simple, every one might be priest in his own family.

The natural desire of pleasing the deity multiplied ceremonies. Hence it followed, that men employed in agriculture became incapable of observing them all and of filling up the number.

Particular places were consecrated to the gods; it then became necessary that they should have ministers to take care of them; in

---

[1] Entering the mosque of Bochara, he took the Koran, and threw it under his horse's feet.—*History of the Tartars,* part III, p. 273.

[2] *Ibid.,* p. 342.

[3] This disposition of mind has been communicated to the Japanese, who, as it may be easily proved, derive their origin from the Tartars.

[4] *Annals,* iii. 60.

[5] Numb., 35, 14.

[6] *Ibid.,* 16, ff.

[7] *De Abstinentia animal.* ii, § 5.

the same manner as every citizen took care of his house and domestic affairs. Hence the people who have no priests are commonly barbarians; such were formerly the Pedalians,[1] and such are still the Wolgusky.[2]

Men consecrated to the deity ought to be honoured, especially among people who have formed an idea of a personal purity necessary to approach the places most agreeable to the gods, and for the performance of particular ceremonies.

The worship of the gods requiring a continual application, most nations were led to consider the clergy as a separate body. Thus, among the Egyptians, the Jews, and the Persians,[3] they consecrated to the deity certain families who performed and perpetuated the service. There have been even religions which have not only estranged ecclesiastics from business, but have also taken away the embarrassments of a family; and this is the practice of the principal branch of Christianity.

I shall not here treat of the consequences of the law of celibacy: it is evident that it may become hurtful in proportion as the body of the clergy may be too numerous; and, in consequence of this, that of the laity too small.

By the nature of the human understanding we love in religion everything which carries the idea of difficulty; as in point of morality we have a speculative fondness for everything which bears the character of severity. Celibacy has been most agreeable to those nations to whom it seemed least adapted, and with whom it might be attended with the most fatal consequences. In the southern countries of Europe, where, by the nature of the climate, the law of celibacy is more difficult to observe, it has been retained; in those of the north, where the passions are less lively, it has been banished. Further, in countries where there are but few inhabitants it has been admitted; in those that are vastly populous it has been rejected. It is obvious that these reflections relate only to the too great extension of celibacy, and not to celibacy itself.

5. *Of the Bounds which the Laws ought to prescribe to the Riches of the Clergy.* As particular families may be extinct, their wealth cannot be a perpetual inheritance. The clergy

is a family which cannot be extinct; wealth is therefore fixed to it for ever, and cannot go out of it.

Particular families may increase; it is necessary then that their wealth should also increase. The clergy is a family which ought not to increase; their wealth ought then to be limited.

We have retained the regulations of the Levitical laws as to the possessions of the clergy, except those relating to the bounds of these possessions; indeed, among us we must ever be ignorant of the limit beyond which any religious community can no longer be permitted to acquire.

These endless acquisitions appear to the people so unreasonable that he who should speak in their defence would be regarded as an idiot.

The civil laws find sometimes many difficulties in altering established abuses, because they are connected with things worthy of respect; in this case an indirect proceeding would be a greater proof of the wisdom of the legislator than another which struck directly at the thing itself. Instead of prohibiting the acquisitions of the clergy, we should seek to give them a distaste for them; to leave them the right and to take away the deed.

In some countries of Europe, a respect for the privileges of the nobility has established in their favour a right of indemnity over immovable goods acquired in mortmain. The interest of the prince has in the same case made him exact a right of amortisation. In Castile, where no such right prevails, the clergy have seized upon everything. In Aragon, where there is some right of amortisation, they have obtained less; in France, where this right and that of indemnity are established, they have acquired less still; and it may be said that the prosperity of this kingdom is in a great measure owing to the exercise of these two rights. If possible, then, increase these rights, and put a stop to the mortmain.

Render the ancient and necessary patrimony of the clergy sacred and inviolable, let it be fixed and eternal like that body itself, but let new inheritances be out of their power.

Permit them to break the rule when the rule has become an abuse; suffer the abuse when it enters into the rule.

They still remember in Rome a certain memorial sent thither on some disputes with the clergy, in which was this maxim: "The clergy ought to contribute to the expenses of the

---

[1] Lilius Giraldus, p. 726.
[2] A people of Siberia. See the account given by Mr. Everard Ysbrant Ides, in the *Collection of Travels to the North,* viii.
[3] Mr. Hyde.

state, let the Old Testament say what it will." They concluded from this passage that the author of this memorial was better versed in the language of the tax-gatherers than in that of religion.

6. *Of Monasteries.* The least degree of common sense will let us see that bodies designed for a perpetual continuance should not be allowed to sell their funds for life, nor to borrow for life; unless we want them to be heirs to all those who have no relatives and to those who do not choose to have any. These men play against the people, but they hold the bank themselves.

7. *Of the Luxury of Superstition.* "Those are guilty of impiety towards the gods," says Plato,[1] "who deny their existence; or who, while they believe it, maintain that they do not interfere with what is done below; or, in fine, who think that they can easily appease them by sacrifices: three opinions equally pernicious." Plato has here said all that the clearest light of nature has ever been able to say in point of religion. The magnificence of external worship has a principal connection with the institution of the state. In good republics, they have curbed not only the luxury of vanity, but even that of superstition. They have introduced frugal laws into religion. Of this number are many of the laws of Solon; many of those of Plato on funerals, adopted by Cicero; and, in fine, some of the laws of Numa on sacrifices.[2]

Birds, says Cicero,[3] and paintings begun and finished in a day are gifts the most divine. We offer common things, says a Spartan, that we may always have it in our power to honour the gods.

The desire of man to pay his worship to the deity is very different from the magnificence of this worship. Let us not offer our treasures to him if we are not proud of showing that we esteem what he would have us despise.

"What must the gods think of the gifts of the impious," said the admirable Plato, "when a good man would blush to receive presents from a villain?"

Religion ought not, under the pretence of gifts, to draw from the people what the necessity of the state has left them; but as Plato says,[4] "The chaste and the pious ought to offer gifts which resemble themselves."

Nor is it proper for religion to encourage expensive funerals. What is there more natural than to take away the difference of fortune in a circumstance and in the very moment which equals all fortunes?

8. *Of the Pontificate.* When religion has many ministers it is natural for them to have a chief and for a sovereign pontiff to be established. In monarchies, where the several orders of the state cannot be kept too distinct, and where all powers ought not to be lodged in the same person, it is proper that the pontificate be distinct from the empire. The same necessity is not to be met with in a despotic government, the nature of which is to unite all the different powers in the same person. But in this case it may happen that the prince may regard religion as he does the laws themselves, as dependent on his own will. To prevent this inconvenience, there ought to be monuments of religion, for instance, sacred books which fix and establish it. The King of Persia is the chief of the religion; but this religion is regulated by the Koran. The Emperor of China is the sovereign pontiff; but there are books in the hands of everybody to which he himself must conform. In vain a certain emperor attempted to abolish them; they triumphed over tyranny.

9. *Of Toleration in point of Religion.* We are here politicians, and not divines; but the divines themselves must allow, that there is a great difference between tolerating and approving a religion.

When the legislator has believed it a duty to permit the exercise of many religions, it is necessary that he should enforce also a toleration among these religions themselves. It is a principle that every religion which is persecuted becomes itself persecuting; for as soon as by some accidental turn it arises from persecution, it attacks the religion which persecuted it; not as religion, but as tyranny.

It is necessary, then, that the laws require from the several religions, not only that they shall not embroil the state, but that they shall not raise disturbances among themselves. A citizen does not fulfil the laws by not disturbing the government; it is requisite that he should not trouble any citizen whomsoever.

[1] *Laws,* x.
[2] *Rogum vino ne respergito.*—Law of the Twelve Tables.
[3] Cicero derives these appropriate words from Plato, *Laws,* xii.—ED.
[4] *Laws,* iv.

10. *The same Subject continued.* As there are scarcely any but persecuting religions that have an extraordinary zeal for being established in other places (because a religion that can tolerate others seldom thinks of its own propagation), it must therefore be a very good civil law, when the state is already satisfied with the established religion, not to suffer the establishment of another.[1]

This is then a fundamental principle of the political laws in regard to religion; that when the state is at liberty to receive or to reject a new religion it ought to be rejected; when it is received it ought to be tolerated.

11. *Of changing a Religion.* A prince who undertakes to destroy or to change the established religion of his kingdom must greatly expose himself. If his government be despotic, he runs a much greater risk of seeing a revolution arise from such a proceeding, than from any tyranny whatsoever, and a revolution is not an uncommon thing in such states. The reason of this is that a state cannot change its religion, manners and customs in an instant, and with the same rapidity as the prince publishes the ordinance which establishes a new religion.

Besides, the ancient religion is connected with the constitution of the kingdom and the new one is not; the former agrees with the climate and very often the new one is opposed to it. Moreover, the citizens become disgusted with their laws, and look upon the government already established with contempt; they conceive a jealousy against the two religions, instead of a firm belief in one; in a word, these innovations give to the state, at least for some time, both bad citizens and bad believers.

12. *Of penal Laws.* Penal laws ought to be avoided in respect to religion: they imprint fear, it is true; but as religion has also penal laws which inspire the same passion, the one is effaced by the other, and between these two different kinds of fear the mind becomes hardened.

The threatenings of religion are so terrible, and its promises so great, that when they actuate the mind, whatever efforts the magistrate may use to oblige us to renounce it, he seems

to leave us nothing when he deprives us of the exercise of our religion, and to bereave us of nothing when we are allowed to profess it.

It is not, therefore, by filling the soul with the idea of this great object, by hastening her approach to that critical moment in which it ought to be of the highest importance, that religion can be most successfully attacked: a more certain way is to tempt her by favours, by the conveniences of life, by hopes of fortune; not by that which revives, but by that which extinguishes the sense of her duty; not by that which shocks her, but by that which throws her into indifference at the time when other passions actuate the mind, and those which religion inspires are hushed into silence. As a general rule in changing a religion the invitations should be much stronger than the penalties.

The temper of the human mind has appeared even in the nature of punishments. If we take a survey of the persecutions in Japan,[2] we shall find that they were more shocked at cruel torments than at long sufferings, which rather weary than affright, which are the more difficult to surmount, from their appearing less difficult.

In a word, history sufficiently informs us that penal laws have never had any other effect than to destroy.

13. *A most humble Remonstrance to the Inquisitors of Spain and Portugal.* A Jewess of ten years of age, who was burned at Lisbon at the last auto-da-fé, gave occasion to the following little piece, the most idle, I believe, that ever was written. When we attempt to prove things so evident we are sure never to convince.

The author declares, that though a Jew he has a respect for the Christian religion; and that he should be glad to take away from the princes who are not Christians, a plausible pretence for persecuting this religion.

"You complain," says he to the Inquisitors, "that the Emperor of Japan caused all the Christians in his dominions to be burned by a slow fire. But he will answer, we treat you who do not believe like us, as you yourselves treat those who do not believe like you; you can only complain of your weakness, which has hindered you from exterminating us, and which has enabled us to exterminate you.

---

[1] I do not mean to speak in this chapter of the Christian religion; for, as I have elsewhere observed, the Christian religion is our chief blessing. See the end of the preceding chapter, and the *Defence of the Spirit of Laws*, part II.

[2] In the *Collection of Voyages that Contributed to the Establishment of the East India Company*, v, part I, p. 192.

"But it must be confessed that you are much more cruel than this emperor. You put us to death who believe only what you believe, because we do not believe *all* that you believe. We follow a religion which you yourselves know to have been formerly dear to God. We think that God loves it still, and you think that he loves it no more: and because you judge thus, you make those suffer by sword and fire who hold an error so pardonable as to believe that God still loves what he once loved.[1]

"If you are cruel to us, you are much more so to our children; you cause them to be burned because they follow the inspirations given them by those whom the law of nature and the laws of all nations teach them to regard as gods.

"You deprive yourselves of the advantage you have over the Mahometans, with respect to the manner in which their religion was established. When they boast of the number of their believers, you tell them that they have obtained them by violence, and that they have extended their religion by the sword; why then do you establish yours by fire?

"When you would bring us over to you, we object to a source from which you glory to have descended. You reply to us, that though your religion is new, it is divine; and you prove it from its growing amidst the persecutions of Pagans, and when watered by the blood of your martyrs; but at present you play the part of the Diocletians, and make us take yours.

"We conjure you, not by the mighty God whom both you and we serve, but by that Christ, who, you tell us, took upon him a human form, to propose himself as an example for you to follow; we conjure you to behave to us as he himself would behave were he upon earth. You would have us become Christians, and you will not be so yourselves.

"But if you will not be Christians, be at least men; treat us as you would, if having only the weak light of justice which nature bestows, you had not a religion to conduct, and a revelation to enlighten you.

"If heaven has had so great a love for you as to make you see the truth, you have received a singular favour; but is it for children who have received the inheritance of their father, to hate those who have not?

"If you have this truth, hide it not from us by the manner in which you propose it. The characteristic of truth is its triumph over hearts and minds, and not that impotency which you confess when you would force us to receive it by tortures.

"If you were wise, you would not put us to death for no other reason than because we are unwilling to deceive you. If your Christ is the son of God, we hope he will reward us for being so unwilling to profane his mysteries; and we believe that the God whom both you and we serve will not punish us for having suffered death for a religion which he formerly gave us, only because we believe that he still continues to give it.

"You live in an age in which the light of nature shines more brightly than it has ever done; in which philosophy has enlightened human understanding; in which the morality of your gospel has been better known; in which the respective rights of mankind with regard to each other and the empire which one conscience has over another are best understood. If you do not therefore shake off your ancient prejudices, which, whilst unregarded, mingle with your passions, it must be confessed that you are incorrigible, incapable of any degree of light or instruction; and a nation must be very unhappy that gives authority to such men.

"Would you have us frankly tell you our thoughts? You consider us rather as your enemies than as the enemies of your religion; for if you loved your religion you would not suffer it to be corrupted by such gross ignorance.

"It is necessary that we should warn you of one thing; that is, if any one in times to come shall dare to assert that in the age in which we live, the people of Europe were civilised, you will be cited to prove that they were barbarians; and the idea they will have of you will be such as will dishonour your age and spread hatred over all your contemporaries."

14. *Why the Christian Religion is so odious in Japan.* We have already mentioned the perverse temper of the people of Japan.[2] The magistrates considered the firmness which Christianity inspires, when they attempted to make the people renounce their faith, as in itself most dangerous; they fancied that it increased their obstinacy. The law of Japan punishes severely the least disobedience. The

---

[1] The source of the blindness of the Jews is their not perceiving that the economy of the Gospel is in the order of the decrees of God and that it is in this light a consequence of his immutability.

[2] Book vi. 13.

people were ordered to renounce the Christian religion; they did not renounce it; this was disobedience; the magistrates punished this crime; and the continuance in disobedience seemed to deserve another punishment.

Punishments among the Japanese are considered as the revenge of an insult done to the prince; the songs of triumph sung by our martyrs appeared as an outrage against him: the title of martyr provoked the magistrates; in their opinion it signified rebel; they did all in their power to prevent their obtaining it. Then it was that their minds were exasperated, and a horrid struggle was seen between the tribunals that condemned and the accused who suffered; between the civil laws and those of religion.

15. *Of the Propagation of Religion.* All the people of the East, except the Mahometans, believe all religions in themselves indifferent. They fear the establishment of another religion no otherwise than as a change in government. Among the Japanese, where there are many sects, and where the state has had for so long a time an ecclesiastical superior, they never dispute on religion.[1] It is the same with the people of Siam.[2] The Calmucks[3] do more; they make it a point of conscience to tolerate every species of religion; at Calicut it is a maxim of the state that every religion is good.[4]

But it does not follow hence, that a religion brought from a far distant country, and quite different in climate, laws, manners, and customs, will have all the success to which its holiness might entitle it. This is more particularly true in great despotic empires: here strangers are tolerated at first, because there is no attention given to what does not seem to strike at the authority of the prince. As they are extremely ignorant, a European may render himself agreeable by the knowledge he communicates: this is very well in the beginning. But as soon as he has any success, when disputes arise and when men who have some interest become informed of it, as their empire, by its very nature, above all things requires tranquillity, and as the least disturbance may overturn it, they proscribe the new religion and those who preach it: disputes between the preachers breaking out, they begin to entertain a distaste for a religion on which even those who propose it are not agreed.

Book XXVI. Of Laws in relation to the Order of Things Which They Determine

1. *Idea of this Book.* Men are governed by several kinds of laws; by the law of nature; by the divine law, which is that of religion; by ecclesiastical, otherwise called canon law, which is that of religious polity; by the law of nations, which may be considered as the civil law of the whole globe, in which sense every nation is a citizen; by the general political law, which relates to that human wisdom whence all societies derive their origin; by the particular political law, the object of which is each society; by the law of conquest founded on this, that one nation has been willing and able, or has had a right to offer violence to another; by the civil law of every society, by which a citizen may defend his possessions and his life against the attacks of any other citizen; in fine, by domestic law, which proceeds from a society's being divided into several families, all which have need of a particular government.

There are therefore different orders of laws, and the sublimity of human reason consists in perfectly knowing to which of these orders the things that are to be determined ought to have a principal relation, and not to throw into confusion those principles which should govern mankind.

2. *Of Laws divine and human.* We ought not to decide by divine laws what should be decided by human laws; nor determine by human what should be determined by divine laws.

These two sorts of laws differ in their origin, in their object, and in their nature.

It is universally acknowledged, that human laws are, in their own nature, different from those of religion; this is an important principle: but this principle is itself subject to others, which must be inquired into.

1. It is in the nature of human laws to be subject to all the accidents which can happen, and to vary in proportion as the will of man changes; on the contrary, by the nature of the

[1] See Kempfer.

[2] Forbin, *Memoirs.*
[3] *History of the Tartars,* part V.
[4] Pirard, *Travels,* 27.

laws of religion, they are never to vary. Human laws appoint for some good; those of religion for the best: good may have another object, because there are many kinds of good; but the best is but one; it cannot therefore change. We may alter laws, because they are reputed no more than good; but the institutions of religion are always supposed to be the best.

2. There are kingdoms in which the laws are of no value as they depend only on the capricious and fickle humour of the sovereign. If in these kingdoms the laws of religion were of the same nature as the human institutions, the laws of religion too would be of no value. It is however, necessary to the society that it should have something fixed; and it is religion that has this stability.

3. The influence of religion proceeds from its being believed; that of human laws from their being feared. Antiquity accords with religion, because we have frequently a firmer belief in things in proportion to their distance; for we have no ideas annexed to them drawn from those times which can contradict them. Human laws, on the contrary, receive advantage from their novelty, which implies the actual and particular attention of the legislator to put them in execution.

3. *Of civil Laws contrary to the Law of Nature.* If a slave, says Plato, defends himself, and kills a freeman, he ought to be treated as a parricide.[1] This is a civil law which punishes self-defence, though dictated by nature.

The law of Henry VIII which condemned a man without being confronted by witnesses was contrary to self-defence. In order to pass sentence of condemnation, it is necessary that the witnesses should know whether the man against whom they make their deposition is he whom they accuse, and that this man be at liberty to say, "I am not the person you mean."

The law passed during the same reign, which condemned every woman, who, having carried on a criminal commerce did not declare it to the king before she married him, violated the regard due to natural modesty. It is as unreasonable to oblige a woman to make this declaration, as to oblige a man not to attempt the defence of his own life.

The law of Henry II which condemned the woman to death who lost her child, in case she did not make known her pregnancy to the magistrate, was not less contrary to self-

defence. It would have been sufficient to oblige her to inform one of her nearest relatives, who might watch over the preservation of the infant.

What other information could she give in this situation, so torturing to natural modesty? Education has heightened the notion of preserving that modesty; and in those critical moments scarcely has she any idea remaining of the loss of life.

There has been much talk of a law in England which permitted girls seven years old to choose a husband.[2] This law was shocking in two ways; it had no regard to the time when nature gives maturity to the understanding, nor to that in which she gives maturity to the body.

Among the Romans, a father might oblige his daughter to repudiate her husband, though he himself had consented to the marriage.[3] But it is contrary to nature for a divorce to be in the power of a third person.

A divorce can be agreeable to nature only when it is by consent of the two parties, or at least of one of them; but when neither consents it is a monstrous separation. In short, the power of divorce can be given only to those who feel the inconveniences of marriage, and who are sensible of the moment when it is for their interest to make them cease.

4. *The same Subject continued.* Gundebald, King of Burgundy, decreed that if the wife or son of a person guilty of robbery did not reveal the crime, they were to become slaves.[4] This was contrary to nature: a wife to inform against her husband! a son to accuse his father! To avenge one criminal action, they ordained another still more criminal.

The law of Recessuinthus permits the children of the adulteress, or those of her husband, to accuse her, and to put the slaves of the house to the torture.[5] How iniquitous the law which, to preserve a purity of morals overturns nature, the origin, the source of all morality!

With pleasure we behold in our theatres a young hero express as much horror against the discovery of his mother-in-law's guilt, as against the guilt itself. In his surprise, though accused, judged, condemned, proscribed, and

[1] *Laws,* ix.
[2] M. Bayle, in his *Criticism on the History of Calvinism,* speaks of this law, p. 263.
[3] See *Leg.* 5, *Cod. de repudiis et judicio de moribus sublato.*
[4] Law of the Burgundians, tit. 47.
[5] In the Code of the Visigoths, iii, tit. 4, § 13.

covered with infamy, he scarcely dares to reflect on the abominable blood whence Phædra sprang; he abandons the most tender object, all that is most dear, all that lies nearest his heart, all that can fill him with rage, to deliver himself up to the unmerited vengeance of the gods. It is nature's voice, the sweetest of all sounds, that inspires us with this pleasure.

5. *Cases in which we may judge by the Principles of the civil Law in limiting the Principles of the Law of Nature.* An Athenian law obliged children to provide for their fathers when fallen into poverty;[1] it excepted those who were born of a courtesan,[2] those whose chastity had been infamously prostituted by their father, and those to whom he had not given any means of gaining a livelihood.[3]

The law considered that, in the first case, the father being uncertain, he had rendered the natural obligation precarious; that in the second, he had sullied the life he had given, and done the greatest injury he could do to his children in depriving them of their reputation; that in the third, he had rendered insupportable a life which had no means of subsistence. The law suspended the natural obligation of children because the father had violated his; it looked upon the father and the son as no more than two citizens, and determined in respect to them only from civil and political views; ever considering that a good republic ought to have a particular regard to manners. I am apt to think that Solon's law was a wise regulation in the first two cases, whether that in which nature has left the son in ignorance with regard to his father, or that in which she even seems to ordain he should not own him; but it cannot be approved with respect to the third, where the father had only violated a civil institution.

6. *That the Order of succession or Inheritance depends on the Principles of political or civil Law, and not on those of the Law of Nature.* The Voconian law ordained that no woman should be left heiress to an estate, not even if she had an only child. Never was there a law, says St. Augustine, more unjust.[4] A formula of Marculfus treats that custom as impious which deprives daughters of the right of succeeding to the estate of their fathers.[5] Justinian gives the appellation of *barbarous* to the right which the males had formerly of succeeding in prejudice to the daughters.[6] These notions proceeded from their having considered the right of children to succeed to their father's possessions as a consequence of the law of nature; which it is not.

The law of nature ordains that fathers shall provide for their children; but it does not oblige them to make them their heirs. The division of property, the laws of this division, and the succession after the death of the person who has had this division can be regulated only by the community, and consequently by political or civil laws.

True it is that a political or civil order frequently demands that children should succeed to their father's estate; but it does not always make this necessary.

There may be some reasons given why the laws of our fiefs appoint that the eldest of the males, or the nearest relatives of the male side, should have all, and the females nothing, and why, by the laws of the Lombards,[7] the sisters, the natural children, the other relatives; and, in their default, the treasury might share the inheritance with the daughters.

It was regulated in some of the dynasties of China that the brothers of the emperor should succeed to the throne, and that the children should not. If they were willing that the prince should have a certain degree of experience, if they feared his being too young, and if it had become necessary to prevent eunuchs from placing children successively on the throne, they might very justly establish a like order of succession, and when some writers have treated these brothers as usurpers, they have judged only by ideas received from the laws of their own countries.[8]

According to the custom of Numidia,[9] Desalces, brother of Gala, succeeded to the kingdom; not Massinissa, his son. And even to this day, among the Arabs in Barbary, where each village has its chief, they adhere to this ancient custom, by choosing the uncle, or some other relative to succeed.[10]

There are monarchies merely elective; and since it is evident that the order of succession ought to be derived from the political or civil

[1] Under pain of infamy, another under pain of imprisonment.
[2] Plutarch, *Solon.*
[3] *Ibid.,* and Gallien, in *Exhort. ad Art.,* 8.
[4] *City of God,* iii. 21.
[5] Book ii. 12.
[6] *Nov.* 21.
[7] Book ii, tit. 14, § 6, 7, and 8.
[8] Father Du Halde on the Second Dynasty.
[9] Livy, xxix. 29.
[10] Shaw, *Travels,* i, p. 402.

laws, it is for these to decide in what cases it is agreeable to reason that the succession be granted to children, and in what cases it ought to be given to others.

In countries where polygamy is established, the prince has many children; and the number of them is much greater in some of these countries than in others. There are states[1] where it is impossible for the people to maintain the children of the king; they might therefore make it a law that the crown shall devolve, not on the king's children, but on those of his sister.

A prodigious number of children would expose the state to the most dreadful civil wars. The order of succession which gives the crown to the children of the sister, the number of whom is not larger than those of a prince who has only one wife, must prevent these inconveniences.

There are people among whom reasons of state, or some maxims of religion, have made it necessary that the crown should be always fixed in a certain family: hence, in India, proceeds the jealousy of their tribes,[2] and the fear of losing the descent; they have there conceived that never to want princes of the blood royal, they ought to take the children of the eldest sister of the king.

A general maxim: it is an obligation of the law of nature to provide for our children; but to make them our successors is an obligation of the civil or political law. Hence are derived the different regulations with respect to bastards in the different countries of the world; these are according to the civil or political laws of each country.

7. *That we ought not to decide by the Precepts of Religion what belongs only to the Law of Nature.* The Abassines have a most severe lent of fifty days, which weakens them to such a degree that for a long time they are incapable of business: the Turks do not fail to attack them after their lent.[3] Religion ought, in favour of the natural right of self-defence, to set bounds to these customs.

The Jews were obliged to keep the Sabbath; but it was an instance of great stupidity in this nation not to defend themselves when their enemies chose to attack them on this day.[4]

Cambyses, laying siege to Pelusium, set in the first rank a great number of those animals which the Egyptians regarded as sacred; the consequence was that the soldiers of the garrison durst not molest them. Who does not see that self-defence is a duty superior to every precept?

8. *That we ought not to regulate by the Principles of the canon Law Things which should be regulated by those of the civil Law.* By the civil law of the Romans,[5] he who took a thing privately from a sacred place was punished only for the guilt of theft; by the canon law, he was punished for the crime of sacrilege.[6] The canon law takes cognizance of the place; the civil laws of the fact. But to attend only to the place is neither to reflect on the nature and definition of a theft, nor on the nature and definition of sacrilege.

As the husband may demand a separation by reason of the infidelity of his wife, the wife might formerly demand it on account of the infidelity of the husband.[7] This custom, contrary to a regulation made in the Roman laws,[8] was introduced into the ecclesiastic court,[9] where nothing was regarded but the maxims of canon law; and indeed, if we consider marriage as a thing merely spiritual, and as relating only to the things of another life, the violation is in both cases the same, but the political and civil laws of almost all nations have, with reason, made a distinction between them. They have required from the women a degree of reserve and continency which they have not exacted from the men, because in women, a violation of chastity supposes a renunciation of all virtue; because women, by violating the laws of marriage, quit the state of their natural dependence; because nature has marked the infidelity of women with certain signs; and, in fine, because the children of

---

[1] See the *Collection of Voyages that Contributed to the Establishment of the East India Company*, iv, part I, p. 114. And Mr. Smith, *Voyage to Guinea*, part II, p. 150, concerning the kingdom of Juida.

[2] See *Edifying Letters*, coll. xiv, and the *Voyages that Contributed to the Establishment of the East India Company*, iii, part II, p. 644.

[3] *Collection of Voyages that Contributed to the Establishment of the East India Company*, iv, part I, pp. 35, 103.

[4] As they did when Pompey besieged the Temple. Dio, xxxvii, 16.

[5] *Leg.*, 5, ff. *ad. leg. Juliam peculatus.*

[6] *Cap. quisquis* 17, *quæstione* 4. Cujas, *Observat.*, xiii. 19, tom. iii.

[7] Beaumanoir, *Ancient Customs of Beauvoisis*, 18, § 6.

[8] *Leg.* 1, *Cod. ad. leg. Jul. de adulteriis.*

[9] At present they do not take cognizance of these things in France.

the wife born in adultery necessarily belong and are an expense to the husband, while the children produced by the adultery of the husband are not the wife's, nor are an expense to the wife.

9. *That Things which ought to be regulated by the Principles of civil Law can seldom be regulated by those of Religion.* The laws of religion have a greater sublimity; the civil laws a greater extent.

The laws of perfection drawn from religion have more in view the goodness of the person that observes them than of the society in which they are observed; the civil laws, on the contrary, have more in view the moral goodness of men in general than that of individuals.

Thus, venerable as those ideas are which immediately spring from religion, they ought not always to serve as a first principle to the civil laws; because these have another, the general welfare of society.

The Romans made regulations among themselves to preserve the morals of their women; these were political institutions. Upon the establishment of monarchy, they made civil laws on this head, and formed them on the principles of their civil government. When the Christian religion became predominant, the new laws that were then made had less relation to the general rectitude of morals than to the holiness of marriage; they had less regard to the union of the two sexes in a civil than in a spiritual state.

At first, by the Roman law, a husband, who brought back his wife into his house after she had been found guilty of adultery, was punished as an accomplice in her debauch.[1] Justinian, from other principles, ordained that during the space of two years he might go and take her again out of the monastery.[2]

Formerly, when a woman, whose husband was gone to war, heard no longer any tidings of him, she might easily marry again, because she had in her hands the power of making a divorce. The law of Constantine obliged the woman to wait four years, after which she might send the bill of divorce to the general; and, if her husband returned, he could not then charge her with adultery.[3] But Justinian decreed that, let the time be never so long

after the departure of her husband, she should not marry unless, by the deposition and oath of the general, she could prove the death of her husband.[4] Justinian had in view the indissolubility of marriage; but we may safely say that he had it too much in view. He demanded a positive proof when a negative one was sufficient; he required a thing extremely difficult to give, an account of the fate of a man at a great distance, and exposed to so many accidents; he presumed a crime, that is, a desertion of the husband, when it was so natural to presume his death. He injured the commonwealth by obliging women to live out of marriage; he injured individuals by exposing them to a thousand dangers.

The law of Justinian, which ranked among the causes of divorce the consent of the husband and wife to enter into a monastery, was entirely opposite to the principles of the civil laws.[5] It is natural that the causes of divorce should have their origin in certain impediments which could not be foreseen before marriage; but this desire of preserving chastity might be foreseen, since it is in ourselves. This law favours inconstancy in a state which is by its very nature perpetual; it shook the fundamental principle of divorce, which permits the dissolution of one marriage only from the hope of another. In short, if we view it in a religious light, it is no more than giving victims to God without a sacrifice.

10. *In what Case we ought to follow the civil Law which permits, and not the Law of Religion which forbids.* When a religion which prohibits polygamy is introduced into a country where it is permitted, we cannot believe (speaking only as a politician) that the laws of the country ought to suffer a man who has many wives to embrace this religion; unless the magistrate or the husband should indemnify them, by restoring them in some way or other to their civil state. Without this their condition would be deplorable; no sooner would they obey the laws than they would find themselves deprived of the greatest advantages of society.

11. *That human Courts of Justice should not be regulated by the Maxims of those Tribunals which relate to the Other Life.* The tribunal of the inquisition, formed by the Christian monks on the idea of the tribunal of peni-

---

[1] *Leg.* 11, § *ult.,* ff. *ad. leg. Jul. de adulteriis.*
[2] *Nov.* 134. *Col. 9,* cap. x, tit. 170.
[3] *Leg.* 7, *Cod. de repudiis, et juricio de morib. sublato.*

[4] Auth. *Hodie quantiscumque, Cod. de repudiis.*
[5] Auth. *Quod hodie, Cod. de repudiis.*

tence, is contrary to all good policy. It has everywhere met with a general dislike, and must have sunk under the oppositions it met with, if those who were resolved to establish it had not drawn advantages even from these oppositions.

This tribunal is insupportable in all governments. In monarchies, it only makes informers and traitors; in republics, it only forms dishonest men; in a despotic state, it is as destructive as the government itself.

12. *The same Subject continued.* It is one abuse of this tribunal that, of two persons accused of the same crime, he who denies is condemned to die; and he who confesses avoids the punishment. This has its source in monastic ideas, where he who denies seems in a state of impenitence and damnation; and he who confesses, in a state of repentance and salvation. But a distinction of this kind can have no relation to human tribunals. Human justice, which sees only the actions, has but one compact with men, namely, that of innocence; divine justice, which sees the thoughts, has two, that of innocence and repentance.

13. *In what Cases, with regard to Marriage, we ought to follow the Laws of Religion; and in what Cases we should follow the civil Laws.* It has happened in all ages and countries, that religion has been blended with marriages. When certain things have been considered as impure or unlawful, and had nevertheless become necessary, they were obliged to call in religion to legitimate in the one case, and to reprove in others.

On the other hand, as marriage is of all human actions that in which society is most interested, it became proper that this should be regulated by the civil laws.

Everything which relates to the nature of marriage, its form, the manner of contracting it, the fruitfulness it occasions, which has made all nations consider it as the object of a particular benediction, a benediction which, not being always annexed to it, is supposed to depend on certain superior graces; all this is within the resort of religion.

The consequences of this union with regard to property, the reciprocal advantages, everything which has a relation to the new family, to that from which it sprang, and to that which is expected to arise; all this relates to the civil laws.

As one of the great objects of marriage is to take away that uncertainty which attends unlawful conjunctions, religion here stamps its seal, and the civil laws join theirs to it, to the end that it may be as authentic as possible. Thus, besides the conditions required by religion to make a marriage valid, the civil laws may still exact others.

The civil laws receive this power from their being additional obligations, and not contradictory ones. The law of religion insists upon certain ceremonies, the civil laws on the consent of fathers; in this case, they demand something more than that of religion, but they demand nothing contrary to it.

It follows hence, that the religious law must decide whether the bond be indissoluble or not; for if the laws of religion had made the bond indissoluble, and the civil laws had declared it might be broken, they would be contradictory to each other.

Sometimes the regulations made by the civil laws with respect to marriage are not absolutely necessary; such are those established by the laws, which, instead of annulling the marriage, only punish those who contract it.

Among the Romans, the Papian law declared those marriages illegal which had been prohibited, and yet only subjected them to a penalty;[1] but a *Senatus Consultum,* made at the instance of the Emperor Marcus Antoninus, declared them void; there then no longer subsisted any such thing as a marriage, wife, dowry, or husband.[2] The civil laws determine according to circumstances: sometimes they are most attentive to repair the evil; at others, to prevent it.

14. *In what instances Marriages between Relatives shall be regulated by the Laws of Nature: and in what instances by the civil Laws.* With regard to the prohibition of marriage between relatives, it is a thing extremely delicate to fix exactly the point at which the laws of nature stop and where the civil laws begin. For this purpose we must establish some principles.

The marriage of the son with the mother confounds the state of things: the son ought to have an unlimited respect for his mother, the wife an unlimited respect for her husband; therefore the marriage of the mother to her son would subvert the natural state of both.

[1] See what has been said on this subject, in book xxiii. 21, in the relation they bear to the number of inhabitants.
[2] See *Leg.* 16, ff. *de ritu nuptiarum,* and *Leg.* 3, § 1; also *Dig. de donationibus inter virum et uxorem.*

Besides, nature has forwarded in women the time in which they are able to have children, but has retarded it in men; and, for the same reason, women sooner lose this ability and men later. If the marriage between the mother and the son were permitted, it would almost always be the case that when the husband was capable of entering into the views of nature, the wife would be incapable.

The marriage between the father and the daughter is contrary to nature, as well as the other; but it is not less contrary, because it has not these two obstacles. Thus the Tartars, who may marry their daughters,[1] never marry their mothers, as we see in the accounts we have of that nation.[2]

It has ever been the natural duty of fathers to watch over the chastity of their children. Entrusted with the care of their education, they are obliged to preserve the body in the greatest perfection, and the mind from the least corruption; to encourage whatever has a tendency to inspire them with virtuous desires, and to nourish a becoming tenderness. Fathers, always employed in preserving the morals of their children, must have a natural aversion to everything that can render them corrupt. Marriage, you will say, is not a corruption; but before marriage they must speak, they must make their persons beloved, they must seduce; it is this seduction which ought to inspire us with horror.

There should be therefore an insurmountable barrier between those who ought to give the education, and those who are to receive it, in order to prevent every kind of corruption, even though the motive be lawful. Why do fathers so carefully deprive those who are to marry their daughters of their company and familiarity?

The horror that arises against the incest of the brother with the sister should proceed from the same source. The desire of fathers and mothers to preserve the morals of their children and families untainted is sufficient to inspire their offspring with a detestation of everything that can lead to the union of the two sexes.

The prohibition of marriage between cousins-german has the same origin. In the early ages, that is, in the times of innocence, in the ages when luxury was unknown, it was customary for children[3] upon their marriage not to remove from their parents, but settle in the same house; as a small habitation was at that time sufficient for a large family; the children of two brothers, or cousins-german,[4] were considered both by others and themselves as brothers. The estrangement then between the brothers and sisters as to marriage subsisted also between the cousins-german.[5] These principles are so strong and no natural that they have had their influence almost over all the earth, independently of any communication. It was not the Romans who taught the inhabitants of Formosa[6] that the marriage of relatives of the fourth degree was incestuous; it was not the Romans that communicated this sentiment to the Arabs;[7] it was not they who taught it to the inhabitants of the Maldivian islands.[8]

But if some nations have not rejected marriages between fathers and children, sisters and brothers, we have seen in the first book, that intelligent beings do not always follow the law of nature. Who could have imagined it! Religious ideas have frequently made men fall into these mistakes. If the Assyrians and the Persians married their mothers, the first were influenced by a religious respect for Semiramis, and the second did it because the religion of Zoroaster gave a preference to these marriages.[9] If the Egyptians married their sisters, it proceeded from the wildness of the Egyptian religion, which consecrated these marriages in honour of Isis. As the spirit of religion leads us to attempt whatever is great and difficult, we cannot infer that a thing is natural from its being consecrated by a false religion.

The principle which informs us that marriages between fathers and children, between brothers and sisters, are prohibited in order to preserve natural modesty in families will

---

[1] This law is very ancient among them. Attila, says Priscus, in his embassy stopped in a certain place to marry Esca his daughter. "A thing permitted," he adds, "by the laws of the Scythians," p. 22.

[2] History of the Tartars, part III, p. 256.

[3] It was thus among the ancient Romans.

[4] Among the Romans they had the same name; the cousins-german were called brothers.

[5] It was thus at Rome in the first ages, till the people made a law to permit them; they were willing to favour a man extremely popular, who had married his cousin-german. Plutarch's treatise entitled Questions Concerning the Affairs of the Romans.

[6] Collection of Voyages to the Indies, v, part I. An account of the state of the isle of Formosa.

[7] Koran, chapter "On Women."

[8] See Francis Pirard.

[9] They were considered as more honourable. See Philo, De Specialibus legib. quæ pertinent ad præcepta decalogi, p. 778, Paris, 1640.

help us to the discovery of those marriages that are forbidden by the law of nature, and of those which can be so only by the civil law.

As children dwell, or are supposed to dwell in their father's house, and consequently the son-in-law with the mother-in-law, the father-in-law with the daughter-in-law, or wife's daughter, the marriage between them is forbidden by the law of nature. In this case the resemblance has the same effect as the reality, because it springs from the same cause; the civil law neither can, nor ought to permit these marriages.

There are nations, as we have already observed, among whom cousins-german are considered as brothers, because they commonly dwell in the same house; there are others where this custom is not known. Among the first the marriage of cousins-german ought to be regarded as contrary to nature; not so among the others.

But the laws of nature cannot be local. Therefore, when these marriages are forbidden or permitted, they are, according to the circumstances, permitted or forbidden by a civil law.

It is not a necessary custom for the brother-in-law and the sister-in-law to dwell in the same house. The marriage between them is not then prohibited to preserve chastity in the family; and the law which forbids or permits it is not a law of nature, but a civil law, regulated by circumstances and dependent on the customs of each country: these are cases in which the laws depend on the morals, or customs of the inhabitants.

The civil laws forbid marriages when by the customs received in a certain country they are found to be in the same circumstances as those forbidden by the law of nature; and they permit them when this is not the case. The prohibitions of the laws of nature are invariable, because the thing on which they depend is invariable; the father, the mother and the children necessarily dwell in the same house. But the prohibitions of the civil laws are accidental because they depend on an accidental circumstance, cousins-german and others dwelling in the house by accident.

This explains why the laws of Moses, those of the Egyptians,[1] and of many other nations permitted the marriage of the brother-in-law with the sister-in-law; whilst these very marriages were disallowed by other nations.

[1] See *Leg. 8, Cod. de incestis et inutilibus nuptiis.*

In the Indies they have a very natural reason for admitting this sort of marriages. The uncle is there considered as the father and is obliged to maintain and educate his nephew as if he were his own child; this proceeds from the disposition of this people, which is good-natured and full of humanity. This law or this custom has produced another; if a husband has lost his wife, he does not fail to marry her sister:[2] which is extremely natural, for his new consort becomes the mother of her sister's children, and not a cruel stepmother.

15. *That we should not regulate by the Principles of political Law those Things which depend on the Principles of civil Law.* As men have given up their natural independence to live under political laws, they have given up the natural community of goods to live under civil laws.

By the first, they acquired liberty; by the second, property. We should not decide by the laws of liberty, which, as we have already said, is only the government of the community, what ought to be decided by the laws concerning property. It is a paralogism to say that the good of the individual should give way to that of the public; this can never take place, except when the government of the community, or, in other words, the liberty of the subject is concerned; this does not affect such cases as relate to private property, because the public good consists in every one's having his property, which was given him by the civil laws, invariably preserved.

Cicero maintains that the Agrarian laws were unjust; because the community was established with no other view than that every one might be able to preserve his property.

Let us, therefore, lay down a certain maxim, that whenever the public good happens to be the matter in question, it is not for the advantage of the public to deprive an individual of his property, or even to retrench the least part of it by a law, or a political regulation. In this case we should follow the rigour of the civil law, which is the Palladium of property.

Thus when the public has occasion for the estate of an individual, it ought never to act by the rigour of political law; it is here that the civil law ought to triumph, which, with the eyes of a mother, regards every individual as the whole community.

If the political magistrate would erect a public edifice, or make a new road, he must

[2] *Edifying Letters,* coll. xiv, p. 403.

indemnify those who are injured by it; the public is in this respect like an individual who treats with an individual. It is fully enough that it can oblige a citizen to sell his inheritance, and that it can strip him of this great privilege which he holds from the civil law, the not being forced to alienate his possessions.

After the nations which subverted the Roman empire had abused their very conquests, the spirit of liberty called them back to that of equity. They exercised the most barbarous laws with moderation: and if any one should doubt the truth of this, he need only read Beaumanoir's admirable work on jurisprudence, written in the twelfth century.

They mended the highways in his time as we do at present. He says, that when a highway could not be repaired, they made a new one as near the old as possible; but indemnified the proprietors at the expense of those who reaped any advantage from the road.[1] They determined at that time by the civil law; in our days, we determine by the law of politics.

16. *That we ought not to decide by the Rules of the civil Law when it is proper to decide by those of the political Law.* Most difficulties on this subject may be easily solved by not confounding the rules derived from property with those which spring from liberty.

Is the demesne of a state or government alienable, or is it not? This question ought to be decided by the political law, and not by the civil. It ought not to be decided by the civil law, because it is as necessary that there should be demesnes for the subsistence of a state, as that the state should have civil laws to regulate the disposal of property.

If then they alienate the demesne, the state will be forced to make a new fund for another. But this expedient overturns the political government, because, by the nature of the thing, for every demesne that shall be established, the subject will always be obliged to pay more, and the sovereign to receive less; in a word, the demesne is necessary, and the alienation is not.

The order of succession is, in monarchies, founded on the welfare of the state; this makes it necessary that such an order should be fixed to avoid the misfortunes, which I have said must arise in a despotic kingdom, where all is uncertain, because all is arbitrary.

The order of succession is not fixed for the sake of the reigning family; but because it is the interest of the state that it should have a reigning family. The law which regulates the succession of individuals is a civil law, whose view is the interest of individuals; that which regulates the succession to monarchy is a political law, which has in view the welfare and preservation of the kingdom.

It follows hence, that when the political law has established an order of succession in government, and this order is at an end, it is absurd to reclaim the succession in virtue of the civil law of any nation whatsoever. One particular society does not make laws for another society. The civil laws of the Romans are no more applicable than any other civil laws. They themselves did not make use of them when they proceeded against kings; and the maxims by which they judged kings are so abominable that they ought never to be revived.

It follows also hence, that when the political law has obliged a family to renounce the succession, it is absurd to insist upon the restitutions drawn from the civil law. Restitutions are in the law, and may be good against those who live in the law: but they are not proper for such as have been raised up for the law, and who live for the law.

It is ridiculous to pretend to decide the rights of kingdoms, of nations, and of the whole globe by the same maxims on which (to make use of an expression of Cicero)[2] we should determine the right of a gutter between individuals.

17. *The same Subject continued.* Ostracism ought to be examined by the rules of politics, and not by those of the civil law; and so far is this custom from rendering a popular government odious, that it is, on the contrary, extremely well adapted to prove its lenity. We should be sensible of this ourselves, if, while banishment is always considered among us as a penalty, we are able to separate the idea of ostracism from that of punishment.

Aristotle[3] tells us, it is universally allowed, that this practice has something in it both humane and popular. If in those times and places where this sentence was executed they found nothing in it that appeared odious; is

---

[1] "The lord appointed collectors to receive the toll from the peasant, the gentlemen were obliged to contribute by the count, and the clergy to the bishop."—Beaumanoir, 25, §§ 13, 17.

[2] *De Leg.*, i.
[3] *Politics*, iii. 13.

it for us who see things at such a distance to think otherwise than the accuser, the judges and the accused themselves?

And if we consider that this judgment of the people loaded the person with glory on whom it was passed; that when at Athens it fell upon a man without merit,[1] from that very moment they ceased to use it;[2] we shall find that numbers of people have obtained a false idea of it; for it was an admirable law that could prevent the ill consequences which the glory of a citizen might produce by loading him with new glory.

18. *That it is necessary to inquire whether the Laws which seem contradictory are of the same Class.* At Rome the husband was permitted to lend his wife to another. Plutarch tells us this in express terms.[3] We know that Cato lent his wife to Hortensius,[4] and Cato was not a man to violate the laws of his country.

On the other hand, a husband who suffered his wife to be debauched, who did not bring her to justice, or who took her again after her condemnation was punished.[5] These laws seem to contradict each other, and yet are not contradictory. The law which permitted a Roman to lend his wife was visibly a Lacedæmonian institution, established with a view of giving the republic children of a good species, if I may be allowed the term; the other had in view the preservation of morals. The first was a law of politics, the second a civil law.

19. *That we should not decide those Things by the civil Law which ought to be decided by domestic Laws.* The law of the Visigoths enjoins that the slaves of the house shall be obliged to bind the man and woman they surprise in adultery, and to present them to the husband and to the judge:[6] a terrible law, which puts into the hands of such mean persons, the care of public, domestic, and private vengeance!

This law can be nowhere proper but in the seraglios of the East, where the slave who has the charge of the enclosure is deemed an accomplice upon the discovery of the least infidelity. He seizes the criminals, not so much with a view to bring them to justice, as to do justice to himself, and to obtain a scrutiny into the circumstances of the action, in order to remove the suspicion of his negligence.

But, in countries where women are not guarded, it is ridiculous to subject those who govern the family to the inquisition of their slaves.

This inquisition may, in certain cases, be at the most a particular domestic regulation, but never a civil law.

20. *That we ought not to decide by the Principles of the civil Laws those Things which belong to the Law of Nations.* Liberty consists principally in not being forced to do a thing, where the laws do not oblige: people are in this state only as they are governed by civil laws; and because they live under those civil laws, they are free.

It follows hence, that princes who live not among themselves under civil laws are not free; they are governed by force; they may continually force, or be forced. Hence it follows that treaties made by force are as obligatory as those made by free consent. When we, who live under civil laws, are, contrary to law, constrained to enter into a contract, we may, by the assistance of the law, recover from the effects of violence: but a prince, who is always in that state in which he forces, or is forced, cannot complain of a treaty which he has been compelled to sign. This would be to complain of his natural state; it would seem as if he would be a prince with respect to other princes, and as if other princes should be subjects with respect to him; that is, it would be contrary to the nature of things.

21. *That we should not decide by political Laws Things which belong to the Law of Nations.* Political laws demand that every man be subject to the natural and civil courts of the country where he resides, and to the censure of the sovereign.

The law of nations requires that princes shall send ambassadors; and a reason drawn from the nature of things does not permit these ambassadors to depend either on the sovereign to whom they are sent, or on his tribunals. They are the voice of the prince who sends them, and this voice ought to be free; no obstacle should hinder the execution of their office: they may frequently offend, because they speak for a man entirely independent; they might be wrongfully accused, if

[1] Hyperbolus. See Plutarch, *Aristides.*
[2] It was found opposite to the spirit of the legislator. See below, xxix. 7.
[3] Plutarch in his comparison between Lycurgus and Numa.
[4] Plutarch, *Cato the Younger.*
[5] *Leg.* 11 § ult., ff. *ad. leg. Jul. de adulteriis.*
[6] Law of the Visigoths, iii, tit. 4, § 6.

they were liable to be punished for crimes: if they could be arrested for debts, these might be forged. Thus a prince, who has naturally a bold and enterprising spirit, would speak by the mouth of a man who had everything to fear. We must then be guided, with respect to ambassadors, by reasons drawn from the law of nations, and not by those derived from political law. But if they make an ill use of their representative character, a stop may be put to it by sending them back. They may even be accused before their master, who becomes either their judge or their accomplice.

22. *The unhappy State of the Inca Athualpa.* The principles we have just been establishing were cruelly violated by the Spaniards. The Inca Athualpa[1] could not be tried by the law of nations: they tried him by political and civil laws; they accused him for putting to death some of his own subjects, for having many wives &c., and to fill up the measure of their stupidity, they condemned him, not by the political and civil laws of his own country, but by the political and civil laws of theirs.

23. *That when, by some Circumstance, the political Law becomes destructive to the State, we ought to decide by such a political Law as will preserve it, which sometimes becomes a Law of Nations.* When that political law which has established in the kingdom a certain order of succession becomes destructive to the body politic for whose sake it was established, there is not the least room to doubt but another political law may be made to change this order; and so far would this law be from opposing the first that it would in the main be entirely conformable to it, since both would depend on this principle, that THE SAFETY OF THE PEOPLE IS THE SUPREME LAW.

I have said[2] that a great state becoming accessory to another is itself weakened, and even weakens the principal. We know that it is for the interest of the state to have the supreme magistrate within itself, that the public revenues be well administered, and that its specie be not sent abroad to enrich another country. It is of importance that he who is to govern has not imbibed foreign maxims; these are less agreeable than those already established. Besides, men have an extravagant fondness for their own laws and customs: these constitute the happiness of every community; and, as we

learn from the histories of all nations, are rarely changed without violent commotions and a great effusion of blood.

It follows hence, that if a great state has for its heir the possessor of a great state, the former may reasonably exclude him, because a change in the order of succession must be of service to both countries. Thus a law of Russia, made in the beginning of the reign of Elizabeth, most wisely excluded from the possession of the crown every heir who possessed another monarchy; thus the law of Portugal disqualifies every stranger who lays claim to the crown by right of blood.

But if a nation may exclude, it may with greater reason be allowed a right to oblige a prince to renounce. If the people fear that a certain marriage will be attended with such consequences as shall rob the nation of its independence, or dismember some of its provinces, it may very justly oblige the contractors and their descendants to renounce all right over them; while he who renounces, and those to whose prejudice he renounces, have the less reason to complain, as the state might originally have made a law to exclude them.

24. *That the Regulations of the Police are of a different Class from other civil Laws.* There are criminals whom the magistrate punishes, there are others whom he reproves. The former are subject to the power of the law, the latter to his authority: those are cut off from society; these they oblige to live according to the rules of society.

In the exercise of the Police, it is rather the magistrate who punishes, than the law; in the sentence passed on crimes, it is rather the law which punishes, than the magistrate. The business of the Police consists in affairs which arise every instant, and are commonly of a trifling nature: there is then but little need of formalities. The actions of the Police are quick; they are exercised over things which return every day: it would be therefore improper for it to inflict severe punishments. It is continually employed about minute particulars; great examples are therefore not designed for its purpose. It is governed rather by regulations than laws; those who are subject to its jurisdiction are incessantly under the eye of the magistrate: it is therefore his fault if they fall into excess. Thus we ought not to confound a flagrant violation of the laws, with a simple breach of the Police; these things are of a different order.

---

[1] See Garcilasso de la Vega, p. 108.
[2] See v. 14; viii. 16–20; ix. 4–7; and x. 9, 10.

Hence it follows, that the laws of an Italian republic,[1] where bearing fire-arms is punished as a capital crime and where it is not more fatal to make an ill use of them than to carry them, is not agreeable to the nature of things.

It follows, moreover, that the applauded action of that emperor who caused a baker to be impaled whom he found guilty of a fraud, was the action of a sultan who knew not how to be just without committing an outrage on justice.

25. *That we should not follow the general Disposition of the civil Law, in things which ought to be subject to particular Rules drawn from their own Nature.* Is it a good law that all civil obligations passed between sailors in a ship in the course of a voyage should be null? Francis Pirard tells us[4] that, in his time, it was not observed by the Portuguese, though it was by the French. Men who are together only for a short time, who have no wants, since they are provided for by the prince; who have only one object in view, that of their voyage; who are no longer in society, but are only the inhabitants of a ship, ought not to contract obligations that were never introduced but to support the burden of civil society.

In the same spirit was the law of the Rhodians, made at a time when they always followed the coasts; it ordained that those who during a tempest stayed in a vessel should have ship and cargo, and those who quitted it should have nothing.

BOOK XXVII

1.*Of the Origin and Revolutions of the Roman Laws on Successions.* This affair derives its establishment from the most distant antiquity, and to penetrate to its foundation, permit me to search among the first laws of the Romans for what, I believe, nobody yet has been so happy as to discover.

We know that Romulus[2] divided the land of his little kingdom among his subjects; it seems to me that hence the laws of Rome on successions were derived.

The law of the division of lands made it necessary that the property of one family should not pass into another: hence it followed that there were but two orders of heirs established by law, the children and all the descendants that lived under the power of the father, whom they called *sui hæredes,* or his natural heirs; and, in their default, the nearest relatives on the male side, whom they called *agnati.*[3]

It followed likewise, that the relatives on the female side, whom they called *cognati,* ought not to succeed; they would have conveyed the estate into another family, which was not allowed.

Thence also it followed that the children ought not to succeed to the mother, nor the mother to her children; for this might carry the estate of one family into another. Thus we see them excluded by the law of the Twelve Tables:[5] it called none to the succession but the *agnati,* and there was no agnation between the son and the mother.

But it was indifferent whether the *suus hæres,* or, in default of such, the nearest by agnation, was male or female; because, as the relatives on the mother's side could not succeed, though a woman who was an heiress should happen to marry, yet the estate always returned into the family whence it came. On this account, the law of the Twelve Tables does not distinguish, whether the person who succeeded was male or female.[6]

This was the cause that, though the grandchildren by the son succeeded to the grandfather, the grandchildren by the daughter did not succeed; for, to prevent the estate from passing into another family, the *agnati* were preferred to them. Hence the daughter, and not her children, succeeded to the father.[7]

Thus among the primitive Romans, the women succeeded, when this was agreeable to the law of the division of lands, and they did not succeed, when this might suffer by it.

Such were the laws of succession among the primitive Romans; and as these had a natural dependence on the constitution, and were derived from the division of lands, it is easy to

---

[1] Venice.
[2] Dionysius Halicarnassus, ii. 3. Plutarch's comparison between Numa and Lycurgus.
[3] *Ast si intestato moritur cui suus hæres nec extabit, agnatus proximus familiam habeto.* Fragment of the law of the Twelve Tables in Ulpian, the last title.

[4] Chapter 14, part XII.
[5] See Ulpian, *Fragment.,* § 8, tit. 26. *Institutes,* tit. 3, *In præmio ad S. C. Tertullianum.*
[6] Paul, *Sentences,* tit. 8, § 3.
[7] *Institutes,* iii, tit. 1, § 15.

perceive that they had not a foreign origin, and were not of the number of those brought into the republic by the deputies sent into the cities of Greece.

Dionysius Halicarnassus tells us[1] that Servius Tullius, finding the laws of Romulus and Numa on the division of lands abolished, restored them, and made new ones to give the old a greater weight. We cannot therefore doubt but that the laws we have been speaking of, made in consequence of this division, were the work of these three Roman legislators.

The order of succession having been established in consequence of a political law, no citizen was allowed to break in upon it by his private will; that is, in the first ages of Rome he had not the power of making a testament. Yet it would have been hard to deprive him, in his last moments, of the friendly commerce of kind and beneficent actions.

They therefore found a method of reconciling, in this respect, the laws with the desires of the individual. He was permitted to dispose of his substance in an assembly of the people; and thus every testament was, in some sort, an act of the legislative power.

The law of the Twelve Tables permitted the person who made his will to choose which citizen he pleased for his heir. The reason that induced the Roman laws so strictly to restrain the number of those who might succeed *ab intestato* was the law of the division of lands; and the reason why they extended so widely the power of the testator was that, as the father might sell his children,[2] he might with greater reason deprive them of his substance. These were therefore different effects, since they flowed from different principles; and such is, in this respect, the spirit of the Roman laws.

The ancient laws of Athens did not suffer a citizen to make a will. Solon permitted it, with an exception to those who had children;[3] and the legislators of Rome, filled with the idea of paternal power, allowed the making a will even to the prejudice of their children. It must be confessed that the ancient laws of Athens were more consistent than those of Rome. The indefinite permission of making a will which had been granted to the Romans,

ruined little by little the political regulation on the division of lands; it was the principal thing that introduced the fatal difference between riches and poverty: many shares were united in the same person; some citizens had too much, and a multitude of others had nothing. Thus the people being continually deprived of their shares were incessantly calling out for a new distribution of lands. They demanded it in an age when the frugality, the parsimony and the poverty of the Romans were their distinguishing characteristics; as well as at a time when their luxury had become still more astonishing.

Testaments being properly a law made in the assembly of the people, those who were in the army were thereby deprived of a testamentary power. The people therefore gave the soldiers the privilege of making before their companions[4] the dispositions which should have been made before them.[5]

The great assembly of the people met but twice a year; besides, both the people and the affairs brought before them were increased; they therefore judged it convenient to permit all the citizens to make their will before some Roman citizens of ripe age, who were to represent the body of the people;[6] they took five citizens,[7] in whose presence the inheritor purchased his family, that is, his inheritance, of the testator;[8] another citizen brought a pair of scales to weigh the value; for the Romans, as yet, had no money.[9]

To all appearance these five citizens were to represent the five classes of the people; and they set no value on the sixth, as being composed of men who had no property.

We ought not to say, with Justinian, that these scales were merely imaginary; they became, indeed, imaginary in time, but were not so originally. Most of the laws, which afterwards regulated wills, were built on the reality of these scales: we find sufficient proof of this

---

[1] Book iv, p. 276.

[2] Dionysius Halicarnassus proves, by a law of Numa, that the law which permitted a father to sell his son three times was made by Romulus, and not by the Decemvirs.—Book ii.

[3] See Plutarch, *Solon*.

[4] This testament, called *in procinctu*, was different from that which they styled military, which was established only by the constitutions of the emperors. *Leg.* 1, ff. *de militari testamento.* This was one of the artifices by which they cajoled the soldiers.

[5] This testament was not in writing, and it was without formality, *sine librâ et tabulis*, as Cicero says, *De Orat.*, i.

[6] *Institutes*, ii, tit. 10, § 1. Aulus Gellius, xv. 27. They called this form of testament *per æs et libram.*

[7] Ulpian, tit. 10, § 2.

[8] Theophilus, *Institutes*, ii, tit. 10.

[9] Livy, iv, *Nondum argentum signatum erat.* He speaks of the time of the siege of Veii.

in the fragments of Ulpian.[1] The deaf, the dumb, the prodigal, could not make a will: the deaf, because he could not hear the words of the buyer of the inheritance; the dumb, because he could not pronounce the terms of nomination; the prodigal, because as he was excluded from the management of all affairs, he could not sell his inheritance. I omit any further examples.

Wills being made in the assembly of the people were rather the acts of political than of civil laws, a public rather than a private right; whence it followed that the father, while his son was under his authority, could not give him leave to make a will.

Among most nations, wills are not subject to greater formalities than ordinary contracts; because both the one and the other are only expressions of the will of him who makes the contract, and both are equally a private right. But among the Romans, where testaments were derived from the public law, they were attended with much greater formalities than other affairs;[2] and this is still the case in those provinces of France which are governed by the Roman law.

Testaments being, as I have said, a law of the people, they ought to be made with the force of a command, and in such terms as are called *direct and imperative*.[3] Hence a rule was formed, that they could neither give nor transmit an inheritance without making use of the imperative words: whence it followed, that they might very justly in certain cases make a substitution;[4] and ordain, that the inheritance should pass to another heir; but that they could never make a fiduciary bequest,[5] that is, charge any one in terms of entreaty to restore an inheritance, or a part of it, to another.

When the father neither instituted his son his heir, nor disinherited him, the will was annulled; but it was valid, though he did not disinherit his daughter, nor institute her his heiress. The reason is plain: when he neither instituted nor disinherited his son, he did an injury to his grandson, who might have succeeded *ab intestato* to his father; but in neither instituting nor disinheriting his daughter,

he did no injury to his daughter's children, who could not succeed *ab intestato* to their mother, because they were neither *sui hæredes*, nor *agnati*.[6]

The laws of the ancient Romans concerning successions, being formed with the same spirit which dictated the division of lands, did not sufficiently restrain the riches of women; thus a door was left open to luxury, which is always inseparable from this sort of opulence. Between the second and third Punic war, they began to perceive the evil and made the Voconian law;[7] but as they were induced to this by the most important considerations; as but few monuments have reached us that take notice of this law, and as it has hitherto been spoken of in a most confused manner, I shall endeavour to clear it up.

Cicero has preserved a fragment, which forbids the instituting a woman an heiress, whether she was married or unmarried.[8]

The *Epitome of Livy*, where he speaks of this law, says no more:[9] it appears from Cicero[10] and St. Augustine[11] that the daughter, though an only child, was comprehended in the prohibition.

Cato, the elder, contributed all in his power to get this law passed.[12] Aulus Gellius cites a fragment of a speech,[13] which he made on this occasion. By preventing the succession of women, his intent was to take away the source of luxury; as by undertaking the defence of the Oppian law, he intended to put a stop to luxury itself.

In the Institutes of Justinian[14] and Theophilus,[15] mention is made of a chapter of the Voconian law which limits the power of bequeathing. In reading these authors, everybody would imagine that this chapter was made to prevent the inheritance from being

---

[1] Tit. 20, § 13.
[2] *Institutes*, ii, tit. 10, § 1.
[3] Let Titus be my heir.
[4] Vulgar, pupillary, and exemplary.
[5] Augustus, for particular reasons, first began to authorise the fiduciary bequest, which, in the Roman law, was called *fidei commissum*. *Institutes*, ii, tit. 23, § 1.

[6] *Ad liberos matris intestatæ hæredit as*, leg. 12 Tab., *non pertinebat, quia, fœminæ suos hæredes non habent*. Ulpian, *Fragment.*, tit. 26, § 7.
[7] It was proposed by Quintus Voconius, tribune of the people, in the year 585 of Rome, 169 B.C. See Cicero, *Second Oration against Verres*. In the *Epitome of Livy*, xli we should read *Voconius*, instead of *Voluminus*.
[8] *Sanxit . . . . . ne quis hæredem virginem neve mulierem faceret.*—Cicero, *Second Oration against Verres*, 107.
[9] *Legem tulit, ne quis hæredem mulierem institueret.*—Book xli.
[10] *Second Oration against Verres.*
[11] *City of God*, iii. 21.
[12] *Epitome of Livy*, xli.
[13] Book xvii, 6.
[14] *Institutes*, ii, tit. 22
[15] *Ibid.*

so exhausted by legacies as to render it unworthy of the heir's acceptance. But this was not the spirit of the Voconian law. We have just seen that they had in view the hindering women from inheriting an estate. The article of this law, which set bounds to the power of bequeathing entered into this view: for if people had been possessed of the liberty to bequeath as much as they pleased, the women might have received as legacies what they could not receive by succession.

The Voconian law was made to hinder the women from growing too wealthy; for this end it was necessary to deprive them of large inheritances, and not of such as were incapable of supporting luxury. The law fixed a certain sum to be given to the women whom it deprived of the succession. Cicero,[1] from whom we have this particular, does not tell us what was the sum; but by Dio we are informed it was a hundred thousand sesterces.[2]

The Voconian law was made to regulate opulence, not to lay a restraint upon poverty; hence Cicero[3] informs us that it related only to those whose names were registered in the censors' books.

This furnished a pretence for eluding the law: it is well known that the Romans were extremely fond of set forms; and we have already taken notice that it was the spirit of the republic to follow the letter of the law. There were fathers who would not give in their names to be enrolled by the censors, because they would have it in their power to leave the succession to a daughter: and the prætors determined that this was no violation of the Voconian law since it was not contrary to the letter of it.

One Anius Asellus had appointed his daughter his sole heir and executrix. He had a right to make this disposition, says Cicero;[4] he was not restrained by the Voconian law, since he was not included in the census. Verres, during the time of his prætorship, had deprived Anius' daughter of the succession; and Cicero maintains that Verres had been bribed, otherwise he would not have annulled a disposition which all the other prætors had confirmed.

What kind of citizens then must those have been, who were not registered in the census in which all the freemen of Rome were included? According to the institution of Servius Tullius, mentioned by Dionysius of Halicarnassus,[5] every citizen not enrolled in the census became a slave; even Cicero himself observes[6] that such a man forfeited his liberty, and the same thing is affirmed by Zonaras. There must have been therefore a difference between not being in the census according to the spirit of the Voconian law, and not being in it according to the spirit of Servius Tullius' institutions.

They whose names were not registered in the first five classes,[7] in which the inhabitants ranked in proportion to their fortunes, were not comprised in the census according to the spirit of the Voconian law: they who were not enrolled in one of these six classes, or who were not ranked by the censors among such as were called ærarii, were not included in the census according to the spirit of Servius' institutions. Such was the force of nature, that to elude the Voconian law fathers submitted to the disgrace of being confounded in the sixth class with the proletarii and capite censi, or perhaps to have their names entered in the Cærites tabulæ.[8]

We have elsewhere observed that the Roman laws did not admit of fiduciary bequests. The hopes of evading the Voconian law were the cause of their being introduced: they instituted an heir qualified by the law, and they begged he would resign the succession to a person whom the law had excluded; this new method of disposition was productive of very different effects. Some resigned the inheritance; and the conduct of Sextus Peduccus on an occasion of this nature was very remarkable.[9] A considerable succession was left him, and nobody living knew that he was desired to resign it to another, when he waited upon the widow of the testator and made over to her the whole fortune belonging to her late husband.

Others kept possession of the inheritance; and here the example of P. Sextilius Rufus is also famous, having been made use of by Cicero in his disputations against the Epicure-

[1] Nemo censuit plus Fadiæ dandum, quam posset ad eam lege Voconia pervenire. De Finib. boni et mali, ii. 55.
[2] Cum lege Voconia mulieribus prohiberetur, ne qua majorem centum millibus nummum hæreditatem posset adire. Book lvi.
[3] Qui census esset. Second Oration against Verres.
[4] Census non erat. Ibid.

[5] Book iv.
[6] Oratio pro Cæcinna.
[7] These five classes were so considerable, that authors sometimes mention no more than five.
[8] In Cæritum tabulas referri; ærarius fieri.
[9] Cicero, De Finib. boni et mali, ii. 58.

ans.[1] "In my younger days," says he, "I was desired by Sextilius to accompany him to his friends, in order to know whether he ought to restore the inheritance of Quintus Fadius Gallus to his daughter Fadia. There were several young people present, with others of more maturity and judgment; and not one of them was of opinion that he should give more to Fadia than the lady was entitled to by the Voconian law. In consequence of this, Sextilius kept possession of a fine estate, of which he would not have retained a single sestertius had he preferred justice to utility. It is possible, added he, that you would have resigned the inheritance; nay it is possible that Epicurus himself would have resigned it; but you would not have acted according to your own principles." Here I shall pause a little to reflect.

It is a misfortune inherent in humanity that legislators should be sometimes obliged to enact laws repugnant to the dictates of nature: such was the Voconian law. The reason is, the legislature considers the society rather than the citizen, and the citizen rather than the man. The law sacrificed both the citizen and the man, and directed its views to the prosperity of the republic. Suppose a person made a fiduciary bequest in favour of his daughter; the law paid no regard to the sentiments of nature in the father, nor to the filial piety of the daughter; all it had an eye to was the person to whom the bequest was made in trust, and who on such occasion found himself in a terrible dilemma. If he restored the estate, he was a bad citizen; if he kept it, he was a bad man. None but good-natured people thought of eluding the law; and they could pitch upon none but honest men to help them to elude it; for a trust of this kind requires a triumph over avarice and inordinate pleasure, which none but honest men are likely to obtain. Perhaps in this light to look upon them as bad citizens would have savoured too much of severity. It is not impossible but that the legislator carried his point in a great measure, since his law was of such a nature as obliged none but honest men to elude it.

At the time when the Voconian law was passed, the Romans still preserved some remains of their ancient purity of manners. Their conscience was sometimes engaged in favour of the law; and they were made to swear they would observe it:[2] so that honesty in some measure was set in opposition against itself. But latterly their morals were corrupted to such a degree that the fiduciary bequests must have had less efficacy to elude the Voconian law, than that very legislator had to enforce its observance.

The civil wars were the destruction of an infinite number of citizens. Under Augustus, Rome was almost deserted; it was necessary to re-people it. They made the Papian laws, which omitted nothing that could encourage the citizens to marry and procreate children.[3] One of the principal means was to increase, in favour of those who gave in to the views of the law, the hopes of being heirs, and to diminish the expectations of those who refused; and as the Voconian law had rendered women incapable of succeeding, the Papian law, in certain cases, dispensed with this prohibition.[4]

Women,[5] especially those who had children, were rendered capable of receiving in virtue of the will of their husbands; they even might, when they had children, receive in virtue of the will of strangers. All this was in direct opposition to the regulations of the Voconian law: and yet it is remarkable that the spirit of this law was not entirely abandoned. For example, the Papian law, which permitted a man who had one child[6] to receive an entire inheritance by the will of a stranger, granted the same favour to the wife only when she had three children.[7]

It must be remarked that the Papian law did not render the women who had three children capable of succeeding except in virtue of the will of strangers; and that with respect to the succession of relatives, it left the ancient laws, and particularly the Voconian, in all their force.[8] But this did not long subsist.

Rome, corrupted by the riches of every nation, had changed her manners; the putting a stop to the luxury of women was no longer minded. Aulus Gellius, who lived under Adrian,[9] tells us, that in his time the Voconian law

[1] *Ibid.*
[2] Sextilius said he had sworn to observe it.—Cicero, *De Finib. boni et mali*, ii. 55.
[3] See what has been said in xxiii. 21.
[4] The same difference occurs in several regulations of the Papian law. See Ulpian, *Fragment.*, tit. ult., §§ 4, 5, 6.
[5] See Ulpian, *Fragment.*, tit. 15, § 16.
[6] *Quod tibi filiolus, vel filia nascitur ex me, Jura Parentis habes; propter me scriberis hæres.*—Juvenal, *Sat.* ix. 5, 83, 87.
[7] See *Leg.* 9, *Cod. Theod. De bonis proscriptorum*, and Dio, lv. See Ulpian, *Fragment.*, tit. ult., § 6, and tit. 29, § 3.
[8] Ulpian, *Fragment.*, tit. 16, § 1. Sozomenus, i. 29.
[9] Book xx. 1.

was almost abolished; it was buried under the opulence of the city. Thus we find in the sentences of Paulus,[1] who lived under Niger, and in the fragments of Ulpian,[2] who was in the time of Alexander Severus, that the sisters on the father's side might succeed, and that none but the relatives of a more distant degree were in the case of those prohibited by the Voconian law.

The ancient laws of Rome began to be thought severe. The prætors were no longer moved except by reasons of equity, moderation, and decorum.

We have seen, that by the ancient laws of Rome mothers had no share in the inheritance of their children. The Voconian law afforded a new reason for their exclusion. But the Emperor Claudius gave the mother the succession of her children as a consolation for her loss. The Tertullian *senatus consultum,* made under Adrian,[3] gave it them when they had three children if free women, or four if they were freedwomen. It is evident, that this decree of the senate was only an extension of the Papian law, which in the same case had granted to women the inheritance left them by strangers. At length Justinian favoured them with the succession independently of the number of their children.[4]

The same causes which had debilitated the law against the succession of women subverted that, by degrees, which had limited the succession of the relatives on the woman's side.

These laws were extremely conformable to the spirit of a good republic, where they ought to have such an influence as to prevent this sex from rendering either the possession, or the expectation of wealth, an instrument of luxury. On the contrary, the luxury of a monarchy rendering marriage expensive and costly, it ought to be there encouraged, both by the riches which women may bestow, and by the hope of the inheritances it is in their power to procure. Thus when monarchy was established at Rome, the whole system of successions was changed. The prætors called the relatives of the woman's side in default of those of the male side; though by the ancient laws, the relatives on the woman's side were never called. The Orphitian *senatus consultum* called children to the succession of their mother; and the Emperors Valentinian, Theodosius, and Arcadius called the grandchildren by the daughter to the succession of the grandfather.[7] In short, the Emperor Justinian[8] left not the least vestige of the ancient right of successions: he established three orders of heirs, the descendants, the ascendants, and the collaterals, without any distinction between the males and females; between the relatives on the woman's side, and those on the male side; and abrogated all laws of this kind, which were still in force: he believed that he followed nature, even in deviating from what he called the embarrassments of the ancient jurisprudence.

Book XXVIII. Of the Origin and Revolutions of the Civil Laws among the French

1. *Different Character of the Laws of the several People of Germany.* After the Franks had quitted their own country, they made a compilation of the Salic laws with the assistance of the sages of their own nation.[5] The tribe of the Ripuarian Franks having joined itself under Clovis[6] to that of the Salians preserved its own

customs; and Theodoric,[9] King of Austrasia, ordered them to be reduced to writing. He collected likewise the customs of those Bavarians and Germans, who were dependent on his kingdom.[10] For Germany having been weakened by the migration of such a multitude of people, the Franks, after conquering all before them, made a retrograde march and extended their dominion into the forests of their ancestors. Very likely the Thuringian code was given by the same Theodoric, since the Thuringians were also his subjects.[11] As the

[1] Book iv, tit. 8, § 3.
[2] Tit. 26, § 6.
[3] That is, the Emperor Pius who changed his name to that of Adrian by adoption.
[4] *Leg. 2, Cod. de jure liberorum. Institutes,* tit. 3, § 4, *de senatus consult. Tertul.*
[5] See the prologue to the Salic Law. Mr. Leibnitz says, in his treatise of the origin of the Franks, that this law was made before the reign of Clovis: but it could not be before the Franks had quitted Germany, for at that time they did not understand the Latin tongue.
[6] See Gregory of Tours.

[7] *Leg. 9, Cod. de suis et legitimis liberis.*
[8] *Leg. 12, ibid.,* and *Nov.* 118, 127.
[9] See the prologue to the Law of the Bavarians, and that to the Salic Law.
[10] *Ibid.*
[11] *Lex Angliorum Werinorum, hoc est Thuringorum.*

Frisians were subdued by Charles Martel and Pepin, their law cannot be prior to those princes.[1] Charlemagne, the first that reduced the Saxons, gave them the law still extant; and we need only read these last two codes to be convinced they came from the hands of conquerors. As soon as the Visigoths, the Burgundians, and the Lombards had founded their respective kingdoms, they reduced their laws to writing, not with an intent of obliging the vanquished nations to conform to their customs, but with a design of following them themselves.

There is an admirable simplicity in the Salic and Ripuarian laws, as well as in those of the Alemans, Bavarians, Thuringians, and Frisians. They breathe an original coarseness and a spirit which no change or corruption of manners had weakened. They received but very few alterations, because all those people, except the Franks, remained in Germany. Even the Franks themselves laid there the foundation of a great part of their empire, so that they had none but German laws. The same cannot be said of the laws of the Visigoths, of the Lombards and Burgundians; their character considerably altered from the great change which happened in the character of those people after they had settled in their new habitations.

The kingdom of the Burgundians did not last long enough to admit of great changes in the laws of the conquering nation. Gundebald and Sigismond, who collected their customs, were almost the last of their kings. The laws of the Lombards received additions rather than changes. The laws of Rotharis were followed by those of Grimoaldus, Luitprandus, Rachis, and Astulphus, but did not assume a new form. It was not so with the laws of the Visigoths;[2] their kings new-moulded them, and had them also new-moulded by the clergy.

The kings indeed of the first race struck out of the Salic and Ripuarian laws whatever was absolutely inconsistent with Christianity, but left the main part untouched.[3] This cannot be said of the laws of the Visigoths.

The laws of the Burgundians, and especially those of the Visigoths, admitted of corporal punishments; these were not tolerated by the Salic and Ripuarian laws;[4] they preserved their character much better.

The Burgundians and Visigoths, whose provinces were greatly exposed, endeavoured to conciliate the affections of the ancient inhabitants, and to give them the most impartial civil laws;[5] but as the Kings of the Franks had established their power, they had no such considerations.[6]

The Saxons, who lived under the dominion of the Franks, were of an intractable temper, and prone to revolt. Hence we find in their laws the severities of a conqueror,[7] which are not to be met with in the other codes of the laws of the barbarians.

We see the spirit of the German laws in the pecuniary punishments, and the spirit of a conqueror in those of an afflictive nature.

The crimes they commit in their own country are subject to corporal punishment; and the spirit of the German laws is followed only in the punishment of crimes committed beyond the extent of their own territory.

They are plainly told that their crimes shall meet with no mercy, and they are refused even the asylum of churches.

The bishops had an immense authority at the court of the Visigoth Kings, the most important affairs being debated in councils. All the maxims, principles and views of the present inquisition are owing to the code of the Visigoths; and the monks have only copied against the Jews the laws formerly enacted by bishops.

In other respects the laws of Gundebald for the Burgundians seem pretty judicious; and those of Rotharis, and of the other Lombard princes, are still more so. But the laws of the Visigoths, those for instance of Recessuinthus, Chaindasuinthus, and Egigas are puerile, ridiculous and foolish; they attain not their end; they are stuffed with rhetoric and void of sense, frivolous in the substance and bombastic in the style.

2. *That the Laws of the Barbarians were all personal.* It is a distinguishing character of

---

[1] They did not know how to write.

[2] They were made by Euric, and amended by Leovigildus. See Isidorus's chronicle. Chaindasuinthus and Recessuinthus reformed them. Egigas ordered the code now extant to be made, and commissioned bishops for that purpose; nevertheless the laws of Chaindasuinthus and Recessuinthus were preserved, as appears by the sixth council of Toledo.

[3] See the prologue to the Law of the Bavarians.

[4] We find only a few in Childebert's decree.

[5] See the prologue to the Code of the Burgundians, and the code itself, especially tit. 12, § 5, and tit. 38. See also Gregory of Tours, ii. 33, and the code of the Visigoths.

[6] See lower down, chapter 3.

[7] See cap. ii. §§ 8 and 9, and cap. iv. §§ 2 and 7.

these laws of the barbarians that they were not confined to a certain district; the Frank was tried by the law of the Franks, the Aleman by that of the Alemans, the Burgundian by that of the Burgundians, and the Roman by the Roman law; nay, so far were the conquerors in those days from reducing their laws to a uniform system or body, that they did not even think of becoming legislators to the people they had conquered.

The original of this I find in the manners of the Germans. These people were parted asunder by marshes, lakes, and forests; and Cæsar observes[1] they were fond of such separations. Their dread of the Romans brought about their reunion; and yet each individual among these mixed people was still to be tried by the established customs of his own nation. Each tribe apart was free and independent; and when they came to be intermixed, the independence still continued; the country was common, the government peculiar; the territory the same, and the nations different. The spirit of personal laws prevailed therefore among those people before ever they set out from their own homes, and they carried it with them into the conquered provinces.

We find this custom established in the formulas of Marculfus,[2] in the codes of the laws of the barbarians, but chiefly in the law of the Ripuarians[3] and the decrees of the kings of the first race,[4] whence the capitularies on that subject in the second race were derived.[5] The children followed the laws of their father,[6] the wife that of her husband,[7] the widow came back to her own original law,[8] and the freedman was under that of his patron.[9] Besides, every man could make choice of what laws he pleased; but the constitution of Lotharius I[10] required that this choice should be made public.

3. Capital Difference between the Salic Laws and those of the Visigoths and Burgundians.

We have already observed that the laws of the

Burgundians and Visigoths were impartial; but it was otherwise with regard to the Salic law, for it established between the Franks and Romans the most mortifying distinctions. When a Frank, a barbarian, or one living under the Salic law happened to be killed, a composition of 200 sols was to be paid to his relatives;[11] only 100 upon the killing of a Roman proprietor,[12] and no more than forty-five for a Roman tributary. The composition for the murder of one of the king's vassals, if a Frank, was 600 sols;[13] if a Roman, though the king's guest,[14] only 300.[15] The Salic law made therefore a cruel distinction between the Frank and Roman lord, and the Frank and Roman commoner.

Further, if a number of people were got together to assault a Frank in his house,[16] and he happened to be killed, the Salic law ordained a composition of 600 sols; but if a Roman or a freedman was assaulted, only one-half that composition.[17] By the same law,[18] if a Roman put a Frank in irons, he was liable to a composition of 30 sols; but if a Frank had thus used a Roman, he paid only 15. A Frank, stripped by a Roman, was entitled to the composition of 62½ sols, and a Roman stripped by a Frank received only 30. Such unequal treatment must needs have been very grievous to a Roman.

And yet a celebrated author[19] forms a system of the establishment of the Franks in Gaul, on a supposition that they were the best friends of the Romans. The Franks then, the best friends of the Romans, they who did, and they who suffered from the Romans such an infinite deal of mischief![20] The Franks, the friends of the Romans, they who, after subduing them by their arms, oppressed them in cold blood by their laws! They were exactly the friends of the Romans as the Tartars who conquered China were the friends of the Chinese.

If some Catholic bishops thought fit to

[1] De Bello Gall., vi.
[2] Book i, formul. 8.
[3] Chapter 31.
[4] That of Clotarius in the year 560, in the edition of the Capitularies of Baluzius, i, art. 4, ib. in fine.
[5] Capitularies added to the Law of the Lombards, i, tit. 25, 71, ii, tit. 41, 7, and tit. 56, 1, 2.
[6] Ibid., ii, tit. 5.
[7] Ibid., ii, tit. 7, 1.
[8] Ibid., 2.
[9] Ibid., ii, tit. 35, 2.
[10] In the Law of the Lombards, ii, tit. 37.

[11] Salic Law, tit. 44, § 1.
[12] Ibid., tit. 44, §§ 15, 7.
[13] Ibid., tit. 41, § 4.
[14] Ibid., § 6.
[15] The principal Romans followed the court, as may be seen by the lives of several bishops, who were there educated; there were hardly any but Romans that knew how to write.
[16] Salic Law, tit. 45.
[17] Lidus whose condition was better than that of a bondman.—Law of the Alemans, 95.
[18] Tit. 35, §§ 3, 4.
[19] The Abbé du Bos.
[20] Witness the expedition of Arbogastes, in Gregory of Tours, History, ii.

make use of the Franks in destroying the Arian Kings, does it follow that they had a desire of living under those barbarous people? And can we hence conclude that the Franks had any particular regard for the Romans? I should draw quite different consequences; the less the Franks had to fear from the Romans, the less indulgence they showed them.

The Abbé du Bos has consulted but indifferent authorities for his history, such as poets and orators; works of parade and ostentation are improper foundations for building systems.

4. *In what manner the Roman Law came to be lost in the Country subject to the Franks, and preserved in that subject to the Goths and Burgundians.* What has been above said will throw some light upon other things, which have hitherto been involved in great obscurity.

The country at this day called France was under the first race governed by the Roman law, or the Theodosian code, and by the different laws of the Barbarians,[1] who settled in those parts.

In the country subject to the Franks, the Salic law was established for the Franks, and the Theodosian code[2] for the Romans. In that subject to the Visigoths, a compilation of the Theodosian code, made by order of Alaric,[3] regulated disputes among the Romans; and the national customs, which Euric caused to be reduced to writing,[4] determined those among the Visigoths. But how comes it, some will say, that the Salic laws gained almost a general authority in the country of the Franks, and the Roman law gradually declined; whilst in the jurisdiction of the Visigoths the Roman law spread itself, and obtained at last a general sway?

My answer is that the Roman law came to be disused among the Franks because of the great advantages accruing from being a Frank, a Barbarian,[5] or a person living under the Salic law; every one, in that case, readily quitting the Roman to live under the Salic law.

The clergy alone retained it,[6] as a change would be of no advantage to them. The difference of conditions and ranks consisted only in the largeness of the composition, as I shall show in another place. Now particular laws[7] allowed the clergy as favourable compositions as those of the Franks, for which reason they retained the Roman law. This law brought no hardships upon them; and in other respects it was most proper for them, as it was the work of Christian emperors.

On the other hand, in the patrimony of the Visigoths, as the Visigoth law[8] gave no civil advantages to the Visigoths over the Romans, the latter had no reason to discontinue living under their own law in order to embrace another. They retained therefore their own laws without adopting those of the Visigoths.

This is still further confirmed in proportion as we proceed in our inquiry. The law of Gundebald was extremely impartial, not favouring the Burgundians more than the Romans. It appears by the preamble to that law that it was made for the Burgundians, and to regulate the disputes which might arise between them and the Romans; and in the latter case the judges were equally divided of a side. This was necessary for particular reasons, drawn from the political regulations of those times.[9] The Roman law was continued in Burgundy, in order to regulate the disputes of Romans among themselves. The latter had no inducement to quit their own law, as in the country of the Franks; and rather as the Salic law was not established in Burgundy, as appears by the famous letter which Agobard wrote to Louis the Pious.

Agobard[10] desired that prince to establish the Salic law in Burgundy; consequently it had not been established there at that time.

---

[1] The Franks, the Visigoths, and Burgundians.
[2] It was finished in 438.
[3] The 20th year of the reign of this prince, and published two years after by Anian, as appears from the preface to that code.
[4] The year 504 of the Spanish era, the Chronicle of Isidorus.
[5] *Francum, aut Barbarum, aut hominem qui Salica lege vivit.*—Salic Law, tit. 45, § 1.

[6] "According to the Roman law under which the church lives," as is said in the law of the Ripuarians, tit. 58, § 1. See also the numberless authorities on this head pronounced by Du Cange, under the words *Lex Romana.*
[7] See the Capitularies added to the Salic law in Lindembrock, at the end of that law, and the different codes of the laws of the Barbarians concerning the privileges of ecclesiastics in this respect. See also the letter of Charlemagne to his son Pepin, King of Italy, in the year 807, in the edition of Baluzius, i, 462, where it is said, that an ecclesiastic should receive a triple compensation; and the *Collection of the Capitularies,* v, art. 302, i, Edition of Baluzius.
[8] See that law.
[9] Of this I shall speak in another place, xxx. 6–9.
[10] Agobard, *Opera.*

Thus the Roman law did, and still does subsist in so many provinces, which formerly depended on this kingdom.

The Roman and Gothic laws continued likewise in the country of the establishment of the Goths, where the Salic law was never received. When Pepin and Charles Martel expelled the Saracens, the towns and provinces which submitted to these princes petitioned for a continuance of their own laws and obtained it;[1] this, in spite of the usages of those times, when all laws were personal, soon made the Roman law to be considered as a real and territorial law in those countries.

This appears by the edict of Charles the Bald, given at Pistes in the year 864, which distinguishes the countries where causes were decided by the Roman law from where it was otherwise.[2]

The edict of Pistes shows two things; one, that there were countries where causes were decided by the Roman law, and others where they were not; and the other, that those countries where the Roman law obtained were precisely the same where it is still followed at this very day, as appears by the said edict:[3] thus the distinction of the provinces of France *under custom* and those *under written law* was already established at the time of the edict of Pistes.

I have observed that in the beginning of the monarchy all laws were personal; and thus when the edict of Pistes distinguishes the countries of the Roman law from those which were otherwise, the meaning is that, in countries which were not of the Roman law, such a multitude of people had chosen to live under some or other of the laws of the Barbarians that there were scarcely any who would be subject to the Roman law; and that in the countries of the Roman law there were few who would choose to live under the laws of the Barbarians.

I am not ignorant that what is here advanced will be reckoned new; but if the things which I assert be true, surely they are very ancient. After all, what great matter is it, wheth-er they come from me, from the Valesiuses, or from the Bignons?

5. *The same Subject continued.* The law of Gundebald subsisted a long time among the Burgundians, in conjunction with the Roman law; it was still in use under Louis the Pious, as Agobard's letter plainly evinces. In like manner, though the edict of Pistes calls the country occupied by the Visigoths the country of the Roman law, yet the law of the Visigoths was always in force there; as appears by the synod of Troyes held under Louis the Stammerer, in the year 878, that is, fourteen years after the edict of Pistes.

In process of time the Gothic and Burgundian laws fell into disuse even in their own country, which was owing to those general causes that everywhere suppressed the personal laws of the Barbarians.

6. *How the Roman Law kept its Ground in the Demesne of the Lombards.* The facts all coincide with my principles. The law of the Lombards was impartial, and the Romans were under no temptation to quit their own for it. The motive which prevailed with the Romans under the Franks to make choice of the Salic law did not take place in Italy; hence the Roman law maintained itself there, together with that of the Lombards.

It even fell out that the latter gave way to the Roman institutes, and ceased to be the law of the ruling nation; and though it continued to be that of the principal nobility, yet the greatest part of the cities formed themselves into republics, and the nobility mouldered away of themselves, or were destroyed.[4] The citizens of the new republics had no inclination to adopt a law which established the custom of judiciary combats, and whose institutions retained much of the customs and usages of chivalry. As the clergy of those days, a clergy even then so powerful in Italy, lived almost all under the Roman law, the number of those who followed the institutions of the Lombards must have daily diminished.

Besides, the institutions of the Lombards had not that extent, that majesty of the Roman law, by which Italy was reminded of her universal dominion. The institutions of the Lombards and the Roman law could be then of no other use than to furnish out statutes for those cities that were erected into repub-

[1] See Gervais of Tilbury, in Duchesne's Collection, iii, p. 366. And a chronicle of the year 759, produced by Catel, Hist. of Languedoc. And the uncertain author of the Life of Louis the Debonnaire, upon the demand made by the people of Septimania, at the assembly in Carisiaco, in Duchesne's Collection, ii, p. 316.

[2] Art. 16. See also art. 20.

[3] See arts. 12 and 16 of the edict of Pistes *in Cavilono, in Narbona,* &c.

[4] See what Machiavelli says of the ruin of the ancient nobility of Florence.

lics. Now which could better furnish them, the institutions of the Lombards that determined on some particular cases, or the Roman law which embraced them all?

7. *How the Roman Law came to be lost in Spain.* Things happened otherwise in Spain. The law of the Visigoths prevailed, and the Roman law was lost. Chaindasuinthus[1] and Recessuinthus proscribed the Roman laws,[2] and even forbade citing them in their courts of judicature. Recessuinthus was likewise author of the law which took off the prohibition of marriage between the Goths and Romans.[3] It is evident that these two laws had the same spirit; this king wanted to remove the principal causes of separation which subsisted between the Goths and the Romans. Now it was thought that nothing made a wider separation than the prohibition of intermarriages, and the liberty of living under different institutions.

But though the kings of the Visigoths had proscribed the Roman law, it still subsisted in the demesnes they possessed in South Gaul.[4] These countries being distant from the centre of the monarchy lived in a state of great independence. We see from the history of Vamba, who ascended the throne in 672, that the natives of the country had become the prevailing party.[5] Hence the Roman law had greater authority and the Gothic less. The Spanish laws neither suited their manners nor their actual situation; the people might likewise be obstinately attached to the Roman law, because they had annexed to it the idea of liberty. Besides, the laws of Chaindasuinthus and of Recessuinthus contained most severe regulations against the Jews; but these Jews had a vast deal of power in South Gaul. The author of the history of King Vamba calls these provinces the brothel of the Jews. When the Saracens invaded these provinces, it was by invitation; and who could have invited them but the Jews or the Romans? The Goths were the first that were oppressed, because they were the ruling nation. We see in Procopius, that during their calamities they withdrew out of Narbonne Gaul into Spain.[6] Doubtless, under this misfortune, they took refuge in those provinces of Spain which still held out; and the number of those who in South Gaul lived under the law of the Visigoths was thereby greatly diminished.

8. *A false Capitulary.* Did not that wretched compiler Benedictus Levita attempt to transform this Visigoth establishment, which prohibited the use of Roman law, into a capitulary[7] ascribed since to Charlemagne? He made of this particular institution a general one, as if he intended to exterminate the Roman law throughout the universe.

9. *In what manner the Codes of Barbarian Laws and the Capitularies came to be lost.* The Salic, the Ripuarian, Burgundian, and Visigoth laws came, by degrees, to be disused among the French in the following manner:

As fiefs became hereditary, and arrière-fiefs extended, many usages were introduced, to which these laws were no longer applicable. Their spirit indeed was continued, which was to regulate most disputes by fines. But as the value of money was, doubtless, subject to change, the fines were also changed; and we see several charters,[8] where the lords fixed the fines, that were payable in their petty courts. Thus the spirit of the law was followed, without adhering to the law itself.

Besides, as France was divided into a number of petty lordships, which acknowledged rather a feudal than a political dependence, it was very difficult for only one law to be authorised. And, indeed, it would be impossible to see it observed. The custom no longer prevailed of sending extraordinary officers[9] into the provinces to inspect the administration of justice and political affairs; it appears, even by the charters, that when new fiefs were established our kings divested themselves of the right of sending those officers. Thus, when almost everything had become a fief, these officers could not be employed; there was no longer a common law because no one could enforce the observance of it.

The Salic, Burgundian, and Visigoth laws

1 He began to reign in the year 642.
2 "We will no longer be harassed either by foreign or by the Roman laws."—Law of the Visigoths, ii, tit. 1, §§ 9, 10.
3 Law of the Visigoths, iii, tit. 1, 1.
4 See Book iv. 19, 26.
5 The revolt of these provinces was a general defection, as appears by the sentence in the sequel of the history. Paulus and his adherents were Romans; they were even favoured by the bishops. Vamba durst not put to death the rebels whom he had quelled. The author of the history calls Narbonne Gaul the nursery of treason.

6 *De Bello Gothorum,* i. 13.
7 Capitularies, vi, 343, year 1613, edition of Baluzius, i, p. 981.
8 M. de la Thaumassière has collected many of them. See, for instance, chapters 41, 46, and others.
9 *Missi Dominici.*

were, therefore, extremely neglected at the end of the second race; and at the beginning of the third, they were scarcely ever mentioned.

Under the first and second race, the nation was often assembled; that is, the lords and bishops; the commons were not yet thought of. In these assemblies, attempts were made to regulate the clergy, a body which formed itself, if I may so speak, under the conquerors, and established its privileges. The laws made in these assemblies are what we call the Capitularies. Hence four things ensued: the feudal laws were established and a great part of the church revenues was administered by those laws; the clergy effected a wider separation, and neglected those decrees of reformation where they themselves were not the only reformers;[1] a collection was made of the canons of councils and of the decretals of popes;[2] and these the clergy received, as coming from a purer source. Ever since the erection of the grand fiefs, our kings, as we have already observed, had no longer any deputies in the provinces to enforce the observance of their laws; and hence it is that, under the third race, we find no more mention made of Capitularies.

10. *The same Subject continued.* Several capitularies were added to the law of the Lombards, as well as to the Salic and Bavarian laws. The reason of this has been a matter of inquiry; but it must be sought for in the thing itself. There were several sorts of capitularies. Some had relation to political government, others to economical, most of them to ecclesiastical polity, and some few to civil government. Those of the last species were added to the civil law, that is, to the personal laws of each nation; for which reason it is said in the

[1] Let not the bishops, says Charles the Bald, in the Capitulary of 844, art. 8, under pretence of the authority of making canons, oppose this constitution, or neglect the observance of it. It seems he already foresaw the fall thereof .

[2] In the collection of canons a vast number of the decretals of the popes were inserted; they were very few in the ancient collection. Dionysius Exiguus put a great many into his; but that of Isidorus Mercator was stuffed with genuine and spurious decretals. The old collection obtained in France till Charlemagne. This prince received from the hand of Pope Adrian I the collection of Dionysius Exiguus, and caused it to be accepted. The collection of Isidorus Mercator appeared in France about the reign of Charlemagne; people grew passionately fond of it: to this succeeded what we now call *the course of canon law.*

Capitularies that there is nothing stipulated therein contrary to the Roman law.[3] In effect, those capitularies regarding economical, ecclesiastical, or political government had no relation to that law; and those concerning civil government had reference only to the laws of the barbarous people, which were explained, amended, enlarged, or abridged. But the adding of these capitularies to the personal laws occasioned, I imagine, the neglect of the very body of the Capitularies themselves; in times of ignorance, the abridgment of a work often causes the loss of the work itself.

11. *Other Causes of the Disuse of the Codes of Barbarian Laws, as well as of the Roman Law, and of the Capitularies.* When the German nations subdued the Roman empire, they learned the use of writing; and, in imitation of the Romans, they wrote down their own usages, and digested them into codes.[4] The unhappy reigns which followed that of Charlemagne, the invasions of the Normans and the civil wars, plunged the conquering nations again into the darkness out of which they had emerged, so that reading and writing were quite neglected. Hence it is, that in France and Germany the written laws of the Barbarians, as well as the Roman law and the Capitularies fell into oblivion. The use of writing was better preserved in Italy, where reigned the Popes and the Greek Emperors, and where there were flourishing cities, which enjoyed almost the only commerce in those days. To this neighbourhood of Italy it was owing that the Roman law was preserved in the provinces of Gaul, formerly subject to the Goths and Burgundians; and so much the more, as this law was there a territorial institution, and a kind of privilege. It is probable that the disuse of the Visigoth laws in Spain proceeded from the want of writing, and by the loss of so many laws, customs were everywhere established.

Personal laws fell to the ground. Compositions, and what they call *Freda,*[5] were regulated more by custom than by the text of these laws. Thus, as in the establishment of the

[3] See the edict of Pistes, art. 20.
[4] This is expressly set down in some preambles to these codes: we even find in the laws of the Saxons and Frisians different regulations, according to the different districts. To these usages were added some particular regulations suitable to the exigency of circumstances; such were the severe laws against the Saxons.
[5] Of this I shall speak elsewhere (xxx. 14).

monarchy, they had passed from German customs to written laws; some ages after, they came back from written laws to unwritten customs.

12. *Of local Customs. Revolution of the Laws of barbarous Nations, as well as of the Roman Law.* By several memorials it appears, that there were local customs, as early as the first and second race. We find mention made of the "custom of the place,"[1] of the "ancient usage,"[2] of "custom,"[3] of "laws,"[4] and of "customs." It has been the opinion of some authors that what went by the name of customs were the laws of the barbarous nations, and what had the appellation of law were the Roman institutes. This cannot possibly be. King Pepin ordained[5] that wherever there should happen to be no law, custom should be complied with; but that it should never be preferred to the law. Now, to pretend that the Roman law was preferred to the codes of the laws of the Barbarians is subverting all memorials of antiquity, and especially those codes of Barbarian laws, which constantly affirm the contrary.

So far were the laws of the barbarous nations from being those customs, that it was these very laws, as personal institutions, which introduced them. The Salic law, for instance, was a personal law; but generally, or almost generally, in places inhabited by the Salian Franks, this Salic law, how personal soever, became, in respect to those Salian Franks, a territorial institution, and was personal only in regard to those Franks who lived elsewhere. Now if several Burgundians, Alemans, or even Romans should happen to have frequent disputes, in a place where the Salic law was territorial, they must have been determined by the laws of those people; and a great number of decisions agreeable to some of those laws must have introduced new customs into the country. This explains the constitution of Pepin. It was natural that those customs should affect even the Franks who lived on the spot, in cases not decided by the Salic law; but it was not natural that they should prevail over the Salic law itself.

Thus there were in each place an established law and received customs which served as a supplement to that law when they did not contradict it.

They might even happen to supply a law that was in no way territorial; and to continue the same example, if a Burgundian was judged by the law of his own nation, in a place where the Salic law was territorial, and the case happened not to be explicitly mentioned in the very text of this law, there is no manner of doubt but that judgment would have been passed upon him according to the custom of the place.

In the reign of King Pepin, the customs then established had not the same force as the laws; but it was not long before the laws gave way to the customs. And as new regulations are generally remedies that imply a present evil, it may well be imagined that as early as Pepin's time, they began to prefer the customs to the established laws.

What has been said sufficiently explains the manner in which the Roman law began so very early to become territorial, as may be seen in the edict of Pistes; and how the Gothic law continued still in force, as appears by the synod of Troyes above-mentioned.[6] The Roman had become the general personal law, and the Gothic the particular personal law; consequently the Roman law was territorial. But how came it, some will ask, that the personal laws of the Barbarians fell everywhere into disuse, while the Roman law was continued as a territorial institution in the Visigoth and Burgundian provinces? I answer that even the Roman law had very nearly the same fate as the other personal institutions; otherwise we would still have the Theodosian code in those provinces where the Roman law was territorial, whereas we have the Institutes of Justinian. Those provinces retained scarcely anything more than the name of the country under the Roman, or written law, than the natural affection which people have for their own institutions, especially when they consider them as privileges, and a few regulations of the Roman law which were not yet forgotten. This was, however, sufficient to produce such an effect that, when Justinian's compilation appeared, it was received in the provinces of the Gothic and Burgundian demesne as a written law, whereas it was admitted only as written reason in the ancient demesne of the Franks.

13. *Difference between the Salic law, or that of the Salian Franks, and that of the Ripuarian*

[1] Preface to Marculfus, *Formulæ.*
[2] Law of the Lombards, ii, tit. 58, § 3.
[3] *Ibid.*, tit. 41, § 6.
[4] Life of St. Leger.
[5] Law of the Lombards, ii, tit. 41, § 6.
[6] See chapter 5.

Franks and other barbarous Nations. The Salic law did not allow of the custom of negative proofs; that is, if a person brought a demand or charge against another, he was obliged by the Salic law to prove it, and it was not sufficient for the second to deny it, which is agreeable to the laws of almost all nations.

The law of the Ripuarian Franks had quite a different spirit;[1] it was contented with negative proofs, and the person, against whom a demand or accusation was brought, might clear himself, in most cases, by swearing, in conjunction with a certain number of witnesses, that he had not committed the crime laid to his charge. The number of witnesses who were obliged to swear[2] increased in proportion to the importance of the affair; sometimes it amounted to seventy-two.[3] The laws of the Alemans, Bavarians, Thuringians, Frisians, Saxons, Lombards, and Burgundians were formed on the same plan as those of the Ripuarians.

I observed that the Salic law did not allow of negative proofs. There was one case, however, in which they were allowed:[4] but even then they were not admitted alone, and without the concurrence of positive proofs. The plaintiff caused witnesses to be heard,[5] in order to ground his action, the defendant produced also witnesses on his side, and the judge was to come at the truth by comparing those testimonies.[6] This practice was vastly different from that of the Ripuarian, and other barbarous laws, where it was customary for the party accused to clear himself by swearing he was not guilty, and by making his relatives also swear that he had told the truth. These laws could be suitable only to a people remarkable for their natural simplicity and candour; we shall see presently that the legislators were obliged to take proper methods to prevent their being abused.

14. *Another Difference.* The Salic law did not admit of the trial by combat, though it had been received by the laws of the Ripuarians[7]

and of almost all the barbarous nations.[8] To me it seems that the law of combat was a natural consequence and a remedy of the law which established negative proofs. When an action was brought, and it appeared that the defendant was going to elude it by an oath, what other remedy was left to a military man,[9] who saw himself upon the point of being confounded, than to demand satisfaction for the injury done to him: and even for the attempt of perjury? The Salic law, which did not allow the custom of negative proofs, neither admitted nor had any need of the trial by combat; but the laws of the Ripuarians[10] and of the other barbarous nations[11] who had adopted the practice of negative proofs, were obliged to establish the trial by combat.

Whoever will please to examine the two famous regulations of Gundebald, King of Burgundy, concerning this subject will find they are derived from the very nature of the thing.[12] It was necessary, according to the language of the Barbarian laws, to rescue the oath out of the hands of a person who was going to abuse it.

Among the Lombards, the law of Rotharis admits of cases in which a man who had made his defence by oath should not be suffered to undergo the hardship of a duel. This custom spread itself further:[13] we shall presently see the mischiefs that arose from it, and how they were obliged to return to the ancient practice.

15. *A Reflection.* I do not pretend to deny that in the changes made in the code of the Barbarian laws, in the regulations added to that code, and in the body of the Capitularies, it is possible to find some passages where the trial by combat is not a consequence of the negative proof. Particular circumstances might, in

---

[1] This relates to what Tacitus says, *De Moribus Germanorum*, 28, that the Germans had general and particular customs.

[2] Law of the Ripuarians, tit. 6, 7, 8, and others.

[3] *Ibid.*, tit. 11, 12, 17.

[4] It was when an accusation was brought against an Antrustio, that is, the king's vassal, who was supposed to be possessed of a greater degree of liberty. See *Pactus legis Salicæ*, tit. 76.

[5] *Ibid.*

[6] According to the practice now followed in England.

[7] Tit. 32; tit. 57, § 2; tit. 59, § 4.

[8] See the following note.

[9] This spirit appears in the Law of Ripuarians, tit. 59, § 4, and tit. 67, § 5, and in the Capitulary of Louis the Debonnaire, added to the law of the Ripuarians in the year 803, art. 22.

[10] See that law.

[11] The law of the Frisians, Lombards, Bavarians, Saxons, Thuringians, and Burgundians.

[12] In the Law of the Burgundians, tit. 8, §§ 1 and 2, on criminal affairs; and tit. 45, which extends also to civil affairs. See also the law of the Thuringians, tit. 1, § 31; tit. 7, § 6; and tit. 8; and the law of the Alemans, tit. 89; the law of the Bavarians, tit. 8, cap. ii, § 6, and cap. iii, § 1, and tit. 9, cap. iv, § 4; the law of the Frisians, tit. 2, § 3, and tit. 14, § 4; the law of the Lombards, i, tit. 32, § 3, and tit. 35, § 1, and ii, tit. 35, § 2.

[13] See cap. xviii, towards the end.

the course of many ages, give rise to particular laws. I speak only of the general spirit of the laws of the Germans, of their nature and origin; I speak of the ancient customs of those people that were either hinted at or established by those laws; and this is the only matter in question.

16. *Of the Ordeal or Trial by boiling Water, established by the Salic Law.* The Salic law[1] allowed of the ordeal, or trial by boiling water; and as this trial was excessively cruel, the law found an expedient to soften its rigour.[2] It permitted the person, who had been summoned to make the trial with boiling water, to ransom his hand, with the consent of the adverse party. The accuser, for a particular sum determined by the law, might be satisfied with the oath of a few witnesses, declaring that the accused had not committed the crime. This was a particular case, in which the Salic law admitted of the negative proof.

This trial was a thing privately agreed upon, which the law permitted only, but did not ordain. The law gave a particular indemnity to the accuser, who would allow the accused to make his defence by a negative proof: the plaintiff was at liberty to be satisfied with the oath of the defendant, as he was at liberty to forgive him the injury.

The law contrived a middle course,[3] that before sentence passed, both parties, the one through fear of a terrible trial, the other for the sake of a small indemnity, should terminate their disputes, and put an end to their animosities. It is plain, that when once this negative proof was completed, nothing more was requisite; and, therefore, that the practice of legal duels could not be a consequence of this particular regulation of the Salic law.

17. *Particular Notions of our Ancestors.* It is astonishing that our ancestors should thus rest the honour, fortune and life of the subject, on things that depended less on reason than on hazard, and that they should incessantly make use of proofs incapable of convicting, and that had no manner of connection either with innocence or guilt.

The Germans, who had never been subdued,[4] enjoyed an excessive independence.

Different families waged war with each other[5] to obtain satisfaction for murders, robberies or affronts. This custom was moderated by subjecting these hostilities to rules; it was ordained that they should be no longer committed but by the direction and under the eye of the magistrate.[6] This was far preferable to a general licence of annoying each other.

As the Turks in their civil wars look upon the first victory as a decision of heaven in favour of the victor, so the inhabitants of Germany in their private quarrels considered the event of a combat as a decree of Providence, ever attentive to punish the criminal or the usurper.

Tacitus informs us that when one German nation intended to declare war against another, they looked out for a prisoner who was to fight with one of their people, and by the event they judged of the success of the war. A nation who believed that public quarrels could be determined by a single combat might very well think that it was proper also for deciding the disputes of individuals.

Gundebald, King of Burgundy, gave the greatest sanction to the custom of legal duels.[7] The reason he assigns for this law is mentioned in his edict. "It is," says he, "in order to prevent our subjects from attesting by oath what is uncertain, and perjuring themselves about what is certain." Thus, while the clergy declared that an impious law which permitted combats,[8] the Burgundian Kings looked upon that as a sacrilegious law which authorized the taking of an oath.

The trial by combat had some reason for it, founded on experience. In a military nation, cowardice supposes other vices; it is an argument of a person's having deviated from the principles of his education, of his being insensible of honour, and of having refused to be directed by those maxims which govern other men; it shows that he neither fears their contempt, nor sets any value upon their esteem. Men of any tolerable extraction seldom want either the dexterity requisite to co-operate with strength, or the strength necessary to concur with courage; for as they set a value upon honour, they are practised in matters without

---

[1] As also some other laws of the Barbarians.
[2] Tit. 56.
[3] *Ibid.*
[4] This appears by what Tacitus says, *Omnibus idem habitus.—De Moribus Germanorum,* 4.

[5] Velleius Paterculus, ii. 118, says that the Germans decided all their disputes by the sword.
[6] See the codes of Barbarian laws, and in respect to less ancient times, Beaumanoir, *Ancient Custom of Beauvoisis.*
[7] Law of the Burgundians, cap. xlv.
[8] See the works of Agobard.

which this honour cannot be obtained. Besides, in a military nation, where strength, courage and prowess are esteemed, crimes really odious are those which arise from fraud, artifice, and cunning, that is, from cowardice.

With regard to the trial by fire, after the party accused had put his hand on a hot iron, or in boiling water, they wrapped the hand in a bag and sealed it up; if after three days there appeared no mark, he was acquitted. Is it not plain, that among people inured to the handling of arms, the impression made on a rough or callous skin by the hot iron or by boiling water could not be so great as to be seen three days afterwards? And if there appeared any mark, it showed that the person who had undergone the trial was an effeminate fellow. Our peasants are not afraid to handle hot iron with their callous hands; and, with regard to the women, the hands of those who worked hard might be very well able to resist hot iron. The ladies did not want champions to defend their cause; and in a nation where there was no luxury, there was no middle state.[1]

By the law of the Thuringians[2] a woman accused of adultery was condemned to the trial by boiling water only when there was no champion to defend her; and the law of the Ripuarians admits of this trial[3] only when a person had no witnesses to appear in justification. Now a woman that could not prevail upon any one relative to defend her cause, or a man that could not produce one single witness to attest his honesty, was, from those very circumstances, sufficiently convicted.

I conclude, therefore, that under the circumstances of time in which the trial by combat and the trial by hot iron and boiling water obtained, there was such an agreement between those laws and the manners of the people, that the laws were rather unjust in themselves than productive of injustice, that the effects were more innocent than the cause, that they were more contrary to equity than prejudicial to its rights, more unreasonable than tyrannical.

18. *In what manner the Custom of judicial Combats gained Ground.* From Agobard's letter to Louis the Debonnaire, it might be inferred that the custom of judicial combats was not established among the Franks; for having represented to that prince the abuses of the law of Gundebald, he desires that private disputes should be decided in Burgundy by the law of the Franks. But as it is well known from other quarters that the trial by combat prevailed at that time in France, this has been the cause of some perplexity. However, the difficulty may be solved by what I have said; the law of the Salian Franks did not allow of this kind of trial and that of the Ripuarian Franks did.[4]

But, notwithstanding the clamours of the clergy, the custom of judicial combats gained ground continually in France; and I shall presently make it appear that the clergy themselves were in a great measure the occasion of it.

It is the law of the Lombards that furnishes us with this proof. "There has been long since a detestable custom introduced," says the preamble to the constitution of Otho II:[5] "this is, that if the title to an estate was said to be false, the person who claimed under that title made oath upon the Gospel that it was genuine; and without any preceding judgment he took possession of the estate; so that they who would perjure themselves were sure of gaining their point." The Emperor Otho I having caused himself to be crowned at Rome[6] at the very time that a council was there under Pope John XII, all the lords of Italy represented to that prince the necessity of enacting a law to reform this horrible abuse.[7] The Pope and the Emperor were of opinion that the affair should be referred to the council which was to be shortly held at Ravenna.[8] There the lords made the same demands, and redoubled their complaints; but the affair was put off once more, under pretence of the absence of particular persons. When Otho II and Conrad, King of Burgundy, arrived in Italy,[9] they had a conference at Verona[10] with the Italian lords,[11] and at their repeated solicitations, the Emperor, with their unanimous consent, made a law, that whenever there happened any disputes about inheritances, while one of the par-

---

[1] See Beaumanoir, *Ancient Customs of Beauvoisis*, 61. See also the Law of the Angli, cap. xiv, where the trial by boiling water is only a subsidiary proof.
[2] Tit. 14.
[3] Cap. xxxi, § 5.

[4] See this law, tit. 59, § 4, and tit. 67, § 5.
[5] Law of the Lombards, ii, tit. 55, cap. xxxiv.
[6] The year 962.
[7] Law of the Lombards, ii, tit. 55, cap. xxxiv.
[8] It was held in the year 967, in the presence of Pope John XIII and of the Emperor Otho I.
[9] Otho II's uncle, son to Rodolphus, and King of Transjurian Burgundy.
[10] In the year 988.
[11] Law of the Lombards, ii, tit. 55, cap. xxxiv.

ties insisted upon the legality of his title and the other maintained its being false, the affair should be decided by combat; that the same rule should be observed in contests relating to fiefs; and that the clergy should be subject to the same law, but should fight by their champions. Here we see that the nobility insisted on the trial by combat because of the inconvenience of the proof introduced by the clergy; that notwithstanding the clamours of the nobility, the notoriousness of the abuse which called out loudly for redress, and the authority of Otho who came into Italy to speak and act as master, still the clergy held out in two councils; in fine, that the joint concurrence of the nobility and princes having obliged the clergy to submit, the custom of judicial combats must have been considered as a privilege of the nobility, as a barrier against injustice and as a security of property, and from that very moment this custom must have gained ground. And this was effected at a time when the power of the Emperors was great, and that of the popes inconsiderable; at a time when the Othos came to revive the dignity of the empire in Italy.

I shall make one reflection which will corroborate what has been above said, namely, that the institution of negative proofs entailed that of judicial combats. The abuse complained of to the Othos was, that a person who was charged with having a false title to an estate, defended himself by a negative proof, declaring upon the Gospels it was not false. What was done to reform the abuse of a law which had been mutilated? The custom of combat was revived.

I hastened to speak of the constitution of Otho II, in order to give a clear idea of the disputes between the clergy and the laity of those times. There had been indeed a constitution of Lotharius I[1] of an earlier date, a sovereign who, upon the same complaints and disputes, being desirous of securing the just possession of property, had ordained that the notary should make oath that the deed or title was not forged; and if the notary should happen to die, the witnesses should be sworn who had signed it. The evil, however, still continued, till they were obliged at length to have recourse to the remedy above-mentioned.

Before that time I find that, in the general assemblies held by Charlemagne, the nation

represented to him[2] that in the actual state of things it was extremely difficult for either the accuser or the accused to avoid perjuring themselves, and that for this reason it was much better to revive the judicial combat, which was accordingly done.

The usage of judicial combats gained ground among the Burgundians, and that of an oath was limited. Theodoric, King of Italy, suppressed the single combat among the Ostrogoths;[3] and the laws of Chaindasuinthus and Recessuinthus seemed as if they would abolish the very idea of it. But these laws were so little respected in Narbonne Gaul, that they looked upon the legal duel as a privilege of the Goths.[4]

The Lombards who conquered Italy after the Ostrogoths had been destroyed by the Greeks, introduced the custom of judicial combat into that country, but their first laws gave a check to it.[5] Charlemagne,[6] Louis the Debonnaire, and the Othos made divers general constitutions, which we find inserted in the laws of the Lombards and added to the Salic laws, whereby the practice of legal duels, at first in criminal, and afterwards in civil cases, obtained a greater extent. They knew not what to do. The negative proof by oath had its inconveniences; that of legal duels had its inconveniences also; hence they often changed, according as the one or the other affected them most.

On the one hand, the clergy were pleased to see that in all secular affairs people were obliged to have recourse to the altar,[7] and, on the other, a haughty nobility were fond of maintaining their rights by the sword.

I would not have it inferred that it was the clergy who introduced the custom so much complained of by the nobility. This custom was derived from the spirit of the Barbarian laws, and from the establishment of negative

[2] *Ibid.*, § 23.
[3] Cassiodorus, iii. 23, 24.
[4] The anonymous author of the life of Louis the Debonnaire.
[5] See in the Law of the Lombards, i, tit. 4, and tit. 9, § 23, and ii, tit. 35 §§ 4 and 5, and tit. 55 §§ 1, 2, 3. The regulations of Rotharis; and in § 15, that of Luitprandus.
[6] *Ibid.*, ii, tit. 55, § 23.
[7] The judicial oaths were made at that time in the churches, and during the first race of our kings there was a chapel set apart in the royal palace for the affairs that were to be thus decided. See Marculfus, *Formulæ* i. 38. The Law of the Ripuarians, tit. 59, § 4, tit. 65, § 5. The *History* of Gregory of Tours; and the Capitulary of the year 803, added to the Salic Law.

[1] *Ibid.*, § 33. In the copy that Muratori made use of it is attributed to the Emperor Guido.

proofs. But a practice that contributed to the impunity of such a number of criminals, having given some people reason to think it was proper to make use of the sanctity of the churches in order to strike terror into the guilty, and to intimidate perjurers, the clergy maintained this usage and the practice which attended it: for in other respects they were absolutely averse to negative proofs. We find in Beaumanoir[1] that this kind of proof was never allowed in ecclesiastic courts, which contributed greatly, without doubt, to its suppression, and to weaken in this respect the regulation of the codes of the Barbarian laws.

This will convince us more strongly of the connection between the usage of negative proofs and that of judicial combats, of which I have said so much. The lay tribunals admitted of both, and both were rejected by the ecclesiastic courts.

In choosing the trial by duel the nation followed its military spirit; for while this was established as a divine decision, the trials by the cross, by cold or boiling waters, which had been also regarded in the same lights, were abolished.

Charlemagne ordained that, if any difference should arise between his children, it should be terminated by the judgment of the cross. Louis the Debonnaire[2] limited this judgment to ecclesiastic affairs; his son Lotharius abolished it in all cases; nay, he suppressed even the trial by cold water.[3]

I do not pretend to say that, at a time when so few usages were universally received, these trials were not revived in some churches, especially as they are mentioned in a charter of Philip Augustus,[4] but I affirm that they were very seldom practised. Beaumanoir,[5] who lived at the time of St. Louis and a little after, enumerating the different kinds of trial, mentions that of judicial combat, but not a word of the others.

19. *A new Reason of the Disuse of the Salic and Roman Laws, as also of the Capitularies.* I have already mentioned the reasons that had destroyed the authority of the Salic and Roman laws, as also of the Capitularies; here I shall add that the principal cause was the great extension given to judiciary combats.

As the Salic laws did not admit of this custom, they became in some measure useless, and fell into oblivion. In like manner the Roman laws, which also rejected this custom, were laid aside; their whole attention was then taken up in establishing the law of judicial combats, and in forming a proper digest of the several cases that might happen on those occasions. The regulations of the Capitularies became likewise of no manner of service. Thus it is that such a number of laws lost all their authority, without our being able to tell the precise time in which it was lost; they fell into oblivion, and we cannot find any others that were substituted in their place.

Such a nation had no need of written laws; hence its written laws might very easily fall into disuse.

If there happened to be any disputes between two parties, they had only to order a single combat. For this no great knowledge or abilities were requisite.

All civil and criminal actions are reduced to facts. It is upon these facts they fought; and not only the substance of the affair, but likewise the incidents and imparlances were decided by combat, as Beaumanoir observes, who produces several instances.[6]

I find that, towards the commencement of the third race, the jurisprudence of those times related entirely to precedents; everything was regulated by the point of honour. If the judge was not obeyed, he insisted upon satisfaction from the person that contemned his authority. At Bourges, if the provost had summoned a person and he refused to come, his way of proceeding was to tell him, "I sent for thee, and thou didst not think it worth thy while to come; I demand therefore satisfaction for this thy contempt." Upon which they fought.[7] Louis the Fat reformed this custom.[8]

The custom of legal duels prevailed at Orleans, even in all demands of debt.[9] Louis the Young declared that this custom should take place only when the demand exceeded five sous. This ordinance was a local law; for in St. Louis' time it was sufficient that the value was more than twelve deniers.[10] Beaumanoir[11] had

[1] Chapter 39, p. 212.
[2] We find his Constitutions inserted in the Law of the Lombards, and at the end of the Salic Laws.
[3] In a constitution inserted in the Law of the Lombards, ii, tit. 55, § 31.
[4] In the year 1200.
[5] *Ancient Custom of Beauvoisis,* 39.

[6] *Ibid.,* 61, pp. 309, 310.
[7] Charter of Louis the Fat in the year 1145, in the Collection of Ordinances.
[8] *Ibid.*
[9] Charter of Louis the Young, in 1168, in the Collection of Ordinances.
[10] See Beaumanoir, 63, p. 325.
[11] See the *Ancient Custom of Beauvoisis,* 28, p. 203.

heard a gentleman of the law affirm that formerly there had been a bad custom in France of hiring a champion for a certain time to fight their battles in all causes. This shows that the custom of judiciary combat must have prevailed at that time to a wonderful extent.

20. *Origin of the Point of Honour.* We meet with inexplicable enigmas in the codes of laws of the Barbarians. The law of the Frisians[1] allows only half a sou in composition to a person that had been beaten with a stick, and yet for ever so small a wound it allows more. By the Salic law, if a freeman gave three blows with a stick to another freeman, he paid three sous; if he drew blood, he was punished as if he had wounded him with steel, and he paid fifteen sous: thus the punishment was proportioned to the greatness of the wound. The law of the Lombards established different compositions for one, two, three, four blows, and so on.[2] At present, a single blow is equivalent to a hundred thousand.

The constitution of Charlemagne, inserted in the law of the Lombards, ordains that those who were allowed the trial by combat should fight with bastons.[3] Perhaps this was out of regard to the clergy; or probably, as the usage of legal duels gained ground, they wanted to render them less sanguinary. The capitulary of Louis the Debonnaire allows the liberty of choosing to fight either with the sword or baston.[4] In process of time none but bondmen fought with the baston.[5]

Here I see the first rise and formation of the particular articles of our point of honour. The accuser began by declaring in the presence of the judge that such a person had committed such an action, and the accused made answer that he lied,[6] upon which the judge gave orders for the duel. It became then an established rule that whenever a person had the lie given him, it was incumbent on him to fight.

Upon a man's declaring that he would fight,[7] he could not afterwards depart from his word; if he did, he was condemned to a penalty. Hence this rule ensued, that whenever a person had engaged his word, honour forbade him to recall it.

Gentlemen fought one another on horse-back, and armed at all points;[8] villains fought on foot and with bastons.[9] Hence it followed that the baston was looked upon as the instrument of insults and affronts,[10] because to strike a man with it was treating him like a villain.

None but villains fought with their faces uncovered,[11] so that none but they could receive a blow on the face. Therefore, a box on the ear became an injury that must be expiated with blood, because the person who received it had been treated as a villain.

The several people of Germany were no less sensible than we of the point of honour; nay, they were more so. Thus the most distant relatives took a very considerable share to themselves in every affront, and on this all their codes are founded. The law of the Lombards ordains[12] that whosoever goes attended with servants to beat a man unawares, in order to load him with shame and to render him ridiculous, should pay half the composition which he would owe if he had killed him;[13] and if through the same motive he tied or bound him, he would pay three-quarters of the same composition.

Let us then conclude that our forefathers were extremely sensible of affronts; but that affronts of a particular kind, such as being struck with a certain instrument on a certain part of the body, and in a certain manner, were as yet unknown to them. All this was included in the affront of being beaten, and in this case the amount of violence determined the magnitude of the outrage.

21. *A new Reflection upon the Point of Honour among the Germans.* "It was a great infamy," says Tacitus,[14] "among the Germans for a person to leave his buckler behind him in battle; for which reason many after a misfortune of this kind have destroyed themselves." Thus the ancient Salic law[15] allows a composition of fifteen sous to any person that had been injuriously reproached with having left his buckler behind him.

---

[1] *Additio sapientium Wilemari*, tit. 5.
[2] Book i, tit. 6, § 3.
[3] Book ii, tit. 5, § 23.
[4] Added to the Salic law in 819.
[5] See Beaumanoir, 64, p. 328.
[6] *Ibid.*, p. 329.
[7] See Beaumanoir, 3, p. 25 and 329.
[8] See in regard to the arms of the combatants, Beaumanoir, 61, p. 308, and 64, p. 328.
[9] *Ibid.*, 74, p. 328. See also the Charters of St. Aubin of Anjou, quoted by Galland, p. 263.
[10] Among the Romans, it was not infamous to be beaten with a stick.
[11] They had only the baston and buckler.—Beaumanoir, 64, p. 328.
[12] Book i, tit. 6, § 1.
[13] *Ibid.*, § 2.
[14] *De Moribus Germanorum*, 6.
[15] In the *Pactus legis Salicæ*, 6.

When Charlemagne amended the Salic law,[1] he allowed in this case no more than three sous in composition. As this prince cannot be suspected of having had a design to enervate the military discipline, it is manifest that such an alteration was due to a change of weapons, and that from this change of weapons a great number of usages derive their origin.

22. *Of the Manners in relation to judicial Combats.* Our connections with the fair sex are founded on the pleasure of enjoyment; on the happiness of loving and being loved; and likewise on the ambition of pleasing the ladies, because they are the best judges of some of those things which constitute personal merit. This general desire of pleasing produces gallantry, which is not love itself, but the delicate, the volatile, the perpetual simulation of love.

According to the different circumstances of every country and age, love inclines more to one of those three things than to the other two. Now I maintain that the prevailing spirit at the time of our judicial combats must have been that of gallantry.

I find in the law of the Lombards,[2] that if one of the two champions was found to have any magic herbs about him, the judge ordered them to be taken from him, and obliged him to swear he had no more. This law could be founded only on the vulgar opinion; it was fear, the alleged inventor of much that made them imagine this kind of prestige. As in single combats the champions were armed at all points, and as with heavy arms, both of the offensive and defensive kind, those of a particular temper and strength gave immense advantages, the notion of some champions having enchanted arms must certainly have turned the brains of a great many people.

Hence arose the marvellous system of chivalry. The minds of all sorts of people quickly imbibed these extravagant ideas. In romances are found knights-errant, necromancers, and fairies, winged or intelligent horses, invisible or invulnerable men, magicians who concerned themselves in the birth and education of great personages, enchanted and disenchanted palaces, a new world in the midst of the old one, the usual course of nature being left only to the lower class of mankind.

Knights-errant ever in armour, in a part of the world abounding in castles, forts, and robbers, placed all their glory in punishing injustice, and in protecting weakness. Hence our romances are full of gallantry founded on the idea of love joined to that of strength and protection.

Such was the origin of gallantry, when they formed the notion of an extraordinary race of men who at the sight of a virtuous and beautiful lady in distress were inclined to expose themselves to all hazards for her sake, and to endeavour to please her in the common actions of life.

Our romances of chivalry flattered this desire of pleasing, and communicated to a part of Europe that spirit of gallantry which we may venture to affirm was very little known to the ancients.

The prodigious luxury of that immense city of Rome encouraged sensuous pleasures. The tranquillity of the plains of Greece gave rise to the description of the sentiments of love.[3] The idea of knights-errant, protectors of the virtue and beauty of the fair sex, led to that of gallantry.

This spirit was continued by the custom of tournaments, which, uniting the rights of valour and love, added still a considerable importance to gallantry.

23. *Of the Code of Laws on judicial Combats.* Some perhaps will have a curiosity to see this abominable custom of judiciary combat reduced to principles and to find the groundwork of such an extraordinary code of laws. Men, though reasonable in the main, reduce their very prejudices to rule. Nothing was more contrary to good sense, than those combats, and yet when once this point was laid down, a kind of prudential management was used in carrying it into execution.

In order to be thoroughly acquainted with the jurisprudence of those times, it is necessary to read with attention the regulations of St. Louis, who made such great changes in the judiciary order. Défontaines was contemporary with that prince; Beaumanoir wrote after him,[4] and the rest lived since his time. We must, therefore, look for the ancient practice in the amendments that have been made of it.

24. *Rules established in the judicial Combat.* When there happened to be several accusers, they were obliged to agree among themselves

[1] We have both the ancient law and that which was amended by this prince.
[2] Book ii, tit. 55, § 11.
[3] See the Greek romances of the middle age.
[4] In the year 1283.

that the action might be carried on by a single prosecutor; and, if they could not agree, the person before whom the action was brought, appointed one of them to prosecute the quarrel.[1]

When a gentleman challenged a villain, he was obliged to present himself on foot with buckler and baston; but if he came on horseback and armed like a gentleman, they took his horse and his arms from him and, stripping him to his shirt, they compelled him to fight in that condition with the villain.[2]

Before the combat the magistrates ordered three bans to be published. By the first the relatives of the parties were commanded to retire; by the second the people were warned to be silent; and the third prohibited the giving of any assistance to either of the parties, under severe penalties, nay, even on pain of death if by this assistance either of the combatants should happen to be vanquished.[3]

The officers belonging to the civil magistrate[4] guarded the list or enclosure where the battle was fought; and in case either of the parties declared himself desirous of peace, they took particular notice of the actual state in which they mutually stood at that very moment, to the end that they might be restored to the same situation in case they did not come to an understanding.[5]

When the pledges were received either for a crime or for false judgment, the parties could not make up the matter without the consent of the lord; and when one of the parties was overcome, there could be no accommodation without the permission of the count, which had some analogy to our letters of grace.[6]

But if it happened to be a capital crime, and the lord, corrupted by presents, consented to an accommodation, he was obliged to pay a fine of sixty livres, and the right he had of punishing the malefactor devolved upon the count.[7]

There were a great many people incapable either of offering, or of accepting battle. But liberty was given them, on cause being shown, to choose a champion; and that he might have

a stronger interest in defending the party in whose behalf he appeared, his hand was cut off if he lost the battle.[8]

When capital laws were made in the last century against duels, perhaps it would have been sufficient to have deprived a warrior of his military capacity by the loss of his hand; nothing in general being a greater mortification to mankind than to survive the loss of their character.

When, in capital cases, the duel was fought by champions, the parties were placed where they could not behold the battle; each was bound with the cord that was to be used at his execution in case his champion was overcome.[9]

The person overcome in battle did not always lose the point contested; if, for instance, they fought on an imparlance, he lost only the imparlance.[10]

25. *Of the Bounds prescribed to the Custom of judicial Combats.* When pledges of battle had been received upon a civil affair of small importance, the lord obliged the parties to withdraw them.

If a fact was notorious; for instance, if a man had been assassinated in the open market-place, then there was neither a trial by witnesses, nor by combat; the judge gave his decision from the notoriety of the fact.[11]

When the court of a lord had often determined after the same manner, and the usage was thus known,[12] the lord refused to grant the parties the privilege of duelling, to the end that the usages might not be altered by the different success of the combats.

They were not allowed to insist upon duelling but for themselves, for some one belonging to their family, or for their liege lord.[13]

When the accused had been acquitted, another relative could not insist on fighting him; otherwise disputes would never be terminated.[14]

If a person appeared again in public whose relatives, upon a supposition of his being murdered, wanted to revenge his death, there was then no room for a combat; the same may

[1] Beaumanoir, 6, pp. 40, 41.
[2] *Ibid.*, 64, p. 328.
[3] *Ibid.*, p. 330.
[4] *Ibid.*
[5] *Ibid.*
[6] The great vassals had particular privileges.
[7] Beaumanoir, 64, p. 330, says he lost his jurisdiction: these words in the authors of those days have not a general signification, but a signification limited to the affair in question. Défontaines, 21, art. 29.

[8] This custom, which we meet with in the Capitularies, was still subsisting at the time of Beaumanoir. See 61, p. 315.
[9] Beaumanoir, 64, p. 330.
[10] *Ibid.*, 61, p. 309.
[11] *Ibid.*, p. 308; 43, p. 239.
[12] *Ibid.*, 61, p. 314. See also Défontaines, 22, art. 24.
[13] Beaumanoir, 63, p. 322.
[14] *Ibid.*

be said if by a notorious absence the fact was proved to be impossible.[1]

If a man who had been mortally wounded had exculpated before his death the person accused and named another, they did not proceed to a duel; but if he had mentioned nobody his declaration was looked upon as a forgiveness on his death-bed; the prosecution was continued, and even among gentlemen they could make war against each other.[2]

When there was a conflict, and one of the relatives had given or received pledges of battle, the right of contest ceased; for then it was thought that the parties wanted to pursue the ordinary course of justice; therefore he that would have continued the contest would have been sentenced to make good all the losses.

Thus the practice of judiciary combat had this advantage, that it was apt to change a general into an individual quarrel, to restore the courts of judicature to their authority, and to bring back into the civil state those who were no longer governed but by the law of nations.

As there are an infinite number of wise things that are managed in a very foolish manner; so there are many foolish things that are very wisely conducted.

When a man who was challenged with a crime visibly showed that it had been committed by the challenger himself, there could be then no pledges of battle; for there is no criminal but would prefer a duel of uncertain event to a certain punishment.[3]

There were no duels in affairs decided by arbiters,[4] nor by ecclesiastical courts, nor in cases relating to women's dowries.

"A woman," says Beaumanoir, "cannot fight." If a woman challenged a person without naming her champion, the pledges of battle were not accepted. It was also requisite that a woman should be authorised by her baron, that is, by her husband, to challenge; but she might be challenged without this authority.[5]

If either the challenger or the person challenged were under fifteen years of age, there could be no combat.[6] They might order it, indeed, in disputes relating to orphans when their guardians or trustees were willing to run the risk of this procedure.

The cases in which a bondman was allowed to fight are, I think, as follows. He was allowed to fight another bondman; to fight a freedman, or even a gentleman, in case he were challenged; but if he himself challenged, the other might refuse to fight; and even the bondman's lord had a right to take him out of the court.[7] The bondman might by his lord's charter or by usage fight with any freeman;[8] and the church claimed this right for her bondmen[9] as a mark of respect due to her by the laity.[10]

26. *On the judiciary Combat between one of the Parties and one of the Witnesses.* Beaumanoir informs us[11] that a person who saw a witness going to swear against him might elude the other by telling the judges that his adversary produced a false and slandering witness; and if the witness was willing to maintain the quarrel, he gave pledges of battle. The inquiry was no longer the question; for if the witness was overcome, it was decided that the adversary had produced a false witness, and he lost his cause.

It was necessary that the second witness should not be heard; for if he had made his attestation, the affair would have been decided by the deposition of two witnesses. But by staying the second, the deposition of the first witness became void.

The second witness being thus rejected, the party was not allowed to produce any others, but he lost his cause; in case, however, there had been no pledges of battle, he might produce other witnesses.

Beaumanoir observes[12] that the witness might say to the party he appeared for, before he made his deposition: "I do not care to fight for your quarrel, nor to enter into any debate; but if you are willing to stand by me, I am ready to tell the truth." The party was then obliged to fight for the witness, and if he happened to be overcome, he did not lose his cause,[13] but the witness was rejected.

This, I believe, was a modification of the ancient custom; and what makes me think so is that we find this usage of challenging the witnesses established in the laws of the Bava-

[1] *Ibid.*
[2] *Ibid.*, p. 323.
[3] *Ibid.*, 63, p. 324.
[4] *Ibid.*, p. 325.
[5] *Ibid.*
[6] *Ibid.*, p. 323. See also what I have said in book xviii.

[7] *Ibid.*, p. 327.
[8] Défontaines, 22, art. 7.
[9] Charter of Louis the Fat, in the year 1118.
[10] *Ibid.*
[11] Chapter 61, p. 315.
[12] Chapter 6, p. 40.
[13] But if the battle was fought by champions, the champion that was overcome had his hand cut off.

rians[1] and Burgundians[2] without any restriction.

I have already made mention of the constitution of Gundebald, against which Agobard[3] and St. Avitus[4] made such loud complaints. "When the accused," says this prince, "produces witnesses to swear that he has not committed the crime, the accuser may challenge one of the witnesses to a combat; for it is very just that the person who has offered to swear, and has declared that he was certain of the truth, should make no difficulty of maintaining it by combat." Thus the witnesses were deprived by this king of every kind of subterfuge to avoid the judiciary combat.

27. *Of the judicial Combat between one of the Parties and one of the Lords' Peers. Appeal of false Judgment.* As the nature of judicial combats was to terminate the affair for ever, and was incompatible with a new judgment and new prosecutions,[5] an appeal, such as is established by the Roman and Canon laws, that is, to a superior court in order to rejudge the proceedings of an inferior, was a thing unknown in France.

This is a form of proceeding to which a warlike nation, governed solely by the point of honour, was quite a stranger; and agreeably to this very spirit, the same methods were used against the judges as were allowed against the parties.[6]

An appeal among the people of this nation was a challenge to fight with arms, a challenge to be decided by blood; and not that invitation to a paper quarrel, the knowledge of which was reserved for succeeding ages.

Thus St. Louis, in his *Institutions*,[7] says that an appeal includes both felony and iniquity. Thus Beaumanoir tells us that if a vassal wanted to make his complaint of an outrage committed against him by his lord,[8] he was first obliged to announce that he quitted his fief; after which he appealed to his lord paramount, and offered pledges of battle. In like manner the lord renounced the homage of his vassal, if he challenged him before the count.

For a vassal to challenge his lord of false judgment was as much as to say to him that his sentence was unjust and malicious; now to utter such words against his lord was in some measure committing the crime of felony.

Hence, instead of bringing a challenge of false judgment against the lord who appointed and directed the court, they challenged the peers of whom the court itself was formed, by which means they avoided the crime of felony, for they insulted only their peers, with whom they could always account for the affront.

It was a very dangerous thing to challenge the peers of false judgment.[9] If the party waited till judgment was pronounced, he was obliged to fight them all when they offered to make good their judgment.[10] If the appeal was made before all the judges had given their opinion, he was obliged to fight all who had agreed in their judgment. To avoid this danger, it was usual to petition the lord to direct that each peer should give his opinion aloud;[11] and when the first had pronounced, and the second was going to do the same, the party told him that he was a liar, a knave and a slanderer, and then he had to fight only with that peer.

Défontaines[12] would have it that, before a challenge was made of false judgment, it was customary to let three judges pronounce; and he does not say that it was necessary to fight them all three; much less that there was any obligation to fight all those who had declared themselves of the same opinion. These differences arose from this, that in those times there were few usages exactly in all parts the same; Beaumanoir gives an account of what passed in the county of Clermont; and Défontaines of what was practised in Vermandois.

When one of the peers or a vassal had declared that he would maintain the judgment, the judge ordered pledges of battle to be given, and likewise took security of the challenger that he would maintain his case.[13] But the peer who was challenged gave no security, because he was the lord's vasal, and was obliged to defend the challenge, or to pay the lord a fine of sixty livres.

If he who challenged did not prove that the judgment was bad,[14] he paid the lord a fine of sixty livres, the same fine to the peer whom he

[1] Tit. 16, § 2.
[2] Tit. 45.
[3] Letter to Louis the Debonnaire.
[4] Life of St. Avitus.
[5] Beaumanoir, 2, p. 22.
[6] *Ibid.*, 61, p. 312, and 67, p. 338.
[7] Book ii. 15.
[8] Beaumanoir, 61, pp. 310 and 311, and 67, p. 337.

[9] *Ibid.*, 61, p. 313.
[10] *Ibid.*, p. 314.
[11] *Ibid.*
[12] Chapter 22, art. 1, 10, and 11, he says only that each of them was allowed a small fine.
[13] Beaumanoir, 61, p. 314.
[14] *Ibid.* Défontaines, 22, art. 9.

had challenged, and as much to every one of those who had openly consented to the judgment.[1]

When a person, strongly suspected of a capital crime, had been taken and condemned, he could make no appeal of false judgment:[2] for he would always appeal either to prolong his life, or to get an absolute discharge.

If a person said that the judgment was false and bad and did not offer to prove it so, that is, to fight, he was condemned to a fine of ten sous if a gentleman, and to five sous if a bondman, for the injurious expressions he had uttered.[3]

The judges or peers who were overcome forfeited neither life nor limbs,[4] but the person who challenged them was punished with death, if it happened to be a capital crime.[5]

This manner of challenging the vassals with false judgment was to avoid challenging the lord himself. But if the lord had no peers,[6] or had not a sufficient number, he might at his own expense borrow peers of his lord paramount;[7] but these peers were not obliged to pronounce judgment if they did not like it; they might declare that they were come only to give their opinion: in that particular case, the lord himself judged and pronounced sentence as judge;[8] and if an appeal of false judgment was made against him, it was his business to answer to the challenge.

If the lord happened to be so very poor as not to be able to hire peers of his paramount,[9] or if he neglected to ask for them, or the paramount refused to give them, then, as the lord could not judge by himself, and as nobody was obliged to plead before a tribunal where judgment could not be given, the affair was brought before the lord paramount.

This, I believe, was one of the principal causes of the separation between the jurisdiction and the fief, whence arose the maxim of the French lawyers, "The fief is one thing, and the jurisdiction is another." For as there were a vast number of peers who had no subordinate vassals under them, they were incapable of holding their court; all affairs were then brought before their lord paramount, and they lost the privilege of pronouncing judgment, because they had neither power nor will to claim it.

All the judges who had been at the judgment were obliged to be present when it was pronounced, that they might follow one another, and say aye to the person who, wanting to make an appeal of false judgment, asked them whether they followed;[10] for Défontaines says[11] that it is an affair of courtesy and loyalty, and there is no such thing as evasion or delay. Hence, I imagine, arose the custom still followed in England of obliging the jury to be all unanimous in their verdict in cases relating to life and death.

Judgment was therefore given, according to the opinion of the majority; and if there was an equal division, sentence was pronounced, in criminal cases, in favour of the accused; in cases of debt, in favour of the debtor; and in cases of inheritance, in favour of the defendant.

Défontaines observes[12] that a peer could not excuse himself by saying that he would not sit in court if there were only four,[13] or if the whole number, or at least the wisest part, were not present. This is just as if he were to say, in the heat of an engagement, that he would not assist his lord because he had not all his vassals with him. But it was the lord's business to cause his court to be respected, and to choose the bravest and most knowing of his tenants. This I mention, in order to show the duty of vassals, which was to fight, and to give judgment: and such, indeed, was this duty, that to give judgment was all the same as to fight.

It was lawful for a lord, who went to law with his vassal in his own court, and was cast, to challenge one of his tenants with false judgment. But as the latter owed a respect to his lord for the fealty he had vowed, and the lord, on the other hand, owed benevolence to his vassal for the fealty accepted, it was customary to make a distinction between the lord's affirming in general that the judgment was

[1] *Ibid.*
[2] Beaumanoir, 61, p. 316, and Défontaines, 22, art. 21.
[3] Beaumanoir, 61, p. 314.
[4] Défontaines, 22, art. 7.
[5] See Défontaines, 21, arts. 11 and 12, and following, who distinguishes the cases in which the appellant of false judgment loses his life, the point contested, or only the imparlance.
[6] Beaumanoir, 62, p. 322. Défontaines, 22, art. 3.
[7] The count was not obliged to lend any. Beaumanoir, 67, p. 337.
[8] Nobody can pass judgment in his court. *Ibid.*, pp. 336, 337.
[9] *Ibid.*, 62, p. 322.

[10] Défontaines, 21, arts. 27 and 28.
[11] *Ibid.*, art. 28.
[12] Chapter 21, art. 37.
[13] This number at least was necessary. Défontaines, 21, art. 36.

false and unjust,[1] and imputing personal prevarications to his tenant.[2] In the former case he affronted his own court, and in some measure himself, so that there was no room for pledges of battle. But there was room in the latter, because he attacked his vassal's honour; and the person overcome was deprived of life and property, in order to maintain the public tranquillity.

This distinction, which was necessary in that particular case, had afterwards a greater extent. Beaumanoir says that when the challenger of false judgment attacked one of the peers by personal imputation, battle ensued; but if he attacked only the judgment, the peer challenged was at liberty to determine the dispute either by battle or by law.[3] But as the prevailing spirit in Beaumanoir's time was to restrain the usage of judicial combats, and as this liberty, which had been granted to the peer challenged, of defending the judgment by combat or not is equally contrary to the ideas of honour established in those days, and to the obligation the vassal lay under of defending his lord's jurisdiction, I am apt to think that this distinction of Beaumanoir's was a novelty in French jurisprudence.

I would not have it thought that all appeals of false judgment were decided by battle; it fared with this appeal as with all others. The reader may recollect the exceptions mentioned in the 25th chapter. Here it was the business of the superior court to examine whether it was proper to withdraw the pledges of battle or not.

There could be no appeal of false judgment against the king's court, because, as there was no one equal to the king, no one could challenge him; and as the king had no superior, none could appeal from his court.

This fundamental regulation, which was necessary as a political law, diminished also as a civil law the abuses of the judicial proceedings of those times. When a lord was afraid that his court would be challenged with false judgment, or perceived that they were determined to challenge, if the interests of justice required that it should not be challenged, he might demand from the king's court men whose judgment could not be set aside.[4] Thus King Philip, says Défontaines,[5] sent his whole

council to judge an affair in the court of the Abbot of Corbey.

But if the lord could not have judges from the king, he might remove his court into the king's, if he held immediately of him; and if there were intermediate lords, he had recourse to his suzerain, removing from one lord to another till he came to the sovereign.

Thus, notwithstanding they had in those days neither the practice nor even the idea of our modern appeals, yet they had recourse to the king, who was the source whence all those rivers flowed, and the sea into which they returned.

28. *Of the Appeal of Default of Justice.* The appeal of default of justice was, when the court of a particular lord deferred, evaded, or refused to do justice to the parties.

During the time of our princes of the second race, though the count had several officers under him, their person was subordinate, but not their jurisdiction. These officers in their court days, assizes, or *Placita,* gave judgment in the last resort as the count himself; all the difference consisted in the division of the jurisdiction. For instance, the count had the power of condemning to death, of judging of liberty, and of the restitution of goods, which the *centenarii* had not.[6]

For the same reason there were greater cases which were reserved to the king; namely, those which directly concerned the political order of the state.[7] Such were the disputes between bishops, abbots, counts, and other grandees, which were determined by the king together with the great vassals.[8]

What some authors have advanced, namely, that an appeal lay from the count to the king's commissary, or *Missus Dominicus,* is not well-grounded. The count and the *Missus* had an equal jurisdiction, independent of each other.[9] The whole difference was that the *Missus* held his *Placita,* or assizes, four months in the year,[10] and the count the other eight.

If a person, who had been condemned at an assize, demanded to have his cause tried over

---

[1] Beaumanoir, 67, p. 337.
[2] *Ibid.*
[3] *Ibid.*, pp. 337, 338.
[4] Défontaines, 22, art. 14.
[5] *Ibid.*

[6] Third capitulary of the year 812, art. 3, edition of Baluzius, p. 497, and of Charles the Bald, added to the law of the Lombards, ii, art. 3.
[7] Third capitulary of the year 812, art. 2, edition of Baluzius, p. 497.
[8] Capitulary of Louis the Debonnaire, edition of Baluzius, p. 667.
[9] See the Capitulary of Charles the Bald, added to the law of the Lombards, ii, art. 3.
[10] Third capitulary of the year 812, art. 8.

again, and was afterwards cast, he paid a fine of fifteen sous, or received fifteen blows from the judges who had decided the affair.[1]

When the counts, or the king's commissaries did not find themselves able to bring the great lords to reason, they made them give bail or security[2] that they would appear in the king's court: this was to try the cause, and not to rejudge it. I find in the capitulary of Metz[3] a law by which the appeal of false judgment to the king's court is established, and all other kinds of appeal are proscribed and punished.

If they refused to submit to the judgment of the sheriffs[4] and made no complaint, they were imprisoned till they had submitted, but if they complained, they were conducted under a proper guard before the king, and the affair was examined in his court.

There could be hardly any room then for an appeal of default of justice. For instead of its being usual in those days to complain that the counts and others who had a right of holding assizes were not exact in discharging this duty,[5] it was a general complaint that they were too exact. Hence we find such numbers of ordinances, by which the counts and all other officers of justice are forbidden to hold their assizes above thrice a year. It was not so necessary to chastise their indolence, as to check their activity.

But, after an infinite number of petty lordships had been formed, and different degrees of vassalage established, the neglect of certain vassals in holding their courts gave rise to this kind of appeal;[6] especially as very considerable profits accrued to the lord paramount from the several fines.

As the custom of judicial combats gained every day more ground, there were places, cases, and times, in which it was difficult to assemble the peers, and consequently in which justice was delayed. The appeal of default of justice was therefore introduced, an appeal that has been often a remarkable era in our history; because most of the wars of those days were imputed to a violation of the political law; as

the cause, or at least the pretence, of our modern wars is the infringement of the laws of nations.

Beaumanoir says[7] that, in case of default of justice, battle was not allowed: the reasons are these: 1. They could not challenge the lord himself, because of the respect due to his person; neither could they challenge the lord's peers, because the case was clear, and they had only to reckon the days of the summons, or of the other delays; there had been no judgment passed, consequently there could be no appeal of false judgment: in fine, the crime of the peers offended the lord as well as the party, and it was against rule that there should be battle between the lord and his peers.

But as the default was proved by witnesses before the superior court,[8] the witnesses might be challenged, and then neither the lord nor his court were offended.

In case the default was owing to the lord's tenants or peers, who had delayed to administer justice, or had avoided giving judgment after past delays, then these peers were appealed of default of justice before the paramount; and if they were cast, they paid a fine to their lord.[9] The latter could not give them any assistance; on the contrary, he seized their fief, till they had each paid a fine of sixty livres.

2. When the default was owing to the lord, which was the case whenever there happened not to be a sufficient number of peers in his court to pass judgment, or when he had not assembled his tenants or appointed somebody in his place to assemble them, an appeal might be made of the default before the lord paramount; but then the party and not the lord was summoned, because of the respect due to the latter.[10]

The lord demanded to be tried before the paramount, and if he was acquitted of the default, the cause was remanded to him, and he was likewise paid a fine of sixty livres.[11] But if the default was proved, the penalty inflicted on him was to lose the trial of the cause,[12] which was to be then determined in the superior court. And, indeed, the complaint of default was made with no other view.

3. If the lord was sued in his own court,[13]

[1] Placitum.
[2] This appears by the formulas, charters, and the capitularies.
[3] In the year 757, edition of Baluzius, p. 180, arts. 9 and 10, and the Synod apud Vernas, in the year 755, art. 29, edition of Baluzius, p. 175. These two capitularies were made under King Pepin.
[4] The officers under the count, Scabini.
[5] See the Law of the Lombards, ii, tit. 52, art. 22.
[6] There are instances of appeals of default of justice as early as the time of Philip Augustus.

[7] Chapter 61, p. 315.
[8] Ibid.
[9] Défontaines, 21, art. 24.
[10] Ibid., art. 32.
[11] Beaumanoir, 61, p. 312.
[12] Défontaines, 21, art. 29.
[13] This was the case in the famous difference between the Lord of Nesle and Joan, Countess of

which never happened but upon disputes in relation to the fief, after letting all the delays pass, the lord himself was summoned before the peers in the sovereign's name,[1] whose permission was necessary on that occasion. The peers did not make the summons in their own name, because they could not summon their lord, but they could summon for their lord.[2]

Sometimes the appeal of default of justice was followed by an appeal of false judgment, when the lord had caused judgment to be passed, notwithstanding the default.[3]

The vassal who had wrongfully challenged his lord of default of justice was sentenced to pay a fine according to his lord's pleasure.[4]

The inhabitants of Gaunt had challenged the Earl of Flanders of default of justice before the king, for having delayed to give judgment in his own court.[5] Upon examination it was found that he had used fewer delays than even the custom of the country allowed. They were therefore remanded to him; upon which their effects to the value of sixty thousand livres were seized. They returned to the king's court in order to have the fine moderated; but it was decided that the earl might insist upon the fine, and even upon more if he pleased. Beaumanoir was present at those judgments.

4. In other disputes which the lord might have with his vassal, in respect to the person or honour of the latter, or to property that did not belong to the fief, there was no room for a challenge of default of justice; because the cause was not tried in the lord's court, but in that of the paramount: vassals, says Défontaines,[6] having no power to give judgment on the person of their lord.

I have been at some trouble to give a clear idea of those things, which are so obscure and confused in ancient authors that to disentangle them from the chaos in which they were involved may be reckoned a new discovery.

29. *Epoch of the Reign of St. Louis.* St. Louis abolished the judicial combats in all the courts of his demesne, as appears by the ordinance he published thereupon,[7] and by the *Institutions.*[8]

But he did not suppress them in the courts of his barons, except in the case of challenge of false judgment.[9]

A vassal could not challenge the court of his lord of false judgment, without demanding a judicial combat against the judges who pronounced sentence. But St. Louis introduced the practice of challenging of false judgment without fighting, a change that may be reckoned a kind of revolution.[10]

He declared[11] that there should be no challenge of false judgment in the lordships of his demesnes, because it was a crime of felony. In reality, if it was a kind of felony against the lord, by a much stronger reason it was felony against the king. But he consented that they might demand an amendment[12] of the judgments passed in his courts; not because they were false or iniquitous, but because they did some prejudice.[13] On the contrary, he ordained that they should be obliged to make a challenge of false judgment against the courts of the barons,[14] in case of any complaint.

It was not allowed by the *Institutions,* as we have already observed, to bring a challenge of false judgment against the courts in the king's demesnes. They were obliged to demand an amendment before the same court; and in case the bailiff refused the amendment demanded, the king gave leave to make an appeal to his court;[15] or rather, interpreting the *Institutions* by themselves, to present him a request or petition.[16]

With regard to the courts of the lords, St. Louis, by permitting them to be challenged of false judgment, would have the cause brought before the royal tribunal,[17] or that of the lord paramount, not to be decided by duel[18] but by

---

Flanders, during the reign of Louis VIII. He called upon her to have it tried within forty days, and thereupon challenged her at the king's court with default of justice. She answered that she would have it tried by her peers in Flanders. The king's court determined that it should not be sent there and that the countess should be cited.

[1] Défontaines, 21, art. 34.
[2] *Ibid.,* art. 9.
[3] Beaumanoir, 61, p. 311.
[4] *Ibid.,* 61, p. 312. But he that was neither tenant nor vassal to the lord paid only a fine of sixty livres.—*Ibid.*
[5] *Ibid.,* p. 318.
[6] Chapter 21, art. 35.

[7] In the year 1260.
[8] Book i. 2, 7, and ii. 10, 11.
[9] As appears everywhere in the *Institutions,* &c., and Beaumanoir, 61, p. 309.
[10] *Institutions,* i. 6, ii. 15.
[11] *Ibid.,* ii. 15.
[12] *Ibid.,* i. 78, ii. 15.
[13] *Ibid.,* i. 78.
[14] *Ibid.,* ii. 15.
[15] *Ibid.,* i. 78.
[16] *Ibid.,* ii. 15.
[17] But if they wanted to appeal without falsifying the judgment, the appeal was not admitted.—*Ibid.*
[18] *Ibid.,* i. 6, 67; ii. 15; and Beaumanoir, 11, p. 58.

witnesses, pursuant to a certain form of proceeding, the rules of which he laid down in the
Institutions.[1]

Thus, whether they could falsify the judgment, as in the court of the barons; or whether
they could not falsify, as in the court of his
demesnes, he ordained that they might appeal
without the hazard of a duel.

Défontaines[2] gives us the first two examples
he ever saw, in which they proceeded thus
without a legal duel: one, in a cause tried at
the court of St. Quentin, which belonged to
the king's demesne; and the other, in the court
of Ponthieu, where the count, who was present, opposed the ancient jurisprudence: but
these two causes were decided by law.

Here, perhaps, it will be asked why St. Louis
ordained for the courts of his barons a different form of proceeding from that which he had
established in the courts of his demesnes? The
reason is this: when St. Louis made the regulation for the courts of his demesnes, he was not
checked or limited in his views: but he had
measures to keep with the lords who enjoyed
this ancient prerogative, that causes should
not be removed from their courts, unless the
party was willing to expose himself to the dangers of an appeal of false judgment. St. Louis
preserved the usage of this appeal; but he ordained that it should be made without a judicial combat; that is, in order to make the
change less felt, he suppressed the thing, and
continued the terms.

This regulation was not universally received
in the courts of the lords. Beaumanoir says[3]
that in his time there were two ways of trying
causes; one according to the king's establishment, and the other pursuant to the ancient
practice; that the lords were at liberty to follow which way they pleased; but when they
had pitched upon one in any cause, they could
not afterwards have recourse to the other. He
adds,[4] that the Count of Clermont followed
the new practice, while his vassals kept to the
old one; but that it was in his power to re-
establish the ancient practice whenever he
pleased, otherwise he would have less authority than his vassals.

It is proper here to observe that France was
at that time divided into the country of the
king's demesne, and that which was called the
country of the barons, or the baronies; and, to
make use of the terms of St. Louis' *Institutions*, into the country under obedience to the
king, and the country out of his obedience.[5]
When the king made ordinances for the country of his demesne, he employed his own single authority. But when he published any ordinances that concerned also the country of
his barons, these were made in concert with
them,[6] or sealed and subscribed by them: otherwise the barons received or refused them, according as they seemed conducive to the good
of their baronies. The rear-vassals were upon
the same terms with the great-vassals. Now the
Institutions were not made with the consent
of the lords, though they regulated matters
which to them were of great importance: but
they were received only by those who believed
they would redound to their advantage. Robert, son of St. Louis, received them in his
county of Clermont; yet his vassals did not
think proper to conform to this practice.

30. *Observation on Appeals.* I apprehend that
appeals, which were challenges to a combat,
must have been made immediately on the spot.
"If the party leaves the court without appealing," says Beaumanoir,[7] "he loses his appeal,
and the judgment stands good." This continued still in force, even after all the restrictions of judicial combat.[8]

31. *The same Subject continued.* The villain
could not bring a challenge of false judgment
against the court of his lord. This we learn
from Défontaines,[9] and he is confirmed moreover by the *Institutions*.[10] Hence Défontaines
says,[11] "between the lord and his villain there
is no other judge but God."

It was the custom of judicial combats that
deprived the villains of the privilege of challenging their lord's court of false judgment.

[1] Book i. 1–3.
[2] Chapter 22, arts. 16, 17.
[3] Chapter 61, p. 309.
[4] *Ibid.*

[5] See Beaumanoir, Défontaines, and the *Institutions*, ii. 10, 11, 15, and others.
[6] See the ordinances at the beginning of the
third race, in the collection of Laurière, especially
those of Philip Augustus, on ecclesiastic jurisdiction; that of Louis VIII concerning the Jews; and
the charters related by Mr. Brussel; particularly
that of St. Louis, on the release and recovery of
lands, and the feudal majority of young women,
ii, book iii, p. 35, and *ibid.*, the ordinance of
Philip Augustus, p. 7.
[7] Chapter 63, p. 327; chapter 61, p. 312.
[8] See the *Institutions* of St. Louis, ii. 15, and the
Ordinance of Charles VII in the year 1453.
[9] Chapter 21, arts. 21, 22.
[10] Book i. 136.
[11] Chapter 2, art. 8.

And so true is this, that those villains[1] who by charter or custom had a right to fight had also the privilege of challenging their lord's court of false judgment, even though the peers who tried them were gentlemen;[2] and Défontaines proposes expedients to gentlemen in order to avoid the scandal of fighting with a villain by whom they had been challenged of false judgment.[3]

As the practice of judicial combats began to decline, and the usage of new appeals to be introduced, it was reckoned unfair that freemen should have a remedy against the injustice of the courts of their lords, and the villains should not; hence the parliament received their appeals all the same as those of freemen.

32. *The same Subject continued.* When a challenge of false judgment was brought against the lord's court, the lord appeared in person before his paramount to defend the judgment of his court. In like manner, in the appeal of default of justice, the party summoned before the lord paramount brought his lord along with him, to the end that if the default was not proved, he might recover his jurisdiction.[4]

In process of time as the practice observed in these two particular cases became general, by the introduction of all sorts of appeals, it seemed very extraordinary that the lord should be obliged to spend his whole life in strange tribunals, and for other people's affairs. Philip of Valois ordained[5] that none but the bailiffs should be summoned; and when the usage of appeals became still more frequent, the parties were obliged to defend the appeal: the deed of the judge became that of the party.[6]

I took notice that in the appeal of default of justice,[7] the lord lost only the privilege of having the cause tried in his own court. But if the lord himself was sued as party,[8] which be-

came a very common practice,[9] he paid a fine of sixty livres to the king, or to the paramount, before whom the appeal was brought. Thence arose the usage, after appeals had been generally received, of making the fine payable to the lord upon the reversal of the sentence of his judge; a usage which lasted a long time, and was confirmed by the ordinance of Rousillon, but fell, at length, to the ground through its own absurdity.

33. *The same Subject continued.* In the practice of judicial combats, the person who had challenged one of the judges of false judgment might lose his cause by the combat, but could not possibly gain it.[10] And, indeed, the party who had a judgment in his favour ought not to have been deprived of it by another man's act. The appellant, therefore, who had gained the battle was obliged to fight likewise against the adverse party: not in order to know whether the judgment was good or bad (for this judgment was out of the case, being reversed by the combat), but to determine whether the demand was just or not; and it was on this new point they fought. Thence proceeds our manner of pronouncing decrees, "The court annuls the appeal; the court annuls the appeal and the judgment against which the appeal was brought." In effect, when the person who had made the challenge of false judgment happened to be overcome, the appeal was reversed: when he proved victorious, both the judgment and the appeal were reversed; then they were obliged to proceed to a new judgment.

This is so far true that, when the cause was tried by inquests, this manner of pronouncing did not take place: witness what M. de la Roche Flavin says,[11] namely, that the chamber of inquiry could not use this form at the beginning of its existence.

34. *In what Manner the Proceedings at Law became secret.* Duels had introduced a public form of proceeding, so that both the attack and the defence were equally known. "The witnesses," says Beaumanoir,[12] "ought to give their testimony in open court."

Boutillier's commentator says he had learned of ancient practitioners, and from some old manuscript law books, that criminal

---

[1] *Ibid.*, 22, art. 7. This article, and the 21st of the 22nd chapter of the same author, have been hitherto very badly explained. Défontaines does not oppose the judgment of the lord to that of the gentleman, because it was the same thing; but he opposes the common villain to him who had the privilege of fighting.
[2] Gentlemen may always be appointed judges. *Ibid.*, 21, art. 48.
[3] *Ibid.*, 22, art. 14.
[4] *Ibid.*, 21, art. 33.
[5] In the year 1332.
[6] See the situation of things in Boutillier's time, who lived in the year 1402.—*Somme Rurale*, i, pp. 19, 20.
[7] See chapter 30.
[8] Beaumanoir, 61, pp. 312 and 318.

[9] *Ibid.*
[10] Défontaines, 21, art. 14.
[11] *Of the Parliaments of France*, i. 16.
[12] Chapter 61, p. 315.

processes were anciently carried on in public, and in a form not very different from the public judgments of the Romans. This was owing to their not knowing how to write; a thing in those days very common. The usage of writing fixes the ideas, and keeps the secret; but when this usage is laid aside, nothing but the notoriety of the proceeding is capable of fixing those ideas.

And as uncertainty might easily arise in respect to what had been adjudicated by vassals, or pleaded before them, they could, therefore, refresh their memory[1] every time they held a court by what were called proceedings on record.[2] In that case, it was not allowed to challenge the witnesses to combat; for then there would be no end of disputes.

In process of time a private form of proceeding was introduced. Everything before had been public; everything now became secret; the interrogatories, the informations, the re-examinations, the confronting of witnesses, the opinion of the attorney-general; and this is the present practice. The first form of proceeding was suitable to the government of that time, as the new form was proper to the government since established.

Boutillier's commentator fixes the epoch of this change to the ordinance in the year 1539. I am apt to believe that the change was made insensibly, and passed from one lordship to another, in proportion as the lords renounced the ancient form of judging, and that derived from the *Institutions* of St. Louis was improved. And indeed, Beaumanoir says[3] that witnesses were publicly heard only in cases in which it was allowed to give pledges of battle: in others they were heard in secret, and their depositions were reduced to writing. The proceedings became, therefore, secret, when they ceased to give pledges of battle.

35. *Of the Costs.* In former times no one was condemned in the lay courts of France to the payment of costs.[4] The party cast was sufficiently punished by pecuniary fines to the lord and his peers. From the manner of proceeding by judicial combat it followed, that the party condemned and deprived of life and fortune was punished as much as he could be: and in the other cases of the judicial combat, there

were fines sometimes fixed, and sometimes dependent on the disposition of the lord, which were sufficient to make people dread the consequences of suits. The same may be said of causes that were not decided by combat. As the lord had the chief profits, so he was also at the chief expense, either to assemble his peers, or to enable them to proceed to judgment. Besides, as disputes were generally determined at the same place, and almost always at the same time, without that infinite multitude of writings which afterwards followed, there was no necessity of allowing costs to the parties.

The custom of appeals naturally introduced that of giving costs. Thus Défontaines says,[5] that when they appealed by written law, that is, when they followed the new laws of St. Louis, they gave costs; but that in the ordinary practice, which did not permit them to appeal without falsifying the judgment, no costs were allowed. They obtained only a fine, and the possession for a year and a day of the thing contested, if the cause was remanded to the lord.

But when the number of appeals increased from the new facility of appealing;[6] when by the frequent usage of those appeals from one court to another, the parties were continually removed from the place of their residence; when the new method of procedure multiplied and prolonged the suits; when the art of eluding the very justest demands became refined; when the parties at law knew how to fly only in order to be followed; when plaints were ruinous and defence easy; when the arguments were lost in whole volumes of words and writings; when the kingdom was filled with limbs of the law, who were strangers to justice; when knavery found encouragement at the very place where it did not find protection; then it was necessary to deter litigious people by the fear of costs. They were obliged to pay costs for the judgment and for the means they had employed to elude it. Charles the Fair made a general ordinance on that subject.[7]

36. *Of the public Prosecutor.* As by the Salic, Ripuarian, and other barbarous laws, crimes were punished with pecuniary fines; they had not in those days, as we have at present, a pub-

---

[1] As Beaumanoir says, chapter 39, p. 209.
[2] They proved by witnesses what had been already done, said, or decreed in court.
[3] Chapter 39, p. 218.
[4] Défontaines in his counsel, chapter 22, arts. 3, 8: and Beaumanoir, 33. *Institutions*, i. 90.

[5] Chapter 22, art. 8.
[6] At present when they are so inclined to appeal, says Boutillier—*Somme Rurale*, i, tit. 3, p. 16, Paris, 1621.
[7] In the year 1324.

lic officer who had the care of criminal prosecutions. And, indeed, the issue of all causes
being reduced to the reparation of injuries,
every prosecution was in some measure civil,
and might be managed by any one. On the
other hand, the Roman law had popular
forms for the prosecution of crimes which
were inconsistent with the functions of a public prosecutor.

The custom of judicial combats was no less
opposite to this idea; for who is it that would
choose to be a public prosecutor and to make
himself every man's champion against all the
world?

I find in the collection of formulas, inserted
by Muratori in the laws of the Lombards, that
under our princes of the second race there was
an advocate for the public prosecutor.[1] But
whoever pleases to read the entire collection
of these formulas will find that there was a total difference between such officers and those we
now call the public prosecutor, our attorneys-
general, our king's solicitors, or our solicitors for the nobility. The former were rather
agents to the public for the management of
political and domestic affairs, than for the civil. And, indeed, we did not find in those formulas that they were entrusted with criminal prosecutions, or with causes relating to minors, to
churches, or to the condition of any one.

I said that the establishment of a public
prosecutor was repugnant to the usage of judicial combats. I find, notwithstanding, in one
of those formulas, an advocate for the public
prosecutor, who had the liberty to fight. Muratori has placed it just after the constitution of
Henry I, for which it was made.[2] In this constitution it is said, "That if any man kills his
father, his brother, or any of his other relatives, he shall lose their succession, which shall
pass to the other relatives, and his own property shall go to the exchequer." Now it was in
suing for the estate which had devolved to the
exchequer, that the advocate for the public
prosecutor, by whom its rights were defended,
had the privilege of fighting: this case fell
within the general rule.

We see in those formulas the advocate for
the public prosecutor proceeding against a
person who had taken a robber, but had not
brought him before the count;[3] against another who had raised an insurrection or tumult
against the count;[4] against another who had
saved a man's life whom the count had ordered to be put to death;[5] against the advocate
of some churches, whom the count had commanded to bring a robber before him, but had
not obeyed;[6] against another who had revealed the king's secret to strangers;[7] against
another, who with open violence had attacked
the emperor's commissary;[8] against another
who had been guilty of contempt to the emperor's rescripts, and he was prosecuted either
by the emperor's advocate or by the emperor
himself;[9] against another who refused to accept of the prince's coin;[10] in fine, this advocate sued for things which by the law were
adjudged to the exchequer.[11]

But in criminal causes, we never meet with
the advocate for the public prosecutor; not
even where duels are used;[12] not even in the
case of incendiaries;[13] not even when the judge
is killed on his bench;[14] not even in causes relating to the conditions of persons,[15] to liberty and slavery.[16]

These formulas are made, not only for the
laws of the Lombards, but likewise for the capitularies added to them, so that we have no
reason to doubt of their giving us the practice
observed with regard to this subject under our
princes of the second race.

It is obvious that these advocates for a public prosecutor must have ended with our second race of kings, in the same manner as the
king's commissioners in the provinces; because there was no longer a general law nor
general exchequer, and because there were no
longer any counts in the provinces to hold the
assizes, and, of course, there were no more of
those officers whose principal function was to
support the authority of the counts.

As the usage of combats became more frequent under the third race, it did not allow of
any such thing as a public prosecutor. Hence
Boutillier, in his *Somme Rurale*, speaking of
the officers of justice, takes notice only of the

---

[1] *Advocatus de parte publicâ.*

[2] See this constitution and this formula. in the
second volume of the *Historians of Italy*, p. 175.

[3] Collection of Muratori, p. 104, on the 88th law
of Charlemagne, i, tit. 26, § 78.

[4] Another formula, *ibid.*, p. 87.

[5] *Ibid.*, p. 104.

[6] *Ibid.*, p. 95.

[7] *Ibid.*, p. 88.

[8] *Ibid.*, p. 98.

[9] *Ibid.*, p. 132.

[10] *Ibid.*

[11] *Ibid.*, p. 137.

[12] *Ibid.*, p. 147.

[13] *Ibid.*

[14] *Ibid.*, p. 168.

[15] *Ibid.*, p. 134.

[16] *Ibid.*, p. 107.

bailiffs, the peers and serjeants. See the *Institutions*[1] and Beaumanoir[2] concerning the manner in which prosecutions were managed in those days.

I find in the laws of James II, King of Majorca,[3] a creation of the office of king's attorney-general, with the very same functions as are exercised at present by the officers of that name among us. It is manifest that this office was not instituted till we had changed the form of our judiciary proceedings.

37. *In what Manner the Institutions of St. Louis fell into Oblivion.* It was the fate of the *Institutions* that their origin, progress, and decline were comprised within a very short period.

I shall make a few reflections upon this subject. The code we have now under the name of St. Louis' *Institutions* was never designed as a law for the whole kingdom, though such a design is mentioned in the preface. The compilation is a general code, which determines all points relating to civil affairs, to the disposal of property by will or otherwise, the dowries and privileges of women, and emoluments and privileges of fiefs, with the affairs in relation to the police, &c. Now, to give a general body of civil laws, at a time when each city, town, or village, had its customs, was attempting to subvert in one moment all the particular laws then in force in every part of the kingdom. To reduce all the particular customs to a general one would be a very inconsiderate thing, even at present when our princes find everywhere the most passive obedience. But if it be true that we ought not to change when the inconveniences are equal to the advantages, much less should we change when the advantages are small and the inconveniences immense. Now, if we attentively consider the situation which the kingdom was in at that time, when every lord was puffed up with the notion of his sovereignty and power, we shall find that to attempt a general alteration of the received laws and customs must be a thing that could never enter into the heads of those who were then in the administration.

What I have been saying proves likewise that this code of institutions was not confirmed in parliament by the barons and magistrates of the kingdom, as is mentioned in a manuscript of the town-hall of Amiens, quoted by M. Du Cange.[4] We find in other manuscripts that this code was given by St. Louis in the year 1270, before he set out for Tunis. But this fact is not truer than the other; for St. Louis set out upon that expedition in 1269, as M. Du Cange observes: whence he concludes that this code might have been published in his absence. But this I say is impossible. How can St. Louis be imagined to have pitched upon the time of his absence for transacting an affair which would have been a sowing of troubles, and might have produced not only changes, but revolutions? An enterprise of that kind had need, more than any other, of being closely pursued, and could not be the work of a feeble regency, composed moreover of lords, whose interest it was that it should not succeed. These were Mathieu, Abbot of St. Denis, Simon of Clermont, Count of Nesle, and, in case of death, Philip, Bishop of Evreux, and Jean, Count of Ponthieu. We have seen above[5] that the Count of Ponthieu opposed the execution of a new judiciary order in his lordship.

Thirdly, I affirm it to be very probable that the code now extant is quite a different thing from St. Louis' *Institutions*. It cites the *Institutions;* therefore it is a comment upon the *Institutions,* and not the institutions themselves. Besides, Beaumanoir, who frequently makes mention of St. Louis' *Institutions,* quotes only some particular laws of that prince, and not this compilation. Défontaines,[6] who wrote in that prince's reign, makes mention of the first two times that his *Institutions* on judicial proceedings were put in execution, as of a thing long since elapsed. The institutions of St. Louis were prior, therefore, to the compilation I am now speaking of, which from their rigour, and their adopting the erroneous prefaces inserted by some ignorant persons in that work, could not have been published before the last year of St. Louis or even not till after his death.

38. *The same Subject continued.* What is this compilation then which goes at present under the name of St. Louis' *Institutions?* What is this obscure, confused, and ambiguous code, where the French law is continually mixed with the Roman, where a legislator speaks and yet we see a civilian, where we find a complete

[1] Book i, 1; ii, 11, 13.
[2] Chapters 1, 61.
[3] See these laws in the *Lives of the Saints,* of the month of June, iii, p. 26.

[4] Preface to the *Institutions.*
[5] Chapter 29.
[6] See above, chapter 29.

digest of all cases and points of the civil law? To understand this thoroughly, we must transfer ourselves in imagination to those times.

St. Louis, seeing the abuses in the jurisprudence of his time, endeavoured to give the people a dislike to it. With this view he made several regulations for the court of his demesnes, and for those of his barons. And such was his success that Beaumanoir, who wrote a little after the death of that prince, informs us[1] that the manner of trying causes which had been established by St. Louis obtained in a great number of the courts of the barons.

Thus this prince attained his end, though his regulations for the courts of the lords were not designed as a general law for the kingdom, but as a model which every one might follow, and would even find his advantage in it. He removed the bad practice by showing them a better. When it appeared that his courts, and those of some lords, had chosen a form of proceeding more natural, more reasonable, more conformable to morality, to religion, to the public tranquillity, and to the security of person and property, this form was soon adopted, and the other rejected.

To allure when it is rash to constrain, to win by pleasing means when it is improper to exert authority, shows the man of abilities. Reason has a natural, and even a tyrannical sway; it meets with resistance, but this very resistance constitutes its triumph; for after a short struggle it commands an entire submission.

St. Louis, in order to give a distaste of the French jurisprudence, caused the books of the Roman law to be translated; by which means they were made known to the lawyers of those times. Défontaines, who is the oldest law writer we have, made great use of those Roman laws.[2] His work is, in some measure, a result from the ancient French jurisprudence, of the laws or Institutions of St. Louis, and of the Roman law. Beaumanoir made very little use of the latter; but he reconciled the ancient French laws to the regulations of St. Louis.

I have a notion, therefore, that the law book known by the name of the Institutions was compiled by some bailiffs, with the same design as that of the authors of those two works, and especially of Défontaines. The title of this work mentions that it is written according to the usage of Paris, Orleans, and court of Barony; and the preamble says that it

treats of the usage of the whole kingdom, of Anjou and of the court of Barony. It is plain that this work was made for Paris, Orleans and Anjou, as the works of Beaumanoir and Défontaines were framed for the counties of Clermont and Vermandois; and as it appears from Beaumanoir that divers laws of St. Louis had been received in the courts of Barony, the compiler was in the right to say that his work related also to those courts.[3]

It is manifest that the person who composed this work compiled the customs of the country together with the laws and Institutions of St. Louis. This is a very valuable work, because it contains the ancient customs of Anjou, the Institutions of St. Louis, as they were then in use; and, in fine, the whole practice of the ancient French law.

The difference between this work and those of Défontaines and Beaumanoir is its speaking in imperative terms as a legislator; and this might be right, since it was a medley of written customs and laws.

There was an intrinsic defect in this compilation; it formed an amphibious code, in which the French and Roman laws were mixed, and where things were joined that were in no relation, but often contradictory to each other.

I am not ignorant that the French courts of vassals or peers, the judgments without power of appealing to another tribunal, the manner of pronouncing sentence by these words "I condemn" or "I absolve,"[4] had some conformity to the popular judgments of the Romans. But they made very little use of that ancient jurisprudence; they rather chose that which was afterwards introduced by the emperor, in order to regulate, limit, correct, and extend the French jurisprudence.

39. *The same Subject continued.* The judiciary forms introduced by St. Louis fell into disuse. This prince had not so much in view the thing itself, that is, the best manner of trying causes, as the best manner of supplying the ancient practice of trial. The principal intent was to give a disrelish of the ancient jurisprudence, and the next to form a new one. But

[1] Chapter 61, p. 309.
[2] As he says himself, in his prologue.

[3] Nothing so vague as the title and prologue. At first they are the customs of Paris, Orleans, and the court of Barony; then they are the customs of all the lay courts of the kingdom, and of the provostships of France; at length, they are the customs of the whole kingdom, Anjou, and the court of Barony.
[4] *Institutions*, ii. 15.

when the inconveniences of the latter appeared, another soon succeeded.

The *Institutions* of St. Louis did not, therefore, so much change the French jurisprudence as they afforded the means of changing it; they opened new tribunals, or rather ways to come at them. And when once the public had easy access to the superior courts, the judgments which before constituted only the usages of a particular lordship formed a universal digest. By means of the *Institutions,* they had obtained general decisions, which were entirely wanting in the kingdom; when the building was finished, they let the scaffold fall to the ground.

Thus the *Institutions* produced effects which could hardly be expected from a masterpiece of legislation. To prepare great changes whole ages are sometimes requisite; the events ripen, and the revolutions follow.

The parliament judged in the last resort of almost all the affairs of the kingdom. Before,[1] it took cognizance only of disputes between the dukes, counts, barons, bishops, abbots, or between the king and his vassals,[2] rather in the relation they bore to the political than to the civil order. They were soon obliged to render it permanent, whereas it used to be held only a few times in a year: and, in fine, a great number were created, in order to be sufficient for the decision of all manner of causes.

No sooner had the parliament become a fixed body, than they began to compile its decrees. Jean de Monluc, in the reign of Philip the Fair, made a collection which at present is known by the name of the Olim registers.[3]

40. *In what Manner the judiciary Forms were borrowed from the Decretals.* But how comes it, some will ask, that when the *Institutions* were laid aside, the judicial forms of the canon law should be preferred to those of the Roman? It was because they had constantly before their eyes the ecclesiastic courts, which followed the forms of the canon law, and they knew of no court that followed those of the Roman law. Besides, the limits of the spiritual and temporal jurisdiction were at that time very little understood; there were people who sued indifferently[4] and causes that were tried

indifferently, in either court.[5] It seems[6] as if the temporal jurisdiction reserved no other cases exclusively to itself than the judgment of feudal matters,[7] and of such crimes committed by laymen as did not relate to religion. For[8] if on the account of conventions and contracts, they had occasion to sue in a temporal court, the parties might of their own accord proceed before the spiritual tribunals; and as the latter had not a power to oblige the temporal court to execute the sentence, they commanded submission by means of excommunications. Under those circumstances, when they wanted to change the course of proceedings in the temporal court, they took that of the spiritual tribunals, because they knew it; but did not meddle with that of the Roman law, by reason they were strangers to it: for in point of practice people know only what is really practised.

41. *Flux and Reflux of the ecclesiastic and temporal Jurisdiction.* The civil power being in the hands of an infinite number of lords, it was an easy matter for the ecclesiastic jurisdiction to gain daily a greater extent. But as the ecclesiastic courts weakened those of the lords, and contributed thereby to give strength to the royal jurisdiction, the latter gradually checked the jurisdiction of the clergy. The parliament, which in its form of proceedings had adopted whatever was good and useful in the spiritual courts, soon perceived nothing else but the abuses which had crept into those tribunals; and as the royal jurisdiction gained ground every day, it grew every day more capable of correcting those abuses. And, indeed, they were intolerable; without enumerating them I shall refer the reader to Beaumanoir, to Boutillier and to the ordinances of our kings.[9] I shall mention only two in which the public interest was more directly concerned. These abuses we know by the de-

5 Widows, croises, &c.—*Ibid.*
6 See the whole eleventh chapter of Beaumanoir.
7 The spiritual tribunals had even laid hold of these, under the pretext of the oath, as may be seen by the famous Concordat between Philip Augustus, the clergy, and the barons, which is to be found in the ordinances of Laurière.
8 Beaumanoir, 11, p. 60.
9 See Boutillier, *Somme Rurale,* tit. 9, what persons are incapable of suing in a temporal court; and Beaumanoir, 11, p. 56, and the regulations of Philip Augustus upon this subject; as also the regulation between Philip Augustus, the clergy, and the barons.

1 See Du Tillet on the court of peers. See also Laroche, Flavin, Budeus and Paulus Æmilius, i. 3.
2 Other causes were decided by the ordinary tribunals.
3 See the Président Henault's excellent abridgment of the history of France in the year 1313.
4 Beaumanoir, 11, p. 58.

crees that reformed them; they had been introduced in the times of the darkest ignorance, and upon the breaking out of the first gleam of light, they vanished. From the silence of the clergy it may be presumed that they forwarded this reformation: which, considering the nature of the human mind, deserves commendation. Every man that died without bequeathing a part of his estate to the church, which was called dying "without confession," was deprived of the sacrament and of Christian burial. If he died intestate, his relatives were obliged to prevail upon the bishop that he would, jointly with them, name proper arbiters to determine what sum the deceased ought to have given, in case he had made a will. People could not lie together the first night of their nuptials, or even the two following nights, without having previously purchased leave; these, indeed, were the best three nights to choose; for as to the others, they were not worth much. All this was redressed by the parliament: we find in the glossary of the French law,[1] by Ragau, the decree which it published against the Bishop of Amiens.[2]

I return to the beginning of my chapter. Whenever we observe in any age or government the different bodies of the state endeavouring to increase their authority, and to take particular advantages of each other, we should be often mistaken were we to consider their encroachments as an evident mark of their corruption. Through a fatality inseparable from human nature, moderation in great men is very rare: and as it is always much easier to push on force in the direction in which it moves than to stop its movement, so in the superior class of the people, it is less difficult, perhaps, to find men extremely virtuous, than extremely prudent.

The human mind feels such an exquisite pleasure in the exercise of power; even those who are lovers of virtue are so excessively fond of themselves that there is no man so happy as not still to have reason to mistrust his honest intentions; and, indeed, our actions depend on so many things that it is infinitely easier to do good, than to do it well.

42. *The Revival of the Roman Law, and the Result thereof. Change of Tribunals.* Upon the discovery of Justinian's digest towards the year 1137, the Roman law seemed to rise out

[1] In the word "testamentary Executors."
[2] March 19, 1409.

of its ashes. Schools were then established in Italy, where it was publicly taught; they had already the Justinian code and the *Novellæ*. I mentioned before that this code had been so favourably received in that country as to eclipse the law of the Lombards.

The Italian doctors brought the law of Justinian into France, where they had only the Theodosian code;[3] because Justinian's laws were not made till after the settlement of the Barbarians in Gaul.[4] This law met with some opposition: but it stood its ground notwithstanding the excommunications of the popes, who supported their own canons.[5] St Louis endeavoured to bring it into repute by the translations of Justinian's works, made according to his orders, which are still in manuscript in our libraries; and I have already observed that they made great use of them in compiling the *Institutions*. Philip the Fair ordered the Laws of Justinian to be taught only as written reason in those provinces of France that were governed by customs; and they were adopted as a law in those provinces where the Roman law had been received.[6]

I have already noticed that the manner of proceeding by judicial combat required very little knowledge in the judges; disputes were decided according to the usage of each place, and to a few simple customs received by tradition. In Beaumanoir's time there were two different ways of administering justice;[7] in some places they tried by peers,[8] in others by bailiffs: in following the former way, the peers gave judgment according to the practice of their court; in the latter, it was the *prud'-hommes,* or old men, who pointed out this same practice to the bailiffs.[9] This whole proceeding required neither learning, capacity,

[3] In Italy they followed Justinian's code; hence Pope John VIII, in his constitution published after the Synod of Troyes, makes mention of this code, not because it was known in France, but because he knew it himself, and his constitution was general.
[4] This emperor's code was published towards the year 530.
[5] *Decretals,* v. tit. *de privilegiis,* cap. 28, *super specula.*
[6] By a charter in the year 1312, in favour of the university of Orleans, quoted by Du Tillet.
[7] *Ancient Custom of Beauvoisis,* 1, "Of the Office of Bailiffs."
[8] Among the common people the burghers were tried by burghers, as the feudatory tenants were tried by one another. See La Thaumassière, 19.
[9] Thus all requests began with these words: "My lord judge, it is customary that in your court," &c., as appears from the formula quoted by Boutillier, *Somme Rurale,* i, tit. xxi.

nor study. But when the dark code of the *Institutions* made its appearance; when the Roman law was translated and taught in public schools; when a certain art of procedure and jurisprudence began to be formed; when practitioners and civilians were seen to rise, the peers and the *prud'hommes* were no longer capable of judging: the peers began to withdraw from the lords' tribunals; and the lords were very little inclined to assemble them; especially as the new form of trial, instead of being a solemn proceeding, agreeable to the nobility and interesting to a warlike people, had become a course of pleading which they neither understood, nor cared to learn. The custom of trying by peers began to be less used;[1] that of trying by bailiffs to be more so; the bailiffs did not give judgment themselves,[2] they summed up the evidence and pronounced the judgment of the *prud'hommes;* but the latter being no longer capable of judging, the bailiffs themselves gave judgment.

This was effected so much the easier, as they had before their eyes the practice of the ecclesiastic courts; the canon and new civil law both concurred alike to abolish the peers.

Thus fell the usage hitherto constantly observed in the French monarchy, that judgment should not be pronounced by a single person, as may be seen in the Salic laws, the capitularies, and in the first law-writers under the third race.[3] The contrary abuse which obtains only in local jurisdictions has been moderated, and in some measure redressed, by introducing in many places a judge's deputy, whom he consults, and who represents the ancient *prud'hommes* by the obligation the judge is under of taking two graduates in cases that deserve a corporal punishment; and, in fine, it has become of no effect by the extreme facility of appeals.

43. *The same Subject continued.* Thus there was no law to prohibit the lords from holding their courts themselves; none to abolish the functions of their peers; none to ordain the creation of bailiffs; none to give them the power of judging. All this was effected insensibly, and by the very necessity of the thing. The knowledge of the Roman law, the decrees of the courts, the new digest of the customs, required a study of which the nobility and illiterate people were incapable.

The only ordinance we have upon this subject is that which obliged the lords to choose their bailiffs from among the laity.[4] It is a mistake to look upon this as a law of their creation; for it says no such thing. Besides, the intention of the legislator is determined by the reasons assigned in the ordinance: "to the end that the bailiffs may be punished for their prevarications, it is necessary they be taken from the order of the laity." The immunities of the clergy in those days are very well known.

We must not imagine that the privileges which the nobility formerly enjoyed, and of which they are now divested, were taken from them as usurpations; no, many of those privileges were lost through neglect, and others were given up because, as various changes had been introduced in the course of so many ages, they were inconsistent with those changes.

44. *Of the Proof by Witnesses.* The judges, who had no other rule to go by than the usages, inquired very often by witnesses into every cause that was brought before them.

The usage of judicial combats beginning to decline, they made their inquests in writing. But a verbal proof committed to writing is never more than a verbal proof; so that this only increased the expenses of law proceedings. Regulations were then made which rendered most of those inquests useless;[5] public registers were established, which ascertained most facts, as nobility, age, legitimacy, and marriage. Writing is a witness very hard to corrupt; the customs were therefore reduced to writing. All this is very reasonable; it is much easier to go and see in the baptismal register whether Peter is the son of Paul than to prove this fact by a tedious inquest. When

---

[1] The change was insensible: we meet with trials by peers, even in Boutillier's time, who lived in the year 1402, which is the date of his will: Yet nothing but feudal matters were tried any longer by the peers. *Ibid.*, i, tit. i, p. 16.

[2] As appears by the formula of the letters which their lord used to give them, quoted by Boutillier, *Somme Rurale,* I, tit. xiv, which is proved likewise by Beaumanoir, *Ancient Custom of Beauvoisis,* 1, of the bailiffs: they only directed the proceedings. "The bailiff is obliged in the presence of the peers to take down the words of those who plead, and to ask the parties whether they are willing to have judgment given according to the reasons alleged; and if they say, yes, my lord; the bailiff ought to oblige the peers to give judgment." See also the *Institutions* of St. Louis, i. 105, ii. 15.

[3] Beaumanoir, 67, p. 336, and 61, pp. 315 and 316. The *Institutions,* ii. 15.

[4] It was published in the year 1287.

[5] See in what manner age and parentage were proved.—*Institutions,* i. 71, 72.

there are a number of usages in a country, it is much easier to write them all down in a code, than to oblige individuals to prove every usage. At length the famous ordinance was made which prohibited the admitting of the proof by witnesses for a debt exceeding an hundred livres, except there was the beginning of a proof in writing.

45. *Of the Customs of France.* France, as we have already observed, was governed by written customs, and the particular usages of each lordship constituted the civil law. Every lordship had its civil law, according to Beaumanoir,[1] and so particular a law, that this author, who is looked upon as a luminary, and a very great luminary of those times, says he does not believe that throughout the whole kingdom there were two lordships entirely governed by the same law.

This prodigious diversity had a twofold origin. With regard to the first, the reader may recollect what has been already said concerning it in the chapter of local customs:[2] and as to the second, we meet with it in the different events of legal duels, it being natural that a continual series of fortuitous cases must have been productive of new usages.

These customs were preserved in the memory of old men, but insensibly laws or written customs were formed.

1. At the commencement of the third race, the kings gave not only particular charters, but likewise general ones, in the manner above explained; such are the institutions of Philip Augustus and those made by St. Louis. In like manner the great vassals, in concurrence with the lords who held under them, granted certain charters or establishments, according to particular circumstances at the assizes of their duchies or counties; such were the assize of Godfrey, Count of Brittany, on the division of the nobles; the customs of Normandy, granted by Duke Ralph; the customs of Champagne, given by King Theobald; the laws of Simon, Count of Montfort, and others. This produced some written laws, and even more general ones than those they had before.

2. At the beginning of the third race, almost all the common people were bondmen; but there were several reasons which afterwards determined the kings and lords to enfranchise them.

The lords by enfranchising their bondmen gave them property; it was necessary therefore to give them civil laws, in order to regulate the disposal of that property. But by enfranchising their bondmen, they likewise deprived themselves of their property; there was a necessity, therefore, of regulating the rights which they reserved to themselves, as an equivalent for that property. Both these things were regulated by the charters of enfranchisement; those charters formed a part of our customs, and this part was reduced to writing.[3]

3. Under the reign of St. Louis, and of the succeeding princes, some able practitioners, such as Défontaines, Beaumanoir, and others, committed the customs of their bailiwicks to writing. Their design was rather to give the course of judicial proceedings, than the usages of their time in respect to the disposal of property. But the whole is there, and though these particular authors have no authority but what they derive from the truth and notoriety of the things they speak of, yet there is no manner of doubt but that they contributed greatly to the restoration of our ancient French jurisprudence. Such was in those days our common law.

We have come now to the grand epoch. Charles VII and his successors caused the different local customs throughout the kingdom to be reduced to writing, and prescribed set forms to be observed to their digesting. Now, as this digesting was made through all the provinces, and as people came from each lordship to declare in the general assembly of the province the written or unwritten usages of each place, endeavours were made to render the customs more general, as much as possible, without injuring the interests of individuals, which were carefully preserved.[4] Thus our customs were characterised in a threefold manner; they were committed to writing, they were made more general, and they received the stamp of the royal authority.

Many of these customs having been digested anew, several changes were made either in suppressing whatever was incompatible with the actual practice of the law, or in adding several things drawn from this practice.

Though the common law is considered among us as in some measure opposite to the

[1] Prologue to the *Ancient Custom of Beauvoisis.*
[2] Chapter 12.

[3] See the *Collection of Ordinances,* by Laurière.
[4] This was observed at the digesting of the customs of Berry and of Paris. See La Thaumassière, 3.

Roman, insomuch that these two laws divide the different territories, it is, notwithstanding, true that several regulations of the Roman law entered into our customs, especially when they made the new digests, at a time not very distant from ours, when this law was the principal study of those who were designed for civil employments, at a time when it was not usual for people to boast of not knowing what it was their duty to know, and of knowing what they ought not to know, at a time when a quickness of understanding was made more subservient to learning than pretending to a profession, and when a continual pursuit of amusements was not even the characteristic of women.

I should have been more diffuse at the end of this book, and, entering into the several details, should have traced all the insensible changes which from the opening of appeals have formed the great corpus of our French jurisprudence. But this would have been ingrafting one large work upon another. I am like that antiquarian[4] who set out from his own country, arrived in Egypt, cast an eye on the pyramids and returned home.

Book XXIX. Of the Manner of Composing Laws

1. *Of the Spirit of a Legislator.* I say it, and methinks I have undertaken this work with no other view than to prove it, the spirit of a legislator ought to be that of moderation; political, like moral good, lying always between two extremes.[1] Let us produce an example.

The set forms of justice are necessary to liberty, but the number of them might be so great as to be contrary to the end of the very laws that established them; processes would have no end; property would be uncertain; the goods of one of the parties would be adjudged to the other without examining, or they would both be ruined by examining too much.

The citizens would lose their liberty and security, the accusers would no longer have any means to convict, nor the accused to justify themselves.

2. *The same Subject continued.* Cecilius, in Aulus Gellius,[2] speaking of the law of the Twelve Tables which permitted the creditor to cut the insolvent debtor into pieces, justifies it even by its cruelty, which hindered people from borrowing beyond their ability of paying.[3] Shall then the cruellest laws be the best? Shall goodness consist in excess, and all the relations of things be destroyed?

3. *That the Laws which seem to deviate from the Views of the Legislator are frequently agreeable to them.* The law of Solon which declared those persons infamous who espoused no side in an insurrection seemed very extraordinary; but we ought to consider the circumstances in which Greece was at that time. It was divided into very small states; and there was reason to apprehend lest in a republic torn by intestine divisions the soberest part should keep retired, in consequence of which things might be carried to extremity.

In the seditions raised in those petty states the bulk of the citizens either made or engaged in the quarrel. In our large monarchies parties are formed by a few, and the people choose to live quietly. In the latter case it is natural to call back the seditious to the bulk of the citizens, and not these to the seditious; in the other it is necessary to oblige the small number of prudent people to enter among the seditious; it is thus the fermentation of one liquor may be stopped by a single drop of another.

4. *Of the Laws contrary to the Views of the Legislator.* There are laws so little understood by the legislator as to be contrary to the very end he proposed. Those who made this regulation among the French, that when one of the two competitors died the benefice should devolve to the survivor, had in view, without doubt, the extinction of quarrels; but the very reverse falls out; we see the clergy at variance every day, and like English mastiffs worrying one another to death.

5. *The same Subject continued.* The law I am going to speak of is to be found in this oath

1 Aristotle, *Politics*, iv. 11.
2 Book xx. 1.
3 Cecilius says that he never saw nor read of an instance in which this punishment had been inflicted; but it is likely that no such punishment was ever established: the opinion of some civilians, that the law of the Twelve Tables meant only the division of the money arising from the sale of the debtor, seems very probable.
4 In the *Spectator.*

preserved by Æschines:[1] "I swear that I will never destroy a town of the Amphictyones, and that I will not divert the course of its running waters; if any nation shall presume to do such a thing, I will declare war against them and will destroy their towns." The last article of this law, which seems to confirm the first, is really contrary to it. Amphictyon is willing that the Greek towns should never be destroyed, and yet his law paves the way for their destruction. In order to establish a proper law of nations among the Greeks, they ought to have been accustomed early to think it a barbarous thing to destroy a Greek town; consequently they ought not even to ruin the destroyers. Amphictyon's law was just, but it was not prudent; this appears even from the abuse made of it. Did not Philip assume the power of demolishing towns, under the pretence of their having infringed the laws of the Greeks? Amphictyon might have inflicted other punishments; he might have ordained, for example, that a certain number of the magistrates of the destroying town, or of the chiefs of the infringing army, should be punished with death; that the destroying nation should cease for a while to enjoy the privileges of the Greeks; that they should pay a fine till the town was rebuilt. The law ought, above all things, to aim at the reparation of damages.

6. *The Laws which appear the same have not always the same Effect.* Cæsar made a law to prohibit people from keeping above sixty sesterces in their houses.[2] This law was considered at Rome as extremely proper for reconciling the debtors to their creditors, because, by obliging the rich to lend to the poor, they enabled the latter to pay their debts. A law of the same nature made in France at the time of the System proved extremely fatal, because it was enacted under a most frightful situation. After depriving people of all possible means of laying out their money, they stripped them even of the last resource of keeping it at home, which was the same as taking it from them by open violence. Cæsar's law was intended to make the money circulate; the French minister's design was to draw all the money into one hand. The former gave either lands or mortgages on private people for the money; the latter proposed in lieu of money nothing but effects which were of no value, and could have none by their very na-

ture, because the law compelled people to accept of them.

7. *The same Subject continued. Necessity of composing Laws in a proper Manner.* The law of ostracism was established at Athens, at Argos,[3] and at Syracuse. At Syracuse it was productive of a thousand mischiefs, because it was imprudently enacted. The principal citizens banished one another by holding the leaf of a fig-tree in their hands, so that those who had any kind of merit withdrew from public affairs.[4] At Athens, where the legislator was sensible of the proper extent and limits of his law, ostracism proved an admirable regulation. They never condemned more than one person at a time; and such a number of suffrages were requisite for passing this sentence that it was extremely difficult for them to banish a person whose absence was not necessary to the state.[5]

The power of banishing was exercised only every fifth year: and indeed, as the ostracism was designed against none but great personages who threatened the state with danger, it ought not to have been the transaction of every day.

8. *That Laws which appear the same were not always made through the same Motive.* In France they have received most of the Roman laws on substitutions, but through quite a different motive from the Romans. Among the latter the inheritance was accompanied with certain sacrifices[6] which were to be performed by the inheritor and were regulated by the pontifical law; hence it was that they reckoned it a dishonour to die without heirs, that they made slaves their heirs, and that they devised substitutions. Of this we have a very strong proof in the vulgar substitution, which was the first invented, and took place only when the heir appointed did not accept of the inheritance. Its view was not to perpetuate the estate in a family of the same name, but to find somebody that would accept of it.

9. *That the Greek and Roman Laws punished Suicide, but not through the same Motive.* A man, says Plato, who has killed one nearly re-

---

[1] *De Falsa legatione.*
[2] Dio, xli.

[3] Aristotle, *Politics*, v. 13.
[4] Plutarch, *Dionysius.*
[5] See xxvi. 17, p. 223, above.
[6] When the inheritance was too much encumbered they eluded the pontifical law by certain sales, whence come the words *sine sacris hæreditas.*

lated to him, that is, himself, not by an order of the magistrate, not to avoid ignomiy, but through pusillanimity shall be punished.[1] The Roman law punished this action when it was not committed through pusillanimity, through weariness of life, through impatience in pain, but from a criminal despair. The Roman law acquitted where the Greek condemned, and condemned where the other acquitted.

Plato's law was formed upon the Lacedæmonian institutions, where the orders of the magistrate were absolute, where shame was the greatest of miseries, and pusillanimity the greatest of crimes. The Romans had no longer those refined ideas; theirs was only a fiscal law.

During the time of the republic, there was no law at Rome against suicides; this action is always considered by their historians in a favourable light, and we never meet with any punishment inflicted upon those who committed it.

Under the first emperors, the great families of Rome were continually destroyed by criminal prosecutions. The custom was then introduced of preventing judgment by a voluntary death. In this they found a great advantage: they had an honourable interment, and their wills were executed, because there was no law against suicides.[2] But when the emperors became as avaricious as cruel, they deprived those who destroyed themselves of the means of preserving their estates by rendering it criminal for a person to make away with himself through a criminal remorse.

What I have been saying of the motive of the emperors is so true, that they consented that the estates of suicides should not be confiscated when the crime for which they killed themselves was not punished with confiscation.[3]

10. *That Laws which seem contrary proceed sometimes from the same Spirit.* In our time we give summons to people in their own houses; but this was not permitted among the Romans.[4]

A summons was a violent action,[5] and a

kind of warrant for seizing the body;[6] hence it was no more allowed to summon a person in his own house than it is now allowed to arrest a person in his own house for debt.

Both the Roman and our laws admit of this principle alike, that every man ought to have his own house for an asylum, where he should suffer no violence.[7]

11. *How to compare two different Systems of Laws.* In France the punishment for false witnesses is capital; in England it is not. Now, to be able to judge which of these two laws is the best, we must add that in France the rack is used for criminals, but not in England; that in France the accused is not allowed to produce his witnesses, and that they very seldom admit of what are called justifying circumstances in favour of the prisoner; in England they allow of witnesses on both sides. These three French laws form a close and well-connected system; and so do the three English laws. The law of England, which does not allow of the racking of criminals, has but very little hope of drawing from the accused a confession of his crime; for this reason it invites witnesses from all parts, and does not venture to discourage them by the fear of a capital punishment. The French law, which has one resource more, is not afraid of intimidating the witnesses; on the contrary, reason requires they should be intimidated; it listens only to the witnesses on one side, which are those produced by the attorney-general, and the fate of the accused depends entirely on their testimony.[8] But in England they admit of witnesses on both sides, and the affair is discussed in some measure between them; consequently false witness is there less dangerous, the accused having a remedy against the false witness which he has not in France. Wherefore, to determine which of those systems is most agreeable to reason, we must take them each as a whole and compare them in their entirety.

12. *That Laws which appear the same are sometimes really different.* The Greek and Roman laws inflicted the same punishment on

---

[1] *Laws* ix.
[2] Tacitus, *Annals*, vi. 29.
[3] Rescript of the Emperor Pius in *Leg.* 3, §§ 1, 2, ff. *de bonis eorum qui ante sententiam mortem sibi consciverunt.*
[4] *Leg.* 18, ff. *de in jus vocando.*
[5] See the Law of the Twelve Tables.

[6] *Rapit in jus.*—Horace, *Sat.,* i. 9. Hence they could not summon those to whom a particular respect was due.
[7] See *Leg.* 18, ff. *de in jus vocando.*
[8] By the ancient French law, witnesses were heard on both sides; hence we find in the *Institutions* of St. Louis, i. 7, that there was only a pecuniary punishment against false witnesses.

CHAP. 14 THE SPIRIT OF LAWS 265

the receiver as on the thief;[1] the French law does the same. The former acted rationally, but the latter does not. Among the Greeks and Romans the thief was condemned to a pecuniary punishment, which ought also to be inflicted on the receiver; for every man that contributes in what shape soever to a damage is obliged to repair it. But as the punishment of theft is capital with us, the receiver cannot be punished like the thief without carrying things to excess. A receiver may act innocently on a thousand occasions: the thief is always culpable; one hinders the conviction of a crime, the other commits it; in one the whole is passive, the other is active; the thief must surmount more obstacles, and his soul must be more hardened against the laws.

The civilians have gone further; they look upon the receiver as more odious than the thief,[2] for were it not for the receiver the theft, say they, could not be long concealed. But this again might be right when there was only a pecuniary punishment; the affair in question was a damage done, and the receiver was generally better able to repair it; but when the punishment became capital, they ought to have been directed by other principles.

13. *That we must not separate Laws from the End for which they were made: of the Roman Laws on Theft.* When a thief was caught in the act, this was called by the Romans a manifest theft; when he was not detected till some time afterwards, it was a non-manifest theft.

The law of the Twelve Tables ordained that a manifest thief should be whipped with rods and condemned to slavery if he had attained the age of puberty; or only whipped if he was not of ripe age; but as for the non-manifest thief, he was only condemned to a fine of double the value of what he had stolen.

When the Porcian laws abolished the custom of whipping the citizens with rods, and of reducing them to slavery, the manifest thief was condemned to a payment of fourfold, and they still continued to condemn the non-manifest thief to a payment of double.[3]

It seems very odd that these laws should make such a difference in the quality of those two crimes, and in the punishments they inflicted. And, indeed, whether the thief was detected either before or after he had carried the stolen goods to the place intended, this was a

circumstance which did not alter the nature of the crime. I do not at all question that the whole theory of the Roman laws in relation to theft was borrowed from the Lacedæmonian institutions. Lycurgus, with a view of rendering the citizens dextrous and cunning, ordained that children should be practised in thieving, and that those who were caught in the act should be severely whipped. This occasioned among the Greeks, and afterwards among the Romans, a great difference between a manifest and a non-manifest theft.[4]

Among the Romans, a slave who had been guilty of stealing was thrown from the Tarpeian rock. Here the Lacedæmonian institutions were out of the question; the laws of Lycurgus in relation to theft were not made for slaves; to deviate from them in this respect was in reality conforming to them.

At Rome, when a person of unripe age happened to be caught in the act, the prætor ordered him to be whipped with rods according to his pleasure, as was practised at Sparta. All this had a more remote origin. The Lacedæmonians had derived these usages from the Cretans; and Plato,[5] who wants to prove that the Cretan institutions were designed for war, cites the following, namely, the power of bearing pain in individual combats, and in thefts which have to be concealed.

As the civil laws depend on the political institutions, because they are made for the same society, whenever there is a design of adopting the civil law of another nation, it would be proper to examine beforehand whether they have both the same institutions and the same political law.

Thus when the Cretan laws on theft were adopted by the Lacedæmonians, as their constitution and government were adopted at the same time, these laws were equally reasonable in both nations. But when they were carried from Lacedæmon to Rome, as they did not find there the same constitution, they were always thought strange, and had no manner of connection with the other civil laws of the Romans.

14. *That we must not separate the Laws from the Circumstances in which they were made.* It was decreed by a law at Athens that when the city was besieged, all the useless people should

---

[1] *Leg.* 1, ff. *de receptatoribus.*
[2] *Ibid.*
[3] See what Favorinus says in Aulus Gellius, xx. 1.

[4] Compare what Plutarch says in the *Lycurgus* with the laws of the *Digest*, title *De furtis;* and the *Institutes*, iv, tit. 1, §§ 1, 2, 3.
[5] *Laws*, i.

be put to death.[1] This was an abominable political law, in consequence of an abominable law of nations. Among the Greeks, the inhabitants of a town taken lost their civil liberty and were sold as slaves. The taking of a town implied its entire destruction, which is the source not only of those obstinate defences, and of those unnatural actions, but likewise of those shocking laws which they sometimes enacted.

The Roman laws ordained that physicians should be punished for neglect or unskilfulness.[2] In those cases, if the physician was a person of any fortune or rank, he was only condemned to deportation, but if he was of a low condition he was put to death. By our institutions it is otherwise. The Roman laws were not made under the same circumstances as ours: at Rome every ignorant pretender intermeddled with physic; but among us, physicians are obliged to go through a regular course of study, and to take their degrees, for which reason they are supposed to understand their profession.

15. *That sometimes it is proper the Law should amend itself.* The law of the Twelve Tables allowed people to kill a night-thief as well as a day-thief,[3] if upon being pursued he attempted to make a defence; but it required that the person who killed the thief should cry out and call his fellow-citizens. This is indeed what those laws, which permit people to do justice to themselves, ought always to require. It is the cry of innocence which in the very moment of the action calls in witnesses and appeals to judges. The people ought to take cognizance of the action, and at the very instant of its being done; an instant when everything speaks, even air, countenance, passions, silence; and when every word either condemns or absolves. A law which may become so opposed to the security and liberty of the citizens ought to be executed in their presence.[4]

16. *Things to be observed in the composing of Laws.* They who have a genius sufficient to enable them to give laws to their own, or to another nation, ought to be particularly attentive to the manner of forming them.

The style ought to be concise. The laws of the Twelve Tables are a model of conciseness;

the very children used to learn them by heart.[5] Justinian's *Novellæ* were so very diffuse that they were obliged to abridge them.[6]

The style should also be plain and simple, a direct expression being better understood than an indirect one. There is no majesty at all in the laws of the lower empire; princes are made to speak like rhetoricians. When the style of laws is inflated, they are looked upon only as a work of parade and ostentation.

It is an essential article that the words of the laws should excite in everybody the same ideas. Cardinal Richelieu[7] agreed that a minister might be accused before the king, but he would have the accuser punished if the facts he proved were not matters of moment. This was enough to hinder people from telling any truth whatsoever against the minister, because a matter of moment is entirely relative, and what may be of moment to one is not so to another.

The law of Honorius punished with death any person that purchased a freedman as a slave, or that gave him molestation.[8] He should not have made use of so vague an expression; the molestation given a man depends entirely on the degree of his sensibility.

When the law has to impose a penalty, it should avoid as much as possible the estimating it in money. The value of money changes from a thousand causes, and the same denomination continues without the same thing. Every one knows the story of that impudent fellow at Rome[9] who used to give those he met a box on the ear, and afterwards tendered them the five-and-twenty pence of the law of the Twelve Tables.

When the law has once fixed the idea of things, it should never return to vague expressions. The ordinance of Louis XIV[10] concerning criminal matters, after an exact enumeration of the causes in which the king is immediately concerned, adds these words, "and those which in all times have been subject to the determination of the king's judges"; this again renders arbitrary what had just been fixed.

Charles VII says[11] he has been informed that

[1] Syrian., in Hermog.
[2] The Cornelian law *De Sicariis, Institutes,* iv, tit. 3, *de lege Aquilia,* § 7.
[3] See *Leg.* 4, ff. *ad leg. Aquil.*
[4] *Ibid.;* see the decree of Tassillon added to the law of the Bavarians, *de popularib. Legib.* art. 4.

[5] *Ut carmen necessarium.*—Cicero, *De Leg.* ii, 23.
[6] It is the work of Irnerius.
[7] *Testament. Polit.*
[8] Appendix to the Theodosian code in the first volume of Father Sirmond's works, p. 737.
[9] Aulus Gellius, xx. 1.
[10] We find in the verbal process of this ordinance the motives that determined him.
[11] In his ordinance of Montel-les-Tours, in the year 1453.

the parties appeal three, four, and six months after judgment, contrary to the custom of the kingdom in a country where custom prevailed; he therefore ordains that they shall appeal forthwith, unless there happens to be some fraud or deceit on the part of the attorney,[1] or unless there be a great or evident cause to discharge the appeal. The end of this law destroys the beginning, and it destroys it so effectually, that they used afterwards to appeal during the space of thirty years.[2]

The law of the Lombards does not allow a woman that has taken a religious habit,[3] though she has made no vow, to marry; because, says this law, "if a spouse who has been contracted to a woman only by a ring cannot without guilt be married to another, for a much stronger reason the spouse of God or of the blessed Virgin." Now, I say, that in laws the arguments should be drawn from one reality to another, and not from reality to figure, or from figure to reality.

A law enacted by Constantine[4] ordains that the single testimony of a bishop should be sufficient without listening to any other witnesses. This prince took a very short method; he judged of affairs by persons, and of persons by dignities.

The laws ought not to be subtle; they are designed for people of common understanding, not as an art of logic, but as the plain reason of a father of a family.

When there is no necessity for exceptions and limitations in a law, it is much better to omit them: details of that kind throw people into new details.

No alteration should be made in a law without sufficient reason. Justinian ordained that a husband might be repudiated and yet the wife not lose her portion, if for the space of two years he had been incapable of consummating the marriage.[5] He altered his law afterwards, and allowed the poor wretch three years.[6] But in a case of that nature two years are as good as three, and three are not worth more than two.

When a legislator condescends to give the

reason of his law it ought to be worthy of its majesty. A Roman law decrees that a blind man is incapable to plead, because he cannot see the ornaments of the magistracy.[7] So bad a reason must have been given on purpose, when such a number of good reasons were at hand.

Paul, the jurist, says[8] that a child grows perfect in the seventh month, and that the ratio of Pythagoras' numbers seems to prove it. It is very extraordinary that they should judge of those things by the ratio of Pythagoras' numbers.

Some French lawyers have asserted that when the king made an acquisition of a new country, the churches became subject to the *Regale*, because the king's crown is round. I shall not examine here into the king's rights, or whether in this case the reason of the civil or ecclesiastic law ought to submit to that of the law of politics; I shall only say that those august rights ought to be defended by grave maxims. Was there ever such a thing known as the real rights of a dignity founded on the figure of that dignity's sign?

Davila says[9] that Charles IX was declared of age in the parliament of Rouen at the commencement of his fourteenth year, because the laws require every moment of the time to be reckoned, in cases relating to the restitution and administration of a ward's estate; whereas it considers the year commenced as a year complete, when the case is concerning the acquisition of honours. I am very far from censuring a regulation which has been hitherto attended with no inconvenience; I shall only notice that the reason alleged is not the true one; it is false, that the government of a nation is only an honour.

In point of presumption, that of the law is far preferable to that of the man. The French law considers every act of a merchant during the ten days preceding his bankruptcy as fraudulent:[10] this is the presumption of the law. The Roman law inflicted punishments on the husband who kept his wife after she had been guilty of adultery, unless he was induced to do it through fear of the event of a lawsuit, or through contempt of his own shame; this is the presumption of the man. The judge must have presumed the motives of the husband's conduct, and must have determined a

---

[1] They might punish the attorney, without there being any necessity of disturbing the public order.

[2] The ordinance of the year 1667 has made some regulations upon this head.

[3] Book ii, tit. 37.

[4] In Father Sirmond's appendix to the Theodosian code, i.

[5] *Leg.* 1, *Cod. de repudiis.*

[6] See the authentic *sed hodie,* in the *Cod. de repudiis.*

[7] *Leg.* 1, ff. *de Postulando.*

[8] *Sentences,* iv. 9.

[9] *Della guerra civile di Francia,* p. 96.

[10] It was made on November 18, 1702.

very obscure and ambiguous point; when the law presumes, it gives a fixed rule to the judge.

Plato's law,[1] as I have observed already, required that a punishment should be inflicted on the person who killed himself not with a design of avoiding shame, but through pusillanimity. This law was so far defective that in the only case in which it was impossible to draw from the criminal an acknowledgment of the motive upon which he had acted, it required the judge to determine concerning these motives.

As useless laws debilitate such as are necessary, so those that may be easily eluded weaken the legislation. Every law ought to have its effect, and no one should be suffered to deviate from it by a particular exception.

The Falcidian law ordained among the Romans, that the heir should always have the fourth part of the inheritance; another law suffered the testator to prohibit the heir from retaining this fourth part.[2] This is making a jest of the laws. The Falcidian law became useless: for if the testator had a mind to favour his heir, the latter had no need of the Falcidian law; and if he did not intend to favour him, he forbad him to make use of it.

Care should be taken that the laws be worded in such a manner as not to be contrary to the very nature of things. In the proscription of the Prince of Orange, Philip II promises to any man that will kill the prince to give him, or his heirs, five-and-twenty thousand crowns, together with the title of nobility; and this upon the word of a king, and as a servant of God. To promise nobility for such an action! to ordain such an action in the quality of a servant of God! This is equally subversive of the ideas of honour, morality, and religion.

There very seldom happens to be a necessity of prohibiting a thing which is not bad under pretence of some imaginary perfection.

There ought to be a certain simplicity and candour in the laws; made to punish the iniquity of men, they themselves should be clad with the robes of innocence. We find in the law of the Visigoths[3] that ridiculous request, by which the Jews were obliged to eat everything dressed with pork, provided they did not eat the pork itself. This was a very great cruelty: they were obliged to submit to a law contrary to their own; and they were obliged to retain nothing more of their own than what might serve as a mark to distinguish them.

17. *A bad Method of giving Laws.* The Roman Emperors manifested their will, like our princes, by decrees and edicts; but they permitted, which our princes do not, both the judges and private people to interrogate them by letters in their several differences; and their answers were called rescripts. The decretals of the popes are rescripts, strictly speaking. It is plain that this is a bad method of legislation. Those who thus apply for laws are improper guides to the legislator; the facts are always wrongly stated. Julius Capitolinus says[4] that Trajan often refused to give this kind of rescripts, lest a single decision, and frequently a particular favour, should be extended to all cases. Macrinus had resolved to abolish all those rescripts;[5] he could not bear that the answers of Commodus, Caracalla, and all those other ignorant princes, should be considered as laws. Justinian thought otherwise, and he filled his compilation with them.

I would advise those who read the Roman laws to distinguish carefully between this sort of hypothesis, and the *Senatus Consulta,* the *Plebiscita,* the general constitutions of the emperors, and all the laws founded on the nature of things, on the frailty of women, the weakness of minors, and the public utility.

18. *Of the Ideas of Uniformity.* There are certain ideas of uniformity, which sometimes strike great geniuses (for they even affected Charlemagne), but infallibly make an impression on little souls. They discover therein a kind of perfection, which they recognize because it is impossible for them not to see it; the same authorized weights, the same measures in trade, the same laws in the state, the same religion in all its parts. But is this always right and without exception? Is the evil of changing constantly less than that of suffering? And does not a greatness of genius consist rather in distinguishing between those cases in which uniformity is requisite, and those in which there is a necessity for differences? In China the Chinese are governed by the Chinese ceremonial and the Tartars by theirs; and yet there is no nation in the world that aims so much at tranquillity. If the people observe the laws, what signifies it whether these laws are the same?

---

[1] *Laws,* ix.
[2] It is the authentic *sed cum testator.*
[3] Book xii, tit. 2, § 16.

[4] See Julius Capitolinus, in Macrinus, 13.
[5] *Ibid.*

19. *Of Legislators.* Aristotle wanted to indulge sometimes his jealousy against Plato, and sometimes his passion for Alexander. Plato was incensed against the tyranny of the people of Athens. Machiavel was full of his idol, the Duke of Valentinois. Sir Thomas More, who spoke rather of what he had read than of what he thought, wanted to govern all states with the simplicity of a Greek city.[1] Harrington was full of the idea of his favourite republic of England, while a crowd of writers saw nothing but confusion where monarchy is abolished. The laws always conform to the passions and prejudices of the legislator; sometimes the latter pass through, and only tincture them; sometimes they remain, and are incorporated with them.

Book XXX. Theory of the Feudal Laws among the Franks in the Relation They Bear to the Establishment of the Monarchy

1. *Of Feudal Laws.* I should think my work imperfect were I to pass over in silence an event which never again, perhaps, will happen; were I not to speak of those laws which suddenly appeared over all Europe without being connected with any of the former institutions; of those laws which have done infinite good and infinite mischief; which have suffered rights to remain when the demesne has been ceded; which by vesting several with different kinds of seignory over the same things or persons have diminished the weight of the whole seignory; which have established different limits in empires of too great extent; which have been productive of rule with a bias to anarchy, and of anarchy with a tendency to order and harmony.

This would require a particular work to itself; but considering the nature of the present undertaking, the reader will here meet rather with a general survey than with a complete treatise of those laws.

The feudal laws form a very beautiful prospect. A venerable old oak raises its lofty head to the skies, the eye sees from afar its spreading leaves; upon drawing nearer, it perceives the trunk but does not discern the root; the ground must be dug up to discover it.[2]

2. *Of the Source of Feudal Laws.* The conquerors of the Roman empire came from Germany. Though few ancient authors have described their manners, yet we have two of very great weight. Cæsar making war against the Germans describes the manners of that nation;[3] and upon these he regulated some of his enterprises.[4] A few pages of Cæsar upon this subject are equal to whole volumes.

Tacitus has written an entire work on the manners of the Germans. This work is short, but it comes from the pen of Tacitus, who was always concise, because he saw everything at one glance.

These two authors agree so perfectly with the codes still extant of the laws of the Barbarians, that reading Cæsar and Tacitus we imagine we are perusing these codes, and perusing these codes we fancy we are reading Cæsar and Tacitus.

But if in this research into the feudal laws I should find myself entangled and lost in a dark labyrinth, I fancy I have the clue in my hand, and that I shall be able to find my way through.

3. *The Origin of Vassalage.* Cæsar says[5] that, "The Germans neglected agriculture; that the greatest part of them lived upon milk, cheese and flesh; that no one had lands or boundaries of his own; that the princes and magistrates of each nation allotted what portion of land they pleased to individuals, and obliged them the year following to remove to some other part." Tacitus says[6] that, "Each prince had a multitude of men, who were attached to his service, and followed him wherever he went." This author gives them a name in his language in accordance with their state, which is that of companions.[7] They had a strong emulation to obtain the prince's esteem; and the princes had the same emulation to distinguish themselves in the bravery and number of their companions. "Their dignity and power," continues Tacitus, "consist in being constantly surrounded by a multitude of young and

[1] In his *Utopia.*
[2] *Quantum vertice ad oras Æthereas, tantum radice ad Tartara tendit.*— Virgil, *Georg.,* ii. 292; *Æneid,* iv. 446.
[3] Book iv.
[4] For instance, his retreat from Germany.—*Ibid.*

[5] *De Bello Gall.,* vi. 21; Tacitus, *De Moribus Germanorum,* 31.
[6] *De Moribus Germanorum,* 13.
[7] *Comites.*

chosen people; this they reckon their ornament in peace, this their defence and support in war. Their name becomes famous at home, and among neighbouring nations, when they excel all others in the number and courage of their companions: they receive presents and embassies from all parts. Reputation frequently decides the fate of war. In battle it is infamy in the prince to be surpassed in courage; it is infamy in the companions not to follow the brave example of their prince; it is an eternal disgrace to survive him. To defend him is their most sacred engagement. If a city be at peace, the princes go to those who are at war; and it is thus they retain a great number of friends. To these they give the war horse and the terrible javelin. Their pay consists in coarse but plentiful repasts. The prince supports his liberality merely by war and plunder. You might more easily persuade them to attack an enemy and to expose themselves to the dangers of war, than to cultivate the land, or to attend to the cares of husbandry; they refuse to acquire by sweat what they can purchase with blood."

Thus, among the Germans, there were vassals, but no fiefs; they had no fiefs, because the princes had no lands to give; or rather their fiefs consisted in horses trained for war, in arms, and feasting. There were vassals, because there were trusty men who being bound by their word engaged to follow the prince to the field, and did very nearly the same service as was afterwards performed for the fiefs.

4. *The same Subject continued.* Cæsar says[1] that "when any of the princes declared to the assembly that he intended to set out upon an expedition and asked them to follow him, those who approved the leader and the enterprise stood up and offered their assistance. Upon which they were commended by the multitude. But, if they did not fulfil their engagements, they lost the public esteem, and were looked upon as deserters and traitors."

What Cæsar says in this place, and what we have extracted in the preceding chapter from Tacitus, are the substance of the history of our princes of the first race.

We must not therefore be surprised that our kings should have new armies to raise upon every expedition, new troops to encourage, new people to engage; that to acquire much they were obliged to incur great expenses; that they should be constant gainers by the division of lands and spoils, and yet give these lands and spoils incessantly away: that their demesne should continually increase and diminish; that a father upon settling a kingdom on one of his children[2] should always give him a treasure with it: that the king's treasure should be considered as necessary to the monarchy; and that one king could not give part of it to foreigners, even in portion with his daughter, without the consent of the other kings.[3] The monarchy moved by springs, which they were continually obliged to wind up.

5. *Of the Conquests of the Franks.* It is not true that the Franks upon entering Gaul took possession of the whole country to turn it into fiefs. Some have been of this opinion because they saw the greatest part of the country towards the end of the second race converted into fiefs, rear-fiefs, or other dependencies; but such a disposition was owing to particular causes which we shall explain hereafter.

The consequence which sundry writers would infer thence, that the barbarians made a general regulation for establishing in all parts the state of villainage is as false as the principle from which it is derived. If at a time when the fiefs were precarious, all the lands of the kingdom had been fiefs, or dependencies of fiefs; and all the men in the kingdom vassals or bondmen subordinate to vassals; as the person that has property is ever possessed of power, the king, who would have continually disposed of the fiefs, that is, of the only property then existing; would have had a power as arbitrary as that of the Sultan is in Turkey; which is contradictory to all history.

6. *Of the Goths, Burgundians, and Franks.* Gaul was invaded by German nations. The Visigoths took possession of the province of Narbonne, and of almost all the south; the Burgundians settled in the east; and the Franks subdued very nearly all the rest.

No doubt but these Barbarians retained in their respective conquests the manners, inclinations, and usages of their own country; for no nation can change in an instant their manner of thinking and acting. These people in

[1] *De Bello Gall.*, vi. 22.

[2] See the Life of Dagobert.
[3] See Gregory of Tours, vi, on the marriage of the daughter of Chilperic. Childebert sends ambassadors to tell him that he should not give the cities of his father's kingdom to his daughter, nor his treasures, nor his bondmen, nor horses, nor horsemen, nor teams of oxen, &c.

Germany neglected agriculture. It seems by Cæsar and Tacitus that they applied themselves greatly to a pastoral life; hence the regulations of the codes of Barbarian laws almost all relate to their flocks. Roricon, who wrote a history among the Franks, was a shepherd.

7. *Different Ways of dividing the Land.* After the Goths and Burgundians had, under various pretences, penetrated into the heart of the empire, the Romans, in order to put a stop to their devastations, were obliged to provide for their subsistence. At first they allowed them corn,[1] but afterwards chose to give them lands. The emperors, or the Roman magistrates, in their name, made particular conventions with them concerning the division of lands,[2] as we find in the chronicles and in the codes of the Visigoths[3] and Burgundians.[4]

The Franks did not follow the same plan. In the Salic and Ripuarian laws, we find not the least vestige of any such division of lands; they had conquered the country, and so took what they pleased, making no regulations but among themselves.

Let us, therefore, distinguish between the conduct of the Burgundians and Visigoths in Gaul, of those same Visigoths in Spain, of the auxiliary troops under Augustulus and Odoacer in Italy,[5] and that of the Franks in Gaul, as also of the Vandals in Africa.[6] The former entered into conventions with the ancient inhabitants, and in consequence thereof made a division of lands between them; the latter did no such thing.

8. *The same Subject continued.* What has induced some to think that the Roman lands were entirely usurped by the Barbarians is their finding in the laws of the Visigoths and the Burgundians that these two nations had two-thirds of the lands; but this they took only in certain quarters or districts assigned them.

Gundebald says, in the law of the Burgundians, that his people at their establishment

had two-thirds of the lands allowed them;[7] and the second supplement to this law notices that only a moiety would be allowed to those who should hereafter come to live in that country.[8] Therefore, all the lands had not been divided in the beginning between the Romans and the Burgundians.

In those two regulations we meet with the same expressions in the text, consequently they explain one another; and as the latter cannot mean a universal division of lands, neither can this signification be given to the former.

The Franks acted with the same moderation as the Burgundians; they did not strip the Romans wherever they extended their conquests. What would they have done with so much land? They took what suited them, and left the remainder.

9. *A just Application of the Law of the Burgundians, and of that of the Visigoths, in relation to the Division of Lands.* It is to be considered that those divisions of land were not made with a tyrannical spirit; but with a view of relieving the reciprocal wants of two nations that were to inhabit the same country.

The law of the Burgundians ordains that a Burgundian shall be received in an hospitable manner by a Roman. This is agreeable to the manners of the Germans, who, according to Tacitus,[9] were the most hospitable people in the world.

By the law of the Burgundians, it is ordained that the Burgundians shall have two-thirds of the lands, and one-third of the bondmen. In this it considered the genius of two nations, and conformed to the manner in which they procured their subsistence. As the Burgundians kept herds and flocks, they wanted a great deal of land and few bondmen, and the Romans, from their application to agriculture, had need of less land, and of a greater number of bondmen. The woods were equally divided, because their wants in this respect were the same.

We find in the code of the Burgundians[10] that each Barbarian was placed near a Roman. The division therefore was not general; but the Romans who gave the division were equal in number to the Burgundians who received it. The Roman was injured least. The Burgun-

---

[1] The Romans obliged themselves to this by treaties. See Zozimus, v, upon the distribution of corn demanded by Alaric.—Ed.
[2] Marius' Chronicle in the year 456.
[3] Book x, tit. 1, §§ 8, 9, & 16.
[4] Chapter 54, §§ 1, 2. This division was still subsisting in the time of Louis the Debonnaire, as appears by his Capitulary of the year 829, which has been inserted in the law of the Burgundians, tit. 79, § 1.
[5] See Procopius, *War of the Goths.*
[6] See Procopius, *War of the Vandals.*

[7] Law of the Burgundians, tit. 54, § 1.
[8] Art. 11.
[9] *De Moribus Germanorum,* 21.
[10] And in that of the Visigoths.

dians as a martial people, fond of hunting and of a pastoral life, did not refuse to accept of the fallow grounds; while the Romans kept such lands as were properest for culture: the Burgundian's flock fattened the Roman's field.

10. *Of Servitudes.* The law of the Burgundians notices[1] that when those people settled in Gaul, they were allowed two-thirds of the land, and one-third of the bondmen. The state of villainage was therefore established in that part of Gaul before it was invaded by the Burgundians.[2]

The law of the Burgundians, in points relating to the two nations, makes a formal distinction in both, between the nobles, the freeborn and the bondmen.[3] Servitude was not therefore a thing peculiar to the Romans; nor liberty and nobility to the Barbarians.

This very same law says,[4] that if a Burgundian freedman had not given a certain sum to his master, nor received a third share of a Roman, he was always supposed to belong to his master's family. The Roman proprietor was therefore free, since he did not belong to another person's family; he was free, because his third portion was a mark of liberty.

We need only open the Salic and Ripuarian laws to be satisfied that the Romans were no more in a state of servitude among the Franks than among the other conquerors of Gaul.

The Count de Boulainvilliers is mistaken in the capital point of his system: he has not proved that the Franks made a general regulation which reduced the Romans into a kind of servitude.

As this author's work is penned without art, and as he speaks with the simplicity, frankness, and candour of that ancient nobility whence he descends, every one is capable of judging of the good things he says, and of the errors into which he has fallen. I shall not, therefore, undertake to criticise him; I shall only observe that he had more wit than enlightenment, more enlightenment than learning; though his learning was not contemptible, for he was well acquainted with the most valuable part of our history and laws.

The Count de Boulainvilliers and the Abbé du Bos have formed two different systems, one of which seems to be a conspiracy against the commons, and the other against the nobility. When the sun gave leave to Phaëton to drive his chariot, he said to him, "If you ascend too high, you will burn the heavenly mansions; if you descend too low, you will reduce the earth to ashes; do not drive to the right, you will meet there with the constellation of the Serpent; avoid going too much to the left, you will there fall in with that of the Altar: keep in the middle."[5]

11. *The same Subject continued.* What first gave rise to the notion of a general regulation made at the time of the conquest was our meeting with an immense number of forms of servitude in France, towards the beginning of the third race; and as the continual progression of these forms of servitude was not perceived, people imagined in an age of obscurity a general law which was never framed.

Towards the commencement of the first race we meet with an infinite number of freemen, both among the Franks and the Romans; but the number of bondmen increased to that degree, that at the beginning of the third race all the husbandmen and almost all the inhabitants of towns had become bondmen:[6] and whereas, at the first period, there was very nearly the same administration in the cities as among the Romans, namely, a corporation, a senate, and courts of judicature; at the other we hardly meet with anything but a lord and his bondmen.

When the Franks, Burgundians, and Goths made their several invasions, they seized upon gold, silver, movables, clothes, men, women, boys, and whatever the army could carry; the whole was brought to one place, and divided among the army.[7] History shows that after the first settlement, that is, after the first devastation, they entered into an agreement with the inhabitants, and left them all their political and civil rights. This was the law of nations in those days; they plundered everything in time of war, and granted everything in time of peace. Were it not so, how should we find both in the Salic and Burgundian laws such a number of regulations absolutely contrary to a general servitude of the people?

But though the conquest was not immediately productive of servitude, it arose never-

---

[1] Tit. 54.
[2] This is confirmed by the whole title of the code *de Agricolis et Censitis, et Colonis.*
[3] Tit. 26, §§ 1, 2.
[4] Tit. 57.

[5] Ovid, *Met.* ii. 134.
[6] While Gaul was under the dominion of the Romans they formed particular bodies; these were generally freedmen, or the descendants of freedmen.
[7] See Gregory of Tours, ii, 27. Aimoin, i. 12.

theless from the same law of nations which subsisted after the conquest.[1] Opposition, revolts and the taking of towns were followed by the slavery of the inhabitants. And, not to mention the wars which the conquering nations made against one another, as there was this peculiarity among the Franks, that the different partitions of the monarchy gave rise continually to civil wars between brothers or nephews, in which this law of nations was constantly practised, servitudes, of course, became more general in France than in other countries: and this is, I believe, one of the causes of the difference between our French laws and those of Italy and Spain, in respect to the right of seigniories.

The conquest was soon over, and the law of nations then in force was productive of some servile dependences. The custom of the same law of nations, which obtained for many ages, gave a prodigious extent to those servitudes.

Theodoric[2] imagining that the people of Auvergne were not faithful to him, thus addressed the Franks of his division: "Follow me, and I will carry you into a country where you shall have gold, silver, captives, clothes, and flocks in abundance; and you shall remove all the people into your own country."

After the conclusion of the peace between Gontram and Chilperic, the troops employed in the siege of Bourges, having had orders to return, carried such a considerable booty away with them that they hardly left either men or cattle in the country.[3]

Theodoric, King of Italy, whose spirit and policy it was ever to distinguish himself from the other barbarian kings, upon sending an army into Gaul, wrote thus to the general:[4] "It is my will that the Roman laws be followed, and that you restore the fugitive slaves to their right owners. The defender of liberty ought not to encourage servants to desert their masters. Let other kings delight in the plunder and devastation of the towns which they have subdued; we are desirous to conquer in such a manner that our subjects shall lament their having fallen too late under our government." It is evident that his intention was to cast odium on the kings of the Franks and the Burgundians, and that he alluded in the above passage to their particular law of nations.

Yet this law of nations continued in force

1 See the *Lives of the Saints*, footnote 7, below.
2 Gregory of Tours, ii.
3 *Ibid.*, vi. 31.
4 Cassiodorus, iii. 43.

under the second race. King Pepin's army, having penetrated into Aquitaine, returned to France loaded with an immense booty, and with a number of bondmen, as we are informed by the annals of Metz.[5]

Here might I quote numberless authorities;[6] and as the public compassion was raised at the sight of those miseries, as several holy prelates, beholding the captives in chains, employed the treasure belonging to the church, and sold even the sacred utensils, to ransom as many as they could; and as several holy monks exerted themselves on that occasion, it is in the *Lives of the Saints* that we meet with the best explanations on the subject.[7] And, although it may be objected to the authors of those lives that they have been sometimes a little too credulous in respect to things which God has certainly performed, if they were in the order of his providence; yet we draw considerable light thence with regard to the manners and usages of those times.

When we cast an eye upon the monuments of our history and laws, the whole seems to be an immense expanse, a boundless ocean;[8] all those frigid, dry, insipid, and hard writings must be read and devoured in the same manner as Saturn is fabled to have devoured the stones.

A vast quantity of land which had been in the hands of freemen[9] was changed into mortmain. When the country was stripped of its free inhabitants, those who had a great multitude of bondmen either took large territories by force, or had them yielded by agreement, and built villages, as may be seen in different charters. On the other hand, the freemen who cultivated the arts found themselves reduced to exercise those arts in a state of servitude; thus the servitudes restored to the arts and to agriculture whatever they had lost.

It was a customary thing with the proprietors of lands, to give them to the churches, in order to hold them themselves by a quit-rent, thinking to partake by their servitude of the sanctity of the churches.

5 In the year 763.
6 See the annals of Fuld, in the year 739, Paulus Diaconus, *De gestis Longobardorum*, iii. 30, iv. 1, and the *Lives of the Saints* in the next footnote.
7 See the lives of St. Epiphanius, St. Eptadius, St. Cæsarius, St. Fidolus, St. Porcian, St. Treverius, St. Eusichius, and of St. Leger; the miracles of St. Julian, &c.
8 Ovid, *Met.*, i. 293.
9 Even the husbandmen themselves were not all slaves; see the *Leg.* 18, 23, *Cod. de Agricolis, et Censitis, et Colonis*, and *Leg.* 20 of the same title.

12. *That the Lands belonging to the Division of the Barbarians paid no Taxes.* A people remarkable for their simplicity and poverty, a free and martial people, who lived without any other industry than that of tending their flocks, and who had nothing but rush cottages to attach them to their lands,[1] such a people, I say, must have followed their chiefs for the sake of booty, and not to pay or to raise taxes. The art of tax-gathering was invented later, and when men began to enjoy the blessings of other arts.

The temporary tax of a pitcher of wine for every acre,[2] which was one of the exactions of Chilperic and Fredegonda, related only to the Romans. And indeed it was not the Franks that tore the rolls of those taxes, but the clergy, who in those days were all Romans.[3] The burden of this tax lay chiefly on the inhabitants of the towns;[4] now these were almost all inhabited by Romans.

Gregory of Tours relates[5] that a certain judge was obliged, after the death of Chilperic, to take refuge in a church, for having under the reign of that prince ordered taxes to be levied on several Franks who in the reign of Childebert were *ingenui,* or free-born: *Multos de Francis, qui tempore Childeberti regis ingenui fuerant, publico tributo subegit.* Therefore the Franks who were not bondmen paid no taxes.

There is not a grammarian but would turn pale to see how the Abbé du Bos has interpreted this passage.[6] He observes that in those days the freedmen were also called *ingenui.* Upon this supposition he renders the Latin word *ingenui,* by the words *"freed from taxes";* a phrase which we indeed may use in French, as we say *"freed from cares,"* *"freed from punishments";* but in the Latin tongue such expressions as *ingenui a tributis, libertini a tributis, manumissi tributorum,* would be quite monstrous.

Parthenius, says Gregory of Tours,[7] had like to have been put to death by the Franks for subjecting them to taxes. The Abbé du Bos finding himself hard pressed by this passage[8] very coolly assumes the thing in question; it

was, says he, a surcharge.

We find in the law of the Visigoths[9] that when a Barbarian had seized upon the estate of a Roman, the judge obliged him to sell it, to the end that this estate might continue to be tributary; consequently the Barbarians paid no land taxes.[10]

The Abbé du Bos,[11] who would fain have the Visigoths subjected to taxes,[12] quits the literal and spiritual sense of the law, and pretends, upon no other indeed than an imaginary foundation, that between the establishment of the Goths and this law, there had been an augmentation of taxes which related only to the Romans. But none but Father Harduin are allowed thus to exercise an arbitrary power over facts.

This learned author[13] has rummaged Justinian's Code[14] in search of laws to prove that, among the Romans, the military benefices were subject to taxes. Whence he would infer that the same held good with regard to fiefs or benefices among the Franks. But the opinion that our fiefs derive their origin from that *Institution* of the Romans is at present exploded; it obtained only at a time when the Roman history, not ours, was well understood, and our ancient records lay buried in obscurity and dust.

But the Abbé is in the wrong to quote Cassiodorus, and to make use of what was transacting in Italy, and in the part of Gaul subject to Theodoric, in order to acquaint us with the practice established among the Franks; these are things which must not be confounded. I propose to show, some time or other, in a certain work, that the plan of the monarchy of the Ostrogoths was entirely different from that of any other government founded in those days by the other Barbarian nations; and that so far from our being entitled to affirm that a practice obtained among the Franks because it was established among the Ostrogoths, we

---

[1] See Gregory of Tours, ii.
[2] *Ibid.,* v. 28.
[3] *Ibid.,* viii. 36.
[4] Life of St. Aridius.
[5] Book vii.
[6] *Establishment of the French Monarchy,* iii. 14, p. 515.
See Baluzius, ii, p. 187.
[7] Book iii. 36.
[8] Book iii, p. 514.

[9] Book x, tit. 1, cap. xiv.
[10] The Vandals paid none in Africa.—Procopius, *War of the Vandals,* i, ii. *Historia Miscella,* xvi, p. 106. Observe that the conquerors of Africa were a mixture of Vandals, Alans, and Franks. *Historia Miscella,* xiv, p. 94.
[11] *Establishment of the Franks in Gaul,* iii. 14, p. 510.
[12] He lays a stress upon another law of the Visigoths, x, tit. 1, art. 11, which proves nothing at all; it says only that he who received of a lord a piece of land on condition of a rent or service ought to pay it.
[13] Book iii, p. 511.
[14] *Leg.* 3, xi, tit. 74.

have on the contrary just reason to think that a custom of the Ostrogoths was not in force among the Franks.

The hardest task for persons of extensive erudition is to seek their proofs in such passages as bear upon the subject, and to find, if we may be allowed to express ourselves in astronomical terms, the position of the sun.

The same author makes a wrong use of the capitularies, as well as of the historians and laws of the barbarous nations. When he wants the Franks to pay taxes, he applies to freemen what can be understood only of bondmen;[1] when he speaks of their military service, he applies to bondmen what can never relate but to freemen.[2]

13. *Of Taxes paid by the Romans and Gauls in the Monarchy of the Franks.* I might here examine whether, after the Gauls and Romans were conquered, they continued to pay the taxes to which they were subject under the emperors. But, for the sake of brevity, I shall be satisfied with observing that, if they paid them in the beginning, they were soon after exempted, and that those taxes were changed into a military service. For, I confess, I can hardly conceive how the Franks should have been at first such great friends, and afterwards such sudden and violent enemies, to taxes.

A capitulary[3] of Louis the Debonnaire explains extremely well the situation of the freemen in the monarchy of the Franks. Some troops of Goths or Iberians, flying from the oppression of the Moors, were received into Louis' dominions. The agreement made with them was that, like other freemen, they should follow their count to the army; and that upon a march they should mount guard and patrol under the command also of their count; and that they should furnish horses and carriages for baggage to the king's commissaries,[4] and to the ambassadors in their way to or from court; and that they should not be compelled to pay any further impost, but should be treated as the other freemen.

It cannot be said that these were new usages introduced at the commencement of the second race. This must be referred at least to the middle or to the end of the first. A capitulary of the year 864[5] says in express terms that it was the ancient custom for freemen to perform military service, and to furnish likewise the horses and carriages above-mentioned; duties particular to themselves, and from which those who possessed the fiefs were exempt, as I shall prove hereafter.

This is not all; there was a regulation which hardly permitted the imposing of taxes on those freemen.[6] He who had four manors was obliged to march against the enemy:[7] he who had but three was joined with a freeman that had only one; the latter bore the fourth part of the other's charges, and stayed at home. In like manner, they joined two freemen who had each two manors; he who went to the army had half his charges borne by him who stayed at home.

Again, we have an infinite number of charters, in which the privileges of fiefs are granted to lands or districts possessed by freemen, and of which I shall make further mention hereafter.[8] These lands are exempted from all the duties or services which were required of them by the counts, and by the rest of the king's officers; and as all these services are particularly enumerated without making any mention of taxes, it is manifest that no taxes were imposed upon them.

It was very natural that the Roman system of taxation should of itself fall out of use in the monarchy of the Franks; it was a most complicated device, far above the conception, and wide from the plan of those simple people. Were the Tartars to overrun Europe, we should find it very difficult to make them comprehend what is meant by our financiers.

The anonymous author of the life of Louis the Debonnaire,[9] speaking of the counts and other officers of the nation of the Franks, whom Charlemagne established in Aquitania, says, that he entrusted them with the care of

---

[1] *Establishment of the French Monarchy*, iii. 14, p. 513, where he quotes the 28th article of the edict of Pistes. See farther on.

[2] *Ibid.* iii. 4, p. 298.

[3] In the year 815, cap. i, which is agreeable to the Capitulary of Charles the Bald, in the year 844, arts. 1, 2.

[4] They were not obliged to furnish any to the count.—*Ibid.*, art. 5.

[5] The counts are forbidden to deprive them of their horses, *ut hostem facere, et debitos paraveredos secundum antequam consuetudinem exsolvere possint.*—Edict of Pistes, in Baluzius, p. 186.

[6] Capitulary of Charlemagne, 1, in the year 812. Edict of Pistes in the year 864, art. 27.

[7] *Quatuor mansos.* I fancy that what they called *Mansus* was a particular portion of land belonging to a farm where there were bondmen; witness the capitulary of the year 853, *apud Sylvacum*, tit. 14, against those who drove the bondmen from their *Mansus.*

[8] See below, chapter 20 of this book.

[9] In Duchesne, ii, p. 287.

defending the frontiers, as also with the military power and the direction of the demesnes belonging to the crown. This shows the state of the royal revenues under the second race. The prince had kept his demesnes in his own hands, and employed his bondmen in improving them. But the indictions, the capitations and other imposts raised at the time of the emperors on the persons or goods of freemen had been changed into an obligation of defending the frontiers and marching against the enemy.

In the same history,[1] we find that Louis the Debonnaire, having been to wait upon his father in Germany, this prince asked him, why he, who was a crowned head, came to be so poor: to which Louis made answer that he was only a nominal king, and that the great lords were possessed of almost all his demesnes; that Charlemagne, being apprehensive lest this young prince should forfeit their affection, if he attempted himself to resume what he had inconsiderately granted, appointed commissaries to restore things to their former situation.

The bishops, writing[2] to Louis, brother of Charles the Bald, used these words: "Take care of your lands, that you may not be obliged to travel continually by the houses of the clergy, and to tire their bondmen with carriages. Manage your affairs," continue they, "in such a manner that you may have enough to live upon, and to receive embassies." It is evident that the king's revenues in those days consisted of their demesnes.[3]

14. *Of what they called Census.* After the Barbarians had quitted their own country, they were desirous of reducing their usages into writing; but as they found difficulty in writing German words with Roman letters, they published these laws in Latin.

In the confusion and rapidity of the conquest, most things changed their nature; in order, however, to express them, they were obliged to make use of such old Latin words as were most analogous to the new usages. Thus, whatever was likely to revive the idea of the ancient census of the Romans they called by the name of *census tributum,*[4] and when

things had no relation at all to the Roman census, they expressed, as well as they could, the German words by Roman letters; thus they formed the word *fredum,* on which I shall have occasion to descant in the following chapters.

The words *census* and *tributum* having been employed in an arbitrary manner, this has thrown some obscurity on the signification in which these words were used under our princes of the first and second race. And modern authors[5] who have adopted particular systems, having found these words in the writings of those days, imagined that what was then called census was exactly the census of the Romans; and thence they inferred this consequence, that our kings of the first two races had put themselves in the place of the Roman emperors, and made no change in their administration.[6] Besides, as particular duties raised under the second race were by change and by certain restrictions converted into others,[7] they inferred thence that these duties were the census of the Romans; and as, since the modern regulations, they found that the crown demesnes were absolutely unalienable, they pretended that those duties which represented the Roman census, and did not form a part of the demesnes, were mere usurpation. I omit the other consequences.

To apply the ideas of the present time to distant ages is the most fruitful source of error. To those people who want to modernize all the ancient ages, I shall say what the Egyptian priests said to Solon, "O Athenians, you are mere children!"[8]

15. *That what they called Census was raised only on the Bondmen and not on the Freemen.* The king, the clergy, and the lords raised regular taxes, each on the bondmen of their respective demesnes. I prove it with respect to the king, by the capitulary *de Villis;* with regard to the clergy, by the codes of the laws of

---

[1] *Ibid.,* p. 89.

[2] See the Capitulary of the year 858, art. 14.

[3] They levied also some duties on rivers, where there happened to be a bridge or a passage.

[4] The *census* was so generical a word, that they made use of it to express the tolls of rivers, when there was a bridge or ferry to pass. See the third Capitulary, in the year 803, edition of Baluzius, p.

395, art. 1; and the 5th in the year 819, p. 616. They gave likewise this name to the carriages furnished by the freemen to the king, or to his commissaries, as appeals by the Capitulary of Charles the Bald in the year 865, art. 8.

[5] The Abbé du Bos, and his followers.

[6] See the weakness of the arguments produced by the Abbé du Bos, in the Establishment of the French Monarchy, iii, book VI. 14; especially in the inference he draws from a passage of Gregory of Tours, concerning a dispute between his church and King Charibert.

[7] For instance, by enfranchisements.

[8] Plato, *Timæus.*—ED.

the Barbarians[1] and in relation to the lords, by the regulations which Charlemagne made concerning this subject.[2]

These taxes were called *census;* they were economical and not fiscal claims, entirely private dues and not public taxes.

I affirm that what they called *census* at that time was a tax raised upon the bondmen. This I prove by a formulary of Marculfus containing a permission from the king to enter into holy orders, provided the persons be freeborn,[3] and not enrolled in the register of the *census.* I prove it also by a commission from Charlemagne to a count[4] whom he had sent into Saxony, which contains the enfranchisement of the Saxons for having embraced Christianity, and is properly a charter of freedom.[5] This prince restores them to their former civil liberty,[6] and exempts them from paying the census. It was, therefore, the same thing to be a bondman as to pay the census, to be free as not to pay it.

By a kind of letters patent of the same prince in favour of the Spaniards,[7] who had been received into the monarchy, the counts are forbidden to demand any census of them, or to deprive them of their lands. That strangers upon their coming to France were treated as bondmen is a thing well known; and Charlemagne being desirous they should be considered as freemen, since he would have them be proprietors of their lands, forbad the demanding any census of them.

A capitulary of Charles the Bald,[8] given in favour of those very Spaniards, orders them to be treated like the other Franks, and forbids the requiring any census of them; consequently this census was not paid by freemen.

The thirtieth article of the edict of Pistes reforms the abuse by which several of the husbandmen belonging to the king or to the church sold the lands dependent on their manors to ecclesiastics or to people of their condition, reserving only a small cottage to themselves; by which means they avoided paying the census; and it ordains that things should be restored to their primitive situation: the census was, therefore, a tax peculiar to bondmen.

Thence also it follows that there was no general census in the monarchy; and this is clear from a great number of passages. For what could be the meaning of this capitulary?[9] "We ordain that the royal census should be levied in all places where formerly it was lawfully levied."[10] What could be the meaning of that in which Charlemagne[11] orders his commissaries in the provinces to make an exact inquiry into all the census that belonged in former times to the king's demesne?[12] And of that[13] in which he disposes of the census paid by those[14] of whom they are demanded? What can that other capitulary mean[15] in which we read, "If any person has acquired a tributary land[16] on which we were accustomed to levy the census?" And that other, in fine,[17] in which Charles the Bald[18] makes mention of feudal lands whose census had from time immemorial belonged to the king.

Observe that there are some passages which seem at first sight to be contrary to what I have said, and yet confirm it. We have already seen that the freemen in the monarchy were obliged only to furnish particular carriages; the capitulary just now cited gives to this the name of census, and opposes it to the census paid by the bondmen.

Besides, the edict of Pistes[19] notices those freemen who are obliged to pay the royal census for their head and for their cottages,[20] and who had sold themselves during the famine. The king orders them to be ransomed. This is because those who were manumitted by the king's letters[21] did not, generally speaking,

[1] Law of the Alemans, cap. xxii; and the Law of the Bavarians, tit. 1, cap. iv., where the regulations are to be found which the clergy made concerning their order.
[2] Capitularies, v. 303.
[3] Book i, form. 19.
[4] In the year 789, edition of the Capitularies by Baluzius, i, p. 250.   [5] *Ibid.*   [6] *Ibid.*
[7] *Præceptum pro Hispanis,* in the year 812, ed. Baluzius, i, p. 500.
[8] In the year 844, ed. Baluzius, ii, arts. 1 and 2, p. 27.
[9] Third Capitulary of the year 805, arts. 20 and 22, inserted in the Collection of Angezise, iii, art. 15. This is agreeable to that of Charles the Bald, in the year 854, *apud Attiniacum,* art. 6.   [10] *Ibid.*
[11] In the year 812, arts. 10 and 11, ed. Baluzius, i, p. 498.
[12] Capitulary of the year 812, arts. 10 and 11.
[13] In the year 813, art. 6, ed. Baluzius, i, p. 508.
[14] Capitulary of the year 813, art. 6.
[15] Book iv of the Capitularies, art. 37, and inserted in the law of the Lombards.
[16] Book iv of the Capitularies, art. 37.
[17] In the year 805, art. 8.
[18] Capitulary of the year 805, art. 8.
[19] In the year 864, art. 34, ed. Baluzius, p. 192.
[20] *Ibid.*
[21] The 28th article of the same edict explains this extremely well; it even makes a distinction between a Roman freedman and a Frank freedman: and we likewise see there that the census was not general; it deserves to be read.

acquire a full and perfect liberty,[1] but they paid *censum in capite;* and these are the people here meant.

We must, therefore, waive the idea of a general and universal census, derived from that of the Romans, from which the rights of the lords are also supposed to have been derived by usurpation. What was called *census* in the French monarchy, independently of the abuse made of that word, was a particular tax imposed on the bondmen by their masters.

I beg the reader to excuse the trouble I must give him with such a number of citations. I should be more concise did I not meet with the Abbé du Bos' book on the establishment of the French monarchy in Gaul, continually in my way. Nothing is a greater obstacle to our progress in knowledge than a bad performance of a celebrated author; because, before we instruct, we must begin with undeceiving.

16. *Of the feudal Lords or Vassals.* I have noticed those volunteers among the Germans, who have followed their princes in their several expeditions. The same usage continued after the conquest. Tacitus mentions them by the name of companions;[2] the Salic law by that of men who have vowed fealty to the king;[3] the formularies of Marculfus[4] by that of the king's *Antrustios;*[5] the earliest French historians by that of *Leudes,*[6] faithful and loyal; and those of later date by that of vassals and lords.[7]

In the Salic and Ripuarian laws we meet with an infinite number of regulations in regard to the Franks, and only with a few for the Antrustios. The regulations concerning the Antrustios are different from those which were made for the other Franks; they are full of what relates to the settling of the property of the Franks, but mention not a word concerning that of the Antrustios. This is because the property of the latter was regulated rather by the political than by the civil law, and was the share that fell to an army, and not the patrimony of a family.

The goods reserved for the feudal lords

were called fiscal goods, benefices, honours, and fiefs, by different authors, and in different times.[8]

There is no doubt but the fiefs at first were at will.[9] We find in Gregory of Tours[10] that Sunegisilus and Gallomanus were deprived of all they held of the exchequer, and no more was left them than their real property. When Gontram raised his nephew Childebert to the throne, he had a private conference with him, in which he named the persons who ought to be honoured with, and those who ought to be deprived of, the fiefs.[11] In a formulary of Marculfus,[12] the king gives in exchange, not only the benefices held by his exchequer, but likewise those which had been held by another. The law of the Lombards opposes the benefices to property.[13] In this, our historians, the formularies, the codes of the different barbarous nations and all the monuments of those days are unanimous. In fine, the writers of the book of fiefs inform us[14] that at first the lords could take them back when they pleased, that afterwards they granted them for the space of a year,[15] and that at length they gave them for life.

17. *Of the military Service of Freemen.* Two sorts of people were bound to military service; the great and lesser vassals, who were obliged in consequence of their fief; and the freemen, whether Franks, Romans, or Gauls, who served under the count and were commanded by him and his officers.

The name of freemen was given to those, who on the one hand had no benefits or fiefs, and on the other were not subject to the base services of villainage; the lands they possessed were what they called allodial estates.

The counts assembled the freemen,[16] and led

[1] As appears by the Capitulary of Charlemagne in the year 813, which we have already quoted.
[2] *Comites. De Moribus Germanorum,* 13.
[3] *Qui sunt in truste regis,* tit. 44, art. 4.
[4] Book i, form. 18.
[5] From the word *trew,* which signifies faithful among the Germans.
[6] *Leudes, fideles.*
[7] *Vassalli, seniores.*

[8] *Fiscalia.* See Marculfus, i. form. 14. It is mentioned in the Life of St. Maur, *dedit fiscum unum:* and in the annals of Metz, in the year 747, *dedit illi comitatus et fiscos plurimos.* The goods designed for the support of the royal family were called *regalia.*
[9] See i, tit. 1, of the fiefs; and Cujas on that book.
[10] Book ix. 38.
[11] *Ibid.,* vii.
[12] Book i, form. 30.
[13] Book iii, tit. 8, § 3.
[14] *Feudorum,* i, tit. 1.
[15] It was a kind of precarious tenure which the lord consented or refused to renew every year; as Cujas has observed.
[16] See the Capitulary of Charlemagne in the year 812, arts. 3 and 4, ed. Baluzius, i, p. 491; and the edict of Pistes in the year 864, art. 26, ii, p. 186.

them against the enemy; they had officers under them who were called vicars;[1] and as all the freemen were divided into hundreds, which constituted what they called a borough, the counts had also officers under them, who were denominated *centenarii,* and led the freemen of the borough, or their hundreds, to the field.[2]

This division into hundreds is posterior to the establishment of the Franks in Gaul. It was made by Clotharius and Childebert, with a view of obliging each district to answer for the robberies committed in their division; this we find in the decrees of those princes.[3] A regulation of this kind is to this very day observed in England.

As the counts led the freemen against the enemy, the feudal lords commanded also their vassals or rear-vassals; and the bishops, abbots, or their advocates[4] likewise commanded theirs.[5]

The bishops were greatly embarrassed and inconsistent with themselves;[6] they requested Charlemagne not to oblige them any longer to military service; and when he granted their request, they complained that he had deprived them of the public esteem; so that this prince was obliged to justify his intentions upon this head. Be that as it may, when they were exempted from marching against the enemy, I do not find that their vassals were led by the counts; on the contrary, we see that the kings or the bishops chose one of their feudatories to conduct them.[7]

In a Capitulary of Louis the Debonnaire,[8] this prince distinguishes three sorts of vassals, those belonging to the king, those to the bishops, and those to the counts. The vassals of a feudal lord were not led against the enemy by the count, except some employment in the king's household hindered the lord himself from commanding them.[9]

But who is it that led the feudal lords into the field? No doubt the king himself, who was always at the head of his faithful vassals. Hence we constantly find in the capitularies a distinction made between the king's vassals and those of the bishops.[10] Such brave and magnanimous princes as our kings did not take the field to put themselves at the head of an ecclesiastic militia; these were not the men they chose to conquer or to die with.

But these lords likewise carried their vassals and rear-vassals with them, as we can prove by the capitulary in which Charlemagne ordains that every freeman who has four manors, either in his own property or as a benefice from somebody else, should march against the enemy or follow his lord.[11] It is evident that Charlemagne means that the person who had a manor of his own should march under the count and he who held a benefice of a lord should set out along with him.

And yet the Abbé du Bos pretends[12] that, when mention is made in the capitularies of tenants who depended on a particular lord, no others are meant than bondmen; and he grounds his opinion on the law of the Visigoths and the practice of that nation. It is much better to rely on the capitularies themselves; that which I have just quoted says expressly the contrary. The treaty between Charles the Bald and his brothers notices also those freemen who might choose to follow either a lord or the king; and this regulation is conformable to a great many others.

We may, therefore, conclude that there were three sorts of military services; that of the king's vassals, who had other vassals under them; that of the bishops or of the other clergy and their vassals, and, in fine, that of the count, who commanded the freemen.

Not but the vassals might be also subject to the count; as those who have a particular command are subordinate to him who is invested with a more general authority.

We even find that the count and the king's commissaries might oblige them to pay the fine when they had not fulfilled the engagements of their fief. In like manner, if the king's vassals committed any outrage[13] they

---

[1] Book ii of the Capitularies, art. 28.
[2] They were called *Compagenses.*
[3] Published in the year 595, art. 1. See the Capitularies, ed. Baluzius, p. 20. These regulations were undoubtedly made by agreement.
[4] *Advocati.*
[5] Capitulary of Charlemagne, in the year 812, art. 1 and 5, ed. Baluzius, i, p. 490.
[6] See the Capitulary of the year 803, published at Worms, ed Baluzius, pp. 408, 410.
[7] Capitulary of Worms in the year 803, edition of Baluzius, p. 409; and the council in the year 845, under Charles, the Bald, *in verno palatio,* edition of Baluzius, ii, p. 17, art. 8.
[8] The fifth Capitulary of the year 819, art. 27, edition of Baluzius, p. 618.
[9] Capitulary II in the year 812, art. 7, edition of Baluzius, i, p. 494.

[10] Capitulary i of the year 812, art. 5, edition of Baluzius, i, p. 490.
[11] In the year 812, cap. i, edition of Baluzius, p. 490.
[12] *Establishment of the French Monarchy,* iii, book VI, cap. iv, p. 299.
[13] Capitulary of the year 882, art. 11, *apud vernis palatium,* edition of Baluzius, ii, p. 289.

were subject to the correction of the count, unless they choose to submit rather to that of the king.

18. *Of the double Service.* It was a fundamental principle of the monarchy that whosoever was subject to the military power of another person was subject also to his civil jurisdiction. Thus the Capitulary of Louis the Debonnaire,[1] in the year 815, makes the military power of the count and his civil jurisdiction over the freemen keep always an equal pace. Thus the *placita*[2] of the count who carried the freemen against the enemy were called the *placita* of the freemen;[3] whence undoubtedly came this maxim, that the questions relating to liberty could be decided only in the count's *placita*, and not in those of his officers. Thus the count never led the vassals[4] belonging to the bishops, or to the abbots, against the enemy, because they were not subject to his civil jurisdiction. Thus he never commanded the rear-vassals belonging to the king's vassals. Thus the glossary of the English laws informs us[5] that those to whom the Saxons gave the name of *Coples*[6] were by the Normans called *counts,* or *companions,* because they shared the justiciary fines with the king. Thus we see that at all times the duty of a vassal towards his lord[7] was to bear arms[8] and to try his peers in his court.

One of the reasons which produced this connection between the judiciary right and that of leading the forces against the enemy was because the person who led them exacted at the same time the payment of the fiscal duties, which consisted in some carriage services due by the freemen, and in general, in certain judiciary profits, of which we shall treat hereafter. The lords had the right of administering justice in their fief, by the same principle as the counts had it in their counties. And, indeed, the counties in the several variations

that happened at different times always followed the variations of the fiefs; both were governed by the same plan, and by the same principles. In a word, the counts in their counties were lords, and the lords in their seignories were counts.

It has been a mistake to consider the counts as civil officers, and the dukes as military commanders. Both were equally civil and military officers:[9] the whole difference consisted in the duke's having several counts under him, though there were counts who had no duke over them, as we learn from Fredegarius.[10]

It will be imagined, perhaps, that the government of the Franks must have been very severe at that time, since the same officers were invested with a military and civil power, nay, even with a fiscal authority, over the subjects; which in the preceding books I have observed to be distinguishing marks of despotism.

But we must not believe that the counts pronounced judgment by themselves, and administered justice in the same manner as the bashaws in Turkey; in order to judge affairs, they assembled a kind of assizes, where the principal men appeared.

To the end we may thoroughly understand what relates to the judicial proceedings in the formulas, in the laws of the Barbarians and in the capitularies, it is proper to observe that the functions of the count, of the *Grafio* or fiscal judge and the *Centenarius* were the same; that the judges, the *Rathimburghers,* and the aldermen were the same persons under different names. These were the count's assistants, and were generally seven in number; and as he was obliged to have twelve persons to judge,[11] he filled up the number with the principal men.[12]

But whoever had the jurisdiction, the king, the count, the *Grafio,* the *Centenarius,* the lords, or the clergy, they never tried causes alone; and this usage, which derived its origin from the forests of Germany, was still continued even after the fiefs had assumed a new form.

[1] Art. 1, 2, and the council in *verno palatio* of the year 845, art. 8, edition of Baluzius, ii, p. 17.
[2] Or assizes.
[3] Capitularies, book iv of the *Collection of Angezise,* art. 57; and the fifth capitulary of Louis the Debonnaire, in the year 819, art. 14, edition of Baluzius, i, p. 615.
[4] See the 8th note of the preceding chapter.
[5] It is to be found in the Collection of William Larabard, *De Priscis Anglorum legibus.*
[6] In the word *Satrapia.*
[7] This is well explained by the assizes of Jerusalem, 221, 222.
[8] The advowees of the church (*advocati*) were equally at the head of their *placita* and of their militia.

[9] See Marculfus, i, form. 8, which contains the letters given to a duke, patrician, or count; and invests them with the civil jurisdiction, and the fiscal administration.
[10] *Chronicle,* 78, in the year 636.
[11] See concerning this subject the capitularies of Louis the Debonnaire added to the Salic law, art. 2, and the formula of judgments given by Du Cange in the word *boni homines.*
[12] *Per bonos homines,* sometimes there were none but principal men. See the appendix to the formularies of Marculfus, 51.

With regard to the fiscal power, its nature was such that the count could hardly abuse it. The rights of the prince in respect to the freemen were so simple that they consisted only, as we have already observed, in certain carriages which were demanded of them on some public occasions.[1] And as for the judiciary rights, there were laws which prevented misdemeanors.[2]

19. *Of Compositions among the barbarous Nations.* Since it is impossible to gain any insight into our political law unless we are thoroughly acquainted with the laws and manners of the German nations, I shall, therefore, pause here awhile, in order to inquire into those manners and laws.

It appears by Tacitus that the Germans knew only two capital crimes; they hanged traitors, and drowned cowards; these were the only public crimes among that people. When a man had injured another, the relatives of the person injured took share in the quarrel, and the offence was cancelled by a satisfaction.[3] This satisfaction was made to the person offended, when capable of receiving it; or to the relatives if they had been injured in common, or if by the decease of the party aggrieved or injured the satisfaction had devolved to them.

In the manner mentioned by Tacitus, these satisfactions were made by the mutual agreement of the parties; hence in the codes of the barbarous nations these satisfactions are called compositions.

The law of the Frisians[4] is the only one I find that has left the people in that situation in which every family at variance was in some measure in the state of nature, and in which, being unrestrained either by a political or civil law, they might give freedom to their revenge till they had obtained satisfaction. Even this law was moderated; a regulation was made[5] that the person whose life was sought after should be unmolested in his own house, as also in going and coming from church and the court where causes were tried.

The compilers of the Salic law[6] cite an an-

cient usage of the Franks, by which a person who had dug a corpse out of the ground, in order to strip it, should be banished from society till the relatives had consented to his being re-admitted. And as before that time strict orders were issued to every one, even to the offender's own wife, not to give him a morsel of bread, or to receive him under their roofs, such a person was in respect to others, and others in respect to him, in a state of savagery till an end was put to this state by a composition.

This excepted, we find that the sages of the different barbarous nations thought of determining by themselves what would have been too long and too dangerous to expect from the mutual agreement of the parties. They took care to fix the value of the composition which the party wronged or injured was to receive. All those barbarian laws are in this respect most admirably exact; the several cases are minutely distinguished,[7] the circumstances are weighed, the law substitutes itself in the place of the person injured and insists upon the same satisfaction as he himself would have demanded in cold blood.

By the establishing of those laws, the German nations quitted that state of nature in which they seemed to have lived in Tacitus' time.

Rotharis declares, in the law of the Lombards,[8] that he had increased the compositions allowed by ancient custom for wounds, to the end that, the wounded person being fully satisfied, all enmities should cease. And indeed as the Lombards, from a very poor people had grown rich by the conquest of Italy, the ancient compositions had become frivolous, and reconcilements prevented. I do not question but this was the motive which obliged the other chiefs of the conquering nations to make the different codes of laws now extant.

The principal composition was that which the murderer paid to the relatives of the deceased. The difference of conditions produced a difference in the compositions.[9] Thus in the law of the Angli, there was a composition of six hundred sous for the murder of an adeling, two hundred for that of a freeman, and thirty for killing a bondman. The largeness there-

---

[1] And some tolls on rivers, of which I have spoken already.

[2] See the law of the Ripuarians, tit. 89; and the law of the Lombards, ii, tit. 52, § 9.

[3] Tacitus, *De Moribus Germanorum*, 21.

[4] See this law in the 2nd title on murders; and Vulemar's addition on robberies.

[5] Tit. i, § 1.

[6] Salic Law, tit. 8, § 1; tit. 17, § 3.

[7] The Salic laws are admirable in this respect, see especially the titles 3, 4, 5, 6, and 7, which related to the stealing of cattle.

[8] Book i, tit. 7, § 15.

[9] See the law of the Angli, tit. 1, §§ 1, 2, and 4; *ibid.* tit. 5, § 6; the law of the Bavarians, tit. 1, cap. 8, 9, and the law of the Frisians, tit. 15.

fore of the composition for the life of a man was one of his chief privileges; for besides the distinction it made of his person, it likewise established a greater security in his favour among rude and boisterous nations.

This we are made sensible of by the law of the Bavarians:[1] it gives the names of the Bavarian families who received a double composition, because they were the first after the Agilolfings.[2] The Agilolfings were of the ducal race, and it was customary with this nation to choose a duke out of that family; these had a quadruple composition. The composition for a duke exceeded by a third that which had been established for the Agilolfings. "Because he is a duke," says the law, "a greater honour is paid to him than to his relatives."

All these compositions were valued in money. But as those people, especially when they lived in Germany, had very little specie, they might pay it in cattle, corn, movables, arms, dogs, hawks, lands, &c.[3] The law itself frequently determined the value of those things; which explains how it was possible for them to have such a number of pecuniary punishments with so very little money.[4]

These laws were therefore employed in exactly determining the difference of wrongs, injuries and crimes; to the end that every one might know how far he had been injured or offended, the reparation he was to receive, and especially that he was to receive no more.

In this light it is easy to conceive that a person who had taken revenge after having received satisfaction was guilty of a heinous crime. This contained a public as well as a private offence; it was a contempt of the law of itself; a crime which the legislators never failed to punish.[5]

There was another crime which above all others was considered as dangerous, when those people lost something of their spirit of independence, and when the kings endea-

voured to establish a better civil administration; this was the refusing to give or to receive satisfaction.[6] We find in the different codes of the laws of the Barbarians that the legislators were peremptory on this article.[7] In effect, a person who refused to receive satisfaction wanted to preserve his right of prosecution; he who refused to give it left the right of prosecution to the person injured; and this is what the sages had reformed in the institutions of the Germans, whereby people were invited but not compelled to compositions.

I have just now made mention of a text of the Salic law, in which the legislator left the party offended at liberty to receive or to refuse satisfaction; it is the law by which a person who had stripped a dead body was expelled from society till the relatives upon receiving satisfaction petitioned for his being re-admitted.[8] It was owing to the respect they had for sacred things that the compilers of the Salic laws did not meddle with the ancient usage.

It would have been absolutely unjust to grant a composition to the relatives of a robber killed in the act, or to the relatives of a woman who had been repudiated for the crime of adultery. The law of the Bavarians allowed no compositions in the like cases, but punished the relatives who sought revenge.[9]

It is no rare thing to meet with compositions for involuntary actions in the codes of the laws of the Barbarians. The law of the Lombards is generally very prudent; it ordained[10] that in those cases the compositions should be according to the person's generosity; and that the relatives should no longer be permitted to pursue their revenge.

Clotharius II made a very wise decree; he forbad the person robbed to receive any

[1] Tit. 2, cap. xx.

[2] Hozidra, Ozza, Sagana, Habalingua, Anniena. —*Ibid.*

[3] Thus the law of Ina valued life by a certain sum of money, or by a certain portion of land. *Leges Inæ regis, titulo de villico regio de priscis Anglorum legibus.*—Cambridge, 1644.

[4] See the law of the Saxons, which makes this same regulation for several people, cap. xviii. See also the law of the Ripuarians, tit. 36, § 11; the law of the Bavarians, tit. 1, §§ 10 and 11.

[5] See the law of the Lombards, i, tit. 25 § 21; *ibid.*, i, tit. 9, §§ 8, 34; *ibid.*, § 38, and the Capitulary of Charlemagne in the year 802, cap. xxxii, containing an instruction given to those whom he sent into the provinces.

[6] See in Gregory of Tours, vii. 47, the detail of a process, wherein a party loses half the composition that had been adjudged to him, for having done justice to himself, instead of receiving satisfaction, whatever injury he might have afterwards received.

[7] See the law of the Saxons, cap. iii, § 4; the law of the Lombards, i, tit. 37, §§ 1 and 2; and the law of the Alemans, tit. 45, §§ 1 and 2. This last law gave leave to the party injured to right himself upon the spot, and in the first transport of passion. See also the Capitularies of Charlemagne in the year 779, cap. xxii, in the year 802, cap. xxxii, and also that of the year 805, cap. v.

[8] The compilers of the law of the Ripuarians seem to have softened this. See the 85th title of those laws.

[9] See the decree of Tassillon, *De Popularibus legibus*, art. 3, 4, 10, 16, 19; the law of the Angli, tit. vii. § 4.

[10] Book i, tit. ix, § 4.

clandestine composition, and without an order from the judge.[1] We shall presently see the motive of this law.

20. *Of what was afterwards called the Jurisdiction of the Lords.* Besides the composition which they were obliged to pay to the relatives for murders or injuries, they were also under a necessity of paying a certain duty which the codes of the barbarian laws called *fredum.*[2] I intend to treat of it at large; and in order to give an idea of it, I begin with defining it as a recompense for the protection granted against the right of vengeance. Even to this day, *fred* in the Swedish language signifies peace.

The administration of justice among those rude and unpolished nations was nothing more than granting to the person who had committed an offence a protection against the vengeance of the party offended, and obliging the latter to accept of the satisfaction due to him: insomuch that among the Germans, contrary to the practice of all other nations, justice was administered in order to protect the criminal against the party injured.

The codes of the Barbarian laws have given us the cases in which the *freda* might be demanded. When the relatives could not prosecute, they allowed of no *fredum;* and indeed, when there was no prosecution there could be no composition for a protection against it. Thus, in the law of the Lombards,[3] if a person happened to kill a freeman by accident, he paid the value of the man killed, without the *fredum;* because, as he had killed him involuntarily, it was not the case in which the relatives were allowed the right of prosecution. Thus in the law of the Ripuarians,[4] when a person was killed with a piece of wood, or with any instrument made by man, the instrument or the wood were deemed culpable, and the relatives seized upon them for their own use, but were not allowed to demand the *fredum.*

In like manner, when a beast happened to kill a man, the same law established a composition without the *fredum,* because the relatives of the deceased were not offended.[5]

In fine, it was ordained by the Salic law,[6] that a child who had committed a fault before the age of twelve should pay the composition without the *fredum:* as he was not yet able to bear arms, he could not be in the case in which the party injured, or his relatives, had a right to demand satisfaction.

It was the criminal that paid the *fredum* for the peace and security of which he had been deprived by his crime, and which he might recover by protection. But a child did not lose this security; he was not a man, and consequently could not be expelled from human society.

This *fredum* was a local right in favour of the person who was judge of the district.[7] Yet the law of the Ripuarians[8] forbade him to demand it himself: it ordained that the party who had gained the cause should receive it and carry it to the exchequer, to the end that there might be a lasting peace, says the law among the Ripuarians.

The greatness of the *fredum* was proportioned to the degree of protection: thus the *fredum* for the king's protection was greater than what was granted for the protection of the count, or of the other judges.[9]

Here I see the origin of the jurisdiction of the lords. The fiefs comprised very large territories, as appears from a vast number of records. I have already proved that the kings raised no taxes on the lands belonging to the division of the Franks; much less could they reserve to themselves any duties on the fiefs. Those who obtained them had in this respect a full and perfect enjoyment, reaping every possible emolument from them. And as one of the most considerable emoluments was the justiciary profits (*freda*),[10] which were received according to the usage of the Franks, it followed thence that the person seized of the fief

---

[1] *Pactus pro tenore pacis inter Childebertum et Clotarium, anno* 593, *et decretio Clotarii* 2 *regis, circa annum* 595, cap. xi.

[2] When it was not determined by the law, it was generally the third of what was given for the composition, as appears in the law of the Ripuarians, cap. lxxxix, which is explained by the third Capitulary of the year 813.—Edition of Baluzius, i, p. 512.

[3] Book i, tit. 9, § 17, ed. Lindembrock.

[4] Tit. 70.

[5] Tit. 46. See also the law of the Lombards, i. cap. xxi, § 3, Lindembrock's edition, *si caballus cum pede,* &c.

[6] Tit. 28, § 6.

[7] As appears by the decree of Clotharius II in the year 595.

[8] Tit. 89.

[9] *Capitulare incerti anni,* 57, in Baluzius, i, p. 515, and it is to be observed, that what was called *fredum* or *faida,* in the monuments of the first race, is known by the name of *bannum* in those of the second race, as appears from the Capitulary *de partibus Saxoniæ,* in the year 789.

[10] See the Capitulary of Charlemagne, *de villis,* where he ranks these *freda* among the great revenues of what was called *villæ,* or the king's demesnes.

was also seized of the jurisdiction, the exercise of which consisted of the compositions made to the relatives, and of the profits accruing to the lord; it was nothing more than ordering the payment of the compositions of the law, and demanding the legal fines. We find by the formularies containing confirmation of the perpetuity of a fief in favour of a feudal lord,[1] or of the privileges of fiefs in favour of churches,[2] that the fiefs were possessed of this right. This appears also from an infinite number of charters[3] mentioning a prohibition to the king's judges or officers of entering upon the territory in order to exercise any act of judicature whatsoever, or to demand any judiciary emolument. When the king's judges could no longer make any demand in a district, they never entered it; and those to whom this district was left performed the same functions as had been exercised before by the judges.

The king's judges are forbidden also to oblige the parties to give security for their appearing before them; it belonged therefore to the person who had received the territory in fief to demand this security. They mention also that the king's commissaries shall not insist upon being accommodated with a lodging; in effect, they no longer exercised any function in those districts.

The administration therefore of justice, both in the old and new fiefs, was a right inherent in the very fief itself, a lucrative right which constituted a part of it. For this reason it had been considered at all times in this light; whence this maxim arose, that jurisdictions are patrimonial in France.

Some have thought that the jurisdictions derived their origin from the manumissions made by the kings and lords in favour of their bondmen. But the German nations, and those descended from them, are not the only people who manumitted their bondmen, and yet they are the only people that established patrimonial jurisdictions. Besides, we find by the formularies of Marculfus[4] that there were freemen dependent on these jurisdictions in the earliest times: the bondmen were therefore subject to the jurisdiction, because they were upon the territory; and they did not give rise to the fiefs for having been annexed to the fief.

Others have taken a shorter cut; the lords, say they (and this is all they say), usurped the jurisdictions. But are the nations descended from Germany the only people in the world that usurped the rights of princes? We are sufficiently informed by history that several other nations have encroached upon their sovereigns, and yet we find no other instance of what we call the jurisdiction of the lords. The origin of it is therefore to be traced in the usages and customs of the Germans.

Whoever has the curiosity to look into Loyseau[5] will be surprised at the manner in which this author supposes the lords to have proceeded in order to form and usurp their different jurisdictions. They must have been the most artful people in the world; they must have robbed and plundered, not after the manner of a military nation, but as the country justices and the attornies rob one another. Those brave warriors must be said to have formed a general system of politics throughout all the provinces of the kingdom, and in so many other countries in Europe; Loyseau makes them reason as he himself reasoned in his closet.

Once more; if the jurisdiction was not a dependence of the fief, how come we everywhere to find that the service of the fief was to attend the king or the lord, both in their courts and in the army?[6]

21. *Of the Territorial Jurisdiction of the Churches.* The churches acquired very considerable property. We find that our kings gave them great seigniories, that is, great fiefs; and we find jurisdictions established at the same time in the demesnes of those churches. Whence could so extraordinary a privilege derive its origin? It must certainly have been in the nature of the grant. The church land had this privilege because it had not been taken from it. A seigniory was given to the church; and it was allowed to enjoy the same privileges as if it had been granted to a vassal. It was also subjected to the same service as it would have paid to the state if it had been given to a layman, according to what we have already observed.

The churches had therefore the right of demanding the payment of compositions in their

---

[1] See Marculfus, i, form. 3, 4, 17.
[2] See Marculfus, i, form. 2, 3, 4.
[3] See the Collections of those charters, especially that at the end of the 5th volume of the historians of France, published by the Benedictine monks.
[4] See the 3rd, 4th, and 14th of the first book, and the charter of Charlemagne, in the year 771, in Martene, *Anecdot. collect.*, i, 11.

[5] Treatise of village jurisdictions, Loyseau.
[6] See Du Cange on the word *hominium*.

territory, and of insisting upon the *fredum;* and as those rights necessarily implied that of hindering the king's officers from entering upon the territory to demand these *freda* and to exercise acts of judicature, the right which ecclesiastics had of administering justice in their own territory was called immunity, in the style of the formularies, of the charters, and of the capitularies.[1]

The law of the Ripuarians[2] forbids the freedom of the churches[3] to hold the assembly for administering justice in any other place than in the church where they were manumitted.[4] The churches had therefore jurisdictions even over freemen, and held their *placita* in the earliest times of the monarchy.

I find in the *Lives of the Saints*[5] that Clovis gave to a certain holy person power over a district of six leagues, and exempted it from all manner of jurisdiction. This, I believe, is a falsity, but it is a falsity of a very ancient date; both the truth and the fiction contained in that life are in relation to the customs and laws of those times, and it is these customs and laws we are investigating.[6]

Clotharius II orders the bishops or the nobility who are possessed of estates in distant parts, to choose upon the very spot those who are to administer justice, or to receive the judiciary emoluments.[7]

The same prince regulates the judiciary power between the ecclesiastic courts and his officers.[8] The Capitulary of Charlemagne in the year 802 prescribes to the bishops and abbots the qualifications necessary for their officers of justice. Another capitulary of the same prince inhibits the royal officers[9] to exercise any jurisdiction over those who are employed in cultivating church lands, except they entered into that state by fraud, and to exempt themselves from contributing to the public charges.[10] The bishops assembled at Rheims made a declaration that the vassals belonging to the respective churches are within their immunity.[11] The Capitulary of Charlemagne in the year 806 ordains that the churches should have both criminal and civil jurisdiction over those who live upon their lands.[12] In fine, as the capitulary of Charles the Bald[13] distinguishes between the king's jurisdiction, that of the lords, and that of the church, I shall say nothing further upon this subject.

22. *That the Jurisdictions were established before the End of the Second Race.* It has been pretended that the vassals usurped the jurisdiction in their seigniories, during the confusion of the second race. Those who choose rather to form a general proposition than to examine it found it easier to say that the vassals did not possess than to discover how they came to possess. But the jurisdictions do not owe their origin to usurpations; they are derived from the primitive establishment, and not from its corruption.

"He who kills a freeman," says the law of the Bavarians, "shall pay a composition to his relatives if he has any; if not, he shall pay it to the duke, or to the person under whose protection he had put himself in his lifetime."[14] It is well known what it was to put oneself under the protection of another for a benefice.

"He who had been robbed of his bondman," says the law of the Alemans, "shall have recourse to the prince to whom the robber is subject; to the end that he may obtain a composition."[15]

"If a *centenarius*," says the decree of Childebert, "finds a robber in another hundred than his own, or in the limits of our faithful vassals, and does not drive him out, he shall be answerable for the robber, or purge himself by oath."[16] There was therefore a difference between the district of the *centenarii* and that of the vassals.

This decree of Childebert[17] explains the constitution of Clotharius of the same year, which being given for the same occasion and on the same matter differs only in the terms; the constitution calling *in truste* what by the decree

---

[1] See Marculfus, i, form. 3, 4.

[2] *Ne aliubi nisi ad ecclesiam, ubi relaxati sunt, mallum teneant,* tit. 58, § 1. See also § 19. Lindembrock's edition.

[3] *Tabulariis.*

[4] *Mallum.*

[5] *Vita S. Germeri, Episcopi Tolosani apud Bollandianos* 16 *Maii.*

[6] See also the life of St. Melanius, and that of St. Deicola.

[7] In the council of Paris, in the year 615, art. 19. See also art. 12.

[8] *Ibid.,* art. 5.

[9] In the law of the Lombards, ii, tit. 44, cap ii. Lindembrock's edition.

[10] *Ibid.*

[11] Letter in the year 858, art. 7 in the Capitularies, p. 108.

[12] It is added to the law of the Bavarians, art. 7. See also art. 3. Lindembrock's edition, p. 444.

[13] In the year 857, *in synodo apud Carisiacum,* art. 4, edition of Baluzius, p. 96.

[14] Tit. 3, cap. xiii. Lindembrock's edition.

[15] Tit. 85.

[16] In the year 595, arts. 11 and 12, edition of the Capitularies by Baluzius, p. 19.

[17] Arts. 2 and 3.

is styled *in terminis fidelium nostrorum*. Messieurs Bignon and Ducange, who pretend that *in truste* signified another king's demesne, are mistaken in their conjecture.[1]

Pepin, King of Italy, in a constitution that had been made as well for the Franks as for the Lombards,[2] after imposing penalties on the counts and other royal officers for prevarications or delays in the administration of justice, ordains that if it happens that a Frank or a Lombard, possessed of a fief, is unwilling to administer justice, the judge to whose district he belongs shall suspend the exercise of his fief, and in the meantime, either the judge or his commissary shall administer justice.[3]

It appears by a Capitulary of Charlemagne,[4] that the kings did not levy the *freda* in all places. Another capitulary of the same prince shows the feudal laws[5] and feudal court to have been already established. Another of Louis the Debonnaire ordains that when a person possessed of a fief does not administer justice,[6] or hinders it from being administered, the king's commissaries shall live in his house at discretion, till justice be administered. I shall likewise quote two capitularies of Charles the Bald; one of the year 861,[7] where we find the particular jurisdictions established, with judges and subordinate officers; and the other of the year 864,[8] where he makes a distinction between his own seigniories and those of private persons.

We have not the original grants of the fiefs, because they were established by the partition which is known to have been made among the conquerors. It cannot, therefore, be proved by original contracts that the jurisdictions were at first annexed to the fiefs: but if in the formularies of the confirmations, or of the translations of those fiefs in perpetuity, we find, as already has been observed, that the jurisdiction was there established, this judiciary right must certainly have been inherent in the fief and one of its chief privileges.

We have a far greater number of records that establish the patrimonial jurisdiction of the clergy in their districts than there are to prove that the benefices or fiefs of the feudal lords; for which two reasons may be assigned. The first, that most of the records now extant were preserved or collected by the monks, for the use of their monasteries. The second, that the patrimony of the several churches having been formed by particular grants, and by a kind of derogation from the order established, they were obliged to have charters granted to them; whereas the concessions made to the feudal lords being consequences of the political order, they had no occasion to demand, and much less to preserve, a particular charter. Nay the kings were oftentimes satisfied with making a simple delivery with the sceptre, as appears from the *Life of St. Maur.*

But the third formulary of Marculfus sufficiently proves that the privileges of immunity, and consequently that of jurisdiction, were common to the clergy and the laity, since it is made for both.[9] The same may be said of the constitution of Clotharius II.[10]

23. *General Idea of the Abbé du Bos' Book on the Establishment of the French Monarchy in Gaul.* Before I finish this book, it will not be improper to write a few strictures on the Abbé du Bos' performance, because my notions are perpetually contrary to his; and if he has hit on the truth, I must have missed it.

This performance has imposed upon a great many because it is penned with art; because the point in question is constantly supposed; because the more it is deficient in proofs the more it abounds in probabilities; and, in fine, because an infinite number of conjectures are laid down as principles, and thence other conjectures are inferred as consequences. The reader forgets he has been doubting in order to begin to believe. And as a prodigious fund of erudition is interspersed, not in the system but around it, the mind is taken up with the appendages, and neglects the principal. Besides, such a vast multitude of researches hardly permits one to imagine that nothing has been found; the length of the way makes us think that we have arrived at our journey's end.

---

[1] See Du Cange, *Glossary*, on the word *trustis*.
[2] Inserted in the Law of the Lombards, ii. tit. 52, §14. It is the Capitulary of the year 793, in Baluzius, p. 544, art. 10.
[3] See also the same law of the Lombards, ii, tit. 52, § 2, which relates to the Capitulary of Charlemagne of the year 779, art. 21.
[4] The third of the year 812, art. 10.
[5] The second of the year 813, arts. 14, 20, Baluzius' edition, p. 509.
[6] *Capitulare quintum anni* 819 art. 23, Baluzius' edition, p. 617.
[7] *Edictum in Carisiaco* in Baluzius, ii, p. 152.
[8] *Edictum Pistense*, art. 18, Baluzius' edition, ii, p. 181.

[9] Lib. 1.
[10] I have already quoted it in the preceding chapter, *Episcopi vel potentes.*

But when we examine the matter thoroughly, we find an immense colossus with earthen feet; and it is the earthen feet that render the colossus immense. If the Abbé du Bos' system had been well grounded, he would not have been obliged to write three tedious volumes to prove it; he would have found everything within his subject, and without wandering on every side in quest of what was extremely foreign to it; even reason itself would have undertaken to range this in the same chain with the other truths. Our history and laws would have told him, "Do not take so much trouble, we shall be your vouchers."

24. *The same Subject continued. Reflection on the main Part of the System.* The Abbé du Bos endeavours by all means to explode the opinion that the Franks made the conquest of Gaul. According to his system, our kings were invited by the people, and only substituted themselves in the place and succeeded to the rights of the Roman Emperors.

This pretension cannot be applied to the time when Clovis, upon his entering Gaul, took and plundered the towns; neither is it applicable to the period when he defeated Syagrius, the Roman commander, and conquered the country which he held; it can, therefore, be referred only to the period when Clovis, already master of a great part of Gaul by open force, was called by the choice and affection of the people to the sovereignty over the rest. And it is not enough that Clovis was received, he must have been called; the Abbé du Bos must prove that the people chose rather to live under Clovis than under the domination of the Romans or under their own laws. Now the Romans belonging to that part of Gaul not yet invaded by the Barbarians were, according to this author, of two sorts: the first were of the Armorican confederacy, who had driven away the emperor's officers in order to defend themselves against the Barbarians, and to be governed by their own laws; the second were subject to the Roman officers. Now, does the Abbé produce any convincing proofs that the Romans, who were still subject to the empire, called in Clovis? Not one. Does he prove that the republic of the Armoricans invited Clovis; or even concluded any treaty with him? Not at all. So far from being able to tell us the fate of this republic, he cannot even so much as prove its existence; and notwithstanding he pretends to trace it from the time of Honorius to the conquest of Clovis, notwithstanding he relates with most admirable exactness all the events of those times; still this republic remains invisible in ancient authors. For there is a wide difference between proving by a passage of Zozimus[1] that under the Emperor Honorius, the country of Armorica[2] and the other provinces of Gaul revolted and formed a kind of republic, and showing us that notwithstanding the different pacifications of Gaul, the Armoricans formed always a particular republic, which continued till the conquest of Clovis; and yet this is what he should have demonstrated by strong and substantial proofs, in order to establish his system. For when we behold a conqueror entering a country, and subduing a great part of it by force and open violence, and soon after find the whole country subdued, without any mention in history of the manner of its being effected, we have sufficient reason to believe that the affair ended as it began.

When we find he has mistaken this point, it is easy to perceive that his whole system falls to the ground; and as often as he infers a consequence from these principles that Gaul was not conquered by the Franks, but that the Franks were invited by the Romans, we may safely deny it.

This author proves his principle by the Roman dignities with which Clovis was invested: he insists that Clovis succeeded to Childeric his father in the office of *magister militiæ*. But these two offices are merely of his own creation. St. Remigius' letter to Clovis, on which he grounds his opinion, is only a congratulation upon his accession to the crown.[3] When the intent of a writing is so well known, why should we give it another turn?

Clovis, towards the end of the reign, was made consul by the Emperor Anastasius: but what right could he receive from an authority that lasted only one year? It is very probable, says our author, that in the same diploma the Emperor Anastasius made Clovis proconsul. And, I say, it is very probable he did not. With regard to a fact for which there is no foundation, the authority of him who denies is equal to that of him who affirms. But I have also a reason for denying it. Gregory of Tours, who mentions the consulate, says never a word concerning the proconsulate. And even this proconsulate could have lasted only about six

[1] *History*, vi.
[2] *Ibid.*
[3] Vol. ii, book III, 18, p. 270.

months. Clovis died a year and a half after he was created consul; and we cannot pretend to make the pro-consulate an hereditary office. In fine, when the consulate, and, if you will, the proconsulate, were conferred upon him, he was already master of the monarchy, and all his rights were established.

The second proof alleged by the Abbé du Bos is the renunciation made by the Emperor Justinian, in favour of the children and grandchildren of Clovis, of all the rights of the empire over Gaul. I could say a great deal concerning this renunciation. We may judge of the regard shown to it by the kings of the Franks, from the manner in which they performed the conditions of it. Besides, the kings of the Franks were masters and peaceable sovereigns of Gaul; Justinian had not one foot of ground in that country; the western empire had been destroyed a long time before, and the eastern empire had no right to Gaul, but as representing the emperor of the west. These were rights upon rights; the monarchy of the Franks was already founded; the regulation of their establishment was made; the reciprocal rights of the persons and of the different nations who lived in the monarchy were admitted, the laws of each nation were given and even reduced to writing. What, therefore, could that foreign renunciation avail to a government already established?

What can the Abbé mean by making such a parade of the declamations of all those bishops, who, amidst the confusion and total subversion of the state, endeavour to flatter the conqueror? What else is implied by flattering but the weakness of him who is obliged to flatter? What do rhetoric and poetry prove but the use of those very arts? Is it possible to help being surprised at Gregory of Tours, who, after mentioning the assassinations committed by Clovis, says that God laid his enemies every day at his feet, because he walked in his ways? Who doubts but the clergy were glad of Clovis's conversion, and that they even reaped great advantages from it? But who doubts at the same time that the people experienced all the miseries of conquest and that the Roman government submitted to that of the Franks? The Franks were neither willing nor able to make a total change; and few conquerors were ever seized with so great a degree of madness. But to render all the Abbé du Bos' consequences true, they must not only have made no change among the Romans, but they must even have changed themselves.

I could undertake to prove, by following this author's method, that the Greeks never conquered Persia. I should set out with mentioning the treaties which some of their cities concluded with the Persians; I should mention the Greeks who were in Persian pay, as the Franks were in the pay of the Romans. And if Alexander entered the Persian territories, besieged, took, and destroyed the city of Tyre, it was only a particular affair like that of Syagrius. But, behold the Jewish pontiff goes forth to meet him. Listen to the oracle of Jupiter Ammon. Recollect how he had been predicted at Gordium. See what a number of towns crowd, as it were, to submit to him; and how all the satraps and grandees come to pay him obeisance. He put on the Persian dress; this is Clovis' consular robe. Does not Darius offer him one half of his kingdom? Is not Darius assassinated like a tyrant? Do not the mother and wife of Darius weep at the death of Alexander? Were Quintius Curtius, Arrian, or Plutarch, Alexander's contemporaries? Has not the invention of printing afforded us great light which those authors wanted?[1] Such is the history of the *Establishment of the French Monarchy in Gaul.*

25. *Of the French Nobility.* The Abbé du Bos maintains that at the commencement of our monarchy there was only one order of citizens among the Franks. This assertion, so injurious to the noble blood of our principal families, is equally affronting to the three great houses which successively governed this realm. The origin of their grandeur would not, therefore, have been lost in the obscurity of time. History might point out the ages when they were plebeian families; and to make Childeric, Pepin, and Hugh Capet gentlemen, we should be obliged to trace their pedigree among the Romans or Saxons, that is, among the conquered nations.

This author grounds his opinion on the Salic law.[2] By that law, he says, it plainly appears that there were not two different orders of citizens among the Franks: it allowed a composition of two hundred sous for the murder of any Frank whatsoever;[3] but among the Romans it distinguished the king's guest, for whose death it gave a composition of three

[1] See the preliminary discourse of the Abbé du Bos.

[2] See the *Establishment of the French Monarchy*, iii, book VI, 4, p. 304.

[3] He cites the 44th title of this law, and the law of the Ripuarians, tit. 7 and 36.

hundred sous, from the Roman proprietor to whom it granted a hundred, and from the Roman tributary to whom it gave only a composition of forty-five. And as the difference of the compositions formed the principal distinction, he concludes that there was but one order of citizens among the Franks, and three among the Romans.

It is astonishing that his very mistake did not set him right. And, indeed, it would have been very extraordinary that the Roman nobility who lived under the domination of the Franks should have had a larger composition, and been persons of much greater importance than the most illustrious among the Franks, and their greatest generals. What probability is there that the conquering nation should have so little respect for themselves, and so great a regard for the conquered people? Besides, our author quotes the laws of other barbarous nations which prove that they had different orders of citizens. Now it would be a matter of astonishment that this general rule should have failed only among the Franks. Hence he ought to have concluded either that he did not rightly understand or that he misapplied the passages of the Salic law, which is actually the case.

Upon opening this law, we find that the composition for the death of an Antrustio,[1] that is, of the king's vassal, was six hundred sous; and that for the death of a Roman, who was the king's guest, was only three hundred.[2] We find there likewise that the composition[3] for the death of an ordinary Frank was two hundred sous;[4] and for the death of an ordinary Roman, was only one hundred.[5] For the death of a Roman tributary,[6] who was a kind of bondman or freedman, they paid a composition of forty-five sous: but I shall take no notice of this, any more than of the composition for the murder of a Frank bondman or of a Frank freedman, because this third order of persons is out of the question.

What does our author do? He is quite silent with respect to the first order of persons among the Franks, that is the article relating

to the Antrustios; and afterwards upon comparing the ordinary Frank, for whose death they paid a composition of two hundred sous, with those whom he distinguishes under three orders among the Romans, and for whose death they paid different compositions, he finds that there was only one order of citizens among the Franks, and that there were three among the Romans.

As the Abbé is of opinion that there was only one order of citizens among the Franks, it would have been lucky for him that there had been only one order also among the Burgundians, because their kingdom constituted one of the principal branches of our monarchy. But in their codes we find three sorts of compositions, one for the Burgundians or Roman nobility, the other for the Burgundians or Romans of a middling condition, and the third for those of a lower rank in both nations.[7] He has not quoted this law.

It is very extraordinary to see in what manner he evades those passages which press him hard on all sides.[8] If you speak to him of the grandees, lords, and the nobility, these, he says, are mere distinctions of respect, and not of order; they are things of courtesy, and not legal privileges; or else, he says, those people belonged to the king's council; nay, they possibly might be Romans: but still there was only one order of citizens among the Franks. On the other hand, if you speak to him of some Franks of an inferior rank,[9] he says they are bondmen; and thus he interprets the decree of Childebert. But I must stop here a little, to inquire farther into this decree. Our author has rendered it famous by availing himself of it in order to prove two things: the one that all the compositions we meet with in the laws of the Barbarians were only civil fines added to corporal punishments, which entirely subverts all the ancient records;[10] the other, that all freemen were judged directly and immediately by the king,[11] which is contradicted by an infinite number of passages and authorities informing us of the judiciary order of those times.[12]

This decree, which was made in an assembly

[1] *Qui in truste dominicâ est,* tit. 44, § 4, and this relates to the 13th formulary of Marculfus, *de regis Antrustione.* See also tit. 66, of the Salic law, §§ 3 and 4, and tit. 74; and the law of the Ripuarians, tit. 11, and the Capitulary of Charles the Bald, *apud Carisiacum,* in the year 877, cap. xx.
[2] Salic law, tit. 44, § 6.
[3] Tit. 44, § 4.
[4] Tit. 44, § 1.
[5] Tit. 44, § 15.
[6] Tit. 44, § 7.

[7] Arts. 1, 2, and 3, of tit. 26, of the law of the Burgundians.
[8] *Establishment of the French Monarchy,* iii, book VI. 4, 5.
[9] *Ibid.,* iii. 5, pp. 319, 320.
[10] *Ibid.,* iii, book VI, 4, pp. 307, 308.
[11] *Ibid.,* p. 309, and in the following chapter, pp. 310, 320.
[12] See xxviii. 28 of this work; and xxxi. 8.

of the nation,[1] says that, if the judge finds a
notorious robber, he must command him to be
tied, in order to be carried before the king,
si Francus fuerit; but if he is a weaker person
(debilior persona), he shall be hanged on the
spot. According to the Abbé du Bos, Francus
is a freeman, debilior persona is a bondman.
I shall defer entering for a moment into the
signification of the word Francus, and begin
with examining what can be understood by
these words, a weaker person. In all languages
whatsoever, every comparison necessarily supposes three terms, the greatest, the less degree,
and the least. If none were here meant but
freemen and bondmen, they would have said
a bondman, and not a man of less power.
Therefore debilior persona does not signify a
bondman, but a person of a superior condition to a bondman. Upon this supposition,
Francus cannot mean a freeman, but a powerful man; and this word is taken here in that
acceptation, because among the Franks there
were always men who had greater power than
others in the state, and it was more difficult
for the judge or count to chastise them. This
construction agrees very well with many capitularies[2] where we find the cases in which the
criminals were to be carried before the king,
and those in which it was otherwise.

It is mentioned in the Life of Louis the Debonnaire,[3] written by Tegan, that the bishops
were the principal cause of the humiliation of
that emperor, especially those who had been
bondmen and such as were born among the
Barbarians. Tegan thus addresses Hebo,
whom this prince had drawn from the state of
servitude, and made Archbishop of Rheims:
"What recompense did the Emperor receive
from you for so many benefits? He made you a
freeman, but did not ennoble you, because he
could not give you nobility after having given
you your liberty."[4]

This passage, which proves so strongly the
two orders of citizens, does not at all confound
the Abbé du Bos. He answers thus:[5] "The
meaning of this passage is not that Louis the
Debonnaire was incapable of introducing Hebo into the order of the nobility. Hebo, as
Archbishop of Rheims, must have been of the
first order, superior to that of the nobility." I
leave the reader to judge whether this be not

the meaning of that passage; I leave him to
judge whether there be any question here concerning a precedence of the clergy over the
nobility. "This passage proves only," continues the same writer,[6] "that the free-born
subjects were qualified as noblemen; in the
common acceptation, noblemen and men who
are free-born have for this long time signified
the same thing." What! because some of our
burghers have lately assumed the quality of
noblemen, shall a passage of the Life of Louis
the Debonnaire be applied to this sort of
people? "And perhaps," continues he still,[7]
"Hebo had not been a bondman among the
Franks, but among the Saxons, or some other
German nation, where the people were divided into several orders." Then, because of
the Abbé du Bos' "perhaps," there must have
been no nobility among the nation of the
Franks. But he never applied a "perhaps" so
badly. We have seen that Tegan distinguishes
the bishops,[8] who had opposed Louis the Debonnaire, some of whom had been bondmen,
and others of a barbarous nation. Hebo belonged to the former and not to the latter.
Besides, I do not see how a bondman, such as
Hebo, can be said to have been a Saxon or a
German; a bondman has no family, and consequently no nation. Louis the Debonnaire
manumitted Hebo; and as bondmen after
their manumission embraced the law of their
master, Hebo had become a Frank, and not a
Saxon or German.

I have been hitherto acting offensively; it
is now time to defend myself. It will be objected to me that indeed the body of the Antrustios formed a distinct order in the state
from that of the freemen; but as the fiefs were
at first precarious, and afterwards for life, this
could not form a nobleness of descent, since
the privileges were not annexed to an hereditary fief. This is the objection which induced
M. de Valois to think that there was only one
order of citizens among the Franks; an opinion which the Abbé du Bos has borrowed of
him, and which he has absolutely spoiled with
so many bad arguments. Be that as it may, it
is not the Abbé du Bos that could make this
objection. For after having given three orders
of Roman nobility, and the quality of the
king's guest for the first, he could not pretend
to say that this title was a greater mark of a
noble descent than that of Antrustio. But I

[1] Capitulary, Baluzius's edition, i, p. 19.
[2] See xxviii. 28 of this work, and xxxi. 8.
[3] Chapters 43, 44.
[4] Ibid.
[5] Establishment of the French Monarchy, iii, book VI, 4, p. 316.
[6] Ibid., p. 316.
[7] Ibid.
[8] De Gestis Ludovici Pii, 43, 44.

must give a direct answer. The Antrustios or trusty men were not such because they were possessed of a fief, but that they had a fief given them because they were Antrustios or trusty men. The reader may please to recollect what has been said in the beginning of this book. They had not at that time, as they had afterwards, the same fief: but if they had not that, they had another, because the fiefs were given at their birth, and because they were often granted in the assemblies of the nation, and, in fine, because as it was the interest of the nobility to receive them it was likewise the king's interest to grant them. These families were distinguished by their dignity of trusty men, and by the privilege of being qualified to swear allegiance for a fief. In the following book[1] I shall demonstrate how, from the circumstances of the time, there were freemen who were permitted to enjoy this great privilege, and consequently to enter into the order of nobility. This was not the case at the time of Gontram, and his nephew Childebert; but so it was at the time of Charlemagne. But though in that prince's reign the freemen were not incapable of possessing fiefs, yet it appears, by the above-cited passage of Tegan, that the emancipated serfs were absolutely excluded. Will the Abbé du Bos, who carries us to Turkey to give us an idea of the ancient French nobility;[3] will he, I say, pretend that they ever complained among the Turks of the elevation of people of low birth to the honours and dignities of the state, as they complained under Louis the Debonnaire and Charles the Bald? There was no complaint of that kind under Charlemagne, because this prince always distinguished the ancient from the new families; which Louis the Debonnaire, and Charles the Bald did not.

The public should not forget the obligation it owes to the Abbé du Bos for several excellent performances. It is by these works, and not by his history of the *Establishment of the French Monarchy*, we ought to judge of his merit. He committed very great mistakes, because he had more in view the Count of Boulainvilliers' work than his own subject.

From all these strictures I shall draw only one reflection: if so great a man was mistaken, how cautiously ought I to tread?

Book XXXI. Theory of the Feudal Laws among the Franks, in the Relation They Bear to the Revolutions of their Monarchy

1. *Changes in the Offices and in the Fiefs.* The counts at first were sent into their districts only for a year; but they soon purchased the continuation of their offices. Of this we have an example in the reign of Clovis' grandchildren. A person named Peonius was count in the city of Auxerre;[2] he sent his son Mummolus with money to Gontram, to prevail upon him to continue him in his employment; the son gave the money for himself, and obtained the father's place. The kings had already begun to spoil their own favours.

Though by the laws of the kingdom the fiefs were precarious, yet they were neither given nor taken away in a capricious and arbitrary manner: nay, they were generally one of the principal subjects debated in the national assemblies. It is natural, however, to imagine that corruption crept into this as well as the other case; and that the possession of the fiefs, like that of the counties, was continued for money.

I shall show in the course of this book,[4] that, independently of the grants which the princes made for a certain time, there were others in perpetuity. The court wanted to revoke the former grants; this occasioned a general discontent in the nation, and was soon followed by that famous revolution in French history, whose first epoch was the amazing spectacle of the execution of Brunehault.

That this queen, who was daughter, sister and mother of so many kings, a queen to this very day celebrated for public monuments worthy of a Roman ædile or proconsul, born with an admirable genius for affairs, and endowed with qualities so long respected, should see herself of a sudden exposed to so slow, so ignominious and cruel a torture,[5] by a king whose authority was but indifferently established in the nation,[6] would appear very extraordinary, had she not incurred that nation's

[1] Chapter 23.
[2] Gregory of Tours, iv. 42.

[3] *Establishment of the French Monarchy*, iii, book VI. 4, p. 302.
[4] Chapter 7.
[5] Fredegarius, *Chronicle*, 42.
[6] Clotharius II, son of Chilperic, and the father of Dagobert.

displeasure for some particular cause. Clotharius reproached her with the murder of ten kings; but two of them he had put to death himself; the death of some of the others was owing to chance, or to the villainy of another queen;[1] and a nation that had permitted Fredegunda to die in her bed,[2] that had even opposed the punishment of her flagitious crimes, ought to have been very different with respect to those of Brunehault.

She was put upon a camel, and led ignominiously through the army; a certain sign that she had given great offence to those troops. Fredegarius relates that Protarius,[3] Brunehault's favourite, stripped the lords of their property, and filled the exchequer with the plunder; that he humbled the nobility, and that no person could be sure of continuing in any office or employment. The army conspired against him, and he was stabbed in his tent; but Brunehault, either by revenging his death, or by pursuing the same plan,[4] became every day more odious to the nation.[5]

Clotharius, ambitious of reigning alone, inflamed moreover with the most furious revenge, and sure of perishing if Brunehault's children got the upper hand, entered into a conspiracy against himself; and whether it was owing to ignorance, or to the necessity of his circumstances, he became Brunehault's accuser, and made a terrible example of that princess.

Warnacharius had been the very soul of the conspiracy formed against Brunehault. Being at that time mayor of Burgundy, he made Clotharius consent that he should not be displaced while he lived.[6] By this step the mayor could no longer be in the same case as the French lords before that period; and this authority began to render itself independent of the regal dignity.

It was Brunehault's unhappy regency which had exasperated the nation. So long as the laws subsisted in their full force, no one could grumble at having been deprived of a fief, since the law did not bestow it upon him in perpetuity. But when fiefs came to be acquired by avarice, by bad practices and corruption, they complained of being divested, by irregular means, of things that had been irregularly acquired. Perhaps if the public good had been the motive of the revocation of those

grants, nothing would have been said; but they pretended a regard for order while they were openly abetting the principles of corruption; the fiscal rights were claimed in order to lavish the public treasure; and grants were no longer the reward or the encouragement of services. Brunehault, from a corrupt spirit, wanted to reform the abuses of the ancient corruption. Her caprices were not owing to weakness; the vassals and the great officers, thinking themselves in danger, prevented their own by her ruin.

We are far from having all the records of the transactions of those days; and the writers of chronicles, who understood very nearly as much of the history of their time as our peasants know of ours, are extremely barren. Yet we have a constitution of Clotharius, given in the council of Paris,[7] for the reformation of abuses,[8] which shows that this prince put a stop to the complaints that had occasioned the revolution. On the one hand, he confirms all the grants that had been made or confirmed by the kings his predecessors;[9] and on the other, he ordains that whatever had been taken from his vassals should be restored to them.[10]

This was not the only concession the king made in that council; he enjoined that whatever had been innovated, in opposition to the privileges of the clergy, should be redressed; and he moderated the influence of the court in the election of bishops.[11] He even reformed the fiscal affairs, ordaining that all the new censuses should be abolished,[12] and that they should not levy any toll established since the deaths of Gontram, Sigebert, and Chilperic;[13] that is, he abolished whatever had been done during the regencies of Fredegunda and Brunehault. He forbad the driving of his cattle to graze in private people's grounds;[14] and we shall presently see that the reformation was still more general, so as to extend even to civil affairs.

2. *How the Civil Government was reformed.* Hitherto the nation had given marks of impatience and levity with regard to the choice or

---

[1] Fredegarius, *Chronicle,* 42.
[2] See Gregory of Tours, viii. 31.
[3] Fredegarius, *Chronicle,* 27, in the year 605.
[4] *Ibid.,* 28, in the year 607.
[5] *Ibid.,* 41, in the year 613.
[6] *Ibid.,* 42, in the year 613.

[7] Some time after Brunehault's execution, in the year 615. See Baluzius's edition of the *Capitularies,* p. 21.
[8] *Ibid.,* art. 16.
[9] *Ibid.*
[10] *Ibid.,* art. 17.
[11] *Ibid.,* art. 1.
[12] *Ibid.,* art. 8.
[13] *Ibid.,* art. 9.
[14] *Ibid.,* art. 21.

conduct of her masters; she had regulated their differences and obliged them to come to an agreement among themselves. But now she did what before was quite unexampled; she cast her eyes on her actual situation, examined the laws coolly, provided against their insufficiency, repressed violence, and moderated the regal power.

The bold and insolent regencies of Fredegunda and Brunehault had less surprised than roused the nation. Fredegunda had defended her horried cruelties, her poisonings and assassinations, by a repetition of the same crimes; and had behaved in such a manner that her outrages were rather of a private than public nature. Fredegunda did more mischief: Brunehault threatened more. In this crisis the nation was not satisfied with rectifying the feudal system; she was also determined to secure her civil government. For the latter was rather more corrupt than the former; a corruption the more dangerous as it was more inveterate, and connected rather with the abuse of manners than with that of laws.

The history of Gregory of Tours exhibits, on the one hand, a fierce and barbarous nation; and on the other, kings remarkable for the same ferocity of temper. Those princes were bloody, iniquitous and cruel, because such was the character of the whole nation. If Christianity appeared sometimes to soften their manners, it was only by the circumstances of terror with which this religion alarms the sinner; the church supported herself against them by the miraculous operations of her saints. The kings would not commit sacrilege, because they dreaded the punishments inflicted on that species of guilt: but this excepted, either in the riot of passion or in the coolness of deliberation, they perpetrated the most horrid crimes and barbarities where divine vengeance did not appear so immediately to overtake the criminal. The Franks, as I have already observed, bore with cruel kings, because they were of the same disposition themselves; they were not shocked at the iniquity and extortions of their princes, because this was the national characteristic. There had been many laws established, but it was usual for the king to defeat them all, by a kind of letter called *precepts*,[1] which rendered them of no effect; they were somewhat similar to the rescripts of the Roman Emperors; whether it be that our kings borrowed this usage from those princes,

or whether it was owing to their own natural temper. We see in Gregory of Tours, that they perpetrated murder in cool blood, and put the accused to death unheard; how they gave precepts for illicit marriages;[2] for transferring successions; for depriving relatives of their right; and, in fine, marrying consecrated virgins. They did not, indeed, assume the whole legislative power, but they dispensed with the execution of the laws.

Clotharius' constitution redressed all these grievances: no one could any longer be condemned without being heard:[3] relatives were made to succeed, according to the order established by law;[4] all precepts for marrying religious women were declared null;[5] and those who had obtained and made use of them were severely punished. We might know perhaps more exactly his determinations with regard to these *precepts,* if the thirteenth and the next two articles of this decree had not been lost through the injury of time. We have only the first words of this thirteenth article, ordaining that the *precepts* shall be observed, which cannot be understood of those he had just abolished by the same law. We have another constitution by the same prince,[6] which is in relation to his decree, and corrects in the same manner every article of the abuses of the *precepts.*

True it is that Baluzius, finding this constitution without date and without the name of the place where it was given, attributes it to Clotharius I. But I say it belongs to Clotharius II, for three reasons: 1. It says that the king will preserve the immunities granted to the churches by his father and grandfather.[7] What immunities could the churches receive from Childeric, grandfather of Clotharius I, who was not a Christian, and who lived even before the foundation of the monarchy? But if we attribute this decree to Clotharius II, we shall find his grandfather to have been this

[1] They were orders which the king sent to the judges to do or to tolerate things contrary to law.

[2] See Gregory of Tours, iv, p. 227. Both our history and the charters are full of this; and the extent of these abuses appears especially in Clotharius' constitution, inserted in the edition of the Capitularies made to reform them. Baluzius's edition, p. 7.
[3] *Ibid.,* art. 22.
[4] *Ibid.,* art 6.
[5] *Ibid.,* art. 18.
[6] In Baluzius's edition of the Capitularies, i. p. 7.
[7] In the preceding book I have made mention of these immunities, which were grants of judicial rights, and contained prohibitions to the regal judges to perform any function in the territory, and were equivalent to the erection or grant of a fief.

very Clotharius I, who made immense donations to the church with a view of expiating
the murder of his son Cramne, whom he had
ordered to be burned, together with his wife
and children.

2. The abuses redressed by this constitution
were still subsisting after the death of Clotharius I and were even carried to their highest
extravagance during the weak reign of Gontram, the cruel administration of Chilperic, and
the execrable regencies of Fredegunda
and Brunehault. Now, can we imagine that
the nation would have borne with grievances
so solemnly proscribed, without complaining
of their continual repetition? Can we imagine
she would not have taken the same step as she
did afterwards under Childeric II,[1] when, upon a repetition of the old grievances, she
pressed him to ordain that law and customs in
regard to judicial proceedings should be complied with as formerly.[2]

In fine, as this constitution was made to redress grievances, it cannot relate to Clotharius
I, since there were no complaints of that kind
in his reign, and his authority was perfectly
established throughout the kingdom, especially at the time in which they place this constitution; whereas it agrees extremely well with
the events that happened during the reign of
Clotharius II, which produced a revolution in
the political state of the kingdom. History
must be illustrated by the laws, and the laws
by history.

3. *Authority of the Mayors of the Palace.* I noticed that Clotharius II had promised not to
deprive Warnacharius of his mayor's place
during life; a revolution productive of another effect. Before that time the mayor was
the king's officer, but now he became the officer of the people; he was chosen before by
the king, and now by the nation. Before the
revolution Protarius had been made mayor by
Theodoric, and Landeric by Fredegunda;[3] but
after that the mayors[4] were chosen by the nation.[5]

We must not therefore confound, as some

authors have done, these mayors of the palace
with such as were possessed of this dignity before the death of Brunehault; the king's mayors with those of the kingdom. We see by the
law of the Burgundians that among them
the office of mayor was not one of the most respectable in the state;[6] nor was it one of the
most eminent under the first Kings of the
Franks.[7]

Clotharius removed the apprehensions of
those who were possessed of employments and
fiefs; and when, after the death of Warnacharius,[8] he asked the lords assembled at Troyes,
who is it they would put in his place, they
cried out they would choose no one, but suing
for his favour committed themselves entirely
into his hands.

Dagobert reunited the whole monarchy in
the same manner as his father; the nation had
a thorough confidence in him, and appointed
no mayor. This prince, finding himself at liberty and elated by his victories, resumed
Brunehault's plan. But he succeeded so ill
that the vassals of Austrasia let themselves be
beaten by the Sclavonians, and returned
home; so that the marches of Austrasia were
left to prey to the barbarians.[9]

He determined then to make an offer to the
Austrasians of resigning that country, together
with a provincial treasure, to his son Sigebert,
and to put the government of the kingdom
and of the palace into the hands of Cunibert,
Bishop of Cologne, and of the Duke Adalgi-
sus. Fredegarius does not enter into the particulars of the conventions then made; but the
king confirmed them all by charters, and Austrasia was immediately secured from danger.[10]

Dagobert, finding himself near his end, recommended his wife Nentechildis and his son
Clovis to the care of Æga. The vassals of Neustria and Burgundy chose this young prince for
their king.[11] Æga and Nentechildis had the
government of the palace;[12] they restored whatever Dagobert had taken;[13] and complaints
ceased in Neustria and Burgundy, as they had
ceased in Austrasia.

After the death of Æga, Queen Nentechildis
engaged the lords of Burgundy to choose Floa-

[1] He began to reign towards the year 670.
[2] See the *Life of St. Leger.*
[3] *Instigante Brunihault, Theodorico jubente,*
&c.—Fredegarius, 27, in the year 605.
[4] *Gesta regum Francorum,* 36.
[5] See Fredegarius, *Chronicle,* 54, in the year 626,
and his anonymous continuator, 101, in the year
695, and 105, in the year 715. Aimoin, iv. 15, Eginhard, Life of Charlemagne, 48. *Gesta regum Francorum,* 45.

[6] See the Law of the Burgundians, pref., and the
second supplement to this law, tit. 13.
[7] See Gregory of Tours, ix. 36.
[8] Fredegarius, *Chronicle,* 44, in the year 626.
[9] Fredegarius, *Chronicle,* 68, in the year 630.
[10] Fredegarius, *Chronicle,* 75, in the year 632.
[11] Fredegarius, *Chronicle,* 79, in the year 638.
[12] *Ibid.*
[13] *Ibid.,* 80, in the year 639.

chatus for their mayor.[1] The latter dispatched letters to the bishops and chief lords of the kingdom of Burgundy, by which he promised to preserve their honours and dignities for ever, that is, during life.[2] He confirmed his word by oath. This is the period at which the author of the *Treatise on the Mayors of the Palace* fixes the administration of the kingdom by those officers.[3]

Fredegarius, being a Burgundian, has entered into a more minute detail as to what concerns the Mayors of Burgundy at the time of the revolution of which we are speaking, than with regard to the mayors of Austrasia and Neustria. But the conventions made in Burgundy were, for the very same reasons, agreed to in Neustria and Austrasia.

The nation thought it safer to lodge the power in the hands of a mayor whom she chose herself, and to whom she might prescribe conditions, than in those of a king whose power was hereditary.

4. *Of the Genius of the Nation in regard to the Mayors.* A government in which a nation that had an hereditary king chose a person to exercise the regal authority seems very extraordinary; but, independently of the circumstances of the times, I apprehend that the notions of the Franks in this respect were derived from a remote source.

The Franks were descended from the Germans, of whom Tacitus says[4] that in the choice of their king they were determined by his noble extraction, and in that of their leader, by his valour. This gives us an idea of the kings of the first race, and of the mayors of the palace; the former were hereditary, the latter elective.

No doubt but those princes who stood up in the national assembly and offered themselves as the conductors of a public enterprise to such as were willing to follow them, united generally in their own person both the power of the mayor and the king's authority. By the splendour of their descent they had attained the regal dignity; and their military abilities having recommended them to the command of armies, they rose to the power of mayor. By the regal dignity, our first kings presided in the courts and assemblies, and enacted laws with the national consent; by the dignity of duke or leader, they undertook expeditions and commanded the armies.

In order to be acquainted with the genius of the primitive Franks in this respect, we have only to cast an eye on the conduct of Argobastes,[5] a Frank by nation, on whom Valentinian had conferred the command of the army. He confined the emperor to his own palace, where he would suffer nobody to speak to him, concerning either civil or military affairs. Argobastes did at that time what was afterwards practised by the Pepins.

5. *In what Manner the Mayors obtained the Command of the Armies.* So long as the kings commanded their armies in person, the nation never thought of choosing a leader. Clovis and his four sons were at the head of the Franks, and led them on through a series of victories. Theobald, son of Theodobert, a young, weak, and sickly prince, was the first of our kings who confined himself to his palace.[6] He refused to undertake an expedition into Italy against Narses, and had the mortification of seeing the Franks choose for themselves two chiefs, who led them against the enemy.[7] Of the four sons of Clotharius I, Gontram was the least fond of commanding his armies;[8] the other kings followed this example; and, in order to entrust the command without danger into other hands, they conferred it upon several chiefs or dukes.[9]

Innumerable were the inconveniences which thence arose; all discipline was lost, no one would any longer obey. The armies were dreadful only to their own country; they were laden with spoils before they had reached the enemy. Of these miseries we have a very lively picture in Gregory of Tours.[10] "How shall we be able to obtain a victory," said Gontram,[11] "we who do not so much as keep what our ancestors acquired? Our nation is no longer the same." . . . . Strange that it should be on the decline so early as the reign of Clovis' grandchildren!

[5] See Sulpicius Alexander, in Gregory of Tours, ii.

[6] In the year 552.

[7] Agathias, i. Gregory of Tours, iv. 9.

[8] Gontram did not even march against Gondovald, who styled himself son of Clotharius, and claimed his share of the kingdom.

[9] Sometimes to the number of twenty. See Gregory of Tours, v. 27, viii. 28 and 30, x. 3. Dagobert, who had no mayor in Burgundy, observed the same policy, and sent against the Gascons ten dukes and several counts who had no dukes over them.—Fredegarius, *Chronicle*, 78, in the year 636.

[10] Gregory of Tours, viii. 30, and x. 3.

[11] *Ibid.*, viii. 30.

[1] Fredegarius, *Chronicle*, 89, in the year 641.
[2] *Ibid.*
[3] *De Majoribus Domus Regiæ.*
[4] *De Moribus Germanorum,* 7.

It was therefore natural they should determine at last upon an only duke, a duke invested with an authority over this prodigious multitude of feudal lords and vassals who had now become strangers to their own engagements; a duke who was to establish the military discipline, and to put himself at the head of a nation unhappily practised in making war against itself. This power was conferred on the mayors of the palace.

The original function of the mayors of the palace was the management of the king's household. They had afterwards, in conjunction with other officers, the political government of fiefs; and at length they obtained the sole disposal of them.[1] They had also the administration of military affairs, and the command of the armies; employments necessarily connected with the other two. In those days it was much more difficult to raise than to command the armies; and who but the dispenser of favours could have this authority? In this martial and independent nation, it was prudent to invite rather than to compel; prudent to give away or to promise the fiefs that should happen to be vacant by the death of the possessor; prudent, in fine, to reward continually, and to raise a jealousy with regard to preferences. It was therefore right that the person who had the superintendence of the palace should also be general of the army.

6. *Second Epoch of the Humiliation of our Kings of the first Race.* After the execution of Brunehault, the mayors were administrators of the kingdom under the sovereigns; and though they had the conduct of the war, the kings were always at the head of the armies, while the mayor and the nation fought under their command. But the victory of Duke Pepin over Theodoric and his mayor[2] completed the degradation of our princes;[3] and that which Charles Martel obtained over Chilperic and his mayor Rainfroy confirmed it.[4] Austrasia triumphed twice over Neustria and Burgundy; and the mayoralty of Austrasia being annexed as it were to the family of the Pepins, this mayoralty and family became greatly superior to all the rest. The conquerors were then afraid lest some person of credit should seize the king's person, in order to excite disturb-

ances. For this reason they kept them in the royal palace as in a kind of prison, and once a year showed them to the people.[5] There they made ordinances, but these were such as were dictated by the mayor;[6] they answered ambassadors, but the mayor made the answers. This is the time mentioned by historians of the government of the mayors over the kings whom they held in subjection.[7]

The extravagant passion of the nation for Pepin's family went so far that they chose one of his grandsons, who was yet an infant, for mayor;[8] and put him over one Dagobert, that is, one phantom over another.

7. *Of the great Offices and Fiefs under the Mayors of the Palace.* The mayors of the palace were little disposed to establish the uncertain tenure of places and offices; for, indeed, they ruled only by the protection which in this respect they granted to the nobility. Hence the great offices continued to be given for life, and this usage was every day more firmly established.

But I have some particular reflections to make here in respect of fiefs: I do not question but most of them became hereditary from this time.

In the treaty of Andeli,[9] Gontram and his nephew Childebert engage to maintain the donations made to the vassals and churches by the kings their predecessors; and leave is given to the wives, daughters, and widows of kings to dispose by will, and in perpetuity, of whatever they hold of the exchequer.

Marculfus wrote his formularies at the time of the mayors.[10] We find several in which the kings make donations both to the person and to his heirs:[11] and as the formularies represent the common actions of life, they prove that part of the fiefs had become hereditary towards the end of the first race. They were far from having in those days the idea of an un-

---

[1] See the second supplement to the law of the Burgundians, tit. 13, and Gregory of Tours, ix. 36.

[2] See the *Annals of Metz,* years 687 and 688.

[3] *Ibid.*, year 695.

[4] *Ibid.*, year 719.

[5] *Ibid.*

[6] *Ex chronico Centulensi,* ii.

[7] *Annals of Metz,* year 691. Annals of Fulda, or of Laurishan, *Pippinus dux Francorum obtinuit regnum Francorum per annos 27, cum regibus sibi subjectis.*

[8] The anonymous continuator of Fredegarius, 104, in the year 714.

[9] Cited by Gregory of Tours, ix. See also the edict of Clotharius II, in the year 615, art. 16.

[10] See the 24th and the 34th of the first book.

[11] See the 14th formula of the first book, which is equally applicable to the fiscal estates given direct in perpetuity, or given at first as a benefice, and afterwards in perpetuity. See also the 17th formula, *ibid.*

alienable demesne; this is a modern thing, which they knew neither in theory nor practice.

In proof hereof we shall presently produce positive fact; and if we can point out a time in which there were no longer any benefices for the army, nor any funds for its support, we must certainly conclude that the ancient benefices had been alienated. The time I mean is that of Charles Martel, who founded some new fiefs, which we should carefully distinguish from those of the earliest date.

When the kings began to make grants in perpetuity, either through the corruption which crept into the government or by reason of the constitution itself, which continually obliged those princes to confer rewards, it was natural they should begin with giving the perpetuity of the fiefs, rather than of the counties. For to deprive themselves of some acres of land was no great matter; but to renounce the right of disposing of the great offices was divesting themselves of their very power.

8. *In what Manner the Allodial Estates were changed into Fiefs.* The manner of changing an allodial estate into a fief may be seen in a formulary of Marculfus.[1] The owner of the land gave it to the king, who restored it to the donor by way of usufruct, or benefice, and then the donor nominated his heirs to the king.

In order to find out the reasons which induced them thus to change the nature of the allodia, I must trace the source of the ancient privileges of our nobility, a nobility which for these eleven centuries has been enveloped with dust, with blood, and with the marks of toil.

They who were seized of fiefs enjoyed very great advantages. The composition for the injuries done them was greater than that of freemen. It appears by the formularies of Marculfus that it was a privilege belonging to a king's vassal, that whoever killed him should pay a composition of six hundred sous. This privilege was established by the Salic law,[2] and by that of the Ripuarians;[3] and while these two laws ordained a composition of six hundred sous for the murder of a king's vassal, they gave but two hundred sous for the murder of a person freeborn, if he was a Frank or

Barbarian, or a man living under the Salic law;[4] and only a hundred for a Roman.

This was not the only privilege belonging to the king's vassals. We ought to know that when a man was summoned in court, and did not make his appearance nor obey the judge's orders, he was called before the king;[5] and if he persisted in his contumacy, he was excluded from the royal protection,[6] and no one was allowed to entertain him, nor even to give him a morsel of bread. Now, if he was a person of an ordinary condition, his goods were confiscated;[7] but if he was the king's vassal, they were not.[8] The first by his contumacy was deemed sufficiently convicted of the crime, the second was not; the former for the smallest crimes was obliged to undergo the trial by boiling water,[9] the latter was condemned to this trial only in the case of murder.[10] In fine, the king's vassal could not be compelled to swear in court against another vassal.[11] These privileges were continually increasing, and the Capitulary of Carloman does this honour to the king's vassals, that they should not be obliged to swear in person, but only by the mouth of their own vassals.[12] Moreover, when a person, having these honours, did not repair to the army, his punishment was to abstain from flesh-meat and wine as long as he had been absent from the service; but a freeman[13] who neglected to follow his count was fined sixty sous,[14] and was reduced to a state of servitude till he had paid it.

It is very natural, therefore, to believe that those Franks who were not the king's vassals, and much more the Romans, became fond of entering into the state of vassalage: and that they might not be deprived of their demesnes, they devised the usage of giving their *allodium* to the king, of receiving it from him afterwards as a fief, and of nominating their heirs. This usage was continued, and took place especially during the times of confusion under the second race, when every man being in

[1] Book i, form. 13.
[2] Tit. 44. See also tit. 66, §§ 3, 4; and tit. 74.
[3] Tit. 11.

[4] See also the law of the Ripuarians, tit. 7; and the Salic law, tit. 44, art. 1 and 4.
[5] Salic law, tit. 59 and 76.
[6] *Ibid.*
[7] *Ibid.*, tit. 59, § 1.
[8] *Ibid.*, tit. 76, § 1.
[9] *Ibid.*, tit. 56 and 59.
[10] *Ibid.*, tit. 76, § 1.
[11] *Ibid.*, § 2.
[12] *Apud vernis palatium*, in the year 883, art. 4 and 11.
[13] *Capitulary* of Charlemagne, second of the year 812, art. 1 and 3.
[14] *Heribannum.*

want of a protector was desirous of incorporating himself with the other lords, and of entering, as it were, into the feudal monarchy, because the political no longer existed.[1]

This continued under the third race, as we find by several charters;[2] whether they gave their allodium, and resumed it by the same act; or whether it was declared an allodium, and afterwards acknowledged as a fief. These were called *fiefs of resumption*.

This does not imply that those who were seized of fiefs administered them as a prudent father of a family would; for though the freemen grew desirous of being possessed of fiefs, yet they managed this sort of estates as usufructs are managed in our days. This is what induced Charlemagne, the most vigilant and considerate prince we ever had, to make a great many regulations in order to hinder the fiefs from being demeaned in favour of allodial estates.[3] It proves only that in his time most benefices were but for life, and consequently that they took more care of the freeholds than of the benefices; and yet for all that, they did not choose rather to be the king's vassals than freemen. They might have reasons for disposing of some particular part of a fief, but they were not willing to be stripped of their dignity likewise.

I know, likewise, that Charlemagne laments in a certain capitulary, that in some places there were people who gave away their fiefs in property, and redeemed them afterwards in the same manner.[4] But I do not say that they were not fonder of the property than of the usufruct; I mean only, that when they could convert an allodium into a fief, which was to descend to their heirs, as is the case of the formulary above-mentioned, they had very great advantages in doing it.

9. *How the Church Lands were converted into Fiefs.* The use of the fiscal lands should have been only to serve as a donation by which the kings were to encourage the Franks to undertake new expeditions, and by which, on the other hand, these fiscal lands were increased. This, as I have already observed, was the spirit of the nation; but these donations took another turn. There is still extant a speech of Chilperic,[5] grandson of Clovis, in which he complains that almost all these lands had been already given away to the church. "Our exchequer," says he, "is impoverished, and our riches are transferred to the clergy;[6] none reign now but the bishops, who live in grandeur while we are quite eclipsed."

This was the reason that the mayors, who durst not attack the lords, stripped the churches; and one of the motives alleged by Pepin for entering Neustria[7] was his having been invited thither by the clergy to put a stop to the encroachments of the kings, that is, of the mayors, who deprived the church of all her possessions.

The Mayors of Austrasia, that is the family of the Pepins, had behaved towards the clergy with more moderation than those of Neustria and Burgundy. This is evident from our chronicles,[8] in which we see the monks perpetually extolling the devotion and liberality of the Pepins. They themselves had been possessed of the first places in the church. "One crow does not pull out the eyes of another"; as Chilperic said to the bishops.[9]

Pepin subdued Neustria and Burgundy; but as his pretence for destroying the mayors and kings was the grievances of the clergy, he could not strip the latter without acting inconsistently with his cause, and showing that he made a jest of the nation. However, the conquest of two great kingdoms and the destruction of the opposite party afforded him sufficient means of satisfying his generals.

Pepin made himself master of the monarchy by protecting the clergy; his son, Charles Martel, could not maintain his power but by oppressing them. This prince, finding that part of the regal and fiscal lands had been given either for life, or in perpetuity, to the nobility, and that the church by receiving both from rich and poor had acquired a great part even of the allodial estates, he resolved to strip the clergy; and as the fiefs of the first di-

---

[1] *Non infirmis reliquit hæredibus*, says Lambert d'Ardres in Du Cange, on the word *alodis*.

[2] See those quoted by Du Cange, in the word *alodis*, and those produced by Galland, in his *Treatise on Allodial Lands*, p. 14, ff.

[3] Second Capitulary of the year 802, art. 10; and the seventh Capitulary of the year 803, art. 3; the first Capitulary, *incerti anni*, art. 49; the fifth Capitulary of the year 806, art. 7; the Capitulary of the year 779, art. 29; the Capitulary of Louis the Pious, in the year 829, art. 1.

[4] The fifth of the year 806, art. 8.

[5] In Gregory of Tours, vi. 46.

[6] This is what induced him to annul the testaments made in favour of the clergy, and even the donations of his father; Gontram re-established them, and even made new donations.—Gregory of Tours, vii. 7.

[7] See the *Annals of Metz*, year 687.

[8] See the *Annals of Metz*.

[9] In Gregory of Tours.

vision were no longer in being, he formed a second.[1] He took for himself and for his officers the church-lands and the churches themselves; thus he remedied an evil which differed from ordinary diseases, as its extremity rendered it the more easy to cure.

10. *Riches of the Clergy*. So great were the donations made to the clergy that under the three races of our princes they must have several times received the full property of all the lands of the kingdom. But if our kings, the nobility, and the people found the way of giving them all their estates, they found also the method of getting them back again. The spirit of devotion established a great number of churches under the first race; but the military spirit was the cause of their being given away afterwards to the soldiery, who divided them among their children. What a number of lands must have then been taken from the clergy's *mensalia!* The kings of the second race opened their hands, and made new donations to them; but the Normans, who came afterwards, plundered and ravaged all before them, wreaking their vengeance chiefly on the priests and monks, and devoting every religious house to destruction. For they charged those ecclesiastics with the destruction of their idols, and with all the oppressive measures of Charlemagne by which they had been successively obliged to take shelter in the north. These were animosities which the space of forty or fifty years had not been able to obliterate. In this situation, what losses must the clergy have sustained! There were hardly ecclesiastics left to demand the estates of which they had been deprived. There remained, therefore, for the religious piety of the third race, foundations enough to make, and lands to bestow. The opinions which were spread abroad and believed in those days would have deprived the laity of all their estates, if they had been but virtuous enough. But if the clergy were actuated by ambition, the laity were not without theirs; if dying persons gave their estates to the church, their heirs would fain resume them. We meet with continual quarrels between the lords and the bishops, the gentlemen and the abbots; and the clergy must have been very hard pressed, since they were obliged to put themselves under the protection of certain lords, who granted them a momentary defence, and afterwards joined their oppressors.

[1] From *Chronica Centulensi*, ii.

But a better administration having been established under the third race gave the clergy leave to augment their possessions; when the Calvinists started up, and having plundered the churches, they turned all the sacred plate into specie. How could the clergy be sure of their estates, when they were not even safe in their persons? They were debating on controversial subjects while their archives were in flames. What did it avail them to demand back of an impoverished nobility those estates which were no longer in possession of the latter, but had been conveyed into other hands by different mortgages? The clergy have been long acquiring, and have often refunded, and still there is no end of their acquisitions.

11. *State of Europe at the Time of Charles Martel*. Charles Martel, who undertook to strip the clergy, found himself in a most happy situation. He was both feared and beloved by the soldiery; he worked for them, having the pretext of his wars against the Saracens. He was hated, indeed, by the clergy, but he had no need of their assistance.[2] The Pope, to whom he was necessary, stretched out his arms to him. Every one knows the famous embassy he received from Gregory III.[3] These two powers were strictly united, because they could not do without each other: the Pope stood in need of the Franks to assist him against the Lombards and the Greeks; Charles Martel had occasion for the Pope, to humble the Greeks, to embarrass the Lombards, to make himself more respectable at home, and to guarantee the titles which he had, and those which he or his children might take. It was impossible, therefore, for his enterprise to miscarry.

St. Eucherius, Bishop of Orleans, had a vision which frightened all the princes of that time. I shall produce on this occasion the letter written by the bishops assembled at Rheims to Louis, King of Germany, who had invaded the territories of Charles the Bald;[4] because it will give us an insight into the situation of things in those times, and the temper of the people. They say[5] that "St. Eucherius, having been snatched up into heaven, saw Charles Martel tormented in the bottom of

[2] See the *Annals of Metz*.
[3] *Ibid.*, year 741.
[4] Year 858, in Carisiacus; Baluzius's edition, ii, p. 101.
[5] *Ibid.*, ii, art. 7, p. 109.

hell by order of the saints, who are to sit with Christ at the last judgment; that he had been condemned to this punishment before his time, for having stripped the church of her possessions and thereby charged himself with the sins of all those who founded these livings; that King Pepin held a council upon this occasion, and had ordered all the church-lands he could recover to be restored; that as he could get back only a part of them, because of his disputes with Vaifre, Duke of Acquitaine, he issued letters called *precaria*[1] for the remainder, and made a law that the laity should pay a tenth part of the church-lands they possessed, and twelve deniers for each house; that Charlemagne did not give the church-lands away; on the contrary, that he published a capitulary, by which he engaged both for himself and for his successors never to make any such grant; that all they say is committed to writing, and that a great many of them heard the whole related by Louis the Debonnaire, the father of those two kings."

King Pepin's regulation, mentioned by the bishops, was made in the council held at Leptines.[2] The church found this advantage in it, that such as had received those lands held them no longer but in a precarious manner; and moreover that she received the tithe or tenth part, and twelve deniers for every house that had belonged to her. But this was only a palliative, and did not remove the disorder.

Nay, it met with opposition, and Pepin was obliged to make another capitulary,[3] in which he enjoins those who held any of those benefices to pay this tithe and duty, and even to keep up the houses belonging to the bishopric or monastery, under the penalty of forfeiting those possessions. Charlemagne renewed the regulations of Pepin.[4]

That part of the same letter which says that Charlemagne promised both for himself and for his successors never to divide again the church-lands among the soldiery is agreeable to the capitulary of this prince, given at Aix-la-Chapelle in the year 803, with a view of removing the apprehensions of the clergy upon this subject. But the donations already made were still in force.[5] The bishops very justly add that Louis the Debonnaire followed the example of Charlemagne, and did not give away the church-lands to the soldiery.

And yet the old abuses were carried to such a pitch, that the laity under the children of Louis the Debonnaire preferred ecclesiastics to benefices, or turned them out of their livings[6] without the consent of the bishops. The benefices were divided among the next heirs,[7] and when they were held in an indecent manner the bishops had no other remedy left than to remove the relics.[8]

By the Capitulary of Compiègne[9] it is enacted that the king's commissary shall have a right to visit every monastery, together with the bishop, by the consent and in presence of the person who holds it; and this shows that the abuse was general.

Not that there were laws wanting for the restitution of the church-lands. The Pope having reprimanded the bishops for their neglect in regard to the re-establishment of the monasteries, they wrote to Charles the Bald that they were not affected by this reproach, because they were not culpable;[10] and they reminded him of what had been promised, resolved and decreed in so many national assemblies. In point of fact, they quoted nine.

Still they went on disputing; till the Normans came and made them all agree.

12. *Establishment of the Tithes.* The regulations made under King Pepin had given the church rather hopes of relief than effectually relieved her; and as Charles Martel found all

---

[1] *Precaria, quod precibus utendum conceditur,* says Cujas, in his notes upon the first Book of Fiefs. I find in a diploma of King Pepin, dated the third year of his reign, that this prince was not the first who established these *precaria;* he cites one made by the Mayor *Ebroin,* and continued after his time. See the diploma of the king, in the *Historians of France* by the Benedictines, v, art. 6.

[2] In the year 743, see the 5th book of the *Capitularies,* art. 3, Baluzius's edition, p. 825.

[3] That of Metz, in the year 736, art. 4.

[4] See his Capitulary, in the year 803, given at Worms; Baluzius's edition, p. 411, where he regulates the *precarious* contract, and that of Frankfort, in the year 794, p. 267, art. 24, in relation to the repairing of the houses; and that of the year 800, p. 330.

[5] As appears by the preceding note, and by the Capitulary of Pepin, King of Italy, where it says, that the king would give the monasteries in fief to those who would swear allegiance for fiefs: it is added to the law of the Lombards, iii, tit. 1, § 30; and to the Salic Law, *Collection of Pepin's Laws* in Echard, p. 195, tit. 26, art. 4.

[6] See the constitution of Lotharius I, in the law of the Lombards, iii. *Leg.* 1, § 43.

[7] *Ibid.,* § 44.

[8] *Ibid.*

[9] Given the 28th year of the reign of Charles the Bald, in the year 868. Baluzius's edition, p. 203.

[10] *Concilium apud Bonoilum,* the 16th year of Charles the Bald, in the year 856, Baluzius's edition, p. 78.

the landed estates of the kingdom in the hands of the clergy, Charlemagne found all the church-lands in the hands of the soldiery. The latter could not be compelled to restore a voluntary donation, and the circumstances of that time rendered the thing still more impracticable than it seemed to be of its own nature. On the other hand, Christianity ought not to have been lost for want of ministers, churches, and instruction.[1]

This was the reason of Charlemagne's establishing the tithes,[2] a new kind of property which had this advantage in favour of the clergy, that as they were given particularly to the church, it was easier in process of time to know when they were usurped.

Some have attempted to make this institution of a still remoter date, but the authorities they produce seem rather, I think, to prove the contrary. The constitution of Clotharius says[3] only that they shall not raise certain tithes on church-lands;[4] so far then was the church from exacting tithes at that time, that its whole pretension was to be exempted from paying them. The second council of Mâcon,[5] which was held in 585, and ordains the payment of tithes, says, indeed, that they were paid in ancient times, but it says also that the custom of paying them was then abolished.

No one questions but that the clergy opened the Bible before Charlemagne's time, and preached the gifts and offerings in Leviticus. But I say that before that prince's reign, though the tithes might have been preached, they were never established.

I noticed that the regulations made under King Pepin had subjected those who were seized of church lands in fief to the payment of tithes, and to the repairing of the churches.

It was a great deal to induce by a law, whose equity could not be disputed, the principal men of the nation to set the example.

Charlemagne did more; and we find by the capitulary *de Villis*[6] that he obliged his own demesnes to the payment of the tithes; this was a still more striking example.

But the commonalty are rarely influenced by example to sacrifice their interests. The synod of Frankfort furnished them with a more cogent motive to pay the tithes.[7] A capitulary was made in that synod, wherein it is said that in the last famine the spikes of corn were found to contain no seed,[8] the infernal spirits having devoured it all, and that those spirits had been heard to reproach them with not having paid the tithes; in consequence of which it was ordained that all those who were seized of church lands should pay the tithes; and the next consequence was that the obligation extended to all.

Charlemagne's project did not succeed at first, for it seemed too heavy a burden.[9] The payment of the tithes among the Jews was connected with the plan of the foundation of their republic; but here it was a burden quite independent of the other charges of the establishment of the monarchy. We find by the regulations added to the law of the Lombards[10] the difficulty there was in causing the tithes to be accepted by the civil laws; and as for the opposition they met with before they were admitted by the ecclesiastic laws, we may easily judge of it from the different canons of the councils.

The people consented at length to pay the tithes, upon condition that they might have the power of redeeming them. This the constitution of Louis the Debonnaire[11] and that of the Emperor Lotharius, his son, would not allow.[12]

The laws of Charlemagne, in regard to the establishment of tithes, were a work of necessity, not of superstition—a work, in short, in which religion only was concerned.

His famous division of the tithes into four

[1] In the civil wars which broke out at the time of Charles Martel, the lands belonging to the church of Rheims were given away to laymen; "the clergy were left to shift as well as they could," says the life of Remigius, Surius, i, p. 279.
[2] Law of the Lombards, iii, tit. 3, §§ 1 and 2.
[3] It is that on which I have descanted in the 4th chapter of this book, and which is to be found in Baluzius's edition of the Capitularies, i, art. 11, p. 9.
[4] The Capitulary of Charlemagne in the year 800, Baluzius's edition, p. 336, explains extremely well what is meant by that sort of tithe from which the church is exempted by Clotharius; it was the tithe of the swine which were put into the king's forests to fatten; and Charlemagne enjoins his judges to pay it, as well as other people, in order to set an example: it is plain that this was a right of seigniory or economy.
[5] *Canone 5, ex tomo 1, conciliorum antiquorum Galliæ opera Jacobi Sirmundi.*

[6] Art. 6, Baluzius's edition, p. 332. It was given in the year 800.
[7] Held under Charlemagne, in the year 794.
[8] Baluzius's edition, p. 267, art. 23.
[9] See among the rest the capitulary of Louis the Debonnaire in the year 829, Baluzius's edition. p. 663; against those who, to avoid paying tithes neglected to cultivate the lands, &c., art. 5.
[10] Among others, that of Lotharius, iii, tit. 3, cap. vi.
[11] In the year 829, art. 7, in Baluzius, i, p. 663.
[12] In the law of the Lombards, iii, tit. 3, § 8.

parts, for the repairing of the churches, for the poor, for the bishop, and for the clergy, manifestly proves that he wished to give the church that fixed and permanent status which she had lost.

His will shows that he was desirous of repairing the mischief done by his grandfather, Charles Martel.[1] He made three equal shares of his movable goods; two of these he would have divided each into one-and-twenty parts, for the one-and-twenty metropolitan sees of his empire; each part was to be sub-divided between the metropolitan and the dependent bishoprics. The remaining third he distributed into four parts; one he gave to his children and grandchildren, another was added to the two-thirds already bequeathed, and the other two were assigned to charitable uses. It seems as if he looked upon the immense donation he was making to the church less as a religious act than as a political distribution.

13. *Of the Election of Bishops and Abbots.* As the church had grown poor, the kings resigned the right of nominating to bishoprics and other ecclesiastic benefices.[2] The princes gave themselves less trouble about the ecclesiastic ministers; and the candidates were less solicitous in applying to their authorities. Thus the church received a kind of compensation for the possessions she had lost.

Hence, if Louis the Debonnaire left the people of Rome in possession of the right of choosing their popes, it was owing to the general spirit that prevailed in his time;[3] he behaved in the same manner to the see of Rome as to other bishoprics.

14. *Of the Fiefs of Charles Martel.* I shall not pretend to determine whether Charles Martel, in giving the church-lands in fief, made a grant of them for life or in perpetuity. All I know is that under Charlemagne[4] and Lotharius I[5] there were possessions of that

kind which descended to the next heirs, and were divided among them.

I find, moreover, that one part of them was given as allodia, and the other as fiefs.[6]

I noticed that the proprietors of the allodia were subject to service all the same as the possessors of the fiefs. This, without doubt, was partly the reason that Charles Martel made grants of allodial lands as well as of fiefs.

15. *The same Subject continued.* We must observe that the fiefs having been changed into church-lands, and these again into fiefs, they borrowed something of each other. Thus the church-lands had the privileges of fiefs, and these had the privileges of church-lands. Such were the honorary rights of churches, which began at that time.[7] And as those rights have ever been annexed to the judiciary power, in preference to what is still called the fief, it follows that the patrimonial jurisdictions were established at the same time as those very rights.

16. *Confusion of the Royalty and Mayoralty. The Second Race.* The connection of my subject has made me invert the order of time, so as to speak of Charlemagne before I had mentioned the famous epoch of the translation of the crown to the Carlovingians under King Pepin; a revolution, which, contrary to the nature of ordinary events, is more remarked perhaps in our days than when it happened.

The kings had no authority; they had only an empty name. The regal title was hereditary, and that of mayor elective. Though it was latterly in the power of the mayors to place any of the Merovingians on the throne, they had not yet taken a king of another family; and the ancient law which fixed the crown in a particular family was not yet erased from the hearts of the Franks. The king's person was almost unknown in the monarchy; but royalty was not. Pepin, son of Charles Martel, thought it would be proper to confound those

---

[1] It is a kind of codicil produced by Eginhard, and different from the will itself, which we find in Goldastus and Baluzius.

[2] See the Capitulary of Charlemagne in the year 803, art. 2, Baluzius's edition, p. 379; and the edict of Louis the Debonnaire in the year 834, in Goldast, *Constit. Impérial.*, i.

[3] This is mentioned in the famous canon, *ego Ludovicus*, which is a palpable forgery; it is Baluzius's edition, p. 591, in the year 817.

[4] As appears by his Capitulary, in the year 801, art. 17, in Baluzius, i, p. 360.

[5] See his constitution, inserted in the code of the Lombards, iii, tit. 1, § 44.

[6] See the above constitution, and the Capitulary of Charles the Bald, in the year 846, cap. xx. *in Villa Sparnaco*, Baluzius's edition, ii. p. 31, and that of the year 853, cap. iii and v, in the Synod of Soissons, Baluzius's edition, ii, p. 54; and that of the year 854, *apud Attiniacum*, cap. x. Baluzius's edition, ii, p. 70. See also the first Capitulary of Charlemagne, *incerti anni*, art. 49 and 56. Baluzius's edition, i, p. 519.

[7] See the Capitularies, v. art. 44, and the edict of Pistes in the year 869, art. 8 and 9, where we find the honorary rights of the lords established, in the same manner as they are at this very day.

two titles, a confusion which would leave it a moot point whether the new royalty was hereditary or not; and this was sufficient for him who to the regal dignity had joined a great power. The mayor's authority was then blended with that of the king. In the mixture of these two authorities a kind of reconciliation was made; the mayor had been elective, and the king hereditary; the crown at the beginning of the second race was elective, because the people chose; it was hereditary, because they always chose in the same family.[1]

Father le Cointe, in spite of the authority of all ancient records,[2] denies that the Pope authorised this great change; and one of his reasons is that he would have committed an injustice.[3] A fine thing to see a historian judge of that which men have done by that which they ought to have done; by this mode of reasoning we should have no more history.

Be that as it may, it is very certain that immediately after Duke Pepin's victory, the Merovingians ceased to be the reigning family. When his grandson, Pepin, was crowned king, it was only one ceremony more, and one phantom less; he acquired nothing thereby but the royal ornaments; there was no change made in the nation.

This I have said in order to fix the moment of the revolution, that we may not be mistaken in looking upon that as a revolution which was only a consequence of it.

When Hugh Capet was crowned king at the beginning of the third race, there was a much greater change, because the kingdom passed from a state of anarchy to some kind of government; but when Pepin took the crown, there was only a transition from one government to another, which was identical.

When Pepin was crowned king there was only a change of name; but when Hugh Capet was crowned there was a change in the nature of the thing, because by uniting a great fief to the crown the anarchy ceased.

When Pepin was crowned the title of king was united to the highest office; when Hugh Capet was crowned it was annexed to the greatest fief.

17. A particular Circumstance in the Election of the Kings of the Second Race.

We find by the formulary of Pepin's coronation that Charles and Carloman were also anointed,[4] and blessed, and that the French nobility bound themselves, on pain of interdiction and excommunication, never to choose a prince of another family.[5]

It appears by the wills of Charlemagne and Louis the Debonnaire, that the Franks made a choice among the king's children, which agrees with the above-mentioned clause. And when the empire was transferred from Charlemagne's family, the election, which before had been restricted and conditional, became pure and simple, so that the ancient constitution was departed from.

Pepin, perceiving himself near his end, assembled the lords, both temporal and spiritual, at St. Denis, and divided his kingdom between his two sons, Charles and Carloman.[6] We have not the acts of this assembly, but we find what was there transacted in the author of the ancient historical collection, published by Canisius, and in the writer of the annals of Metz,[7] according to the observation of Baluzius.[8] Here I meet with two things in some measure contradictory; that he made this division with the consent of the nobility, and afterwards that he made it by his paternal authority. This proves what I said, that the people's right in the second race was to choose in the same family; it was, properly speaking, rather a right of exclusion than that of election.

This kind of elective right is confirmed by the records of the second race. Such is this capitulary of the division of the empire made by Charlemagne among his three children, in which, after settling their shares, he says,[9] "That if one of the three brothers happens to have a son, such as the people shall be willing to choose as a fit person to succeed to his father's kingdom, his uncles shall consent to it."

This same regulation is to be met with in the partition which Louis the Debonnaire made among his three children, Pepin, Louis, and Charles, in the year 837, at the assembly of Aix-la-Chapelle;[10] and likewise in another

[1] See the will of Charlemagne, and the division which Louis the Debonnaire made to his children in the assembly of the states held at Quierzy, related to Goldast.
[2] The anonymous Chronicle in the year 752; and *Chronic. Centul.*, in the year 754.
[3] *Ecclesiastic Annals of the French*, ii, p. 319.
[4] *Historians of France* by the Benedictines, v, p. 9.
[5] *Ibid.*, p. 10.
[6] In the year 768.
[7] Tom. ii, *lectionis antiquæ*.
[8] Edition of the Capitularies, i, p. 188.
[9] In the 1st Capitulary of the year 806. Baluzius's edition, p. 439, art. 5.
[10] In Goldast, *Constit. Impérial.*, ii, p. 19.

partition, made twenty years before, by the same emperor, in favour of Lotharius, Pepin, and Louis.[1] We may likewise see the oath which Louis the Stammerer took at Compiègne at his coronation. "I, Louis, by the divine mercy, and the people's election, appointed king, do promise"[2]. . . . What I say is confirmed by the acts of the Council of Valence, held in the year 890, for the election of Louis, son of Bo-on, to the kingdom of Arles.[3] Louis was there elected, and the principal reason they gave for choosing him is that he was of the imperial family,[4] that Charles the Fat had conferred upon him the dignity of king, and that the Emperor Arnold had invested him by the sceptre, and by the ministry of his ambassadors. The kingdom of Arles, like the other dismembered or dependent kingdoms of Charlemagne, was elective and hereditary.

18. *Charlemagne.* Charlemagne's intention was to restrain the power of the nobility within proper bounds, and to hinder them from oppressing the freemen and the clergy. He balanced the several orders of the state, and remained perfect master of them all. The whole was united by the strength of his genius. He led the nobility continually from one expedition to another, giving them no time to form conspiracies, but employing them entirely in the execution of his designs. The empire was supported by the greatness of its chief; the prince was great, but the man was greater. The kings, his children, were his first subjects, the instruments of his power and patterns of obedience. He made admirable laws; and, what is more, he took care to see them executed. His genius diffused itself through every part of the empire. We find in this prince's laws a comprehensive spirit of foresight, and a certain force which carries all before it. All pretexts for evading the duties are removed, neglects are corrected, abuses reformed or prevented.[5] He knew how to punish, but he understood much better how to pardon. He was great in his designs, and simple in the execu-

tion of them. No prince ever possessed in a higher degree the art of performing the greatest things with ease, and the most difficult with expedition. He was continually visiting the several parts of his vast empire, and made them feel the weight of his hand wherever it fell. New difficulties sprang up on every side, and on every side he removed them. Never prince had more resolution in facing dangers; never prince knew better how to avoid them. He mocked all manner of perils, and particularly those to which great conquerors are generally subject, namely, conspiracies. This wonderful prince was extremely moderate, of a very mild character, plain and simple in his behaviour. He loved to converse freely with the lords of his court. He indulged, perhaps, too much his passion for the fair sex; a failing, however, which in a prince who always governed by himself, and who spent his life in a continual series of toils, may merit some allowance. He was wonderfully exact in his expenses, administering his demesnes with prudence, attention, and economy. A father might learn from his laws how to govern his family; and we find in his capitularies the pure and sacred source whence he derived his riches.[6] I shall add only one word more: he gave orders that the eggs in the bartons on his demesnes, and the superfluous garden-stuff, should be sold;[7] he distributed among his people all the riches of the Lombards, and the immense treasures of those Huns that had plundered the whole world.

19. *The same Subject continued.* Charlemagne and his immediate successors were afraid lest those whom they placed in distant parts should be inclined to revolt, and thought they should find more docility among the clergy. For this reason they erected a great number of bishoprics in Germany and endowed them with very large fiefs.[8] It appears by some charters that the clauses containing the prerogatives of those fiefs were not different from such as were commonly inserted in those grants,[9] though at present we find the

[1] Baluzius's edition, p. 574, art. 14.
[2] Capitulary of the year 877. Baluzius's edition, p. 272.
[3] In Father Labbe's Councils, ix, col. 424; and in Dumont's *Corp. Diplomat.*, i, art. 36.
[4] By the mother's side.
[5] See his third Capitulary of the year 811, p. 486, art. 1, 2, 3, 4, 5, 6, 7, and 8; and the first Capitulary of the year 812, p. 490, art. 1; and the Capitulary of the year 812, p. 494, art. 9 and 11, etc.

[6] See the Capitulary *de Villis* in the year 800; his second Capitulary of the year 813, art. 6 and 19; and the fifth book of the Capitularies, art. 303.
[7] Capitulary *de Villis*, art. 39. See this whole Capitulary, which is a masterpiece of prudence, good administration, and economy.
[8] See among others the foundation of the Archbishopric of Bremen, in the Capitulary of the year 789. Baluzius's edition, p. 245.
[9] For instance, the prohibition of the king's judges against entering upon the territory to de-

principal ecclesiastics of Germany invested with a sovereign power. Be that as it may, these were some of the contrivances they used against the Saxons. That which they could not expect from the indolence or supineness of vassals they thought they ought to expect from the sedulous attention of a bishop. Besides, a vassal of that kind, far from making use of the conquered people against them, would rather stand in need of their assistance to support themselves against their own people.

20. *Louis the Debonnaire.* When Augustus Cæsar was in Egypt he ordered Alexander's tomb to be opened; and upon their asking him whether he was willing they should open the tombs of the Ptolemies, he made answer that he wanted to see the king, and not the dead. Thus, in the history of the second race, we are continually looking for Pepin and Charlemagne; we want to see the kings, and not the dead.

A prince who was the sport of his passions, and a dupe even to his virtues; a prince who never understood rightly either his own strength or weakness; a prince who was incapable of making himself either feared or beloved; a prince, in fine, who with few vices in his heart had all manner of defects in his understanding, took into his hands the reins of the empire which had been held by Charlemagne.

At a time when the whole world is in tears for the death of his father, at a time of surprise and alarm, when the subjects of that extensive empire all call upon Charles and find him no more; at a time when he is advancing with all expedition to take possession of his father's throne, he sends some trusty officers before him in order to seize the persons of those who had contributed to the irregular conduct of his sisters. This step was productive of the most terrible catastrophes.[1] It was imprudent and precipitate. He began with punishing domestic crimes before he reached the palace; and with alienating the minds of his subjects before he ascended the throne.

His nephew, Bernard, King of Italy, having come to implore his clemency, he ordered his eyes to be put out, which proved the cause of that prince's death a few days after, and created Louis a great many enemies. His apprehension of the consequence induced him to shut his brothers up in a monastery; by which means the number of his enemies increased. These two last transactions were afterwards laid to his charge in a judicial manner,[2] and his accusers did not fail to tell him that he had violated his oath and the solemn promises which he had made to his father on the day of his coronation.[3]

After the death of the Empress Hermengarde, by whom he had three children, he married Judith, and had a son by that princess; but soon mixing all the indulgence of an old husband, with all the weakness of an old king, he flung his family into a disorder which was followed by the downfall of the monarchy.

He was continually altering the partitions he had made among his children. And yet these partitions had been confirmed each in their turn by his own oath, and by those of his children and the nobility. This was as if he wanted to try the fidelity of his subjects; it was endeavouring by confusion, scruples, and equivocation, to puzzle their obedience; it was confounding the different rights of those princes, and rendering their titles dubious, especially at a time when there were but few fortresses, and when the principal bulwark of authority was the fealty sworn and accepted.

The Emperor's children, in order to preserve their shares, courted the clergy, and granted them privileges till then unheard. These privileges were specious; and the clergy in return were made to warrant the revolution in favour of those princes. Agobard[4] represents to Louis the Debonnaire his having sent Lotharius to Rome, in order to have him declared emperor; and that he had made a division of his dominions among his children, after having consulted heaven by three days fasting and praying. What defence could such a weak prince make against the attack of superstition? It is easy to perceive the shock which the supreme authority must have twice received from his imprisonment, and from his public penance; they would fain degrade

mand the *freda*, and other duties. I have said a good deal concerning this in the preceding book, 20, 21, 22.

[1] The anonymous author of the Life of Louis the Debonnaire in Duchesne's Collection, tom. ii, p. 295.

[2] See his trial and the circumstances of his deposition, in Duchesne's Collection, tom. ii, p. 333.

[3] He directed him to show unlimited clemency (*indeficientem misericordiam*) to his sisters, his brothers, and his nephews. Tegan in the collection of Duchesne, ii, p. 276.

[4] See his letters.

the king, and they degraded the regal dignity.

We find difficulty at first in conceiving how a prince who was possessed of several good qualities, who had some knowledge, who had a natural disposition to virtue, and who in short was the son of Charlemagne, could have such a number of enemies,[1] so impetuous and implacable as even to insult him in his humiliation and to be determined upon his ruin: and, indeed they would have utterly completed it, if his children, who in the main were more honest than they, had been steady in their design, and could have agreed among themselves.

21. *The same Subject continued.* The strength and solidity for which the kingdom was indebted to Charlemagne still subsisted under Louis the Debonnaire in such a degree as enabled the state to support its grandeur, and to command respect from foreign nations. The prince's understanding was weak, but the nation was warlike. His authority declined at home, though there seemed to be no diminution of power abroad.

Charles Martel, Pepin, and Charlemagne were in succession rulers of the monarchy. The first flattered the avarice of the soldiers: the other two that of the clergy. Louis the Debonnaire displeased both.

In the French constitution, the whole power of the state was lodged in the hands of the king, the nobility, and clergy. Charles Martel, Pepin, and Charlemagne joined sometimes their interest with one of those parties to check the other and generally with both; but Louis the Debonnaire could gain the affection of neither. He disobliged the bishops by publishing regulations which had the air of severity, because he carried things to a greater length than was agreeable to their inclination. Very good laws may be ill-timed. The bishops in those days, being accustomed to take the field against the Saracens and the Saxons, had very little of the spirit of religion.[2] On the other hand, as he had no longer any confidence in the nobility, he promoted mean people,[3] turning the nobles out of their

employments at court to make room for strangers and upstarts.[4] By this means the affections of the two great bodies of the nobility and clergy were alienated from their prince, the consequence of which was a total desertion.

22. *The same Subject continued.* But what chiefly contributed to weaken the monarchy was the extravagance of this prince in alienating the crown demesnes.[5] And here it is that we ought to listen to the account of Nitard, one of our most judicious historians, a grandson of Charlemagne, strongly attached to Louis the Debonnaire and who wrote his history by order of Charles the Bald.

He says, "that one Adelhard for some time gained such an ascendant over the Emperor, that this prince conformed to his will in everything; that at the instigation of this favourite, he had granted the crown lands to everybody that asked them,[6] by which means the state was ruined."[7] Thus he did the same mischief throughout the empire as I observed he had done in Aquitaine;[8] the former Charlemagne redressed, but the latter was past all remedy.

The state was reduced to the same debility in which Charles Martel found it upon his accession to the mayoralty; and so desperate were its circumstances that no exertion of authority was any longer capable of saving it.

The treasury was so exhausted that in the reign of Charles the Bald, no one could continue in his employments, nor be safe in his person without paying for it.[9] When they had it in their power to destroy the Normans, they took money to let them escape:[10] and the first advice which Hincmar gives to Louis the Stammerer is to ask of the assembly of the nation a sufficient allowance to defray the expenses of his household.

23. *The same Subject continued.* The clergy had reason to repent the protection they had granted to the children of Louis the Debonnaire. This prince, as I have already observed,

---

[1] See his trial and the circumstances of his deposition, in Duchesne's Collection, ii, p. 331. See also his life written by Tegan: "*Tanto enim odio laborabat, ut tæderet eos vita ipsius,*" says this anonymous author in Duchesne, ii, p. 307.

[2] The anonymous author of the Life of Louis the Debonnaire in Duchesne's Collection, ii, p. 298.

[3] Tegan says that what seldom happened under Charlemagne was a common practice under Louis.

[4] Being desirous to check the nobility, he promoted one Bernard to the place of chamberlain, by which the great lords were exasperated to the highest pitch.

[5] Tegan, *De Gestis Ludovici pii.*

[6] Nitard, iv, *prope finem.*

[7] *Ibid.*

[8] See book xxx. 13.

[9] Hincmar, let. 1, to Louis the Stammerer.

[10] See the fragment of the Chronicle of the Monastery of St. Sergius of Angers, in Duchesne, ii, p. 401.

had never given any of the church-lands by *precepts* to the laity;[1] but it was not long before Lotharius in Italy, and Pepin in Aquitaine, quitted Charlemagne's plan, and resumed that of Charles Martel. The clergy had recourse to the Emperor against his children, but they themselves had weakened the authority to which they appealed. In Aquitaine some condescension was shown, but none in Italy.

The civil wars with which the life of Louis the Debonnaire had been embroiled were the seed of those which followed his death. The three brothers, Lotharius, Louis, and Charles, endeavoured each to bring over the nobility to their party and to make them their tools. To such as were willing therefore to follow them they granted church-lands by *precepts;* so that to gain the nobility, they sacrificed the clergy.

We find in the Capitularies[2] that those princes were obliged to yield to the importunity of demands, and that what they would not often have freely granted was extorted from them: we find that the clergy thought themselves more oppressed by the nobility than by the kings. It appears that Charles the Bald[3] became the greatest enemy of the patrimony of the clergy, whether he was most incensed against them for having degraded his father on their account, or whether he was the most timorous. Be that as it may, we meet with continual quarrels in the Capitularies,[4] between the clergy who demanded their estates, and the nobility who refused or deferred to restore them; and the kings acting as mediators.

The situation of affairs at that time is a spectacle really deserving of pity. While Louis the Debonnaire made immense donations out of his demesnes to the clergy, his children distributed the church-lands among the laity. The same prince with one hand founded new abbeys and despoiled old ones. The clergy had no fixed state; one moment they were plundered, another they received satisfaction; but the crown was continually losing.

Toward the close of the reign of Charles the Bald, and from that time forward, there was an end of the disputes of the clergy and laity concerning the restitution of church-lands. The bishops indeed breathed out still a few sighs in their remonstrances to Charles the Bald, which we find in the Capitulary of the year 856, and in the letter they wrote to Louis, King of Germany, in the year 858,[5] but they proposed things, and challenged promises, so often eluded, that we plainly see they had no longer any hopes of obtaining their desire.

All that could be expected then was to repair in general the injuries done both to church and state.[6] The kings engaged not to deprive the nobility of their freemen, and not to give away any more church-lands by *precepts,*[7] so that the interests of the clergy and nobility seemed then to be united.

The dreadful depredations of the Normans, as I have already observed, contributed greatly to put an end to those quarrels.

The authority of our kings diminishing every day, both for the reasons already given and those which I shall mention hereafter, they imagined they had no better resource left, than to resign themselves into the hands of the clergy. But the ecclesiastics had weakened the power of the kings, and these had diminished the influence of the ecclesiastics.

In vain did Charles the Bald and his succes-

---

[1] See what the bishops say in the synod of the year 845, *apud Teudonis villam*, art. 4.

[2] See the synod in the year 845, *apud Teudonis villam*, art. 3 and 4, which gives a very exact description of things; as also, that of the same year, held at the palaces of Vernes, art. 12, and the synod of Beauvais, also in the same year, art. 3, 4, and 6, in the Capitulary *in villa Sparnaco*, in the year 846, art. 20, and the letter which the bishops assembled at Rheims wrote in 858, to Louis, King of Germany, art. 8.

[3] See the Capitulary *in villa Sparnaco*, in the year 846. The nobility had set the King against the bishops, insomuch that he expelled them from the assembly; a few of the canons enacted in council were picked out, and the prelates were told that these were the only ones which should be observed; nothing was granted them that could be refused. See art. 20, 21 and 22. See also the letter which the bishops assembled at Rheims wrote in the year 858 to Louis, King of Germany, art. 8, and the edict of Pistes, in the year 864, art. 5.

[4] See this very Capitulary in the year 846, *in villa Sparnaco*. See also the Capitulary of the assembly held *apud Marsnam* in the year 847, art. 4, wherein the clergy reduced themselves to demand only the restitution of what they had been possessed of under Louis the Debonnaire. See also the Capitulary of the year 851, *apud Marsnam*, art. 6, and 7, which confirms the nobility and clergy in their several possessions, and that *apud Bonoilum*, in the year 856, which is a remonstrance of the bishops to the king, because the evils, after so many laws, had not been redressed; and, in fine, the letter which the bishops assembled at Rheims wrote in the year 858, to Louis, King of Germany, art. 8.

[5] Art. 8.

[6] See the Capitulary of the year 851, art. 6 and 7.

[7] Charles the Bald, in the Synod of Soissons, says, that he had promised the bishops not to issue any more precepts relating to church-lands. Capitulary of the year 853, art. 11, Baluzius's edition, ii, p. 56.

sors call in the church to support the state, and to prevent its ruin; in vain did they make use of the respect which the commonalty had for that body,[1] to maintain that which they should also have for their prince;[2] in vain did they endeavour to give an authority to their laws by that of the canons; in vain did they join the ecclesiastic with the civil punishments;[3] in vain to counterbalance the authority of the count did they give to each bishop the title of their commissary in the several provinces;[4] it was impossible to repair the mischief they had done; and a terrible misfortune, which I shall presently mention, proved the ruin of the monarchy.

24. *That the Freemen were rendered capable of holding Fiefs.* I said that the freemen were led against the enemy by their count, and the vassals by their lord. This was the reason that the several orders of the state balanced each other, and though the king's vassals had other vassals under them, yet they might be overawed by the count, who was at the head of all the freemen of the monarchy.

The freemen were not allowed at first to do homage for a fief; but in process of time this was permitted:[5] and I find that this change was made during the period that elapsed from the reign of Gontram to that of Charlemagne. This I prove by the comparison which may be made between the treaty of Andelot,[6] by Gontram, Childebert, and Queen Brunehault, and the partition made by Charlemagne among his children, as well as a like partition by Louis the Debonnaire.[7] These three acts contain nearly the same regulations with regard to the vassals; and as they determine the very same points, under almost the same circum-

stances, the spirit as well as the letter of those three treaties in this respect are very much alike.

But as to what concerns the freemen, there is a vital difference. The treaty of Andelot does not say that they might do homage for a fief; whereas we find in the divisions of Charlemagne and Louis the Debonnaire express clauses to empower them to do homage. This shows that a new usage had been introduced after the treaty of Andelot, whereby the freemen had become capable of this great privilege.

This must have happened when Charles Martel, after distributing the church-lands to his soldiers, partly in fief, and partly as allodia, made a kind of revolution in the feudal laws. It is very probable that the nobility who were seized already of fiefs found a greater advantage in receiving the new grants as allodia; and that the freemen thought themselves happy in accepting them as fiefs.

THE PRINCIPAL CAUSE OF THE HUMILIATION OF THE SECOND RACE

25. *Changes in the Allodia.* Charlemagne in the partition[8] mentioned in the preceding chapter ordained that after his death the vassals belonging to each king should be permitted to receive benefices in their own sovereign's dominion, and not in those of another;[9] whereas they may keep their allodial estates in any of their dominions.[10] But he adds [11] that every freeman might, after the death of his lord, do homage in any of three kingdoms he pleased, as well as he that never had been subject to a lord. We find the same regulations in the partition which Louis the Debonnaire made among his children in the year 817.

But though the freeman had done homage for a fief, yet the count's militia was not thereby weakened: the freeman was still obliged to contribute for his *allodium,* and to get people ready for the service belonging to it, at the proportion of one man to four manors; or else to procure a man that should do the duty of

---

[1] See the Capitulary of Charles the Bald, *apud Saponarias,* in the year 859, art. 3. "Venilon, whom I made Archbishop of Sens, has consecrated me; and I ought not to be expelled the kingdom by anybody."

[2] See the Capitulary of Charles the Bald, *De Carisiaco,* in the year 857, Baluzius's edition, ii, p. 88, §§ 1, 2, 3, 4, and 7.

[3] See the synod of Pistes in the year 862, art. 4, and the Capitulary of Lewis II, *apud Vernis palatium,* in the year 883, art. 4 and 5.

[4] Capitulary of the year 876, under Charles, the Bald, *in synodo Pontigonensi,* Baluzius's edition, art. 12.

[5] See what has been said already, book xxx, last chapter, towards the end.

[6] In the year 587, in Gregory of Tours, ix.

[7] See the following chapter, where I shall speak more diffusely of those partitions; and the notes in which they are quoted.

[8] In the year 806, between Charles, Pepin, and Louis, it is quoted by Goldast, and by Baluzius, ii, p. 439.

[9] Art. 9, p. 443, which is agreeable to the treaty of Andelot, in Gregory of Tours, ix.

[10] Art. 10, and there is no mention made of this in the treaty of Andelot.

[11] In Baluzius, i, p. 174, art. 9. See also the division made by the same emperor in the year 837, art. 6, Baluzius's edition, p. 686.

the fief in his stead. And when some abuses had been introduced upon this head, they were redressed, as appears by the constitutions of Charlemagne,[1] and by that of Pepin, King of Italy, which explain each other.[2]

The remark made by historians that the battle of Fontenay was the ruin of the monarchy, is very true; but I beg leave to cast an eye on the unhappy consequences of that day.

Some time after the battle, the three brothers, Lothairius, Louis, and Charles, made a treaty,[3] wherein I find some clauses which must have altered the whole political system of the French government.

1. In the declaration[4] which Charles made to the people of the part of the treaty relating to them, he says that every freeman might choose whom he pleased for his lord,[5] whether the king or any of the nobility. Before this treaty the freeman might do homage for a fief; but his allodium still continued under the immediate power of the king, that is, under the count's jurisdiction; and he depended on the lord to whom he vowed fealty, only on account of the fief which he had obtained. After that treaty every freeman had a right to subject his allodium to the king, or to any other lord, as he thought proper. The question is not in regard to those who put themselves under the protection of another for a fief, but to such as changed their allodial into a feudal land, and withdrew themselves, as it were, from the civil jurisdiction to enter under the power of the king, or of the lord whom they thought proper to choose.

Thus it was that those who formerly were only under the king's power, as freemen under the count, became insensibly vassals one of another, since every freeman might choose whom he pleased for his lord, the king or any of the nobility.

2. If a man changed an estate which he possessed in perpetuity into a fief, this new fief could no longer be only for life. Hence we see, a short time after, a general law for giving the fiefs to the children of the present possessor:[6]

it was made by Charles the Bald, one of the three contracting princes.

What has been said concerning the liberty every freeman had in the monarchy, after the treaty of the three brothers, of choosing whom he pleased for his lord, the king or any of the nobility, is confirmed by the acts subsequent to that time.

In the reign of Charlemagne,[7] when the vassal had received a present of a lord, were it worth only a sou, he could not afterwards quit him. But under Charles the Bald, the vassals might follow what was agreeable to their interests or their inclination with entire safety;[8] and so strongly does this prince explain himself on the subject that he seems rather to encourage them in the enjoyment of this liberty than to restrain it. In Charlemagne's time, benefices were rather personal than real; afterwards they became rather real than personal.

26. *Changes in the Fiefs.* The same changes happened in the fiefs as in the *allodia*. We find by the Capitulary of Compiègne,[9] under King Pepin, that those who had received a benefice from the king gave a part of this benefice to different bondmen; but these parts were not distinct from the whole. The king revoked them when he revoked the whole; and at the death of the king's vassal, the rear-vassal lost also his rear-fief: and a new beneficiary succeeded, who likewise established new rear-vassals. Thus it was the person and not the rear-fief that depended on the fief; on the one hand, the rear-vassal returned to the king because he was not tied for ever to the vassal; and the rear-fief returned also to the king because it was the fief itself and not a dependence of it.

Such was the rear-vassalage, while the fiefs were during pleasure; and such was it also while they were for life. This was altered when the fiefs descended to the next heirs, and the rear-fiefs the same. That which was held before immediately of the king was held now

---

[1] In the year 811, Baluzius's edition, i, p. 486, art. 7 and 8, and that of the year 812, *ibid.* p. 490, art. 1. See also the Capitulary of the year 807, Baluzius's edition, i, p. 458.

[2] In the year 793, inserted in the law of the Lombards, iii, tit. 9, cap. ix.

[3] In the year 847, quoted by Aubert le Mire, and Baluzius, ii, page 42.

[4] *Adnunciatio.*

[5] Art. 2, of the Declaration of Charles.

[6] Capitulary of the year 877, tit. 53, art. 9 and 10, *apud Carisiacum, similiter et de nostris vas-*

sallis faciendum est, &c. This Capitulary relates to another of the same year, and of the same place, art. 3.

[7] Capitulary of Aix la Chapelle, in the year 813, art. 16, and the Capitulary of Pepin, in the year 783, art. 5.

[8] See the capitulary *de Carisiaco*, in the year 856, art. 10 and 13. Baluzius's edition, tom. ii, p. 83, in which the king, together with the lords spiritual and temporal, agreed to this.

[9] In the year 757, art. 6, Baluzius's edition, p. 181.

mediately; and the regal power was thrown back, as it were, one degree, sometimes two; and oftentimes more.

We find in the books of fiefs[1] that, though the king's vassals might give away in fief, that is, in rear-fief, to the king, yet these rear-vassals, or petty vavasors, could not give also in fief; so that whatever they had given, they might always resume. Besides, a grant of that kind did not descend to the children like the fiefs, because it was not supposed to have been made according to the feudal laws.

If we compare the situation in which the rear-vassalage was at the time when the two Milanese senators wrote those books, with what it was under King Pepin, we shall find that the rear-fiefs preserved their primitive nature longer than the fiefs.[2]

But when those senators wrote, such general exceptions had been made to this rule as had almost abolished it. For if a person who had received a fief of a rear-vassal happened to follow him upon an expedition to Rome, he was entitled to all the privileges of a vassal.[3] In like manner, if he had given money to the rear-vassal to obtain the fief, the latter could not take it from him, nor hinder him from transmitting it to his son, till he returned him his money: in fine, this rule was no longer observed by the senate of Milan.[4]

27. *Another change which happened in the Fiefs.* In Charlemagne's time they were obliged,[5] under great penalties, to repair to the general meeting in case of any war whatsoever; they admitted of no excuses, and if the count exempted any one, he was liable himself to be punished. But the treaty of the three brothers[6] made a restriction upon this head which rescued the nobility, as it were, out of the king's hands; they were no longer obliged to serve him in time of war, except when the war was defensive.[7] In others, they were at liberty to follow their lord, or to mind their own business. This treaty relates to another,[8] concluded, five years before, between the two brothers, Charles the Bald and Louis, King of

Germany, by which these princes release their vassals from serving them in war, in case they should attempt hostilities against each other; an agreement which the two princes confirmed by oath, and at the same time made their armies swear to it.

The death of a hundred thousand French, at the battle of Fontenay, made the remains of the nobility imagine that by the private quarrels of their kings about their respective shares, their whole body would be exterminated, and that the ambition and jealousy of those princes would end in the destruction of all the best families of the kingdom. A law was therefore passed that the nobility should not be obliged to serve their princes in war unless it was to defend the state against a foreign invasion. This law obtained for several ages.[9]

28. *Changes which happened in the great Offices, and in the Fiefs.* The many changes introduced into the fiefs in particular cases seemed to spread so widely as to be productive of general corruption. I noticed that in the beginning several fiefs had been alienated in perpetuity; but those were particular cases, and the fiefs in general preserved their nature; so that if the crown lost some fiefs it substituted others in their stead. I observed, likewise, that the crown had never alienated the great offices in perpetuity.[10]

But Charles the Bald made a general regulation, which equally affected the great offices and the fiefs. He ordained, in his capitularies, that the counties should be given to the children of the count, and that this regulation should also take place in respect to the fiefs.[11]

We shall see presently that this regulation received a wider extension, insomuch that the great offices and fiefs went even to distant relatives. Thence it followed that most of the lords who before this time had held immediately of the crown, held now mediately. Those

[1] Book i, 1.
[2] At least in Italy and Germany.
[3] Book i, of fiefs, 1.
[4] *Ibid.*
[5] Capitulary of the year 802, art. 7, Baluzius's edition, p. 365.
[6] *Apud Marsnam,* in the year 847, Baluzius's edition, p. 42.
[7] Art. 5, *ibid.,* p. 44.
[8] *Apud Argentoratum,* in Baluzius, *Capitularies,* ii, p. 39.

[9] See the law of Guy, King of the Romans, among those which were added to the Salic law, and to that of the Lombards, tit. 6, § 2 in Echard.
[10] Some authors pretend that the County of Toulouse had been given away by Charles Martel, and passed by inheritance down to Raymond, the last count; but, if this be true, it was owing to some circumstances which might have been an inducement to choose the Counts of Toulouse from among the children of the last possessor.
[11] See his Capitulary of the year 877, tit. 53, art. 9 and 10, *apud Carisiacum.* This Capitulary bears relation to another of the same year and place, art. 3.

counts who formerly administered justice in the king's *placita,* and who led the freemen against the enemy, found themselves situated between the king and his freemen; and the king's power was removed farther off another degree.

Again, it appears from the capitularies,[1] that the counts had benefices annexed to their counties, and vassals under them. When the counties became hereditary, the count's vassals were no longer the immediate vassals of the king; and the benefices annexed to the counties were no longer the king's benefices; the counts grew powerful because the vassals whom they had already under them enabled them to procure others.

In order to be convinced how much the monarchy was thereby weakened towards the end of the second race we have only to cast an eye on what happened at the beginning of the third, when the multiplicity of rear-fiefs flung the great vassals into despair.

It was a custom of the kingdom[2] that when the elder brothers had given shares to their younger brothers, the latter paid homage to the elder; so that those shares were held of the lord paramount only as a rear-fief. Philip Augustus, the Duke of Burgundy, the Counts of Nevers, Boulogne, St. Paul, Dampierre, and other lords declared[3] that henceforward, whether the fiefs were divided by succession or otherwise, the whole should be always of the same lord, without any intermediation. This ordinance was not generally followed; for, as I have elsewhere observed, it was impossible to make general ordinances at that time; but many of our customs were regulated by them.

29. *Of the Nature of the Fiefs after the Reign of Charles the Bald.* We have observed that Charles the Bald ordained that when the possessor of a great office or of a fief left a son at his death, the office or fief should devolve to him. It would be a difficult matter to trace the progress of the abuses which thence resulted, and of the extension given to that law in each country. I find in the books of fiefs,[4] that towards the beginning of the reign of the Em-

peror Conrad II, the fiefs situated in his dominions did not descend to the grandchildren: they descended only to one of the last possessor's children, who had been chosen by the lord:[5] thus the fiefs were given by a kind of election, which the lord made among the children.

In the seventeenth chapter of this book we have explained in what manner the crown was in some respects elective, and in others hereditary under the second race. It was hereditary, because the kings were always taken from that family, and because the children succeeded; it was elective, by reason that the people chose from among the children. As things proceed step by step, and one political law has constantly some relation to another political law, the same spirit was followed in the succession of fiefs, as had been observed in the succession to the crown.[6] Thus the fiefs were transmitted to the children by the right of succession, as well as of election; and each fief became both elective and hereditary, like the crown.

This right of election[7] in the person of the lord was not subsisting at the time of the authors[8] of the book of fiefs, that is, in the reign of the Emperor Frederick I.

30. *The same Subject continued.* It is mentioned in the books of fiefs, that when the Emperor Conrad set out for Rome, the vassals in his service presented a petition to him that he would please to make a law that the fiefs which descended to the children should descend also to the grandchildren; and that he whose brother died without legitimate heirs might succeed to the fief which had belonged to their common father.[9] This was granted.

In the same place it is said (and we are to remember that those writers lived at the time of the Emperor Frederick I)[10] "that the ancient jurists had always been of opinion[11] that the succession of fiefs in a collateral line did not extend farther than to brothers-german, though of late it was carried as far as the seventh degree, and by the new code they had extended it in a direct line *in infinitum.*" It is thus that Conrad's law was insensibly extended.

All these things being supposed, the bare

[1] The third Capitulary of the year 812, art. 7, and that of the year 815, art. 6, on the Spaniards. The collection of the Capitularies, book 5, art. 288, and the Capitulary of the year 869, art. 2, and that of the year 877, art. 13, Baluzius's edition.

[2] As appears from Otho of Frissingue, *Of the Actions of Frederic,* ii. 29.

[3] See the ordinance of Philip Augustus in the year 1209, in the new collection.

[4] Book i, tit. 1.

[5] *Ibid.*

[6] At least in Italy and Germany.

[7] Book i, of fiefs, tit. 1.

[8] Gerardus Niger and Aubertus de Orto.

[9] Book i, of fiefs, tit. 1.

[10] Cujas has proved it extremely well.

[11] *Ibid.*

perusal of the history of France is sufficient to demonstrate that the pepetuity of fiefs was established earlier in this kingdom than in Germany. Towards the commencement of the reign of the Emperor Conrad II in 1024, things were upon the same footing still in Germany, as they had been in France during the reign of Charles the Bald, who died in 877. But such were the changes made in this kingdom after the reign of Charles the Bald, that Charles the Simple found himself unable to dispute with a foreign house his incontestable rights to the empire; and, in fine, that in Hugh Capet's time the reigning family, stripped of all its demesnes, was no longer in a condition to maintain the crown.

The weak understanding of Charles the Bald produced an equal weakness in the French monarchy. But as his brother, Louis, King of Germany, and some of that prince's successors were men of better parts, their government preserved its vigour much longer.

But what do I say? Perhaps the phlegmatic constitution, and, if I dare use the expression, the immutability of spirit peculiar to the German nation made a longer stand than the volatile temper of the French against that disposition of things, which perpetuated the fiefs by a natural tendency, in families.

Besides, the kingdom of Germany was not laid waste and annihilated, as it were, like that of France, by that particular kind of war with which it had been harassed by the Normans and Saracens. There were less riches in Germany, fewer cities to plunder, less extent of coast to scour, more marshes to get over, more forests to penetrate. As the dominions of those princes were less in danger of being ravaged and torn to pieces, they had less need of their vassals and consequently less dependence on them. And in all probability, if the Emperors of Germany had not been obliged to be crowned at Rome, and to make continual expeditions into Italy, the fiefs would have preserved their primitive nature much longer in that country.

31. *In what Manner the Empire was transferred from the Family of Charlemagne.* The empire, which, in prejudice to the branch of Charles the Bald had been already given to the bastard line of Louis, King of Germany,[1] was transferred to a foreign house by the election of Conrad, Duke of Franconia, in 912. The reigning branch in France, being hardly

[1] Arnold and his son Louis IV.

able to contest a few villages, was much less in a situation to contest the empire. We have an agreement entered into between Charles the Simple and the Emperor Henry I, who had succeeded to Conrad. It is called the Compact of Bonn.[2] These two princes met in a vessel which had been placed in the middle of the Rhine, and swore eternal friendship. They used on this occasion an excellent *middle term.* Charles took the title of King of West France, and Henry that of King of East France. Charles contracted with the King of Germany, and not with the Emperor.

32. *In what Manner the Crown of France was transferred to the House of Hugh Capet.* The inheritance of the fiefs, and the general establishment of rear-fiefs, extinguished the political and formed a feudal government. Instead of that prodigious multitude of vassals who were formerly under the king, there were now a few only, on whom the others depended. The kings had scarcely any longer a direct authority; a power which was to pass through so many other and through such great powers either stopped or was lost before it reached its term. Those great vassals would no longer obey; and they even made use of their rear-vassals to withdraw their obedience. The kings, deprived of their demesnes and reduced to the cities of Rheims and Laon, were left exposed to their mercy; the tree stretched out its branches too far, and the head was withered. The kingdom found itself without a demesne, as the empire is at present. The crown was, therefore, given to one of the most potent vassals.

The Normans ravaged the kingdom; they sailed in open boats or small vessels, entered the mouths of rivers, and laid the country waste on both sides. The cities of Orleans and Paris put a stop to those plunderers, so that they could not advance farther, either on the Seine, or on the Loire.[3] Hugh Capet, who was master of those cities, held in his hands the two keys of the unhappy remains of the kingdom; the crown was conferred upon him as the only person able to defend it. It is thus the empire was afterwards given to a family whose dominions form so strong a barrier against the Turks.

[2] In the year 926, quoted by Aubert le Mire, *Cod. donationum piarum,* 27.
[3] See the Capitulary of Charles the Bald, in the year 877, *apud Carisiacum,* on the importance of Paris, St. Denis, and the castles on the Loire, in those days.

The empire went from Charlemagne's family at a time when the inheritance of fiefs was established only as a mere condescendence. It even appears that this inheritance obtained much later among the Germans than among the French;[1] which was the reason that the empire, considered as a fief, was elective. On the contrary, when the crown of France went from the family of Charlemagne, the fiefs were really hereditary in this kingdom; and the crown, as a great fief, was also hereditary.

But it is very wrong to refer to the very moment of this revolution all the changes which happened, either before or afterwards. The whole was reduced to two events; the reigning family changed, and the crown was united to a great fief.

33. *Some Consequences of the Perpetuity of Fiefs.* From the perpetuity of fiefs it followed that the right of seniority or primogeniture was established among the French. This right was quite unknown under the first race;[2] the crown was divided among the brothers, the allodia were shared in the same manner; and as the fiefs, whether precarious or for life, were not an object of succession, there could be no partition in regard to those tenures.

Under the second race, the title of emperor, which Louis the Debonnaire enjoyed, and with which he honoured his eldest son, Lotharius, made him think of giving this prince a kind of superiority over his younger brothers. The two kings were obliged to wait upon the emperor every year, to carry him presents, and to receive much greater from him; they were also to consult with him upon common affairs.[3] This is what inspired Lotharius with those pretences which met with such bad success. When Agobard wrote in favour of this prince,[4] he alleged the emperor's own intention, who had associated Lotharius with the empire after he had consulted the Almighty by a three days' fast, by the celebration of the holy mysteries, and by prayers and almsgiving; after the nation had sworn allegiance to him, which they could not refuse without perjuring themselves; and after he had sent Lotharius to Rome to be confirmed by the Pope. Upon all this he lays a stress, and not upon his right of primogeniture. He says, indeed, that the emperor had designed a partition among the younger brothers, and that he had given the preference to the elder; but saying he had preferred the elder was saying at the same time that he might have given the preference to his younger brothers.

But as soon as the fiefs became hereditary, the right of seniority was established in the feudal succession; and for the same reason in that of the crown, which was the great fief. The ancient law of partitions was no longer subsisting; the fiefs being charged with a service, the possessor must have been enabled to discharge it. The law of primogeniture was established, and the right of the feudal law was superior to that of the political or civil institution.

As the fiefs descended to the children of the possessor, the lords lost the liberty of disposing of them; and, in order to indemnify themselves, they established what they called the right of redemption, whereof mention is made in our customs, which at first was paid in a direct line, and by usage came afterwards to be paid only in a collateral line.

The fiefs were soon rendered transferable to strangers as a patrimonial estate. This gave rise to the right of lord's dues, which were established almost throughout the kingdom. These rights were arbitrary in the beginning; but when the practice of granting such permissions became general, they were fixed in every district.

The right of redemption was to be paid at every change of heir, and at first was paid even in a direct line.[5] The most general custom had fixed it to one year's income. This was burdensome and inconvenient to the vassal, and affected in some measure the fief itself. It was often agreed in the act of homage that the lord should no longer demand more than a certain sum of money for the redemption, which, by the changes incident to money, became afterwards of no manner of importance.[6] Thus the right of redemption is in our days reduced almost to nothing, while that of the lord's dues is continued in its full extent. As this right concerned neither the vassal nor his

---

[1] See above, chapter 30.
[2] See the Salic law, and the law of the Ripuarians, in the title of *Allodia.*
[3] See the Capitulary of the year 817, which contains the first partition made by Louis the Debonnaire among his children.
[4] See his two letters upon this subject, the title of one of which is *De Divisione imperii.*

[5] See the ordinance of Philip Augustus, in the year 1209, on the fiefs.
[6] We find several of these conventions in the charters, as in the register book of Vendôme, and that of the abbey, in St. Cyprian in Poitou, of which Mr. Galland has given some extracts, p. 55.

heirs, but was a fortuitous case which no one was obliged to foresee or expect, these stipulations were not made, and they continued to pay a certain part of the price.

When the fiefs were for life, they could not give a part of a fief to hold in perpetuity as a rear-fief; for it would have been absurd that a person who had only the usufruct of a thing should dispose of the property of it. But when they became perpetual, this was permitted,[1] with some restrictions made by the customs, which was what they call dismembering their fief.[2]

The perpetuity of feudal tenures having established the right of redemption, the daughters were rendered capable of succeeding to a fief, in default of male issue. For when the lord gave the fief to his daughter, he multiplied the cases of his right of redemption, because the husband was obliged to pay it as well as the wife.[3] This regulation could not take place in regard to the crown, for as it was not held of any one, there could be no right of redemption over it.

The daughter of William V, Count of Toulouse, did not succeed to the county. But Eleanor succeeded to Aquitaine, and Matilda to Normandy; and the right of the succession of females seemed so well established in those days, that Louis the Young, after his divorce from Eleanor, made no difficulty in restoring Guienne to her. But as these two last instances followed close on the first, the general law by which the women were called to the succession of fiefs must have been introduced much later into the county of Toulouse than into the other provinces of France.[4]

The constitution of several kingdoms of Europe has been directed by the state of feudal tenures at the time when those kingdoms were founded. The women succeeded neither to the crown of France nor to the empire, because at the foundation of those two monarchies they were incapable of succeeding to fiefs. But they succeeded in kingdoms whose foundation was posterior to that of the perpetuity of the fiefs, such as those founded by the Normans, those by the conquests made on the Moors, and others, in fine, which were beyond the limits of Germany, and in later times received in some measure a second birth by the establishment of Christianity.

When these fiefs were at will, they were given to such as were capable of doing service for them, and, therefore, were never bestowed on minors; but when they became perpetual, the lords took the fief into their own hands, till the pupil came of age, either to increase their own emoluments, or to train the ward to the use of arms.[5] This is what our customs call *the guardianship of a nobleman's children*, which is founded on principles different from those of tutelage, and is entirely a distinct thing from it.

When the fiefs were for life, it was customary to vow fealty for a fief; and the real delivery, which was made by a sceptre, confirmed the fief, as it is now confirmed by homage. We do not find that the counts, or even the king's commissaries, received the homage in the provinces; nor is this ceremony to be met with in the commissions of those officers which have been handed down to us in the Capitularies. They sometimes, indeed, made all the king's subjects take an oath of allegiance;[6] but so far was this oath from being of the same nature as the service afterwards established by the name of homage, that it was only a ceremony of less solemnity, occasionally used, either before or after that act of obeisance; in short, it was quite a distinct thing from homage.[7]

The counts and the king's commissaries further made those vassals whose fidelity was suspected give occasionally a security, which was

---

[1] But they could not abridge the fiefs, that is, abolish a portion of it.

[2] They fixed the portion which they could dismember.

[3] This was the reason that the lords obliged the widow to marry again.

[4] Most of the great families had their particular laws of succession. See what M. de la Thaumassière says concerning the families of Berri.

[5] We see in the Capitulary of the year 817, *apud Carisiacum*, art. 3, Baluzius's edition, ii, p. 269, the moment in which the kings caused the fiefs to be administered in order to preserve them for the minors; an example followed by the lords, and which gave rise to what we have mentioned by the name of *the guardianship of a nobleman's children*.

[6] We find the formula thereof in the second Capitulary of the year 802. See also that of the year 854, art. 13, and others.

[7] M. Du Cange in the word *hominium*, p. 1163, and in the word *fidelitas*, p. 474, cites the charters of the ancient homages where these differences are found, and a great number of authorities which may be seen. In paying homage, the vassal put his hand on that of his lord, and took his oath; the oath of fealty was made by swearing on the gospels. The homage was performed kneeling, the oath of fealty standing. None but the lord could receive homage, but his officers might take the oath of fealty.—See Littleton, §§ 91, 92, faith and homage, that is, fidelity and homage.

called *firmitas*,[1] but this security could not be an homage, since kings gave it to each other.[2]

And though the Abbot Suger[3] makes mention of a chair of Dagobert, in which according to the testimony of antiquity, the kings of France were accustomed to receive the homage of the nobility, it is plain that he expresses himself agreeably to the ideas and language of his own time.

When the fiefs descended to the heirs, the acknowledgment of the vassal, which at first was only an occasional service, became a regular duty. It was performed in a more splendid manner, and attended with more formalities, because it was to be a perpetual memorial of the reciprocal duties of the lord and vassal.

I should be apt to think that homages began to be established under King Pepin, which is the time I mentioned that several benefices were given in perpetuity, but I should not think thus without caution, and only upon a supposition that the authors of the ancient annals of the Franks were not ignorant pretenders,[4] who in describing the fealty professed by Tassillon, Duke of Bavaria, to King Pepin, spoke according to the usages of their own time.[5]

34. *The same Subject continued.* When the fiefs were either precarious or for life, they seldom bore a relation to any other than the political laws; for which reason in the civil institutions of those times there is very little mention made of the laws of fiefs. But when they became hereditary, when there was a power of giving, selling, and bequeathing them, they bore a relation both to the political and the civil laws. The fief, considered as an obligation of performing military service, depended on the political law; considered as a kind of commercial property, it depended on the civil law. This gave rise to the civil regulations concerning feudal tenures.

When the fiefs became hereditary, the law relating to the order of succession must have been in relation to the perpetuity of fiefs. Hence this rule of the French law, *estates of inheritance do not ascend,*[6] was established in spite of the Roman and Salic laws.[7] It was necessary that service should be paid for the fief; but a grandfather or a great-uncle would have been too old to perform any service; this rule thus held good at first only in regard to the feudal tenures, as we learn from Boutillier.[8]

When the fiefs became hereditary, the lords who were to see that service was paid for the fief, insisted that the females who were to succeed to the feudal estate, and I fancy sometimes the males, should not marry without their consent; insomuch that the marriage contracts became in respect to the nobility both of a feudal and a civil regulation.[9] In an act of this kind under the lord's inspection, regulations were made for the succession, with the view that the heirs might pay service for the fief: hence none but the nobility at first had the liberty of disposing of successions by marriage contract, as Boyer[10] and Aufrerius[11] have observed.

It is needless to mention that the power of redemption, founded on the old right of the relatives, a mystery of our ancient French jurisprudence I have not time to unravel, could not take place with regard to the fiefs till they became perpetual.

Italiam, Italiam . . .[12]

I finish my treatise of fiefs at a period where most authors commence theirs.

[1] Capitularies of Charles the Bald, in the year 860, *post reditum a Confluentibus,* art. 3, Baluzius's edition, p. 145.

[2] *Ibid.,* art. 1.

[3] Suger, *Lib. de administratione sua.*

[4] Year 757, cap. xvii.

[5] One would think that here was an homage and an oath of fealty. See note 6, p. 314.

[6] Book iv, *de feudis,* tit. 59.

[7] In the title of *Allodia.*

[8] *Somme Rurale,* i, tit. 76, p. 447.

[9] According to an ordinance of St. Louis, in the year 1246 to settle the customs of Anjou and Maine; those who shall have the care of the heiress of a fief shall give security to the lord, that she shall not be married without his consent.

[10] Decision 155, No. 8; and 204, No. 38.

[11] In *Capell. Thol.,* decision 453.

[12] *Æneid,* iii, 523.

ROUSSEAU

BIOGRAPHICAL NOTE
Jean Jacques Rousseau, 1712–1778

THE Rousseau family, which had fled from France at the time of the religious wars, had been in Geneva for more than a century when Jean Jacques was born, June 28, 1712. His mother died in childbirth. His father, a watchmaker, taught him to read when he was five or six and before he was ten they had read together the "romances" his mother had left; from them, he later declared, "I date my uninterrupted self-consciousness . . . and my odd, romantic notions of human life." He also read history, particularly Plutarch, who "became my favorite author, . . . cured me a little of my taste for romance, . . . and formed in me the free and republican spirit." When he was about ten, his father, as the result of a quarrel, had to leave Geneva, and Rousseau was put in the care of an uncle, who entrusted his education to the pastor of Boissy.

At the age of twelve or thirteen, when Rousseau had completed his elementary education, he was placed as an apprentice, first to a notary and, when that proved unsuccessful, to an engraver. In 1728 he abandoned his master, left town, and began the series of adventures and wanderings which are recorded in the first six books of his Confessions. After a few days he appealed for charity to a Catholic priest in Savoy, who recommended him to a Madame de Warens, known for her good works. Aided by her, he went to Turin and presented himself to a hospice, where he was provided with food and lodging for nine days while being instructed in the Catholic faith. Although he later remarked that his renunciation of Protestantism was "at bottom the act of a bandit," Rousseau continued to regard himself as a Catholic until 1754. After serving a few months as a lackey, he re-visited Annecy and appealed to Madame de Warens, who took him into her house and after some years became his mistress.

During the nine or ten years that he was with Madame de Warens, Rousseau made several efforts to fit himself for an occupation. For a while he considered the priesthood and studied with the priests of St. Lazare. Then, thinking that he was better fitted for music, he took lessons from the choir-master of the cathedral; although not very proficient, he never afterwards lost interest in music, and it was several times his sole source of support. The only systematic studying he did during these years was at the rural retreat of Les Charmettes, where, prompted by Voltaire's Philosophical Letters, he undertook to make a survey of all the sciences. In a more or less desultory manner he read the seventeenth century philosophers and worked at mathematics, astronomy, anatomy, the Latin poets, history, and theology. His life with Madame de Warens was interrupted by frequent wanderings. On one occasion he returned to find that his place in the household had been taken by another. Rousseau then accepted the position of a tutor with a noble family of Lyons. After a few months he found that teaching was not to his liking, and in 1741 he went to Paris.

Rousseau's plans for establishing himself in the capital rested upon a new system of musical notation which he had developed. Although he succeeded in presenting it before the Academy of Sciences, it won no adherents. He was compelled to accept the post of secretary to the French Ambassador at Venice, which he obtained through one of the leading families he had become acquainted with at Paris. Returning to the city in 1745, he copied music for a living, cultivated the society of the literary circles, and through Diderot became a contributor on music to the Encyclopédie. His opera, Les Muses galantes, which was privately produced, won him some measure of fame. At about the same time, he began to live with Thérèse le Vasseur, a plain and ignorant servant girl at his hotel. He remained with her throughout his life, and according to his account, which is sometimes questioned, she bore him five children, all of whom were consigned at birth to the foundling hospital.

While at Venice in 1743 Rousseau planned a book on "political institutions" which would "set the seal upon my reputation"; but it was not until 1749 that he actually began to write upon politics. In that year he entered the contest held by the Academy of Dijon for the best essay on the subject: "Has the progress of the arts and sciences contributed more to the corruption or purification of morals?" Rousseau's essay, attacking civilization as corrupting the goodness of nature, won him the prize and immediate literary fame. The salons honored him, the office of the receiver-general provided him with a lucrative post, another of his operas was presented at court, and he had the opportunity of obtaining a royal pension, although after some hesitation he turned it down. Diderot asked him for an article on politics, and he wrote the *Discourse on Political Economy,* which first appeared in the *Encyclopédie* in 1755. In the same year he published the *Discourse on the Origin of Inequality,* which also had been written for a Dijon Academy contest.

Shortly after his first literary success Rousseau began to apply to himself his teachings on the simple life, and in 1756 he retired to the country near Paris to live at the Hermitage, which had been set up for him by Madame d'Épinay. Here he wrote *La Nouvelle Héloïse* and became involved in an obscure and bitter quarrel with Diderot and Frederick Melchior Grimm, the lover of Madame d'Épinay. He left the Hermitage in 1758 and settled at Montlouis, where he wrote both *Émile, on Education,* and the *Social Contract,* which were published in 1762.

Rousseau's quarrel with Diderot and Grimm embittered his relations with all of the Encyclopaedists. He angered them still more by his attack upon D'Alembert and Voltaire for their defense of theatrical representations. By his views on politics and religion he incurred the enmity of the French authorities. *Émile,* shortly after its appearance, was condemned by the parliament of Paris, and Rousseau learned that he would be arrested if he did not go into exile.

The first years of his exile were passed in Neuchâtel, which then belonged to Prussia. His controversial writings with those who condemned him continually embroiled him in public disputes, and he was finally compelled to flee again. He went first to the territory of Berne, but the same fate awaited him there. Finally in 1766 he accepted the invitation of Hume and accompanied him to England, leaving Thérèse to follow later in the company of Boswell. At first he enjoyed some popularity; he met the great men of the day and received a pension from the King. But he soon quarreled with Hume, and in 1767 he fled back to France, where he had learned he would be unmolested. After wandering about for some time, he settled in Paris in 1770, resumed his former occupation of music-copying, and completed his *Confessions* and other auto-biographical works. He could not rid himself, however, of his suspicions of secret enemies, which had tormented him since his quarrel with Diderot, and in 1778 he gladly accepted the offer of a cottage at Ermenonville. He died suddenly on July 2 in circumstances that gave rise to rumors of suicide, although later inquiries failed to bear them out.

CONTENTS

A DISCOURSE

ON A SUBJECT PROPOSED BY THE ACADEMY OF DIJON:

WHAT IS THE ORIGIN OF INEQUALITY AMONG MEN,

AND IS IT AUTHORISED BY NATURAL LAW?

> We should consider what is natural not in things depraved but in those which are rightly ordered according to nature.   Aristotle, *Politics*, Bk. i, ch. 5

DEDICATION TO THE REPUBLIC OF GENEVA

MOST HONOURABLE, MAGNIFICENT AND SOVEREIGN LORDS, convinced that only a virtuous citizen can confer on his country honours which it can accept, I have been for thirty years past working to make myself worthy to offer you some public homage; and, this fortunate opportunity supplementing in some degree the insufficiency of my efforts, I have thought myself entitled to follow in embracing it the dictates of the zeal which inspires me, rather than the right which should have been my authorisation. Having had the happiness to be born among you, how could I reflect on the equality which nature has ordained between men, and the inequality which they have introduced, without reflecting on the profound wisdom by which both are in this State happily combined and made to coincide, in the manner that is most in conformity with natural law, and most favourable to society, to the maintenance of public order and to the happiness of individuals? In my researches after the best rules common sense can lay down for the constitution of a government, I have been so struck at finding them all in actuality in your own, that even had I not been born within your walls I should have thought it indispensable for me to offer this picture of human society to that people, which of all others seems to be possessed of its greatest advantages, and to have best guarded against its abuses.

If I had had to make choice of the place of my birth, I should have preferred a society which had an extent proportionate to the limits of the human faculties; that is, to the possibility of being well governed: in which every person being equal to his occupation, no one should be obliged to commit to others the functions with which he was entrusted: a State, in which all the individuals being well known to one another, neither the secret machinations of vice, nor the modesty of virtue should be able to escape the notice and judgment of the public; and in which the pleasant custom of seeing and knowing one another should make the love of country rather a love of the citizens than of its soil.

I should have wished to be born in a country in which the interest of the Sovereign and that of the people must be single and identical; to the end that all the movements of the machine might tend always to the general happiness. And as this could not be the case, unless the Sovereign and the people were one and the same person, it follows that I should have wished to be born under a democratic government, wisely tempered.

I should have wished to live and die free: that is, so far subject to the laws that neither I, nor anybody else, should be able to cast off their honourable yoke: the easy and salutary yoke which the haughtiest necks bear with the greater docility, as they are made to bear no other.

I should have wished then that no one within the State should be able to say he was above the law; and that no one without should be able to dictate so that the State should be obliged to recognise his authority. For, be the constitution of a government what it may, if there be within its jurisdiction a single man who is not subject to the law, all the rest are necessarily at his discretion. And if there be a national ruler within, and a foreign ruler without, however they may divide their authority, it is impossible that both should be duly obeyed, or that the State should be well governed.

I should not have chosen to live in a republic of recent institution, however excellent its laws; for fear the government, being perhaps otherwise framed than the circumstances of the moment might require, might disagree with the new citizens, or they with it, and the State run the risk of overthrow and destruction almost as soon as it came into being. For it is with liberty as it is with those solid and succulent foods, or with those generous wines which are well adapted to nourish and fortify robust constitutions that are used to them, but ruin and intoxicate weak and delicate constitutions to which they are not suited. Peoples once accustomed to masters are not in a condition to do without them. If they attempt to shake off the yoke, they still more estrange themselves from freedom, as, by mistaking for it an unbridled license to which it is diametrically opposed, they nearly always manage, by their revolutions, to hand themselves over to seducers, who only make their chains heavier than before. The Roman people itself, a model for all free peoples, was wholly incapable of governing itself when it escaped from the oppression of the Tarquins. Debased by slavery, and the ignominious tasks which had been imposed upon it, it was at first no better than a stupid mob, which it was necessary to control and govern with the greatest wisdom; in order that, being accustomed by degrees to breathe the health-giving air of liberty, minds which had been enervated or rather brutalised under tyranny, might gradually acquire that severity of morals and spirit of fortitude which made it at length the people of all most worthy of respect. I should, then, have sought out for my country some peaceful and happy Republic, of an antiquity that lost itself, as it were, in the night of time: which had experienced only such shocks as served to manifest and strengthen the courage and patriotism of its subjects; and whose citizens, long accustomed to a wise independence, were not only free, but worthy to be so.

I should have wished to choose myself a country, diverted, by a fortunate impotence, from the brutal love of conquest, and secured, by a still more fortunate situation, from the fear of becoming itself the conquest of other States: a free city situated between several nations, none of which should have any interest in attacking it, while each had an interest in preventing it from being attacked by the others; in short, a Republic which should have nothing to tempt the ambition of its neighbours, but might reasonably depend on their assistance in case of need. It follows that a republican State so happily situated could have nothing to fear but from itself; and that, if its members trained themselves to the use of arms, it would be rather to keep alive that military ardour and courageous spirit which are so proper among freemen, and tend to keep up their taste for liberty, than from the necessity of providing for their defence.

I should have sought a country, in which the right of legislation was vested in all the citizens; for who can judge better than they of the conditions under which they had best dwell together in the same society? Not that I should have approved of Plebiscita, like those among the Romans; in which the rulers in the State, and those most interested in its preservation, were excluded from the deliberations on which in many cases its security depended; and in which, by the most absurd inconsistency, the magistrates were deprived of rights which the meanest citizens enjoyed.

On the contrary, I should have desired that, in order to prevent self-interested and ill-conceived projects, and all such dangerous innovations as finally ruined the Athenians, each man should not be at liberty to propose new laws at pleasure; but that this right should belong exclusively to the magistrates; and that even they should use it with so much caution, the people, on its side, be so reserved in giving its consent to such laws, and the promulgation of them be attended with so much solemnity, that before the constitution could be upset by them, there might be time enough for all to be convinced, that it is above all the great antiquity of the laws which makes them sacred and venerable, that men soon learn to despise laws which they see daily altered, and that States, by accustoming themselves to neglect their ancient customs under the pretext of improvement, often introduce greater evils than those they endeavour to remove.

I should have particularly avoided, as necessarily ill-governed, a Republic in which the people, imagining themselves in a position to do without magistrates, or at least to leave them with only a precarious authority, should imprudently have kept for themselves the administration of civil affairs and the execution of their own laws. Such must have been the rude constitution of primitive governments, directly emerging from a state of nature; and this was another of the vices that contributed to the downfall of the Republic of Athens.

But I should have chosen a community in which the individuals, content with sanctioning their laws, and deciding the most important public affairs in general assembly and on the motion of the rulers, had established honoured tribunals, carefully distinguished the several departments, and elected year by year some of the most capable and upright of their fellow-citizens to administer justice and govern the State; a community, in short, in which the virtue of the magistrates thus bearing witness to the wisdom of the people, each class reciprocally did the other honour. If in such a case any fatal misunderstandings arose to disturb the public peace, even these intervals of blindness and error would bear the marks of moderation, mutual esteem, and a common respect for the laws; which are sure signs and pledges of a reconciliation as lasting as sincere. Such are the advantages, most honourable, magnificent and sovereign lords, which I should have sought in the country in which I should have chosen to be born. And if providence had added to all these a delightful situation, a temperate climate, a fertile soil, and the most beautiful countryside under Heaven, I should have desired only, to complete my felicity, the peaceful enjoyment of all these blessings, in the bosom of this happy country; to live at peace in the sweet society of my fellow-citizens, and practising towards them, from their own example, the duties of friendship, humanity, and every other virtue, to leave behind me the honourable memory of a good man, and an upright and virtuous patriot.

But, if less fortunate or too late grown wise, I had seen myself reduced to end an infirm and languishing life in other climates, vainly regretting that peaceful repose which I had forfeited in the imprudence of youth, I should at least have entertained the same feelings in my heart, though denied the opportunity of making use of them in my native country. Filled with a tender and disinterested love for my distant fellow-citizens, I should have addressed them from my heart, much in the following terms.

"My dear fellow-citizens, or rather my brothers, since the ties of blood, as well as the laws, unite almost all of us, it gives me pleasure that I cannot think of you, without thinking, at the same time, of all the blessings you enjoy, and of which none of you, perhaps, more deeply feels the value than I who have lost them. The more I reflect on your civil and political condition, the less can I conceive that the nature of human affairs could admit of a better. In all other governments, when there is a question of ensuring the greatest good of the State, nothing gets beyond projects and ideas, or at best bare possibilities. But as for you, your happiness is complete, and you have nothing to do but enjoy it; you require nothing more to be made perfectly happy, than to know how to be satisfied with being so. Your sovereignty, acquired or recovered by the sword, and maintained for two centuries past by your valour and wisdom, is at length fully and universally acknowledged. Your boundaries are fixed, your rights confirmed and your repose secured by honourable treaties. Your constitution is excellent, being not only dictated by the profoundest wisdom, but guaranteed by great and friendly powers. Your State enjoys perfect tranquillity; you have neither wars nor conquerors to fear; you have no other master than the wise laws you have yourselves made; and these are administered by upright magistrates of your own choosing. You are neither so wealthy as to be enervated by effeminacy, and thence to lose, in the pursuit of frivolous pleasures, the taste for real happiness and solid virtue; nor poor enough to require more assistance from abroad than your own industry is sufficient to procure you. In the meantime the precious privilege of liberty, which in great nations is maintained only by submission to the most exorbitant impositions, costs you hardly anything for its preservation.

May a Republic, so wisely and happily constituted, last for ever, for an example to other nations, and for the felicity of its own citizens! This is the only prayer you have left to make, the only precaution that remains to be taken. It depends, for the future, on yourselves alone (not to make you happy, for your ancestors have saved you that trouble), but to render that happiness lasting, by your wisdom in its enjoyment. It is on your constant union, your obedience to the laws, and your respect for their ministers, that your preservation depends. If there remains among you the smallest trace of bitterness or distrust, hasten to destroy it, as an accursed leaven which sooner or later must bring misfortune and ruin on the State. I conjure you all to look into your hearts, and to hearken to the secret voice of conscience. Is there any among you who can find, throughout the universe, a more upright, more enlightened and more honourable body than your magistracy? Do not all its members set you an example of moderation, of simplicity of manners, of respect for the laws, and of the most sincere harmony? Place, therefore, without reserve, in such wise superiors, that salutary confidence which reason ever owes to virtue. Consider that they are your own choice, that they justify that choice, and that the honours due to those whom you have dignified are necessarily yours by reflexion. Not one of you is so ignorant as not to know that, when the laws lose their force and those who defend them their authority, security and liberty are universally impossible. Why, therefore, should you hesitate to do that cheerfully and with just confidence which you would all along have been bound to do by your true interest, your duty and reason itself?

Let not a culpable and pernicious indifference to the maintenance of the constitution ever induce you to neglect, in case of need, the prudent advice of the most enlightened and zealous of your fellow-citizens; but let equity, moderation and firmness of resolution continue to regulate all your proceedings, and to exhibit you to the whole universe as the example of a valiant and modest people, jealous equally of their honour and of their liberty. Beware particularly, as the last piece of advice I shall give you, of sinister constructions and venomous rumours, the secret motives of which are often more dangerous than the actions at which they are levelled. A whole house will be awake and take the first alarm given by a good and trusty watch-dog, who barks only at the approach of thieves; but we hate the importunity of those noisy curs, which are perpetually disturbing the public repose, and whose continual ill-timed warnings prevent our attending to them, when they may perhaps be necessary."

And you, most honourable and magnificent lords, the worthy and revered magistrates of a free people, permit me to offer you in particular my duty and homage. If there is in the world a station capable of conferring honour on those who fill it, it is undoubtedly that which virtue and talents combine to bestow, that of which you have made yourselves worthy, and to which you have been promoted by your fellow-citizens. Their worth adds a new lustre to your own; while, as you have been chosen, by men capable of governing others, to govern themselves, I cannot but hold you as much superior to all other magistrates, as a free people, and particularly that over which you have the honour to preside, is by its wisdom and its reason superior to the populace of other States.

Be it permitted me to cite an example of which there ought to have existed better records, and one which will be ever near to my heart. I cannot recall to mind, without the sweetest emotions, the memory of that virtuous citizen, to whom I owe my being, and by whom I was often instructed, in my infancy, in the respect which is due to you. I see him still, living by the work of his hands, and feeding his soul on the sublimest truths. I see the works of Tacitus, Plutarch, and Grotius lying before him in the midst of the tools of his trade. At his side stands his dear son, receiving, alas with too little profit, the tender instructions of the best of fathers. But, if the follies of youth made me for a while forget his wise lessons, I have at length the happiness to be conscious that, whatever propensity one may have to vice, it is not easy for an education, with which love has mingled, to be entirely thrown away.

Such, my most honourable and magnificent lords, are the citizens, and even the common inhabitants of the State which you govern; such are those intelligent and sensible men, of whom, under the name of workmen and the people, it is usual, in other nations, to have a low and false opinion. My father, I own with pleasure, was in no way distinguished among his fellow-citizens. He was only such as they all are; and yet, such as he was, there is no country, in which his acquaintance would not have been coveted, and cultivated even with advantage by men of the highest character. It would not become me, nor is it, thank Heaven, at all necessary for me to remind you of the regard which such men have a right to expect of their magistrates, to whom they are equal both by education and by the rights of nature and birth, and inferior only, by their own will, by that preference which they owe to your merit, and, for giving you, can claim some sort of acknowledgment on your side. It is with a lively satisfaction I understand that the greatest candour and condescension attend, in all your behaviour towards them, on that gravity which becomes the ministers of the law; and that you so well repay them, by your esteem and attention, the respect and obedience which they owe to you. This conduct is not only just but prudent; as it happily tends to obliterate the memory of many unhappy events, which ought to be buried in eternal oblivion. It is also so much the more judicious, as it tends to make this generous and equitable people find a pleasure in their duty; to make them naturally love to do you honour, and to cause those who are the most zealous in the maintenance of their own rights to be at the same time the most disposed to respect yours.

It ought not to be thought surprising that the rulers of a civil society should have the welfare and glory of their communities at heart: but it is uncommonly fortunate for the peace of men, when those persons who look upon themselves as the magistrates, or rather the masters of a more holy and sublime country, show some love for the earthly country which maintains them. I am happy in having it in my power to make so singular an exception in our favour, and to be able to rank, among its best citizens, those zealous depositaries of the sacred articles of faith established by the laws, those venerable shepherds of souls whose powerful and captivating eloquence are so much the better calculated to bear to men's hearts the maxims of the gospel, as they are themselves the first to put them into practice. All the world knows of the great success with which the art of the pulpit is cultivated at Geneva; but men are so used to hearing divines preach one thing and practise another, that few have a chance of knowing how far the spirit of Christianity, holiness of manners, severity towards themselves and indulgence towards their neighbours, prevail throughout the whole body of our ministers. It is, perhaps, given to the city of Geneva alone, to produce the edifying example of so perfect a union between its clergy and men of letters. It is in great measure on their wisdom, their known moderation, and their zeal for the prosperity of the State that I build my hopes of its perpetual tranquillity. At the same time, I notice, with a pleasure mingled with surprise and veneration, how much they detest the frightful maxims of those accursed

and barbarous men, of whom history furnishes us with more than one example; who, in order to support the pretended rights of God, that is to say their own interests, have been so much the less greedy of human blood, as they were more hopeful their own in particular would be always respected.

I must not forget that precious half of the Republic, which makes the happiness of the other; and whose sweetness and prudence preserve its tranquillity and virtue. Amiable and virtuous daughters of Geneva, it will be always the lot of your sex to govern ours. Happy are we, so long as your chaste influence, solely exercised within the limits of conjugal union, is exerted only for the glory of the State and the happiness of the public. It was thus the female sex commanded at Sparta; and thus you deserve to command at Geneva. What man can be such a barbarian as to resist the voice of honour and reason, coming from the lips of an affectionate wife? Who would not despise the vanities of luxury, on beholding the simple and modest attire which, from the lustre it derives from you, seems the most favourable to beauty? It is your task to perpetuate, by your insinuating influence and your innocent and amiable rule, a respect for the laws of the State, and harmony among the citizens. It is yours to reunite divided families by happy marriages; and, above all things, to correct, by the persuasive sweetness of your lessons and the modest graces of your conversation, those extravagancies which our young people pick up in other countries, whence, instead of many useful things by which they might profit, they bring home hardly anything, besides a puerile air and a ridiculous manner, acquired among loose women, but an admiration for I know not what so-called grandeur, and paltry recompenses for being slaves, which can never come near the real greatness of liberty. Continue, therefore, always to be what you are, the chaste guardians of our morals, and the sweet security for our peace, exerting on every occasion the privileges of the heart and of nature, in the interests of duty and virtue.

I flatter myself that I shall never be proved to have been mistaken, in building on such a foundation my hopes of the general happiness of the citizens and the glory of the Republic. It must be confessed, however, that with all these advantages, it will not shine with that lustre, by which the eyes of most men are dazzled; a puerile and fatal taste for which is the most mortal enemy of happiness and liberty.

Let our dissolute youth seek elsewhere light pleasures and long repentances. Let our pretenders to taste admire elsewhere the grandeur of palaces, the beauty of equipages, sumptuous furniture, the pomp of public entertainments, and all the refinements of luxury and effeminacy. Geneva boasts nothing but men; such a sight has nevertheless a value of its own, and those who have a taste for it are well worth the admirers of all the rest.

Deign, most honourable, magnificent and sovereign lords, to receive, and with equal goodness, this respectful testimony of the interest I take in your common prosperity. And,

if I have been so unhappy as to be guilty of any indiscreet transport in this glowing effusion of my heart, I beseech you to pardon me, and to attribute it to the tender affection of a true patriot, and to the ardent and legitimate zeal of a man, who can imagine for himself no greater felicity than to see you happy.

Most honourable, magnificent and sovereign lords, I am, with the most profound respect,

Your most humble and obedient servant and fellow-citizen.

J. J. ROUSSEAU

Chambéry, June 12, 1754

PREFACE

OF all human sciences the most useful and most imperfect appears to me to be that of mankind: and I will venture to say, the single inscription on the Temple of Delphi contained a precept more difficult and more important than is to be found in all the huge volumes that moralists have ever written. I consider the subject of the following discourse as one of the most interesting questions philosophy can propose, and unhappily for us, one of the most thorny that philosophers can have to solve. For how shall we know the source of inequality between men, if we do not begin by knowing mankind? And how shall man hope to see himself as nature made him, across all the changes which the succession of place and time must have produced in his original constitution? How can he distinguish what is fundamental in his nature from the changes and additions which his circumstances and the advances he has made have introduced to modify his primitive condition? Like the statue of Glaucus, which was so disfigured by time, seas and tempests, that it looked more like a wild beast than a god, the human soul, altered in society by a thousand causes perpetually recurring, by the acquisition of a multitude of truths and errors, by the changes happening to the constitution of the body, and by the continual jarring of the passions, has, so to speak, changed in appearance, so as to be hardly recognisable. Instead of a being, acting constantly from fixed and invariable principles, instead of that celestial and majestic simplicity, impressed on it by its divine Author, we find in it only the frightful contrast of passion mistaking itself for reason, and of understanding grown delirious.

It is still more cruel that, as every advance made by the human species removes it still farther from its primitive state, the more discoveries we make, the more we deprive ourselves of the means of making the most important of all. Thus it is, in one sense, by our very study of man, that the knowledge of him is put out of our power.

It is easy to perceive that it is in these successive changes in the constitution of man that we must look for the origin of those differences which now distinguish men, who, it is allowed, are as equal among themselves as were the animals of every kind, before physical causes had introduced those varieties which are now observable among some of them.

It is, in fact, not to be conceived that these primary changes, however they may have arisen, could have altered, all at once and in the same manner, every individual of the species. It is natural to think that, while the condition of some of them grew better or worse, and they were acquiring various good or bad qualities not inherent in their nature, there were others who continued a longer time in their original condition. Such was doubtless the first source of the inequality of mankind, which it is much easier to point out thus in general terms, than to assign with precision to its actual causes.

Let not my readers therefore imagine that I flatter myself with having seen what it appears to me so difficult to discover. I have here entered upon certain arguments, and risked some conjectures, less in the hope of solving the difficulty, than with a view to throwing some light upon it, and reducing the question to its proper form. Others may easily proceed farther on the same road, and yet no one find it very easy to get to the end. For it is by no means a light undertaking to distinguish properly between what is original and what is artificial in the actual nature of man, or to form a true idea of a state which no longer exists, perhaps never did exist, and probably never will exist; and of which, it is, nevertheless, necessary to have true ideas, in order to form a proper judgment of our present state. It requires, indeed, more philosophy than can be imagined to enable any one to determine exactly what precautions he ought to take, in order to make solid observations on this subject; and it appears to me that a good solution of the following problem would be not unworthy of the Aristotles and Plinys of the present age. *What experiments would have to be made, to discover the natural man? And how are those experiments to be made in a state of society?*

So far am I from undertaking to solve this problem, that I think I have sufficiently considered the subject, to venture to declare beforehand that our greatest philosophers would not be too good to direct such experiments, and our most powerful sovereigns to make them. Such a combination we have very little reason to expect, especially attended with the perseverance, or rather succession of intelligence and goodwill necessary on both sides to success.

These investigations, which are so difficult to make, and have been hitherto so little thought of, are, nevertheless, the only means that remain of obviating a multitude of difficulties which deprive us of the knowledge of the real foundations of human society. It is this ignorance of the nature of man, which casts so much uncertainty and obscurity on the true definition of natural right: for, the idea of right, says Burlamaqui, and more particularly that of natural right, are ideas manifestly relative to the nature of man. It is then from this very nature itself, he goes on, from the constitution and state of man, that we must deduce the first principles of this science.

We cannot see without surprise and disgust how little agreement there is between the different authors who have treated this great subject. Among the more important writers there are scarcely two of the same mind about it. Not to speak of the ancient philosophers, who seem to have done their best purposely to contradict one another on the most fundamental principles, the Roman jurists subjected man and the other animals indiscriminately to the same natural law, because they considered, under that name, rather the law which nature imposes on herself than that which she prescribes to others; or rather because of the particular acceptation of the term law among those jurists; who seem on this occasion to have understood nothing more by it than the general relations established by nature between all animated beings, for their common preservation. The moderns, understanding, by the term law, merely a rule prescribed to a moral being, that is to say intelligent, free and considered in his relations to other beings, consequently confine the jurisdiction of natural law to man, as the only animal endowed

with reason. But, defining this law, each after his own fashion, they have established it on such metaphysical principles, that there are very few persons among us capable of comprehending them, much less of discovering them for themselves. So that the definitions of these learned men, all differing in everything else, agree only in this, that it is impossible to comprehend the law of nature, and consequently to obey it, without being a very subtle casuist and a profound metaphysician. All which is as much as to say that mankind must have employed, in the establishment of society, a capacity which is acquired only with great difficulty, and by very few persons, even in a state of society.

Knowing so little of nature, and agreeing so ill about the meaning of the word *law,* it would be difficult for us to fix on a good definition of natural law. Thus all the definitions we meet with in books, setting aside their defect in point of uniformity, have yet another fault, in that they are derived from many kinds of knowledge, which men do not possess naturally, and from advantages of which they can have no idea until they have already departed from that state. Modern writers begin by inquiring what rules it would be expedient for men to agree on for their common interest, and then give the name of natural law to a collection of these rules, without any other proof than the good that would result from their being universally practised. This is undoubtedly a simple way of making definitions, and of explaining the nature of things by almost arbitrary conveniences.

But as long as we are ignorant of the natural man, it is in vain for us to attempt to determine either the law originally prescribed to him, or that which is best adapted to his constitution. All we can know with any certainty respecting this law is that, if it is to be a law, not only the wills of those it obliges must be sensible of their submission to it; but also, to be natural, it must come directly from the voice of nature.

Throwing aside, therefore, all those scientific books, which teach us only to see men such as they have made themselves, and contemplating the first and most simple operations of the human soul, I think I can perceive in it two principles prior to reason, one of them deeply interesting us in our own welfare and preservation, and the other exciting a natural repugnance at seeing any other sensible being, and particularly any of our own species, suffer pain or death. It is from the agreement and combination which the understanding is in a position to establish between these two principles, without its being necessary to introduce that of sociability, that all the rules of natural right appear to me to be derived—rules which our reason is afterwards obliged to establish on other foundations, when by its successive developments it has been led to suppress nature itself.

In proceeding thus, we shall not be obliged to make man a philosopher before he is a man. His duties toward others are not dictated to him only by the later lessons of wisdom; and, so long as he does not resist the internal impulse of compassion, he will never hurt any other man, nor even any sentient being, except on those lawful occasions on which his own preservation is concerned and he is obliged to give himself the preference. By this method also we put an end to the time-honoured disputes concerning the participation of animals in natural law: for it is clear that, being destitute of intelligence and liberty, they cannot recognise that law; as they partake, however, in some measure of our nature, in consequence of the sensibility with which they are endowed, they ought to partake of natural right; so that mankind is subjected to a kind of obligation even toward the brutes. It appears, in fact, that if I am bound to do no injury to my fellow-creatures, this is less because they are rational than because they are sentient beings: and this quality, being common both to men and beasts, ought to entitle the latter at least to the privilege of not being wantonly ill-treated by the former.

The very study of the original man, of his real wants, and the fundamental principles of his duty, is besides the only proper method we can adopt to obviate all the difficulties which the origin of moral inequality presents, on the true foundations of the body politic, on the reciprocal rights of its members, and on many other similar topics equally important and obscure.

If we look at human society with a calm and disinterested eye, it seems, at first, to show us only the violence of the powerful and the oppression of the weak. The mind is shocked at the cruelty of the one, or is induced to lament the blindness of the other; and as nothing is less permanent in life than those external relations, which are more frequently produced by accident than wisdom, and which are called weakness or power, riches or poverty, all human institutions seem at first glance to be founded merely on banks of shifting sand. It is only by taking a closer look, and removing the dust and sand that surround the edifice, that we perceive the immovable basis on which it is raised, and learn to respect its foundations. Now, without a serious study of man, his natural faculties and their successive development, we shall never be able to make these necessary distinctions, or to separate, in the actual constitution of things, that which is the effect of the divine will, from the innovations attempted by human art. The political and moral investigations, therefore, to which the important question before us leads, are in every respect useful; while the hypothetical history of governments affords a lesson equally instructive to mankind.

In considering what we should have become, had we been left to ourselves, we should learn to bless Him, whose gracious hand, correcting our institutions, and giving them an immovable basis, has prevented those disorders which would otherwise have arisen from them, and caused our happiness to come from those very sources which seemed likely to involve us in misery.

•   •   ○

A DISSERTATION
ON THE ORIGIN AND FOUNDATION OF
THE INEQUALITY OF MANKIND

It is of man that I have to speak; and the question I am investigating shows me that it is to men that I must address myself: for questions of this sort are not asked by those who are afraid to honour truth. I shall then confidently uphold the cause of humanity before the wise men who invite me to do so, and shall not be dissatisfied if I acquit myself in a manner worthy of my subject and of my judges.

I conceive that there are two kinds of inequality among the human species; one, which I call natural or physical, because it is established by nature, and consists in a difference of age, health, bodily strength, and the qualities of the mind or of the soul: and another, which may be called moral or political inequality, because it depends on a kind of convention, and is established, or at least authorised by the consent of men. This latter consists of the different privileges, which some men enjoy to the prejudice of others; such as that of being more rich, more honoured, more powerful or even in a position to exact obedience.

It is useless to ask what is the source of natural inequality, because that question is answered by the simple definition of the word. Again, it is still more useless to inquire whether there is any essential connection between the two inequalities; for this would be only asking, in other words, whether those who command are necessarily better than those who obey, and if strength of body or of mind, wisdom or virtue are always found in particular individuals, in proportion to their power or wealth: a question fit perhaps to be discussed by slaves in the hearing of their masters, but highly unbecoming to reasonable and free men in search of the truth.

The subject of the present discourse, therefore, is more precisely this. To mark, in the progress of things, the moment at which right took the place of violence and nature became subject to law, and to explain by what sequence of miracles the strong came to submit to serve the weak, and the people to purchase imaginary repose at the expense of real felicity.

The philosophers, who have inquired into the foundations of society, have all felt the necessity of going back to a state of nature; but not one of them has got there. Some of them have not hesitated to ascribe to man, in such a state, the idea of just and unjust, without troubling themselves to show that he must be possessed of such an idea, or that it could be of any use to him. Others have spoken of the natural right of every man to keep what belongs to him, without explaining what they meant by *belongs*. Others again, beginning by giving the strong authority over the weak, proceeded directly to the birth of government, without regard to the time that must have elapsed before the meaning of the words authority and government could have existed among men. Every one of them, in short, constantly dwelling on wants, avidity, oppression, desires and pride, has transferred to the state of nature ideas which were acquired in society; so that, in speaking of the savage, they described the social man. It has not even entered into the heads of most of our writers to doubt whether the state of nature ever existed; but it is clear from the Holy Scriptures that the first man, having received his understanding and commandments immediately from God, was not himself in such a state; and that, if we give such credit to the writings of Moses as every Christian philosopher ought to give, we must deny that, even before the deluge, men were ever in the pure state of nature; unless, indeed, they fell back into it from some very extraordinary circumstance; a paradox which it would be very embarrassing to defend, and quite impossible to prove.

Let us begin then by laying facts aside, as

they do not affect the question. The investigations we may enter into, in treating this subject, must not be considered as historical truths, but only as mere conditional and hypothetical reasonings, rather calculated to explain the nature of things, than to ascertain their actual origin; just like the hypotheses which our physicists daily form respecting the formation of the world. Religion commands us to believe that, God Himself having taken men out of a state of nature immediately after the creation, they are unequal only because it is His will they should be so: but it does not forbid us to form conjectures based solely on the nature of man, and the beings around him, concerning what might have become of the human race, if it had been left to itself. This then is the question asked me, and that which I propose to discuss in the following discourse. As my subject interests mankind in general, I shall endeavour to make use of a style adapted to all nations, or rather, forgetting time and place, to attend only to men to whom I am speaking. I shall suppose myself in the Lyceum of Athens, repeating the lessons of my masters, with Plato and Xenocrates for judges, and the whole human race for audience.

O man, of whatever country you are, and whatever your opinions may be, behold your history, such as I have thought to read it, not in books written by your fellow-creatures, who are liars, but in nature, which never lies. All that comes from her will be true; nor will you meet with anything false, unless I have involuntarily put in something of my own. The times of which I am going to speak are very remote: how much are you changed from what you once were! It is, so to speak, the life of your species which I am going to write, after the qualities which you have received, which your education and habits may have depraved, but cannot have entirely destroyed. There is, I feel, an age at which the individual man would wish to stop: you are about to inquire about the age at which you would have liked your whole species to stand still. Discontented with your present state, for reasons which threaten your unfortunate descendants with still greater discontent, you will perhaps wish it were in your power to go back; and this feeling should be a panegyric on your first ancestors, a criticism of your contemporaries, and a terror to the unfortunates who will come after you.

THE FIRST PART

IMPORTANT as it may be, in order to judge rightly of the natural state of man, to consider him from his origin, and to examine him, as it were, in the embryo of his species; I shall not follow his organisation through its successive developments, nor shall I stay to inquire what his animal system must have been at the beginning, in order to become at length what it actually is. I shall not ask whether his long nails were at first, as Aristotle supposes, only crooked talons; whether his whole body, like that of a bear, was not covered with hair; or whether the fact that he walked upon all fours, with his looks directed toward the earth, confined to a horizon of a few paces, did not at once point out the nature and limits of his ideas. On this subject I could form none but vague and almost imaginary conjectures. Comparative anatomy has as yet made too little progress, and the observations of naturalists are too uncertain to afford an adequate basis for any solid reasoning. So that, without having recourse to the supernatural information given us on this head, or paying any regard to the changes which must have taken place in the internal, as well as the external, conformation of man, as he applied his limbs to new uses, and fed himself on new kinds of food, I shall suppose his conformation to have been at all times what it appears to us at this day; that he always walked on two legs, made use of his hands as we do, directed his looks over all nature, and measured with his eyes the vast expanse of Heaven.

If we strip this being, thus constituted, of all the supernatural gifts he may have received, and all the artificial faculties he can have acquired only by a long process; if we consider him, in a word, just as he must have come from the hands of nature, we behold in him an animal weaker than some, and less agile than others; but, taking him all round, the most advantageously organised of any. I see him satisfying his hunger at the first oak, and slaking his thirst at the first brook; finding his bed at the foot of the tree which afforded him a repast; and, with that, all his wants supplied.

While the earth was left to its natural fertility and covered with immense forests, whose trees were never mutilated by the axe, it would present on every side both sustenance and shelter for every species of animal. Men, dispersed up and down among the rest, would observe and imitate their industry, and thus attain even to the instinct of the beasts, with the advantage that, whereas every species of brutes was confined to one particular instinct, man, who perhaps has not any one peculiar to himself, would appropriate them all, and live upon most of those different foods which other animals shared among themselves; and thus would find his subsistence much more easily than any of the rest.

Accustomed from their infancy to the inclemencies of the weather and the rigour of the seasons, inured to fatigue, and forced, naked and unarmed, to defend themselves and their prey from other ferocious animals, or to escape them by flight, men would acquire a robust and almost unalterable constitution. The children, bringing with them into the world the excellent constitution of their parents, and fortifying it by the very exercises which first produced it, would thus acquire all the vigour of which the human frame is capable. Nature in this case treats them exactly as Sparta treated the children of her citizens: those who come well formed into the world she renders strong and robust, and all the rest she destroys; differing in this respect from our modern communities, in which the State, by making children a burden to their parents, kills them indiscriminately before they are born.

The body of a savage man being the only instrument he understands, he uses it for various purposes, of which ours, for want of practice, are incapable: for our industry deprives us of that force and agility, which necessity obliges him to acquire. If he had had an axe, would he have been able with his naked arm to break so large a branch from a tree? If he had had a sling, would he have been able to throw a stone with so great velocity? If he had had a ladder, would he have been so nimble in climbing a tree? If he had had a horse, would he have been himself so swift of foot? Give civilised man time to gather all his machines about him, and he will no doubt easily beat the savage; but if you would see a still more unequal contest, set them together naked and unarmed, and you will soon see the advantage of having all our forces constantly at our disposal, of being always prepared for every event, and of carrying one's self, as it were, perpetually whole and entire about one.

Hobbes contends that man is naturally intrepid, and is intent only upon attacking and fighting. Another illustrious philosopher holds the opposite, and Cumberland and Puffendorf also affirm that nothing is more timid and fearful than man in the state of nature; that he is always in a tremble, and ready to fly at the least noise or the slightest movement. This may be true of things he does not know; and I do not doubt his being terrified by every novelty that presents itself, when he neither knows the physical good or evil he may expect from it, nor can make a comparison between his own strength and the dangers he is about to encounter. Such circumstances, however, rarely occur in a state of nature, in which all things proceed in a uniform manner, and the face of the earth is not subject to those sudden and continual changes which arise from the passions and caprices of bodies of men living together. But savage man, living dispersed among other animals, and finding himself betimes in a situation to measure his strength with theirs, soon comes to compare himself with them; and, perceiving that he surpasses them more in adroitness than they surpass him in strength, learns to be no longer afraid of them. Set a bear, or a wolf, against a robust, agile, and resolute savage, as they all are, armed with stones and a good cudgel, and you will see that the danger will be at least on both sides, and that, after a few trials of this kind, wild beasts, which are not fond of attacking each other, will not be at all ready to attack man, whom they will have found to be as wild and ferocious as themselves. With regard to such animals as have really more strength than man has adroitness, he is in the same situation as all weaker animals, which notwithstanding are still able to subsist; except indeed that he has the advantage that, being equally swift of foot, and finding an almost certain place of refuge in every tree, he is at liberty to take or leave it at every encounter, and thus to fight or fly, as he chooses. Add to this that it does not appear that any animal naturally makes war on man, except in case of self-defence or excessive hunger, or betrays any of those violent antipathies, which seem to indicate that one species is intended by nature for the food of another.

This is doubtless why negroes and savages are so little afraid of the wild beasts they may meet in the woods. The Caraibs of Venezuela among others live in this respect in absolute security and without the smallest inconvenience. Though they are almost naked, Francis Corréal tells us, they expose themselves freely in the woods, armed only with bows and arrows; but no one has ever heard of one of them being devoured by wild beasts.

But man has other enemies more formidable, against which is is not provided with such means of defence: these are the natural infirmities of infancy, old age, and illness of every kind, melancholy proofs of our weakness, of which the two first are common to all animals, and the last belongs chiefly to man in a state of society. With regard to infancy, it is observable that the mother, carrying her child always with her, can nurse it with much greater ease than the females of many other animals, which are forced to be perpetually going and coming, with great fatigue, one way to find subsistence, and another to suckle or feed their young. It is true that if the woman happens to perish, the infant is in great danger of perishing with her; but this risk is common to many other species of animals, whose young take a long time before they are able to provide for themselves. And if our infancy is longer than theirs, our lives are longer in proportion; so that all things are in this respect fairly equal; though there are other rules to be considered regarding the duration of the first period of life, and the number of young, which do not affect the present subject. In old age, when men are less active and perspire little, the need for food diminishes with the ability to provide it. As the savage state also protects them from gout and rheumatism, and old age is, of all ills, that which human aid can least alleviate, they cease to be, without others perceiving that they are no more, and almost without perceiving it themselves.

With respect to sickness, I shall not repeat the vain and false declamations which most healthy people pronounce against medicine; but I shall ask if any solid observations have been made from which it may be justly concluded that, in the countries where the art of medicine is most neglected, the mean duration of man's life is less than in those where it is most cultivated. How indeed can this be the case, if we bring on ourselves more diseases than medicine can furnish remedies? The great inequality in manner of living, the extreme idleness of some, and the excessive labour of others, the easiness of exciting and gratifying our sensual appetites, the too exquisite foods of the wealthy which overheat and fill them with indigestion, and, on the other hand, the unwholesome food of the poor, often, bad as it is, insufficient for their needs, which induces them, when opportunity offers, to eat voraciously and overcharge their stomachs; all these, together with sitting up late, and excesses of every kind, immoderate transports of every passion, fatigue, mental exhaustion, the innumerable pains and anxieties inseparable from every condition of life, by which the mind of man is incessantly tormented; these are too fatal proofs that the greater part of our ills are of our own making, and that we might have avoided them nearly all by adhering to that simple, uniform and solitary manner of life which nature prescribed. If she destined man to be healthy, I venture to declare that a state of reflection is a state contrary to nature, and that a thinking man is a depraved animal. When we think of the good constitution of the savages, at least of those whom we have not ruined with our spirituous liquors, and reflect that they are troubled with hardly any disorders, save wounds and old age, we are tempted to believe that, in following the history of civil society, we shall be telling also that of human sickness. Such, at least, was the opinion of Plato, who inferred from certain remedies prescribed, or approved, by Podalirius and Machaon at the siege of Troy, that several sicknesses which these remedies gave rise to in his time, were not then known to mankind: and Celsus tells us that diet, which is now so necessary, was first invented by Hippocrates.

Being subject therefore to so few causes of sickness, man, in the state of nature, can have no need of remedies, and still less of physicians: nor is the human race in this respect worse off than other animals, and it is easy to learn from hunters whether they meet with many infirm animals in the course of the chase. It is certain they frequently meet with such as carry the marks of having been considerably wounded, with many that have had bones or even limbs broken, yet have been healed without any other surgical assistance than that of time, or any other regimen than that of their ordinary life. At the same time their cures seem not to have been less perfect, for their not having been tortured by incisions, poisoned with drugs, or wasted by fasting. In short, however useful medicine, properly administered, may be among us, it is certain that, if the savage, when he is sick and left to himself, has nothing to hope but from nature, he has, on the other hand, nothing to fear but from his disease; which renders his situation often preferable to our own.

We should beware, therefore, of confounding the savage man with the men we have daily before our eyes. Nature treats all the animals left to her care with a predilection that seems to show how jealous she is of that right. The horse, the cat, the bull, and even the ass are generally of greater stature, and always more robust, and have more vigour, strength and courage, when they run wild in the forests than when bred in the stall. By becoming domesticated, they lose half these advantages; and it seems as if all our care to feed and treat them well serves only to deprave them. It is thus with man also: as he becomes sociable and a slave, he grows weak, timid and servile; his effeminate way of life totally enervates his strength and courage. To this it may be added that there is still a greater difference between savage and civilised man, than between wild and tame beasts: for men and brutes having been treated alike by nature, the several conveniences in which men indulge themselves still more than they do their beasts, are so many additional causes of their deeper degeneracy.

It is not therefore so great a misfortune to these primitive men, nor so great an obstacle to their preservation, that they go naked, have no dwellings and lack all the superfluities which we think so necessary. If their skins are not covered with hair, they have no need of such covering in warm climates; and, in cold countries, they soon learn to appropriate the skins of the beasts they have overcome. If they have but two legs to run with, they have two arms to defend themselves with, and provide for their wants. Their children are slowly and with difficulty taught to walk; but their mothers are able to carry them with ease; an advantage which other animals lack, as the mother, if pursued, is forced either to abandon her young, or to regulate her pace by theirs. Unless, in short, we suppose a singular and fortuitous concurrence of circumstances of which I shall speak later, and which would be unlikely to exist, it is plain in every state of the case, that the man who first made himself clothes or a dwelling was furnishing himself with things not at all necessary; for he had till then done without them, and there is no reason why he should not have been able to put up in manhood with the same kind of life as had been his in infancy.

Solitary, indolent, and perpetually accompanied by danger, the savage cannot but be fond of sleep; his sleep too must be light, like that of the animals, which think but little and may be said to slumber all the time they do not think. Self-preservation being his chief and almost sole concern, he must exercise most those faculties which are most concerned with attack or defence, either for overcoming his prey, or for preventing him from becoming the prey of other animals. On the other hand, those organs which are perfected only by softness and sensuality will remain in a gross and imperfect state, incompatible with any sort of delicacy; so that, his senses being divided on this head, his touch and taste will be extremely coarse, his sight, hearing and smell exceedingly fine and subtle. Such in general is the animal condition, and such, according to the narratives of travellers, is that of most savage nations. It is therefore no matter for surprise that the Hottentots of the Cape of Good Hope distinguish ships at sea, with the naked eye, at as great a distance as the Dutch can do with their telescopes; or that the savages of America should trace the Spaniards, by their smell, as well as the best dogs could have done; or that these barbarous peoples feel no pain in going naked, or that they use large quantities of piemento with their food, and drink the strongest European liquors like water.

Hitherto I have considered merely the physical man; let us now take a view of him on his metaphysical and moral side.

I see nothing in any animal but an ingenious machine, to which nature hath given senses to wind itself up, and to guard itself, to a certain degree, against anything that might tend to disorder or destroy it. I perceive exactly the same things in the human machine, with this difference, that in the operations of the brute, nature is the sole agent, whereas man has some share in his own operations, in his character as a free agent. The one chooses and refuses by instinct, the other from an act of free-will: hence the brute cannot deviate from the rule prescribed to it, even when it would be advantageous for it to do so; and, on the contrary, man frequently deviates from such rules to his own prejudice. Thus a pigeon would be starved to death by the side of a dish of the choicest meats, and a cat on a heap of fruit or grain; though it is certain that either might find nourishment in the foods which it thus rejects with disdain, did it think of trying them. Hence it is that dissolute men run into excesses which bring on fevers and death; because the mind depraves the senses, and the will continues to speak when nature is silent.

Every animal has ideas, since it has senses; it even combines those ideas in a certain degree; and it is only in degree that man differs, in this respect, from the brute. Some philosophers have even maintained that there is a greater difference between one man and another than between some men and some beasts. It is not, therefore, so much the understanding that constitutes the specific difference between the man and the brute, as the human quality of free-agency. Nature lays her commands on every animal, and the brute obeys her voice. Man receives the same impulsion, but at the same time knows himself at liberty to acquiesce or resist: and it is particularly in his consciousness of this liberty that the spirituality of his soul is displayed. For physics may explain, in some measure, the mechanism of the senses and the formation of ideas; but in the power of willing or rather of choosing, and in the feeling of this power, nothing is to be found but acts which are purely spiritual and wholly inexplicable by the laws of mechanism.

However, even if the difficulties attending all these questions should still leave room for difference in this respect between men and brutes, there is another very specific quality which distinguishes them, and which will admit of no dispute. This is the faculty of self-improvement, which, by the help of circumstances, gradually develops all the rest of our faculties, and is inherent in the species as in the individual: whereas a brute is, at the end of a few months, all he will ever be during his whole life, and his species, at the end of a thousand years, exactly what it was the first year of that thousand. Why is man alone liable to grow into a dotard? Is it not because he returns, in this, to his primitive state; and that, while the brute, which has acquired nothing and has therefore nothing to lose, still retains the force of instinct, man, who loses, by age or accident, all that his *perfectibility* had enabled him to gain, falls by this means lower than the brutes themselves? It would be melancholy, were we forced to admit that this distinctive and almost unlimited faculty is the source of all human misfortunes; that it is this which, in time, draws man out of his original state, in which he would have spent his days insensibly in peace and innocence; that it is

this faculty, which, successively producing in different ages his discoveries and his errors, his vices and his virtues, makes him at length a tyrant both over himself and over nature.[1] It would be shocking to be obliged to regard as a benefactor the man who first suggested to the Oroonoko Indians the use of the boards they apply to the temples of their children, which secure to them some part at least of their imbecility and original happiness.

Savage man, left by nature solely to the direction of instinct, or rather indemnified for what he may lack by faculties capable at first of supplying its place, and afterwards of raising him much above it, must accordingly begin with purely animal functions: thus seeing and feeling must be his first condition, which would be common to him and all other animals. To will, and not to will, to desire and to fear, must be the first, and almost the only operations of his soul, till new circumstances occasion new developments of his faculties.

Whatever moralists may hold, the human understanding is greatly indebted to the passions, which, it is universally allowed, are also much indebted to the understanding. It is by the activity of the passions that our reason is improved; for we desire knowledge only because we wish to enjoy; and it is impossible to conceive any reason why a person who has neither fears nor desires should give himself the trouble of reasoning. The passions, again, originate in our wants, and their progress depends on that of our knowledge; for we cannot desire or fear anything, except from the idea we have of it, or from the simple impulse of nature. Now savage man, being destitute of every species of intelligence, can have no passions save those of the latter kind: his desires never go beyond his physical wants. The only goods he recognises in the universe are food, a female, and sleep: the only evils he fears are pain and hunger. I say pain, and not death: for no animal can know what it is to die; the knowledge of death and its terrors being one of the first acquisitions made by man in departing from an animal state.

It would be easy, were it necessary, to support this opinion by facts, and to show that, in all the nations of the world, the progress of the understanding has been exactly proportionate to the wants which the peoples had received from nature, or been subjected to by circumstances, and in consequence to the passions that induced them to provide for those

[1] See Appendix, p. 363.

necessities. I might instance the arts, rising up in Egypt and expanding with the inundation of the Nile. I might follow their progress into Greece, where they took root afresh, grew up and towered to the skies, among the rocks and sands of Attica, without being able to germinate on the fertile banks of the Eurotas: I might observe that in general, the people of the North are more industrious than those of the South, because they cannot get on so well without being so: as if nature wanted to equalise matters by giving their understandings the fertility she had refused to their soil.

But who does not see, without recurring to the uncertain testimony of history, that everything seems to remove from savage man both the temptation and the means of changing his condition? His imagination paints no pictures; his heart makes no demands on him. His few wants are so readily supplied, and he is so far from having the knowledge which is needful to make him want more, that he can have neither foresight nor curiosity. The face of nature becomes indifferent to him as it grows familiar. He sees in it always the same order, the same successions: he has not understanding enough to wonder at the greatest miracles; nor is it in his mind that we can expect to find that philosophy man needs, if he is to know how to notice for once what he sees every day. His soul, which nothing disturbs, is wholly wrapped up in the feeling of its present existence, without any idea of the future, however near at hand; while his projects, as limited as his views, hardly extend to the close of day. Such, even at present, is the extent of the native Caribbean's foresight: he will improvidently sell you his cotton-bed in the morning, and come crying in the evening to buy it again, not having foreseen he would want it again the next night.

The more we reflect on this subject, the greater appears the distance between pure sensation and the most simple knowledge: it is impossible indeed to conceive how a man, by his own powers alone, without the aid of communication and the spur of necessity, could have bridged so great a gap. How many ages may have elapsed before mankind were in a position to behold any other fire than that of the heavens. What a multiplicity of chances must have happened to teach them the commonest uses of that element! How often must they have let it out before they acquired the art of reproducing it? and how often may not such a secret have died with him who had dis-

covered it? What shall we say of agriculture, an art which requires so much labour and foresight, which is so dependent on others that it is plain it could only be practised in a society which had at least begun, and which does not serve so much to draw the means of subsistence from the earth—for these it would produce of itself—but to compel it to produce what is most to our taste? But let us suppose that men had so multiplied that the natural produce of the earth was no longer sufficient for their support; a supposition, by the way, which would prove such a life to be very advantageous for the human race; let us suppose that, without forges or workshops, the instruments of husbandry had dropped from the sky into the hands of savages; that they had overcome their natural aversion to continual labour; that they had learnt so much foresight for their needs; that they had divined how to cultivate the earth, to sow grain and plant trees; that they had discovered the arts of grinding corn, and of setting the grape to ferment—all being things that must have been taught them by the gods, since it is not to be conceived how they could discover them for themselves—yet after all this, what man among them would be so absurd as to take the trouble of cultivating a field, which might be stripped of its crop by the first comer, man or beast, that might take a liking to it; and how should each of them resolve to pass his life in wearisome labour, when, the more necessary to him the reward of his labour might be, the surer he would be of not getting it? In a word, how could such a situation induce men to cultivate the earth, till it was regularly parcelled out among them; that is to say, till the state of nature had been abolished?

Were we to suppose savage man as trained in the art of thinking as philosophers make him; were we, like them, to suppose him a very philosopher capable of investigating the sublimest truths, and of forming, by highly abstract chains of reasoning, maxims of reason and justice, deduced from the love of order in general, or the known will of his Creator; in a word, were we to suppose him as intelligent and enlightened, as he must have been, and is in fact found to have been, dull and stupid, what advantage would accrue to the species, from all such metaphysics, which could not be communicated by one to another, but must end with him who made them? What progress could be made by mankind, while dispersed in the woods among other animals? and how far could men improve or mutually enlighten one another, when, having no fixed habitation, and no need of one another's assistance, the same persons hardly met twice in their lives, and perhaps then, without knowing one another or speaking together?

Let it be considered how many ideas we owe to the use of speech; how far grammar exercises the understanding and facilitates its operations. Let us reflect on the inconceivable pains and the infinite space of time that the first invention of languages must have cost. To these reflections add what preceded, and then judge how many thousand ages must have elapsed in the successive development in the human mind of those operations of which it is capable.

I shall here take the liberty for a moment, of considering the difficulties of the origin of languages, on which subject I might content myself with a simple repetition of the Abbé Condillac's investigations, as they fully confirm my system, and perhaps even first suggested it. But it is plain, from the manner in which this philosopher solves the difficulties he himself raises, concerning the origin of arbitrary signs, that he assumes what I question, viz., that a kind of society must already have existed among the first inventors of language. While I refer, therefore, to his observations on this head, I think it right to give my own, in order to exhibit the same difficulties in a light adapted to my subject. The first which presents itself is to conceive how language can have become necessary; for as there was no communication among men and no need for any, we can neither conceive the necessity of this invention, nor the possibility of it, if it was not somehow indispensable. I might affirm, with many others, that languages arose in the domestic intercourse between parents and their children. But this expedient would not obviate the difficulty, and would besides involve the blunder made by those who, in reasoning on the state of nature, always import into it ideas gathered in a state of society. Thus they constantly consider families as living together under one roof, and the individuals of each as observing among themselves a union as intimate and permanent as that which exists among us, where so many common interests unite them: whereas, in this primitive state, men had neither houses, nor huts, nor any kind of property whatever; every one lived where he could, seldom for more than a single night; the sexes united without

design, as accident, opportunity or inclination brought them together, nor had they any great need of words to communicate their designs to each other; and they parted with the same indifference. The mother gave suck to her children at first for her own sake; and afterwards, when habit had made them dear, for theirs: but as soon as they were strong enough to go in search of their own food, they forsook her of their own accord; and, as they had hardly any other method of not losing one another than that of remaining continually within sight, they soon became quite incapable of recognising one another when they happened to meet again. It is farther to be observed that the child, having all his wants to explain, and of course more to say to his mother than the mother could have to say to him, must have borne the brunt of the task of invention, and the language he used would be of his own device, so that the number of languages would be equal to that of the individuals speaking them, and the variety would be increased by the vagabond and roving life they led, which would not give time for any idiom to become constant. For to say that the mother dictated to her child the words he was to use in asking her for one thing or another, is an explanation of how languages already formed are taught, but by no means explains how languages were originally formed.

We will suppose, however, that this first difficulty is obviated. Let us for a moment then take ourselves as being on this side of the vast space which must lie between a pure state of nature and that in which languages had become necessary, and, admitting their necessity, let us inquire how they could first be established. Here we have a new and worse difficulty to grapple with; for if men need speech to learn to think, they must have stood in much greater need of the art of thinking, to be able to invent that of speaking. And though we might conceive how the articulate sounds of the voice came to be taken as the conventional interpreters of our ideas, it would still remain for us to inquire what could have been the interpreters of this convention for those ideas, which, answering to no sensible objects, could not be indicated either by gesture or voice; so that we can hardly form any tolerable conjectures about the origin of this art of communicating our thoughts and establishing a correspondence between minds: an art so sublime, that far distant as it is from its origin, philosophers still behold it at such an immeasurable distance from perfection, that there is none rash enough to affirm it will ever reach it, even though the revolutions time necessarily produces were suspended in its favour, though prejudice should be banished from our academies or condemned to silence, and those learned societies should devote themselves uninterruptedly for whole ages to this thorny question.

The first language of mankind, the most universal and vivid, in a word the only language man needed, before he had occasion to exert his eloquence to persuade assembled multitudes, was the simple cry of nature. But as this was excited only by a sort of instinct on urgent occasions, to implore assistance in case of danger, or relief in case of suffering, it could be of little use in the ordinary course of life, in which more moderate feelings prevail. When the ideas of men began to expand and multiply, and closer communication took place among them, they strove to invent more numerous signs and a more copious language. They multiplied the inflections of the voice, and added gestures, which are in their own nature more expressive, and depend less for their meaning on a prior determination. Visible and movable objects were therefore expressed by gestures, and audible ones by imitative sounds: but, as hardly anything can be indicated by gestures, except objects actually present or easily described, and visible actions; as they are not universally useful—for darkness or the interposition of a material object destroys their efficacy—and as besides they rather request than secure our attention; men at length bethought themselves of subsituting for them the articulate sounds of the voice, which, without bearing the same relation to any particular ideas, are better calculated to express them all, as conventional signs. Such an institution could only be made by common consent, and must have been effected in a manner not very easy for men whose gross organs had not been accustomed to any such exercise. It is also in itself still more difficult to conceive, since such a common agreement must have had motives, and speech seems to have been highly necessary to establish the use of it.

It is reasonable to suppose that the words first made use of by mankind had a much more extensive signification than those used in languages already formed, and that ignorant as they were of the division of discourse into its constituent parts, they at first gave every single word the sense of a whole proposition. When they began to distinguish subject and attribute, and noun and verb, which was itself no common effort of genius, substantives were first only so many proper names; the present infinitive was the only tense of verbs; and the very idea of adjectives must have been developed with great difficulty; for every adjective is an abstract idea, and abstractions are painful and unnatural operations.

Every object at first received a particular name without regard to genus or species, which these primitive originators were not in a position to distinguish; every individual presented itself to their minds in isolation, as they are in the picture of nature. If one oak was called A, another was called B; for the primitive idea of two things is that they are not the same, and it often takes a long time for what they have in common to be seen: so that, the narrower the limits of their knowledge of things, the more copious their dictionary must have been. The difficulty of using such a vocabulary could not be easily removed; for, to arrange beings under common and generic denominations, it became necessary to know their distinguishing properties: the need arose for observation and definition, that is to say, for natural history and metaphysics of a far more developed kind than men can at that time have possessed.

Add to this, that general ideas cannot be introduced into the mind without the assistance of words, nor can the understanding seize them except by means of propositions. This is one of the reasons why animals cannot form such ideas, or ever acquire that capacity for self-improvement which depends on them. When a monkey goes from one nut to another, are we to conceive that he entertains any general idea of that kind of fruit, and compares its archetype with the two individual nuts? Assuredly he does not; but the sight of one of these nuts recalls to his memory the sensations which he received from the other, and his eyes, being modified after a certain manner, give information to the palate of the modification it is about to receive. Every general idea is purely intellectual; if the imagination meddles with it ever so little, the idea immediately becomes particular. If you endeavour to trace in your mind the image of a tree in general, you never attain to your end. In spite of all you can do, you will have to see it as great or little, bare or leafy, light or dark, and were you capable of seeing nothing in it but what is common to all trees, it would no longer be like a tree at all. Purely abstract beings are perceivable in the same manner, or are only conceivable by the help of language. The definition of a triangle alone gives you a true idea of it: the moment you imagine a triangle in your mind, it is some particular triangle and not another, and you cannot avoid giving it sensible lines and a coloured area. We must then make use of propositions and of language in order to form general ideas. For no sooner does the imagination cease to operate than the understanding proceeds only by the help of words. If then the first inventors of speech could give names only to ideas they already had, it follows that the first substantives could be nothing more than proper names.

But when our new grammarians, by means of which I have no conception, began to extend their ideas and generalise their terms, the ignorance of the inventors must have confined this method within very narrow limits; and, as they had at first gone too far in multiplying the names of individuals, from ignorance of their genus and species, they made afterwards too few of these, from not having considered beings in all their specific differences. It would indeed have needed more knowledge and experience than they could have, and more pains and inquiry than they would have bestowed, to carry these distinctions to their proper length. If, even to-day, we are continually discovering new species, which have hitherto escaped observation, let us reflect how many of them must have escaped men who judged things merely from their first appearance! It is superfluous to add that the primitive classes and the most general notions must necessarily have escaped their notice also. How, for instance, could they have understood or thought of the words matter, spirit, substance, mode, figure, motion, when even our philosophers, who have so long been making use of them, have themselves the greatest difficulty in understanding them; and when, the ideas attached to them being purely metaphysical, there are no models of them to be found in nature?

But I stop at this point, and ask my judges to suspend their reading a while, to consider, after the invention of physical substantives, which is the easiest part of language to invent, that there is still a great way to go, before the thoughts of men will have found perfect expression and constant form, such as would answer the purposes of public speaking, and produce their effect on society. I beg of them to consider how much time must have been spent, and how much knowledge needed, to find out numbers, abstract terms, aorists and all the tenses of verbs, particles, syntax, the method of connecting propositions, the forms of reasoning, and all the logic of speech. For myself, I am so aghast at the increasing difficulties which present themselves, and so well convinced of the almost demonstrable impossibility that languages should owe their original institution to merely human means, that I leave, to any one who will undertake it, the discussion of the difficult problem, which was most necessary, the existence of society to the invention of language, or the invention of language to the establishment of society. But be the origin of language and society what they may, it may be at least inferred, from the little care which nature has taken to unite mankind by mutual wants, and to facilitate the use of speech, that she has contributed little to make them sociable, and has put little of her own into all they have done to create such bonds of union. It is in fact impossible to conceive why, in a state of nature, one man should stand more in need of the assistance of another, than a monkey or a wolf of the assistance of another of its kind: or, granting that he did, what motives could induce that other to assist him; or, even then, by what means they could agree about the conditions. I know it is incessantly repeated that man would in such a state have been the most miserable of creatures; and indeed, if it be true, as I think I have proved, that he must have lived many ages, before he could have either desire or an opportunity of emerging from it, this would only be an accusation against nature, and not against the being which she had thus unhappily constituted. But as I understand the word *miserable,* it either has no meaning at all, or else signifies only a painful privation of something, or a state of suffering either in body or soul. I should be glad to have explained to me, what kind of misery a free being, whose heart is at ease and whose body is in health, can possibly suffer. I would ask also, whether a social or a natural life is most likely to become insupportable to those who enjoy it. We see around us hardly a creature in civil society, who does not lament his existence: we even see many deprive themselves of as much of it as they can, and laws human and divine together can hardly put a stop to the disorder. I ask, if it was ever known that a savage took it into his head, when at liberty, to complain of life or to make away with himself. Let us therefore judge, with less vanity, on which side the real misery is found. On the other hand, nothing could be more unhappy than savage man, dazzled by science, tormented by his passions, and reasoning about a state different from his own. It appears that Providence most wisely determined that the faculties, which he potentially possessed, should develop themselves only as occasion offered to exercise them, in order that they might not be superfluous or perplexing to him, by appearing before their time, nor slow and useless when the need for them arose. In instinct alone, he had all he required for living in the state of nature; and with a developed understanding he has only just enough to support life in society.

It appears, at first view, that men in a state of nature, having no moral relations or determinate obligations one with another, could not be either good or bad, virtuous or vicious; unless we take these terms in a physical sense, and call, in an individual, those qualities vices which may be injurious to his preservation, and those virtues which contribute to it; in which case, he would have to be accounted most virtuous, who put least check on the pure impulses of nature. But without deviating from the ordinary sense of the words, it will be proper to suspend the judgment we might be led to form on such a state, and be on our guard against our prejudices, till we have weighed the matter in the scales of impartiality, and seen whether virtues or vices preponderate among civilised men; and whether their virtues do them more good than their vices do harm; till we have discovered, whether the progress of the sciences sufficiently indemnifies them for the mischiefs they do one another, in proportion as they are better informed of the good they ought to do; or whether they would not be, on the whole, in a much happier condition if they had nothing to fear or to hope from any one, than as they are, subjected to universal dependence, and obliged to take everything from those who engage to give them nothing in return.

Above all, let us not conclude, with Hobbes, that because man has no idea of goodness, he must be naturally wicked; that he is vicious because he does not know virtue; that he always refuses to do his fellow-creatures services which he does not think they have a right to demand; or that by virtue of the right he truly claims to everything he needs, he foolishly imagines himself the sole proprietor of the whole universe. Hobbes had seen clearly the defects of all the modern definitions of natural right: but the consequences which he deduces from his own show that he understands it in an equally false sense. In reasoning on the principles he lays down, he ought to have said that the state of nature, being that in which the care for our own preservation is the least prejudicial to that of others, was consequently the best calculated to promote peace, and the most suitable for mankind. He does say the exact opposite, in consequence of having improperly admitted, as a part of savage man's care for self-preservation, the gratification of a multitude of passions which are the work of society, and have made laws necessary. A bad man, he says, is a robust child. But it remains to be proved whether man in a state of nature is this robust child: and, should we grant that he is, what would he infer? Why truly, that if this man, when robust and strong, were dependent on others as he is when feeble, there is no extravagance he would not be guilty of; that he would beat his mother when she was too slow in giving him her breast; that he would strangle one of his younger brothers, if he should be troublesome to him, or bite the arm of another, if he put him to any inconvenience. But that man in the state of nature is both strong and dependent involves two contrary suppositions. Man is weak when he is dependent, and is his own master before he comes to be strong. Hobbes did not reflect that the same cause, which prevents a savage from making use of his reason, as our jurists hold, prevents him also from abusing his faculties, as Hobbes himself allows: so that it may be justly said that savages are not bad merely because they do not know what it is to be good: for it is neither the development of the understanding nor the restraint of law that hinders them from doing ill; but the peacefulness of their passions, and their ignorance of vice: *tanto plus in illis proficit vitiorum ignoratio, quam in his cognitio virtutis.*[1]

There is another principle which has escaped Hobbes; which, having been bestowed on mankind, to moderate, on certain occasions, the impetuosity of egoism, or, before its birth, the desire of self-preservation, tempers the ardour with which he pursues his own welfare, by an innate repugnance at seeing a

[1] Justin, *Hist.* ii. 2. So much more does the ignorance of vice profit the one sort than the knowledge of virtue the other.

fellow-creature suffer.[1] I think I need not fear contradiction in holding man to be possessed of the only natural virtue, which could not be denied him by the most violent detractor of human virtue. I am speaking of compassion, which is a disposition suitable to creatures so weak and subject to so many evils as we certainly are: by so much the more universal and useful to mankind, as it comes before any kind of reflection; and at the same time so natural, that the very brutes themselves sometimes give evident proofs of it. Not to mention the tenderness of mothers for their offspring and the perils they encounter to save them from danger, it is well known that horses show a reluctance to trample on living bodies. One animal never passes by the dead body of another of its species: there are even some which give their fellows a sort of burial; while the mournful lowings of the cattle when they enter the slaughter-house show the impressions made on them by the horrible spectacle which meets them. We find, with pleasure, the author of the Fable of the Bees obliged to own that man is a compassionate and sensible being, and laying aside his cold subtlety of style, in the example he gives, to present us with the pathetic description of a man who, from a place of con-

finement, is compelled to behold a wild beast tear a child from the arms of its mother, grinding its tender limbs with its murderous teeth, and tearing its palpitating entrails with its claws. What horrid agitation must not the eyewitness of such a scene experience, although he would not be personally concerned! What anxiety would he not suffer at not being able to give any assistance to the fainting mother and the dying infant!

Such is the pure emotion of nature, prior to all kinds of reflection! Such is the force of natural compassion, which the greatest depravity of morals has as yet hardly been able to destroy! for we daily find at our theatres men affected, nay shedding tears at the sufferings of a wretch who, were he in the tyrant's place, would probably even add to the torments of his enemies; like the bloodthirsty Sulla, who was so sensitive to ills he had not caused, or that Alexander of Pheros who did not dare to go and see any tragedy acted, for fear of being seen weeping with Andromache and Priam, though he could listen without emotion to the cries of all the citizens who were daily strangled at his command.

> *Mollissima corda*
> *Humano generi dare se natura fatetur,*
> *Quæ lacrimas dedit.*
>
> Juvenal, *Satires,* xv. 151[2]

Mandeville well knew that, in spite of all their morality, men would have never been better than monsters, had not nature bestowed on them a sense of compassion, to aid their reason: but he did not see that from this quality alone flow all those social virtues, of which he denied man the possession. But what is generosity, clemency or humanity but compassion applied to the weak, to the guilty, or to mankind in general? Even benevolence and friendship are, if we judge rightly, only the effects of compassion, constantly set upon a particular object: for how is it different to wish that another person may not suffer pain and uneasiness and to wish him happy? Were it even true that pity is no more than a feeling, which puts us in the place of the sufferer, a feeling, obscure yet lively in a savage, developed yet feeble in civilised man; this truth would have no other consequence than to confirm my argument. Compassion must, in fact, be the stronger, the more the animal beholding any kind of distress identifies himself with the animal that

---

[1] Egoism must not be confused with self-respect: for they differ both in themselves and in their effects. Self-respect is a natural feeling which leads every animal to look to its own preservation, and which, guided in man by reason and modified by compassion, creates humanity and virtue. Egoism is a purely relative and factitious feeling, which arises in the state of society, leads each individual to make more of himself than of any other, causes all the mutual damage men inflict one on another, and is the real source of the "sense of honour." This being understood, I maintain that, in our primitive condition, in the true state of nature, egoism did not exist; for as each man regarded himself as the only observer of his actions, the only being in the universe who took any interest in him, and the sole judge of his deserts, no feeling arising from comparisons he could not be led to make could take root in his soul; and for the same reason, he could know neither hatred nor the desire for revenge, since these passions can spring only from a sense of injury: and as it is the contempt or the intention to hurt, and not the harm done, which constitutes the injury, men who neither valued nor compared themselves could do one another much violence, when it suited them, without feeling any sense of injury. In a word, each man, regarding his fellows almost as he regarded animals of different species, might seize the prey of a weaker or yield up his own to a stronger, and yet consider these acts of violence as mere natural occurrences, without the slightest emotion of insolence or despite, or any other feeling than the joy or grief of success or failure.

[2] Nature avows she gave the human race the softest hearts, who gave them tears.

suffers. Now, it is plain that such identification must have been much more perfect in a state of nature than it is in a state of reason. It is reason that engenders self-respect, and reflection that confirms it: it is reason which turns man's mind back upon itself, and divides him from everything that could disturb or afflict him. It is philosophy that isolates him, and bids him say, at sight of the misfortunes of others: "Perish if you will, I am secure." Nothing but such general evils as threaten the whole community can disturb the tranquil sleep of the philosopher, or tear him from his bed. A murder may with impunity be committed under his window; he has only to put his hands to his ears and argue a little with himself, to prevent nature, which is shocked within him, from identifying itself with the unfortunate sufferer. Uncivilised man has not this admirable talent; and for want of reason and wisdom, is always foolishly ready to obey the first promptings of humanity. It is the populace that flocks together at riots and street-brawls, while the wise man prudently makes off. It is the mob and the market-women, who part the combatants, and hinder gentle-folks from cutting one another's throats.

It is then certain that compassion is a natural feeling, which, by moderating the violence of love of self in each individual, contributes to the preservation of the whole species. It is this compassion that hurries us without reflection to the relief of those who are in distress: it is this which in a state of nature supplies the place of laws, morals and virtues, with the advantage that none are tempted to disobey its gentle voice: it is this which will always prevent a sturdy savage from robbing a weak child or a feeble old man of the sustenance they may have with pain and difficulty acquired, if he sees a possibility of providing for himself by other means: it is this which, instead of inculcating that sublime maxim of rational justice, *Do to others as you would have them do unto you,* inspires all men with that other maxim of natural goodness, much less perfect indeed, but perhaps more useful; *Do good to yourself with as little evil as possible to others.* In a word, it is rather in this natural feeling than in any subtle arguments that we must look for the cause of that repugnance, which every man would experience in doing evil, even independently of the maxims of education. Although it might belong to Socrates and other minds of the like craft to acquire virtue by reason, the human race would

long since have ceased to be, had its preservation depended only on the reasonings of the individuals composing it.

With passions so little active, and so good a curb, men, being rather wild than wicked, and more intent to guard themselves against the mischief that might be done them, than to do mischief to others, were by no means subject to very perilous dissensions. They maintained no kind of intercourse with one another, and were consequently strangers to vanity, deference, esteem and contempt; they had not the least idea of *meum* and *tuum,* and no true conception of justice; they looked upon every violence to which they were subjected, rather as an injury that might easily be repaired than as a crime that ought to be punished; and they never thought of taking revenge, unless perhaps mechanically and on the spot, as a dog will sometimes bite the stone which is thrown at him. Their quarrels therefore would seldom have very bloody consequences; for the subject of them would be merely the question of subsistence. But I am aware of one greater danger, which remains to be noticed.

Of the passions that stir the heart of man, there is one which makes the sexes necessary to each other, and is extremely ardent and impetuous; a terrible passion that braves danger, surmounts all obstacles, and in its transports seems calculated to bring destruction on the human race which it is really destined to preserve. What must become of men who are left to this brutal and boundless rage, without modesty, without shame, and daily upholding their amours at the price of their blood?

It must, in the first place, be allowed that, the more violent the passions are, the more are laws necessary to keep them under restraint. But, setting aside the inadequacy of laws to effect this purpose, which is evident from the crimes and disorders to which these passions daily give rise among us, we should do well to inquire if these evils did not spring up with the laws themselves; for in this case, even if the laws were capable of repressing such evils, it is the least that could be expected from them, that they should check a mischief which would not have arisen without them.

Let us begin by distinguishing between the physical and moral ingredients in the feeling of love. The physical part of love is that general desire which urges the sexes to union with each other. The moral part is that which determines and fixes this desire exclusively upon one particular object; or at least gives it a greater degree of energy toward the object thus preferred. It is easy to see that the moral part of love is a factitious feeling, born of social usage, and enhanced by the women with much care and cleverness, to establish their empire, and put in power the sex which ought to obey. This feeling, being founded on certain ideas of beauty and merit which a savage is not in a position to acquire, and on comparisons which he is incapable of making, must be for him almost non-existent; for, as his mind cannot form abstract ideas of proportion and regularity, so his heart is not susceptible of the feelings of love and admiration, which are even insensibly produced by the application of these ideas. He follows solely the character nature has implanted in him, and not tastes which he could never have acquired; so that every woman equally answers his purpose.

Men in a state of nature being confined merely to what is physical in love, and fortunate enough to be ignorant of those excellences, which whet the appetite while they increase the difficulty of gratifying it, must be subject to fewer and less violent fits of passion, and consequently fall into fewer and less violent disputes. The imagination, which causes such ravages among us, never speaks to the heart of savages, who quietly await the impulses of nature, yield to them involuntarily, with more pleasure than ardour, and, their wants once satisfied, lose the desire. It is therefore incontestable that love, as well as all other passions, must have acquired in society that glowing impetuosity, which makes it so often fatal to mankind. And it is the more absurd to represent savages as continually cutting one another's throats to indulge their brutality, because this opinion is directly contrary to experience; the Caribbeans, who have as yet least of all deviated from the state of nature, being in fact the most peaceable of people in their amours, and the least subject to jealousy, though they live in a hot climate which seems always to inflame the passions.

With regard to the inferences that might be drawn, in the case of several species of animals, the males of which fill our poultry-yards with blood and slaughter, or in spring make the forests resound with their quarrels over their females; we must begin by excluding all those species, in which nature has plainly established, in the comparative power of the sexes, relations different from those which exist among us: thus we can base no conclusion

about men on the habits of fighting cocks. In those species where the proportion is better observed, these battles must be entirely due to the scarcity of females in comparison with males; or, what amounts to the same thing, to the intervals during which the female constantly refuses the advances of the male: for if each female admits the male but during two months in the year, it is the same as if the number of females were five-sixths less. Now, neither of these two cases is applicable to the human species, in which the number of females usually exceeds that of males, and among whom it has never been observed, even among savages, that the females have, like those of other animals, their stated times of passion and indifference. Moreover, in several of these species, the individuals all take fire at once, and there comes a fearful moment of universal passion, tumult and disorder among them; a scene which is never beheld in the human species, whose love is not thus seasonal. We must not then conclude from the combats of such animals for the enjoyment of the females, that the case would be the same with mankind in a state of nature: and, even if we drew such a conclusion, we see that such contests do not exterminate other kinds of animals, and we have no reason to think they would be more fatal to ours. It is indeed clear that they would do still less mischief than is the case in a state of society; especially in those countries in which, morals being still held in some repute, the jealousy of lovers and the vengeance of husbands are the daily cause of duels, murders, and even worse crimes; where the obligation of eternal fidelity only occasions adultery, and the very laws of honour and continence necessarily increase debauchery and lead to the multiplication of abortions.

Let us conclude then that man in a state of nature, wandering up and down the forests, without industry, without speech, and without home, an equal stranger to war and to all ties, neither standing in need of his fellow-creatures nor having any desire to hurt them, and perhaps even not distinguishing them one from another; let us conclude that, being self-sufficient and subject to so few passions, he could have no feelings or knowledge but such as befitted his situation; that he felt only his actual necessities, and disregarded everything he did not think himself immediately concerned to notice, and that his understanding made no greater progress than his vanity. If by accident he made any discovery, he was the less able to communicate it to others, as he did not know even his own children. Every art would necessarily perish with its inventor, where there was no kind of education among men, and generations succeeded generations without the least advance; when, all setting out from the same point, centuries must have elapsed in the barbarism of the first ages; when the race was already old, and man remained a child.

If I have expatiated at such length on this supposed primitive state, it is because I had so many ancient errors and inveterate prejudices to eradicate, and therefore thought it incumbent on me to dig down to their very root, and show, by means of a true picture of the state of nature, how far even the natural inequalities of mankind are from having that reality and influence which modern writers suppose.

It is in fact easy to see that many of the differences which distinguish men are merely the effect of habit and the different methods of life men adopt in society. Thus a robust or delicate constitution, and the strength or weakness attaching to it, are more frequently the effects of a hardy or effeminate method of education than of the original endowment of the body. It is the same with the powers of the mind; for education not only makes a difference between such as are cultured and such as are not, but even increases the differences which exist among the former, in proportion to their respective degrees of culture: as the distance between a giant and a dwarf on the same road increases with every step they take. If we compare the prodigious diversity, which obtains in the education and manner of life of the various orders of men in the state of society, with the uniformity and simplicity of animal and savage life, in which every one lives on the same kind of food and in exactly the same manner, and does exactly the same things, it is easy to conceive how much less the difference between man and man must be in a state of nature than in a state of society, and how greatly the natural inequality of mankind must be increased by the inequalities of social institutions.

But even if nature really affected, in the distribution of her gifts, that partiality which is imputed to her, what advantage would the greatest of her favourites derive from it, to the detriment of others, in a state that admits of hardly any kind of relation between them? Where there is no love, of what advantage is beauty? Of what use is wit to those who do not converse, or cunning to those who have no business with others? I hear it constantly repeated that, in such a state, the strong would oppress the weak; but what is here meant by oppression? Some, it is said, would violently domineer over others, who would groan under a servile submission to their caprices. This indeed is exactly what I observe to be the case among us; but I do not see how it can be inferred of men in a state of nature, who could not easily be brought to conceive what we mean by dominion and servitude. One man, it is true, might seize the fruits which another had gathered, the game he had killed, or the cave he had chosen for shelter; but how would he ever be able to exact obedience, and what ties of dependence could there be among men without possessions? If, for instance, I am driven from one tree, I can go to the next; if I am disturbed in one place, what hinders me from going to another? Again, should I happen to meet with a man so much stronger than myself, and at the same time so depraved, so indolent, and so barbarous, as to compel me to provide for his sustenance while he himself remains idle; he must take care not to have his eyes off me for a single moment; he must bind me fast before he goes to sleep, or I shall certainly either knock him on the head or make my escape. That is to say, he must in such a case voluntarily expose himself to much greater trouble than he seeks to avoid, or can give me. After all this, let him be off his guard ever so little; let him but turn his head aside at any sudden noise, and I shall be instantly twenty paces off, lost in the forest, and, my fetters burst asunder, he would never see me again.

Without my expatiating thus uselessly on these details, every one must see that as the bonds of servitude are formed merely by the mutual dependence of men on one another and the reciprocal needs that unite them, it is impossible to make any man a slave, unless he be first reduced to a situation in which he cannot do without the help of others: and, since such a situation does not exist in a state of nature, every one is there his own master, and the law of the strongest is of no effect.

Having proved that the inequality of mankind is hardly felt, and that its influence is next to nothing in a state of nature, I must next show its origin and trace its progress in the successive developments of the human mind. Having shown that human *perfectibility,* the social virtues, and the other faculties which natural man potentially possessed, could never develop of themselves, but must require the fortuitous concurrence of many foreign causes that might never arise, and without which he would have remained for ever in his primitive condition, I must now collect and consider the different accidents which may have improved the human understanding while depraving the species, and made man wicked while making him sociable; so as to bring him and the world from that distant period to the point at which we now behold them.

I confess that, as the events I am going to describe might have happened in various ways, I have nothing to determine my choice but conjectures: but such conjectures become reasons, when they are the most probable that can be drawn from the nature of things, and the only means of discovering the truth. The consequences, however, which I mean to deduce will not be barely conjectural; as, on the principles just laid down, it would be impossible to form any other theory that would not furnish the same results, and from which I could not draw the same conclusions.

This will be a sufficient apology for my not dwelling on the manner in which the lapse of time compensates for the little probability in the events; on the surprising power of trivial causes, when their action is constant; on the impossibility, on the one hand, of destroying certain hypotheses, though on the other we cannot give them the certainty of known matters of fact; on its being within the province of history, when two facts are given as real, and have to be connected by a series of intermediate facts, which are unknown or supposed to be so, to supply such facts as may connect them; and on its being in the province of philosophy when history is silent, to determine similar facts to serve the same end; and lastly, on the influence of similarity, which, in the case of events, reduces the facts to a much smaller number of different classes than is commonly imagined. It is enough for me to offer these hints to the consideration of my judges, and to have so arranged that the general reader has no need to consider them at all.

THE SECOND PART

THE first man who, having enclosed a piece of ground, bethought himself of saying *This is mine,* and found people simple enough to believe him, was the real founder of civil society. From how many crimes, wars and murders, from how many horrors and misfortunes might not any one have saved mankind, by pulling up the stakes, or filling up the ditch, and crying to his fellows, "Beware of listening to this impostor; you are undone if you once forget that the fruits of the earth belong to us all, and the earth itself to nobody." But there is great probability that things had then already come to such a pitch, that they could no longer continue as they were; for the idea of property depends on many prior ideas, which could only be acquired successively, and cannot have been formed all at once in the human mind. Mankind must have made very considerable progress, and acquired considerable knowledge and industry which they must also have transmitted and increased from age to age, before they arrived at this last point of the state of nature. Let us then go farther back, and endeavour to unify under a single point of view that slow succession of events and discoveries in the most natural order.

Man's first feeling was that of his own existence, and his first care that of self-preservation. The produce of the earth furnished him with all he needed, and instinct told him how to use it. Hunger and other appetites made him at various times experience various modes of existence; and among these was one which urged him to propagate his species—a blind propensity that, having nothing to do with the heart, produced a merely animal act. The want once gratified, the two sexes knew each other no more; and even the offspring was nothing to its mother, as soon as it could do without her.

Such was the condition of infant man; the life of an animal limited at first to mere sensations, and hardly profiting by the gifts nature bestowed on him, much less capable of entertaining a thought of forcing anything from her. But difficulties soon presented themselves, and it became necessary to learn how to surmount them: the height of the trees, which prevented him from gathering their fruits, the competition of other animals desirous of the same fruits, and the ferocity of those who needed them for their own preservation, all obliged him to apply himself to bodily exercises. He had to be active, swift of foot, and vigorous in fight. Natural weapons, stones and sticks, were easily found: he learnt to surmount the obstacles of nature, to contend in case of necessity with other animals, and to dispute for the means of subsistence even with other men, or to indemnify himself for what he was forced to give up to a stronger.

In proportion as the human race grew more numerous, men's cares increased. The difference of soils, climates and seasons, must have introduced some differences into their manner of living. Barren years, long and sharp winters, scorching summers which parched the fruits of the earth, must have demanded a new industry. On the seashore and the banks of rivers, they invented the hook and line, and became fishermen and eaters of fish. In the forests they made bows and arrows, and became huntsmen and warriors. In cold countries they clothed themselves with the skins of the beasts they had slain. The lightning, a volcano, or some lucky chance acquainted them with fire, a new resource against the rigours of winter: they next learned how to preserve this element, then how to reproduce it, and finally how to prepare with it the flesh of animals which before they had eaten raw.

This repeated relevance of various beings to himself, and one to another, would naturally give rise in the human mind to the perceptions of certain relations between them. Thus the relations which we denote by the terms, great, small, strong, weak, swift, slow, fearful, bold, and the like, almost insensibly compared at need, must have at length produced in him a kind of reflection, or rather a mechanical prudence, which would indicate to him the precautions most necessary to his security.

The new intelligence which resulted from this development increased his superiority over other animals, by making him sensible of it. He would now endeavour, therefore, to ensnare them, would play them a thousand tricks, and though many of them might surpass him in swiftness or in strength, would in time become the master of some and the scourge of others. Thus, the first time he looked into himself, he felt the first emotion of pride; and, at a time when he scarce knew how to distinguish the different orders of beings, by looking upon his species as of the highest order, he prepared the way for assuming pre-eminence as an individual.

Other men, it is true, were not then to him what they now are to us, and he had no greater intercourse with them than with other animals; yet they were not neglected in his observations. The conformities, which he would in time discover between them, and between himself and his female, led him to judge of others which were not then perceptible; and finding that they all behaved as he himself would have done in like circumstances, he naturally inferred that their manner of thinking and acting was altogether in conformity with his own. This important truth, once deeply impressed on his mind, must have induced him, from an intuitive feeling more certain and much more rapid than any kind of reasoning, to pursue the rules of conduct, which he had best observe towards them, for his own security and advantage.

Taught by experience that the love of well-being is the sole motive of human actions, he found himself in a position to distinguish the few cases, in which mutual interest might justify him in relying upon the assistance of his fellows; and also the still fewer cases in which a conflict of interests might give cause to suspect them. In the former case, he joined in the same herd with them, or at most in some kind of loose association, that laid no restraint on its members, and lasted no longer than the transitory occasion that formed it. In the latter case, every one sought his own private advantage, either by open force, if he thought himself strong enough, or by address and cunning, if he felt himself the weaker.

In this manner, men may have insensibly acquired some gross ideas of mutual undertakings, and of the advantages of fulfilling them: that is, just so far as their present and apparent interest was concerned: for they were perfect strangers to foresight, and were so far from troubling themselves about the distant future, that they hardly thought of the morrow. If a deer was to be taken, every one saw that, in order to succeed, he must abide faithfully by his post: but if a hare happened to come within the reach of any one of them, it is not to be doubted that he pursued it without scruple, and, having seized his prey, cared very little, if by so doing he caused his companions to miss theirs.

It is easy to understand that such intercourse would not require a language much more refined than that of rooks or monkeys, who associate together for much the same purpose. Inarticulate cries, plenty of gestures and some imitative sounds, must have been for a long time the universal language; and by the addition, in every country, of some conventional articulate sounds (of which, as I have already intimated, the first institution is not too easy to explain) particular languages were produced; but these were rude and imperfect, and nearly such as are now to be found among some savage nations.

Hurried on by the rapidity of time, by the abundance of things I have to say, and by the almost insensible progress of things in their beginnings, I pass over in an instant a multitude of ages; for the slower the events were in their succession, the more rapidly may they be described.

These first advances enabled men to make others with greater rapidity. In proportion as they grew enlightened, they grew industrious. They ceased to fall asleep under the first tree, or in the first cave that afforded them shelter; they invented several kinds of implements of hard and sharp stones, which they used to dig up the earth, and to cut wood; they then made huts out of branches, and afterwards learnt to plaster them over with mud and clay. This was the epoch of a first revolution, which established and distinguished families, and introduced a kind of property, in itself the source of a thousand quarrels and conflicts. As, however, the strongest were probably the first to build themselves huts which they felt themselves able to defend, it may be concluded that the weak found it much easier and safer to imitate, than to attempt to dislodge them: and of those who were once provided with huts, none could have any inducement to appropriate that of his neighbour; not indeed so much because it did not belong to him, as because it could be of no use, and he could not make himself master of it without exposing himself to a desperate battle with the family which occupied it.

The first expansions of the human heart were the effects of a novel situation, which united husbands and wives, fathers and children, under one roof. The habit of living together soon gave rise to the finest feelings known to humanity, conjugal love and paternal affection. Every family became a little society, the more united because liberty and reciprocal attachment were the only bonds of its union. The sexes, whose manner of life had been hitherto the same, began now to adopt different ways of living. The women became

more sedentary, and accustomed themselves to mind the hut and their children, while the men went abroad in search of their common subsistence. From living a softer life, both sexes also began to lose something of their strength and ferocity: but, if individuals became to some extent less able to encounter wild beasts separately, they found it, on the other hand, easier to assemble and resist in common.

The simplicity and solitude of man's life in this new condition, the paucity of his wants, and the implements he had invented to satisfy them, left him a great deal of leisure, which he employed to furnish himself with many conveniences unknown to his fathers: and this was the first yoke he inadvertently imposed on himself, and the first source of the evils he prepared for his descendants. For, besides continuing thus to enervate both body and mind, these conveniences lost with use almost all their power to please, and even degenerated into real needs, till the want of them became far more disagreeable than the possession of them had been pleasant. Men would have been unhappy at the loss of them, though the possession did not make them happy.

We can here see a little better how the use of speech became established, and insensibly improved in each family, and we may form a conjecture also concerning the manner in which various causes may have extended and accelerated the progress of language, by making it more and more necessary. Floods or earthquakes surrounded inhabited districts with precipices or waters: revolutions of the globe tore off portions from the continent, and made them islands. It is readily seen that among men thus collected and compelled to live together, a common idiom must have arisen much more easily than among those who still wandered through the forests of the continent. Thus it is very possible that after their first essays in navigation the islanders brought over the use of speech to the continent: and it is at least very probable that communities and languages were first established in islands, and even came to perfection there before they were known on the mainland.

Everything now begins to change its aspect. Men, who have up to now been roving in the woods, by taking to a more settled manner of life, come gradually together, form separate bodies, and at length in every country arises a distinct nation, united in character and manners, not by regulations or laws, but by uniformity of life and food, and the common influence of climate. Permanent neighbourhood could not fail to produce, in time, some connection between different families. Among young people of opposite sexes, living in neighbouring huts, the transient commerce required by nature soon led, through mutual intercourse, to another kind not less agreeable, and more permanent. Men began now to take the difference between objects into account, and to make comparisons; they acquired imperceptibly the ideas of beauty and merit, which soon gave rise to feelings of preference. In consequence of seeing each other often, they could not do without seeing each other constantly. A tender and pleasant feeling insinuated itself into their souls, and the least opposition turned it into an impetuous fury: with love arose jealousy; discord triumphed, and human blood was sacrificed to the gentlest of all passions.

As ideas and feelings succeeded one another, and heart and head were brought into play, men continued to lay aside their original wildness; their private connections became every day more intimate as their limits extended. They accustomed themselves to assemble before their huts round a large tree; singing and dancing, the true offspring of love and leisure, became the amusement, or rather the occupation, of men and women thus assembled together with nothing else to do. Each one began to consider the rest, and to wish to be considered in turn; and thus a value came to be attached to public esteem. Whoever sang or danced best, whoever was the handsomest, the strongest, the most dexterous, or the most eloquent, came to be of most consideration; and this was the first step towards inequality, and at the same time towards vice. From these first distinctions arose on the one side vanity and contempt and on the other shame and envy: and the fermentation caused by these new leavens ended by producing combinations fatal to innocence and happiness.

As soon as men began to value one another, and the idea of consideration had got a footing in the mind, every one put in his claim to it, and it became impossible to refuse it to any with impunity. Hence arose the first obligations of civility even among savages; and every intended injury became an affront; because, besides the hurt which might result from it, the party injured was certain to find in it a contempt for his person, which was often more insupportable than the hurt itself.

Thus, as every man punished the contempt shown him by others, in proportion to his opinion of himself, revenge became terrible, and men bloody and cruel. This is precisely the state reached by most of the savage nations known to us: and it is for want of having made a proper distinction in our ideas, and see how very far they already are from the state of nature, that so many writers have hastily concluded that man is naturally cruel, and requires civil institutions to make him more mild; whereas nothing is more gentle than man in his primitive state, as he is placed by nature at an equal distance from the stupidity of brutes, and the fatal ingenuity of civilised man. Equally confined by instinct and reason to the sole care of guarding himself against the mischiefs which threaten him, he is restrained by natural compassion from doing any injury to others, and is not led to do such a thing even in return for injuries received. For, according to the axiom of the wise Locke, *There can be no injury, where there is no property.*

But it must be remarked that the society thus formed, and the relations thus established among men, required of them qualities different from those which they possessed from their primitive constitution. Morality began to appear in human actions, and every one, before the institution of law, was the only judge and avenger of the injuries done him, so that the goodness which was suitable in the pure state of nature was no longer proper in the newborn state of society. Punishments had to be made more severe, as opportunities of offending became more frequent, and the dread of vengeance had to take the place of the rigour of the law. Thus, though men had become less patient, and their natural compassion had already suffered some diminution, this period of expansion of the human faculties, keeping a just mean between the indolence of the primitive state and the petulant activity of our egoism, must have been the happiest and most stable of epochs. The more we reflect on it, the more we shall find that this state was the least subject to revolutions, and altogether the very best man could experience; so that he can have departed from it only through some fatal accident, which, for the public good, should never have happened. The example of savages, most of whom have been found in this state, seems to prove that men were meant to remain in it, that it is the real youth of the world, and that all subsequent advances have been apparently so many steps towards the perfection of the individual, but in reality towards the decrepitude of the species.

So long as men remained content with their rustic huts, so long as they were satisfied with clothes made of the skins of animals and sewn together with thorns and fish-bones, adorned themselves only with feathers and shells, and continued to paint their bodies different colours, to improve and beautify their bows and arrows and to make with sharp-edged stones fishing boats or clumsy musical instruments; in a word, so long as they undertook only what a single person could accomplish, and confined themselves to such arts as did not require the joint labour of several hands, they lived free, healthy, honest and happy lives, so long as their nature allowed, and as they continued to enjoy the pleasures of mutual and independent intercourse. But from the moment one man began to stand in need of the help of another; from the moment it appeared advantageous to any one man to have enough provisions for two, equality disappeared, property was introduced, work became indispensable, and vast forests became smiling fields, which man had to water with the sweat of his brow, and where slavery and misery were soon seen to germinate and grow up with the crops.

Metallurgy and agriculture were the two arts which produced this great revolution. The poets tell us it was gold and silver, but, for the philosophers, it was iron and corn, which first civilised men, and ruined humanity. Thus both were unknown to the savages of America, who for that reason are still savage: the other nations also seem to have continued in a state of barbarism while they practised only one of these arts. One of the best reasons, perhaps, why Europe has been, if not longer, at least more constantly and highly civilised than the rest of the world, is that it is at once the most abundant in iron and the most fertile in corn.

It is difficult to conjecture how men first came to know and use iron; for it is impossible to suppose they would of themselves think of digging the ore out of the mine, and preparing it for smelting, before they knew what would be the result. On the other hand, we have the less reason to suppose this discovery the effect of any accidental fire, as mines are only formed in barren places, bare of trees and plants; so that it looks as if nature had taken pains to keep that fatal secret from us. There remains, therefore, only the extraordinary accident of some volcano which, by ejecting metallic substances already in fusion, suggested to the spectators the idea of imitating the natural operation. And we must further conceive them as possessed of uncommon courage and foresight, to undertake so laborious a work, with so distant a prospect of drawing advantage from it; yet these qualities are united only in minds more advanced than we can suppose those of these first discoverers to have been.

With regard to agriculture, the principles of it were known long before they were put in practice; and it is indeed hardly possible that men, constantly employed in drawing their subsistence from plants and trees, should not readily acquire a knowledge of the means made use of by nature for the propagation of vegetables. It was in all probability very long, however, before their industry took that turn, either because trees, which together with hunting and fishing afforded them food, did not require their attention; or because they were ignorant of the use of corn, or without instruments to cultivate it; or because they lacked foresight to future needs; or lastly, because they were without means of preventing others from robbing them of the fruit of their labour.

When they grew more industrious, it is natural to believe that they began, with the help of sharp stones and pointed sticks, to cultivate a few vegetables or roots around their huts; though it was long before they knew how to prepare corn, or were provided with the implements necessary for raising it in any large quantity; not to mention how essential it is, for husbandry, to consent to immediate loss, in order to reap a future gain—a precaution very foreign to the turn of a savage's mind; for, as I have said, he hardly foresees in the morning what he will need at night.

The invention of the other arts must therefore have been necessary to compel mankind to apply themselves to agriculture. No sooner were artificers wanted to smelt and forge iron, than others were required to maintain them; the more hands that were employed in manufactures, the fewer were left to provide for the common subsistence, though the number of mouths to be furnished with food remained the same: and as some required commodities in exchange for their iron, the rest at length discovered the method of making iron serve for the multiplication of commodities. By this means the arts of husbandry and agriculture were established on the one hand, and the art of working metals and multiplying their uses on the other.

The cultivation of the earth necessarily brought about its distribution; and property, once recognised, gave rise to the first rules of justice; for, to secure each man his own, it had to be possible for each to have something. Besides, as men began to look forward to the future, and all had something to lose, every one had reason to apprehend that reprisals would follow any injury he might do to another. This origin is so much the more natural, as it is impossible to conceive how property can come from anything but manual labour: for what else can a man add to things which he does not originally create, so as to make them his own property? It is the husbandman's labour alone that, giving him a title to the produce of the ground he has tilled, gives him a claim also to the land itself, at least till harvest, and so, from year to year, a constant possession which is easily transformed into property. When the ancients, says Grotius, gave to Ceres the title of Legislatrix, and to a festival celebrated in her honour the name of Thesmophoria, they meant by that that the distribution of lands had produced a new kind of right: that is to say, the right of property, which is different from the right deducible from the law of nature.

In this state of affairs, equality might have been sustained, had the talents of individuals been equal, and had, for example, the use of iron and the consumption of commodities always exactly balanced each other; but, as there was nothing to preserve this balance, it was soon disturbed; the strongest did most work; the most skilful turned his labour to best account; the most ingenious devised methods of diminishing his labour: the husbandman wanted more iron, or the smith more corn, and, while both laboured equally, the one gained a great deal by his work, while the other could hardly support himself. Thus natural inequality unfolds itself insensibly with that of combination, and the difference between men, developed by their different circumstances, becomes more sensible and permanent in its effects, and begins to have an influence, in the same proportion, over the lot of individuals.

Matters once at this pitch, it is easy to imagine the rest. I shall not detain the reader with a description of the successive invention of other arts, the development of language, the trial and utilisation of talents, the inequality of fortunes, the use and abuse of riches, and all the details connected with them which the reader can easily supply for himself. I shall confine myself to a glance at mankind in this new situation.

Behold then all human faculties developed, memory and imagination in full play, egoism interested, reason active, and the mind almost at the highest point of its perfection. Behold all the natural qualities in action, the rank and condition of every man assigned him; not merely his share of property and his power to serve or injure others, but also his wit, beauty, strength or skill, merit or talents: and these being the only qualities capable of commanding respect, it soon became necessary to possess or to affect them.

It now became the interest of men to appear what they really were not. To be and to seem became two totally different things; and from this distinction sprang insolent pomp and cheating trickery, with all the numerous vices that go in their train. On the other hand, free and independent as men were before, they were now, in consequence of a multiplicity of new wants, brought into subjection, as it were, to all nature, and particularly to one another; and each became in some degree a slave even in becoming the master of other men: if rich, they stood in need of the services of others; if poor, of their assistance; and even a middle condition did not enable them to do without one another. Man must now, therefore, have been perpetually employed in getting others to interest themselves in his lot, and in making them, apparently at least, if not really, find their advantage in promoting his own. Thus he must have been sly and artful in his behaviour to some, and imperious and cruel to others; being under a kind of necessity to ill-use all the persons of whom he stood in need, when he could not frighten them into compliance, and did not judge it his interest to be useful to them. Insatiable ambition, the thirst of raising their respective fortunes, not so much from real want as from the desire to surpass others, inspired all men with a vile propensity to injure one another, and with a secret jealousy, which is the more dangerous, as it puts on the mask of benevolence, to carry its point with greater security. In a word, there arose rivalry and competition on the one hand, and conflicting interests on the other, together with a secret desire on both of profiting at the expense of others. All these evils were the first effects of property, and the inseparable attendants of growing inequality.

Before the invention of signs to represent

riches, wealth could hardly consist in anything but lands and cattle, the only real possessions men can have. But, when inheritances so increased in number and extent as to occupy the whole of the land, and to border on one another, one man could aggrandise himself only at the expense of another; at the same time the supernumeraries, who had been too weak or too indolent to make such acquisitions, and had grown poor without sustaining any loss, because, while they saw everything change around them, they remained still the same, were obliged to receive their subsistence, or steal it, from the rich; and this soon bred, according to their different characters, dominion and slavery, or violence and rapine. The wealthy, on their part, had no sooner begun to taste the pleasure of command, than they disdained all others, and, using their old slaves to acquire new, thought of nothing but subduing and enslaving their neighbours; like ravenous wolves, which, having once tasted human flesh, despise every other food and thenceforth seek only men to devour.

Thus, as the most powerful or the most miserable considered their might or misery as a kind of right to the possessions of others, equivalent, in their opinion, to that of property, the destruction of equality was attended by the most terrible disorders. Usurpations by the rich, robbery by the poor, and the unbridled passions of both, suppressed the cries of natural compassion and the still feeble voice of justice, and filled men with avarice, ambition and vice. Between the title of the strongest and that of the first occupier, there arose perpetual conflicts, which never ended but in battles and bloodshed. The new-born state of society thus gave rise to a horrible state of war; men thus harassed and depraved were no longer capable of retracing their steps or renouncing the fatal acquisitions they had made, but, labouring by the abuse of the faculties which do them honour, merely to their own confusion, brought themselves to the brink of ruin.

Attonitus novitate mali, divesque miserque,
Effugere optat opes; et quæ modo voverat odit.[1]

It is impossible that men should not at length have reflected on so wretched a situation, and on the calamities that overwhelmed

<hr/>

[1] Ovid, *Metamorphoses*, xi. 127.
 Both rich and poor, shocked at their new-found ills,
 Would fly from wealth, and lose what they had sought.

them. The rich, in particular, must have felt how much they suffered by a constant state of war, of which they bore all the expense; and in which, though all risked their lives, they alone risked their property. Besides, however speciously they might disguise their usurpations, they knew that they were founded on precarious and false titles; so that, if others took from them by force what they themselves had gained by force, they would have no reason to complain. Even those who had been enriched by their own industry, could hardly base their proprietorship on better claims. It was in vain to repeat, "I built this well; I gained this spot by my industry." Who gave you your standing, it might be answered, and what right have you to demand payment of us for doing what we never asked you to do? Do you not know that numbers of your fellow-creatures are starving, for want of what you have too much of? You ought to have had the express and universal consent of mankind, before appropriating more of the common subsistence than you needed for your own maintenance. Destitute of valid reasons to justify and sufficient strength to defend himself, able to crush individuals with ease, but easily crushed himself by a troop of bandits, one against all, and incapable, on account of mutual jealousy, of joining with his equals against numerous enemies united by the common hope of plunder, the rich man, thus urged by necessity, conceived at length the profoundest plan that ever entered the mind of man: this was to employ in his favour the forces of those who attacked him, to make allies of his adversaries, to inspire them with different maxims, and to give them other institutions as favourable to himself as the law of nature was unfavourable.

With this view, after having represented to his neighbours the horror of a situation which armed every man against the rest, and made their possessions as burdensome to them as their wants, and in which no safety could be expected either in riches or in poverty, he readily devised plausible arguments to make them close with his design. "Let us join," said he, "to guard the weak from oppression, to restrain the ambitious, and secure to every man the possession of what belongs to him: let us institute rules of justice and peace, to which all without exception may be obliged to conform; rules that may in some measure make amends for the caprices of fortune, by subjecting equally the powerful and the weak to the observance of reciprocal obligations. Let us, in a word, instead of turning our forces against ourselves, collect them in a supreme power which may govern us by wise laws, protect and defend all the members of the association, repulse their common enemies, and maintain eternal harmony among us."

Far fewer words to this purpose would have been enough to impose on men so barbarous and easily seduced; especially as they had too many disputes among themselves to do without arbitrators, and too much ambition and avarice to go long without masters. All ran headlong to their chains, in hopes of securing their liberty; for they had just wit enough to perceive the advantages of political institutions, without experience enough to enable them to foresee the dangers. The most capable of foreseeing the dangers were the very persons who expected to benefit by them; and even the most prudent judged it not inexpedient to sacrifice one part of their freedom to ensure the rest; as a wounded man has his arm cut off to save the rest of his body.

Such was, or may well have been, the origin of society and law, which bound new fetters on the poor, and gave new powers to the rich; which irretrievably destroyed natural liberty, eternally fixed the law of property and inequality, converted clever usurpation into unalterable right, and, for the advantage of a few ambitious individuals, subjected all mankind to perpetual labour, slavery and wretchedness. It is easy to see how the establishment of one community made that of all the rest necessary, and how, in order to make head against united forces, the rest of mankind had to unite in turn. Societies soon multiplied and spread over the face of the earth, till hardly a corner of the world was left in which a man could escape the yoke, and withdraw his head from beneath the sword which he saw perpetually hanging over him by a thread. Civil right having thus become the common rule among the members of each community, the law of nature maintained its place only between different communities, where, under the name of the right of nations, it was qualified by certain tacit conventions, in order to make commerce practicable, and serve as a substitute for natural compassion, which lost, when applied to societies, almost all the influence it had over individuals, and survived no longer except in some great cosmopolitan spirits, who, breaking down the imaginary barriers that separate different peoples, follow the example of our Sovereign Creator, and include the whole human race in their benevolence.

But bodies politic, remaining thus in a state of nature among themselves, presently experienced the inconveniences which had obliged individuals to forsake it; for this state became still more fatal to these great bodies than it had been to the individuals of whom they were composed. Hence arose national wars, battles, murders, and reprisals, which shock nature and outrage reason; together with all those horrible prejudices which class among the virtues the honour of shedding human blood. The most distinguished men hence learned to consider cutting each other's throats a duty; at length men massacred their fellow-creatures by thousands without so much as knowing why, and committed more murders in a single day's fighting, and more violent outrages in the sack of a single town, than were committed in the state of nature during whole ages over the whole earth. Such were the first effects which we can see to have followed the division of mankind into different communities. But let us return to their institutions.

I know that some writers have given other explanations of the origin of political societies, such as the conquest of the powerful, or the association of the weak. It is, indeed, indifferent to my argument which of these causes we choose. That which I have just laid down, however, appears to me the most natural for the following reasons. First: because, in the first case, the right of conquest, being no right in itself, could not serve as a foundation on which to build any other; the victor and the vanquished people still remained with respect to each other in the state of war, unless the vanquished, restored to the full possession of their liberty, voluntarily made choice of the victor for their chief. For till then, whatever capitulation may have been made being founded on violence, and therefore *ipso facto* void, there could not have been on this hypothesis either a real society or body politic, or any law other than that of the strongest. Secondly: because the words *strong* and *weak* are, in the second case, ambiguous; for during the interval between the establishment of a right of property, or prior occupancy, and that of political government, the meaning of these words is better expressed by the terms *rich* and *poor*: because, in fact, before the institution of laws, men had no other way of reducing their equals to submission, than by attacking their goods, or making some of their own over to them. Thirdly: because, as the poor had nothing but their freedom to lose, it would have been in the highest degree absurd for them to resign voluntarily the only good they still enjoyed, without getting anything in exchange: whereas the rich having feelings, if I may so express myself, in every part of their possessions, it was much easier to harm them, and therefore more necessary for them to take precautions against it; and, in short, because it is more reasonable to suppose a thing to have been invented by those to whom it would be of service, than by those whom it must have harmed.

Government had, in its infancy, no regular and constant form. The want of experience and philosophy prevented men from seeing any but present inconveniences, and they thought of providing against others only as they presented themselves. In spite of the endeavours of the wisest legislators, the political state remained imperfect, because it was little more than the work of chance; and, as it had begun ill, though time revealed its defects and suggested remedies, the original faults were never repaired. It was continually being patched up, when the first task should have been to get the site cleared and all the old materials removed, as was done by Lycurgus at Sparta, if a stable and lasting edifice was to be erected. Society consisted at first merely of a few general conventions, which every member bound himself to observe; and for the performance of covenants the whole body went security to each individual. Experience only could show the weakness of such a constitution, and how easily it might be infringed with impunity, from the difficulty of convicting men of faults, where the public alone was to be witness and judge: the laws could not but be eluded in many ways; disorders and inconveniences could not but multiply continually, till it became necessary to commit the dangerous trust of public authority to private persons, and the care of enforcing obedience to the deliberations of the people to the magistrate. For to say that chiefs were chosen before the confederacy was formed, and that the administrators of the laws were there before the laws themselves, is too absurd a supposition to consider seriously.

It would be as unreasonable to suppose that men at first threw themselves irretrievably and unconditionally into the arms of an absolute master, and that the first expedient which proud and unsubdued men hit upon for their common security was to run headlong into slavery. For what reason, in fact, did they take to themselves superiors, if it was not in order that they might be defended from oppression, and have protection for their lives, liberties and properties, which are, so to speak, the constituent elements of their being? Now, in the relations between man and man, the worst that can happen is for one to find himself at the mercy of another, and it would have been inconsistent with common-sense to begin by bestowing on a chief the only things they wanted his help to preserve. What equivalent could he offer them for so great a right? And if he had presumed to exact it under pretext of defending them, would he not have received the answer recorded in the fable: "What more can the enemy do to us?" It is therefore beyond dispute, and indeed the fundamental maxim of all political right, that people have set up chiefs to protect their liberty, and not to enslave them. *If we have a prince,* said Pliny to Trajan, *it is to save ourselves from having a master.*

Politicians indulge in the same sophistry about the love of liberty as philosophers about the state of nature. They judge, by what they see, of very different things, which they have not seen; and attribute to man a natural propensity to servitude, because the slaves within their observation are seen to bear the yoke with patience; they fail to reflect that it is with liberty as with innocence and virtue; the value is known only to those who possess them, and the taste for them is forfeited when they are forfeited themselves. "I know the charms of your country," said Brasidas to a satrap, who was comparing the life at Sparta with that at Persepolis, "but you cannot know the pleasures of mine."

An unbroken horse erects his mane, paws the ground and starts back impetuously at the sight of the bridle; while one which is properly trained suffers patiently even whip and spur: so savage man will not bend his neck to the yoke to which civilised man submits without a murmur, but prefers the most turbulent state of liberty to the most peaceful slavery. We cannot therefore, from the servility of nations already enslaved, judge of the natural disposition of mankind for or against slavery; we should go by the prodigious efforts of every free people to save itself from oppression. I know that the former are for ever holding forth in praise of the tranquillity they enjoy in their chains, and that they call a state of wretched servitude a state of peace: *miserri-*

mam servitutem pacem appellant.[1] But when I observe the latter sacrificing pleasure, peace, wealth, power and life itself to the preservation of that one treasure, which is so disdained by those who have lost it; when I see free-born animals dash their brains out against the bars of their cage, from an innate impatience of captivity; when I behold numbers of naked savages, that despise European pleasures, braving hunger, fire, the sword and death, to preserve nothing but their independence, I feel that it is not for slaves to argue about liberty.

With regard to paternal authority, from which some writers have derived absolute government and all society, it is enough, without going back to the contrary arguments of Locke and Sidney, to remark that nothing on earth can be further from the ferocious spirit of despotism than the mildness of that authority which looks more to the advantage of him who obeys than to that of him who commands; that, by the law of nature, the father is the child's master no longer than his help is necessary; that from that time they are both equal, the son being perfectly independent of the father, and owing him only respect and not obedience. For gratitude is a duty which ought to be paid, but not a right to be exacted: instead of saying that civil society is derived from paternal authority, we ought to say rather that the latter derives its principal force from the former. No individual was ever acknowledged as the father of many, till his sons and daughters remained settled around him. The goods of the father, of which he is really the master, are the ties which keep his children in dependence, and he may bestow on them, if he pleases, no share of his property, unless they merit it by constant deference to his will. But the subjects of an arbitrary despot are so far from having the like favour to expect from their chief, that they themselves and everything they possess are his property, or at least are considered by him as such; so that they are forced to receive, as a favour, the little of their own he is pleased to leave them. When he despoils them, he does but justice, and mercy in that he permits them to live.

By proceeding thus to test fact by right, we should discover as little reason as truth in the voluntary establishment of tyranny. It would also be no easy matter to prove the validity of a contract binding on only one of the parties, where all the risk is on one side, and none on the other; so that no one could suffer but he who bound himself. This hateful system is indeed, even in modern times, very far from being that of wise and good monarchs, and especially of the kings of France; as may be seen from several passages in their edicts; particularly from the following passage in a celebrated edict published in 1667 in the name and by order of Louis XIV.

"Let it not, therefore, be said that the Sovereign is not subject to the laws of his State; since the contrary is a true proposition of the right of nations, which flattery has sometimes attacked but good princes have always defended as the tutelary divinity of their dominions. How much more legitimate is it to say with the wise Plato, that the perfect felicity of a kingdom consists in the obedience of subjects to their prince, and of the prince to the laws, and in the laws being just and constantly directed to the public good!"[2]

I shall not stay here to inquire whether, as liberty is the noblest faculty of man, it is not degrading our very nature, reducing ourselves to the level of the brutes, which are mere slaves of instinct, and even an affront to the Author of our being, to renounce without reserve the most precious of all His gifts, and to bow to the necessity of committing all the crimes He has forbidden, merely to gratify a mad or a cruel master; or if this sublime craftsman ought not to be less angered at seeing His workmanship entirely destroyed than thus dishonoured. I will waive (if my opponents please) the authority of Barbeyrac, who, following Locke, roundly declares that no man can so far sell his liberty as to submit to an arbitrary power which may use him as it likes. *For,* he adds, *this would be to sell his own life, of which he is not master.* I shall ask only what right those who were not afraid thus to debase themselves could have to subject their posterity to the same ignominy, and to renounce for them those blessings which they do not owe to the liberality of their progenitors, and without which life itself must be a burden to all who are worthy of it.

Puffendorf says that we may divest ourselves of our liberty in favour of other men, just as we transfer our property from one to another by contracts and agreements. But this seems a very weak argument. For in the first place, the property I alienate becomes quite foreign to me, nor can I suffer from the abuse of it; but it

---

[1] Tacitus, *Hist.* iv. 17. The most wretched slavery they call peace.

[2] Of the Rights of the Most Christian Queen over Various States of the Monarchy of Spain, 1667.

very nearly concerns me that my liberty should not be abused, and I cannot without incurring the guilt of the crimes I may be compelled to commit, expose myself to become an instrument of crime. Besides, the right of property being only a convention of human institution, men may dispose of what they possess as they please: but this is not the case with the essential gifts of nature, such as life and liberty, which every man is permitted to enjoy, and of which it is at least doubtful whether any have a right to divest themselves. By giving up the one, we degrade our being; by giving up the other, we do our best to annul it; and, as no temporal good can indemnify us for the loss of either, it would be an offence against both reason and nature to renounce them at any price whatsoever. But, even if we could transfer our liberty, as we do our property, there would be a great difference with regard to the children, who enjoy the father's substance only by the transmission of his right; whereas, liberty being a gift which they hold from nature as being men, their parents have no right whatever to deprive them of it. As then, to establish slavery, it was necessary to do violence to nature, so, in order to perpetuate such a right, nature would have to be changed. Jurists, who have gravely determined that the child of a slave comes into the world a slave, have decided, in other words, that a man shall come into the world not a man.

I regard it then as certain, that government did not begin with arbitrary power, but that this is the depravation, the extreme term, of government, and brings it back, finally, to just the law of the strongest, which it was originally designed to remedy. Supposing, however, it had begun in this manner, such power, being in itself illegitimate, could not have served as a basis for the laws of society, nor, consequently, for the inequality they instituted.

Without entering at present upon the investigations which still remain to be made into the nature of the fundamental compact underlying all government, I content myself with adopting the common opinion concerning it, and regard the establishment of the political body as a real contract between the people and the chiefs chosen by them: a contract by which both parties bind themselves to observe the laws therein expressed, which form the ties of their union. The people having in respect of their social relations concentrated all their wills in one, the several articles, concerning which this will is explained, become so many

fundamental laws, obligatory on all the members of the State without exception, and one of these articles regulates the choice and power of the magistrates appointed to watch over the execution of the rest. This power extends to everything which may maintain the constitution, without going so far as to alter it. It is accompanied by honours, in order to bring the laws and their administrators into respect. The ministers are also distinguished by personal prerogatives, in order to recompense them for the cares and labour which good administration involves. The magistrate, on his side, binds himself to use the power he is entrusted with only in conformity with the intention of his constituents, to maintain them all in the peaceable possession of what belongs to them, and to prefer on every occasion the public interest to his own.

Before experience had shown, or knowledge of the human heart enabled men to foresee, the unavoidable abuses of such a constitution, it must have appeared so much the more excellent, as those who were charged with the care of its preservation had themselves most interest in it; for magistracy and the rights attaching to it being based solely on the fundamental laws, the magistrates would cease to be legitimate as soon as these ceased to exist; the people would no longer owe them obedience; and as not the magistrates, but the laws, are essential to the being of a State, the members of it would regain the right to their natural liberty.

If we reflect with ever so little attention on this subject, we shall find new arguments to confirm this truth, and be convinced from the very nature of the contract that it cannot be irrevocable: for, if there were no superior power capable of ensuring the fidelity of the contracting parties, or compelling them to perform their reciprocal engagements, the parties would be sole judges in their own cause, and each would always have a right to renounce the contract, as soon as he found that the other had violated its terms, or that they no longer suited his convenience. It is upon this principle that the right of abdication may possibly be founded. Now, if, as here, we consider only what is human in this institution, it is certain that, if the magistrate, who has all the power in his own hands, and appropriates to himself all the advantages of the contract, has none the less a right to renounce his authority, the people, who suffer for all the faults of their chief, must have a much better right to renounce their dependence. But the terrible and innumerable quarrels and disorders that would necessarily arise from so dangerous a privilege, show, more than anything else, how much human government stood in need of a more solid basis than mere reason, and how expedient it was for the public tranquillity that the divine will should interpose to invest the sovereign authority with a sacred and inviolable character, which might deprive subjects of the fatal right of disposing of it. If the world had received no other advantages from religion, this would be enough to impose on men the duty of adopting and cultivating it, abuses and all, since it has been the means of saving more blood than fanaticism has ever spilt. But let us follow the thread of our hypothesis.

The different forms of government owe their origin to the differing degrees of inequality which existed between individuals at the time of their institution. If there happened to be any one man among them pre-eminent in power, virtue, riches or personal influence, he became sole magistrate, and the State assumed the form of monarchy. If several, nearly equal in point of eminence, stood above the rest, they were elected jointly, and formed an aristocracy. Again, among a people who had deviated less from a state of nature, and between whose fortune or talents there was less disproportion, the supreme administration was retained in common, and a democracy was formed. It was discovered in process of time which of these forms suited men the best. Some peoples remained altogether subject to the laws; others soon came to obey their magistrates. The citizens laboured to preserve their liberty; the subjects, irritated at seeing others enjoying a blessing they had lost, thought only of making slaves of their neighbours. In a word, on the one side arose riches and conquests, and on the other happiness and virtue.

In these different governments, all the offices were at first elective; and when the influence of wealth was out of the question, the preference was given to merit, which gives a natural ascendancy, and to age, which is experienced in business and deliberate in council. The Elders of the Hebrews, the Gerontes at Sparta, the Senate at Rome, and the very etymology of our word Seigneur, show how old age was once held in veneration. But the more often the choice fell upon old men, the more often elections had to be repeated, and the more they became a nuisance; intrigues set in, factions were formed, party feeling

grew bitter, civil wars broke out; the lives of individuals were sacrificed to the pretended happiness of the State; and at length men were on the point of relapsing into their primitive anarchy. Ambitious chiefs profited by these circumstances to perpetuate their offices in their own families: at the same time the people, already used to dependence, ease, and the conveniences of life, and already incapable of breaking its fetters, agreed to an increase of its slavery, in order to secure its tranquillity. Thus magistrates, having become hereditary, contracted the habit of considering their offices as a family estate, and themselves as proprietors of the communities of which they were at first only the officers, of regarding their fellow-citizens as their slaves, and numbering them, like cattle, among their belongings, and of calling themselves the equals of the gods and kings of kings.

If we follow the progress of inequality in these various revolutions, we shall find that the establishment of laws and of the right of property was its first term, the institution of magistracy the second, and the conversion of legitimate into arbitrary power the third and last; so that the condition of rich and poor was authorised by the first period; that of powerful and weak by the second; and only by the third that of master and slave, which is the last degree of inequality, and the term at which all the rest remain, when they have got so far, till the government is either entirely dissolved by new revolutions, or brought back again to legitimacy.

To understand this progress as necessary we must consider not so much the motives for the establishment of the body politic, as the forms it assumes in actuality, and the faults that necessarily attend it: for the flaws which make social institutions necessary are the same as make the abuse of them unavoidable. If we except Sparta, where the laws were mainly concerned with the education of children, and where Lycurgus established such morality as practically made laws needles—for laws as a rule, being weaker than the passions, restrain men without altering them—it would not be difficult to prove that every government, which scrupulously complied with the ends for which it was instituted, and guarded carefully against change and corruption, was set up unnecessarily. For a country, in which no one either evaded the laws or made a bad use of magisterial power, could require neither laws nor magistrates.

Political distinctions necessarily produce civil distinctions. The growing equality between the chiefs and the people is soon felt by individuals, and modified in a thousand ways according to passions, talents and circumstances. The magistrate could not usurp any illegitimate power, without giving distinction to the creatures with whom he must share it. Besides, individuals only allow themselves to be oppressed so far as they are hurried on by blind ambition, and, looking rather below than above them, come to love authority more than independence, and submit to slavery, that they may in turn enslave others. It is no easy matter to reduce to obedience a man who has no ambition to command; nor would the most adroit politician find it possible to enslave a people whose only desire was to be independent. But inequality easily makes its way among cowardly and ambitious minds, which are ever ready to run the risks of fortune, and almost indifferent whether they command or obey, as it is favourable or adverse. Thus, there must have been a time, when the eyes of the people were so fascinated, that their rules had only to say to the least of men, "Be great, you and all your posterity," to make him immediately appear great in the eyes of every one as well as in his own. His descendants took still more upon them, in proportion to their distance from him; the more obscure and uncertain the cause, the greater the effect: the greater the number of idlers one could count in a family, the more illustrious it was held to be.

If this were the place to go into details, I could readily explain how, even without the intervention of government, inequality of credit and authority became unavoidable among private persons, as soon as their union in a single society made them compare themselves one with another, and take into account the differences which they found out from the continual intercourse every man had to have with his neighbours.[1] These differences are of several kinds; but riches, nobility or rank,

power and personal merit being the principal distinctions by which men form an estimate of each other in society, I could prove that the harmony or conflict of these different forces is the surest indication of the good or bad constitution of a State. I could show that among these four kinds of inequality, personal qualities being the origin of all the others, wealth is the one to which they are all reduced in the end; for, as riches tend most immediately to the prosperity of individuals, and are easiest to communicate, they are used to purchase every other distinction. By this observation we are enabled to judge pretty exactly how far a people has departed from its primitive constitution, and of its progress towards the extreme term of corruption. I could explain how much this universal desire for reputation, honours and advancement, which inflames us all, exercises and holds up to comparison our faculties and powers; how it excites and multiplies our passions, and, by creating universal competition and rivalry, or rather enmity, among men, occasions numberless failures, successes and disturbances of all kinds by making so many aspirants run the same course. I could show that it is to this desire of being talked about, and this unremitting rage of distinguishing ourselves, that we owe the best and the worst

nately among all the citizens, or that which consists in distributing them to each according to his deserts. These able politicians, adds the orator, banishing that unjust inequality which makes no distinction between good and bad men, adhered inviolably to that which rewards and punishes every man according to his deserts.

But in the first place, there never existed a society, however corrupt some may have become, where no difference was made between the good and the bad; and with regard to morality, where no measures can be prescribed by law exact enough to serve as a practical rule for a magistrate, it is with great prudence that, in order not to leave the fortune or quality of the citizens to his discretion, it prohibits him from passing judgment on persons and confines his judgment to actions. Only morals such as those of the ancient Romans can bear censors, and such a tribunal among us would throw everything into confusion. The difference between good and bad men is determined by public esteem; the magistrate being strictly a judge of right alone; whereas the public is the truest judge of morals, and is of such integrity and penetration on this head, that although it may be sometimes deceived, it can never be corrupted. The rank of citizens ought, therefore, to be regulated, not according to their personal merit—for this would put it in the power of the magistrate to apply the law almost arbitrarily—but according to the actual services done to the State, which are capable of being more exactly estimated.

[1] Distributive justice would oppose this rigorous equality of the state of nature, even were it practicable in civil society; as all the members of the State owe it their services in proportion to their talents and abilities, they ought, on their side, to be distinguished and favoured in proportion to the services they have actually rendered. It is in this sense we must understand that passage of Isocrates, in which he extols the primitive Athenians, for having determined which of the two kinds of equality was the most useful, viz., that which consists in dividing the same advantages indiscrimi-

things we possess, both our virtues and our vices, our science and our errors, our conquerors and our philosophers; that is to say, a great many bad things, and a very few good ones. In a word, I could prove that, if we have a few rich and powerful men on the pinnacle of fortune and grandeur, while the crowd grovels in want and obscurity, it is because the former prize what they enjoy only in so far as others are destitute of it; and because, without changing their condition, they would cease to be happy the moment the people ceased to be wretched.

These details alone, however, would furnish matter for a considerable work, in which the advantages and disadvantages of every kind of government might be weighed, as they are related to man in the state of nature, and at the same time all the different aspects, under which inequality has up to the present appeared, or may appear in ages yet to come, according to the nature of the several governments, and the alterations which time must unavoidably occasion in them, might be demonstrated. We should then see the multitude oppressed from within, in consequence of the very precautions it had taken to guard against foreign tyranny. We should see oppression continually gain ground without it being possible for the oppressed to know where it would stop, or what legitimate means was left them of checking its progress. We should see the rights of citizens, and the freedom of nations slowly extinguished, and the complaints, protests and appeals of the weak treated as seditious murmurings. We should see the honour of defending the common cause confined by statecraft to a mercenary part of the people. We should see taxes made necessary by such means, and the disheartened husbandman deserting his fields even in the midst of peace, and leaving the plough to gird on the sword. We should see fatal and capricious codes of honour established; and the champions of their country sooner or later becoming its enemies, and for ever holding their daggers to the breasts of their fellow-citizens. The time would come when they would be heard saying to the oppressor of their country—

Pectore si fratris gladium juguloque parentis
Condere me jubeas, gravidæque in viscera partu
Conjugis, invitâ peragam tamen omnia dextrâ.
Lucan, i. 376

From great inequality of fortunes and conditions, from the vast variety of passions and of talents, of useless and pernicious arts, of vain sciences, would arise a multitude of prejudices equally contrary to reason, happiness and virtue. We should see the magistrates fomenting everything that might weaken men united in society, by promoting dissension among them; everything that might sow in it the seeds of actual division, while it gave society the air of harmony; everything that might inspire the different ranks of people with mutual hatred and distrust, by setting the rights and interests of one against those of another, and so strengthen the power which comprehended them all.

It is from the midst of this disorder and these revolutions, that despotism, gradually raising up its hideous head and devouring everything that remained sound and untainted in any part of the State, would at length trample on both the laws and the people, and establish itself on the ruins of the republic. The times which immediately preceded this last change would be times of trouble and calamity; but at length the monster would swallow up everything, and the people would no longer have either chiefs or laws, but only tyrants. From this moment there would be no question of virtue or morality; for despotism *cui ex honesto nulla est spes,* wherever it prevails, admits no other master; it no sooner speaks than probity and duty lose their weight and blind obedience is the only virtue which slaves can still practise.

This is the last term of inequality, the extreme point that closes the circle, and meets that from which we set out. Here all private persons return to their first equality, because they are nothing; and, subjects having no law but the will of their master, and their master no restraint but his passions, all notions of good and all principles of equity again vanish. There is here a complete return to the law of the strongest, and so to a new state of nature, differing from that we set out from; for the one was a state of nature in its first purity, while this is the consequence of excessive corruption. There is so little difference between the two states in other respects, and the contract of government is so completely dissolved by despotism, that the despot is master only so long as he remains the strongest; as soon as he can be expelled, he has no right to complain of violence. The popular insurrection that ends in the death or deposition of a Sultan is as lawful an act as those by which he disposed, the day before, of the lives and fortunes of his subjects. As he was maintained by force alone, it is force alone that overthrows him. Thus everything takes place according to the natural order; and, whatever may be the result of such frequent and precipitate revolutions, no one man has reason to complain of the injustice of another, but only of his own ill-fortune or indiscretion.

If the reader thus discovers and retraces the lost and forgotten road, by which man must have passed from the state of nature to the state of society; if he carefully restores, along with the intermediate situations which I have just described, those which want of time has compelled me to suppress, or my imagination has failed to suggest, he cannot fail to be struck by the vast distance which separates the two states. It is in tracing this slow succession that he will find the solution of a number of problems of politics and morals, which philosophers cannot settle. He will feel that, men being different in different ages, the reason why Diogenes could not find a man was that he sought among his contemporaries a man of an earlier period. He will see that Cato died with Rome and liberty, because he did not fit the age in which he lived; the greatest of men served only to astonish a world which he would certainly have ruled, had he lived five hundred years sooner. In a word, he will explain how the soul and the passions of men insensibly change their very nature; why our wants and pleasures in the end seek new objects; and why, the original man having vanished by degrees, society offers to us only an assembly of artificial men and factitious passions, which are the work of all these new relations, and without any real foundation in nature. We are taught nothing on this subject, by reflection, that is not entirely confirmed by observation. The savage and the civilised man differ so much in the bottom of their hearts and in their inclinations, that what constitutes the supreme happiness of one would reduce the other to despair. The former breathes only peace and liberty; he desires only to live and be free from labour; even the *ataraxia* of the Stoic falls far short of his profound indifference to every other object. Civilised man, on the other hand, is always moving, sweating, toiling and racking his brains to find still more laborious occupations: he goes on in drudgery to his last moment, and even seeks death to put himself in a position to live, or renounces life to acquire immortality. He pays his court to men in power, whom he hates, and to the wealthy, whom he despises; he stops at nothing to have the honour of serving them; he is not ashamed to value himself on his own meanness and their protection; and, proud of his slavery, he speaks with disdain of those, who have not the honour of sharing it. What a sight would the perplexing and envied labours of a European minister of State present to the eyes of a Caribbean! How many cruel deaths would not this indolent savage prefer to the horrors of such a life, which is seldom even sweetened by the pleasure of doing good! But, for him to see into the motives of all this solicitude, the words *power* and *reputation*, would have to bear some meaning in his mind; he would have to know that there are men who set a value on the opinion of the rest of the world; who can be made happy and satisfied with themselves rather on the testimony of other people than on their own. In reality, the source of all these differences is, that the savage lives within himself, while social man lives constantly outside himself, and only knows how to live in the opinion of others, so that he seems to receive the consciousness of his own existence merely from the judgment of others concerning him. It is not to my present purpose to insist on the indifference to good and evil which arises from this disposition, in spite of our many fine works on morality, or to show how, everything being reduced to appearances, there is but art and mummery in even honour, friendship, virtue, and often vice itself, of which we at length learn the secret of boasting; to show, in short, how, always asking others what we are, and never daring to ask ourselves, in the midst of so much philosophy, humanity and civilisation, and of such sublime codes of morality, we have nothing to show for ourselves but a frivolous and deceitful appearance, honour without virtue, reason without wisdom, and pleasure without happiness. It is sufficient that I have proved that this is not by any means the original state of man, but that it is merely the spirit of society, and the inequality which society produces, that thus transform and alter all our natural inclinations.

I have endeavoured to trace the origin and progress of inequality, and the institution and abuse of political societies, as far as these are capable of being deduced from the nature of man merely by the light of reason, and independently of those sacred dogmas which give the sanction of divine right to sovereign authority. It follows from this survey that, as there is hardly any inequality in the state of nature, all the inequality which now prevails owes its strength and growth to the development of our faculties and the advance of the human mind, and becomes at last permanent and legitimate by the establishment of property and laws. Secondly, it follows that moral inequality, authorised by positive right alone, clashes with natural right, whenever it is not proportionate to physical inequality; a distinction which sufficiently determines what we ought to think of that species of inequality which prevails in all civilised countries; since it is plainly contrary to the law of nature, however defined, that children should command old men, fools wise men, and that the privileged few should gorge themselves with superfluities, while the starving multitude are in want of the bare necessities of life.

.   .   .

APPENDIX[1]

A FAMOUS author, reckoning up the good and evil of human life, and comparing the aggregates, finds that our pains greatly exceed our pleasures: so that, all things considered, human life is not at all a valuable gift. This conclusion does not surprise me; for the writer drew all his arguments from man in civilisation. Had he gone back to the state of nature, his inquiries would clearly have had a different result, and man would have been seen to be subject to very few evils not of his own creation. It has indeed cost us not a little trouble to make ourselves as wretched as we are. When we consider, on the one hand, the immense labours of mankind, the many sciences brought to perfection, the arts invented, the powers employed, the deeps filled up, the mountains levelled, the rocks shattered, the rivers made navigable, the tracts of land cleared, the lakes emptied, the marshes drained, the enormous structures erected on land, and the teeming vessels that cover the sea; and, on the other hand, estimate with ever so little thought, the real advantages that have accrued from all these works to mankind, we cannot help being amazed at the vast disproportion there is between these things, and deploring the infatuation of man, which, to gratify his silly pride and vain self-admiration, induces him eagerly to pursue all the miseries he is capable of feeling, though beneficent nature had kindly placed them out of his way.

That men are actually wicked, a sad and continual experience of them proves beyond doubt: but, all the same, I think I have shown that man is naturally good. What then can have depraved him to such an extent, except the changes that have happened in his constitution, the advances he has made, and the knowledge he has acquired? We may admire human society as much as we please; it will be

[1] See p. 338.

none the less true that it necessarily leads men to hate each other in proportion as their interests clash, and to do one another apparent services, while they are really doing every imaginable mischief. What can be thought of a relation, in which the interest of every individual dictates rules directly opposite to those the public reason dictates to the community in general—in which every man finds his profit in the misfortunes of his neighbour? There is not perhaps any man in a comfortable position who has not greedy heirs, and perhaps even children, secretly wishing for his death; not a ship at sea, of which the loss would not be good news to some merchant or other; not a house, which some debtor of bad faith would not be glad to see reduced to ashes with all the papers it contains; not a nation which does not rejoice at the disasters that befall its neighbours. Thus it is that we find our advantage in the misfortunes of our fellow-creatures, and that the loss of one man almost always constitutes the prosperity of another. But it is still more pernicious that public calamities are the objects of the hopes and expectations of innumerable individuals. Some desire sickness, some mortality, some war, and some famine. I have seen men wicked enough to weep for sorrow at the prospect of a plentiful season; and the great and fatal fire of London, which cost so many unhappy persons their lives or their fortunes, made the fortunes of perhaps ten thousand others. I know that Montaigne censures Demades the Athenian for having caused to be punished a workman who, by selling his coffins very dear, was a great gainer by the deaths of his fellow-citizens; but, the reason alleged by Montaigne being that everybody ought to be punished, my point is clearly confirmed by it. Let us penetrate, therefore, the superficial appearances of benevolence, and survey what passes in the inmost recesses of the heart. Let us reflect what must be the state of things, when men are forced to caress and destroy one another at the same time; when they are born enemies by duty, and knaves by interest. It will perhaps be said that society is so formed that every man gains by serving the rest. That would be all very well, if he did not gain still more by injuring them. There is no legitimate profit so great, that it cannot be greatly exceeded by what may be made illegitimately; we always gain more by hurting our neighbours than by doing them good. Nothing is required but to know how to act with impunity; and to this end the powerful employ all their strength, and the weak all their cunning.

Savage man, when he has dined, is at peace with all nature, and the friend of all his fellow-creatures. If a dispute arises about a meal, he rarely comes to blows, without having first compared the difficulty of conquering his antagonist with the trouble of finding subsistence elsewhere: and, as pride does not come in, it all ends in a few blows; the victor eats, and the vanquished seeks provision somewhere else, and all is at peace. The case is quite different with man in the state of society, for whom first necessaries have to be provided, and then superfluities; delicacies follow next, then immense wealth, then subjects, and then slaves. He enjoys not a moment's relaxation; and what is yet stranger, the less natural and pressing his wants, the more headstrong are his passions, and, still worse, the more he has it in his power to gratify them; so that after a long course of prosperity, after having swallowed up treasures and ruined multitudes, the hero ends up by cutting every throat till he finds himself, at last, sole master of the world. Such is in miniature the moral picture, if not of human life, at least of the secret pretensions of the heart of civilised man.

Compare without partiality the state of the citizen with that of the savage, and trace out, if you can, how many inlets the former has opened to pain and death, besides those of his vices, his wants and his misfortunes. If you reflect on the mental afflictions that prey on us, the violent passions that waste and exhaust us, the excessive labour with which the poor are burdened, the still more dangerous indolence to which the wealthy give themselves up, so that the poor perish of want, and the rich of surfeit; if you reflect but a moment on the heterogeneous mixtures and pernicious seasonings of foods; the corrupt state in which they are frequently eaten; on the adulteration of medicines, the wiles of those who sell them, the mistakes of those who administer them, and the poisonous vessels in which they are prepared; on the epidemics bred by foul air in consequence of great numbers of men being crowded together, or those which are caused by our delicate way of living, by our passing from our houses into the open air and back again, by the putting on or throwing off our clothes with too little care, and by all the precautions which sensuality has converted into necessary habits, and the neglect of which sometimes costs us our life or health; if you take into account the conflagrations and earthquakes, which, devouring or overwhelming whole cities, destroy the inhabitants by thousands; in a word, if you add together all the dangers with which these causes are always threatening us, you will see how dearly nature makes us pay for the contempt with which we have treated her lessons.

I shall not here repeat, what I have elsewhere said of the calamities of war; but wish that those, who have sufficient knowledge, were willing or bold enough to make public the details of the villainies committed in armies by the contractors for commissariat and hospitals: we should see plainly that their monstrous frauds, already none too well concealed, which cripple the finest armies in less than no time, occasion greater destruction among the soldiers than the swords of the enemy.

The number of people who perish annually at sea, by famine, the scurvy, pirates, fire and shipwrecks, affords matter for another shocking calculation. We must also place to the credit of the establishment of property, and consequently to the institution of society, assassinations, poisonings, highway robberies, and even the punishments inflicted on the wretches guilty of these crimes; which, though expedient to prevent greater evils, yet by making the murder of one man cost the lives of two or more, double the loss to the human race.

What shameful methods are sometimes practised to prevent the birth of men, and cheat nature; either by brutal and depraved appetites which insult her most beautiful work—appetites unknown to savages or mere animals, which can spring only from the corrupt imagination of mankind in civilised countries; or by secret abortions, the fitting effects of debauchery and vitiated notions of honour; or by the exposure or murder of multitudes of infants, who fall victims to the poverty of their parents, or the cruel shame of their mothers; or, finally, by the mutilation of unhappy wretches, part of whose life, with their hope of posterity, is given up to vain singing, or, still worse, the brutal jealousy of other men: a mutilation which, in the last case, becomes a double outrage against nature from the treatment of those who suffer it, and from the use to which they are destined. But is it not a thousand times more common and more dangerous for paternal rights openly to offend against humanity? How many talents have not been thrown away, and inclinations forced, by the unwise constraint of fathers? How many men, who would have distinguished themselves in a fitting estate, have died dishonoured and wretched in another for which they had no taste! How many happy, but unequal, marriages have been broken or disturbed, and how many chaste wives have been dishonoured, by an order of things continually in contradiction with that of nature! How many good and virtuous husbands and wives are reciprocally punished for having been ill-assorted! How many young and unhappy victims of their parents' avarice plunge into vice, or pass their melancholy days in tears, groaning in the indissoluble bonds which their hearts repudiate and gold alone has formed! Fortunate sometimes are those whose courage and virtue remove them from life before inhuman violence makes them spend it in crime or in despair. Forgive me, father and mother, whom I shall ever regret: my complaint embitters your griefs; but would they might be an eternal and terrible example to every one who dares, in the name of nature, to violate her most sacred right.

If I have spoken only of those ill-starred unions which are the result of our system, is it to be thought that those over which love and sympathy preside are free from disadvantages? What if I should undertake to show humanity attacked in its very source, and even in the most sacred of all ties, in which fortune is consulted before nature, and, the disorders of society confounding all virtue and vice, continence becomes a criminal precaution, and a refusal to give life to a fellow-creature, an act of humanity? But, without drawing aside the veil which hides all these horrors, let us content ourselves with pointing out the evil which others will have to remedy.

To all this add the multiplicity of unhealthy trades, which shorten men's lives or destroy their bodies, such as working in the mines, and the preparing of metals and minerals, particularly lead, copper, mercury, cobalt, and arsenic: add those other dangerous trades which are daily fatal to many tilers, carpenters, masons and miners: put all these together and we can see, in the establishment and perfection of societies, the reasons for that diminution of our species, which has been noticed by many philosophers.

Luxury, which cannot be prevented among men who are tenacious of their own convenience and of the respect paid them by others, soon completes the evil society had begun, and, under the pretence of giving bread to the poor, whom it should never have made such, impoverishes all the rest, and sooner or later depopulates the State. Luxury is a remedy much worse than the disease it sets up to cure; or rather it is in itself the greatest of all evils, for every State, great or small: for, in order to maintain all the servants and vagabonds it creates, it brings oppression and ruin on the citizen and the labourer; it is like those scorching winds, which, covering the trees and plants with devouring insects, deprive useful animals of their subsistence and spread famine and death wherever they blow.

From society and the luxury to which it gives birth arise the liberal and mechanical arts, commerce, letters, and all those superfluities which make industry flourish, and enrich and ruin nations. The reason for such destruction is plain. It is easy to see, from the very nature of agriculture, that it must be the least lucrative of all the arts; for, its produce being the most universally necessary, the price must be proportionate to the abilities of the very poorest of mankind.

From the same principle may be deduced this rule, that the arts in general are more lucrative in proportion as they are less useful; and that, in the end, the most useful becomes the most neglected. From this we may learn what to think of the real advantages of industry and the actual effects of its progress.

Such are the sensible causes of all the miseries, into which opulence at length plunges the most celebrated nations. In proportion as arts and industry flourish, the despised husbandman, burdened with the taxes necessary for the support of luxury, and condemned to pass his days between labour and hunger, forsakes his native field, to seek in towns the bread he ought to carry thither. The more our capital cities strike the vulgar eye with admiration, the greater reason is there to lament the sight of the abandoned countryside, the large tracts of land that lie uncultivated, the roads crowded with unfortunate citizens turned beggars or highwaymen, and doomed to end their wretched lives either on a dunghill or on the gallows. Thus the State grows rich on the one hand, and feeble and depopulated on the other; the mightiest monarchies, after having taken immense pains to enrich and depopulate themselves, fall at last a prey to some poor nation, which has yielded to the fatal temptation of invading them, and then, growing opulent and weak in its turn, is itself invaded and ruined by some other.

Let any one inform us what produced the swarms of barbarians, who overran Europe, Asia and Africa for so many ages. Was their prodigious increase due to their industry and arts, to the wisdom of their laws, or to the excellence of their political system? Let the learned tell us why, instead of multiplying to such a degree, these fierce and brutal men, without sense or science, without education, without restraint, did not destroy each other hourly in quarrelling over the productions of their fields and woods. Let them tell us how these wretches could have the presumption to oppose such clever people as we were, so well trained in military discipline, and possessed of such excellent laws and institutions: and why, since society has been brought to perfection in northern countries, and so much pains taken to instruct their inhabitants in their social duties and in the art of living happily and peaceably together, we see them no longer produce such numberless hosts as they used once to send forth to be the plague and terror of other nations. I fear some one may at last answer me by saying, that all these fine things, arts, sciences and laws, were wisely invented by men, as a salutary plague, to prevent the too great multiplication of mankind, lest the world, which was given us for a habitation, should in time be too small for its inhabitants.

What, then, is to be done? Must societies be totally abolished? Must *meum* and *tuum* be annihilated, and must we return again to the forests to live among bears? This is a deduction in the manner of my adversaries, which I

would as soon anticipate as let them have the shame of drawing. O you, who have never heard the voice of heaven, who think man destined only to live this little life and die in peace; you, who can resign in the midst of populous cities your fatal acquisitions, your restless spirits, your corrupt hearts and endless desires; resume, since it depends entirely on ourselves, your ancient and primitive innocence: retire to the woods, there to lose the sight and remembrance of the crimes of your contemporaries; and be not apprehensive of degrading your species, by renouncing its advances in order to renounce its vices. As for men like me, whose passions have destroyed their original simplicity, who can no longer subsist on plants or acorns, or live without laws and magistrates; those who were honoured in their first father with supernatural instructions; those who discover, in the design of giving human actions at the start a morality which they must otherwise have been so long in acquiring, the reason for a precept in itself indifferent and inexplicable on every other system; those, in short, who are persuaded that the Divine Being has called all mankind to be partakers in the happiness and perfection of celestial intelligences, all these will endeavour to merit the eternal prize they are to expect from the practice of those virtues, which they make themselves follow in learning to know them. They will respect the sacred bonds of their respective communities; they will love their fellow-citizens, and serve them with all their might: they will scrupulously obey the laws, and all those who make or administer them; they will particularly honour those wise and good princes, who find means of preventing, curing or even palliating all these evils and abuses, by which we are constantly threatened; they will animate the zeal of their deserving rulers, by showing them, without flattery or fear, the importance of their office and the severity of their duty. But they will not therefore have less contempt for a constitution that cannot support itself without the aid of so many splendid characters, much oftener wished for than found; and from which, notwithstanding all their pains and solicitude, there always arise more real calamities than even apparent advantages.

A DISCOURSE

ON POLITICAL ECONOMY

THE word Economy, or Œconomy, is derived from οἶκός, *a house,* and νόμος, *law,* and meant originally only the wise and legitimate government of the house for the common good of the whole family. The meaning of the term was then extended to the government of that great family, the State. To distinguish these two senses of the word, the latter is called *general* or *political* economy, and the former domestic or particular economy. The first only is discussed in the present discourse.

Even if there were as close an analogy as many authors maintain between the State and the family, it would not follow that the rules of conduct proper for one of these societies would be also proper for the other. They differ too much in extent to be regulated in the same manner; and there will always be a great difference between domestic government, in which a father can see everything for himself, and civil government, where the chief sees hardly anything save through the eyes of others. To put both on an equality in this respect, the talents, strength, and all the faculties of the father would have to increase in proportion to the size of his family, and the soul of a powerful monarch would have to be, to that of an ordinary man, as the extent of his empire is to that of a private person's estate.

But how could the government of the State be like that of the family, when the basis on which they rest is so different? The father being physically stronger than his children, his paternal authority, as long as they need his protection, may be reasonably said to be established by nature. But in the great family, all the members of which are naturally equal, the political authority, being purely arbitrary as far as its institution is concerned, can be founded only on conventions, and the Magistrate can have no authority over the rest, except by virtue of the laws. The duties of a father are dictated to him by natural feelings, and in a manner that seldom allows him to neglect them. For rulers there is no such prin-

ciple, and they are really obliged to the people only by what they themselves have promised to do, and the people have therefore a right to require of them. Another more important difference is that since the children have nothing but what they receive from their father, it is plain that all the rights of property belong to him, or emanate from him; but quite the opposite is the case in the great family, where the general administration is established only to secure individual property, which is antecedent to it. The principal object of the work of the whole house is to preserve and increase the patrimony of the father, in order that he may be able some day to distribute it among his children without impoverishing them; whereas the wealth of the exchequer is only a means, often ill understood, of keeping the individuals in peace and plenty. In a word, the little family is destined to be extinguished, and to resolve itself some day into several families of a similar nature; but the great family, being constituted to endure for ever in the same condition, need not, like the small one, increase for the purpose of multiplying, but need only maintain itself; and it can easily be proved that any increase does it more harm than good.

In the family, it is clear, for several reasons which lie in its very nature, that the father ought to command. In the first place, the authority ought not to be equally divided between father and mother; the government must be single, and in every division of opinion there must be one preponderant voice to decide. Secondly, however lightly we may regard the disadvantages peculiar to women, yet, as they necessarily occasion intervals of inaction, this is a sufficient reason for excluding them from this supreme authority: for when the balance is perfectly even, a straw is enough to turn the scale. Besides, the husband ought to be able to superintend his wife's conduct, because it is of importance for him to be assured that the children, whom he is obliged to acknowledge and maintain, belong to no one but himself. Thirdly, children should be obedient to their father, at first of necessity, and afterwards from gratitude: after having had their wants satisfied by him during one half of their lives, they ought to consecrate the other half to providing for his. Fourthly, servants owe him their services in exchange for the provision he makes for them, though they may break off the bargain as soon as it ceases to suit them. I say nothing here of slavery, because it is contrary to nature, and cannot be authorised by any right or law.

There is nothing of all this in political society, in which the chief is so far from having any natural interest in the happiness of the individuals, that it is not uncommon for him to seek his own in their misery. If the magistracy is hereditary, a community of men is often governed by a child. If it be elective, innumerable inconveniences arise from such election; while in both cases all the advantages of paternity are lost. If you have but a single ruler, you lie at the discretion of a master who has no reason to love you: and if you have several, you must bear at once their tyranny and their divisions. In a word, abuses are inevitable and their consequences fatal in every society where the public interest and the laws have no natural force, and are perpetually attacked by personal interest and the passions of the ruler and the members.

Although the functions of the father of a family and those of the chief magistrate ought to make for the same object, they must do so in such different ways, and their duty and rights are so essentially distinct, that we cannot confound them without forming very false ideas about the fundamental laws of society, and falling into errors which are fatal to mankind. In fact, if the voice of nature is the best counsellor to which a father can listen in the discharge of his duty, for the Magistrate it is a false guide, which continually prevents him from performing his, and leads him on sooner or later to the ruin of himself and of the State, if he is not restrained by the most sublime virtue. The only precaution necessary for the father of a family is to guard himself against depravity, and prevent his natural inclinations from being corrupted; whereas it is these themselves which corrupt the Magistrate. In order to act aright, the first has only to consult his heart; the other becomes a traitor the moment he listens to his. Even his own reason should be suspect to him, nor should he follow any rule other than the public reason, which is the law. Thus nature has made a multitude of good fathers of families; but it is doubtful whether, from the very beginning of the world, human wisdom has made ten men capable of governing their peers.

From all that has just been said, it follows that *public* economy, which is my subject, has been rightly distinguished from *private* economy, and that, the State having nothing in common with the family except the obligations which their heads lie under of making both of them happy, the same rules of conduct cannot apply to both. I have considered these few lines enough to overthrow the detestable system which Sir Robert Filmer has endeavoured to establish in his *Patriarcha;* a work to which two celebrated writers have done too much honour in writing books to refute it. Moreover, this error is of very long standing; for Aristotle himself thought proper to combat it with arguments which may be found in the first book of his *Politics.*

I must here ask my readers to distinguish also between *public economy,* which is my subject and which I call *government,* and the supreme authority, which I call *Sovereignty;* a distinction which consists in the fact that the latter has the right of legislation, and in certain cases binds the body of the nation itself, while the former has only the right of execution, and is binding only on individuals.

I shall take the liberty of making use of a very common, and in some respects inaccurate, comparison, which will serve to illustrate my meaning.

The body politic, taken individually, may be considered as an organised, living body, resembling that of man. The sovereign power represents the head; the laws and customs are the brain, the source of the nerves and seat of the understanding, will and senses, of which the Judges and Magistrates are the organs: commerce, industry, and agriculture are the mouth and stomach which prepare the common subsistence; the public income is the blood, which a prudent *economy,* in performing the functions of the heart, causes to distribute through the whole body nutriment and life: the citizens are the body and the members, which make the machine live, move and work; and no part of this machine can be damaged without the painful impression being at once conveyed to the brain, if the animal is in a state of health.

The life of both bodies is the self common

to the whole, the reciprocal sensibility and internal correspondence of all the parts. Where this communication ceases, where the formal unity disappears, and the contiguous parts belong to one another only by juxtaposition, the man is dead, or the State is dissolved.

The body politic, therefore, is also a moral being possessed of a will; and this general will, which tends always to the preservation and welfare of the whole and of every part, and is the source of the laws, constitutes for all the members of the State, in their relations to one another and to it, the rule of what is just or unjust: a truth which shows, by the way, how idly some writers have treated as theft the subtlety prescribed to children at Sparta for obtaining their frugal repasts, as if everything ordained by the law were not lawful.

It is important to observe that this rule of justice, though certain with regard to all citizens, may be defective with regard to foreigners. The reason is clear. The will of the State, though general in relation to its own members, is no longer so in relation to other States and their members, but becomes, for them, a particular and individual will, which has its rule of justice in the law of nature. This, however, enters equally into the principle here laid down; for in such a case, the great city of the world becomes the body politic, whose general will is always the law of nature, and of which the different States and peoples are individual members. From these distinctions, applied to each political society and its members, are derived the most certain and universal rules, by which we can judge whether a government is good or bad, and in general of the morality of all human actions.

Every political society is composed of other smaller societies of different kinds, each of which has its interests and its rules of conduct: but those societies which everybody perceives, because they have an external and authorised form, are not the only ones that actually exist in the State: all individuals who are united by a common interest compose as many others, either transitory or permanent, whose influence is none the less real because it is less apparent, and the proper observation of whose various relations is the true knowledge of public morals and manners. The influence of all these tacit or formal associations causes, by the influence of their will, as many different modifications of the public will. The will of these particular societies has always two relations; for the members of the association, it is a general will; for the great society, it is a particular will; and it is often right with regard to the first object, and wrong as to the second. An individual may be a devout priest, a brave soldier, or a zealous senator, and yet a bad citizen. A particular resolution may be advantageous to the smaller community, but pernicious to the greater. It is true that particular societies being always subordinate to the general society in preference to others, the duty of a citizen takes precedence of that of a senator, and a man's duty of that of a citizen: but unhappily personal interest is always found in inverse ratio to duty, and increases in proportion as the association grows narrower, and the engagement less sacred; which irrefragably proves that the most general will is always the most just also, and that the voice of the people is in fact the voice of God.

It does not follow that the public decisions are always equitable; they may possibly, for reasons which I have given, not be so when they have to do with foreigners. Thus it is not impossible that a Republic, though in itself well governed, should enter upon an unjust war. Nor is it less possible for the Council of a Democracy to pass unjust decrees, and condemn the innocent; but this never happens unless the people is seduced by private interests, which the credit or eloquence of some clever persons substitutes for those of the State: in which case the general will will be one thing, and the result of the public deliberation another. This is not contradicted by the case of the Athenian Democracy; for Athens was in fact not a Democracy, but a very tyrannical Aristocracy, governed by philosophers and orators. Carefully determine what happens in every public deliberation, and it will be seen that the general will is always for the common good; but very often there is a secret division, a tacit confederacy, which, for particular ends, causes the natural disposition of the assembly to be set at nought. In such a case the body of society is really divided into other bodies, the members of which acquire a general will, which is good and just with respect to these new bodies, but unjust and bad with regard to the whole, from which each is thus dismembered.

We see then how easy it is, by the help of these principles, to explain those apparent contradictions, which are noticed in the conduct of many persons who are scrupulously honest in some respects, and cheats and scoundrels in others, who trample under foot the most sacred duties, and yet are faithful to the death to engagements that are often illegitimate. Thus the most depraved of men always pay some sort of homage to public faith; and even robbers, who are the enemies of virtue in the great society, pay some respect to the shadow of it in their secret caves.

In establishing the general will as the first principle of public *economy,* and the fundamental rule of government, I have not thought it necessary to inquire seriously whether the Magistrates belong to the people, or the people to the Magistrates; or whether in public affairs the good of the State should be taken into account, or only that of its rulers. That question indeed has long been decided one way in theory, and another in practice; and in general it would be ridiculous to expect that those who are in fact masters will prefer any other interest to their own. It would not be improper, therefore, further to distinguish public *economy* as popular or tyrannical. The former is that of every State, in which there reigns between the people and the rulers unity of interest and will: the latter will necessarily exist wherever the government and the people have different interests, and, consequently, opposing wills. The rules of the latter are written at length in the archives of history, and in the satires of Machiavelli. The rules of the former are found only in the writings of those philosophers who venture to proclaim the rights of humanity.

I. The first and most important rule of legitimate or popular government, that is to say, of government whose object is the good of the people, is therefore, as I have observed, to follow in everything the general will. But to follow this will it is necessary to know it, and above all to distinguish it from the particular will, beginning with one's self: this distinction is always very difficult to make, and only the most sublime virtue can afford sufficient illumination for it. As, in order to will, it is necessary to be free, a difficulty no less great than the former arises—that of preserving at once the public liberty and the authority of government. Look into the motives which have induced men, once united by their common needs in a general society, to unite themselves still more intimately by means of civil societies: you will find no other motive than that of assuring the property, life and liberty of each member by the protection of all. But can men be forced to defend the liberty of any one among them, without trespassing on that of others? And how can they provide for the public needs, without alienating the individual property of those who are forced to contribute to them? With whatever sophistry all this may be covered over, it is certain that if any constraint can be laid on my will, I am no longer free, and that I am no longer master of my own property, if any one else can lay a hand on it. This difficulty, which would have seemed insurmountable, has been removed, like the first, by the most sublime of all human institutions, or rather by a divine inspiration, which teaches mankind to imitate here below the unchangeable decrees of the Deity. By what inconceivable art has a means been found of making men free by making them subject; of using in the service of the State the properties, the persons and even the lives of all its members, without constraining and without consulting them; of confining their will by their own admission; of overcoming their refusal by that consent, and forcing them to punish themselves, when they act against their own will? How can it be that all should obey, yet nobody take upon him to command, and that all should serve, and yet have no masters, but be the more free, as, in apparent subjection, each loses no part of his liberty but what might be hurtful to that of another? These wonders are the work of law. It is to law alone that men owe justice and liberty. It is this salutary organ of the will of all which establishes, in civil right, the natural equality between men. It is this celestial voice which dictates to each citizen the precepts of public reason, and teaches him to act according to the rules of his own judgment, and not to behave inconsistently with himself. It is with this voice alone that political rulers should speak when they command; for no sooner does one man, setting aside the law, claim to subject another to his private will, than he departs from the state of civil society, and confronts him face to face in the pure state of nature, in which obedience is prescribed solely by necessity.

The most pressing interest of the ruler, and even his most indispensable duty, therefore, is to watch over the observation of the laws of which he is the minister, and on which his whole authority is founded. At the same time, if he exacts the observance of them from others, he is the more strongly bound to observe them himself, since he enjoys all their favour. For his example is of such force, that even if the people were willing to permit him to release himself from the yoke of the law, he ought to be cautious in availing himself of so dangerous a prerogative, which others might soon claim to usurp in their turn, and often use to his prejudice. At bottom, as all social engagements are mutual in nature, it is impossible for any one to set himself above the law, without renouncing its advantages; for nobody is bound by any obligation to one who claims that he is under no obligations to others. For this reason no exemption from the law will ever be granted, on any ground whatsoever, in a well-regulated government. Those citizens who have deserved well of their country ought to be rewarded with honours, but never with privileges: for the Republic is at the eve of its fall, when any one can think it fine not to obey the laws. If the nobility or the soldiery should ever adopt such a maxim, all would be lost beyond redemption.

The power of the laws depends still more on their own wisdom than on the severity of their administrators, and the public will derives its greatest weight from the reason which has dictated it. Hence Plato looked upon it as a very necessary precaution to place at the head of all edicts a preamble, setting forth their justice and utility. In fact, the first of all laws is to respect the laws: the severity of penalties is only a vain resource, invented by little minds in order to substitute terror for that respect which they have no means of obtaining. It has constantly been observed that in those countries where legal punishments are most severe, they are also most frequent; so that the cruelty of such punishments is a proof only of the multitude of criminals, and, punishing everything with equal severity, induces those who are guilty to commit crimes, in order to escape being punished for their faults.

But though the government be not master of the law, it is much to be its guarantor, and to possess a thousand means of inspiring the love of it. In this alone the talent of reigning consists. With force in one's hands, there is no art required to make the whole world tremble, nor indeed much to gain men's hearts; for experience has long since taught the people to give its rulers great credit for all the evil they abstain from doing it, and to adore them if they do not absolutely hate it. A fool, if he be obeyed, may punish crimes as well as another: but the true statesman is he who knows how to prevent them: it is over the wills, even more than the actions, of his subjects that his honourable rule is extended. If he could secure that every one should act aright, he would

no longer have anything to do; and the masterpiece of his labours would be to be able to remain unemployed. It is certain, at least, that the greatest talent a ruler can possess is to disguise his power, in order to render it less odious, and to conduct the State so peaceably as to make it seem to have no need of conductors.

I conclude, therefore, that, as the first duty of the legislator is to make the laws conformable to the general will, the first rule of public *economy* is that the administration of justice should be conformable to the laws. It will even be enough to prevent the State from being ill governed, that the Legislator shall have provided, as he should, for every need of place, climate, soil, custom, neighbourhood, and all the rest of the relations peculiar to the people he had to institute. Not but what there still remains an infinity of details of administration and economy, which are left to the wisdom of the government: but there are two infallible rules for its good conduct on these occasions; one is, that the spirit of the law ought to decide in every particular case that could not be foreseen; the other is that the general will, the source and supplement of all laws, should be consulted wherever they fail. But how, I shall be asked, can the general will be known in cases in which it has not expressed itself? Must the whole nation be assembled together at every unforeseen event? Certainly not. It ought the less to be assembled, because it is by no means certain that its decision would be the expression of the general will; besides, the method would be impractible in a great people, and is hardly ever necessary where the government is well-intentioned: for the rulers well know that the general will is always on the side which is most favourable to the public interest, that is to say, most equitable; so that it is needful only to act justly, to be certain of following the general will. When this is flouted too openly, it makes itself felt, in spite of the formidable restraint of the public authority. I shall cite the nearest possible examples that may be followed in such cases.

In China, it is the constant maxim of the Prince to decide against his officers, in every dispute that arises between them and the people. If bread be too dear in any province, the Intendant of that province is thrown into prison. If there be an insurrection in another, the Governor is dismissed, and every Mandarin answers with his head for all the mischief that happens in his department. Not that these affairs do not subsequently undergo a regular examination; but long experience has caused the judgment to be thus anticipated. There is seldom any injustice to be repaired; in the meantime, the Emperor, being satisfied that public outcry does not arise without cause, always discovers, through the seditious clamours which he punishes, just grievances to redress.

It is a great thing to preserve the rule of peace and order through all the parts of the Republic; it is a great thing that the State should be tranquil, and the law respected: but if nothing more is done, there will be in all this more appearance than reality; for that government which confines itself to mere obedience will find difficulty in getting itself obeyed. If it is good to know how to deal with men as they are, it is much better to make them what there is need that they should be. The most absolute authority is that which penetrates into a man's inmost being, and concerns itself no less with his will than with his actions. It is certain that all peoples become in the long run what the government makes them; warriors, citizens, men, when it so pleases: or merely populace and rabble, when it chooses to make them so. Hence every prince who despises his subjects, dishonours himself, in confessing that he does not know how to make them worthy of respect. Make men, therefore, if you would command men: if you would have them obedient to the laws, make them love the laws, and then they will need only to know what is their duty to do it. This was the great art of ancient governments, in those distant times when philosophers gave laws to men, and made use of their authority only to render them wise and happy. Thence arose the numerous sumptuary laws, the many regulations of morals, and all the public rules of conduct which were admitted or rejected with the greatest care. Even tyrants did not forget this important part of administration, but took as great pains to corrupt the morals of their slaves, as Magistrates took to correct those of their fellow-citizens. But our modern governments, which imagine they have done everything when they have raised money, conceive that it is unnecessary and even impossible to go a step further.

II. The second essential rule of public economy is no less important than the first. If you would have the general will accomplished, bring all the particular wills into conformity with it; in other words, as virtue is nothing more than this conformity of the particular wills with the general will, establish the reign of virtue.

If our politicians were less blinded by their ambition, they would see how impossible it is for any establishment whatever to act in the spirit of its institution, unless it is guided in accordance with the law of duty; they would feel that the greatest support of public authority lies in the hearts of the citizens, and that nothing can take the place of morality in the maintenance of government. It is not only upright men who know how to administer the laws; but at bottom only good men know how to obey them. The man who once gets the better of remorse, will not shrink before punishments which are less severe, and less lasting, and from which there is at least the hope of escaping: whatever precautions are taken, those who only require impunity in order to do wrong will not fail to find means of eluding the law, and avoiding its penalties. In this case, as all particular interests unite against the general interest, which is no longer that of any individual, public vices have a greater effect in enervating the laws than the laws in the repression of such vices: so that the corruption of the people and of their rulers will at length extend to the government, however wise it may be. The worst of all abuses is to pay an apparent obedience to the laws, only in order actually to break them with security. For in this case the best laws soon become the most pernicious; and it would be a hundred times better that they should not exist. In such a situation, it is vain to add edicts to edicts and regulations to regulations. Everything serves only to introduce new abuses, without correcting the old. The more laws are multiplied, the more they are despised, and all the new officials appointed to supervise them are only so many more people to break them, and either to share the plunder with their predecessors, or to plunder apart on their own. The reward of virtue soon becomes that of robbery; the vilest of men rise to the greatest credit; the greater they are the more despicable they become; their infamy appears even in their dignities, and their very honours dishonour them. If they buy the influence of the leaders or the protection of women, it is only that they may sell justice, duty, and the State in their turn: in the meantime, the people, feeling that its vices are not the first cause of its misfortunes, murmurs and complains that all its misfortunes come solely from those whom it pays to protect it from such things.

It is under these circumstances that the voice of duty no longer speaks in men's hearts, and their rulers are obliged to substitute the cry of terror, or the lure of an apparent interest, of which they subsequently trick their creatures. In this situation they are compelled to have recourse to all the petty and despicable shifts which they call *rules of State* and *mysteries of the cabinet*. All the vigour that is left in the government is used by its members in ruining and supplanting one another, while the public business is neglected, or is transacted only as personal interest requires and directs. In short, the whole art of those great politicians lies in so mesmerising those they stand in need of, that each may think he is labouring for his own interest in working for theirs: I say *theirs* on the false supposition that it is the real interest of rulers to annihilate a people in order to make it subject, and to ruin their own property in order to secure their possession of it.

But when the citizens love their duty, and the guardians of the public authority sincerely apply themselves to the fostering of that love by their own example and assiduity, every difficulty vanishes; and government becomes so easy that it needs none of that art of darkness, whose blackness is its only mystery. Those enterprising spirits, so dangerous and so much admired, all those great ministers, whose glory is inseparable from the miseries of the people, are no longer regretted: public morality supplies what is wanting in the genius of the rulers; and the more virtue reigns, the less need there is for talent. Even ambition is better served by duty than by usurpation: when the people is convinced that its rulers are labouring only for its happiness, its deference saves them the trouble of labouring to strengthen their power: and history shows us, in a thousand cases, that the authority of one who is beloved over those whom he loves is a hundred times more absolute than all the tyranny of usurpers. This does not mean that the government ought to be afraid to make use of its power, but that it ought to make use of it only in a lawful manner. We find in history a thousand examples of pusillanimous or ambitious rulers, who were ruined by their slackness or their pride; not one who suffered for having been strictly just. But we ought not to confound negligence with moderation, or clemency with weakness. To be just, it is necessary to be severe; to permit vice, when one has the right and the power to suppress it, is to be oneself vicious.

It is not enough to say to the citizens, *be good;* they must be taught to be so; and even example, which is in this respect the first lesson, is not the sole means to be employed; patriotism is the most efficacious: for, as I have said already, every man is virtuous when his particular will is in all things conformable to the general will, and we voluntarily will what is willed by those whom we love. It appears that the feeling of humanity evaporates and grows feeble in embracing all mankind, and that we cannot be affected by the calamities of Tartary or Japan, in the same manner as we are by those of European nations. It is necessary in some degree to confine and limit our interest and compassion in order to make it active. Now, as this sentiment can be useful only to those with whom we have to live, it is proper that our humanity should confine itself to our fellow-citizens, and should receive a new force because we are in the habit of seeing them, and by reason of the common interest which unites them. It is certain that the greatest miracles of virtue have been produced by patriotism: this fine and lively feeling, which gives to the force of self-love all the beauty of virtue, lends it an energy which, without disfiguring it, makes it the most heroic of all passions. This it is that produces so many immortal actions, the glory of which dazzles our feeble eyes; and so many great men, whose old-world virtues pass for fables now that patriotism is made mock of. This is not surprising; the transports of susceptible hearts appear altogether fanciful to any one who has never felt them; and the love of one's country, which is a hundred times more lively and delightful than the love of a mistress, cannot be conceived except by experiencing it. But it is easy to perceive in every heart that is warmed by it, in all the actions it inspires, a glowing and sublime ardour which does not attend the purest virtue, when separated from it. Contrast Socrates even with Cato; the one was the greater philosopher, the other more of the citizen. Athens was already ruined in the time of Socrates, and he had no other country than the world at large. Cato had the cause of his country always at heart; he lived for it alone, and could not bear to outlive it. The virtue of Socrates was that of the wisest of men; but, compared with Cæsar and Pompey, Cato seems a God among mortals. Socrates instructed a few individuals, opposed the Sophists, and died for truth: but Cato defended his country, its liberty and its laws, against the conquerors of the world, and at length departed from the earth, when he had no longer a country to serve. A worthy pupil of Socrates would be the most virtuous of his contemporaries; but a worthy follower of Cato would be one of the greatest. The virtue of the former would be his happiness; the latter would seek his happiness in that of all. We should be taught by the one, and led by the other; and this alone is enough to determine which to prefer: for no people has ever been made into a nation of philosophers, but it is not impossible to make a people happy.

Do we wish men to be virtuous? Then let us begin by making them love their country: but how can they love it, if their country be nothing more to them than to strangers, and afford them nothing but what it can refuse nobody? It would be still worse, if they did not enjoy even the privilege of social security, and if their lives, liberties and property lay at the mercy of persons in power, without their being permitted, or it being possible for them, to get relief from the laws. For in that case, being subjected to the duties of the state of civil society, without enjoying even the common privileges of the state of nature, and without being able to use their strength in their own defence, they would be in the worst condition in which freemen could possibly find themselves, and the word *country* would mean for them something merely odious and ridiculous. It must not be imagined that a man can break or lose an arm, without the pain being conveyed to his head: nor is it any more credible that the general will should consent that any one member of the State, whoever he might be, should wound or destroy another, than it is that the fingers of a man in his senses should wilfully scratch his eyes out. The security of individuals is so intimately connected with the public confederation that, apart from the regard that must be paid to human weakness, that convention would in point of right be dissolved, if in the State a single citizen who might have been relieved were allowed to perish, or if one were wrongfully confined in prison, or if in one case an obviously unjust sentence were given. For the fundamental conventions being broken, it is impossible to conceive of any right or interest that could retain the people in the social union; unless they were restrained by force, which alone causes the dissolution of the state of civil society.

In fact, does not the undertaking entered into by the whole body of the nation bind it to provide for the security of the least of its members with as much care as for that of all the rest? Is the welfare of a single citizen any less the common cause than that of the whole State? It may be said that it is good that one should perish for all. I am ready to admire such a saying when it comes from the lips of a virtuous and worthy patriot, voluntarily and dutifully sacrificing himself for the good of his country: but if we are to understand by it, that it is lawful for the government to sacrifice an innocent man for the good of the multitude, I look upon it as one of the most execrable rules tyranny ever invented, the greatest falsehood that can be advanced, the most dangerous admission that can be made, and a direct contradiction of the fundamental laws of society. So little is it the case that any one person ought to perish for all, that all have pledged their lives and properties for the defence of each, in order that the weakness of individuals may always be protected by the strength of the public, and each member by the whole State. Suppose we take from the whole people one individual after another, and then press the advocates of this rule to explain more exactly what they mean by the *body of the State,* and we shall see that it will at length be reduced to a small number of persons, who are not the people, but the officers of the people, and who, having bound themselves by personal oath to perish for the welfare of the people, would thence infer that the people is to perish for their own.

Need we look for examples of the protection which the State owes to its members, and the respect it owes to their persons? It is only among the most illustrious and courageous nations that they are to be found; it is only among free peoples that the dignity of man is realised. It is well known into what perplexity the whole republic of Sparta was thrown, when the question of punishing a guilty citizen arose.

In Macedon, the life of a man was a matter of such importance, that Alexander the Great, at the height of his glory, would not have dared to put a Macedonian criminal to death in cold blood, till the accused had appeared to make his defence before his fellow-citizens, and had been condemned by them. But the Romans distinguished themselves above all other peoples by the regard which their government paid to the individual, and by its scrupulous attention to the preservation of the inviolable rights of all the members of the

State. Nothing was so sacred among them as the life of a citizen; and no less than an assembly of the whole people was needed to condemn one. Not even the Senate, nor the Consuls, in all their majesty, possessed the right; but the crime and punishment of a citizen were regarded as a public calamity among the most powerful people in the world. So hard indeed did it seem to shed blood for any crime whatsoever, that by the Lex Porcia, the penalty of death was commuted into that of banishment for all those who were willing to survive the loss of so great a country. Everything both at Rome, and in the Roman armies, breathed that love of fellow-citizens one for another, and that respect for the Roman name, which raised the courage and inspired the virtue of every one who had the honour to bear it. The cap of a citizen delivered from slavery, the civic crown of him who had saved the life of another, were looked upon with the greatest pleasure amid the pomp of their triumphs; and it is remarkable that among the crowns which were bestowed in honour of splendid actions in war, the civic crown and that of the triumphant general alone were of laurel, all the others being merely of gold. It was thus that Rome was virtuous and became the mistress of the world. Ambitious rulers! A herdsman governs his dogs and cattle, and yet is only the meanest of mankind. If it be a fine thing to command, it is when those who obey us are capable of doing us honour. Show respect, therefore, to your fellow-citizens, and you will render yourselves worthy of respect; show respect to liberty, and your power will increase daily. Never exceed your rights, and they will soon become unlimited.

Let our country then show itself the common mother of her citizens; let the advantages they enjoy in their country endear it to them; let the government leave them enough share in the public administration to make them feel that they are at home; and let the laws be in their eyes only the guarantees of the common liberty. These rights, great as they are, belong to all men: but without seeming to attack them directly, the ill-will of rulers may in fact easily reduce their effect to nothing. The law, which they thus abuse, serves the powerful at once as a weapon of offence, and as a shield against the weak; and the pretext of the public good is always the most dangerous scourge of the people. What is most necessary, and perhaps most difficult, in government, is rigid integrity in doing strict justice to all, and above all in protecting the poor against the tyranny of the rich. The greatest evil has already come about, when there are poor men to be defended, and rich men to be restrained. It is on the middle classes alone that the whole force of the law is exerted; they are equally powerless against the treasures of the rich and the penury of the poor. The first mocks them, the second escapes them. The one breaks the meshes, the other passes through them.

It is therefore one of the most important functions of government to prevent extreme inequality of fortunes; not by taking away wealth from its possessors, but by depriving all men of means to accumulate it; not by building hospitals for the poor, but by securing the citizens from becoming poor. The unequal distribution of inhabitants over the territory, when men are crowded together in one place, while other places are depopulated; the encouragement of the arts that minister to luxury and of purely industrial arts at the expense of useful and laborious crafts; the sacrifice of agriculture to commerce; the necessitation of the tax-farmer by the mal-administration of the funds of the State; and in short, venality pushed to such an extreme that even public esteem is reckoned at a cash value, and virtue rated at a market price: these are the most obvious causes of opulence and of poverty, of public interest, of mutual hatred among citizens, of indifference to the common cause, of the corruption of the people, and of the weakening of all the springs of government. Such are the evils, which are with difficulty cured when they make themselves felt, but which a wise administration ought to prevent, if it is to maintain, along with good morals, respect for the laws, patriotism, and the influence of the general will.

But all these precautions will be inadequate, unless rulers go still more to the root of the matter. I conclude this part of public economy where I ought to have begun it. There can be no patriotism without liberty, no liberty without virtue, no virtue without citizens; create citizens, and you have everything you need; without them, you will have nothing but debased slaves, from the rulers of the State downwards. To form citizens is not the work of a day; and in order to have men it is necessary to educate them when they are children. It will be said, perhaps, that whoever has men to govern, ought not to seek, beyond their nature, a perfection of which they are incapable; that he ought not to desire to destroy their passions; and that the execution of such an attempt is no more desirable than it is possible. I will agree, further, that a man without passions would certainly be a bad citizen; but it must be agreed also that, if men are not taught not to love some things, it is impossible to teach them to love one object more than another—to prefer that which is truly beautiful to that which is deformed. If, for example, they were early accustomed to regard their individuality only in its relation to the body of the State, and to be aware, so to speak, of their own existence merely as a part of that of the State, they might at length come to identify themselves in some degree with this greater whole, to feel themselves members of their country, and to love it with that exquisite feeling which no isolated person has save for himself; to lift up their spirits perpetually to this great object, and thus to transform into a sublime virtue that dangerous disposition which gives rise to all our vices. Not only does philosophy demonstrate the possibility of giving feeling these new directions; history furnishes us with a thousand striking examples. If they are so rare among us moderns, it is because nobody troubles himself whether citizens exist or not, and still less does anybody think of attending to the matter soon enough to make them. It is too late to change our natural inclinations, when they have taken their course, and egoism is confirmed by habit: it is too late to lead us out of ourselves when once the human Ego, concentrated in our hearts, has acquired that contemptible activity which absorbs all virtue and constitutes the life and being of little minds. How can patriotism germinate in the midst of so many other passions which smother it? And what can remain, for fellow-citizens, of a heart already divided between avarice, a mistress, and vanity?

From the first moment of life, men ought to begin learning to deserve to live; and, as at the instant of birth we partake of the rights of citizenship, that instant ought to be the beginning of the exercise of our duty. If there are laws for the age of maturity, there ought to be laws for infancy, teaching obedience to others: and as the reason of each man is not left to be the sole arbiter of his duties, government ought the less indiscriminately to abandon to the intelligence and prejudices of fathers the education of their children, as that education is of still greater importance to the State than to the fathers: for, according to the course of nature, the death of the father often deprives him of the final fruits of education; but his country sooner or later perceives its effects. Families dissolve, but the State remains.

Should the public authority, by taking the place of the father, and charging itself with that important function, acquire his rights by discharging his duties, he would have the less cause to complain, as he would only be changing his title, and would have in common, under the name of *citizen*, the same authority over his children, as he was exercising separately under the name of *father*, and would not be less obeyed when speaking in the name of the law, than when he spoke in that of nature. Public education, therefore, under regulations prescribed by the government, and under magistrates established by the Sovereign, is one of the fundamental rules of popular or legitimate government. If children are brought up in common in the bosom of equality; if they are imbued with the laws of the State and the precepts of the general will; if they are taught to respect these above all things; if they are surrounded by examples and objects which constantly remind them of the tender mother who nourishes them, of the love she bears them, of the inestimable benefits they receive from her, and of the return they owe her, we cannot doubt that they will learn to cherish one another mutually as brothers, to will nothing contrary to the will of society, to substitute the actions of men and citizens for the futile and vain babbling of sophists, and to become in time defenders and fathers of the country of which they will have been so long the children.

I shall say nothing of the Magistrates destined to preside over such an education, which is certainly the most important business of the State. It is easy to see that if such marks of public confidence were conferred on slight grounds, if this sublime function were not, for those who have worthily discharged all other offices, the reward of labour, the pleasant and honourable repose of old age, and the crown of all honours, the whole enterprise would be useless and the education void of success. For wherever the lesson is not supported by authority, and the precept by example, all instruction is fruitless; and virtue itself loses its credit in the mouth of one who does not practise it. But let illustrious warriors, bent under the weight of their laurels, preach courage: let upright Magistrates, grown white in the purple and on the bench teach justice. Such teachers as these would thus get themselves virtuous successors, and transmit from age to age, to generations to come, the experience and talents of rulers, the courage and virtue of citizens, and common emulation in all to live and die for their country.

I know of but three peoples which once practised public education, the Cretans, the Lacedemonians, and the ancient Persians: among all these it was attended with the greatest success, and indeed it did wonders among the two last. Since the world has been divided into nations too great to admit of being well governed, this method has been no longer practicable, and the reader will readily perceive other reasons why such a thing has never been attempted by any modern people. It is very remarkable that the Romans were able to dispense with it; but Rome was for five hundred years one continued miracle which the world cannot hope to see again. The virtue of the Romans, engendered by their horror of tyranny and the crimes of tyrants, and by an innate patriotism, made all their houses so many schools of citizenship; while the unlimited power of fathers over their children made the individual authority so rigid that the father was more feared than the Magistrate, and was in his family tribunal both censor of morals and avenger of the laws.

Thus a careful and well-intentioned government, vigilant incessantly to maintain or restore patriotism and morality among the people, provides beforehand against the evils which sooner or later result from the indifference of the citizens to the fate of the Republic, keeping within narrow bounds that personal interest which so isolates the individual that the State is enfeebled by his power, and has nothing to hope from his good-will. Wherever men love their country, respect the laws, and live simply, little remains to be done in order to make them happy; and in public administration, where chance has less influence than in the lot of individuals, wisdom is so nearly allied to happiness, that the two objects are confounded.

III. It is not enough to have citizens and to protect them, it is also necessary to consider their subsistence. Provision for the public wants is an obvious inference from the general will, and the third essential duty of government. This duty is not, we should feel, to fill the granaries of individuals and thereby to grant them a dispensation from labour, but to keep plenty so within their reach that labour

is always necessary and never useless for its acquisition. It extends also to everything regarding the management of the exchequer, and the expenses of public administration. Having thus treated of general economy with reference to the government of persons, we must now consider it with reference to the administration of property.

This part presents no fewer difficulties to solve, and contradictions to remove, than the preceding. It is certain that the right of property is the most sacred of all the rights of citizenship, and even more important in some respects than liberty itself; either because it more nearly affects the preservation of life, or because, property being more easily usurped and more difficult to defend than life, the law ought to pay a greater attention to what is most easily taken away; or finally, because property is the true foundation of civil society, and the real guarantee of the undertakings of citizens: for if property were not answerable for personal actions, nothing would be easier than to evade duties and laugh at the laws. On the other hand, it is no less certain that the maintenance of the State and the government involves costs and outgoings; and as every one who agrees to the end must acquiesce in the means, it follows that the members of a society ought to contribute from their property to its support. Besides, it is difficult to secure the property of individuals on one side, without attacking it on another; and it is impossible that all the regulations which govern the order of succession, will, contracts, &c. should not lay individuals under some constraint as to the disposition of their goods, and should not consequently restrict the right of property.

But besides what I have said above of the agreement between the authority of law and the liberty of the citizen, there remains to be made, with respect to the disposition of goods, an important observation which removes many difficulties. As Puffendorf has shown, the right of property, by its very nature, does not extend beyond the life of the proprietor, and the moment a man is dead his goods cease to belong to him. Thus, to prescribe the conditions according to which he can dispose of them, is in reality less to alter his right as it appears, than to extend it in fact.

In general, although the institution of the laws which regulate the power of individuals in the disposition of their own goods belongs only to the Sovereign, the spirit of these laws, which the government ought to follow in their application, is that, from father to son, and from relation to relation, the goods of a family should go as little out of it and be as little alienated as possible. There is a sensible reason for this in favour of children, to whom the right of property would be quite useless, if the father left them nothing, and who besides, having often contributed by their labour to the acquisition of their father's wealth, are in their own right associates with him in his right of property. But another reason, more distant, though not less important, is that nothing is more fatal to morality and to the Republic than the continual shifting of rank and fortune among the citizens: such changes are both the proof and the source of a thousand disorders, and overturn and confound everything; for those who were brought up to one thing find themselves destined for another; and neither those who rise nor those who fall are able to assume the rules of conduct, or to possess themselves of the qualifications requisite for their new condition, still less to discharge the duties it entails. I proceed to the object of public finance.

If the people governed itself and there were no intermediary between the administration of the State and the citizens, they would have no more to do than to assess themselves occasionally, in proportion to the public needs and the abilities of individuals: and as they would all keep in sight the recovery and employment of such assessments, no fraud or abuse could slip into the management of them; the State would never be involved in debt, or the people over-burdened with taxes; or at least the knowledge of how the money would be used would be a consolation for the severity of the tax. But things cannot be carried on in this manner: on the contrary, however small any State may be, civil societies are always too populous to be under the immediate government of all their members. It is necessary that the public money should go through the hands of the rulers, all of whom have, besides the interests of the State, their own individual interests, which are not the last to be listened to. The people, on its side, perceiving rather the cupidity and ridiculous expenditure of its rulers than the public needs, murmurs at seeing itself stripped of necessaries to furnish others with superfluities; and when once these complaints have reached a certain degree of bitterness, the most upright administration will find it impossible to restore confidence. In such a case, voluntary

contributions bring in nothing, and forced contributions are illegitimate. This cruel alternative of letting the State perish, or of violating the sacred right of property, which is its support, constitutes the great difficulty of just and prudent economy.

The first step which the founder of a republic ought to take after the establishment of laws, is to settle a sufficient fund for the maintenance of the Magistrates and other Officials, and for other public expenses. This fund, if it consist of money, is called *ærarium* or *fisc,* and *public demesne* if it consist of lands. This, for obvious reasons, is much to be preferred. Whoever has reflected on this matter must be of the opinion of Bodin, who looks upon the public demesne as the most reputable and certain means of providing for the needs of the State. It is remarkable also that Romulus, in his division of lands, made it his first care to set apart a third for the use of the State. I confess it is not impossible for the produce of the demesne, if it be badly managed, to be reduced to nothing; but it is not of the essence of public demesnes to be badly administered.

Before any use is made of this fund, it should be assigned or accepted by an assembly of the people, or of the estates of the country, which should determine its future use. After this solemnity, which makes such funds inalienable, their very nature is, in a manner, changed, and the revenues become so sacred, that it is not only the most infamous theft, but actual treason, to misapply them or pervert them from the purpose for which they were destined. It reflects great dishonour on Rome that the integrity of Cato the censor was something so very remarkable, and that an Emperor, on rewarding the talents of a singer with a few crowns, thought it necessary to observe that the money came from his own private purse, and not from that of the State. But if we find few Galbas, where are we to look for a Cato? For when vice is no longer dishonourable, what chiefs will be so scrupulous as to abstain from touching the public revenues that are left to their discretion, and even not in time to impose on themselves, by pretending to confound their own expensive and scandalous dissipations with the glory of the State, and the means of extending their own authority with the means of augmenting its power? It is particularly in this delicate part of the administration that virtue is the only effective instrument, and that the integrity of the Magistrate is the only real check upon his avarice. Books and auditing of accounts, instead of exposing frauds, only conceal them; for prudence is never so ready to conceive new precautions as knavery is to elude them. Never mind, then, about account books and papers; place the management of finance in honest hands: that is the only way to get it faithfully conducted.

When public funds are once established, the rulers of the State become of right the administrators of them: for this administration constitutes a part of government which is always essential, though not always equally so. Its influence increases in proportion as that of other resources is diminished; and it may justly be said that a government has reached the last stage of corruption, when it has ceased to have sinews other than money. Now as every government constantly tends to become lax, this is enough to show why no State can subsist unless its revenues constantly increase.

The first sense of the necessity of this increase is also the first sign of the internal disorder of the State; and the prudent administrator, in his endeavours to find means to provide for the present necessity, will neglect nothing to find out the distant cause of the new need; just as a mariner when he finds the water gaining on his vessel, does not neglect, while he is working the pumps, to discover and stop the leak.

From this rule is deduced the most important rule in the administration of finance, which is, to take more pains to guard against needs than to increase revenues. For, whatever diligence be employed, the relief which only comes after, and more slowly than, the evil, always leaves some injury behind. While a remedy is being found for one evil, another is beginning to make itself felt, and even the remedies themselves produce new difficulties: so that at length the nation is involved in debt and the people oppressed, while the government loses its influence and can do very little with a great deal of money. I imagine it was owing to the recognition of this rule that such wonders were done by ancient governments, which did more with their parsimony than ours do with all their treasures; and perhaps from this comes the common use of the word *economy,* which means rather the prudent management of what one has than ways of getting what one has not.

But apart from the public demesne, which is of service to the State in proportion to the uprightness of those who govern, any one sufficiently acquainted with the whole force of the general administration, especially when it confines itself to legitimate methods, would be astonished at the resources the rulers can make use of for guarding against public needs, without trespassing on the goods of individuals. As they are masters of the whole commerce of the State, nothing is easier for them than to direct it into such channels as to provide for every need, without appearing to interfere. The distribution of provisions, money, and merchandise in just proportions, according to times and places, is the true secret of finance and the source of wealth, provided those who administer it have foresight enough to suffer a present apparent loss, in order really to obtain immense profits in the future. When we see a government paying bounties, instead of receiving duties, on the exportation of corn in time of plenty, and on its importation in time of scarcity, we must have such facts before our eyes if we are to be persuaded of their reality. We should hold such facts to be idle tales, if they had happened in ancient times. Let us suppose that, in order to prevent a scarcity in bad years, a proposal were made to establish public granaries; would not the maintenance of so useful an institution serve in most countries as an excuse for new taxes? At Geneva, such granaries, established and kept up by a prudent administration, are a public resource in bad years, and the principal revenue of the State at all times. *Alit et ditat* is the inscription which stands, rightly and properly, on the front of the building. To set forth in this place the economic system of a good government, I have often turned my eyes to that of this Republic, rejoicing to find in my own country an example of that wisdom and happiness which I should be glad to see prevail in every other.

If we ask how the needs of a State grow, we shall find they generally arise, like the wants of individuals, less from any real necessity than from the increase of useless desires, and that expenses are often augmented only to give a pretext for raising receipts: so that the State would sometimes gain by not being rich, and apparent wealth is in reality more burdensome than poverty itself would be. Rulers may indeed hope to keep the peoples in stricter dependence, by thus giving them with one hand what they take from them with the other; and this was in fact the policy of Joseph towards the Egyptians: but this political sophistry is the more fatal to the State, as the money never returns into the hands it went out of. Such principles only enrich the idle at the expense of the industrious.

A desire for conquest is one of the most evident and dangerous causes of this increase. This desire, occasioned often by a different species of ambition from that which it seems to proclaim, is not always what it appears to be, and has not so much, for its real motive, the apparent desire to aggrandise the Nation as a secret desire to increase the authority of the rulers at home, by increasing the number of troops, and by the diversion which the objects of war occasion in the minds of the citizens.

It is at least certain, that no peoples are so oppressed and wretched as conquering nations, and that their successes only increase their misery. Did not history inform us of the fact, reason would suffice to tell us that, the greater a State grows, the heavier and more burdensome in proportion its expenses become: for every province has to furnish its share to the general expense of government, and besides has to be at the expense of its own administration, which is as great as if it were really independent. Add to this that great fortunes are always acquired in one place and spent in another. Production therefore soon ceases to balance consumption, and a whole country is impoverished merely to enrich a single town.

Another source of the increase of public wants, which depends on the foregoing, is this. There may come a time when the citizens, no longer looking upon themselves as interested in the common cause, will cease to be the defenders of their country, and the Magistrates will prefer the command of mercenaries to that of free-men; if for no other reason than that, when the time comes, they may use them to reduce free-men to submission. Such was the state of Rome towards the end of the Republic and under the Emperors: for all the victories of the early Romans, like those of Alexander, had been won by brave citizens, who were ready, at need, to give their blood in the service of their country, but would never sell it. Only at the siege of Veii did the practice of paying the Roman infantry begin. Marius, in the Jugurthine war, dishonoured the legions by introducing freedmen, vagabonds and other mercenaries. Tyrants, the enemies of the very people it was their duty to make happy, maintained regular troops, apparently to withstand the foreigner, but real-

ly to enslave their countrymen. To form such troops, it was necessary to take men from the land; the lack of their labour then diminished the amount of provisions, and their maintenance introduced those taxes which increased prices. This first disorder gave rise to murmurs among the people; in order to suppress them, the number of troops had to be increased, and consequently the misery of the people also got worse; and the growing despair led to still further increases in the cause in order to guard against its effects. On the other hand, the mercenaries, whose merit we may judge of by the price at which they sold themselves, proud of their own meanness, and despising the laws that protected them, as well as their fellows whose bread they ate, imagined themselves more honoured in being Cæsar's satellites than in being defenders of Rome. As they were given over to blind obedience, their swords were always at the throats of their fellow-citizens, and they were prepared for general butchery at the first sign. It would not be difficult to show that this was one of the principal causes of the ruin of the Roman Empire.

The invention of artillery and fortifications has forced the princes of Europe, in modern times, to return to the use of regular troops, in order to garrison their towns; but, however lawful their motives, it is to be feared the effect may be no less fatal. There is no better reason now than formerly for depopulating the country to form armies and garrisons, nor should the people be oppressed to support them; in a word, these dangerous establishments have increased of late years with such rapidity in this part of the world, that they evidently threaten to depopulate Europe, and sooner or later to ruin its inhabitants.

Be this as it may, it ought to be seen that such institutions necessarily subvert the true economic system, which draws the principal revenue of the State from the public demesne, and leave only the troublesome resource of subsidies and imposts; with which it remains to deal.

It should be remembered that the foundation of the social compact is property; and its first condition, that every one should be maintained in the peaceful possession of what belongs to him. It is true that, by the same treaty, every one binds himself, at least tacitly, to be assessed toward the public wants: but as this undertaking cannot prejudice the fundamental law, and presupposes that the need is clearly recognised by all who contribute to it, it is plain that such assessment, in order to be lawful, must be voluntary; it must depend, not indeed on a particular will, as if it were necessary to have the consent of each individual, and that he should give no more than just what he pleased, but on a general will, decided by vote of a majority, and on the basis of a proportional rating which leaves nothing arbitrary in the imposition of the tax.

That taxes cannot be legitimately established except by the consent of the people or its representatives, is a truth generally admitted by all philosophers and jurists of any repute on questions of public right, not even excepting Bodin. If any of them have laid down rules which seem to contradict this, their particular motives for doing so may easily be seen; and they introduce so many conditions and restrictions that the argument comes at bottom to the same thing: for whether the people has it in its power to refuse, or the Sovereign ought not to exact, is a matter of indifference with regard to right; and if the point in question concerns only power, it is useless to inquire whether it is legitimate or not. Contributions levied on the people are two kinds; real, levied on commodities, and personal, paid by the head. Both are called taxes or subsidies: when the people fixes the sum to be paid, it is called subsidy; but when it grants the product of an imposition, it is called a tax. We are told in *The Spirit of the Laws* that a capitation tax is most suited to slavery, and a real tax most in accordance with liberty. This would be incontestable, if the circumstances of every person were equal; for otherwise nothing can be more disproportionate than such a tax; and it is in the observations of exact proportions that the spirit of liberty consists. But if a tax by heads were exactly proportioned to the circumstances of individuals, as what is called the capitation tax in France might be, it would be the most equitable and consequently the most proper for freemen.

These proportions appear at first very easy to note, because, being relative to each man's position in the world, their incidence is always public: but proper regard is seldom paid to all the elements that should enter into such a calculation, even apart from deception arising from avarice, fraud and self-interest. In the first place, we have to consider the relation of quantities, according to which, *ceteris paribus,* the person who has ten times the property of another man ought to pay ten times as

much to the State. Secondly, the relation of the use made, that is to say, the distinction between necessaries and superfluities. He who possesses only the common necessaries of life should pay nothing at all, while the tax on him who is in possession of superfluities may justly be extended to everything he has over and above mere necessaries. To this he will possibly object that, when his rank is taken into account, what may be superfluous to a man of inferior station is necessary for him. But this is false: for a grandee has two legs just like a cow-herd, and, like him again, but one belly. Besides, these pretended necessaries are really so little necessary to his rank, that if he should renounce them on any worthy occasion, he would only be the more honoured. The populace would be ready to adore a Minister who went to Council on foot, because he had sold off his carriages to supply a pressing need of the State. Lastly, to no man does the law prescribe magnificence; and propriety is no argument against right.

A third relation, which is never taken into account, though it ought to be the chief consideration, is the advantage that every person derives from the social confederacy; for this provides a powerful protection for the immense possessions of the rich, and hardly leaves the poor man in quiet possession of the cottage he builds with his own hands. Are not all the advantages of society for the rich and powerful? Are not all lucrative posts in their hands? Are not all privileges and exemptions reserved for them alone? Is not the public authority always on their side? If man of eminence robs his creditors, or is guilty of other knaveries, is he not always assured of impunity? Are not the assaults, acts of violence, assassinations, and even murders committed by the great, matters that are hushed up in a few months, and of which nothing more is thought? But if a great man himself is robbed or insulted, the whole police force is immediately in motion, and woe even to innocent persons who chance to be suspected. If he has to pass through any dangerous road, the country is up in arms to escort him. If the axle-tree of his chaise breaks, everybody flies to his assistance. If there is a noise at his door, he speaks but a word, and all is silent. If he is incommoded by the crowd, he waves his hand and every one makes way. If his coach is met on the road by a wagon, his servants are ready to beat the driver's brains out, and fifty honest pedestrians going quietly about their business had better be knocked on the head than an idle jackanapes be delayed in his coach. Yet all this respect costs him not a farthing: it is the rich man's right, and not what he buys with his wealth. How different is the case of the poor man! the more humanity owes him, the more society denies him. Every door is shut against him, even when he has a right to its being opened: and if ever he obtains justice, it is with much greater difficulty than others obtain favours. If the militia is to be raised or the highway to be mended, he is always given the preference; he always bears the burden which his richer neighbour has influence enough to get exempted from. On the least accident that happens to him, everybody avoids him: if his cart be overturned in the road, so far is he from receiving any assistance, that he is lucky if he does not get horse-whipped by the impudent lackeys of some young Duke; in a word, all gratuitous assistance is denied to the poor when they need it, just because they cannot pay for it. I look upon any poor man as totally undone, if he has the misfortune to have an honest heart, a fine daughter, and a powerful neighbour.

Another no less important fact is that the losses of the poor are much harder to repair than those of the rich, and that the difficulty of acquisition is always greater in proportion as there is more need for it. "Nothing comes out of nothing," is as true of life as in physics: money is the seed of money, and the first guinea is sometimes more difficult to acquire than the second million. Add to this that what the poor pay is lost to them for ever, and remains in, or returns to, the hands of the rich: and as, to those who share in the government or to their dependents, the whole produce of the taxes must sooner or later pass, although they pay their share, these persons have always a sensible interest in increasing them.

The terms of the social compact between these two estates of men may be summed up in a few words. "You have need of me, because I am rich and you are poor. We will therefore come to an agreement. I will permit you to have the honour of serving me, on condition that you bestow on me the little you have left, in return for the pains I shall take to command you."

Putting all these considerations carefully together, we shall find that, in order to levy taxes in a truly equitable and proportionate manner, the imposition ought not to be in simple ratio to the property of the contributors, but in compound ratio to the difference of their conditions and the superfluity of their possessions. This very important and difficult operation is daily made by numbers of honest clerks, who know their arithmetic; but a Plato or a Montesquieu would not venture to undertake it without the greatest diffidence, or without praying to Heaven for understanding and integrity.

Another disadvantage of personal taxes is that they may be too much felt or raised with too great severity. This, however, does not prevent them from being frequently evaded; for it is much easier for persons to escape a tax than for their possessions.

Of all impositions, that on land, or real taxation, has always been regarded as most advantageous in countries where more attention is paid to what the tax will produce, and to the certainty of recovering the product, than to securing the least discomfort for the people. It has been even maintained that it is necessary to burden the peasant in order to rouse him from indolence, and that he would never work if he had no taxes to pay. But in all countries experience confutes this ridiculous notion. In England and Holland the farmer pays very little, and in China nothing: yet these are the countries in which the land is best cultivated. On the other hand, in those countries where the husbandman is taxed in proportion to the produce of his lands, he leaves them uncultivated, or reaps just as much from them as suffices for bare subsistence. For to him who loses the fruit of his labour, it is some gain to do nothing. To lay a tax on industry is a very singular expedient for banishing idleness.

Taxes on land or corn, especially when they are excessive, lead to two results so fatal in their effect that they cannot but depopulate and ruin, in the long run, all countries in which they are established.

The first of these arises from the defective circulation of specie; for industry and commerce draw all the money from the country into the capitals: and as the tax destroys the proportion there might otherwise be between the needs of the husbandman and the price of his corn, money is always leaving and never returning. Thus the richer the city the poorer the country. The product of the taxes passes from the hands of the Prince or his financial officers into those of artists and traders; and the husbandman, who receives only the smallest part of it, is at length exhausted by paying always the same, and receiving constantly less. How could a human body subsist if it had veins and no arteries, or if its arteries conveyed the blood only within four inches of the heart? Chardin tells us that in Persia the royal dues on commodities are paid in kind: this custom, which, Herodotus informs us, prevailed long ago in the same country down to the time of Darius, might prevent the evil of which I have been speaking. But unless intendants, directors, commissioners, and warehousemen in Persia are a different kind of people from what they are elsewhere, I can hardly believe that the smallest part of this produce ever reaches the king, or that the corn is not spoilt in every granary, and the greater part of the warehouses not consumed by fire.

The second evil effect arises from an apparent advantage, which aggravates the evil before it can be perceived. That is that corn is a commodity whose price is not enhanced by taxes in the country producing it, and which, in spite of its absolute necessity, may be diminished in quantity without the price being increased. Hence, many people die of hunger, although corn remains cheap, and the husbandman bears the whole charge of a tax, for which he cannot indemnify himself by the price of his corn. It must be observed that we ought not to reason about a land-tax in the same manner as about duties laid on various kinds of merchandise; for the effect of such duties is to raise the price, and they are paid by the buyers rather than the sellers. For these duties, however heavy, are still voluntary, and are paid by the merchant only in proportion to the quantity he buys; and as he buys only in proportion to his sale, he himself gives the law its particular application; but the farmer who is obliged to pay his rent at stated times, whether he sells or not, cannot wait till he can get his own price for his commodity: even if he is not forced to sell for mere subsistence, he must sell to pay the taxes; so that it is frequently the heaviness of the tax that keeps the price of corn low.

It is further to be noticed that the resources of commerce and industry are so far from rendering the tax more supportable through abundance of money, that they only render it more burdensome. I shall not insist on what is very evident; i.e., that, although a greater or less quantity of money in a State may give it the greater or less credit in the eye of the foreigner, it makes not the least difference to the real fortune of the citizens, and does not make

their condition any more or less comfortable. But I must make these two important remarks: first, unless a State possesses superfluous commodities, and abundance of money results from foreign trade, only trading cities are sensible of the abundance; while the peasant only becomes relatively poorer. Secondly, as the price of everything is enhanced by the increase of money, taxes also must be proportionately increased; so that the farmer will find himself still more burdened without having more resources.

It ought to be observed that the tax on land is a real duty on the produce. It is universally agreed, however, that nothing is so dangerous as a tax on corn paid by the purchaser: but how comes it we do not see that it is a hundred times worse when the duty is paid by the cultivator himself? Is not this an attack on the substance of the State at its very source? Is it not the directest possible method of depopulating a country, and therefore in the end ruining it? For the worst kind of scarcity a nation can suffer from is lack of inhabitants.

Only the real statesman can rise, in imposing taxes, above the mere financial object: he alone can transform heavy burdens into useful regulations, and make the people even doubtful whether such establishments were not calculated rather for the good of the nation in general, than merely for the raising of money.

Duties on the importation of foreign commodities, of which the natives are fond, without the country standing in need of them; on the exportation of those of the growth of the country which are not too plentiful, and which foreigners cannot do without: on the productions of frivolous and all too lucrative arts; on the importation of all pure luxuries; and in general on all objects of luxury; will answer the two-fold end in view. It is by such taxes, indeed, by which the poor are eased, and the burdens thrown on the rich, that it is possible to prevent the continual increase of inequality of fortune; the subjection of such a multitude of artisans and useless servants to the rich, the multiplication of idle persons in our cities, and the depopulation of the country-side.

It is important that the value of any commodity and the duties laid on it should be so proportioned that the avarice of individuals may not be too strongly tempted to fraud by the greatness of the possible profit. To make smuggling difficult, those commodities should be singled out which are hardest to conceal.

All duties should be rather paid by the consumer of the commodity taxed than by him who sells it: as the quantity of duty he would be obliged to pay would lay him open to greater temptations, and afford him more opportunities for fraud.

This is the constant custom in China, a country where the taxes are greater and yet better paid than in any other part of the world. There the merchant himself pays no duty; the buyer alone, without murmuring or sedition, meets the whole charge; for as the necessaries of life, such as rice and corn, are absolutely exempt from taxation, the common people is not oppressed, and the duty falls only on those who are well-to-do. Precautions against smuggling ought not to be dictated so much by the fear of it occurring, as by the attention which the government should pay to securing individuals from being seduced by illegitimate profits, which first make them bad citizens, and afterwards soon turn them into dishonest men.

Heavy taxes should be laid on servants in livery, on equipages, rich furniture, fine clothes, on spacious courts and gardens, on public entertainments of all kinds, on useless professions, such as dancers, singers, players, and in a word, on all that multiplicity of objects of luxury, amusement and idleness, which strike the eyes of all, and can the less be hidden, as their whole purpose is to be seen, without which they would be useless. We need be under no apprehension of the produce of these taxes being arbitrary, because they are laid on things not absolutely necessary. They must know but little of mankind who imagine that, after they have been once seduced by luxury, they can ever renounce it: they would a hundred times sooner renounce common necessaries, and had much rather die of hunger than of shame. The increase in their expense is only an additional reason for supporting them, when the vanity of appearing wealthy reaps its profit from the price of the thing and the charge of the tax. As long as there are rich people in the world, they will be desirous of distinguishing themselves from the poor, nor can the State devise a revenue less burdensome or more certain than what arises from this distinction.

For the same reason, industry would have nothing to suffer from an economic system which increased the revenue, encouraged agriculture by relieving the husbandman, and insensibly tended to bring all fortunes nearer to that middle condition which constitutes the genuine strength of the State. These taxes might, I admit, bring certain fashionable articles of dress and amusement to an untimely end; but it would be only to substitute others, by which the artificer would gain, and the exchequer suffer no loss. In a word, suppose the spirit of government was constantly to tax only the superfluities of the rich, one of two things must happen: either the rich would convert their superfluous expenses into useful ones, which would redound to the profit of the State, and thus the imposition of taxes would have the effect of the best sumptuary laws, the expenses of the State would necessarily diminish with those of individuals, and the treasury would not receive so much less as it would gain by having less to pay; or, if the rich did not become less extravagant, the exchequer would have such resources in the product of taxes on their expenditure as would provide for the needs of the State. In the first case the treasury would be the richer by what it would save, from having the less to do with its money; and in the second, it would be enriched by the useless expenses of individuals.

We may add to all this a very important distinction in matters of political right, to which governments, constantly tenacious of doing everything for themselves, ought to pay great attention. It has been observed that personal taxes and duties on the necessaries of life, as they directly trespass on the right of property, and consequently on the true foundation of political society, are always liable to have dangerous results, if they are not established with the express consent of the people or its representatives. It is not the same with articles the use of which we can deny ourselves; for as the individual is under no absolute necessity to pay, his contribution may count as voluntary. The particular consent of each contributor then takes the place of the general consent of the whole people: for why should a people oppose the imposition of a tax which falls only on those who desire to pay it? It appears to me certain that everything, which is not proscribed by law, or contrary to morality, and yet may be prohibited by the government, may also be permitted on payment of a certain duty. Thus, for example, if the government may prohibit the use of coaches, it may certainly impose a tax on them; and this is a prudent and useful method of censuring their use without absolutely forbidding it. In this case, the tax may be regarded as a sort of fine, the product of which compensates for the abuse it punishes.

It may perhaps be objected that those, whom Bodin calls *impostors*, i.e., those who impose or contrive the taxes, being in the class of the rich, will be far from sparing themselves to relieve the poor. But this is quite beside the point. If, in every nation, those to whom the Sovereign commits the government of the people, were, from their position, its enemies, it would not be worth while to inquire what they ought to do to make the people happy.

THE SOCIAL CONTRACT

OR

PRINCIPLES OF POLITICAL RIGHT

Fœderis æquas
Dicamus leges. Virgil, *Æneid* XI.

FOREWARD

This little treatise is part of a longer work which I began years ago without realising my limitations, and long since abandoned. Of the various fragments that might have been extracted from what I wrote, this is the most considerable, and, I think, the least unworthy of being offered to the public. The rest no longer exists.

BOOK I

I MEAN to inquire if, in the civil order, there can be any sure and legitimate rule of administration, men being taken as they are and laws as they might be. In this inquiry I shall endeavour always to unite what right sanctions with what is prescribed by interest, in order that justice and utility may in no case be divided.

I enter upon my task without proving the importance of the subject. I shall be asked if I am a prince or a legislator, to write on politics. I answer that I am neither, and that is why I do so. If I were a prince or a legislator, I should not waste time in saying what wants doing; I should do it, or hold my peace.

As I was born a citizen of a free State, and a member of the Sovereign, I feel that, however feeble the influence my voice can have on public affairs, the right of voting on them makes it my duty to study them: and I am happy, when I reflect upon governments, to find my inquiries always furnish me with new reasons for loving that of my own country.

1. SUBJECT OF THE FIRST BOOK

MAN is born free; and everywhere he is in chains. One thinks himself the master of others, and still remains a greater slave than they. How did this change come about? I do not know. What can make it legitimate? That question I think I can answer.

If I took into account only force, and the effects derived from it, I should say: "As long as a people is compelled to obey, and obeys, it does well; as soon as it can shake off the yoke, and shakes it off, it does still better; for, regaining its liberty by the same right as took it away, either it is justified in resuming it, or there was no justification for those who took it away." But the social order is a sacred right which is the basis of all other rights. Nevertheless, this right does not come from nature, and must therefore be founded on conventions. Before coming to that, I have to prove what I have just asserted.

2. THE FIRST SOCIETIES

THE most ancient of all societies, and the only one that is natural, is the family: and even so the children remain attached to the father only so long as they need him for their preservation. As soon as this need ceases, the natural bond is dissolved. The children, released from the obedience they owed to the father, and the father, released from the care he owed his children, return equally to independence. If they remain united, they continue so no longer naturally, but voluntarily;

and the family itself is then maintained only by convention.

This common liberty results from the nature of man. His first law is to provide for his own preservation, his first cares are those which he owes to himself; and, as soon as he reaches years of discretion, he is the sole judge of the proper means of preserving himself, and consequently becomes his own master.

The family then may be called the first model of political societies: the ruler corresponds to the father, and the people to the children; and all, being born free and equal, alienate their liberty only for their own advantage. The whole difference is that, in the family, the love of the father for his children repays him for the care he takes of them, while, in the State, the pleasure of commanding takes the place of the love which the chief cannot have for the peoples under him.

Grotius denies that all human power is established in favour of the governed, and quotes slavery as an example. His usual method of reasoning is constantly to establish right by fact.[1] It would be possible to employ a more logical method, but none could be more favourable to tyrants.

It is then, according to Grotius, doubtful whether the human race belongs to a hundred men, or that hundred men to the human race: and, throughout his book, he seems to incline to the former alternative, which is also the view of Hobbes. On this showing, the human species is divided into so many herds of cattle, each with its ruler, who keeps guard over them for the purpose of devouring them.

As a shepherd is of a nature superior to that of his flock, the shepherds of men, i.e., their rulers, are of a nature superior to that of the peoples under them. Thus, Philo tells us, the Emperor Caligula reasoned, concluding equally well either that kings were gods, or that men were beasts.

The reasoning of Caligula agrees with that of Hobbes and Grotius. Aristotle, before any of them, had said that men are by no means equal naturally, but that some are born for slavery, and others for dominion.

Aristotle was right; but he took the effect for the cause. Nothing can be more certain

than that every man born in slavery is born for slavery. Slaves lose everything in their chains, even the desire of escaping from them: they love their servitude, as the comrades of Ulysses loved their brutish condition.[2] If then there are slaves by nature, it is because there have been slaves against nature. Force made the first slaves, and their cowardice perpetuated the condition.

I have said nothing of King Adam, or Emperor Noah, father of the three great monarchs who shared out the universe, like the children of Saturn, whom some scholars have recognised in them. I trust to getting due thanks for my moderation; for, being a direct descendant of one of these princes, perhaps of the eldest branch, how do I know that a verification of titles might not leave me the legitimate king of the human race? In any case, there can be no doubt that Adam was sovereign of the world, as Robinson Crusoe was of his island, as long as he was its only inhabitant; and this empire had the advantage that the monarch, safe on his throne, had no rebellions, wars, or conspirators to fear.

3. THE RIGHT OF THE STRONGEST

THE strongest is never strong enough to be always the master, unless he transforms strength into right, and obedience into duty. Hence the right of the strongest, which, though to all seeming meant ironically, is really laid down as a fundamental principle. But are we never to have an explanation of this phrase? Force is a physical power, and I fail to see what moral effect it can have. To yield to force is an act of necessity, not of will —at the most, an act of prudence. In what sense can it be a duty?

Suppose for a moment that this so-called "right" exists. I maintain that the sole result is a mass of inexplicable nonsense. For, if force creates right, the effect changes with the cause: every force that is greater than the first succeeds to its right. As soon as it is possible to disobey with impunity, disobedience is legitimate; and, the strongest being always in the right, the only thing that matters is to act so as to become the strongest. But what kind of right is that which perishes when force fails? If we must obey perforce, there is no need to obey because we ought; and if we are not forced to obey, we are under no obligation to do so. Clearly, the word "right" adds

[1] "Learned inquiries into public right are often only the history of past abuses; and troubling to study them too deeply is a profitless infatuation" (*Essay on the Interests of France in Relation to its Neighbours,* by the Marquis d'Argenson). This is exactly what Grotius has done.

[2] See a short treatise of Plutarch's entitled *That Animals Reason.*

nothing to force: in this connection, it means absolutely nothing.

Obey the powers that be. If this means yield to force, it is a good precept, but superfluous: I can answer for its never being violated. All power comes from God, I admit; but so does all sickness: does that mean that we are forbidden to call in the doctor? A brigand surprises me at the edge of a wood: must I not merely surrender my purse on compulsion; but, even if I could withhold it, am I in conscience bound to give it up? For certainly the pistol he holds is also a power.

Let us then admit that force does not create right, and that we are obliged to obey only legitimate powers. In that case, my original question recurs.

4. SLAVERY

SINCE no man has a natural authority over his fellow, and force creates no right, we must conclude that conventions form the basis of all legitimate authority among men.

If an individual, says Grotius, can alienate his liberty and make himself the slave of a master, why could not a whole people do the same and make itself subject to a king? There are in this passage plenty of ambiguous words which would need explaining; but let us confine ourselves to the word *alienate*. To alienate is to give or to sell. Now, a man who becomes the slave of another does not give himself; he sells himself, at the least for his subsistence: but for what does a people sell itself? A king is so far from furnishing his subjects with their subsistence that he gets his own only from them; and, according to Rabelais, kings do not live on nothing. Do subjects then give their persons on condition that the king takes their goods also? I fail to see what they have left to preserve.

It will be said that the despot assures his subjects civil tranquillity. Granted; but what do they gain, if the wars his ambition brings down upon them, his insatiable avidity, and the vexations conduct of his ministers press harder on them than their own dissensions would have done? What do they gain, if the very tranquillity they enjoy is one of their miseries? Tranquillity is found also in dungeons; but is that enough to make them desirable places to live in? The Greeks imprisoned in the cave of the Cyclops lived there very tranquilly, while they were awaiting their turn to be devoured.

To say that a man gives himself gratuitously, is to say what is absurd and inconceivable; such an act is null and illegitimate, from the mere fact that he who does it is out of his mind. To say the same of a whole people is to suppose a people of madmen; and madness creates no right.

Even if each man could alienate himself, he could not alienate his children: they are born men and free; their liberty belongs to them, and no one but they has the right to dispose of it. Before they come to years of discretion, the father can, in their name, lay down conditions for their preservation and well-being, but he cannot give them irrevocably and without conditions: such a gift is contrary to the ends of nature, and exceeds the rights of paternity. It would therefore be necessary, in order to legitimise an arbitrary government, that in every generation the people should be in a position to accept or reject it; but, were this so, the government would be no longer arbitrary.

To renounce liberty is to renounce being a man, to surrender the rights of humanity and even its duties. For him who renounces everything no indemnity is possible. Such a renunciation is incompatible with man's nature; to remove all liberty from his will is to remove all morality from his acts. Finally, it is an empty and contradictory convention that sets up, on the one side, absolute authority, and, on the other, unlimited obedience. Is it not clear that we can be under no obligation to a person from whom we have the right to exact everything? Does not this condition alone, in the absence of equivalence or exchange, in itself involve the nullity of the act? For what right can my slave have against me, when all that he has belongs to me, and, his right being mine, this right of mine against myself is a phrase devoid of meaning?

Grotius and the rest find in war another origin for the so-called right of slavery. The victor having, as they hold, the right of killing the vanquished, the latter can buy back his life at the price of his liberty; and this convention is the more legitimate because it is to the advantage of both parties.

But it is clear that this supposed right to kill the conquered is by no means deducible from the state of war. Men, from the mere fact that, while they are living in their primitive independence, they have no mutual relations stable enough to constitute either the state of peace or the state of war, cannot be naturally enemies. War is constituted by a relation between things, and not between persons; and, as the state of war cannot arise out of simple personal relations, but only out of real relations, private war, or war of man with man, can exist neither in the state of nature, where there is no constant property, nor in the social state, where everything is under the authority of the laws.

Individual combats, duels and encounters, are acts which cannot constitute a state; while the private wars, authorised by the Establishments of Louis IX, King of France, and suspended by the Peace of God, are abuses of feudalism, in itself an absurd system if ever there was one, and contrary to the principles of natural right and to all good polity.

War then is a relation, not between man and man, but between State and State, and individuals are enemies only accidentally, not as men, nor even as citizens,[1] but as soldiers; not as members of their country, but as its defenders. Finally, each State can have for enemies only other States, and not men; for between things disparate in nature there can be no real relation.

Furthermore, this principle is in conformity with the established rules of all times and the constant practice of all civilised peoples. Declarations of war are intimations less to powers than to their subjects. The foreigner, whether king, individual, or people, who robs, kills or detains the subjects, without declaring war on the prince, is not an enemy, but a brigand. Even in real war, a just prince, while laying hands, in the enemy's country, on all that belongs to the public, respects the lives and goods of individuals: he respects rights on which his own are founded. The object of the war being the destruction of the hostile

[1] The Romans, who understood and respected the right of war more than any other nation on earth, carried their scruples on this head so far that a citizen was not allowed to serve as a volunteer without engaging himself expressly against the enemy, and against such and such an enemy by name. A legion in which the younger Cato was seeing his first service under Popilius having been reconstructed, the elder Cato wrote to Popilius that, if he wished his son to continue serving under him, he must administer to him a new military oath, because, the first having been annulled, he was no longer able to bear arms against the enemy. The same Cato wrote to his son telling him to take great care not to go into battle before taking this new oath. I know that the siege of Clusium and other isolated events can be quoted against me; but I am citing laws and customs. The Romans are the people that least often transgressed its laws; and no other people has had such good ones.

State, the other side has a right to kill its defenders, while they are bearing arms; but as soon as they lay them down and surrender, they cease to be enemies or instruments of the enemy, and become once more merely men, whose life no one has any right to take. Sometimes it is possible to kill the State without killing a single one of its members; and war gives no right which is not necessary to the gaining of its object. These principles are not those of Grotius: they are not based on the authority of poets, but derived from the nature of reality and based on reason.

The right of conquest has no foundation other than the right of the strongest. If war does not give the conqueror the right to massacre the conquered peoples, the right to enslave them cannot be based upon a right which does not exist. No one has a right to kill an enemy except when he cannot make him a slave, and the right to enslave him cannot therefore be derived from the right to kill him. It is accordingly an unfair exchange to make him buy at the price of his liberty his life, over which the victor holds no right. Is it not clear that there is a vicious circle in founding the right of life and death on the right of slavery, and the right of slavery on the right of life and death?

Even if we assume this terrible right to kill everybody, I maintain that a slave made in war, or a conquered people, is under no obligation to a master, except to obey him as far as he is compelled to do so. By taking an equivalent for his life, the victor has not done him a favour; instead of killing him without profit, he has killed him usefully. So far then is he from acquiring over him any authority in addition to that of force, that the state of war continues to subsist between them: their mutual relation is the effect of it, and the usage of the right of war does not imply a treaty of peace. A convention has indeed been made; but this convention, so far from destroying the state of war, presupposes its continuance.

So, from whatever aspect we regard the question, the right of slavery is null and void, not only as being illegitimate, but also because it is absurd and meaningless. The words *slave* and *right* contradict each other, and are mutually exclusive. It will always be equally foolish for a man to say to a man or to a people: "I make with you a convention wholly at your expense and wholly to my advantage; I shall keep it as long as I like, and you will keep it as long as I like."

5. THAT WE MUST ALWAYS GO BACK TO A FIRST CONVENTION

EVEN if I granted all that I have been refuting, the friends of despotism would be no better off. There will always be a great difference between subduing a multitude and ruling a society. Even if scattered individuals were successively enslaved by one man, however numerous they might be, I still see no more than a master and his slaves, and certainly not a people and its ruler; I see what may be termed an aggregation, but not an association; there is as yet neither public good nor body politic. The man in question, even if he has enslaved half the world, is still only an individual; his interest, apart from that of others, is still a purely private interest. If this same man comes to die, his empire, after him, remains scattered and without unity, as an oak falls and dissolves into a heap of ashes when the fire has consumed it.

A people, says Grotius, can give itself to a king. Then, according to Grotius, a people is a people before it gives itself. The gift is itself a civil act, and implies public deliberation. It would be better, before examining the act by which a people gives itself to a king, to examine that by which it has become a people; for this act, being necessarily prior to the other, is the true foundation of society.

Indeed, if there were no prior convention, where, unless the election were unanimous, would be the obligation on the minority to submit to the choice of the majority? How have a hundred men who wish for a master the right to vote on behalf of ten who do not? The law of majority voting is itself something established by convention, and presupposes unanimity, on one occasion at least.

6. THE SOCIAL COMPACT

I SUPPOSE men to have reached the point at which the obstacles in the way of their preservation in the state of nature show their power of resistance to be greater than the resources at the disposal of each individual for his maintenance in that state. That primitive condition can then subsist no longer; and the human race would perish unless it changed its manner of existence.

But, as men cannot engender new forces, but only unite and direct existing ones, they have no other means of preserving themselves than the formation, by aggregation, of a sum of forces great enough to overcome the resistance. These they have to bring into play by means of a single motive power, and cause to act in concert.

This sum of forces can arise only where several persons come together: but, as the force and liberty of each man are the chief instruments of his self-preservation, how can he pledge them without harming his own interests, and neglecting the care he owes to himself? This difficulty, in its bearing on my present subject, may be stated in the following terms:

"The problem is to find a form of association which will defend and protect with the whole common force the person and goods of each associate, and in which each, while uniting himself with all, may still obey himself alone, and remain as free as before." This is the fundamental problem of which the *Social Contract* provides the solution.

The clauses of this contract are so determined by the nature of the act that the slightest modification would make them vain and ineffective; so that, although they have perhaps never been formally set forth, they are everywhere the same and everywhere tacitly admitted and recognised, until, on the violation of the social compact, each regains his original rights and resumes his natural liberty, while losing the conventional liberty in favour of which he renounced it.

These clauses, properly understood, may be reduced to one—the total alienation of each associate, together with all his rights, to the whole community; for, in the first place, as each gives himself absolutely, the conditions are the same for all; and, this being so, no one has any interest in making them burdensome to others.

Moreover, the alienation being without reserve, the union is as perfect as it can be, and no associate has anything more to demand: for, if the individuals retained certain rights, as there would be no common superior to decide between them and the public, each, being on one point his own judge, would ask to be so on all; the state of nature would thus continue, and the association would necessarily become inoperative or tyrannical.

Finally, each man, in giving himself to all, gives himself to nobody; and as there is no associate over whom he does not acquire the same right as he yields others over himself, he gains an equivalent for everything he loses, and an increase of force for the preservation of what he has.

If then we discard from the social compact what is not of its essence, we shall find that it reduces itself to the following terms:

"Each of us puts his person and all his power in common under the supreme direction of the general will, and, in our corporate capacity, we receive each member as an indivisible part of the whole."

At once, in place of the individual personality of each contracting party, this act of association creates a moral and collective body, composed of as many members as the assembly contains votes, and receiving from this act its unity, its common identity, its life and its will. This public person, so formed by the union of all other persons formerly took the name of *city*,[1] and now takes that of *Republic* or *body politic;* it is called by its members *State* when passive, *Sovereign* when active, and *Power* when compared with others like itself. Those who are associated in it take collectively the name of *people,* and severally are called *citizens,* as sharing in the sovereign power, and *subjects,* as being under the laws of the State. But these terms are often confused and taken one for another: it is enough to know how to distinguish them when they are being used with precision.

7. THE SOVEREIGN

THIS formula shows us that the act of association comprises a mutual undertaking between the public and the individuals, and that each individual, in making a contract, as we may say, with himself, is bound in a double capacity; as a member of the Sovereign he is

[1] The real meaning of this word has been almost wholly lost in modern times; most people mistake a town for a city, and a townsman for a citizen. They do not know that houses make a town, but citizens a city. The same mistake long ago cost the Carthaginians dear. I have never read of the title of citizens being given to the subjects of any prince, not even the ancient Macedonians or the English of to-day, though they are nearer liberty than any one else. The French alone everywhere familiarly adopt the name of citizens, because, as can be seen from their dictionaries, they have no idea of its meaning; otherwise they would be guilty in usurping it, of the crime of *lèse-majesté:* among them, the name expresses a virtue, and not a right. When Bodin spoke of our citizens and townsmen, he fell into a bad blunder in taking the one class for the other. M. d'Alembert has avoided the error, and, in his article on Geneva, has clearly distinguished the four orders of men (or even five, counting mere foreigners) who dwell in our town, of which two only compose the Republic. No other French writer, to my knowledge, has understood the real meaning of the word citizen.

bound to the individuals, and as a member of the State to the Sovereign. But the maxim of civil right, that no one is bound by undertakings made to himself, does not apply in this case; for there is a great difference between incurring an obligation to yourself and incurring one to a whole of which you form a part.

Attention must further be called to the fact that public deliberation, while competent to bind all the subjects to the Sovereign, because of the two different capacities in which each of them may be regarded, cannot, for the opposite reason, bind the Sovereign to itself; and that it is consequently against the nature of the body politic for the Sovereign to impose on itself a law which it cannot infringe. Being able to regard itself in only one capacity, it is in the position of an individual who makes a contract with himself; and this makes it clear that there neither is nor can be any kind of fundamental law binding on the body of the people—not even the social contract itself. This does not mean that the body politic cannot enter into undertakings with others, provided the contract is not infringed by them; for in relation to what is external to it, it becomes a simple being, an individual.

But the body politic or the Sovereign, drawing its being wholly from the sanctity of the contract, can never bind itself, even to an outsider, to do anything derogatory to the original act, for instance, to alienate any part of itself, or to submit to another Sovereign. Violation of the act by which it exists would be self-annihilation; and that which is itself nothing can create nothing.

As soon as this multitude is so united in one body, it is impossible to offend against one of the members without attacking the body, and still more to offend against the body without the members resenting it. Duty and interest therefore equally oblige the two contracting parties to give each other help; and the same men should seek to combine, in their double capacity, all the advantages dependent upon that capacity.

Again, the Sovereign, being formed wholly of the individuals who compose it, neither has nor can have any interest contrary to theirs; and consequently the sovereign power need give no guarantee to its subjects, because it is impossible for the body to wish to hurt all its members. We shall also see later on that it cannot hurt any in particular. The Sovereign, merely by virtue of what it is, is always what it should be.

This, however, is not the case with the relation of the subjects to the Sovereign, which, despite the common interest, would have no security that they would fulfil their undertakings, unless it found means to assure itself of their fidelity.

In fact, each individual, as a man, may have a particular will contrary or dissimilar to the general will which he has as a citizen. His particular interest may speak to him quite differently from the common interest: his absolute and naturally independent existence may make him look upon what he owes to the common cause as a gratuitous contribution, the loss of which will do less harm to others than the payment of it is burdensome to himself; and, regarding the moral person which constitutes the State as a *persona ficta,* because not a man, he may wish to enjoy the rights of citizenship without being ready to fulfil the duties of a subject. The continuance of such an injustice could not but prove the undoing of the body politic.

In order then that the social compact may not be an empty formula, it tacitly includes the undertaking, which alone can give force to the rest, that whoever refuses to obey the general will shall be compelled to do so by the whole body. This means nothing less than that he will be forced to be free; for this is the condition which, by giving each citizen to his country, secures him against all personal dependence. In this lies the key to the working of the political machine; this alone legitimises civil undertakings, which, without it, would be absurd, tyrannical, and liable to the most frightful abuses.

8. THE CIVIL STATE

THE passage from the state of nature to the civil state produces a very remarkable change in man, by substituting justice for instinct in his conduct, and giving his actions the morality they had formerly lacked. Then only, when the voice of duty takes the place of physical impulses and right of appetite, does man, who so far had considered only himself, find that he is forced to act on different principles, and to consult his reason before listening to his inclinations. Although, in this state, he deprives himself of some advantages which he got from nature, he gains in return others so great, his faculties are so stimulated and developed, his ideas so extended, his feelings so ennobled, and his whole soul so uplifted, that, did not the abuses of this new condition often degrade him below that which he left, he would be bound to bless continually the happy moment which took him from it for ever, and, instead of a stupid and unimaginative animal, made him an intelligent being and a man.

Let us draw up the whole account in terms easily commensurable. What man loses by the social contract is his natural liberty and an unlimited right to everything he tries to get and succeeds in getting; what he gains is civil liberty and the proprietorship of all he possesses. If we are to avoid mistake in weighing one against the other, we must clearly distinguish natural liberty, which is bounded only by the strength of the individual, from civil liberty, which is limited by the general will; and possession, which is merely the effect of force or the right of the first occupier, from property, which can be founded only on a positive title.

We might, over and above all this, add, to what man acquires in the civil state, moral liberty, which alone makes him truly master of himself; for the mere impulse of appetite is slavery, while obedience to a law which we prescribe to ourselves is liberty. But I have already said too much on this head, and the philosophical meaning of the word liberty does not now concern us.

9. REAL PROPERTY

EACH member of the community gives himself to it, at the moment of its foundation, just as he is, with all the resources at his command, including the goods he possesses. This act does not make possession, in changing hands, change its nature, and become property in the hands of the Sovereign; but, as the forces of the city are incomparably greater than those of an individual, public possession is also, in fact, stronger and more irrevocable, without being any more legitimate, at any rate from the point of view of foreigners. For the State, in relation to its members, is master of all their goods by the social contract, which, within the State, is the basis of all rights; but, in relation to other powers, it is so only by the right of the first occupier, which it holds from its members.

The right of the first occupier, though more real than the right of the strongest, becomes a real right only when the right of property has already been established. Every man has naturally a right to everything he needs; but the positive act which makes him proprietor of one thing excludes him from everything else.

Having his share, he ought to keep to it, and can have no further right against the community. This is why the right of the first occupier, which in the state of nature is so weak, claims the respect of every man in civil society. In this right we are respecting not so much what belongs to another as what does not belong to ourselves.

In general, to establish the right of the first occupier over a plot of ground, the following conditions are necessary: first, the land must not yet be inhabited; secondly, a man must occupy only the amount he needs for his subsistence; and, in the third place, possession must be taken, not by an empty ceremony, but by labour and cultivation, the only sign of proprietorship that should be respected by others, in default of a legal title.

In granting the right of first occupancy to necessity and labour, are we not really stretching it as far as it can go? Is it possible to leave such a right unlimited? Is it to be enough to set foot on a plot of common ground, in order to be able to call yourself at once the master of it? Is it to be enough that a man has the strength to expel others for a moment, in order to establish his right to prevent them from ever returning? How can a man or a people seize an immense territory and keep it from the rest of the world except by a punishable usurpation, since all others are being robbed, by such an act, of the place of habitation and the means of subsistence which nature gave them in common? When Nuñez Balboa, standing on the sea-shore, took possession of the South Seas and the whole of South America in the name of the crown of Castile, was that enough to dispossess all their actual inhabitants, and to shut out from them all the princes of the world? On such a showing, these ceremonies are idly multiplied, and the Catholic King need only take possession all at once, from his apartment, of the whole universe, merely making a subsequent reservation about what was already in the possession of other princes.

We can imagine how the lands of individuals, where they were contiguous and came to be united, became the public territory, and how the right of Sovereignty, extending from the subjects over the lands they held, became at once real and personal. The possessors were thus made more dependent, and the forces at their command used to guarantee their fidelity. The advantage of this does not seem to have been felt by ancient monarchs, who called themselves Kings of the Persians, Scythians, or Macedonians, and seemed to regard themselves more as rulers of men than as masters of a country. Those of the present day more cleverly call themselves Kings of France, Spain, England, etc.: thus holding the land, they are quite confident of holding the inhabitants.

The peculiar fact about this alienation is that, in taking over the goods of individuals, the community, so far from despoiling them, only assures them legitimate possession, and changes usurpation into a true right and enjoyment into proprietorship. Thus the possessors, being regarded as depositaries of the public good, and having their rights respected by all the members of the State and maintained against foreign aggression by all its forces, have, by a cession which benefits both the public and still more themselves, acquired, so to speak, all that they gave up. This paradox may easily be explained by the distinction between the rights which the Sovereign and the proprietor have over the same estate, as we shall see later on.

It may also happen that men begin to unite one with another before they possess anything, and that, subsequently occupying a tract of country which is enough for all, they enjoy it in common, or share it out among themselves, either equally or according to a scale fixed by the Sovereign. However the acquisition be made, the right which each individual has to his own estate is always subordinate to the right which the community has over all: without this, there would be neither stability in the social tie, nor real force in the exercise of Sovereignty.

I shall end this chapter and this book by remarking on a fact on which the whole social system should rest: i.e., that, instead of destroying natural inequality, the fundamental compact substitutes, for such physical inequality as nature may have set up between men, an equality that is moral and legitimate, and that men, who may be unequal in strength or intelligence, become every one equal by convention and legal right.[1]

[1] Under bad governments, this equality is only apparent and illusory: it serves only to keep the pauper in his poverty and the rich man in the position he has usurped. In fact, laws are always of use to those who possess and harmful to those who have nothing: from which it follows that the social state is advantageous to men only when all have something and none too much.

BOOK II

1. THAT SOVEREIGNTY IS INALIENABLE

THE first and most important deduction from the principles we have so far laid down is that the general will alone can direct the State according to the object for which it was instituted, i.e., the common good: for if the clashing of particular interests made the establishment of societies necessary, the agreement of these very interests made it possible. The common element in these different interests is what forms the social tie; and, were there no point of agreement between them all, no society could exist. It is solely on the basis of this common interest that every society should be governed.

I hold then that Sovereignty, being nothing less than the exercise of the general will, can never be alienated, and that the Sovereign, who is no less than a collective being, cannot be represented except by himself: the power indeed may be transmitted, but not the will.

In reality, if it is not impossible for a particular will to agree on some point with the general will, it is at least impossible for the agreement to be lasting and constant; for the particular will tends, by its very nature, to partiality, while the general will tends to equality. It is even more impossible to have any guarantee of this agreement; for even if it should always exist, it would be the effect not of art, but of chance. The Sovereign may indeed say: "I now will actually what this man wills, or at least what he says he wills"; but it cannot say: "What he wills tomorrow, I too shall will" because it is absurd for the will to bind itself for the future, nor is it incumbent on any will to consent to anything that is not for the good of the being who wills. If then the people promises simply to obey, by that very act it dissolves itself and loses what makes it a people; the moment a master exists, there is no longer a Sovereign, and from that moment the body politic has ceased to exist.

This does not mean that the commands of the rulers cannot pass for general wills, so long as the Sovereign, being free to oppose them, offers no opposition. In such a case, universal silence is taken to imply the consent of the people. This will be explained later on.

2. THAT SOVEREIGNTY IS INDIVISIBLE

SOVEREIGNTY, for the same reason as makes it inalienable, is indivisible; for will either is, or is not, general;[1] it is the will either of the body of the people, or only of a part of it. In the first case, the will, when declared, is an act of Sovereignty and constitutes law: in the second, it is merely a particular will, or act of magistracy—at the most a decree.

But our political theorists, unable to divide Sovereignty in principle, divide it according to its object: into force and will; into legislative power and executive power; into rights of taxation, justice and war; into internal administration and power of foreign treaty. Sometimes they confuse all these sections, and sometimes they distinguish them; they turn the Sovereign into a fantastic being composed of several connected pieces: it is as if they were making man of several bodies, one with eyes, one with arms, another with feet, and each with nothing besides. We are told that the jugglers of Japan dismember a child before the eyes of the spectators; then they throw all the members into the air one after another, and the child falls down alive and whole. The conjuring tricks of our political theorists are very like that; they first dismember the body politic by an illusion worthy of a fair, and then join it together again we know not how.

This error is due to a lack of exact notions concerning the Sovereign authority, and to taking for parts of it what are only emanations from it. Thus, for example, the acts of declaring war and making peace have been regarded as acts of Sovereignty; but this is not the case, as these acts do not constitute law, but merely the application of a law, a particular act which decides how the law applies, as we shall see clearly when the idea attached to the word *law* has been defined.

If we examined the other divisions in the same manner, we should find that, whenever Sovereignty seems to be divided, there is an illusion: the rights which are taken as being part of Sovereignty are really all subordinate, and always imply supreme wills of which they only sanction the execution.

It would be impossible to estimate the obscurity this lack of exactness has thrown over the decisions of writers who have dealt with political right, when they have used the prin-

---

[1] To be general, a will need not always be unanimous; but every vote must be counted: any exclusion is a breach of generality.

ciples laid down by them to pass judgment on the respective rights of kings and peoples. Every one can see, in Chapters III and IV of the First Book of Grotius, how the learned man and his translator, Barbeyrac, entangle and tie themselves up in their own sophistries, for fear of saying too little or too much of what they think, and so offending the interests they have to conciliate. Grotius, a refugee in France, ill-content with his own country, and desirous of paying his court to Louis XIII, to whom his book is dedicated, spares no pains to rob the peoples of all their rights and invest kings with them by every conceivable artifice. This would also have been much to the taste of Barbeyrac, who dedicated his translation to George I of England. But unfortunately the expulsion of James II, which he called his "abdication," compelled him to use all reserve, to shuffle and to tergiversate, in order to avoid making William out a usurper. If these two writers had adopted the true principles, all difficulties would have been removed, and they would have been always consistent; but it would have been a sad truth for them to tell, and would have paid court for them to no one save the people. Moreover, truth is no road to fortune, and the people dispenses neither ambassadorships, nor professorships, nor pensions.

3. WHETHER THE GENERAL WILL IS FALLIBLE

IT follows from what has gone before that the general will is always right and tends to the public advantage; but it does not follow that the deliberations of the people are always equally correct. Our will is always for our own good, but we do not always see what that is; the people is never corrupted, but it is often deceived, and on such occasions only does it seem to will what is bad.

There is often a great deal of difference between the will of all and the general will; the latter considers only the common interest, while the former takes private interest into account, and is no more than a sum of particular wills: but take away from these same wills the pluses and minuses that cancel one another,[1]

and the general will remains as the sum of the differences.

If, when the people, being furnished with adequate information, held its deliberations, the citizens had no communication one with another, the grand total of the small differences would always give the general will, and the decision would always be good. But when factions arise, and partial associations are formed at the expense of the great association, the will of each of these associations becomes general in relation to its members, while it remains particular in relation to the State: it may then be said that there are no longer as many votes as there are men, but only as many as there are associations. The differences become less numerous and give a less general result. Lastly, when one of these associations is so great as to prevail over all the rest, the result is no longer a sum of small differences, but a single difference; in this case there is no longer a general will, and the opinion which prevails is purely particular.

It is therefore essential, if the general will is to be able to express itself, that there should be no partial society within the State, and that each citizen should think only his own thoughts:[2] which was indeed the sublime and unique system established by the great Lycurgus. But if there are partial societies, it is best to have as many as possible and to prevent them from being unequal, as was done by Solon, Numa and Servius. These precautions are the only ones that can guarantee that the general will shall be always enlightened, and that the people shall in no way deceive itself.

4. THE LIMITS OF THE SOVEREIGN POWER

IF the State is a moral person whose life is in the union of its members, and if the most important of its cares is the care for its own preservation, it must have a universal and compelling force, in order to move and dispose each part as may be most advantageous to the whole. As nature gives each man absolute power over all his members, the social compact gives the body politic absolute power over all its members also; and it is this power which, under the direction of the general will, bears,

---

[1] "Every interest," says the Marquis d'Argenson, "has different principles. The agreement of two particular interests is formed by opposition to a third." He might have added that the agreement of all interests is formed by opposition to that of each. If there were no different interests, the common interest would be barely felt, as it would encounter no obstacle; all would go on of its own accord, and politics would cease to be an art.

[2] "In fact," says Machiavelli, "there are some divisions that are harmful to a Republic and some that are advantageous. Those which stir up sects and parties are harmful; those attended by neither are advantageous. Since, then, the founder of a Republic cannot help enmities arising, he ought at least to prevent them from growing into sects" (*History of Florence*, Book vii).

as I have said, the name of Sovereignty.

But, besides the public person, we have to consider the private persons composing it, whose life and liberty are naturally independent of it. We are bound then to distinguish clearly between the respective rights of the citizens and the Sovereign,[1] and between the duties the former have to fulfil as subjects, and the natural rights they should enjoy as men.

Each man alienates, I admit, by the social compact, only such part of his powers, goods and liberty as it is important for the community to control; but it must also be granted that the Sovereign is sole judge of what is important.

Every service a citizen can render the State he ought to render as soon as the Sovereign demands it; but the Sovereign, for its part, cannot impose upon its subjects any fetters that are useless to the community, nor can it even wish to do so; for no more by the law of reason than by the law of nature can anything occur without a cause.

The undertakings which bind us to the social body are obligatory only because they are mutual; and their nature is such that in fulfilling them we cannot work for others without working for ourselves. Why is it that the general will is always in the right, and that all continually will the happiness of each one, unless it is because there is not a man who does not think of "each" as meaning him, and consider himself in voting for all? This proves that equality of rights and the idea of justice which such equality creates originate in the preference each man gives to himself, and accordingly in the very nature of man. It proves that the general will, to be really such, must be general in its object as well as its essence; that it must both come from all and apply to all; and that it loses its natural rectitude when it is directed to some particular and determinate object, because in such a case we are judging of something foreign to us, and have no true principle of equity to guide us.

Indeed, as soon as a question of particular fact or right arises on a point not previously regulated by a general convention, the matter becomes contentious. It is a case in which the individuals concerned are one party, and the public the other, but in which I can see neither the law that ought to be followed nor the

judge who ought to give the decision. In such a case, it would be absurd to propose to refer the question to an express decision of the general will, which can be only the conclusion reached by one of the parties and in consequence will be, for the other party, merely an external and particular will, inclined on this occasion to injustice and subject to error. Thus, just as a particular will cannot stand for the general will, the general will, in turn, changes its nature, when its object is particular, and, as general, cannot pronounce on a man or a fact. When, for instance, the people of Athens nominated or displaced its rulers, decreed honours to one, and imposed penalties on another, and, by a multitude of particular decrees, exercised all the functions of government indiscriminately, it had in such cases no longer a general will in the strict sense; it was acting no longer as Sovereign, but as magistrate. This will seem contrary to current views; but I must be given time to expound my own.

It should be seen from the foregoing that what makes the will general is less the number of voters than the common interest uniting them; for, under this system, each necessarily submits to the conditions he imposes on others: and this admirable agreement between interest and justice gives to the common deliberations an equitable character which at once vanishes when any particular question is discussed, in the absence of a common interest to unite and identify the ruling of the judge with that of the party.

From whatever side we approach our principle, we reach the same conclusion, that the social compact sets up among the citizens an equality of such a kind, that they all bind themselves to observe the same conditions and should therefore all enjoy the same rights. Thus, from the very nature of the compact, every act of Sovereignty, i.e., every authentic act of the general will, binds or favours all the citizens equally; so that the Sovereign recognises only the body of the nation, and draws no distinctions between those of whom it is made up. What, then, strictly speaking, is an act of Sovereignty? It is not a convention between a superior and an inferior, but a convention between the body and each of its members. It is legitimate, because based on the social contract, and equitable, because common to all; useful, because it can have no other object than the general good, and stable, because guaranteed by the public force and the su-

---

[1] Attentive readers, do not, I pray, be in a hurry to charge me with contradicting myself. The terminology made it unavoidable, considering the poverty of the language; but wait and see.

preme power. So long as the subjects have to submit only to conventions of this sort, they obey no-one but their own will; and to ask how far the respective rights of the Sovereign and the citizens extend, is to ask up to what point the latter can enter into undertakings with themselves, each with all, and all with each.

We can see from this that the sovereign power, absolute, sacred and inviolable as it is, does not and cannot exceed the limits of general conventions, and that every man may dispose at will of such goods and liberty as these conventions leave him; so that the Sovereign never has a right to lay more charges on one subject than on another, because, in that case, the question becomes particular, and ceases to be within its competency.

When these distinctions have once been admitted, it is seen to be so untrue that there is, in the social contract, any real renunciation on the part of the individuals, that the position in which they find themselves as a result of the contract is really preferable to that in which they were before. Instead of a renunciation, they have made an advantageous exchange: instead of an uncertain and precarious way of living they have got one that is better and more secure; instead of natural independence they have got liberty, instead of the power to harm others security for themselves, and instead of their strength, which others might overcome, a right which social union makes invincible. Their very life, which they have devoted to the State, is by it constantly protected; and when they risk it in the State's defence, what more are they doing than giving back what they have received from it? What are they doing that they would not do more often and with greater danger in the state of nature, in which they would inevitably have to fight battles at the peril of their lives in defence of that which is the means of their preservation? All have indeed to fight when their country needs them; but then no one has ever to fight for himself. Do we not gain something by running, on behalf of what gives us our security, only some of the risks we should have to run for ourselves, as soon as we lost it?

5. THE RIGHT OF LIFE AND DEATH

THE question is often asked how individuals, having no right to dispose of their own lives, can transfer to the Sovereign a right which they do not possess. The difficulty of answering this question seems to me to lie in its being wrongly stated. Every man has a right to risk his own life in order to preserve it. Has it ever been said that a man who throws himself out of the window to escape from a fire is guilty of suicide? Has such a crime ever been laid to the charge of him who perishes in a storm because, when he went on board, he knew of the danger?

The social treaty has for its end the preservation of the contracting parties. He who wills the end wills the means also, and the means must involve some risks, and even some losses. He who wishes to preserve his life at others' expense should also, when it is necessary, be ready to give it up for their sake. Furthermore, the citizen is no longer the judge of the dangers to which the law desires him to expose himself; and when the prince says to him: "It is expedient for the State that you should die," he ought to die, because it is only on that condition that he has been living in security up to the present, and because his life is no longer a mere bounty of nature, but a gift made conditionally by the State.

The death-penalty inflicted upon criminals may be looked on in much the same light: it is in order that we may not fall victims to an assassin that we consent to die if we ourselves turn assassins. In this treaty, so far from disposing of our own lives, we think only of securing them, and it is not to be assumed that any of the parties then expects to get hanged.

Again, every malefactor, by attacking social rights, becomes on forfeit a rebel and a traitor to his country; by violating its laws he ceases to be a member of it; he even makes war upon it. In such a case the preservation of the State is inconsistent with his own, and one or the other must perish; in putting the guilty to death, we slay not so much the citizen as an enemy. The trial and the judgment are the proofs that he has broken the social treaty, and is in consequence no longer a member of the State. Since, then, he has recognised himself to be such by living there, he must be removed by exile as a violator of the compact, or by death as a public enemy; for such an enemy is not a moral person, but merely a man; and in such a case the right of war is to kill the vanquished.

But, it will be said, the condemnation of a criminal is a particular act. I admit it: but such condemnation is not a function of the Sovereign; it is a right the Sovereign can confer without being able itself to exert it. All my ideas are consistent, but I cannot expound them all at once.

We may add that frequent punishments are always a sign of weakness or remissness on the part of the government. There is not a single ill-doer who could not be turned to some good. The State has no right to put to death, even for the sake of making an example, any one whom it can leave alive without danger.

The right of pardoning or exempting the guilty from a penalty imposed by the law and pronounced by the judge belongs only to the authority which is superior to both judge and law, i.e., the Sovereign; each its right in this matter is far from clear, and the cases for exercising it are extremely rare. In a well-governed State, there are few punishments, not because there are many pardons, but because criminals are rare; it is when a State is in decay that the multitude of crimes is a guarantee of impunity. Under the Roman Republic, neither the Senate nor the Consuls ever attempted to pardon; even the people never did so, though it sometimes revoked its own decision. Frequent pardons mean that crime will soon need them no longer, and no one can help seeing whither that leads. But I feel my heart protesting and restraining my pen; let us leave these questions to the just man who has never offended, and would himself stand in no need of pardon.

6. LAW

BY the social compact we have given the body politic existence and life; we have now by legislation to give it movement and will. For the original act by which the body is formed and united still in no respect determines what it ought to do for its preservation.

What is well and in conformity with order is so by the nature of things and independently of human conventions. All justice comes from God, who is its sole source; but if we knew how to receive so high an inspiration, we should need neither government nor laws. Doubtless, there is a universal justice emanating from reason alone; but this justice, to be admitted among us, must be mutual. Humanly speaking, in default of natural sanctions, the laws of justice are ineffective among men: they merely make for the good of the wicked and the undoing of the just, when the just man observes them towards everybody and nobody observes them towards him. Conventions and laws are therefore needed to join rights to duties and refer justice to its object. In the state of nature, where everything is common,

I owe nothing to him whom I have promised nothing; I recognise as belonging to others only what is of no use to me. In the state of society all rights are fixed by law, and the case becomes different.

But what, after all, is a law? As long as we remain satisfied with attaching purely metaphysical ideas to the word, we shall go on arguing without arriving at an understanding; and when we have defined a law of nature, we shall be no nearer the definition of a law of the State.

I have already said that there can be no general will directed to a particular object. Such an object must be either within or outside the State. If outside, a will which is alien to it cannot be, in relation to it, general; if within, it is part of the State, and in that case there arises a relation between whole and part which makes them two separate beings, of which the part is one, and the whole minus the part the other. But the whole minus a part cannot be the whole; and while this relation persists, there can be no whole, but only two unequal parts; and it follows that the will of one is no longer in any respect general in relation to the other.

But when the whole people decrees for the whole people, it is considering only itself; and if a relation is then formed, it is between two aspects of the entire object, without there being any division of the whole. In that case the matter about which the decree is made is, like the decreeing will, general. This act is what I call a law.

When I say that the object of laws is always general, I mean that law considers subjects *en masse* and actions in the abstract, and never a particular person or action. Thus the law may indeed decree that there shall be privileges, but cannot confer them on anybody by name. It may set up several classes of citizens, and even lay down the qualifications for membership of these classes, but it cannot nominate such and such persons as belonging to them; it may establish a monarchical government and hereditary succession, but it cannot choose a king, or nominate a royal family. In a word, no function which has a particular object belongs to the legislative power.

On this view, we at once see that it can no longer be asked whose business it is to make laws, since they are acts of the general will; nor whether the prince is above the law, since he is a member of the State; nor whether the law can be unjust, since no one is unjust to himself; nor how we can be both free and subject to the laws, since they are but registers of our wills.

We see further that, as the law unites universality of will with universality of object, what a man, whoever he be, commands of his own motion cannot be a law; and even what the Sovereign commands with regard to a particular matter is no nearer being a law, but is a decree, an act, not of sovereignty, but of magistracy.

I therefore give the name "Republic" to every State that is governed by laws, no matter what the form of its administration may be: for only in such a case does the public interest govern, and the *res publica* rank as a *reality*. Every legitimate government is republican;[1] what government is I will explain later on.

Laws are, properly speaking, only the conditions of civil association. The people, being subject to the laws, ought to be their author: the conditions of the society ought to be regulated solely by those who come together to form it. But how are they to regulate them? Is it to be by common agreement, by a sudden inspiration? Has the body politic an organ to declare its will? Who can give it the foresight to formulate and announce its acts in advance? Or how is it to announce them in the hour of need? How can a blind multitude, which often does not know what it wills, because it rarely knows what is good for it, carry out for itself so great and difficult an enterprise as a system of legislation? Of itself the people wills always the good, but of itself it by no means always sees it. The general will is always in the right, but the judgment which guides it is not always enlightened. It must be got to see objects as they are, and sometimes as they ought to appear to it; it must be shown the good road it is in search of, secured from the seductive influences of individual wills, taught to see times and spaces as a series, and made to weigh the attractions of present and sensible advantages against the danger of distant and hidden evils. The individuals see the good they reject; the public wills the good it does not see. All stand equally in need of guidance. The former must be compelled to bring their wills into conformity with their reason; the latter must be

taught to know what it wills. If that is done, public enlightenment leads to the union of understanding and will in the social body: the parts are made to work exactly together, and the whole is raised to its highest power. This makes a legislator necessary.

7. THE LEGISLATOR

IN order to discover the rules of society best suited to nations, a superior intelligence beholding all the passions of men without experiencing any of them would be needed. This intelligence would have to be wholly unrelated to our nature, while knowing it through and through; its happiness would have to be independent of us, and yet ready to occupy itself with ours; and lastly, it would have, in the march of time, to look forward to a distant glory, and, working in one century, to be able to enjoy in the next.[2] It would take gods to give men laws.

What Caligula argued from the facts, Plato, in the dialogue called the *Politicus,* argued in defining the civil or kingly man, on the basis of right. But if great princes are rare, how much more so are great legislators? The former have only to follow the pattern which the latter have to lay down. The legislator is the engineer who invents the machine, the prince merely the mechanic who sets it up and makes it go. "At the birth of societies," says Montesquieu, "the rulers of Republics establish institutions, and afterwards the institutions mould the rulers."[3]

He who dares to undertake the making of a people's institutions ought to feel himself capable, so to speak, of changing human nature, of transforming each individual, who is by himself a complete and solitary whole, into part of a greater whole from which he in a manner receives his life and being; of altering man's constitution for the purpose of strengthening it; and of substituting a partial and moral existence for the physical and independent existence nature has conferred on us all. He must, in a word, take away from man his own resources and give him instead new ones alien to him, and incapable of being made use of without the help of other men. The more completely these natural resources are annihilated,

---

[1] I understand by this word, not merely an aristocracy or a democracy, but generally any government directed by the general will, which is the law. To be legitimate, the government must be, not one with the Sovereign, but its minister. In such a case even a monarchy is a Republic. This will be made clearer in the following book.

[2] A people becomes famous only when its legislation begins to decline. We do not know for how many centuries the system of Lycurgus made the Spartans happy before the rest of Greece took any notice of it.

[3] Montesquieu, *The Greatness and Decadence of the Romans,* ch. i.

the greater and the more lasting are those which he acquires, and the more stable and perfect the new institutions; so that if each citizen is nothing and can do nothing without the rest, and the resources acquired by the whole are equal or superior to the aggregate of the resources of all the individuals, it may be said that legislation is at the highest possible point of perfection.

The legislator occupies in every respect an extraordinary position in the State. If he should do so by reason of his genius, he does so no less by reason of his office, which is neither magistracy, nor Sovereignty. This office, which sets up the Republic, nowhere enters into its constitution; it is an individual and superior function, which has nothing in common with human empire; for if he who holds command over men ought not to have command over the laws, he who has command over the laws ought not any more to have it over men; or else his laws would be the ministers of his passions and would often merely serve to perpetuate his injustices: his private aims would inevitably mar the sanctity of his work.

When Lycurgus gave laws to his country, he began by resigning the throne. It was the custom of most Greek towns to entrust the establishment of their laws to foreigners. The Republics of modern Italy in many cases followed this example; Geneva did the same and profited by it.[1] Rome, when it was most prosperous, suffered a revival of all the crimes of tyranny, and was brought to the verge of destruction, because it put the legislative authority and the sovereign power into the same hands.

Nevertheless, the decemvirs themselves never claimed the right to pass any law merely on their own authority. "Nothing we propose to you," they said to the people, "can pass into law without your consent. Romans, be yourselves the authors of the laws which are to make you happy."

He, therefore, who draws up the laws has, or should have, no right of legislation, and the people cannot, even if it wishes, deprive itself of this incommunicable right, because, according to the fundamental compact, only the general will can bind the individuals, and there can be no assurance that a particular will is in conformity with the general will, until it has been put to the free vote of the people. This I have said already; but it is worth while to repeat it.

Thus in the task of legislation we find together two things which appear to be incompatible: an enterprise too difficult for human powers, and, for its execution, an authority that is no authority.

There is a further difficulty that deserves attention. Wise men, if they try to speak their language to the common herd instead of its own, cannot possibly make themselves understood. There are a thousand kinds of ideas which it is impossible to translate into popular language. Conceptions that are too general and objects that are too remote are equally out of its range: each individual, having no taste for any other plan of government than that which suits his particular interest, finds it difficult to realise the advantages he might hope to draw from the continual privations good laws impose. For a young people to be able to relish sound principles of political theory and follow the fundamental rules of statecraft, the effect would have to become the cause; the social spirit, which should be created by these institutions, would have to preside over their very foundation; and men would have to be before law what they should become by means of law. The legislator therefore, being unable to appeal to either force or reason, must have recourse to an authority of a different order, capable of constraining without violence and persuading without convincing.

This is what has, in all ages, compelled the fathers of nations to have recourse to divine intervention and credit the gods with their own wisdom, in order that the peoples, submitting to the laws of the State as to those of nature, and recognising the same power in the formation of the city as in that of man, might obey freely, and bear with docility the yoke of the public happiness.

This sublime reason, far above the range of the common herd, is that whose decisions the legislator puts into the mouth of the immortals, in order to constrain by divine authority those whom human prudence could not move.[2]

---

[1] Those who know Calvin only as a theologian much under-estimate the extent of his genius. The codification of our wise edicts, in which he played a large part, does him no less honour than his *Institute*. Whatever revolution time may bring in our religion, so long as the spirit of patriotism and liberty still lives among us, the memory of this great man will be for ever blessed.

[2] "In truth," says Machiavelli, "there has never been, in any country, an extraordinary legislator who has not had recourse to God; for otherwise his laws would not have been accepted: there are, in

But it is not anybody who can make the gods speak, or get himself believed when he proclaims himself their interpreter. The great soul of the legislator is the only miracle that can prove his mission. Any man may grave tablets of stone, or buy an oracle, or feign secret intercourse with some divinity, or train a bird to whisper in his ear, or find other vulgar ways of imposing on the people. He whose knowledge goes no further may perhaps gather round him a band of fools; but he will never found an empire, and his extravagances will quickly perish with him. Idle tricks form a passing tie; only wisdom can make it lasting. The Judaic law, which still subsists, and that of the child of Ishmael, which, for ten centuries, has ruled half the world, still proclaim the great men who laid them down; and, while the pride of philosophy or the blind spirit of faction sees in them no more than lucky impostures, the true political theorist admires, in the institutions they set up, the great and powerful genius which presides over things made to endure.

We should not, with Warburton, conclude from this that politics and religion have among us a common object, but that, in the first periods of nations, the one is used as an instrument for the other.

8. THE PEOPLE

As, before putting up a large building, the architect surveys and sounds the site to see if it will bear the weight, the wise legislator does not begin by laying down laws good in themselves, but by investigating the fitness of the people, for which they are destined, to receive them. Plato refused to legislate for the Arcadians and the Cyrenæans, because he knew that both peoples were rich and could not put up with equality; and good laws and bad men were found together in Crete, because Minos had inflicted discipline on a people already burdened with vice.

A thousand nations have achieved earthly greatness, that could never have endured good laws; even such as could have endured them could have done so only for a very brief period of their long history. Most peoples, like most men, are docile only in youth; as they grow old they become incorrigible. When once

customs have become established and prejudices inveterate, it is dangerous and useless to attempt their reformation; the people, like the foolish and cowardly patients who rave at sight of the doctor, can no longer bear that any one should lay hands on its faults to remedy them.

There are indeed times in the history of States when, just as some kinds of illness turn men's heads and make them forget the past, periods of violence and revolutions do to peoples what these crises do to individuals: horror of the past takes the place of forgetfulness, and the State, set on fire by civil wars, is born again, so to speak, from its ashes, and takes on anew, fresh from the jaws of death, the vigour of youth. Such were Sparta at the time of Lycurgus, Rome after the Tarquins, and, in modern times, Holland and Switzerland after the expulsion of the tyrants.

But such events are rare; they are exceptions, the cause of which is always to be found in the particular constitution of the State concerned. They cannot even happen twice to the same people, for it can make itself free as long as it remains barbarous, but not when the civic impulse has lost its vigour. Then disturbances may destroy it, but revolutions cannot mend it: it needs a master, and not a liberator. Free peoples, be mindful of this maxim: "Liberty may be gained, but can never be recovered."

Youth is not infancy. There is for nations, as for men, a period of youth, or, shall we say, maturity, before which they should not be made subject to laws; but the maturity of a people is not always easily recognisable, and, if it is anticipated, the work is spoilt. One people is amenable to discipline from the beginning; another, not after ten centuries. Russia will never be really civilised, because it was civilised too soon. Peter had a genius for imitation; but he lacked true genius, which is creative and makes all from nothing. He did some good things, but most of what he did was out of place. He saw that his people was barbarous, but did not see that it was not ripe for civilisation: he wanted to civilise it when it needed only hardening. His first wish was to make Germans or Englishmen, when he ought to have been making Russians; and he prevented his subjects from ever becoming what they might have been by persuading them that they were what they are not. In this fashion too a French teacher turns out his pupil to be an infant prodigy, and for the rest of his life to be nothing whatsoever. The empire of Rus-

fact, many useful truths of which a wise man may have knowledge without their having in themselves such clear reasons for their being so as to be able to convince others" (*Discourses on Livy*, Bk. v, ch. xi).

sia will aspire to conquer Europe, and will itself be conquered. The Tartars, its subjects or neighbours, will become its masters and ours, by a revolution which I regard as inevitable. Indeed, all the kings of Europe are working in concert to hasten its coming.

9. THE PEOPLE (*continued*)

As nature has set bounds to the stature of a well-made man, and, outside those limits, makes nothing but giants or dwarfs, similarly, for the constitution of a State to be at its best, it is possible to fix limits that will make it neither too large for good government, nor too small for self-maintenance. In every body politic there is a *maximum* strength which it cannot exceed and which it only loses by increasing in size. Every extension of the social tie means its relaxation; and, generally speaking, a small State is stronger in proportion than a great one.

A thousand arguments could be advanced in favour of this principle. First, long distances make administration more difficult, just as a weight becomes heavier at the end of a longer lever. Administration therefore becomes more and more burdensome as the distance grows greater; for, in the first place, each city has its own, which is paid for by the people: each district its own, still paid for by the people: then comes each province, and then the great governments, satrapies, and vice-royalties, always costing more the higher you go, and always at the expense of the unfortunate people. Last of all comes the supreme administration, which eclipses all the rest. All these over charges are a continual drain upon the subjects; so far from being better governed by all these different orders, they are worse governed than if there were only a single authority over them. In the meantime, there scarce remain resources enough to meet emergencies; and, when recourse must be had to these, the State is always on the eve of destruction.

This is not all; not only has the government less vigour and promptitude for securing the observance of the laws, preventing nuisances, correcting abuses, and guarding against seditious undertakings begun in distant places; the people has less affection for its rulers, whom it never sees, for its country, which, to its eyes, seems like the world, and for its fellow-citizens, most of whom are unknown to it. The same laws cannot suit so many diverse provinces with different customs, situated in the most various climates, and incapable of enduring a uniform government. Different laws lead only to trouble and confusion among peoples which, living under the same rulers and in constant communication one with another, intermingle and intermarry, and, coming under the sway of new customs, never know if they can call their very patrimony their own. Talent is buried, virtue unknown and vice unpunished, among such a multitude of men who do not know one another, gathered together in one place at the seat of the central administration. The leaders, overwhelmed with business, see nothing for themselves; the State is governed by clerks. Finally, the measures which have to be taken to maintain the general authority, which all these distant officials wish to escape or to impose upon, absorb all the energy of the public, so that there is none left for the happiness of the people. There is hardly enough to defend it when need arises, and thus a body which is too big for its constitution gives way and falls crushed under its own weight.

Again, the State must assure itself a safe foundation, if it is to have stability, and to be able to resist the shocks it cannot help experiencing, as well as the efforts it will be forced to make for its maintenance; for all peoples have a kind of centrifugal force that makes them continually act one against another, and tend to aggrandise themselves at their neighbours' expense, like the vortices of Descartes. Thus the weak run the risk of being soon swallowed up; and it is almost impossible for any one to preserve itself except by putting itself in a state of equilibrium with all, so that the pressure is on all sides practically equal.

It may therefore be seen that there are reasons for expansion and reasons for contraction; and it is no small part of the statesman's skill to hit between them the mean that is most favourable to the preservation of the State. It may be said that the reason for expansion, being merely external and relative, ought to be subordinate to the reasons for contraction, which are internal and absolute. A strong and healthy constitution is the first thing to look for; and it is better to count on the vigour which comes of good government than on the resources a great territory furnishes.

It may be added that there have been known States so constituted that the necessity of making conquests entered into their very constitution, and that, in order to maintain themselves, they were forced to expand ceaselessly. It may be that they congratulated themselves greatly on this fortunate necessity, which none the less indicated to them, along with the limits of their greatness, the inevitable moment of their fall.

10. THE PEOPLE (continued)

A BODY politic may be measured in two ways —either by the extent of its territory, or by the number of its people; and there is, between these two measurements, a right relation which makes the State really great. The men make the State, and the territory sustains the men; the right relation therefore is that the land should suffice for the maintenance of the inhabitants, and that there should be as many inhabitants as the land can maintain. In this proportion lies the *maximum* strength of a given number of people; for, if there is too much land, it is troublesome to guard and inadequately cultivated, produces more than is needed, and soon gives rise to wars of defence; if there is not enough, the State depends on its neighbours for what it needs over and above, and this soon gives rise to wars of offence. Every people, to which its situation gives no choice save that between commerce and war, is weak in itself: it depends on its neighbours, and on circumstances; its existence can never be more than short and uncertain. It either conquers others, and changes its situation, or it is conquered and becomes nothing. Only insignificance or greatness can keep it free.

No fixed relation can be stated between the extent of territory and the population that are adequate one to the other, both because of the differences in the quality of land, in its fertility, in the nature of its products, and in the influence of climate, and because of the different tempers of those who inhabit it; for some in a fertile country consume little, and others on an ungrateful soil much. The greater or less fecundity of women, the conditions that are more or less favourable in each country to the growth of population, and the influence the legislator can hope to exercise by his institutions, must also be taken into account. The legislator therefore should not go by what he sees, but by what he foresees; he should stop not so much at the state in which he actually finds the population, as at that to which it ought naturally to attain. Lastly, there are countless cases in which the particular local circumstances demand or allow the acquisition of a greater territory than seems necessary. Thus, expansion will be great in a mountainous country, where the natural products, i.e., woods and pastures, need less labour, where we know from experience that women are more fertile than in the plains, and where a great expanse of slope affords only a small level tract that can be counted on for vegetation. On the other hand, contraction is possible on the coast, even in lands of rocks and nearly barren sands, because there fishing makes up to a great extent for the lack of land-produce, because the inhabitants have to congregate together more in order to repel pirates, and further because it is easier to unburden the country of its superfluous inhabitants by means of colonies.

To these conditions of law-giving must be added one other which, though it cannot take the place of the rest, renders them all useless when it is absent. This is the enjoyment of peace and plenty; for the moment at which a State sets its house in order is, like the moment when a battalion is forming up, that when its body is least capable of offering resistance and easiest to destroy. A better resistance could be made at a time of absolute disorganisation than at a moment of fermentation, when each is occupied with his own position and not with the danger. If war, famine, or sedition arises at this time of crisis, the State will inevitably be overthrown.

Not that many governments have not been set up during such storms; but in such cases these governments are themselves the State's destroyers. Usurpers always bring about or select troublous times to get passed, under cover of the public terror, destructive laws, which the people would never adopt in cold blood. The moment chosen is one of the surest means of distinguishing the work of the legislator from that of the tyrant.

What people, then, is a fit subject for legislation? One which, already bound by some unity of origin, interest, or convention, has never yet felt the real yoke of law; one that has neither customs nor superstitions deeply ingrained, one which stands in no fear of being overwhelmed by sudden invasion; one which, without entering into its neighbours' quarrels, can resist each of them single-handed, or get the help of one to repel another; one in which every member may be known by every other, and there is no need to lay on any man burdens too heavy for a man to bear; one which can do without other peoples, and without which all others can do;[1] one which is neither

[1] If there were two neighbouring peoples, one of which could not do without the other, it would

rich nor poor, but self-sufficient; and, lastly, one which unites the consistency of an ancient people with the docility of a new one. Legislation is made difficult less by what it is necessary to build up than by what has to be destroyed; and what makes success so rare is the impossibility of finding natural simplicity together with social requirements. All these conditions are indeed rarely found united, and therefore few States have good constitutions.

There is still in Europe one country capable of being given laws—Corsica. The valour and persistency with which that brave people has regained and defended its liberty well deserves that some wise man should teach it how to preserve what it has won. I have a feeling that some day that little island will astonish Europe.

11. THE VARIOUS SYSTEMS OF LEGISLATION

IF we ask in what precisely consists the greatest good of all, which should be the end of every system of legislation, we shall find it reduce itself to two main objects, liberty and equality—liberty, because all particular dependence means so much force taken from the body of the State and equality, because liberty cannot exist without it.

I have already defined civil liberty; by equality, we should understand, not that the degrees of power and riches are to be absolutely identical for everybody; but that power shall never be great enough for violence, and shall always be exercised by virtue of rank and law; and that, in respect of riches, no citizen shall ever be wealthy enough to buy another, and none poor enough to be forced to sell himself:[1] which implies, on the part of the great, moderation in goods and position, and,

on the side of the common sort, moderation in avarice and covetousness.

Such equality, we are told, is an unpractical ideal that cannot actually exist. But if its abuse is inevitable, does it follow that we should not at least make regulations concerning it? It is precisely because the force of circumstances tends continually to destroy equality that the force of legislation should always tend to its maintenance.

But these general objects of every good legislative system need modifying in every country in accordance with the local situation and the temper of the inhabitants; and these circumstances should determine, in each case, the particular system of institutions which is best, not perhaps in itself, but for the State for which it is destined. If, for instance, the soil is barren and unproductive, or the land too crowded for its inhabitants, the people should turn to industry and the crafts, and exchange what they produce for the commodities they lack. If, on the other hand, a people dwells in rich plains and fertile slopes, or, in a good land, lacks inhabitants, it should give all its attention to agriculture, which causes men to multiply, and should drive out the crafts, which would only result in depopulation, by grouping in a few localities the few inhabitants there are.[2] If a nation dwells on an extensive and convenient coast-line, let it cover the sea with ships and foster commerce and navigation. It will have a life that will be short and glorious. If, on its coasts, the sea washes nothing but almost inaccessible rocks, let it remain barbarous and ichthyophagous: it will have a quieter, perhaps a better, and certainly a happier life. In a word, besides the principles that are common to all, every nation has in itself something that gives them a particular application, and makes its legislation peculiarly its own. Thus, among the Jews long ago and more recently among the Arabs, the chief object was religion, among the Athenians letters, at Carthage and Tyre commerce, at Rhodes shipping, at Sparta war, at Rome virtue. The author of *The Spirit of the Laws* has shown with many examples by what art the legislator directs the constitution towards each of these objects.

What makes the constitution of a State

---

be very hard on the former, and very dangerous for the latter. Every wise nation, in such a case, would make haste to free the other from dependence. The Republic of Thlascala, enclosed by the Mexican Empire, preferred doing without salt to buying from the Mexicans, or even getting it from them as a gift. The Thlascalans were wise enough to see the snare hidden under such liberality. They kept their freedom, and that little State, shut up in that great Empire, was finally the instrument of its ruin.

[1] If the object is to give the State consistency, bring the two extremes as near to each other as possible; allow neither rich men nor beggars. These two estates, which are naturally inseparable, are equally fatal to the common good; from the one come the friends of tyranny, and from the other tyrants. It is always between them that public liberty is put up to auction; the one buys, and the other sells.

[2] "Any branch of foreign commerce," says M. d'Argenson, "creates on the whole only apparent advantage for the kingdom in general; it may enrich some individuals, or even some towns; but the nation as a whole gains nothing by it, and the people is no better off."

really solid and lasting is the due observance of what is proper, so that the natural relations are always in agreement with the laws on every point, and law only serves, so to speak, to assure, accompany and rectify them. But if the legislator mistakes his object and adopts a principle other than circumstances naturally direct; if his principle makes for servitude while they make for liberty, or if it makes for riches, while they make for populousness, or if it makes for peace, while they make for conquest—the laws will insensibly lose their influence, the constitution will alter, and the State will have no rest from trouble till it is either destroyed or changed, and nature has resumed her invincible sway.

12. The division of the laws

IF the whole is to be set in order, and the commonwealth put into the best possible shape, there are various relations to be considered. First, there is the action of the complete body upon itself, the relation of the whole to the whole, of the Sovereign to the State; and this relation, as we shall see, is made up of the relations of the intermediate terms.

The laws which regulate this relation bear the name of political laws, and are also called fundamental laws, not without reason if they are wise. For, if there is, in each State, only one good system, the people that is in possession of it should hold fast to this; but if the established order is bad, why should laws that prevent men from being good be regarded as fundamental? Besides, in any case, a people is always in a position to change its laws, however good; for, if it choose to do itself harm, who can have a right to stop it?

The second relation is that of the members one to another, or to the body as a whole; and this relation should be in the first respect as unimportant, and in the second as important, as possible. Each citizen would then be perfectly independent of all the rest, and at the same time very dependent on the city; which is brought about always by the same means, as the strength of the State can alone secure the liberty of its members. From this second relation arise civil laws.

We may consider also a third kind of relation between the individual and the law, a relation of disobedience to its penalty. This gives rise to the setting up of criminal laws, which, at bottom, are less a particular class of law than the sanction behind all the rest.

Along with these three kinds of law goes a fourth, most important of all, which is not graven on tablets of marble or brass, but on the hearts of the citizens. This forms the real constitution of the State, takes on every day new powers, when other laws decay or die out, restores them or takes their place, keeps a people in the ways in which it was meant to go, and insensibly replaces authority by the force of habit. I am speaking of morality, of custom, above all of public opinion; a power unknown to political thinkers, on which none the less success in everything else depends. With this the great legislator concerns himself in secret, though he seems to confine himself to particular regulations; for these are only the arc of the arch, while manners and morals, slower to arise, form in the end its immovable keystone.

Among the different classes of laws, the political, which determine the forms of the government, are alone relevant to my subject.

BOOK III

BEFORE speaking of the different forms of government, let us try to fix the exact sense of the word, which has not yet been very clearly explained.

1. Government in general

I WARN the reader that this chapter requires careful reading, and that I am unable to make myself clear to those who refuse to be attentive.

Every free action is produced by the concurrence of two causes; one moral, i.e., the will which determines the act; the other physical, i.e., the power which executes it. When I walk towards an object, it is necessary first that I should will to go there, and, in the second place, that my feet should carry me. If a paralytic wills to run and an active man wills not to, they will both stay where they are. The body politic has the same motive powers; here too force and will are distinguished, will under the name of legislative power and force under that of executive power. Without their concurrence, nothing is, or should be, done.

We have seen that the legislative power belongs to the people, and can belong to it alone. It may, on the other hand, readily be seen, from the principles laid down above, that the executive power cannot belong to the generality as legislature or Sovereign, because it consists wholly of particular acts which fall outside the competency of the law, and consequently of the Sovereign, whose acts must always be laws.

The public force therefore needs an agent of its own to bind it together and set it to work under the direction of the general will, to serve as a means of communication between the State and the Sovereign, and to do for the collective person more or less what the union of soul and body does for man. Here we have what is, in the State, the basis of government, often wrongly confused with the Sovereign, whose minister it is.

What then is government? An intermediate body set up between the subjects and the Sovereign, to secure their mutual correspondence, charged with the execution of the laws and the maintenance of liberty, both civil and political.

The members of this body are called magistrates or *kings*, that is to say *governors*, and the whole body bears the name *prince*.[1] Thus those who hold that the act, by which a people puts itself under a prince, is not a contract, are certainly right. It is simply and solely a commission, an employment, in which the rulers, mere officials of the Sovereign, exercise in their own name the power of which it makes them depositaries. This power it can limit, modify or recover at pleasure; for the alienation of such a right is incompatible with the nature of the social body, and contrary to the end of association.

I call then *government*, or supreme administration, the legitimate exercise of the executive power, and prince or magistrate the man or the body entrusted with that administration.

In government reside the intermediate forces whose relations make up that of the whole to the whole, or of the Sovereign to the State. This last relation may be represented as that between the extreme terms of a continuous proportion, which has government as its mean proportional. The government gets from the Sovereign the orders it gives the people, and, for the State to be properly balanced, there must, when everything is reckoned in, be equality between the product or power of the government taken in itself, and the product or

power of the citizens, who are on the one hand sovereign and on the other subject.

Furthermore, none of these three terms can be altered without the equality being instantly destroyed. If the Sovereign desires to govern, or the magistrate to give laws, or if the subjects refuse to obey, disorder takes the place of regularity, force and will no longer act together, and the State is dissolved and falls into despotism or anarchy. Lastly, as there is only one mean proportional between each relation, there is also only one good government possible for a State. But, as countless events may change the relations of a people, not only may different governments be good for different peoples, but also for the same people at different times.

In attempting to give some idea of the various relations that may hold between these two extreme terms, I shall take as an example the number of a people, which is the most easily expressible.

Suppose the State is composed of ten thousand citizens. The Sovereign can only be considered collectively and as a body; but each member, as being a subject, is regarded as an individual: thus the Sovereign is to the subject as ten thousand to one, i.e., each member of the State has as his share only a ten-thousandth part of the sovereign authority, although he is wholly under its control. If the people numbers a hundred thousand, the condition of the subject undergoes no change, and each equally is under the whole authority of the laws, while his vote, being reduced to a hundred-thousandth part, has ten times less influence in drawing them up. The subject therefore remaining always a unit, the relation between him and the Sovereign increases with the number of the citizens. From this it follows that, the larger the State, the less the liberty.

When I say the relation increases, I mean that it grows more unequal. Thus the greater it is in the geometrical sense, the less relation there is in the ordinary sense of the word. In the former sense, the relation, considered according to quantity, is expressed by the quotient; in the latter, considered according to identity, it is reckoned by similarity.

Now, the less relation the particular wills have to the general will, that is, morals and manners to laws, the more should the repressive force be increased. The government, then, to be good, should be proportionately stronger as the people is more numerous.

On the other hand, as the growth of the

---

[1] Thus at Venice the College, even in the absence of the Doge, is called "Most Serene Prince."

State gives the depositaries of the public authority more temptations and chances of abusing their power, the greater the force with which the government ought to be endowed for keeping the people in hand, the greater too should be the force at the disposal of the Sovereign for keeping the government in hand. I am speaking, not of absolute force, but of the relative force of the different parts of the State.

It follows from this double relation that the continuous proportion between the Sovereign, the prince and the people, is by no means an arbitrary idea, but a necessary consequence of the nature of the body politic. It follows further that, one of the extreme terms, viz., the people, as subject, being fixed and represented by unity, whenever the duplicate ratio increases or diminishes, the simple ratio does the same, and is changed accordingly. From this we see that there is not a single unique and absolute form of government, but as many governments differing in nature as there are States differing in size.

If, ridiculing this system, any one were to say that, in order to find the mean proportional and give form to the body of the government, it is only necessary, according to me, to find the square root of the number of the people, I should answer that I am here taking this number only as an instance; that the relations of which I am speaking are not measured by the number of men alone, but generally by the amount of action, which is a combination of a multitude of causes; and that, further, if, to save words, I borrow for a moment the terms of geometry, I am none the less well aware that moral quantities do not allow of geometrical accuracy.

The government is on a small scale what the body politic which includes it is on a great one. It is a moral person endowed with certain faculties, active like the Sovereign and passive like the State, and capable of being resolved into other similar relations. This accordingly gives rise to a new proportion, within which there is yet another, according to the arrangement of the magistracies, till an indivisible middle term is reached, i.e., a single ruler or supreme magistrate, who may be represented, in the midst of this progression, as the unity between the fractional and the ordinal series.

Without encumbering ourselves with this multiplication of terms, let us rest content with regarding government as a new body within the State, distinct from the people and the Sovereign, and intermediate between them.

There is between these two bodies this essential difference, that the State exists by itself, and the government only through the Sovereign. Thus the dominant will of the prince is, or should be, nothing but the general will or the law; his force is only the public force concentrated in his hands, and, as soon as he tries to base any absolute and independent act on his own authority, the tie that binds the whole together begins to be loosened. If finally the prince should come to have a particular will more active than the will of the Sovereign, and should employ the public force in his hands in obedience to this particular will, there would be, so to speak, two Sovereigns, one rightful and the other actual, the social union would evaporate instantly, and the body politic would be dissolved.

However, in order that the government may have a true existence and a real life distinguishing it from the body of the State, and in order that all its members may be able to act in concert and fulfil the end for which it was set up, it must have a particular personality, a sensibility common to its members, and a force and will of its own making for its preservation. This particular existence implies assemblies, councils, power and deliberation and decision, rights, titles, and privileges belonging exclusively to the prince and making the office of magistrate more honourable in proportion as it is more troublesome. The difficulties lie in the manner of so ordering this subordinate whole within the whole, that it in no way alters the general constitution by affirmation of its own, and always distinguishes the particular force it possesses, which is destined to aid in its preservation, from the public force, which is destined to the preservation of the State; and, in a word, is always ready to sacrifice the government to the people, and never to sacrifice the people to the government.

Furthermore, although the artificial body of the government is the work of another artificial body, and has, we may say, only a borrowed and subordinate life, this does not prevent it from being able to act with more or less vigour or promptitude, or from being, so to speak, in more or less robust health. Finally, without departing directly from the end for which it was instituted, it may deviate more or less from it, according to the manner of its constitution.

From all these differences arise the various relations which the government ought to bear to the body of the State, according to the accidental and particular relations by which the State itself is modified, for often the government that is best in itself will become the most pernicious, if the relations in which it stands have altered according to the defects of the body politic to which it belongs.

2. THE CONSTITUENT PRINCIPLE IN THE VARIOUS FORMS OF GOVERNMENT

To set forth the general cause of the above differences, we must here distinguish between government and its principle, as we did before between the State and the Sovereign.

The body of the magistrate may be composed of a greater or a less number of members. We said that the relation of the Sovereign to the subjects was greater in proportion as the people was more numerous, and, by a clear analogy, we may say the same of the relation of the government to the magistrates.

But the total force of the government, being always that of the State, is invariable; so that, the more of this force it expends on its own members, the less it has left to employ on the whole people.

The more numerous the magistrates, therefore, the weaker the government. This principle being fundamental, we must do our best to make it clear.

In the person of the magistrate we can distinguish three essentially different wills: first, the private will of the individual, tending only to his personal advantage; secondly, the common will of the magistrates, which is relative solely to the advantage of the prince, and may be called corporate will, being general in relation to the government, and particular in relation to the State, of which the government forms part; and, in the third place, the will of the people or the sovereign will, which is general both in relation to the State regarded as the whole, and to the government regarded as a part of the whole.

In a perfect act of legislation, the individual or particular will should be at zero; the corporate will belonging to the government should occupy a very subordinate position; and, consequently, the general or sovereign will should always predominate and should be the sole guide of all the rest.

According to the natural order, on the other hand, these different wills become more active in proportion as they are concentrated. Thus, the general will is always the weakest, the corporate will second, and the individual will strongest of all: so that, in the government, each member is first of all himself, then a magistrate, and then a citizen—in an order exactly the reverse of what the social system requires.

This granted, if the whole government is in the hands of one man, the particular and the corporate will are wholly united, and consequently the latter is at its highest possible degree of intensity. But, as the use to which the force is put depends on the degree reached by the will, and as the absolute force of the government is invariable, it follows that the most active government is that of one man.

Suppose, on the other hand, we unite the government with the legislative authority, and make the Sovereign prince also, and all the citizens so many magistrates: then the corporate will, being confounded with the general will, can possess no greater activity than that will, and must leave the particular will as strong as it can possibly be. Thus, the government, having always the same absolute force, will be at the lowest point of its relative force or activity.

These relations are incontestable, and there are other considerations which still further confirm them. We can see, for instance, that each magistrate is more active in the body to which he belongs than each citizen in that to which he belongs, and that consequently the particular will has much more influence on the acts of the government than on those of the Sovereign; for each magistrate is almost always charged with some governmental function, while each citizen, taken singly, exercises no function of Sovereignty. Furthermore, the bigger the State grows, the more its real force increases, though not in direct proportion to its growth; but, the State remaining the same, the number of magistrates may increase to any extent, without the government gaining any greater real force; for its force is that of the State, the dimension of which remains equal. Thus the relative force or activity of the government decreases, while its absolute or real force cannot increase.

Moreover, it is a certainty that promptitude in execution diminishes as more people are put in charge of it: where prudence is made too much of, not enough is made of fortune; opportunity is let slip, and deliberation results in the loss of its object.

I have just proved that the government

grows remiss in proportion as the number of the magistrates increases; and I previously proved that, the more numerous the people, the greater should be the repressive force. From this it follows that the relation of the magistrates to the government should vary inversely to the relation of the subjects to the Sovereign; that is to say, the larger the State, the more should the government be tightened, so that the number of the rulers diminish in proportion to the increase of that of the people.

It should be added that I am here speaking of the relative strength of the government, and not of its rectitude: for, on the other hand, the more numerous the magistracy, the nearer the corporate will comes to the general will; while, under a single magistrate, the corporate will is, as I said, merely a particular will. Thus, what may be gained on one side is lost on the other, and the art of the legislator is to know how to fix the point at which the force and the will of the government, which are always in inverse proportion, meet in the relation that is most to the advantage of the State.

3. The Division of Governments

We saw in the last chapter what causes the various kinds or forms of government to be distinguished according to the number of the members composing them: it remains in this to discover how the division is made.

In the first place, the Sovereign may commit the charge of the government to the whole people or to the majority of the people, so that more citizens are magistrates than are mere private individuals. This form of government is called *democracy*.

Or it may restrict the government to a small number, so that there are more private citizens than magistrates; and this is named *aristocracy*.

Lastly, it may concentrate the whole government in the hands of a single magistrate from whom all others hold their power. This third form is the most usual, and is called *monarchy*, or royal government.

It should be remarked that all these forms, or at least the first two, admit of degree, and even of very wide differences; for democracy may include the whole people, or may be restricted to half. Aristocracy, in its turn, may be restricted indefinitely from half the people down to the smallest possible number. Even royalty is susceptible of a measure of distribution. Sparta always had two kings, as its constitution provided; and the Roman Empire saw as many as eight emperors at once, without it being possible to say that the Empire was split up. Thus there is a point at which each form of government passes into the next, and it becomes clear that, under three comprehensive denominations, government is really susceptible of as many diverse forms as the State has citizens.

There are even more: for, as the government may also, in certain aspects, be subdivided into other parts, one administered in one fashion and one in another, the combination of the three forms may result in a multitude of mixed forms, each of which admits of multiplication by all the simple forms.

There has been at all times much dispute concerning the best form of government, without consideration of the fact that each is in some cases the best, and in others the worst.

If, in the different States, the number of supreme magistrates should be in inverse ratio to the number of citizens, it follows that, generally, democratic government suits small States, aristocratic government those of middle size, and monarchy great ones. This rule is immediately deducible from the principle laid down. But it is impossible to count the innumerable circumstances which may furnish exceptions.

4. Democracy

He who makes the law knows better than any one else how it should be executed and interpreted. It seems then impossible to have a better constitution than that in which the executive and legislative powers are united; but this very fact renders the government in certain respects inadequate, because things which should be distinguished are confounded, and the prince and the Sovereign, being the same person, form, so to speak, no more than a government without government.

It is not good for him who makes the laws to execute them, or for the body of the people to turn its attention away from a general standpoint and devote it to particular objects. Nothing is more dangerous than the influence of private interests in public affairs, and the abuse of the laws by the government is a less evil than the corruption of the legislator, which is the inevitable sequel to a particular standpoint. In such a case, the State being altered in substance, all reformation becomes impossible. A people that would never misuse governmental powers would never misuse independence; a people that would always govern well would not need to be governed.

If we take the term in the strict sense, there never has been a real democracy, and there never will be. It is against the natural order for the many to govern and the few to be governed. It is unimaginable that the people should remain continually assembled to devote their time to public affairs, and it is clear that they cannot set up commissions for that purpose without the form of administration being changed.

In fact, I can confidently lay down as a principle that, when the functions of government are shared by several tribunals, the less numerous sooner or later acquire the greatest authority, if only because they are in a position to expedite affairs, and power thus naturally comes into their hands.

Besides, how many conditions that are difficult to unite does such a government presuppose! First, a very small State, where the people can readily be got together and where each citizen can with ease know all the rest; secondly, great simplicity of manners, to prevent business from multiplying and raising thorny problems; next, a large measure of equality in rank and fortune, without which equality of rights and authority cannot long subsist; lastly, little or no luxury—for luxury either comes of riches or makes them necessary; it corrupts at once rich and poor, the rich by possession and the poor by covetousness; it sells the country to softness and vanity, and takes away from the State all its citizens, to make them slaves one to another, and one and all to public opinion.

This is why a famous writer has made virtue the fundamental principle of Republics; for all these conditions could not exist without virtue. But, for want of the necessary distinctions, that great thinker was often inexact, and sometimes obscure, and did not see that, the sovereign authority being everywhere the same, the same principle should be found in every well-constituted State, in a greater or less degree, it is true, according to the form of the government.

It may be added that there is no government so subject to civil wars and intestine agitations as democratic or popular government, because there is none which has so strong and continual a tendency to change to another form, or which demands more vigilance and courage for its maintenance as it is. Under such a constitution above all, the citizen

should arm himself with strength and constancy, and say, every day of his life, what a virtuous Count Palatine[1] said in the Diet of Poland: *Malo periculosam libertatem quam quietum servitium.*[2]

Were there a people of gods, their government would be democratic. So perfect a government is not for men.

5. ARISTOCRACY

WE have here two quite distinct moral persons, the government and the Sovereign, and in consequence two general wills, one general in relation to all the citizens, the other only for the members of the administration. Thus, although the government may regulate its internal policy as it pleases, it can never speak to the people save in the name of the Sovereign, that is, of the people itself, a fact which must not be forgotten.

The first societies governed themselves aristocratically. The heads of families took counsel together on public affairs. The young bowed without question to the authority of experience. Hence such names as *priests, elders, senate,* and *gerontes.* The savages of North America govern themselves in this way even now, and their government is admirable.

But, in proportion as artificial inequality produced by institutions became predominant over natural inequality, riches or power[3] were put before age, and aristocracy became elective. Finally, the transmission of the father's power along with his goods to his children, by creating patrician families, made government hereditary, and there came to be senators of twenty.

There are then three sorts of aristocracy—natural, elective and hereditary. The first is only for simple peoples; the third is the worst of all governments; the second is the best, and is aristocracy properly so called.

Besides the advantage that lies in the distinction between the two powers, it presents that of its members being chosen; for, in popular government, all the citizens are born magistrates; but here magistracy is confined to a few, who become such only by election.[4] By

---

[1] The Palatine of Posen, father of the King of Poland, Duke of Lorraine.

[2] I prefer liberty with danger to peace with slavery.

[3] It is clear that the word *optimates* meant, among the ancients, not the best, but the most powerful.

[4] It is of great importance that the form of the election of magistrates should be regulated by

this means uprightness, understanding, experience and all other claims to pre-eminence and public esteem become so many further guarantees of wise government.

Moreover, assemblies are more easily held, affairs better discussed and carried out with more order and diligence, and the credit of the State is better sustained abroad by venerable senators than by a multitude that is unknown or despised.

In a word, it is the best and most natural arrangement that the wisest should govern the many, when it is assured that they will govern for its profit, and not for their own. There is no need to multiply instruments, or get twenty thousand men to do what a hundred picked men can do even better. But it must not be forgotten that corporate interest here begins to direct the public power less under the regulation of the general will, and that a further inevitable propensity takes away from the laws part of the executive power.

If we are to speak of what is individually desirable, neither should the State be so small, nor a people so simple and upright, that the execution of the laws follows immediately from the public will, as it does in a good democracy. Nor should the nation be so great that the rulers have to scatter in order to govern it and are able to play the Sovereign each in his own department, and, beginning by making themselves independent, end by becoming masters.

But if aristocracy does not demand all the virtues needed by popular government, it demands others which are peculiar to itself; for instance, moderation on the side of the rich and contentment on that of the poor; for it seems that thorough-going equality would be out of place, as it was not found even at Sparta.

Furthermore, if this form of government carries with it a certain inequality of fortune, this is justifiable in order that as a rule the administration of public affairs may be entrusted to those who are most able to give them their whole time, but not, as Aristotle maintains, in order that the rich may always be put first. On the contrary, it is of importance that

---

law; for if it is left at the discretion of the prince, it is impossible to avoid falling into hereditary aristocracy, as the Republics of Venice and Berne actually did. The first of these has therefore long been a State dissolved; the second, however, is maintained by the extreme wisdom of the senate, and forms an honourable and highly dangerous exception.

an opposite choice should occasionally teach the people that the deserts of men offer claims to pre-eminence more important than those of riches.

6. MONARCHY

So far, we have considered the prince as a moral and collective person, unified by the force of the laws, and the depositary in the State of the executive power. We have now to consider this power when it is gathered together into the hands of a natural person, a real man, who alone has the right to dispose of it in accordance with the laws. Such a person is called a monarch or king.

In contrast with other forms of administration, in which a collective being stands for an individual, in this form an individual stands for a collective being; so that the moral unity that constitutes the prince is at the same time a physical unity, and all the qualities, which in the other case are only with difficulty brought together by the law, are found naturally united.

Thus the will of the people, the will of the prince, the public force of the State, and the particular force of the government, all answer to a single motive power; all the springs of the machine are in the same hands, the whole moves towards the same end; there are no conflicting movements to cancel one another, and no kind of constitution can be imagined in which a less amount of effort produces a more considerable amount of action. Archimedes, seated quietly on the bank and easily drawing a great vessel afloat, stands to my mind for a skilful monarch, governing vast states from his study, and moving everything while he seems himself unmoved.

But if no government is more vigorous than this, there is also none in which the particular will holds more sway and rules the rest more easily. Everything moves towards the same end indeed, but this end is by no means that of the public happiness, and even the force of the administration constantly shows itself prejudicial to the State.

Kings desire to be absolute, and men are always crying out to them from afar that the best means of being so is to get themselves loved by their people. This precept is all very well, and even in some respects very true. Unfortunately, it will always be derided at court. The power which comes of a people's love is no doubt the greatest; but it is precarious and conditional, and princes will never rest content with it. The best kings desire to be in a position to be wicked, if they please, without forfeiting their mastery: political sermonisers may tell them to their hearts' content that, the people's strength being their own, their first interest is that the people should be prosperous, numerous and formidable; they are well aware that this is untrue. Their first personal interest is that the people should be weak, wretched, and unable to resist them. I admit that, provided the subjects remained always in submission, the prince's interest would indeed be that it should be powerful, in order that its power, being his own, might make him formidable to his neighbours; but, this interest being merely secondary and subordinate, and strength being incompatible with submission, princes naturally give the preference always to the principle that is more to their immediate advantage. This is what Samuel put strongly before the Hebrews, and what Machiavelli has clearly shown. He professed to teach kings; but it was the people he really taught. His *Prince* is the book of Republicans.[1]

We found, on general grounds, that monarchy is suitable only for great States, and this is confirmed when we examine it in itself. The more numerous the public administration, the smaller becomes the relation between the prince and the subjects, and the nearer it comes to equality, so that in democracy the ratio is unity, or absolute equality. Again, as the government is restricted in numbers the ratio increases and reaches its *maximum* when the government is in the hands of a single person. There is then too great a distance between prince and people, and the State lacks a bond of union. To form such a bond, there must be intermediate orders, and princes, personages and nobility to compose them. But no such things suit a small State, to which all class differences mean ruin.

If, however, it is hard for a great State to be well governed, it is much harder for it to be so by a single man; and every one knows what

happens when kings substitute others for themselves.

An essential and inevitable defect, which will always rank monarchical below the republican government, is that in a republic the public voice hardly ever raises to the highest positions men who are not enlightened and capable, and such as to fill them with honour; while in monarchies those who rise to the top are most often merely petty blunderers, petty swindlers, and petty intriguers, whose petty talents cause them to get into the highest positions at Court, but, as soon as they have got there, serve only to make their ineptitude clear to the public. The people is far less often mistaken in its choice than the prince; and a man of real worth among the king's ministers is almost as rare as a fool at the head of a republican government. Thus, when, by some fortunate chance, one of these born governors takes the helm of State in some monarchy that has been nearly overwhelmed by swarms of "gentlemanly" administrators, there is nothing but amazement at the resources he discovers, and his coming marks an era in his country's history.

For a monarchical State to have a chance of being well governed, its population and extent must be proportionate to the abilities of its governor. It is easier to conquer than to rule. With a long enough lever, the world could be moved with a single finger; to sustain it needs the shoulders of Hercules. However small a State may be, the prince is hardly ever big enough for it. When, on the other hand, it happens that the State is too small for its ruler, in these rare cases too it is ill governed, because the ruler, constantly pursuing his great designs, forgets the interests of the people, and makes it no less wretched by misusing the talents he has, than a ruler of less capacity would make it for want of those he had not. A kingdom should, so to speak, expand or contract with each reign, according to the prince's capabilities; but, the abilities of a senate being more constant in quantity, the State can then have permanent frontiers without the administration suffering.

The disadvantage that is most felt in monarchical government is the want of the continuous succession which, in both the other forms, provides an unbroken bond of union. When one king dies, another is needed; elections leave dangerous intervals and are full of storms; and unless the citizens are disinterested and upright to a degree which very seldom

[1] Machiavelli was a proper man and a good citizen; but, being attached to the court of the Medici, he could not help veiling his love of liberty in the midst of his country's oppression. The choice of his detestable hero, Cæsar Borgia, clearly enough shows his hidden aim; and the contradiction between the teaching of the *Prince* and that of the *Discourses on Livy* and the *History of Florence* shows that this profound political thinker has so far been studied only by superficial or corrupt readers. The Court of Rome sternly prohibited his book. I can well believe it; for it is that Court it most clearly portrays.

goes with this kind of government, intrigue and corruption abound. He to whom the State has sold itself can hardly help selling it in his turn and repaying himself, at the expense of the weak, the money the powerful have wrung from him. Under such an administration, venality sooner or later spreads through every part, and peace so enjoyed under a king is worse than the disorders of an interregnum.

What has been done to prevent these evils? Crowns have been made hereditary in certain families, and an order of succession has been set up, to prevent disputes from arising on the death of kings. That is to say, the disadvantages of regency have been put in place of those of election, apparent tranquillity has been preferred to wise administration, and men have chosen rather to risk having children, monstrosities, or imbeciles as rulers to having disputes over the choice of good kings. It has not been taken into account that, in so exposing ourselves to the risks this possibility entails, we are setting almost all the chances against us. There was sound sense in what the younger Dionysius said to his father, who reproached him for doing some shameful deed by asking, "Did I set you the example?" "No," answered his son, "but your father was not king."

Everything conspires to take away from a man who is set in authority over others the sense of justice and reason. Much trouble, we are told, is taken to teach young princes the art of reigning; but their education seems to do them no good. It would be better to begin by teaching them the art of obeying. The greatest kings whose praises history tells were not brought up to reign: reigning is a science we are never so far from possessing as when we have learnt too much of it, and one we acquire better by obeying than by commanding. *"Nam utilissimus idem ac brevissimus bonarum malarumque rerum delectus cogitare quid aut nolueris sub alio principe, aut volueris."*[1]

One result of this lack of coherence is the inconstancy of royal government, which, regulated now on one scheme and now on another, according to the character of the reigning prince or those who reign for him, cannot for long have a fixed object or a consistent policy —and this variability, not found in the other forms of government, where the prince is always the same, causes the State to be always shifting from principle to principle and from project to project. Thus we may say that generally, if a court is more subtle in intrigue, there is more wisdom in a senate, and Republics advance towards their ends by more consistent and better considered policies; while every revolution in a royal ministry creates a revolution in the State; for the principle common to all ministers and nearly all kings is to do in every respect the reverse of what was done by their predecessors.

This incoherence further clears up a sophism that is very familiar to royalist political writers; not only is civil government likened to domestic government, and the prince to the father of a family—this error has already been refuted—but the prince is also freely credited with all the virtues he ought to possess, and is supposed to be always what he should be. This supposition once made, royal government is clearly preferable to all others, because it is incontestably the strongest, and, to be the best also, wants only a corporate will more in conformity with the general will.

But if, according to Plato,[2] the "king by nature" is such a rarity, how often will nature and fortune conspire to give him a crown? And, if royal education necessarily corrupts those who receive it, what is to be hoped from a series of men brought up to reign? It is, then, wanton self-deception to confuse royal government with government by a good king. To see such government as it is in itself, we must consider it as it is under princes who are incompetent or wicked: for either they will come to the throne wicked or incompetent, or the throne will make them so.

These difficulties have not escaped our writers, who, all the same, are not troubled by them. The remedy, they say, is to obey without a murmur: God sends bad kings in His wrath, and they must be borne as the scourges of Heaven. Such talk is doubtless edifying; but it would be more in place in a pulpit than in a political book. What are we to think of a doctor who promises miracles, and whose whole art is to exhort the sufferer to patience? We know for ourselves that we must put up with a bad government when it is there; the question is how to find a good one.

7. MIXED GOVERNMENTS

STRICTLY speaking, there is no such thing as

---

[1] Tacitus, *Histories*, i. 16. "For the best, and also the shortest way of finding out what is good and what is bad is to consider what you would have wished to happen or not to happen, had another than you been Emperor."

[2] In the *Statesman*.

a simple government. An isolated ruler must have subordinate magistrates; a popular government must have a head. There is therefore, in the distribution of the executive power, always a gradation from the greater to the lesser number, with the difference that sometimes the greater number is dependent on the smaller, and sometimes the smaller on the greater.

Sometimes the distribution is equal, when either the constituent parts are in mutual dependence, as in the government of England, or the authority of each section is independent, but imperfect, as in Poland. This last form is bad; for it secures no unity in the government, and the State is left without a bond of union.

Is a simple or a mixed government the better? Political writers are always debating the question, which must be answered as we have already answered a question about all forms of government.

Simple government is better in itself, just because it is simple. But when the executive power is not sufficiently dependent upon the legislative power, i.e., when the prince is more closely related to the Sovereign than the people to the prince, this lack of proportion must be cured by the division of the government; for all the parts have then no less authority over the subjects, while their division makes them all together less strong against the Sovereign.

The same disadvantage is also prevented by the appointment of intermediate magistrates, who leave the government entire, and have the effect only of balancing the two powers and maintaining their respective rights. Government is then not mixed, but moderated.

The opposite disadvantages may be similarly cured, and, when the government is too lax, tribunals may be set up to concentrate it. This is done in all democracies. In the first case, the government is divided to make it weak; in the second, to make it strong: for the *maxima* of both strength and weakness are found in simple governments, while the mixed forms result in a mean strength.

8. That all forms of government do not suit all countries

Liberty, not being a fruit of all climates, is not within the reach of all peoples. The more this principle, laid down by Montesquieu, is considered, the more its truth is felt; the more it is combated, the more chance is given to confirm it by new proofs.

In all the governments that there are, the public person consumes without producing. Whence then does it get what it consumes? From the labour of its members. The necessities of the public are supplied out of the superfluities of individuals. It follows that the civil State can subsist only so long as men's labour brings them a return greater than their needs.

The amount of this excess is not the same in all countries. In some it is considerable, in others middling, in yet others nil, in some even negative. The relation of product to subsistence depends on the fertility of the climate, on the sort of labour the land demands, on the nature of its products, on the strength of its inhabitants, on the greater or less consumption they find necessary, and on several further considerations of which the whole relation is made up.

On the other side, all governments are not of the same nature: some are less voracious than others, and the differences between them are based on this second principle, that the further from their source the public contributions are removed, the more burdensome they become. The charge should be measured not by the amount of the impositions, but by the path they have to travel in order to get back to those from whom they came. When the circulation is prompt and well-established, it does not matter whether much or little is paid; the people is always rich and, financially speaking, all is well. On the contrary, however little the people gives, if that little does not return to it, it is soon exhausted by giving continually: the State is then never rich, and the people is always a people of beggars.

It follows that, the more the distance between people and government increases, the more burdensome tribute becomes: thus, in a democracy, the people bears the least charge; in an aristocracy, a greater charge; and, in monarchy, the weight becomes heaviest. Monarchy therefore suits only wealthy nations; aristocracy, States of middling size and wealth; and democracy, States that are small and poor.

In fact, the more we reflect, the more we find the difference between free and monarchical States to be this: in the former, everything is used for the public advantage; in the latter, the public forces and those of individuals are affected by each other, and either increases as the other grows weak; finally, instead of governing subjects to make them happy, despotism makes them wretched in order to govern them.

We find then, in every climate, natural causes according to which the form of government which it requires can be assigned, and we can even say what sort of inhabitants it should have.

Unfriendly and barren lands, where the product does not repay the labour, should remain desert and uncultivated, or peopled only by savages; lands where men's labour brings in no more than the exact *minimum* necessary to subsistence should be inhabited by barbarous peoples: in such places all polity is impossible. Lands where the surplus of product over labour is only middling are suitable for free peoples; those in which the soil is abundant and fertile and gives a great product for a little labour call for monarchical government, in order that the surplus of superfluities among the subjects may be consumed by the luxury of the prince: for it is better for this excess to be absorbed by the government than dissipated among the individuals. I am aware that there are exceptions; but these exceptions themselves confirm the rule, in that sooner or later they produce revolutions which restore things to the natural order.

General laws should always be distinguished from individual causes that may modify their effects. If all the South were covered with Republics and all the North with despotic States, it would be none the less true that, in point of climate, despotism is suitable to hot countries, barbarism to cold countries, and good polity to temperate regions. I see also that, the principle being granted, there may be disputes on its application; it may be said that there are cold countries that are very fertile, and tropical countries that are very unproductive. But this difficulty exists only for those who do not consider the question in all its aspects. We must, as I have already said, take labour, strength, consumption, etc., into account.

Take two tracts of equal extent, one of which brings in five and the other ten. If the inhabitants of the first consume four and those of the second nine, the surplus of the first product will be a fifth and that of the second a tenth. The ratio of these two surpluses will then be inverse to that of the products, and the tract which produces only five will give a surplus double that of the tract which produces ten.

But there is no question of a double product, and I think no one would put the fertility of cold countries, as a general rule, on an equality with that of hot ones. Let us, however, suppose this equality to exist: let us, if you will, regard England as on the same level as Sicily, and Poland as Egypt—further south, we shall have Africa and the Indies; further north, nothing at all. To get this equality of product, what a difference there must be in tillage: in Sicily, there is only need to scratch the ground; in England, how men must toil! But, where more hands are needed to get the same product, the superfluity must necessarily be less.

Consider, besides, that the same number of men consume much less in hot countries. The climate requires sobriety for the sake of health; and Europeans who try to live there as they would at home all perish of dysentery and indigestion. "We are," says Chardin, "carnivorous animals, wolves, in comparison with the Asiatics. Some attribute the sobriety of the Persians to the fact that their country is less cultivated; but it is my belief that their country abounds less in commodities because the inhabitants need less. If their frugality," he goes on, "were the effect of the nakedness of the land, only the poor would eat little; but everybody does so. Again, less or more would be eaten in various provinces, according to the land's fertility; but the same sobriety is found throughout the kingdom. They are very proud of their manner of life, saying that you have only to look at their hue to recognise how far it excels that of the Christians. In fact, the Persians are of an even hue; their skins are fair, fine and smooth; while the hue of their subjects, the Armenians, who live after the European fashion, is rough and blotchy, and their bodies are gross and unwieldy."

The nearer you get to the equator, the less people live on. Meat they hardly touch; rice, maize, curcur, millet and cassava are their ordinary food. There are in the Indies millions of men whose subsistence does not cost a halfpenny a day. Even in Europe we find considerable differences of appetite between Northern and Southern peoples. A Spaniard will live for a week on a German's dinner. In the countries in which men are more voracious, luxury therefore turns in the direction of consumption. In England, luxury appears in a well-filled table; in Italy, you feast on sugar and flowers.

Luxury in clothes shows similar differences. In climates in which the changes of season are prompt and violent, men have better and simpler clothes; where they clothe themselves only for adornment, what is striking is more thought of than what is useful; clothes themselves are then a luxury. At Naples, you may see daily walking in the Pausilippeum men in gold-embroidered upper garments and nothing else. It is the same with buildings; magnificence is the sole consideration where there is nothing to fear from the air. In Paris and London, you desire to be lodged warmly and comfortably; in Madrid, you have superb salons, but not a window that closes, and you go to bed in a mere hole.

In hot countries foods are much more substantial and succulent; and the third difference cannot but have an influence on the second. Why are so many vegetables eaten in Italy? Because there they are good, nutritious and excellent in taste. In France, where they are nourished only on water, they are far from nutritious and are thought nothing of at table. They take up all the same no less ground, and cost at least as much pains to cultivate. It is a proved fact that the wheat of Barbary, in other respects inferior to that of France, yields much more flour, and that the wheat of France in turn yields more than that of northern countries; from which it may be inferred that a like gradation in the same direction, from equator to pole, is found generally. But is it not an obvious disadvantage for an equal product to contain less nourishment?

To all these points may be added another, which at once depends on and strengthens them. Hot countries need inhabitants less than cold countries, and can support more of them. There is thus a double surplus, which is all to the advantage of despotism. The greater the territory occupied by a fixed number of inhabitants, the more difficult revolt becomes, because rapid or secret concerted action is impossible, and the government can easily unmask projects and cut communications; but the more a numerous people is gathered together, the less can the government usurp the Sovereign's place: the people's leaders can deliberate as safely in their houses as the prince in council, and the crowd gathers as rapidly in the squares as the prince's troops in their quarters. The advantage of tyrannical government therefore lies in acting at great distances. With the help of the rallying-points it establishes, its strength, like that of the lever,[1] grows

with distance. The strength of the people, on the other hand, acts only when concentrated: when spread abroad, it evaporates and is lost, like powder scattered on the ground, which catches fire only grain by grain. The least populous countries are thus the fittest for tyranny: fierce animals reign only in deserts.

9. THE MARKS OF A GOOD GOVERNMENT

THE question "What absolutely is the best government?" is unanswerable as well as indeterminate; or rather, there are as many good answers as there are possible combinations in the absolute and relative situations of all nations.

But if it is asked by what sign we may know that a given people is well or ill governed, that is another matter, and the question, being one of fact, admits of an answer.

It is not, however, answered, because everyone wants to answer it in his own way. Subjects extol public tranquillity, citizens individual liberty; the one class prefers security of possessions, the other that of person; the one regards as the best government that which is most severe, the other maintains that the mildest is the best; the one wants crimes punished, the other wants them prevented; the one wants the State to be feared by its neighbours, the other prefers that it should be ignored; the one is content if money circulates, the other demands that the people shall have bread. Even if an agreement were come to on these and similar points, should we have got any further? As moral qualities do not admit of exact measurement, agreement about the mark does not mean agreement about the valuation.

For my part, I am continually astonished that a mark so simple is not recognised, or that men are of so bad faith as not to admit it. What is the end of political association? The preservation and prosperity of its members. And what is the surest mark of their preservation and prosperity? Their numbers and population. Seek then nowhere else this mark that is in dispute. The rest being equal, the government under which, without external aids, without naturalisation or colonies, the citizens increase and multiply most, is beyond question the best. The government under which a people wanes and diminishes is the worst. Cal-

---

[1] This does not contradict what I said before (Book II, ch. 9) about the disadvantages of great States; for we were then dealing with the authority of the government over the members, while here we are dealing with its force against the subjects. Its scattered members serve it as rallying-points for action against the people at a distance, but it has no rallying-point for direct action on its members themselves. Thus the length of the lever is its weakness in the one case, and its strength in the other.

culators, it is left for you to count, to measure, to compare.[1]

10. THE ABUSE OF GOVERNMENT AND ITS TENDENCY TO DEGENERATE

As the particular will acts constantly in opposition to the general will, the government continually exerts itself against the Sovereignty. The greater this exertion becomes, the more the constitution changes; and, as there is in this case no other corporate will to create an equilibrium by resisting the will of the prince, sooner or later the prince must inevitably suppress the Sovereign and break the social treaty. This is the unavoidable and inherent defect which, from the very birth of the body politic, tends ceaselessly to destroy it, as age and death end by destroying the human body.

[1] On the same principle it should be judged what centuries deserve the preference for human prosperity. Those in which letters and arts have flourished have been too much admired, because the hidden object of their culture has not been fathomed, and their fatal effects not taken into account. *"Idque apud imperitos humanitas vocabatur, cum pars servitutis esset."* (Fools called "humanity" what was a part of slavery, Tacitus, *Agricola*, 31.) Shall we never see in the maxims books lay down the vulgar interest that makes their writers speak? No, whatever they may say, when, despite its renown, a country is depopulated, it is not true that all is well, and it is not enough that a poet should have an income of 100,000 francs to make his age the best of all. Less attention should be paid to the apparent repose and tranquillity of the rulers than to the well-being of their nations as wholes, and above all of the most numerous States. A hail-storm lays several cantons waste, but it rarely makes a famine. Outbreaks and civil wars give rulers rude shocks, but they are not the real ills of peoples, who may even get a respite, while there is a dispute as to who shall tyrannise over them. Their true prosperity and calamities come from their permanent condition: it is when the whole remains crushed beneath the yoke, that decay sets in, and that the rulers destroy them at will, and *"ubi solitudinem faciunt, pacem appellant."* (Where they create solitude, they call it peace, Tacitus, *Agricola*, 31.) When the bickerings of the great disturbed the kingdom of France, and the Coadjutor of Paris took a dagger in his pocket to the Parliament, these things did not prevent the people of France from prospering and multiplying in dignity, ease and freedom. Long ago Greece flourished in the midst of the most savage wars; blood ran in torrents, and yet the whole country was covered with inhabitants. It appeared, says Machiavelli, that in the midst of murder, proscription and civil war, our republic only throve: the virtue, morality and independence of the citizens did more to strengthen it than all their dissensions had done to enfeeble it. A little disturbance gives the soul elasticity; what makes the race truly prosperous is not so much peace as liberty.

There are two general courses by which government degenerates: i.e., when it undergoes contraction, or when the State is dissolved.

Government undergoes contraction when it passes from the many to the few, that is, from democracy to aristocracy, and from aristocracy to royalty. To do so is its natural propensity.[2] If it took the backward course from the few to the many, it could be said that it was relaxed; but this inverse sequence is impossible.

[2] The slow formation and the progress of the Republic of Venice in its lagoons are a notable instance of this sequence; and it is most astonishing that, after more than twelve hundred years' existence, the Venetians seem to be still at the second stage, which they reached with the *Serrar di Consiglio* in 1198. As for the ancient Dukes who are brought up against them, it is proved, whatever the *Squittinio della libertà veneta* may say of them, that they were in no sense sovereigns.

A case certain to be cited against my view is that of the Roman Republic, which, it will be said, followed exactly the opposite course, and passed from monarchy to aristocracy and from aristocracy to democracy. I by no means take this view of it.

What Romulus first set up was a mixed government, which soon deteriorated into despotism. From special causes, the State died an untimely death, as new-born children sometimes perish without reaching manhood. The expulsion of the Tarquins was the real period of the birth of the Republic. But at first it took on no constant form, because, by not abolishing the patriciate, it left half its work undone. For, by this means, hereditary aristocracy, the worst of all legitimate forms of administration, remained in conflict with democracy, and the form of the government, as Machiavelli has proved, was only fixed on the establishment of the tribunate: only then was there a true government and a veritable democracy. In fact, the people was then not only Sovereign, but also magistrate and judge; the senate was only a subordinate tribunal, to temper and concentrate the government, and the consuls themselves, though they were patricians, first magistrates, and absolute generals in war, were in Rome itself no more than presidents of the people.

From that point, the government followed its natural tendency, and inclined strongly to aristocracy. The patriciate, we may say, abolished itself, and the aristocracy was found no longer in the body of patricians as at Venice and Genoa, but in the body of the senate, which was composed of patricians and plebeians, and even in the body of tribunes when they began to usurp an active function: for names do not affect facts, and, when the people has rulers who govern for it, whatever name they bear, the government is an aristocracy.

The abuse of aristocracy led to the civil wars and the triumvirate. Sulla, Julius Cæsar and Augustus became in fact real monarchs; and finally, under the despotism of Tiberius, the State was dissolved. Roman history then confirms, instead of invalidating, the principle I have laid down.

Indeed, governments never change their form except when their energy is exhausted and leaves them too weak to keep what they have. If a government at once extended its sphere and relaxed its stringency, its force would become absolutely nil, and it would persist still less. It is therefore necessary to wind up the spring and tighten the hold as it gives way: or else the State it sustains will come to grief.

The dissolution of the State may come about in either of two ways.

First, when the prince ceases to administer the State in accordance with the laws, and usurps the Sovereign power. A remarkable change then occurs: not the government, but the State, undergoes contraction; I mean that the great State is dissolved, and another is formed within it, composed solely of the members of the government, which becomes for the rest of the people merely master and tyrant. So that the moment the government usurps the Sovereignty, the social compact is broken, and all private citizens recover by right their natural liberty, and are forced, but not bound, to obey.

The same thing happens when the members of the government severally usurp the power they should exercise only as a body; this is as great an infraction of the laws, and results in even greater disorders. There are then, so to speak, as many princes as there are magistrates, and the State, no less divided than the government, either perishes or changes its form.

When the State is dissolved, the abuse of government, whatever it is, bears the common name of *anarchy*. To distinguish, democracy degenerates into *ochlocracy*, and aristocracy into *oligarchy;* and I would add that royalty degenerates into *tyranny;* but this last word is ambiguous and needs explanation.

In vulgar usage, a tyrant is a king who governs violently and without regard for justice and law. In the exact sense, a tyrant is an individual who arrogates to himself the royal authority without having a right to it. This is how the Greeks understood the word "tyrant": they applied it indifferently to good and bad princes whose authority was not legitimate.[1] *Tyrant* and *usurper* are thus per-

fectly synonymous terms.

In order that I may give different things different names, I call him who usurps the royal authority a *tyrant,* and him who usurps the sovereign power a *despot*. The tyrant is he who thrusts himself in contrary to the laws to govern in accordance with the laws; the despot is he who sets himself above the laws themselves. Thus the tyrant cannot be a despot, but the despot is always a tyrant.

11. THE DEATH OF THE BODY POLITIC

SUCH is the natural and inevitable tendency of the best constituted governments. If Sparta and Rome perished, what State can hope to endure for ever? If we would set up a long-lived form of government, let us not even dream of making it eternal. If we are to succeed, we must not attempt the impossible, or flatter ourselves that we are endowing the work of man with a stability of which human conditions do not permit.

The body politic, as well as the human body, begins to die as soon as it is born, and carries in itself the causes of its destruction. But both may have a constitution that is more or less robust and suited to preserve them a longer or a shorter time. The constitution of man is the work of nature; that of the State the work of art. It is not in men's power to prolong their own lives; but it is for them to prolong as much as possible the life of the State, by giving it the best possible constitution. The best constituted State will have an end; but it will end later than any other, unless some unforeseen accident brings about its untimely destruction.

The life-principle of the body politic lies in the sovereign authority. The legislative power is the heart of the State; the executive power is its brain, which causes the movement of all the parts. The brain may become paralysed and the individual still live. A man may remain an imbecile and live; but as soon as the heart ceases to perform its functions, the animal is dead.

The State subsists by means not of the laws, but of the legislative power. Yesterday's law is

[1] *"Omnes enim et habentur et dicuntur tyranni, qui potestate utuntur perpetua in ea civitate quæ libertate usa est"* (Cornelius Nepos, *Life of Miltiades*). (For all those are called and considered tyrants, who hold perpetual power in a State that has known liberty.) It is true that Aristotle (*Ethics,* Book viii, chapter x) distinguishes the ty-

rant from the king by the fact that the former governs in his own interest, and the latter only for the good of his subjects; but not only did all Greek authors in general use the word *tyrant* in a different sense, as appears most clearly in Xenophon's *Hiero,* but also it would follow from Aristotle's distinction that, from the very beginning of the world, there has not yet been a single king.

not binding to-day; but silence is taken for tacit consent, and the Sovereign is held to confirm incessantly the laws it does not abrogate as it might. All that it has once declared itself to will it wills always, unless it revokes its declaration.

Why then is so much respect paid to old laws? For this very reason. We must believe that nothing but the excellence of old acts of will can have preserved them so long: if the Sovereign had not recognised them as throughout salutary, it would have revoked them a thousand times. This is why, so far from growing weak, the laws continually gain new strength in any well constituted State; the precedent of antiquity makes them daily more venerable: while wherever the laws grow weak as they become old, this proves that there is no longer a legislative power, and that the State is dead.

12. How the sovereign authority maintains itself

THE Sovereign, having no force other than the legislative power, acts only by means of the laws; and the laws being solely the authentic acts of the general will, the Sovereign cannot act save when the people is assembled. The people in assembly, I shall be told, is a mere chimera. It is so to-day, but two thousand years ago it was not so. Has man's nature changed?

The bounds of possibility, in moral matters, are less narrow than we imagine: it is our weaknesses, our vices and our prejudices that confine them. Base souls have no belief in great men; vile slaves smile in mockery at the name of liberty.

Let us judge of what can be done by what has been done. I shall say nothing of the Republics of ancient Greece; but the Roman Republic was, to my mind, a great State, and the town of Rome a great town. The last census showed that there were in Rome four hundred thousand citizens capable of bearing arms, and the last computation of the population of the Empire showed over four million citizens, excluding subjects, foreigners, women, children and slaves.

What difficulties might not be supposed to stand in the way of the frequent assemblage of the vast population of this capital and its neighbourhood. Yet few weeks passed without the Roman people being in assembly, and even being so several times. It exercised not only the rights of Sovereignty, but also a part of those of government. It dealt with certain matters, and judged certain cases, and this whole people was found in the public meeting-place hardly less often as magistrates than as citizens.

If we went back to the earliest history of nations, we should find that most ancient governments, even those of monarchical form, such as the Macedonian and the Frankish, had similar councils. In any case, the one incontestable fact I have given is an answer to all difficulties; it is good logic to reason from the actual to the possible.

13. The same (continued)

IT is not enough for the assembled people to have once fixed the constitution of the State by giving its sanction to a body of law; it is not enough for it to have set up a perpetual government, or provided once for all for the election of magistrates. Besides the extraordinary assemblies unforeseen circumstances may demand, there must be fixed periodical assemblies which cannot be abrogated or prorogued, so that on the proper day the people is legitimately called together by law, without need of any formal summoning.

But, apart from these assemblies authorised by their date alone, every assembly of the people not summoned by the magistrates appointed for that purpose, and in accordance with the prescribed forms, should be regarded as unlawful, and all its acts as null and void, because the command to assemble should itself proceed from the law.

The greater or less frequency with which lawful assemblies should occur depends on so many considerations that no exact rules about them can be given. It can only be said generally that the stronger the government the more often should the Sovereign show itself.

This, I shall be told, may do for a single town; but what is to be done when the State includes several? Is the sovereign authority to be divided? Or is it to be concentrated in a single town to which all the rest are made subject?

Neither the one nor the other, I reply. First, the sovereign authority is one and simple, and cannot be divided without being destroyed. In the second place, one town cannot, any more than one nation, legitimately be made subject to another, because the essence of the body politic lies in the reconciliation of obedience and liberty, and the words subject and Sovereign are identical correlatives the idea of which meets in the single word "citizen."

I answer further that the union of several

towns in a single city is always bad, and that, if we wish to make such a union, we should not expect to avoid its natural disadvantages. It is useless to bring up abuses that belong to great States against one who desires to see only small ones; but how can small States be given the strength to resist great ones, as formerly the Greek towns resisted the Great King, and more recently Holland and Switzerland have resisted the House of Austria?

Nevertheless, if the State cannot be reduced to the right limits, there remains still one resource; this is, to allow no capital, to make the seat of government move from town to town, and to assemble by turn in each the Provincial Estates of the country.

People the territory evenly, extend everywhere the same rights, bear to every place in it abundance and life: by these means will the State become at once as strong and as well governed as possible. Remember that the walls of towns are built of the ruins of the houses of the countryside. For every palace I see raised in the capital, my mind's eye sees a whole country made desolate.

14. THE SAME (continued)

THE moment the people is legitimately assembled as a sovereign body, the jurisdiction of the government wholly lapses, the executive power is suspended, and the person of the meanest citizen is as sacred and inviolable as that of the first magistrate; for in the presence of the person represented, representatives no longer exist. Most of the tumults that arose in the comitia at Rome were due to ignorance or neglect of this rule. The consuls were in them merely the presidents of the people; the tribunes were mere speakers;[1] the senate was nothing at all.

These intervals of suspension, during which the prince recognises or ought to recognise an actual superior, have always been viewed by him with alarm; and these assemblies of the people, which are the aegis of the body politic and the curb on the government, have at all times been the horror of rulers: who therefore never spare pains, objections, difficulties, and promises, to stop the citizens from having them. When the citizens are greedy, cowardly, and pusillanimous, and love ease more than

[1] In nearly the same sense as this word has in the English Parliament. The similarity of these functions would have brought the consuls and the tribunes into conflict, even had all jurisdiction been suspended.

liberty, they do not long hold out against the redoubled efforts of the government; and thus, as the resisting force incessantly grows, the sovereign authority ends by disappearing, and most cities fall and perish before their time.

But between the sovereign authority and arbitrary government there sometimes intervenes a mean power of which something must be said.

15. DEPUTIES OR REPRESENTATIVES

As soon as public service ceases to be the chief business of the citizens, and they would rather serve with their money than with their persons, the State is not far from its fall. When it is necessary to march out to war, they pay troops and stay at home: when it is necessary to meet in council, they name deputies and stay at home. By reason of idleness and money, they end by having soldiers to enslave their country and representatives to sell it.

It is through the hustle of commerce and the arts, through the greedy self-interest of profit, and through softness and love of amenities that personal services are replaced by money payments. Men surrender a part of their profits in order to have time to increase them at leisure. Make gifts of money, and you will not be long without chains. The word *finance* is a slavish word, unknown in the city-state. In a country that is truly free, the citizens do everything with their own arms and nothing by means of money; so far from paying to be exempted from their duties, they would even pay for the privilege of fulfilling them themselves. I am far from taking the common view: I hold enforced labour to be less opposed to liberty than taxes.

The better the constitution of a State is, the more do public affairs encroach on private in the minds of the citizens. Private affairs are even of much less importance, because the aggregate of the common happiness furnishes a greater proportion of that of each individual, so that there is less for him to seek in particular cares. In a well-ordered city every man flies to the assemblies: under a bad government no one cares to stir a step to get to them, because no one is interested in what happens there, because it is foreseen that the general will will not prevail, and lastly because domestic cares are all-absorbing. Good laws lead to the making of better ones; bad ones bring about worse. As soon as any man says of the affairs of the State *What does it matter to me?* the State may be given up for lost.

The lukewarmness of patriotism, the activity of private interest, the vastness of States, conquest and the abuse of government suggested the method of having deputies or representatives of the people in the national assemblies. These are what, in some countries, men have presumed to call the Third Estate. Thus the individual interest of two orders is put first and second; the public interest occupies only the third place.

Sovereignty, for the same reason as makes it inalienable, cannot be represented; it lies essentially in the general will, and will does not admit of representation: it is either the same, or other; there is no intermediate possibility. The deputies of the people, therefore, are not and cannot be its representatives: they are merely its stewards, and can carry through no definitive acts. Every law the people has not ratified in person is null and void—is, in fact, not a law. The people of England regards itself as free; but it is grossly mistaken; it is free only during the election of members of parliament. As soon as they are elected, slavery overtakes it, and it is nothing. The use it makes of the short moments of liberty enjoys shows indeed that it deserves to lose them.

The idea of representation is modern; it comes to us from feudal government, from that iniquitous and absurd system which degrades humanity and dishonours the name of man. In ancient republics and even in monarchies, the people never had representatives; the word itself was unknown. It is very singular that in Rome, where the tribunes were so sacrosanct, it was never even imagined that they could usurp the functions of the people, and that in the midst of so great a multitude they never attempted to pass on their own authority a single plebiscitum. We can, however, form an idea of the difficulties caused sometimes by the people being so numerous, from what happened in the time of the Gracchi, when some of the citizens had to cast their votes from the roofs of buildings.

Where right and liberty are everything, disadvantages count for nothing. Among this wise people everything was given its just value, its lictors were allowed to do what its tribunes would never have dared to attempt; for it had no fear that its lictors would try to represent it.

To explain, however, in what way the tribunes did sometimes represent it, it is enough to conceive how the government represents the Sovereign. Law being purely the declaration of the general will, it is clear that, in the exercise of the legislative power, the people cannot be represented; but in that of the executive power, which is only the force that is applied to give the law effect, it both can and should be represented. We thus see that if we looked closely into the matter we should find that very few nations have any laws. However that may be, it is certain that the tribunes, possessing no executive power, could never represent the Roman people by right of the powers entrusted to them, but only by usurping those of the senate.

In Greece, all that the people had to do, it did for itself; it was constantly assembled in the public square. The Greeks lived in a mild climate; they had no natural greed; slaves did their work for them; their great concern was with liberty. Lacking the same advantages, how can you preserve the same rights? Your severer climates add to your needs;[1] for half the year your public squares are uninhabitable; the flatness of your languages unfits them for being heard in the open air; you sacrifice more for profit than for liberty, and fear slavery less than poverty.

What then? Is liberty maintained only by the help of slavery? It may be so. Extremes meet. Everything that is not in the course of nature has its disadvantages, civil society most of all. There are some unhappy circumstances in which we can only keep our liberty at others' expense, and where the citizen can be perfectly free only when the slave is most a slave. Such was the case with Sparta. As for you, modern peoples, you have no slaves, but you are slaves yourselves; you pay for their liberty with your own. It is in vain that you boast of this preference; I find in it more cowardice than humanity.

I do not mean by all this that it is necessary to have slaves, or that the right of slavery is legitimate: I am merely giving the reasons why modern peoples, believing themselves to be free, have representatives, while ancient peoples had none. In any case, the moment a people allows itself to be represented, it is no long free: it no longer exists.

All things considered, I do not see that it is possible henceforth for the Sovereign to preserve among us the exercise of its rights, unless the city is very small. But if it is very small,

---

[1] To adopt in cold countries the luxury and effeminacy of the East is to desire to submit to its chains; it is indeed to bow to them far more inevitably in our case than in theirs.

it will be conquered? No. I will show later on how the external strength of a great people[1] may be combined with the convenient polity and good order of a small State.

16. That the institution of government is not a contract

The legislative power once well established, the next thing is to establish similarly the executive power; for this latter, which operates only by particular acts, not being of the essence of the former, is naturally separate from it. Were it possible for the Sovereign, as such, to possess the executive power, right and fact would be so confounded that no one could tell what was law and what was not; and the body politic, thus disfigured, would soon fall a prey to the violence it was instituted to prevent.

As the citizens, by the social contract, are all equal, all can prescribe what all should do, but no one has a right to demand that another shall do what he does not do himself. It is strictly this right, which is indispensable for giving the body politic life and movement, that the Sovereign, in instituting the government, confers upon the prince.

It has been held that this act of establishment was a contract between the people and the rulers it sets over itself,—a contract in which conditions were laid down between the two parties binding the one to command and the other to obey. It will be admitted, I am sure, that this is an odd kind of contract to enter into. But let us see if this view can be upheld.

First, the supreme authority can no more be modified than it can be alienated; to limit it is to destroy it. It is absurd and contradictory for the Sovereign to set a superior over itself; to bind itself to obey a master would be to return to absolute liberty.

Moreover, it is clear that this contract between the people and such and such persons would be a particular act; and from this is follows that it can be neither a law nor an act of Sovereignty, and that consequently it would be illegitimate.

It is plain too that the contracting parties in relation to each other would be under the law of nature alone and wholly without guarantees of their mutual undertakings, a position

[1] I had intended to do this in the sequel to this work, when in dealing with external relations I came to the subject of confederations. The subject is quite new, and its principles have still to be laid down.

wholly at variance with the civil state. He who has force at his command being always in a position to control execution, it would come to the same thing if the name "contract" were given to the act of one man who said to another: "I give you all my goods, on condition that you give me back as much of them as you please."

There is only one contract in the State, and that is the act of association, which in itself excludes the existence of a second. It is impossible to conceive of any public contract that would not be a violation of the first.

17. The institution of government

Under what general idea then should the act by which government is instituted be conceived as falling? I will begin by stating that the act is complex, as being composed of two others—the establishment of the law and its execution.

By the former, the Sovereign decrees that there shall be a governing body established in this or that form; this act is clearly a law.

By the latter, the people nominates the rulers who are to be entrusted with the government that has been established. This nomination, being a particular act, is clearly not a second law, but merely a consequence of the first and a function of government.

The difficulty is to understand how there can be a governmental act before government exists, and how the people, which is only Sovereign or subject, can, under certain circumstances, become a prince or magistrate.

It is at this point that there is revealed one of the astonishing properties of the body politic, by means of which it reconciles apparently contradictory operations; for this is accomplished by a sudden conversion of Sovereignty into democracy, so that, without sensible change, and merely by virtue of a new relation of all to all, the citizens become magistrates and pass from general to particular acts, from legislation to the execution of the law.

This changed relation is no speculative subtlety without instances in practice: it happens every day in the English Parliament, where, on certain occasions, the Lower House resolves itself into Grand Committee, for the better discussion of affairs, and thus, from being at one moment a sovereign court, becomes at the next a mere commission; so that subsequently it reports to itself, as House of Commons, the result of its proceedings in Grand Committee, and debates over again under one name what it has already settled under another.

It is, indeed, the peculiar advantage of democratic government that it can be established in actuality by a simple act of the general will. Subsequently, this provisional government remains in power, if this form is adopted, or else establishes in the name of the Sovereign the government that is prescribed by law; and thus the whole proceeding is regular. It is impossible to set up government in any other manner legitimately and in accordance with the principles so far laid down.

18. How to check the usurpations of government

WHAT we have just said confirms Chapter 16, and makes it clear that the institution of government is not a contract, but a law; that the depositaries of the executive power are not the people's masters, but its officers; that it can set them up and pull them down when it likes; that for them there is no question of contract, but of obedience and that in taking charge of the functions the State imposes on them they are doing no more than fulfilling their duty as citizens, without having the remotest right to argue about the conditions.

When therefore the people sets up an hereditary government, whether it be monarchical and confined to one family, or aristocratic and confined to a class, what it enters into is not an undertaking; the administration is given a provisional form, until the people chooses to order it otherwise.

It is true that such changes are always dangerous, and that the established government should never be touched except when it comes to be incompatible with the public good; but the circumspection this involves is a maxim of policy and not a rule of right, and the State is no more bound to leave civil authority in the hands of its rulers than military authority in the hands of its generals.

It is also true that it is impossible to be too careful to observe, in such cases, all the formalities necessary to distinguish a regular and legitimate act from a seditious tumult, and the will of a whole people from the clamour of a faction. Here above all no further concession should be made to the untoward possibility than cannot, in the strictest logic, be refused it. From this obligation the prince derives a great advantage in preserving his power despite the people, without it being possible to say he has usurped it; for, seeming to avail himself only of his rights, he finds it very easy to extend them, and to prevent, under the pretext of keeping the peace, assemblies that are destined to the re-establishment of order; with the result that he takes advantage of a silence he does not allow to be broken, or of irregularities he causes to be committed, to assume that he has the support of those whom fear prevents from speaking, and to punish those who dare to speak. Thus it was that the decemvirs, first elected for one year and then kept on in office for a second, tried to perpetuate their power by forbidding the comitia to assemble; and by this easy method every government in the world, once clothed with the public power, sooner or later usurps the sovereign authority.

The periodical assemblies of which I have already spoken are designed to prevent or postpone this calamity, above all when they need no formal summoning; for in that case, the prince cannot stop them without openly declaring himself a law-breaker and an enemy of the State.

The opening of these assemblies, whose sole object is the maintenance of the social treaty, should always take the form of putting two propositions that may not be suppressed, which should be voted on separately.

The first is: "Does it please the Sovereign to preserve the present form of government?"

The second is: "Does it please the people to leave its administration in the hands of those who are actually in charge of it?"

I am here assuming what I think I have shown; that there is in the State no fundamental law that cannot be revoked, not excluding the social compact itself; for if all the citizens assembled of one accord to break the compact, it is impossible to doubt that it would be very legitimately broken. Grotius even thinks that each man can renounce his membership of his own State, and recover his natural liberty and his goods on leaving the country.[1] It would be indeed absurd if all the citizens in assembly could not do what each can do by himself.

[1] Provided, of course, he does not leave to escape his obligations and avoid having to serve his country in the hour of need. Flight in such a case would be criminal and punishable, and would be, not withdrawal, but desertion.

BOOK IV

1. THAT THE GENERAL WILL IS INDESTRUCTIBLE

As long as several men in assembly regard themselves as a single body, they have only a single will which is concerned with their common preservation and general well-being. In this case, all the springs of the State are vigorous and simple and its rules clear and luminous; there are no embroilments or conflicts of interests; the common good is everywhere clearly apparent, and only good sense is needed to perceive it. Peace, unity and equality are the enemies of political subtleties. Men who are upright and simple are difficult to deceive because of their simplicity; lures and ingenious pretexts fail to impose upon them, and they are not even subtle enough to be dupes. When, among the happiest people in the world, bands of peasants are seen regulating affairs of State under an oak, and always acting wisely, can we help scorning the ingenious methods of other nations, which make themselves illustrious and wretched with so much art and mystery?

A State so governed needs very few laws; and, as it becomes necessary to issue new ones, the necessity is universally seen. The first man to propose them merely says what all have already felt, and there is no question of factions or intrigues or eloquence in order to secure the passage into law of what every one has already decided to do, as soon as he is sure that the rest will act with him.

Theorists are led into error because, seeing only States that have been from the beginning wrongly constituted, they are struck by the impossibility of applying such a policy to them. They make great game of all the absurdities a clever rascal or an insinuating speaker might get the people of Paris or London to believe. They do not know that Cromwell would have been put to "the bells" by the people of Berne, and the Duc de Beaufort on the treadmill by the Genevese.

But when the social bond begins to be relaxed and the State to grow weak, when particular interests begin to make themselves felt and the smaller societies to exercise an influence over the larger, the common interest changes and finds opponents: opinion is no longer unanimous; the general will ceases to be the will of all; contradictory views and debates arise; and the best advice is not taken without question.

Finally, when the State, on the eve of ruin, maintains only a vain, illusory and formal existence, when in every heart the social bond is broken, and the meanest interest brazenly lays hold of the sacred name of "public good," the general will becomes mute: all men, guided by secret motives, no more give their views as citizens than if the State had never been; and iniquitous decrees directed solely to private interest get passed under the name of laws.

Does it follow from this that the general will is exterminated or corrupted? Not at all: it is always constant, unalterable and pure; but it is subordinated to other wills which encroach upon its sphere. Each man, in detaching his interest from the common interest, sees clearly that he cannot entirely separate them; but his share in the public mishaps seems to him negligible beside the exclusive good he aims at making his own. Apart from this particular good, he wills the general good in his own interest, as strongly as any one else. Even in selling his vote for money, he does not extinguish in himself the general will, but only eludes it. The fault he commits is that of changing the state of the question, and answering something different from what he is asked. Instead of saying, by his vote, "It is to the advantage of the State," he says, "It is of advantage to this or that man or party that this or that view should prevail." Thus the law of public order in assemblies is not so much to maintain in them the general will as to secure that the question be always put to it, and the answer always given by it.

I could here set down many reflections on the simple right of voting in every act of Sovereignty—a right which no one can take from the citizens—and also on the right of stating views, making proposals, dividing and discussing, which the government is always most careful to leave solely to its members, but this important subject would need a treatise to itself, and it is impossible to say everything in a single work.

2. VOTING

It may be seen, from the last chapter, that the way in which general business is managed may give a clear enough indication of the actual state of morals and the health of the body politic. The more concert reigns in the assemblies, that is, the nearer opinion approaches unanimity, the greater is the dominance of the general will. On the other hand, long debates, dissensions and tumult proclaim the ascendancy of particular interests and the decline of the State.

This seems less clear when two or more orders enter into the constitution, as patricians and plebeians did at Rome; for quarrels between these two orders often disturbed the comitia, even in the best days of the Republic. But the exception is rather apparent than real; for then, through the defect that is inherent in the body politic, there were, so to speak, two States in one, and what is not true of the two together is true of either separately. Indeed, even in the most stormy times, the plebiscita of the people, when the Senate did not interfere with them, always went through quietly and by large majorities. The citizens having but one interest, the people had but a single will.

At the other extremity of the circle, unanimity recurs; this is the case when the citizens, having fallen into servitude, have lost both liberty and will. Fear and flattery then change votes into acclamation; deliberation ceases, and only worship or malediction is left. Such was the vile manner in which the senate expressed its views under the Emperors. It did so sometimes with absurd precautions. Tacitus observes that, under Otho, the senators, while they heaped curses on Vitellius, contrived at the same time to make a deafening noise, in order that, should he ever become their master, he might not know what each of them had said.

On these various considerations depend the rules by which the methods of counting votes and comparing opinions should be regulated, according as the general will is more or less easy to discover, and the State more or less in its decline.

There is but one law which, from its nature, needs unanimous consent. This is the social compact; for civil association is the most voluntary of all acts. Every man being born free and his own master, no one, under any pretext whatsoever, can make any man subject without his consent. To decide that the son of a slave is born a slave is to decide that he is not born a man.

If then there are opponents when the social compact is made, their opposition does not invalidate the contract, but merely prevents them from being included in it. They are foreigners among citizens. When the State is instituted, residence constitutes consent; to dwell within its territory is to submit to the Sovereign.[1]

Apart from this primitive contract, the vote of the majority always binds all the rest. This follows from the contract itself. But it is asked how a man can be both free and forced to conform to wills that are not his own. How are the opponents at once free and subject to laws they have not agreed to?

I retort that the question is wrongly put. The citizen gives his consent to all the laws, including those which are passed in spite of his opposition, and even those which punish him when he dares to break any of them. The constant will of all the members of the State is the general will; by virtue of it they are citizens and free.[2] When in the popular assembly a law is proposed, what the people is asked is not exactly whether it approves or rejects the proposal, but whether it is in conformity with the general will, which is their will. Each man, in giving his vote, states his opinion on that point; and the general will is found by counting votes. When therefore the opinion that is contrary to my own prevails, this proves neither more nor less than that I was mistaken, and that what I thought to be the general will was not so. If my particular opinion had carried the day I should have achieved the opposite of what was my will; and it is in that case that I should not have been free.

This presupposes, indeed, that all the qualities of the general will still reside in the majority: when they cease to do so, whatever side a man may take, liberty is no longer possible.

In my earlier demonstration of how particular wills are substituted for the general will in public deliberation, I have adequately pointed out the practicable methods of avoiding this abuse; and I shall have more to say of them later on. I have also given the principles

---

[1] This should of course be understood as applying to a free State; for elsewhere family, goods, lack of a refuge, necessity, or violence may detain a man in a country against his will; and then his dwelling there no longer by itself implies his consent to the contract or to its violation.

[2] At Genoa, the word *Liberty* may be read over the front of the prisons and on the chains of the galley-slaves. This application of the device is good and just. It is indeed only malefactors of all estates who prevent the citizen from being free. In the country in which all such men were in the galleys, the most perfect liberty would be enjoyed.

for determining the proportional number of votes for declaring that will. A difference of one vote destroys equality; a single opponent destroys unanimity; but between equality and unanimity, there are several grades of unequal division, at each of which this proportion may be fixed in accordance with the condition and the needs of the body politic.

There are two general rules that may serve to regulate this relation. First, the more grave and important the questions discussed, the nearer should the opinion that is to prevail approach unanimity. Secondly, the more the matter in hand calls for speed, the smaller the prescribed difference in the numbers of votes may be allowed to become: where an instant decision has to be reached, a majority of one vote should be enough. The first of these two rules seems more in harmony with the laws, and the second with practical affairs. In any case, it is the combination of them that gives the best proportions for determining the majority necessary.

3. ELECTIONS

In the elections of the prince and the magistrates, which are, as I have said, complex acts, there are two possible methods of procedure, choice and lot. Both have been employed in various republics, and a highly complicated mixture of the two still survives in the election of the Doge at Venice.

"Election by lot," says Montesquieu, "is democratic in nature." I agree that it is so; but in what sense? "The lot," he goes on, "is a way of making choice that is unfair to nobody; it leaves each citizen a reasonable hope of serving his country." These are not reasons.

If we bear in mind that the election of rulers is a function of government, and not of Sovereignty, we shall see why the lot is the method more natural to democracy, in which the administration is better in proportion as the number of its acts is small.

In every real democracy, magistracy is not an advantage, but a burdensome charge which cannot justly be imposed on one individual rather than another. The law alone can lay the charge on him on whom the lot falls. For, the conditions being then the same for all, and the choice not depending on any human will, there is no particular application to alter the universality of the law.

In an aristocracy, the prince chooses the prince, the government is preserved by itself, and voting is rightly ordered.

The instance of the election of the Doge of Venice confirms, instead of destroying, this distinction; the mixed form suits a mixed government. For it is an error to take the government of Venice for a real aristocracy. If the people has no share in the government, the nobility is itself the people. A host of poor Barnabotes never gets near any magistracy, and its nobility consists merely in the empty title of Excellency, and in the right to sit in the Great Council. As this Great Council is as numerous as our General Council at Geneva, its illustrious members have no more privileges than our plain citizens. It is indisputable that, apart from the extreme disparity between the two republics, the *bourgeoisie* of Geneva is exactly equivalent to the *patriciate* of Venice; our *natives* and *inhabitants* correspond to the *townsmen* and the *people* of Venice; our *peasants* correspond to the *subjects* on the mainland; and, however that republic be regarded, if its size be left out of account, its government is no more aristocratic than our own. The whole difference is that, having no life-ruler, we do not, like Venice, need to use the lot.

Election by lot would have few disadvantages in a real democracy, in which, as equality would everywhere exist in morals and talents as well as in principles and fortunes, it would become almost a matter of indifference who was chosen. But I have already said that a real democracy is only an ideal.

When choice and lot are combined, positions that require special talents, such as military posts, should be filled by the former; the latter does for cases, such as judicial offices, in which good sense, justice, and integrity are enough, because in a State that is well constituted, these qualities are common to all the citizens.

Neither lot nor vote has any place in monarchical government. The monarch being by right sole prince and only magistrate, the choice of his lieutenants belongs to none but him. When the Abbé de Saint-Pierre proposed that the Councils of the King of France should be multiplied, and their members elected by ballot, he did not see that he was proposing to change the form of government.

I should now speak of the methods of giving and counting opinions in the assembly of the people; but perhaps an account of this aspect of the Roman constitution will more forcibly illustrate all the rules I could lay down. It is worth the while of a judicious reader to follow in some detail the working of public and private affairs in a Council consisting of two hundred thousand men.

4. THE ROMAN COMITIA

WE are without well-certified records of the first period of Rome's existence; it even appears very probable that most of the stories told about it are fables; indeed, generally speaking, the most instructive part of the history of peoples, that which deals with their foundation, is what we have least of. Experience teaches us every day what causes lead to the revolutions of empires; but, as no new peoples are now formed, we have almost nothing beyond conjecture to go upon in explaining how they were created.

The customs we find established show at least that these customs had an origin. The traditions that go back to those origins, that have the greatest authorities behind them, and that are confirmed by the strongest proofs, should pass for the most certain. These are the rules I have tried to follow in inquiring how the freest and most powerful people on earth exercised its supreme power.

After the foundation of Rome, the new-born republic, that is, the army of its founder, composed of Albans, Sabines and foreigners, was divided into three classes, which, from this division, took the name of *tribes*. Each of these tribes was subdivided into ten *curiæ*, and each *curia* into *decuriæ*, headed by leaders called *curiones* and *decuriones*.

Besides this, out of each tribe was taken a body of one hundred *Equites* or Knights, called a *century*, which shows that these divisions, being unnecessary in a town, were at first merely military. But an instinct for greatness seems to have led the little township of Rome to provide itself in advance with a political system suitable for the capital of the world.

Out of this original division an awkward situation soon arose. The tribes of the Albans (Ramnenses) and the Sabines (Tatienses) remained always in the same condition, while that of the foreigners (Luceres) continually grew as more and more foreigners came to live at Rome, so that it soon surpassed the others in strength. Servius remedied this dangerous fault by changing the principle of cleavage, and substituting for the racial division, which he abolished, a new one based on the quarter of the town inhabited by each tribe. Instead of three tribes he created four, each occupying and named after one of the hills of Rome. Thus, while redressing the inequality of the moment, he also provided for the future; and in order that the division might be one of persons as well as localities, he forbade the inhabitants of one quarter to migrate to another, and so prevented the mingling of the races.

He also doubled the three old centuries of Knights and added twelve more, still keeping the old names, and by this simple and prudent method, succeeded in making a distinction between the body of Knights, and the people, without a murmur from the latter.

To the four urban tribes Servius added fifteen others called rural tribes, because they consisted of those who lived in the country, divided into fifteen cantons. Subsequently, fifteen more were created, and the Roman people finally found itself divided into thirty-five tribes, as it remained down to the end of the Republic.

The distinction between urban and rural tribes had one effect which is worth mention, both because it is without parallel elsewhere, and because to it Rome owed the preservation of her morality and the enlargement of her empire. We should have expected that the urban tribes would soon monopolise power and honours, and lose no time in bringing the rural tribes into disrepute; but what happened was exactly the reverse. The taste of the early Romans for country life is well known. This taste they owed to their wise founder, who made rural and military labours go along with liberty, and, so to speak, relegated to the town arts, crafts, intrigue, fortune and slavery.

Since therefore all Rome's most illustrious citizens lived in the fields and tilled the earth, men grew used to seeking there alone the mainstays of the republic. This condition, being that of the best patricians, was honoured by all men; the simple and laborious life of the villager was preferred to the slothful and idle life of the *bourgeoisie* of Rome; and he who, in the town, would have been but a wretched proletarian, became, as a labourer in the fields, a respected citizen. Not without reason, says Varro, did our great-souled ancestors establish in the village the nursery of the sturdy and valiant men who defended them in time of war and provided for their sustenance in time of peace. Pliny states positively that the country tribes were honoured because of the men of whom they were composed; while cowards men wished to dishonour were transferred, as a public disgrace, to the town tribes. The Sabine Appius Claudius, when he had come to settle in Rome, was loaded with honours and enrolled in a rural tribe, which subsequently took his family name. Lastly, freedmen always entered the urban, and never the rural, tribes: nor is there a single example, throughout the Republic, of a freedman, though he had become a citizen, reaching any magistracy.

This was an excellent rule; but it was carried so far that in the end it led to a change and certainly to an abuse in the political system.

First the censors, after having for a long time claimed the right of transferring citizens arbitrarily from one tribe to another, allowed most persons to enrol themselves in whatever tribe they pleased. This permission certainly did no good, and further robbed the censorship of one of its greatest resources. Moreover, as the great and powerful all got themselves enrolled in the country tribes, while the freedmen who had become citizens remained with the populace in the town tribes, both soon ceased to have any local or territorial meaning, and all were so confused that the members of one could not be told from those of another except by the registers; so that the idea of the word *tribe* became personal instead of real, or rather came to be little more than a chimera.

It happened in addition that the town tribes, being more on the spot, were often the stronger in the comitia and sold the State to those who stooped to buy the votes of the rabble composing them.

As the founder had set up ten *curiæ* in each tribe, the whole Roman people, which was then contained within the walls, consisted of thirty *curiæ*, each with its temples, its gods, its officers, its priests and its festivals, which were called *compitalia* and corresponded to the *paganalia*, held in later times by the rural tribes.

When Servius made his new division, as the thirty *curiæ* could not be shared equally between his four tribes, and as he was unwilling to interfere with them, they became a further division of the inhabitants of Rome, quite independent of the tribes: but in the case of the rural tribes and their members there was no question of *curiæ*, as the tribes had then become a purely civil institution, and, a new system of levying troops having been introduced, the military divisions of Romulus were superfluous. Thus, although every citizen was enrolled in a tribe, there were very many who were not members of a *curia*.

Servius made yet a third division, quite distinct from the two we have mentioned, which became, in its effects, the most important of all. He distributed the whole Roman people into six classes, distinguished neither by place nor by person, but by wealth; the first classes included the rich, the last the poor, and those between persons of moderate means. These six classes were subdivided into one hundred and ninety-three other bodies, called centuries, which were so divided that the first class alone comprised more than half of them, while the last comprised only one. Thus the class that had the smallest number of members had the largest number of centuries, and the whole of the last class only counted as a single subdivision, although it alone included more than half the inhabitants of Rome.

In order that the people might have the less insight into the results of this arrangement, Servius tried to give it a military tone: in the second class he inserted two centuries of armourers, and in the fourth two of makers of instruments of war: in each class, except the last, he distinguished young and old, that is, those who were under an obligation to bear arms and those whose age gave them legal exemption. It was this distinction, rather than that of wealth, which required frequent repetition of the census or counting. Lastly, he ordered that the assembly should be held in the Campus Martius, and that all who were of age to serve should come there armed.

The reason for his not making in the last class also the division of young and old was that the populace, of whom it was composed, was not given the right to bear arms for its country: a man had to possess a hearth to acquire the right to defend it, and of all the troops of beggars who to-day lend lustre to the armies of kings, there is perhaps not one who would not have been driven with scorn out of a Roman cohort, at a time when soldiers were the defenders of liberty.

In this last class, however, *proletarians* were distinguished from *capite censi*. The former, not quite reduced to nothing, at least gave the State citizens, and sometimes, when the need was pressing, even soldiers. Those who had nothing at all, and could be numbered only by counting heads, were regarded as of absolutely no account, and Marius was the first who stooped to enrol them.

Without deciding now whether this third arrangement was good or bad in itself, I think

I may assert that it could have been made practicable only by the simple morals, the disinterestedness, the liking for agriculture and the scorn for commerce and for love of gain which characterised the early Romans. Where is the modern people among whom consuming greed, unrest, intrigue, continual removals, and perpetual changes of fortune, could let such a system last for twenty years without turning the State upside down? We must indeed observe that morality and the censorship, being stronger than this institution, corrected its defects at Rome, and that the rich man found himself degraded to the class of the poor for making too much display of his riches.

From all this it is easy to understand why only five classes are almost always mentioned, though there were really six. The sixth, as it furnished neither soldiers to the army nor votes in the Campus Martius,[1] and was almost without function in the State, was seldom regarded as of any account.

These were the various ways in which the Roman people was divided. Let us now see the effect on the assemblies. When lawfully summoned, these were called *comitia:* they were usually held in the public square at Rome or in the Campus Martius, and were distinguished as *comitia curiata, comitia centuriata,* and *comitia tributa,* according to the form under which they were convoked. The *comitia curiata* were founded by Romulus; the *centuriata* by Servius; and the *tributa* by the tribunes of the people. No law received its sanction and no magistrate was elected, save in the comitia; and as every citizen was enrolled in a *curia,* a century, or a tribe, it follows that no citizen was excluded from the right of voting, and that the Roman people was truly sovereign both *de jure* and *de facto.*

For the comitia to be lawfully assembled, and for their acts to have the force of law, three conditions were necessary. First, the body or magistrate convoking them had to possess the necessary authority; secondly, the assembly had to be held on a day allowed by law; and thirdly, the auguries had to be favourable.

The reason for the first regulation needs no explanation; the second is a matter of policy.

[1] I say "in the Campus Martius" because it was there that the *comitia* assembled by centuries; in its two other forms the people assembled in the *forum* or elsewhere; and then the *capite censi* had as much influence and authority as the foremost citizens.

Thus, the comitia might not be held on festivals or market-days, when the country-folk, coming to Rome on business, had not time to spend the day in the public square. By means of the third, the senate held in check the proud and restive people, and meetly restrained the ardour of seditious tribunes, who, however, found more than one way of escaping this hindrance.

Laws and the election of rulers were not the only questions submitted to the judgment of the comitia: as the Roman people had taken on itself the most important functions of government, it may be said that the lot of Europe was regulated in its assemblies. The variety of their objects gave rise to the various forms these took, according to the matters on which they had to pronounce.

In order to judge of these various forms, it is enough to compare them. Romulus, when he set up *curiæ,* had in view the checking of the senate by the people, and of the people by the senate, while maintaining his ascendancy over both alike. He therefore gave the people, by means of this assembly, all the authority of numbers to balance that of power and riches, which he left to the patricians. But, after the spirit of monarchy, he left all the same a greater advantage to the patricians in the influence of their clients on the majority of votes. This excellent institution of patron and client was a masterpiece of statesmanship and humanity without which the patriciate, being flagrantly in contradiction to the republican spirit, could not have survived. Rome alone has the honour of having given to the world this great example, which never led to any abuse, and yet has never been followed.

As the assemblies by *curiæ* persisted under the kings till the time of Servius, and the reign of the later Tarquin was not regarded as legitimate, royal laws were called generally *leges curiatæ.*

Under the Republic, the *curiæ,* still confined to the four urban tribes, and including only the populace of Rome, suited neither the senate, which led the patricians, nor the tribunes, who, though plebeians, were at the head of the well-to-do citizens. They therefore fell into disrepute, and their degradation was such, that thirty lictors used to assemble and do what the *comitia curiata* should have done.

The division by centuries was so favourable to the aristocracy that it is hard to see at first how the senate ever failed to carry the day in the comitia bearing their name, by which the consuls, the censors and the other curule magistrates were elected. Indeed, of the hundred and ninety-three centuries into which the six classes of the whole Roman people were divided, the first class contained ninety-eight; and, as voting went solely by centuries, this class alone had a majority over all the rest. When all these centuries were in agreement, the rest of the votes were not even taken; the decision of the smallest number passed for that of the multitude, and it may be said that, in the *comitia centuriata*, decisions were regulated far more by depth of purses than by the number of votes.

But this extreme authority was modified in two ways. First, the tribunes as a rule, and always a great number of plebeians, belonged to the class of the rich, and so counterbalanced the influence of the patricians in the first class.

The second way was this. Instead of causing the centuries to vote throughout in order, which would have meant beginning always with the first, the Romans always chose one by lot which proceeded alone to the election; after this all the centuries were summoned another day according to their rank, and the same election was repeated, and as a rule confirmed. Thus the authority of example was taken away from rank, and given to the lot on a democratic principle.

From this custom resulted a further advantage. The citizens from the country had time, between the two elections, to inform themselves of the merits of the candidate who had been provisionally nominated, and did not have to vote without knowledge of the case. But, under the pretext of hastening matters, the abolition of this custom was achieved, and both elections were held on the same day.

The *comitia tributa* were properly the council of the Roman people. They were convoked by the tribunes alone; at them the tribunes were elected and passed their plebiscita. The senate not only had no standing in them, but even no right to be present; and the senators, being forced to obey laws on which they could not vote, were in this respect less free than the meanest citizens. This injustice was altogether ill-conceived, and was alone enough to invalidate the decrees of a body to which all its members were not admitted. Had all the patricians attended the comitia by virtue of the right they had as citizens, they would not, as mere private individuals, have had any considerable influence on a vote reckoned by counting heads, where the meanest proletarian was as good as the *princeps senatus*.

It may be seen, therefore, that besides the order which was achieved by these various ways of distributing so great a people and taking its votes, the various methods were not reducible to forms indifferent in themselves, but the results of each were relative to the objects which caused it to be preferred.

Without going here into further details, we may gather from what has been said above that the *comitia tributa* were the most favourable to popular government, and the *comitia centuriata* to aristocracy. The *comitia curiata,* in which the populace of Rome formed the majority, being fitted only to further tyranny and evil designs, naturally fell into disrepute, and even seditious persons abstained from using a method which too clearly revealed their projects. It is indisputable that the whole majesty of the Roman people lay solely in the *comitia centuriata*, which alone included all; for the *comitia curiata* excluded the rural tribes, and the *comitia tributa* the senate and the patricians.

As for the method of taking the vote, it was among the ancient Romans as simple as their morals, although not so simple as at Sparta. Each man declared his vote aloud, and a clerk duly wrote it down; the majority in each tribe determined the vote of the tribe, the majority of the tribes that of the people, and so with *curiæ* and centuries. This custom was good as long as honesty was triumphant among the citizens, and each man was ashamed to vote publicly in favour of an unjust proposal or an unworthy subject; but, when the people grew corrupt and votes were bought, it was fitting that voting should be secret in order that purchasers might be restrained by mistrust, and rogues be given the means of not being traitors.

I know that Cicero attacks this change, and attributes partly to it the ruin of the Republic. But though I feel the weight Cicero's authority must carry on such a point, I cannot agree with him; I hold, on the contrary, that, for want of enough such changes, the destruction of the State must be hastened. Just as the regimen of health does not suit the sick, we should not wish to govern a people that has been corrupted by the laws that a good people requires. There is no better proof of this rule than the long life of the Republic of Venice, of which the shadow still exists, solely because its laws are suitable only for men who are wicked.

The citizens were provided, therefore, with tablets by means of which each man could vote without any one knowing how he voted: new methods were also introduced for collecting the tablets, for counting voices, for comparing numbers, etc.; but all these precautions did not prevent the good faith of the officers charged with these functions[1] from being often suspect. Finally, to prevent intrigues and trafficking in votes, edicts were issued; but their very number proves how useless they were.

Towards the close of the Republic, it was often necessary to have recourse to extraordinary expedients in order to supplement the inadequacy of the laws. Sometimes miracles were supposed; but this method, while it might impose on the people, could not impose on those who governed. Sometimes an assembly was hastily called together, before the candidates had time to form their factions: sometimes a whole sitting was occupied with talk, when it was seen that the people had been won over and was on the point of taking up a wrong position. But in the end ambition eluded all attempts to check it; and the most incredible fact of all is that, in the midst of all these abuses, the vast people, thanks to its ancient regulations, never ceased to elect magistrates, to pass laws, to judge cases, and to carry through business both public and private, almost as easily as the senate itself could have done.

5. THE TRIBUNATE

WHEN an exact proportion cannot be established between the constituent parts of the State, or when causes that cannot be removed continually alter the relation of one part to another, recourse is had to the institution of a peculiar magistracy that enters into no corporate unity with the rest. This restores to each term its right relation to the others, and provides a link or middle term between either prince and people, or prince and Sovereign, or, if necessary, both at once.

This body, which I shall call the *tribunate,* is the preserver of the laws and of the legislative power. It serves sometimes to protect the Sovereign against the government, as the tribunes of the people did at Rome; sometimes to uphold the government against the people, as the Council of Ten now does at Venice; and sometimes to maintain the balance between the two, as the Ephors did at Sparta.

[1] *Custodes, diribitores, rogatores suffragiorum.*

The tribunate is not a constituent part of the city, and should have no share in either legislative or executive power; but this very fact makes its own power the greater: for, while it can do nothing, it can prevent anything from being done. It is more sacred and more revered, as the defender of the laws, than the prince who executes them, or than the Sovereign which ordains them. This was seen very clearly at Rome, when the proud patricians, for all their scorn of the people, were forced to bow before one of its officers, who had neither auspices nor jurisdiction.

The tribunate, wisely tempered, is the strongest support a good constitution can have; but if its strength is ever so little excessive, it upsets the whole State. Weakness, on the other hand, is not natural to it: provided it is something, it is never less than it should be.

It degenerates into tyranny when it usurps the executive power, which it should confine itself to restraining, and when it tries to dispense with the laws, which it should confine itself to protecting. The immense power of the Ephors, harmless as long as Sparta preserved its morality, hastened corruption when once it had begun. The blood of Agis, slaughtered by these tyrants, was avenged by his successor; the crime and the punishment of the Ephors alike hastened the destruction of the republic, and after Cleomenes Sparta ceased to be of any account. Rome perished in the same way: the excessive power of the tribunes, which they had usurped by degrees, finally served, with the help of laws made to secure liberty, as a safeguard for the emperors who destroyed it. As for the Venetian Council of Ten, it is a tribunal of blood, an object of horror to patricians and people alike; and, so far from giving a lofty protection to the laws, it does nothing, now they have become degraded, but strike in the darkness blows of which no one dare take note.

The tribunate, like the government, grows weak as the number of its members increases. When the tribunes of the Roman people, who first numbered only two, and then five, wished to double that number, the senate let them do so, in the confidence that it could use one to check another, as indeed it afterwards freely did.

The best method of preventing usurpations by so formidable a body, though no government has yet made use of it, would be not to make it permanent, but to regulate the periods during which it should remain in abeyance. These intervals, which should not be long enough to give abuses time to grow strong, may be so fixed by law that they can easily be shortened at need by extraordinary commissions.

This method seems to me to have no disadvantages, because, as I have said, the tribunate, which forms no part of the constitution, can be removed without the constitution being affected. It seems to be also efficacious, because a newly restored magistrate starts not with the power his predecessor exercised, but with that which the law allows him.

6. THE DICTATORSHIP

THE inflexibility of the laws, which prevents them from adapting themselves to circumstances, may, in certain cases, render them disastrous, and make them bring about, at a time of crisis, the ruin of the State. The order and slowness of the forms they enjoin require a space of time which circumstances sometimes withhold. A thousand cases against which the legislator has made no provision may present themselves, and it is a highly necessary part of foresight to be conscious that everything cannot be foreseen.

It is wrong therefore to wish to make political institutions so strong as to render it impossible to suspend their operation. Even Sparta allowed its laws to lapse.

However, none but the greatest dangers can counterbalance that of changing the public order, and the sacred power of the laws should never be arrested save when the existence of the country is at stake. In these rare and obvious cases, provision is made for the public security by a particular act entrusting it to him who is most worthy. This commitment may be carried out in either of two ways, according to the nature of the danger.

If increasing the activity of the government is a sufficient remedy, power is concentrated in the hands of one or two of its members: in this case the change is not in the authority of the laws, but only in the form of administering them. If, on the other hand, the peril is of such a kind that the paraphernalia of the laws are an obstacle to their preservation, the method is to nominate a supreme ruler, who shall silence all the laws and suspend for a moment the sovereign authority. In such a case, there is no doubt about the general will, and it is clear that the people's first intention is that the State shall not perish. Thus the suspension of the legislative authority is in no sense its abolition; the magistrate who silences it cannot make it speak; he dominates it, but cannot represent it. He can do anything, except make laws.

The first method was used by the Roman senate when, in a consecrated formula, it charged the consuls to provide for the safety of the Republic. The second was employed when one of the two consuls nominated a dictator:[1] a custom Rome borrowed from Alba.

During the first period of the Republic, recourse was very often had to the dictatorship, because the State had not yet a firm enough basis to be able to maintain itself by the strength of its constitution alone. As the state of morality then made superfluous many of the precautions which would have been necessary at other times, there was no fear that a dictator would abuse his authority, or try to keep it beyond his term of office. On the contrary, so much power appeared to be burdensome to him who was clothed with it, and he made all speed to lay it down, as if taking the place of the laws had been too troublesome and too perilous a position to retain.

It is therefore the danger not of its abuse, but of its cheapening, that makes me attack the indiscreet use of this supreme magistracy in the earliest times. For as long as it was freely employed at elections, dedications and purely formal functions, there was danger of its becoming less formidable in time of need, and of men growing accustomed to regarding as empty a title that was used only on occasions of empty ceremonial.

Towards the end of the Republic, the Romans, having grown more circumspect, were as unreasonably sparing in the use of the dictatorship as they had formerly been lavish. It is easy to see that their fears were without foundation, that the weakness of the capital secured it against the magistrates who were in its midst; that a dictator might, in certain cases, defend the public liberty, but could never endanger it; and that the chains of Rome would be forged, not in Rome itself, but in her armies. The weak resistance offered by Marius to Sulla, and by Pompey to Cæsar, clearly showed what was to be expected from authority at home against force from abroad.

This misconception led the Romans to make great mistakes; such, for example, as the

---

[1] The nomination was made secretly by night, as if there were something shameful in setting a man above the laws.

failure to nominate a dictator in the Catilinarian conspiracy. For, as only the city itself, with at most some province in Italy, was concerned, the unlimited authority the laws gave to the dictator would have enabled him to make short work of the conspiracy, which was, in fact, stifled only by a combination of lucky chances human prudence had no right to expect.

Instead, the senate contented itself with entrusting its whole power to the consuls, so that Cicero, in order to take effective action, was compelled on a capital point to exceed his powers; and if, in the first transports of joy, his conduct was approved, he was justly called, later on, to account for the blood of citizens spilt in violation of the laws. Such a reproach could never have been levelled at a dictator. But the consul's eloquence carried the day; and he himself, Roman though he was, loved his own glory better than his country, and sought, not so much the most lawful and secure means of saving the State, as to get for himself the whole honour of having done so.[1] He was therefore justly honoured as the liberator of Rome, and also justly punished as a law-breaker. However brilliant his recall may have been, it was undoubtedly an act of pardon.

However this important trust be conferred, it is important that its duration should be fixed at a very brief period, incapable of being ever prolonged. In the crises which lead to its adoption, the State is either soon lost, or soon saved; and, the present need passed, the dictatorship becomes either tyrannical or idle. At Rome, where dictators held office for six months only, most of them abdicated before their time was up. If their term had been longer, they might well have tried to prolong it still further, as the decemvirs did when chosen for a year. The dictator had only time to provide against the need that had caused him to be chosen; he had none to think of further projects.

7. The censorship

As the law is the declaration of the general will, the censorship is the declaration of the public judgment: public opinion is the form of law which the censor administers, and, like the prince, only applies to particular cases.

The censorial tribunal, so far from being the arbiter of the people's opinion, only declares it, and, as soon as the two part company, its decisions are null and void.

It is useless to distinguish the morality of a nation from the objects of its esteem; both depend on the same principle and are necessarily indistinguishable. There is no people on earth the choice of whose pleasures is not decided by opinion rather than nature. Right men's opinions, and their morality will purge itself. Men always love what is good or what they find good; it is in judging what is good that they go wrong. This judgment, therefore, is what must be regulated. He who judges of morality judges of honour; and he who judges of honour finds his law in opinion.

The opinions of a people are derived from its constitution; although the law does not regulate morality, it is legislation that gives it birth. When legislation grows weak, morality degenerates; but in such cases the judgment of the censors will not do what the force of the laws has failed to effect.

From this it follows that the censorship may be useful for the preservation of morality, but can never be so for its restoration. Set up censors while the laws are vigorous; as soon as they have lost their vigour, all hope is gone; no legitimate power can retain force when the laws have lost it.

The censorship upholds morality by preventing opinion from growing corrupt, by preserving its rectitude by means of wise applications, and sometimes even by fixing it when it is still uncertain. The employment of seconds in duels, which had been carried to wild extremes in the kingdom of France, was done away with merely by these words in a royal edict: "As for those who are cowards enough to call upon seconds." This judgment, in anticipating that of the public, suddenly decided it. But when edicts from the same source tried to pronounce duelling itself an act of cowardice, as indeed it is, then, since common opinion does not regard it as such, the public took no notice of a decision on a point on which its mind was already made up.

I have stated elsewhere[2] that as public opinion is not subject to any constraint, there need be no trace of it in the tribunal set up to represent it. It is impossible to admire too much the art with which this resource, which we

---

[1] That is what he could not be sure of, if he proposed a dictator; for he dared not nominate himself, and could not be certain that his colleague would nominate him.

[2] I merely call attention in this chapter to a subject with which I have dealt at greater length in my *Letter to M. d'Alembert*.

moderns have wholly lost, was employed by the Romans, and still more by the Lacedæmonians.

A man of bad morals having made a good proposal in the Spartan Council, the Ephors neglected it, and caused the same proposal to be made by a virtuous citizen. What an honour for the one, and what a disgrace for the other, without praise or blame of either! Certain drunkards from Samos[1] polluted the tribunal of the Ephors: the next day, a public edict gave Samians permission to be filthy. An actual punishment would not have been so severe as such an impunity. When Sparta has pronounced on what is or is not right, Greece makes no appeal from her judgments.

8. CIVIL RELIGION

AT first men had no kings save the gods, and no government save theocracy. They reasoned like Caligula, and, at that period, reasoned aright. It takes a long time for feeling so to change that men can make up their minds to take their equals as masters, in the hope that they will profit by doing so.

From the mere fact that God was set over every political society, it followed that there were as many gods as peoples. Two peoples that were strangers the one to the other, and almost always enemies, could not long recognise the same master: two armies giving battle could not obey the same leader. National divisions thus led to polytheism, and this in turn gave rise to theological and civil intolerance, which, as we shall see hereafter, are by nature the same.

The fancy the Greeks had for rediscovering their gods among the barbarians arose from the way they had of regarding themselves as the natural Sovereigns of such peoples. But there is nothing so absurd as the erudition which in our days identifies and confuses gods of different nations. As if Moloch, Saturn, and Chronos could be the same god! As if the Phœnician Baal, the Greek Zeus, and the Latin Jupiter could be the same! As if there could still be anything common to imaginary beings with different names!

If it is asked how in pagan times, where each State had its cult and its gods, there were no wars of religion, I answer that it was precisely because each State, having its own cult as well as its own government, made no distinction

between its gods and its laws. Political war was also theological; the provinces of the gods were, so to speak, fixed by the boundaries of nations. The god of one people had no right over another. The gods of the pagans were not jealous gods; they shared among themselves the empire of the world: even Moses and the Hebrews sometimes lent themselves to this view by speaking of the God of Israel. It is true, they regarded as powerless the gods of the Canaanites, a proscribed people condemned to destruction, whose place they were to take; but remember how they spoke of the divisions of the neighbouring peoples they were forbidden to attack! "Is not the possession of what belongs to your god Chamos lawfully your due?" said Jephthah to the Ammonites. "We have the same title to the lands our conquering God has made his own."[2] Here, I think, there is a recognition that the rights of Chamos and those of the God of Israel are of the same nature.

But when the Jews, being subject to the Kings of Babylon, and, subsequently, to those of Syria, still obstinately refused to recognise any god save their own, their refusal was regarded as rebellion against their conqueror, and drew down on them the persecutions we read of in their history, which are without parallel till the coming of Christianity.[3]

Every religion, therefore, being attached solely to the laws of the State which prescribed it, there was no way of converting a people except by enslaving it, and there could be no missionaries save conquerors. The obligation to change cults being the law to which the vanquished yielded, it was necessary to be victorious before suggesting such a change. So far from men fighting for the gods, the gods, as in Homer, fought for men; each asked his god for victory, and repaid him with new altars. The Romans, before taking a city, summoned its gods to quit it; and, in leaving the Tarentines their outraged gods, they regarded

[1] They were from another island, which the delicacy of our language forbids me to name on this occasion.

[2] *Nonne ea quæ possidet Chamos deus tuus, tibi jure debentur?* (Judges, 11. 24.) Such is the text in the Vulgate. Father de Carrières translates: "Do you not regard yourselves as having a right to what your god possesses?" I do not know the force of the Hebrew text: but I perceive that, in the Vulgate, Jephthah positively recognises the right of the god Chamos, and that the French translator weakened this admission by inserting an "according to you," which is not in the Latin.

[3] It is quite clear that the Phocian War, which was called "the Sacred War," was not a war of religion. Its object was the punishment of acts of sacrilege, and not the conquest of unbelievers.

them as subject to their own and compelled to do them homage. They left the vanquished their gods as they left them their laws. A wreath to the Jupiter of the Capitol was often the only tribute they imposed.

Finally, when, along with their empire, the Romans had spread their cult and their gods, and had themselves often adopted those of the vanquished, by granting to both alike the rights of the city, the peoples of that vast empire insensibly found themselves with multitudes of gods and cults, everywhere almost the same; and thus paganism throughout the known world finally came to be one and the same religion.

It was in these circumstances that Jesus came to set up on earth a spiritual kingdom, which, by separating the theological from the political system, made the State no longer one, and brought about the internal divisions which have never ceased to trouble Christian peoples. As the new idea of a kingdom of the other world could never have occurred to pagans, they always looked on the Christians as really rebels, who, while feigning to submit, were only waiting for the chance to make themselves independent and their masters, and to usurp by guile the authority they pretended in their weakness to respect. This was the cause of the persecutions.

What the pagans had feared took place. Then everything changed its aspect: the humble Christians changed their language, and soon this so-called kingdom of the other world turned, under a visible leader, into the most violent of earthly despotisms.

However, as there have always been a prince and civil laws, this double power and conflict of jurisdiction have made all good polity impossible in Christian States; and men have never succeeded in finding out whether they were bound to obey the master or the priest.

Several peoples, however, even in Europe and its neighbourhood, have desired without success to preserve or restore the old system: but the spirit of Christianity has everywhere prevailed. The sacred cult has always remained or again become independent of the Sovereign, and there has been no necessary link between it and the body of the State. Mahomet held very sane views, and linked his political system well together; and, as long as the form of his government continued under the caliphs who succeeded him, that government was indeed one, and so far good. But the Arabs, having grown prosperous, lettered, civ-

ilised, slack and cowardly, were conquered by barbarians: the division between the two powers began again; and, although it is less apparent among the Mahometans than among the Christians, it none the less exists, especially in the sect of Ali, and there are States, such as Persia, where it is continually making itself felt.

Among us, the Kings of England have made themselves heads of the Church, and the Czars have done the same: but this title has made them less its masters than its ministers; they have gained not so much the right to change it, as the power to maintain it: they are not its legislators, but only its princes. Wherever the clergy is a corporate body,[1] it is master and legislator in its own country. There are thus two powers, two Sovereigns, in England and in Russia, as well as elsewhere.

Of all Christian writers, the philosopher Hobbes alone has seen the evil and how to remedy it, and has dared to propose the reunion of the two heads of the eagle, and the restoration throughout of political unity, without which no State or government will ever be rightly constituted. But he should have seen that the masterful spirit of Christianity is incompatible with his system, and that the priestly interest would always be stronger than that of the State. It is not so much what is false and terrible in his political theory, as what is just and true, that has drawn down hatred on it.[2]

I believe that if the study of history were developed from this point of view, it would be easy to refute the contrary opinions of Bayle and Warburton, one of whom holds that religion can be of no use to the body politic, while the other, on the contrary, maintains that Christianity is its strongest support. We should demonstrate to the former that no

[1] It should be noted that the clergy find their bond of union not so much in formal assemblies, as in the communion of Churches. Communion and excommunication are the social compact of the clergy, a compact which will always make them masters of peoples and kings. All priests who communicate together are fellow-citizens, even if they come from opposite ends of the earth. This invention is a masterpiece of statesmanship: there is nothing like it among pagan priests; who have therefore never formed a clerical corporate body.

[2] See, for instance, in a letter from Grotius to his brother (April 11, 1643), what that learned man found to praise and to blame in the *De Cive*. It is true that, with a bent for indulgence, he seems to pardon the writer the good for the sake of the bad; but all men are not so forgiving.

State has ever been founded without a religious basis, and to the latter, that the law of Christianity at bottom does more harm by weakening than good by strengthening the constitution of the State. To make myself understood, I have only to make a little more exact the too vague ideas of religion as relating to this subject.

Religion, considered in relation to society, which is either general or particular, may also be divided into two kinds: the religion of man, and that of the citizen. The first, which has neither temples, nor altars, nor rites, and is confined to the purely internal cult of the supreme God and the eternal obligations of morality, is the religion of the Gospel pure and simple, the true theism, what may be called natural divine right or law. The other, which is codified in a single country, gives it its gods, its own tutelary patrons; it has its dogmas, its rites, and its external cult prescribed by law; outside the single nation that follows it, all the world is in its sight infidel, foreign and barbarous; the duties and rights of man extend for it only as far as its own altars. Of this kind were all the religions of early peoples, which we may define as civil or positive divine right or law.

There is a third sort of religion of a more singular kind, which gives men two codes of legislation, two rulers, and two countries, renders them subject to contradictory duties, and makes it impossible for them to be faithful both to religion and to citizenship. Such are the religions of the Lamas and of the Japanese, and such is Roman Christianity, which may be called the religion of the priest. It leads to a sort of mixed and anti-social code which has no name.

In their political aspect, all these three kinds of religion have their defects. The third is so clearly bad, that it is waste of time to stop to prove it such. All that destroys social unity is worthless; all institutions that set man in contradiction to himself are worthless.

The second is good in that it unites the divine cult with love of the laws, and, making country the object of the citizens' adoration, teaches them that service done to the State is service done to its tutelary god. It is a form of theocracy, in which there can be no pontiff save the prince, and no priests save the magistrates. To die for one's country then becomes martyrdom; violation of its laws, impiety; and to subject one who is guilty to public execra-

tion is to condemn him to the anger of the gods: *Sacer estod.*

On the other hand, it is bad in that, being founded on lies and error, it deceives men, makes them credulous and superstitious, and drowns the true cult of the Divinity in empty ceremonial. It is bad, again, when it becomes tyrannous and exclusive, and makes a people bloodthirsty and intolerant, so that it breathes fire and slaughter, and regards as a sacred act the killing of every one who does not believe in its gods. The result is to place such a people in a natural state of war with all others, so that its security is deeply endangered.

There remains therefore the religion of man or Christianity—not the Christianity of to-day, but that of the Gospel, which is entirely different. By means of this holy, sublime, and real religion all men, being children of one God, recognise one another as brothers, and the society that unites them is not dissolved even at death.

But this religion, having no particular relation to the body politic, leaves the laws in possession of the force they have in themselves without making any addition to it; and thus one of the great bonds that unite society considered in severalty fails to operate. Nay, more, so far from binding the hearts of the citizens to the State, it has the effect of taking them away from all earthly things. I know of nothing more contrary to the social spirit.

We are told that a people of true Christians would form the most perfect society imaginable. I see in this supposition only one great difficulty: that a society of true Christians would not be a society of men.

I say further that such a society, with all its perfection, would be neither the strongest nor the most lasting: the very fact that it was perfect would rob it of its bond of union; the flaw that would destroy it would lie in its very perfection.

Every one would do his duty; the people would be law-abiding, the rulers just and temperate; the magistrates upright and incorruptible; the soldiers would scorn death; there would be neither vanity nor luxury. So far, so good; but let us hear more.

Christianity as a religion is entirely spiritual, occupied solely with heavenly things; the country of the Christian is not of this world. He does his duty, indeed, but does it with profound indifference to the good or ill success of his cares. Provided he has nothing to reproach himself with, it matters little to him whether things go well or ill here on earth. If the State is prosperous, he hardly dares to share in the public happiness, for fear he may grow proud of his country's glory; if the State is languishing, he blesses the hand of God that is hard upon His people.

For the State to be peaceable and for harmony to be maintained, all the citizens without exception would have to be good Christians; if by ill hap there should be a single self-seeker or hypocrite, a Catiline or a Cromwell, for instance, he would certainly get the better of his pious compatriots. Christian charity does not readily allow a man to think hardly of his neighbours. As soon as, by some trick, he has discovered the art of imposing on them and getting hold of a share in the public authority, you have a man established in dignity; it is the will of God that he be respected: very soon you have a power; it is God's will that it be obeyed: and if the power is abused by him who wields it, it is the scourge wherewith God punishes His children. There would be scruples about driving out the usurper: public tranquillity would have to be disturbed, violence would have to be employed, and blood spilt; all this accords ill with Christian meekness; and after all, in this vale of sorrows, what does it matter whether we are free men or serfs? The essential thing is to get to heaven, and resignation is only an additional means of doing so.

If war breaks out with another State, the citizens march readily out to battle; not one of them thinks of flight; they do their duty, but they have no passion for victory; they know better how to die than how to conquer. What does it matter whether they win or lose? Does not Providence know better than they what is meet for them? Only think to what account a proud, impetuous and passionate enemy could turn their stoicism! Set over against them those generous peoples who were devoured by ardent love of glory and of their country, imagine your Christian republic face to face with Sparta or Rome: the pious Christians will be beaten, crushed and destroyed, before they know where they are, or will owe their safety only to the contempt their enemy will conceive for them. It was to my mind a fine oath that was taken by the soldiers of Fabius, who swore, not to conquer or die, but to come back victorious—and kept their oath. Christians would never have taken such an oath; they would have looked on it as tempting God.

But I am mistaken in speaking of a Chris-

tian republic; the terms are mutually exclusive. Christianity preaches only servitude and dependence. Its spirit is so favourable to tyranny that it always profits by such a *régime*. True Christians are made to be slaves, and they know it and do not much mind: this short life counts for too little in their eyes.

I shall be told that Christian troops are excellent. I deny it. Show me an instance. For my part, I know of no Christian troops. I shall be told of the Crusades. Without disputing the valour of the Crusaders, I answer that, so far from being Christians, they were the priests' soldiery, citizens of the Church. They fought for their spiritual country, which the Church had, somehow or other, made temporal. Well understood, this goes back to paganism: as the Gospel sets up no national religion, a holy war is impossible among Christians.

Under the pagan emperors, the Christian soldiers were brave; every Christian writer affirms it, and I believe it: it was a case of honourable emulation of the pagan troops. As soon as the emperors were Christian, this emulation no longer existed, and, when the Cross had driven out the eagle, Roman valour wholly disappeared.

But, setting aside political considerations, let us come back to what is right, and settle our principles on this important point. The right which the social compact gives the Sovereign over the subjects does not, we have seen, exceed the limits of public expediency.[1] The subjects then owe the Sovereign an account of their opinions only to such an extent as they matter to the community. Now, it matters very much to the community that each citizen should have a religion. That will make him love his duty; but the dogmas of that religion concern the State and its members only so far as they have reference to morality and to the duties which he who professes them is bound to do to others. Each man may have, over and above, what opinions he pleases, without it being the Sovereign's business to take cognisance of them; for, as the Sovereign has no authority in the other world, whatever the lot of its sub-

[1] "In the republic," says the Marquis d'Argenson, "each man is perfectly free in what does not harm others." This is the invariable limitation, which it is impossible to define more exactly. I have not been able to deny myself the pleasure of occasionally quoting from this manuscript, though it is unknown to the public, in order to do honour to the memory of a good and illustrious man, who had kept even in the Ministry the heart of a good citizen, and views on the government of his country that were sane and right.

jects may be in the life to come, that is not its business, provided they are good citizens in this life.

There is therefore a purely civil profession of faith of which the Sovereign should fix the articles, not exactly as religious dogmas, but as social sentiments without which a man cannot be a good citizen or a faithful subject.[1] While it can compel no one to believe them, it can banish from the State whoever does not believe them—it can banish him, not for impiety, but as an anti-social being, incapable of truly loving the laws and justice, and of sacrificing, at need, his life to his duty. If any one, after publicly recognising these dogmas, behaves as if he does not believe them, let him be punished by death: he has committed the worst of all crimes, that of lying before the law.

The dogmas of civil religion ought to be few, simple, and exactly worded, without explanation or commentary. The existence of a mighty, intelligent and beneficent Divinity, possessed of foresight and providence, the life to come, the happiness of the just, the punishment of the wicked, the sanctity of the social contract and the laws: these are its positive dogmas. Its negative dogmas I confine to one, intolerance, which is a part of the cults we have rejected.

Those who distinguish civil from theological intolerance are, to my mind, mistaken. The two forms are inseparable. It is impossible to live at peace with those we regard as damned; to love them would be to hate God who punishes them: we positively must either reclaim or torment them. Wherever theological intolerance is admitted, it must inevitably have some civil effect;[2] and as soon as it has

[1] Cæsar, pleading for Catiline, tried to establish the dogma that the soul is mortal: Cato and Cicero, in refutation, did not waste time in philosophising. They were content to show that Cæsar spoke like a bad citizen, and brought forward a doctrine that would have a bad effect on the State. This, in fact, and not a problem of theology, was what the Roman senate had to judge.

[2] Marriage, for instance, being a civil contract, has civil effects without which society cannot even subsist. Suppose a body of clergy should claim the sole right of permitting this act, a right which every intolerant religion must of necessity claim, is

such an effect, the Sovereign is no longer Sovereign even in the temporal sphere: thenceforce priests are the real masters, and kings only their ministers.

Now that there is and can be no longer an exclusive national religion, tolerance should be given to all religions that tolerate others, so long as their dogmas contain nothing contrary to the duties of citizenship. But whoever dares to say: *Outside the Church is no salvation,* ought to be driven from the State, unless the State is the Church, and the prince the pontiff. Such a dogma is good only in a theocratic government; in any other, it is fatal. The reason for which Henry IV is said to have embraced the Roman religion ought to make every honest man leave it, and still more any prince who knows how to reason.

9. Conclusion

Now that I have laid down the true principles of political right, and tried to give the State a basis of its own to rest on, I ought next to strengthen it by its external relations, which would include the law of nations, commerce, the right of war and conquest, public right, leagues, negotiations, treaties, etc.. But all this forms a new subject that is far too vast for my narrow scope. I ought throughout to have kept to a more limited sphere.

---

it not clear that in establishing the authority of the Church in this respect, it will be destroying that of the prince, who will have thenceforth only as many subjects as the clergy choose to allow him? Being in a position to marry or not to marry people according to their acceptance of such and such a doctrine, their admission or rejection of such and such a formula, their greater or less piety, the Church alone, by the exercise of prudence and firmness, will dispose of all inheritances, offices and citizens, and even of the State itself, which could not subsist if it were composed entirely of bastards? But, I shall be told, there will be appeals on the ground of abuse, summonses and decrees; the temporalities will be seized. How sad! The clergy, however little, I will not say courage, but sense it has, will take no notice and go its way: it will quietly allow appeals, summonses, decrees and seizures, and, in the end, will remain the master. It is not, I think, a great sacrifice to give up a part, when one is sure of securing all.

THE GREAT IDEAS, Volumes 2 and 3

••••••••••••••••••••••••••••••••••	FAMILY
ANGEL	FATE
ANIMAL	FORM
ARISTOCRACY	GOD
ART	GOOD AND EVIL
ASTRONOMY	GOVERNMENT
BEAUTY	HABIT
BEING	HAPPINESS
CAUSE	HISTORY
CHANCE	HONOR
CHANGE	HYPOTHESIS
CITIZEN	IDEA
CONSTITUTION	IMMORTALITY
COURAGE	INDUCTION
CUSTOM AND	INFINITY
CONVENTION	JUDGMENT
DEFINITION	JUSTICE
DEMOCRACY	KNOWLEDGE
DESIRE	LABOR
DIALECTIC	LANGUAGE
DUTY	LAW
EDUCATION	LIBERTY
ELEMENT	LIFE AND DEATH
EMOTION	LOGIC
ETERNITY	LOVE
EVOLUTION	MAN
EXPERIENCE	MATHEMATICS